Numerical Methods
with MATLAB

Numerical Methods with MATLAB

Implementations and Applications

Gerald W. Recktenwald

Prentice Hall
Upper Saddle River, New Jersey 07458

Library of Congress Cataloging-in-Publication Data
Recktenwald, Gerald W., 1958–
    Numerical methods with MATLAB : implementations and applications / Gerald W. Recktenwald.
       p.   cm.
    Includes bibliographical references and index.
    ISBN 0-201-30860-6 (alk. paper)
     1. Engineering mathematics—Data processing.   2. MATLAB.   3. Numerical
analysis—Data processing.   I. Title.
    TA345 .R43   2000
    620'001'51—dc21   00-042758

Vice president and editorial director: *Marcia Horton*
Acquisitions editor: *Eric Frank*
Editorial assistant: *Jennifer DiBlasi*
Marketing manager: *Danny Hoyt*
Production editor: *Leslie Galen*
Executive managing editor: *Vince O'Brien*
Managing editor: *David A. George*
Art director: *Jayne Conte*
Cover design: *Bruce Kenselaar*
Manufacturing manager: *Trudy Pisciotti*
Compositor: *Integre Technical Publishing Co., Inc.*
Manufacturing buyer: *Dawn Murrin*
Assistant vice president of production and manufacturing: *David W. Riccardi*

Photograph courtesy of The Time Museum, Rockford, Illinois.

Prentice
Hall   © 2000 by Prentice-Hall, Inc.
           Upper Saddle River, New Jersey 07458

The author and publisher of this book have used their best efforts in preparing this book. These efforts include the development, research, and testing of the theories and programs to determine their effectiveness.

Printed in the United States of America

10 9 8 7 6 5 4 3

ISBN 0-201-30860-6

Prentice-Hall International (UK) Limited, *London*
Prentice-Hall of Australia Pty. Limited, *Sydney*
Prentice-Hall of Canada Inc., *Toronto*
Prentice-Hall Hispanoamericana, S.A., *Mexico*
Prentice-Hall of India Private Limited, *New Delhi*
Prentice-Hall of Japan, Inc., *Tokyo*
Pearson Education Asia Pte. Ltd., *Singapore*
Editora Prentice-Hall do Brasil, Ltda., *Rio de Janeiro*

To Elsbeth

Preface

This book is about using MATLAB to obtain numerical solutions to problems in engineering and science. The emphasis is on the application of standard numerical techniques, not on the analysis of those techniques. Mathematical theory is used primarily to develop the logic of the algorithms and to identify the strengths and weaknesses of different numerical methods. In most cases, the behavior of the methods is exposed by numerical experiment.

The intended audience is students in engineering and science learning how to use numerical methods in their own disciplines. I also hope the book will be useful to practicing engineers and scientists who have a specific numerical task and wish to implement a solution in MATLAB. The reader needs no previous experience in numerical analysis. A solid understanding of basic calculus is assumed, as is some previous exposure to linear algebra, differential equations, and computer programming.

This is not a "how to ... " book. Although there are many examples that show how to use MATLAB to solve practical problems, the "how" is accompanied by a strong dose of "why." The basic theory of each method is developed before that method is implemented in MATLAB. If you are interested in a set of recipes for plugging numbers into MATLAB statements, you should put this book down and select another one from the shelf. If you are interested in developing an understanding of how certain numerical methods work and how different methods used to accomplish the same task compare, read on.

Not every routine presented here is recommended for solving practical problems. Elementary algorithms are implemented and their performance is investigated. Advanced techniques are then developed as improvements on the elementary algorithms. By progressing from the simple to the sophisticated, the reader is given an understanding of the fundamentals, as well as guidance on how to apply more reliable and efficient algorithms to practical problems. Numerous sample problems are provided in each chapter. Where applicable, the same problem is solved with different methods, and the results are compared. Simple examples allow the reader to focus on the fundamental aspects of the numerical methods. More sophisticated examples demonstrate the solution to realistic and complicated practical problems.

The first part of the book provides an introduction to MATLAB as an interactive computing system and as a programming language. It is assumed that the reader has some prior experience with computer programming. The material is presented as a first course in numerical methods, not a first course in programming. An ambitious and determined person with significant computer experience could probably use this material as a condensed introduction to programming, although, for that purpose, there are better books.

The routines and data files presented in the book constitute the Numerical Methods with MATLAB (NMM) toolbox, which is available at `http://www.prenhall.com/recktenwald`. Once the NMM toolbox is installed on your computer, you will be able to interactively execute all of the sample problems in this book, as well as apply the NMM toolbox routines to practical problems in your own work.

To the Student

Learning to use computers can be an extremely frustrating experience. It is very easy, in a state of exhaustion and despair, to conclude that numerical methods are (choose one or all of the following) (1) a waste of effort, (2) solely a means of torture, (3) only to be learned by computer geeks, (4) making me less, not more, productive. When I teach numerical methods, I warn my students that they can expect an initial drop in their productivity as they learn a new tool such as MATLAB. It is inevitable that mastering something as powerful and multifaceted as MATLAB will take patience and commitment. The rewards, however, are significant.

The best way to learn a computer tool is to use it. With the knowledge that it may at times be frustrating, jump in. Try it. Let mistakes happen. You will not damage the computer by entering an incorrect MATLAB command. Have this book open when you are running MATLAB. Enter the commands that appear in the text, and explain the outcome in your own words. Try not to rush through the examples. Do not treat them as recipes that must never be altered. Experiment. See if you can break the examples by changing the input parameters. The failure of a numerical solution is a learning experience. Why does one set of inputs work when another does not? What is the smallest difference between two set of inputs that differentiates success from failure? Does the method fail because of an inherent weakness, or are the inputs not valid? Will a more powerful method work for the same inputs?

Use the study guides, lecture notes, solutions to selected end-of-chapter exercises, and other supplemental learning material at `http://www.prenhall.com/recktenwald` to complement the information in the book. The study guides are designed to help you master the material presented in each chapter, and contain learning goals that will be most useful if consulted after reading the chapter. Your instructor may highlight specific learning goals from the study guides. In each chapter solutions to selected end-of-chapter exercises, designated by $\overline{\text{SOLUTION}}$, are provided.

To the Instructor

Various subsets of the material in this book may be organized into college-level courses. To help orient the reader, the beginning of each chapter contains a brief outline of the major topics covered. Study guides for each chapter provide a series of learning objectives divided into basic, intermediate, and advanced topics. Recognizing that the classification of topics is subjective, I am making the study guides available as PDF and as plain text documents at `http://www.prenhall.com/recktenwald`. Instructors are encouraged to download and adapt the study guides to their own selection of topics. Other course materials, including transparency masters, are also available at `http://www.prenhall.com/recktenwald`.

Some very important practical areas of numerical computation are not covered in the book: iterative methods for linear systems of equations, the fast Fourier transform, partial differential equations, and minimization (optimization). These topics were included in the original outline, but as the manuscript evolved, and the sabbatical allocated for writing expired, it became clear that not everything in my plan would make it into the final draft. The absence of some numerical methods will be viewed as a limitation by some instructors. This has not been a problem for the course that was the impetus for writing the book. I believe that undergraduate students are better served by providing a sound foundation in the fundamentals than by a quickly paced survey of many numerical methods. The focus of this book is on providing such a foundation.

I believe that it is counterproductive to require engineering students to develop all of their own programs from pseudocode. This is not to suggest that numerical methods should be treated superficially or that the reader use the NMM toolbox routines as black boxes. The source code for the NMM toolbox is provided with the intention that it is to be read as an integral part of the text. Many of the end-of-chapter assignments require modifications to the source code presented in the chapter, or application of the codes to new problems. Starting with working codes allows you to challenge your students through the *application* of numerical methods to your discipline. This frees you to focus on the behavior of each numerical method without having to guide students as they reinvent standard methods. Having a library of working codes at their disposal, students are also more likely to apply numerical methods in other classes. This provides an opportunity for integrating numerical methods into the undergraduate curriculum.

A Few Words of Caution

As with any work of this scope and size, there is certainly room for improvement. If you find errors or have suggestions, I would be grateful if you take the time to point them out to me. Send all corrections and suggestions for improvements via e-mail. I will maintain errata at `http://www.prenhall.com/recktenwald`.

I cannot, of course, in any way be responsible for negative (or positive!) outcomes from the application of the techniques presented here. There are many ways to apply a correct algorithm to the wrong problem. There are also limits to applying any technique to the problems for which it was designed. Though I have tried to offer guidance, you assume all the risk of using any of the algorithms, codes, and recommendations provided in the book.

Thanks

I have accumulated many debts on the path toward completion of this book. The writers and researchers that I have drawn upon have provided a rich background that I have synthesized into my own writing. The creators of MATLAB have produced a useful and beautiful tool that has significantly advanced my understanding of numerical mathematics. I have benefited immensely from the NA-net and NA-teach electronic digests. My teachers were inspiring and patient as I began my training in engineering and numerical problem-solving. My students endured experiments in my development of the draft manuscript. My colleagues at Portland State provided much encouragement and stimulation. In particular, I would like to thank Dave Turcic for providing feedback on the book as I was writing it and for using an early draft as a textbook in a course on numerical methods for engineers.

Many people at Prentice Hall have given me encouragement, sound advice, and judicious prodding. I am indebted to Denise Penrose and Rob Merino for encouragement at the beginning of this project. I am grateful to Susan Slater and Michael Slaughter for editorial advice and gentle prodding in the middle phase of manuscript development. I am especially appreciative of Eric Frank for his sound understanding of textbooks, and his enthusiastic support of my vision for what this book could become. I owe many thanks to Lisa Bell-Greer and the worker bees at Revolution Publishing in Portland for making exceptional-quality, small production runs of the draft manuscript. Final thanks, chronologically speaking, go to the staff at Integre Technical Publishing, and in particular to Leslie Galen (the midwife), for polishing my prose and Don DeLand for putting sparkle into my LaTeX source.

The following people read drafts and provided valuable feedback: Ron Buckmire (Occidental College), Anand Cousins (Seattle University), John D'Errico (Kodak Corporation), Bahram Shahian (California State University, Long Beach), and Howard Wilson (University of Alabama, Huntsville). I am responsible, of course, for any mistakes in the book.

On a personal level, I am very grateful for my parents' support of my intellectual and geographic journeys. I am also lucky to have good friends that have encouraged me and shared a lot of fun. My son Cullen has given me abundant inspiration and joy. My wife and dear companion, Elsbeth, has given much support and affection to help me toward this and other goals. I dedicate this book to her.

Gerald Recktenwald
gerry@me.pdx.edu

Contents

1   *INTRODUCTION*   *1*

    1.1   Terminology   1
          1.1.1   Numerical and Symbolic Calculation, 1
          1.1.2   Numerical Methods and Algorithms, 4
          1.1.3   Numerical Methods and Numerical Analysis, 5
    1.2   MATLAB Overview   6
    1.3   Organization of the Book   7
          1.3.1   MATLAB Basics, 8
          1.3.2   Numerical Techniques, 8
          1.3.3   Cross-referencing of MATLAB Programs, 10
    1.4   Rating System for Exercises   10

Part 1   MATLAB **Basics**   **13**

   2   *INTERACTIVE COMPUTING WITH* MATLAB   **15**

      2.1   Running MATLAB   15

2.1.1 MATLAB as an Expression Evaluator, 18
2.1.2 MATLAB Variables, 20
2.1.3 Built-in Variables and Functions, 21
2.1.4 Functions and Commands, 22
2.1.5 On-line Help, 23

2.2 Matrices and Vectors 24
2.2.1 Creating Matrices, 26
2.2.2 Subscript Notation for Matrix Elements, 31
2.2.3 Colon Notation, 33
2.2.4 Deleting Elements from Vectors and Matrices, 35
2.2.5 Mathematical Operations with Matrices, 36
2.2.6 Reshaping Matrices, 42

2.3 Additional Types of Variables 45
2.3.1 Complex Numbers, 45
2.3.2 Strings, 48
2.3.3 Polynomials, 51

2.4 Managing the Interactive Environment 52
2.4.1 The MATLAB Workspace, 52
2.4.2 Working with Data from External Files, 53

2.5 Plotting in MATLAB 63
2.5.1 Line Plots, 63
2.5.2 Annotating Plots, 66
2.5.3 Subplots, 68
2.5.4 Surface Plots, 69
2.5.5 Contour Plots, 74

2.6 Summary 77

3 MATLAB PROGRAMMING **85**

3.1 Script m-Files 86
3.1.1 Creating m-Files, 88
3.1.2 Script Side Effects, 91
3.1.3 Comment Statements, 93

3.2 Function m-Files 93
3.2.1 Function Syntax, 94
3.2.2 Input and Output Parameters, 94
3.2.3 Primary and Secondary Functions, 98

3.3 Input and Output 100
3.3.1 Prompting for User Input, 100
3.3.2 Text Output, 101

3.4 Flow Control 105
3.4.1 Relational Operators, 105

3.4.2   Operator Precedence, 107
3.4.3   if ... else ... , 108
3.4.4   Case Selection with switch Structure, 109
3.4.5   for Loops, 110
3.4.6   while loops, 114
3.4.7   The break Command, 115
3.4.8   The return Command, 117
3.5   Vectorization   118
3.5.1   Using Vector Operations instead of Loops, 119
3.5.2   Preallocating Memory for Vectors and Matrices, 120
3.5.3   Vectorized Indexing and Logical Functions, 121
3.6   Deus ex Machina   128
3.6.1   Variable Number of Input and Output Parameters, 129
3.6.2   Global Variables, 133
3.6.3   The feval Function, 134
3.6.4   Inline Function Objects, 137
3.7   Summary   139

4   ORGANIZING AND DEBUGGING MATLAB PROGRAMS   151

4.1   Organizing and Documenting m-files   152
4.1.1   Use of a Consistent Style, 153
4.1.2   Visual Blocking and Whitespace, 154
4.1.3   Meaningful Variable Names, 155
4.1.4   Documentation, 156
4.2   Organizing a Numerical Solution   159
4.2.1   Stepwise Refinement, 160
4.2.2   Implementation: One Program, Multiple m-files, 162
4.2.3   Testing, 169
4.3   Debugging   173
4.3.1   Defensive Programming, 174
4.3.2   Debugging Tools, 176
4.4   Summary   180

Part 2   Numerical Techniques   185

5   UNAVOIDABLE ERRORS IN COMPUTING   187

5.1   Digital Representation of Numbers   191
5.1.1   Bits, Bytes, and Words, 191
5.1.2   Integers, 192
5.1.3   Floating-point Numbers, 193

5.1.4   Numerical versus Symbolic Calculations, 201
5.2   Finite Precision Arithmetic   202
    5.2.1   Machine Precision, 209
    5.2.2   Implications for Routine Calculations, 210
    5.2.3   Measuring Errors, 211
    5.2.4   Convergence of Iterative Sequences, 213
    5.2.5   Relative and Absolute Convergence Criteria, 216
5.3   Truncation Error of Algorithms   217
    5.3.1   Taylor Series, 221
    5.3.2   Order Notation, 223
5.4   Summary   232

6   FINDING THE ROOTS OF $f(x) = 0$ **240**

6.1   Preliminaries   243
    6.1.1   General Considerations, 243
    6.1.2   The Basic Root-finding Procedure, 244
    6.1.3   Bracketing, 245
6.2   Fixed-point Iteration   250
    6.2.1   Convergence of Fixed-point Iteration, 253
6.3   Bisection   253
    6.3.1   Analysis of the Bisection Method, 256
    6.3.2   Convergence Criteria, 257
    6.3.3   A General Implementation of Bisection, 259
6.4   Newton's Method   261
    6.4.1   Convergence of Newton's Method, 264
    6.4.2   A General Implementation of Newton's Method, 265
6.5   The Secant Method   268
6.6   Hybrid Methods   273
    6.6.1   The `fzero` Function, 273
6.7   Roots of Polynomials   279
    6.7.1   The `roots` Function, 280
6.8   Summary   283

7   A REVIEW OF LINEAR ALGEBRA   **293**

7.1   Vectors   294
    7.1.1   Vector Operations, 296
    7.1.2   Vector Norms, 301
    7.1.3   Orthogonal Vectors, 308
7.2   Matrices   309
    7.2.1   The Rows and Columns of a Matrix Are Vectors, 309

      7.2.2   Matrix Operations, 310
      7.2.3   Operation Counts for Matrix and Vector Operations, 331
      7.2.4   Matrix Norms, 333
  7.3   Mathematical Properties of Vectors and Matrices   334
      7.3.1   Linear Independence, 335
      7.3.2   Vector Spaces, 336
      7.3.3   Subspaces Associated with Matrices, 339
      7.3.4   Matrix Rank, 341
      7.3.5   Matrix Determinant, 342
  7.4   Special Matrices   346
      7.4.1   Diagonal Matrices, 346
      7.4.2   The Identity Matrix, 347
      7.4.3   The Matrix Inverse, 348
      7.4.4   Symmetric Matrices, 349
      7.4.5   Tridiagonal Matrices, 349
      7.4.6   Positive Definite Matrices, 351
      7.4.7   Orthogonal Matrices, 351
      7.4.8   Permutation Matrices, 352
  7.5   Summary   353

8 SOLVING SYSTEMS OF EQUATIONS   **363**

  8.1   Basic Concepts   365
      8.1.1   Matrix Formulation, 365
      8.1.2   Requirements for a Solution, 369
  8.2   Gaussian Elimination   379
      8.2.1   Solving Diagonal Systems, 379
      8.2.2   Solving Triangular Systems, 380
      8.2.3   Gaussian Elimination without Pivoting, 382
      8.2.4   Gaussian Elimination with Pivoting, 387
      8.2.5   Solving Systems with the Backslash Operator, 396
  8.3   Limitations on Numerical Solutions to $Ax = b$ 398
      8.3.1   Computational Work, 398
      8.3.2   Sensitivity to Inputs, 399
      8.3.3   Computational Stability, 405
      8.3.4   The Residual, 407
      8.3.5   Rules of Thumb, 407
      8.3.6   Computing $\kappa(A)$, 408
  8.4   Factorization Methods   410
      8.4.1   LU Factorization, 410
      8.4.2   Cholesky Factorization, 422
      8.4.3   The Backslash Operator Reconsidered, 426

8.5   Nonlinear Systems of Equations   427
       8.5.1   Iterative Methods for Nonlinear Systems, 427
       8.5.2   Successive Substitution, 429
       8.5.3   Newton's Method, 432
8.6   Summary   443

9   LEAST-SQUARES FITTING OF A CURVE TO DATA   455
9.1   Fitting a Line to Data   458
       9.1.1   Minimizing the Residual, 460
       9.1.2   An Overdetermined System of Equations, 461
       9.1.3   Implementation of Line Fitting, 463
       9.1.4   The R^2 Statistic, 464
       9.1.5   Fitting Lines to Apparently Nonlinear Functions, 468
       9.1.6   Summary of Fitting Data to a Line, 472
9.2   Least-Squares Fit to a Linear Combination of Functions   473
       9.2.1   Basis Functions, 474
       9.2.2   Least-Squares Fit via Solution to the Normal
                Equations, 475
       9.2.3   Least-Squares Approximation with QR Factorization, 485
       9.2.4   Polynomial Curve Fitting, 495
9.3   Multivariate Linear Least-Squares Fitting   500
9.4   Summary   508

10   INTERPOLATION   521
10.1   Basic Ideas   524
        10.1.1   Interpolation versus Curve Fitting, 525
        10.1.2   Interpolation and Extrapolation, 525
10.2   Interpolating Polynomials of Arbitrary Degree   527
        10.2.1   Polynomial Interpolation with a Monomial Basis, 527
        10.2.2   Polynomial Interpolation with a Lagrange Basis, 532
        10.2.3   Polynomial Interpolation with a Newton Basis, 538
        10.2.4   Polynomial Wiggle, 552
10.3   Piecewise Polynomial Interpolation   554
        10.3.1   Piecewise-Linear Interpolation, 556
        10.3.2   Searching for Support Points, 557
        10.3.3   The linterp Function, 559
        10.3.4   Piecewise-Cubic Hermite Interpolation, 560
        10.3.5   Cubic Spline Interpolation, 568
10.4   MATLAB's Built in Interpolation Functions   583
        10.4.1   One-dimensional Interpolation with interp1 and
                  spline, 584
10.5   Summary   586

11 NUMERICAL INTEGRATION   597

11.1 Basic Ideas and Nomenclature   600
    11.1.1 Symbolic versus Numerical Integration, 602
11.2 Newton–Cotes Rules   603
    11.2.1 Trapezoid Rule, 603
    11.2.2 Simpson's Rule, 612
    11.2.3 Catalog of Newton–Cotes Rules, 616
11.3 Gaussian Quadrature   620
    11.3.1 Theoretical Basis, 622
    11.3.2 The Basic Rule for Gauss–Legendre Quadrature, 626
    11.3.3 Table Lookup for Nodes and Weights, 628
    11.3.4 Computing the Nodes and Weights, 629
    11.3.5 Composite Rule for Gauss–Legendre Quadrature, 634
11.4 Adaptive Quadrature   644
    11.4.1 Adaptive Integration Based on Simpson's Rule, 646
    11.4.2 Built-in quad and quad8 Functions, 654
    11.4.3 New quad and quadl Functions, 659
11.5 Improper Integrals and Other Complications   660
    11.5.1 Integrals with Infinite Limits, 660
11.6 Summary   666

12 NUMERICAL INTEGRATION OF ORDINARY DIFFERENTIAL EQUATIONS   674

12.1 Basic Ideas and Nomenclature   676
    12.1.1 Ordinary Differential Equations, 676
    12.1.2 Overview of Numerical Solution Strategy, 679
12.2 Euler's Method   681
    12.2.1 Implementation of Euler's Method, 683
    12.2.2 Analysis of Euler's Method, 686
    12.2.3 Generalization: One-Step Methods, 691
    12.2.4 Summary of §12.2, 692
12.3 Higher Order One-step Methods   692
    12.3.1 Midpoint Method, 693
    12.3.2 Heun's Method, 696
    12.3.3 Fourth-order Runge–Kutta Method, 697
12.4 Adaptive Stepsize Algorithms   700
    12.4.1 The ode23 and ode45 Routines, 701
12.5 Coupled ODEs   710
    12.5.1 The RK-4 Algorithm for Coupled ODEs, 713
    12.5.2 Higher Order Differential Equations, 720

12.6   Additional Topics   724
12.7   Summary   725

BIBLIOGRAPHY   735

APPENDIX A   EIGENVALUES AND EIGENSYSTEMS   741

A.1   Eigenvectors Map onto Themselves   742
A.2   Mathematical Preliminaries   745
    A.2.1   Characteristic Polynomial, 745
    A.2.2   Companion Matrix, 746
    A.2.3   Eigenfacts, 746
A.3   The Power Method   748
    A.3.1   Power Iterations, 749
    A.3.2   Inverse-Power Iterations, 751
A.4   Built-in Functions for Eigenvalue Computation   753
    A.4.1   The eig Function, 753
    A.4.2   The eigs Function, 755
A.5   Singular Value Decomposition   755
    A.5.1   The svd Function, 756

APPENDIX B   SPARSE MATRICES   757

B.1   Storage and Flop Savings   758
B.2   MATLAB Sparse Matrix Format   758
    B.2.1   Creating Sparse Matrices, 759
    B.2.2   Operations on Sparse Matrices, 766

MATLAB TOOLBOX FUNCTIONS   769

LISTINGS FOR NMM TOOLBOX m-FILES   773

SUBJECT INDEX   775

List of Figures

2.1   Primary topics discussed in Chapter 2.   16
2.2   Response of an underdamped second-order system.   42
2.3   Euler notation for complex numbers.   47
2.4   Directory structures for the MATLAB and NMM toolboxes.   59
2.5   Line plot example.   64
2.6   Semilog plot example.   65
2.7   Demonstration of plot annotation functions.   67
2.8   Four subplots in a figure window.   68
2.9   Surface plot example.   71
2.10 Four types of surface plots.   72
2.11 Viewing angle for three-dimensional plots.   72
2.12 Contour plot example.   74
2.13 Sketch of source–sink pair.   75
2.14 Surface plot of source–sink pair.   76

3.1   Primary topics discussed in Chapter 3.   86
3.2   Plots created with the `trigplot` script.   91
3.3   Visual representation of difference between the `break` and
      `return` statements.   117

3.4   Rules for array and logical indexing.   122
3.5   Bypassing input–output parameters with global variables.   133

4.1   Primary topics discussed in Chapter 4.   152
4.2   Basic structure of an m-file function.   153
4.3   Annotation of an m-file prologue.   158
4.4   Plot of river flow data.   169
4.5   keyboard command demonstration.   180

5.1   Primary topics discussed in Chapter 5.   189
5.2   Discrete approximation to the real number line.   196
5.3   Graphical interpretation of ε_m.   210
5.4   Plot of series approximations to e^{-10}.   221
5.5   Plot of Taylor series approximations to $f(x) = 1/(1-x)$.   224
5.6   Polygons inscribed in a circle as a method of calculating π.   227
5.7   Relative error in finite-difference approximations to $d(e^x)/dx$.   231

6.1   Primary topics discussed in Chapter 6.   241
6.2   A picnic table.   242
6.3   Dimensions of picnic table legs.   242
6.4   Roots of a generic scalar function $f(x) = 0$.   244
6.5   Sign change of $f(x)$ brackets either a root or singularity.   245
6.6   Bracket intervals for $\sin(x) = 0$.   248
6.7   Plot of the function $f(x) = x - x^{1/3} - 2$.   249
6.8   Plot of the function $f(x) = x - 12x^{1/3} + 12$.   252
6.9   Two steps of the bisection method.   254
6.10 Stopping criteria for a root-finding procedure.   257
6.11 Two steps of Newton's method.   262
6.12 Pathological failure of Newton's method.   263
6.13 Bypassing I/O parameters of newton with global variables.   270
6.14 Two steps of the secant method.   271
6.15 Pathological failure of the secant method.   272
6.16 Inverse quadratic interpolation.   273
6.17 Polynomials with distinct real roots, repeated real roots, and
      imaginary roots.   279
6.18 Solid spheres floating in water.   282

7.1   Primary topics discussed in Chapter 7.   294
7.2   Vectors in $\mathbf{R}^2$.   298
7.3   Comparing the lengths of two-dimensional vectors.   302
7.4   Convergence of $[x]^k$ in the L_1, L_2 and L_∞ norms.   307

7.5	Graphical depiction of the triangle inequality for two-dimensional vectors.	308
7.6	Levels of abstraction for matrix and vector operations.	311
7.7	Summary of products involving matrices and vectors.	325
7.8	Graphical representation of the column view of the matrix–matrix product.	327
7.9	Graphical representation of the row view for the matrix–matrix product.	328
7.10	Three-element vectors in a subspace of $\mathbf{R}^3$.	338
7.11	Minors of a 3×3 matrix.	343
8.1	Primary topics discussed in Chapter 8.	364
8.2	Typical performance curve for a centrifugal pump.	364
8.3	IC package on a heat spreader.	367
8.4	Shapes and applications of matrices with m rows and n columns.	369
8.5	Inconsistent and consistent systems from fitting three data points to a line.	371
8.6	Solution scenarios for a 2×2 system of equations.	375
8.7	Wheatstone bridge.	377
8.8	Cartoon version of Gaussian elimination.	384
8.9	Solution scenarios for the system of nonlinear equations in Example 8.10.	429
8.10	Three-reservoir problem.	438
9.1	Primary topics discussed in Chapter 9.	456
9.2	Measuring the voltage across a discharging capacitor.	457
9.3	Conductivity of copper at low temperatures.	458
9.4	Least-squares fit of data to a line.	459
9.5	Least-squares fit of four data points to a line.	465
9.6	Graphical interpretation of quantities used to compute R^2.	466
9.7	Line fit to bulk modulus of SiC versus temperature.	467
9.8	Fit of data to $y = c_1 x e^{-c_2 x}$.	472
9.9	Plot of curve fit in Example 9.7.	477
9.10	Least-squares fit of thermal conductivity data in file `cucon1.dat`.	483
9.11	Least-squares fit of thermal conductivity data in files `cucon2.dat` and `cucon3.dat`.	485
9.12	Polynomial curve fits to thermocouple calibration data.	499
9.13	Residuals for polynomial curve fits of thermocouple calibration data.	499
9.14	Fitting data to a plane.	502
9.15	(a) Vane-axial fan and (b) typical fan curve.	503

9.16   Surface fit to fan curve data at a range of voltages.   504

10.1   Primary topics discussed in Chapter 10.   522
10.2   Visual interpolation in reading a speedometer and a wristwatch.   523
10.3   Viscosity of glycerin as a function of temperature.   524
10.4   Contrast interpolation and curve fitting.   525
10.5   Contrast interpolation and extrapolation.   526
10.6   Extrapolation of airport passenger data.   527
10.7   Interpolation of gasoline price data with a monomial basis.   531
10.8   Interpolation of gas data with shifted dates.   532
10.9   Linear interpolation and the corresponding Lagrange basis.   533
10.10 Lagrange basis polynomials of degree 1 through 4.   535
10.11 Flop counts for interpolation with different polynomial bases.   552
10.12 Polynomial wiggle and extrapolation.   554
10.13 Continuity conditions for piecewise interpolation.   555
10.14 Piecewise-cubic Hermite interpolating polynomials.   561
10.15 Location of appropriate segment for piecewise polynomial
       interpolation.   565
10.16 Piecewise-cubic Hermite approximations to $y = xe^{-x}$.   567
10.17 Cubic-spline interpolating functions.   568
10.18 End conditions for a draftsman's spline.   577
10.19 Spline approximations with different end conditions.   583
10.20 Interpolation methods used by `interp1`.   585

11.1   Primary topics discussed in Chapter 11.   598
11.2   Forming of an elliptical tube from a sheet.   599
11.3   Numerical integration of a piecewise-linear interpolant.   600
11.4   Basic and composite rules.   601
11.5   Trapezoid rule integration for two points.   604
11.6   Trapezoid rule integration for three nodes.   605
11.7   Plot of the trapezoid rule approximation to $\int_0^5 xe^{-x}\,dx$.   610
11.8   Simpson's rule for three nodes.   612
11.9   Simpson's rule for n points.   613
11.10 Plot of the Simpson's rule approximation to $\int_0^5 xe^{-x}\,dx$.   617
11.11 Closed and open intervals for three-point Newton–Cotes rules.   619
11.12 Location of nodes and value of weights for Gauss–Legendre
       quadrature.   628
11.13 Transformation of a panel for Gauss–Legendre quadrature.   636
11.14 Efficiency of trapezoid rule, Simpson's rule and Gauss–Legendre
       quadrature.   644
11.15 Refinement for the adaptive Simpson quadrature algorithm.   646

11.16   Demonstration of the adaptSimpson function.   652
11.17   Performance of built-in quad and quad8 functions.   658

12.1   Primary topics covered in Chapter 12.   675
12.2   Cooling of an object by a flowing fluid.   678
12.3   Numerical approximation to $dy/dt = f(t, y)$, $y(t_0) = y_0$.   680
12.4   Reducing step size with Euler's method.   687
12.5   Continuous and approximate solutions used in analysis of
        Euler's method.   689
12.6   Graphical representation of the midpoint method.   693
12.7   Graphical representation of the Heun's method.   696
12.8   Graphical representation of the fourth-order Runge–Kutta method.   698
12.9   Heat treating of steel rods.   709
12.10   Heat-treating simulation results.   712
12.11   Plot of solution to coupled system of first-order ODEs.   717
12.12   Results of the predator–prey model.   718
12.13   A generic spring–mass–damper system.   721
12.14   Step response of a second-order mechanical system.   724

B.1   Four examples of sparse matrices.   759

List of Tables

2.1 Built-in variables in MATLAB.   21
2.2 Some built-in functions for creating matrices.   27
2.3 Built-in functions for working with complex numbers.   46
2.4 Built-in functions for manipulating polynomials.   51
2.5 File permissions commonly used with the `fopen` function.   60
2.6 Plot symbols, line types, and colors.   64
2.7 Annotation functions.   66

3.1 Demonstration of `format` commands.   102
3.2 Summary of format codes for use with `fprintf` and `fscanf`.   104
3.3 Effect of formatting codes on values displayed by `fprintf`.   104
3.4 Relational and logical operators in MATLAB.   106
3.5 Precedence of arithmetic operators.   108
3.6 A sample of built-in logical functions.   123
3.7 NMM toolbox functions used to introduce programming concepts.   139

4.1 NMM toolbox functions used to introduce program organization
     and debugging.   181

5.1   Base 10 and binary (base 2) numbers.   191
5.2   Ranges of floating-point data types.   195
5.3   NMM toolbox functions used to demonstrate numerical errors.   233

6.1   Reduction of bracket size during bisections.   257
6.2   NMM toolbox functions for root finding.   283

7.1   Typographical convention for scalars, vectors, and matrices.   295
7.2   Flop counts for vector and matrix products.   333
7.3   NMM functions for linear algebra review.   354
7.4   Summary of restrictions on basic operations involving two vectors.   355
7.5   Summary of restrictions on basic operations involving
      two matrices.   355

8.1   Operation counts for solving linear systems.   399
8.2   Commonly used matrix factorizations.   410
8.3   NMM Toolbox functions for solving linear systems of equations.   444

9.1   Data transformations for use with linear least-squares fitting.   469
9.2   NMM functions for curve-fitting.   509

10.1 Divided-difference table.   544
10.2 Built-in MATLAB functions for interpolation of data.   584
10.3 NMM functions for interpolation.   587

11.1 NMM functions for numerical integration.   667

12.1 Nomenclature for numerical solution of ODEs.   680
12.2 NMM toolbox functions for ODE integration.   726
12.3 MATLAB's built-in ODE integration routines.   726
12.4 NMM toolbox functions for evaluating the right-hand sides
      of ODEs.   727

B.1   Sparse matrix functions.   760

1

Introduction

Being able to automate calculations with a computer is an essential skill for engineers, mathematicians, and scientists. Although there is a wide variety of practical problems to which computers are applied, there is also a core of ideas common to many computer calculations and many professional disciplines. This book is about the core ideas of applied numerical computation and their implementation in a particular computing system called MATLAB.

1.1 TERMINOLOGY

It is useful to define terminology, not so much for the sake of semantic purity, but as a guide to the reader. The following subsections present working definitions of some terms in an attempt to establish a context for the rest of the book.

1.1.1 Numerical and Symbolic Calculation

A numerical calculation involves numbers directly, as opposed to the symbols by which the numbers are represented in an equation. A numerical calculation, there-

1

fore, produces a numerical result, not a mathematical expression. When we evaluate a formula such as

$$\frac{(17.36)^2 - 1}{17.36 + 1} = 16.36,$$

we perform a numerical computation. In contrast, a symbolic calculation involves the manipulation of mathematical symbols without any necessary reference to the numerical values those symbols might take. Thus,

$$\frac{x^2 - 1}{x + 1} = x - 1$$

is a symbolic calculation that is true for any $x \neq -1$.

An important aspect of numerical computation is the use of approximations instead of exact numerical values. Indeed, one working definition of numerical computation is the evaluation of approximations to quantities that cannot be computed exactly with a finite number of digits. Consider the fraction 1/3 and the fundamental constant π:

Symbolic	Numerical
$\dfrac{1}{3}$	0.33333...
π	3.14159265358979...

The fraction 1/3 is a symbolic formula representing the division of the integer 1 by the integer 3. The " ... " in "0.33333..." is a reminder that the exact numerical value of 1/3 requires an infinite number of decimal digits. When the expression "one divided by three" is evaluated on a computer (or on a hand-held calculator), the result is truncated to 0.3333333, 0.3333333333, 0.3333333333333333, or some other value, depending on how many decimal digits are allocated to each number.[1] Similarly, the value of π used in a computer program will be a truncated approximation to the exact, symbolic value. When a human or a computer program performs a mathematical operation with numerical quantities such as 0.3333 instead of 1/3, the process is called numerical computation. Symbolic computation can involve symbols such as x, rational numbers such as 1/3, or transcendental numbers such as π, without any limit to the number of digits associated with these symbols.

---

[1]Binary representations of floating-point values are addressed in Chapter 5.

Example 1.1: Symbolic and Numeric Calculations with Rational Numbers

Consider the simple calculation

$$\frac{1}{2} + \frac{1}{3} + \frac{1}{4} - 1 = \frac{1}{12}. \tag{1.1}$$

The symbols $1/2$, $1/3$, and $1/4$ have the numerical values 0.5, $0.33333\ldots$, and 0.25. Both $1/2$ and $1/4$ can be represented with a finite number of decimal digits, but $1/3$ cannot. If the preceding calculations were performed to four significant digits, the result would be

$$0.5000 + 0.3333 + 0.2500 - 1.000 = 0.0833. \tag{1.2}$$

For most practical purposes, the difference between 0.0833 and $1/12 = 0.0833\ldots$ is insignificant, though, clearly, these numerical values are not exactly equal. One of the essential features of a numerical calculation is that exact symbolic quantities—in this case, the rational number $1/3$—are represented by an approximate numerical value.

Numerical computations are performed with programming languages such as Fortran, Basic, Pascal, C, C++, and Java. These languages involve the manipulation of variables that refer to locations in computer memory. At the level of electronic circuits, all values stored in a computer are represented by a sequence of ones and zeros. The *binary* (i.e., 1 or 0) representation corresponds to "on" and "off" states of circuit components. Whenever a program variable is assigned a numerical value, it is converted to a binary number so that it can be stored in computer memory. Since not all decimal (base-10) numbers can be represented exactly in base 2, the very act of assigning a value to a program variable introduces an approximation. The error in this approximation contributes to subsequent errors in the evaluation of formulas using the variables. The errors inherent in working with numerical values are usually small. In some situations, small numerical errors can be significant, as described in Chapter 5.

Symbolic computations are performed by computer programs such as Derive®, Macsyma®, Maple®, and Mathematica®. MATLAB also supports symbolic computation through the Symbolic Mathematics toolbox, which uses the symbolic routines of Maple. Symbolic calculations can be performed without the approximations that are necessary for numerical calculations. The avoidance of these approximations comes at a cost in speed. In general, *numerical* results are obtained much more quickly with a numerical computation than with the numerical evaluation of a symbolic calculation.

Symbolic computation is an important and complementary aspect of computing. In this book, however, symbolic calculations are used only to highlight the fundamental behavior of numerical calculations.

1.1.2 Numerical Methods and Algorithms

Although "numerical method" is often considered to be synonymous with "numerical algorithm," we will make a distinction here that allows the introduction of a critical idea. A numerical method is a mathematical description of the calculations to be performed; an algorithm is a precise sequence of actions taken to obtain a desired result. This distinction implicitly acknowledges that a good method (i.e., one that has desirable mathematical properties) may be implemented with different algorithms. Furthermore, it is possible that one algorithm is better, by some measure, than another algorithm embodying the same method.

Much of human enterprise involves algorithms. A particular goal can often be obtained with different methods, and each method might be realizable with different algorithms. Consider, for example, the goal of making a cup of coffee. There are several practical methods for doing so: One could use a percolator, a drip coffeemaker, an espresso machine, or some other device. Once the "drip machine method" is chosen, one can use two possible algorithms for making the coffee:

Algorithm 1

1. Grind fresh beans
2. Place new filter in filter holder and carefully measure ground coffee into the filter.
3. Wash and carefully rinse the coffeepot.
4. Fill drip machine with bottled spring water and press the "on" switch.
5. While waiting, carefully wash and rinse a coffee cup.

6. Fill coffee cup and add some half-and-half.

Algorithm 2

1. Take can of coffee from cupboard
2. Place new filter in filter holder and pour some coffee in filter.
3. Empty old coffee from pot.
4. Fill drip machine with tap water and press the "on" switch.
5. While waiting, find a coffee cup from the kitchen counter and dump out old coffee.
6. Fill coffee cup and add some non-dairy creamer.

Whether or not the choice of coffee algorithm makes a significant difference depends on the precision and accuracy of your taste buds. The choice of algorithm will also be influenced by the the "application" for the coffee: Algorithm 1 is appropriate for preparing coffee to accompany a fine dessert or an elegant breakfast, whereas Algorithm 2 is a suitable means of ingesting caffeine during a late-night study break.

The chapters in Part II of this book present a variety of numerical methods. In the interest of economy of space, and to avoid testing your patience, only one algorithm is given for each method. The algorithm is chosen by a highly subjective balance of three criteria: ease of understanding; reliability in performing the stated objective; and efficiency in the use of computer resources.

Once an algorithm is chosen, it must be implemented in a computer code, or simply, a code. A code is a translation of an algorithm into a sequence of statements in a particular computer language. Just as a given method can be implemented by different algorithms, so, too, can a given algorithm be implemented by different codes. The practice of implementing numerical algorithms in effective MATLAB code is the subject of Chapter 4.

You are strongly encouraged to experiment with and modify the codes given in this book. Some end-of-chapter exercises require doing just that. Direct experimentation with working codes is an important part of learning numerical methods.

1.1.3 Numerical Methods and Numerical Analysis

Numerical analysis is the mathematical study of numerical methods. It is possible to perform significant numerical analysis without ever using a computer. In fact, many of the techniques presented in this book were developed long before the current digital age. Mathematicians, engineers, and scientists who could not find a closed-form analytical solution to some pressing practical problem developed sequential procedures for computing approximations to the analytical solution. In the days of hands-only computation, the importance of minimizing effort while maximizing accuracy led to the development of numerical analysis as a branch of mathematics. The emphasis of numerical analysis is more on understanding the general behavior of numerical methods and less on how to apply these methods to a specific problem. The invention of the modern digital computer and its application to all aspects of science and industry have only increased the importance of numerical analysis.

The results of numerical analysis help the practitioner choose an appropriate method and algorithm. They also provide important a priori information on the limits of the method and an estimate of the accuracy of the computed result. By using the results of numerical analysis, a programmer can increase the likelihood that the computed result will be close to the "true" solution. Without analysis, programmers would have to discover the merits of each method by experimentation. Not only would this be time consuming, but also, it would make it very difficult to generalize the knowledge gained during the development of any one program.

This book is focused on the implementation, rather than the analysis, of numerical techniques. The results of analysis are used to anticipate the performance of numerical methods and to explain the differences between related methods. Numerical experiments are used to demonstrate the behavior of numerical methods in concrete terms. Although experimentation can be used to motivate understanding, it can never be a complete substitute for analysis. It is hoped that, having solid implementations in hand, the curious reader will pursue a better theoretical understanding. A good book on numerical analysis such as [9, 10, 11, 64] will provide useful mathematical background to supplement the approach taken in this text. More specific references are provided as each method is discussed. The goal is not to minimize the importance of numerical analysis, but to use direct numerical experimentation as a teaching device.

1.2 MATLAB OVERVIEW

The name "MATLAB" is an abbreviation of "Matrix Laboratory." The first version of MATLAB was an interface to the routines in the LINPACK and EISPACK libraries[2] for the analysis of linear systems of equations. As MATLAB evolved, routines were added for many tasks beyond linear algebra. At its heart, MATLAB is still an interactive analysis tool that relies on commands typed into a command-line environment. The interactive environment can be extended by user-written programs in a language resembling Fortran. Programs exist as modules that are immediately available as commands from within the interactive environment.

The MATLAB user interface includes a modest set of drop-down menus and dialog boxes that will be familiar to any user of a personal computer. These menu commands primarily support file manipulation, printing, basic editing of programs, and customization of the user interface. The vast majority numerical computations in MATLAB are performed by entering commands in the command window, not by making menu selections.

MATLAB software exists as a primary application program and a large library of program modules called the standard toolbox. Most of the numerical methods described in this book are implemented in one form or another in the toolbox. The MATLAB toolbox contains an extensive library for solving many practical numerical problems, such as root-finding, interpolation, numerical integration, solving systems of linear and nonlinear equations, and solving ordinary differential equations. As a result of its LINPACK, EISPACK, and LAPACK legacy, MATLAB is a highly optimized and extremely reliable system for numerical linear algebra. Many numerical tasks can be concisely expressed in the language of linear algebra. The

---

[2]Superseded by LAPACK, which is available at netlib, www.netlib.org. Version 6 of MATLAB is based on LAPACK.

deep affinity between MATLAB and linear algebra allows programmers to perform complicated numerical tasks in short sequences of MATLAB statements.

The standard toolbox also includes an extensive graphics library for data visualization, from simple line plots to complex three-dimensional graphics and animation. These functions are available to all MATLAB programs, making it possible to perform the analysis and create publication-quality plots all in the same program or set of programs. Having immediate access to graphical results can dramatically increase a user's productivity. Diagnostic plots can be incorporated to help debug a program or verify that an algorithm is behaving as expected. In addition, low-level graphics functions allow the development of custom graphical user interfaces for analysis codes.

In addition to the standard toolbox, additional toolboxes are available for signal processing, image processing, optimization, statistical analysis, the solution of partial differential equations, and many other specialized areas of numerical computation.

Student and Professional Versions   MATLAB is a commercial product available on different computer platforms. For personal computers, both a student and a professional version are available. In mid-1999, the MathWorks (creators of MATLAB) began selling the *Student Version of* MATLAB for Windows and Linux. Up until mid-1999, a *Student Edition of* MATLAB was sold by Prentice-Hall. The *Student Version* includes Simulink and the symbolic math toolbox, is based on MATLAB 5.3, and has no limit on the size of matrices. Owners of the *Student Version* get a one-time discount on upgrades to the professional version.

The professional version is much more expensive than the *Student Version*, which costs roughly as much as an engineering textbook. The professional version of MATLAB includes only the standard toolbox (the subject of this book). All other toolboxes must be purchased separately. The size of matrices that can be used in the professional edition is limited only by the memory available on the computer running MATLAB. Owners of the professional version may upgrade as new releases of MATLAB are produced.

Readers seeking more information on these products should contact the MathWorks at the address given at the back of the title page of this book.

3 ORGANIZATION OF THE BOOK

The book is divided into two parts. Following this introductory chapter, Part I, "MATLAB Basics," attempts to give the reader a solid background in the use of MATLAB. It is extensive, but not exhaustive. In Part I, no specific consideration to numerical methods is given, other than a presentation of the basic logical structures that can be combined into useful algorithms. Part I assumes that the reader has experience in some programming language. Users already familiar with MATLAB can skim Part I, treating it as a reference. Readers new to MATLAB should take time to study Chapters 2 through 4 and then proceed in a logical progression through the rest of the book.

1.3.1 MATLAB Basics

Chapters 2 and 3 should be read at a computer while running MATLAB. Do not worry about memorizing the commands. Try them out. Experiment. Try to learn the basic syntax of commands (Chapter 2), and learn how MATLAB calculations can be organized into user-defined functions (Chapter 3).

Chapter 4, "Organizing and Debugging MATLAB Programs," presents strategies for writing effective programs. Modular programming is stressed and demonstrated with examples. A style for documenting programs is presented. Basic techniques for debugging programs as well as anticipating the existence of bugs are described.

1.3.2 Numerical Techniques

Part II, "Numerical Techniques," contains fundamental numerical methods organized into separate chapters. The development of the material in each chapter involves a progression from simple to more sophisticated algorithms. While it may be possible to stop midway through a chapter, it will be somewhat difficult to start at the midpoint.

Chapter 5, "Unavoidable Errors in Computing," sets the stage for many algorithmic decisions made in later chapters. The basic features of floating-point arithmetic are described. Roundoff and truncation errors are discussed, and practical advice for performing calculations in floating-point arithmetic is given.

Chapter 6, "Finding the Roots of $f(x)$," is the first chapter to deal with methods dedicated to a specific task. Root-finding is the process of determining a value of x that gives $f(x) = 0$. Any scalar equation in one variable can be put into the form $f(x) = 0$. Beginning with fixed-point iteration and bisection, the chapter progresses through Newton's method, the secant method, and the hybrid methods provided in the MATLAB toolbox. Roots of polynomials are considered as a separate case at the end of the chapter.

Chapter 7, "A Review of Linear Algebra," provides a foundation for the use of matrix calculations throughout the remainder of the book. Readers already confident in their understanding of linear algebra, but unfamiliar with MATLAB, should not skip this chapter. Performing linear algebra with MATLAB requires an understanding of linear algebra *and* an appreciation for MATLAB syntax.

Chapter 8, "Solving Linear Systems," deals with a central part of many numerical methods, namely, the solution of $Ax = b$, where A is a matrix (usually square), x is a column vector of unknowns, and b is a column vector of known values. The material begins with an overview of the mathematical conditions necessary for solving $Ax = b$, which is followed by an exposition of the classical Gaussian elimination algorithm. The condition number is introduced as a way to quantify the numerical errors that arise during Gaussian elimination and back substitution. Chapter 8 also covers LU and Cholesky factorization methods for solving $Ax = b$. In MATLAB, the solution of linear systems is achieved with \, the "backslash operator," which uses LU factorization, Cholesky factorization, or QR factorization, depending on the properties of the A matrix. This single keystroke has immense power and significance in MATLAB, and an important goal of Chapter 8 is to show how to use the backslash operator correctly and with confidence. The chapter ends with a brief discussion of solving nonlinear systems of equations.

Chapter 9, "Fitting a Curve to Data," covers the least squares method as it applies to the modeling of data. The chapter begins with a simple algorithm for fitting a line to (x, y) data and proceeds to the more general problem of fitting an arbitrary (but linear) combination of functions to a data set. One of the highlights of the chapter is an explanation of how MATLAB's built-in backslash operator can be used to obtain the least squares solution via QR factorization. Multivariate least squares fitting is also covered.

Chapter 10, "Interpolation," deals with the interpolation of discrete data. Two basic approaches are considered: interpolation with polynomials of arbitrary degree and interpolation with piecewise polynomials. Different algorithms for one-dimensional polynomial and spline interpolation are presented and related to MATLAB's built-in `interp` functions.

Chapter 11, "Integration," discusses techniques for evaluating definite integrals that have no closed-form expression. The trapezoid rule and Simpson's rule are derived and implemented as general-purpose routines. The basic theory of Gaussian quadrature is explained, and a routine for composite Gaussian quadrature of any order is given. Adaptive quadrature methods are discussed, and the built-in `quad` and `quad8` routines are demonstrated.

Chapter 12, "Numerical Solution of Ordinary Differential Equations," describes several techniques for initial-value problems. Fundamental concepts are examined via Euler's method. A sequence of more accurate and efficient methods, culminating with adaptive step-size Runge–Kutta methods, is presented. The methods are developed for first-order ordinary differential equations (ODEs) and then are extended to coupled systems of equations and higher order ODEs.

1.3.3 Cross-referencing of MATLAB Programs

MATLAB programs are listed in boxed displays with descriptive captions. A table at the end of each chapter lists the programs developed in that chapter. In addition, three indexes are provided at the end of the book. The first index lists the page numbers where built-in MATLAB functions are used or discussed. The second index provides the page numbers where programs developed in the book are listed. The third index is a comprehensive cross-reference for the book.

1.4 RATING SYSTEM FOR EXERCISES

Each end-of-chapter exercise is rated according to the amount of skill and effort required to complete it. One might be tempted to call this a degree-of-difficulty rating, but I prefer to think in terms of the level of mastery of the subject matter. The greater one's proficiency with numerical methods, the easier the problems become. Any such rating is subjective, of course, but my intention is to provide some guidance to an instructor choosing an exercise for a homework problem and to individuals using the exercises for self-study. The system used here is modeled on that used to rate rivers that are run by kayakers and rafters.[3]

The skill and effort required to complete an exercise are expressed by its "class":

Class 1 Straightforward application of a concept or MATLAB function discussed in the text. Though a class 1 exercise can be completed with minimal effort, the concepts dealt with in the exercise should not be dismissed as unimportant.

Class 2 Application of a method to a new problem requiring minimal or no modification to the method as presented in the text. Some thought is required to formulate the problem so that it may be used with a standard method.

Class 3 Solution requires adaptation of methods and codes presented in the text. The method must be well understood, as its misapplication will result in a potentially serious error. Some effort is required to validate the result.

Class 4 Development of a solution requires extension of the techniques presented in the book. The solution will likely involve false starts that require changes of direction. A degree of intellectual nimbleness, therefore, is of advantage. Additional data from outside sources may be required. Significant program development is to be expected. The development of a means of validating the solution will also require a significant effort.

---

[3]For more information on the American Whitewater Affiliation International Scale of River Difficulty, see www.awa.org.

As is the case with river ratings, the ratings for the exercises are modified by appending plus and minus signs to the numerical class values. Thus, a class 3− exercise is an easier class 3, and a class 4+ is a more difficult class 4.

Readers familiar with the river rating system will note the absence of Class 5 and Class 6 exercises. These correspond to "navigable only by experts who can execute without error," and "the extreme limit for experts, no margin whatsoever for error." In river boating, mistakes on any class of water, but especially on class 5 and class 6 water, can be fatal. There is no point in providing class 5 and class 6 in this book.

The rating system for rivers appeals to me for two reasons. First of all, I enjoy white-water boating. Second, as boaters become more proficient and as equipment advances, some rivers that were once considered class 4, say, migrate to class 4− and then 3+ and so on. I expect that with the continued development of numerical software such as MATLAB and with progress in numerical analysis, problems that are difficult today will seem more manageable, and even routine, in the not-too-distant future.

The danger of such optimism is that having successfully navigated a difficult problem, a novice user may assume that he is capable of sustained performance at a high level. Worse yet, ready access to powerful software, fancy graphics, and fast computers can easily seduce the undisciplined user into the belief that she *understands* the computation merely because the steps were executed in the right order and with the proper inputs. In light of these potential distractions, let the goal be to develop solid ability at a particular level, while stretching ones ability on higher class problems. As a teacher of numerical methods, I like to encourage students to jump into the deep water, ever mindful that it is my responsibility to stand by with a rope.

2

Interactive Computing
with MATLAB

This chapter is concerned with MATLAB fundamentals: entering commands, defining and using variables, and creating two- and three-dimensional plots. These operations are performed interactively by typing one command at a time. Since many sophisticated numerical tasks can be performed with just a few concise commands, using MATLAB interactively is highly productive. All interactive commands can be used in programs as well. Thus, the material presented in this chapter is essential to any use of MATLAB. Figure 2.1 summarizes the major topics covered in the chapter.

2.1 RUNNING MATLAB

The details of installing and starting MATLAB depend on the type of computer being used. Once MATLAB is running, however, it presents a consistent interface utilizing drop-down menus, and one or more windows in which commands are entered and output is displayed. The menus are primarily used to manage files, assist command window editing, and control the display. This menu system is relatively small compared with that of most other computer programs. Virtually all numerical computations in MATLAB are performed by typing commands, not by manipulating menus.

Topics Covered in This Chapter

1. Running MATLAB

The use of MATLAB as an interactive expression evaluator is demonstrated. User-defined variables, built-in variables, and a small sample of built-in functions are introduced. The On-line Help system is described.

2. Matrices and Vectors

All MATLAB variables, including scalars and vectors, are treated as matrices. This section describes how to define and manipulate matrix variables. The use of subscripts and **colon notation** to extract and manipulate matrix elements is explained, along with a technique for deleting elements from a matrix.

A **vectorized** operation efficiently performs a mathematical operation on all elements of a vector or matrix. The use of vectorized statements and **array operators** for element-by-element operations on matrices is described.

3. Additional Types of Variables

MATLAB functions for manipulating complex numbers, polynomials, and strings are described and demonstrated by examples.

4. Managing the Interactive Environment

This section shows how to manage, save and reload variables that are used during an interactive session. Reading data from disk files into MATLAB variables is described.

5. Plotting in MATLAB

Functions for creating line, surface, and contour plots are listed and demonstrated. The annotation of plots with axis labels and legends is described.

Figure 2.1   Primary topics discussed in Chapter 2.

The best way to learn MATLAB is to experiment by entering commands in the command window. It would be a good idea to have MATLAB running and enter the commands presented in the text as you read. When MATLAB starts, it opens a single window called the command window and displays the command prompt

```
>>
```

If you are running the educational version of MATLAB, the prompt is

```
EDU>
```

The prompt indicates that MATLAB is ready for input. The basic procedure is to type commands at the prompt and press the return key. Depending on the nature of the command, MATLAB will either respond with a text message in the command window or create another window for graphical output. After the command is executed, another prompt symbol is displayed. This mode of using MATLAB is interactive. (That is, as each command is entered, a response is returned.) In some cases, the response will be just the display of another command prompt, indicating that MATLAB is ready to accept the next command.

Typographical Conventions   Throughout this book, commands will be presented in monospaced font, as in

```
>> help matfun
```

When the prompt symbol precedes the command, it is valid as written, and the command may be directly entered into the command window. When the purpose of the text is to discuss the input and output parameters of a function, no command prompt will be shown, and representative names will be used for the input and output parameters. The parameter names are displayed in a slanted monospace font. For example,

```
ones(nrows,ncols)
```

indicates that the ones function takes two parameters: *nrows* and *ncols*. Since the command did not include a prompt symbol, it is not to be entered exactly as written. A version of the ones function that *can* be entered at the command prompt is

```
>> ones(3,5)
```

Sometimes, comment statements will be used to provide additional information about a function. Comments begin with the % character and extend to the end of the line, as in

```
>> x = sqrt(-4)  %  MATLAB automatically computes with complex numbers
```

When entering a command at the command prompt, one may omit the comments.
       Variables (described in § 2.1.2) are also displayed in monospaced font. If variables are used, they are defined first:

```
>> nr = 2
>> nc = 2
>> ones(nr,nc)
```

Text output resulting from an interactive command is displayed in monospaced font immediately after the command that created the output. The display of commands, variables, and output is intended to mimic the display created by MATLAB on the computer screen. Thus, the preceding commands would be typeset as

```
>> nr = 2
nr =
    2

>> nc = 3
nc =
    3

>> ones(nr,nc)
ans =
    1  1  1
    1  1  1
```

where extra vertical space has been removed for compactness.

2.1.1 MATLAB as an Expression Evaluator

MATLAB can be used to evaluate simple mathematical expressions. To perform a calculation, simply type it into the command window and press return:

```
>> 2 + 6 - 4
ans =
    4
```

The response is in the form `ans = ...` , where `ans` is an automatically defined variable used when an expression is not assigned to a user-defined variable. To continue a calculation, the value stored in `ans` can be recalled:

```
>> ans/2
ans =
    2
```

Instead of merely evaluating an expression, one can assign its value to a variable, as in

```
>> a = 5
a =
    5
```

```
>> b = 6
b =
    6

>> c = b/a
c =
    1.2000
```

where the `ans = ...` response has been replaced with `variableName = ...`, as one would expect.

MATLAB has many built-in functions and a handful of predefined variables. Common trigonometric functions are included in the function set. The input parameters to all functions are enclosed in parentheses, as in

```
>> sin(pi/4)
ans =
    0.7071
```

where the built-in variable `pi` has been used to compute the input argument. All trigonometric functions assume that the arguments are in radians. There is no "degrees mode."

A simple way to display the value of any variable, either built-in or user defined, is to enter the name of the variable at the command prompt and press return:

```
>> pi
ans =
    3.1416
```

In a sequence of commands, the intermediate values may not be interesting, or the echoing of values to the command window might be distracting. The output of individual commands may be suppressed by appending a semicolon to the end of the expression:

```
>> x = 5;
>> y = sqrt(59);
>> z = log(y) + x^0.25
z =
    3.5341
```

The semicolon is not required; it merely indicates to MATLAB that no immediate output is desired. To save space, multiple expressions can be entered on one line. This *requires* that the individual expressions be separated by semicolons or commas. The commas allow more than one command to be entered on a line without suppressing the output:

```
>> a = 5;   b = sin(a),   c = cosh(a)
b =
   -0.9589

c =
   74.2099
```

2.1.2 MATLAB Variables

As the preceding examples illustrate, variables are created as they are used. If a variable does not already exist, it is created whenever it appears on the left-hand side of an equals sign. The value stored in a variable can be changed, of course, by a subsequent assignment:

```
>> t = 5;
>> t = t + 2
t =
     7
```

Any variable appearing on the right-hand side of the equals sign must already be defined. The statement

```
>> x = 2*z
??? Undefined function or variable 'z'.
```

results in an error (in this example) because z has not been previously defined with its own assignment statement.

The names of variables can be up to 31 characters long in MATLAB version 5. Variable names are case sensitive. For example, x and X are two different variables. Variable names must begin with the alphabetic characters a–z or A–Z. After the first character, the remainder of the name can be any combination of the alphanumeric characters, including the underscore, "_". The use of long variable names can be advantageous in documenting code. (See § 4.1.3.) The following statements, for example, perform a familiar geometric calculation that needs no further explanation:

```
>> radius = 5.2;
>> area = pi*radius^2;
```

Very long variable names, on the other hand, can be cumbersome.

TABLE 2.1   BUILT-IN VARIABLES IN MATLAB.

Variable	Meaning
ans	value of an expression when that expression is not assigned to a variable
eps	floating-point precision
i, j	unit imaginary numbers, $i = j = \sqrt{-1}$
pi	$\pi, 3.14159265\ldots.$
realmax	largest positive floating-point number
realmin	smallest positive floating-point number
Inf	∞, a number larger than realmax, the result of evaluating $1/0$
NaN	not a number (e.g., the result of evaluating $0/0$)

2.1.3 Built-in Variables and Functions

MATLAB uses a small number of names for built-in variables. An example is the ans variable, which is automatically created whenever a mathematical expression is not assigned to another variable. Table 2.1 lists the built-in variables and their meanings. Although you can reassign the values of these built-in variables, it is not a good idea to do so, because they are used by the built-in functions. The exceptions to this rule are the built-in variables i and j, which are often reassigned integer values for use as matrix subscripts. (See § 2.2.2.)

The built-in eps variable is called machine epsilon and is used in constructing tolerances. Machine epsilon is discussed in detail in Chapter 5. The realmax, realmin, Inf, and NaN variables are used to handle floating-point exceptions. The realmax and realmin values are the magnitudes of the largest and smallest numbers, respectively, that can be stored in double precision.[1] The Inf ("infinity") and NaN ("not a number") values appear if a floating-point exception has occurred during the calculations. The following calculations are handled in a predictable and reliable way with the values of Inf and NaN:

```
>> x = 0;
>> 5/x
Warning: Divide by zero
ans =
     Inf

>> x/x
Warning: Divide by zero
ans =
   NaN
```

---

[1]The precision of floating-point numbers and its relation to realmax and realmin are discussed in Chapter 5.

The eps, Inf, realmin, and realmax variables are discussed further in Chapter 5.

MATLAB has many very powerful built-in functions. It is good practice to avoid using variables with the same names as built-in functions. This is not always easy, because there are so many MATLAB functions. One might not realize, for example, that gamma is a built-in function to evaluate

$$\Gamma(x) = \int_0^\infty t^{x-1} e^{-t} \, dt.$$

A statement such as

```
>> gamma = 1.4
```

which creates a variable named gamma is not illegal; it merely hides the gamma function from use in the current MATLAB session.

2.1.4 Functions and Commands

It is helpful to make a semantic distinction between *functions* and *commands* that are entered in the command window. A function has input arguments and usually has output arguments. For example, the expression

```
>> y = sin(pi/6)
```

uses the sin function with the input argument pi/6 and assigns the result to the variable y. The help command, in contrast, is used with a space between the command name and its argument, as, for example, in

```
>> help sin
```

In general, commands are used to manipulate the state of the current MATLAB session, whereas functions are used to manipulate MATLAB variables.

The distinction between commands and functions is somewhat artificial, because all commands can be used as functions if the command argument is supplied as a string input, as in

```
>> help('sin')
```

Although commands can be treated as functions, functions can not be treated as commands. The expression

```
>> sin pi
ans =
   -0.8900 -0.9705
```

produces an unexpected result.

Working with MATLAB primarily involves using functions. The difference in syntax between functions and commands is a minor complication, because there are only a small handful of commands, and these all deal with nonnumerical tasks.

2.1.5 On-line Help

The printed manuals for MATLAB provide extensive documentation of all built-in functions. The HTML and PDF versions[2] of the manuals may also be viewed on-screen. In many situations, however, the manuals are not as convenient as the on-line help available directly through the MATLAB command window. On-line help is particularly useful when you need information on how to use a specific built-in function.

To get on-line help for *functionName*, enter

```
help functionName
```

or

```
helpwin('functionName')
```

at the command prompt. The only difference between these two commands is how MATLAB displays the information. The "help *functionName*" command causes the information to be displayed in the command window, whereas "helpwin('*functionName*')" opens up a separate window called the *help browser*.

Suppose, for example, that you cannot remember whether the log function computes the natural logarithm or the base-10 logarithm. Rather than look up "log" in the manual, simply type

```
>> help log
```

and MATLAB responds with

```
LOG Natural logarithm.
 LOG(X) is the natural logarithm of the elements of X.
  Complex results are produced if X is not positive.

 See also LOG10, EXP, LOGM.
```

This concise output provides the necessary information, including references to the related functions log10, exp, and logm.

---

[2]Information on the Adobe Portable Document Format is available at www.adobe.com.

The `lookfor` command can help find functions related to a particular topic. This is especially useful if you want to know whether MATLAB has a function for performing an operation, but you do not know what that function might be called. Typing

```
lookfor searchString
```

initiates a search through all of the functions available to MATLAB. If the `searchString` is part of a function name or part of the first comment line for the function, then the first comment line is printed to the command window. Suppose, for example, you would like to know whether MATLAB has a built-in function to evaluate the hyperbolic cosine function. Using `lookfor` to find "hyperbolic" or "cosine" will return the names of the related MATLAB functions. For example,

```
>> lookfor cosine
ACOS    Inverse cosine.
ACOSH   Inverse hyperbolic cosine.
COS     Cosine.
COSH    Hyperbolic cosine.
```

The output is a list of functions (printed in capital letters) and a short description of what each does. The advantage of using the `lookfor` command is that you do not need to know the name of the function. Once the name is found with `lookfor`, more detailed information is obtained with the `help` command. Specific information on using the `cosh` function, for example, can then be found with

```
>> help cosh
```

2.2 MATRICES AND VECTORS

In the preceding examples, the variables appeared to be scalars. In fact, all MATLAB variables are *arrays*. An array is a collection of values referred to by a single variable name. Individual elements of an array are stored and extracted by specifying the *index* of the element from the beginning of the array. In MATLAB version 5 and later, arrays can be created with any number of indices. For applications dealt with in this book, the arrays have one or two indices that contain either numerical values or characters. (Character arrays, or *strings*, are described in § 2.3.2 beginning on page 48.)

A matrix is a two-dimensional array of numerical values that obeys the rules of linear algebra as described in Chapter 7. Although a little linear algebra is used in this chapter, here we are primarily concerned with defining and using MATLAB matrix variables for simple computational tasks. A scalar is considered to be a matrix with one row and one column. A vector is a matrix with either one row or one column. When a mathematical expression is entered, the MATLAB interpreter parses the expression and evaluates it using the rules of linear algebra. Scalar expressions such as

```
>> a = 2; b = 3;
>> c = a*b
c =
    6
```

are covered by these rules.

Square brackets, [ ], are used to delimit vectors and matrices when they are entered at the command prompt. The following expression creates a row vector with three elements:

```
>> v = [7 3 9]
v =
    7   3   9
```

Elements in a row are separated by spaces or commas. Semicolons separate the rows. An example of a three-element column vector is

```
>> w = [2; 6; 1]
w =
    2
    6
    1
```

and an example of 3 × 3 matrix is

```
>> A = [1 2 3; 5 7 11; 13 17 19]
A =
    1    2    3
    5    7   11
   13   17   19
```

It is also possible to separate rows with a carriage return when a matrix is entered manually:

```
>> B = [ 11    12    13      % press "return" after "13" is typed
         14    15    16
         17    18    19 ]
```

```
B =
    11    12    13
    14    15    16
    17    18    19
```

The dimension of the matrix (or vector) is not specified explicitly.[3] MATLAB automatically keeps track of the number of rows and columns.

2.2.1 Creating Matrices

Matrix variables in MATLAB can be created in any one of the following ways:

- Manual entry
- Expressions that evaluate to a matrix
- Built-in functions that return matrices
- User-written functions that return matrices
- Importing matrix data from files on disk

The preceding examples show how to enter matrices manually. When entering vectors, it is important to distinguish between row and column vectors. According to the rules of linear algebra, row and column vectors are not interchangeable, and the MATLAB interpreter will not allow illegal expressions. A row vector may be converted to a column vector, and vice versa, with the *transpose operator*. In conventional mathematical notation, if v is a vector, then v^T is its transpose. For example,

$$v = \begin{bmatrix} 2 & 4 & 1 & 7 \end{bmatrix} \quad \text{and} \quad v^T = \begin{bmatrix} 2 \\ 4 \\ 1 \\ 7 \end{bmatrix}$$

The MATLAB transpose operator is the single quote appended to a matrix or vector. Corresponding to the preceding mathematical notation, the vector v and its transpose are created in MATLAB with

```
>> v = [2 4 1 7]
v =
    2   4   1   7
```

---

[3]It is possible to "preallocate" matrices to improve efficiency, although this is not necessary. (Refer to § 3.5.2 beginning on page 120.)

```
>> v'
ans =
     2
     4
     1
     7
```

A matrix transpose uses the same notation:

```
>> A = [1 2 3; 4 5 6; 7 8 9 ];
>> A'
ans =
     1    4    7
     2    5    8
     3    6    9
```

The single quote is a small character that is easy to miss. As a result, errors caused by extraneous or missing transpose operators can be literally hard to see.

There are several built-in functions for creating vectors and matrices. A few of these are listed in Table 2.2. The eye function takes either one or two input arguments and creates a matrix with ones on the main diagonal. The single input form of the eye function creates a square identity matrix with the dimension determined by the value of the input parameter, as in

```
>> C = eye(4)
C =
     1    0    0    0
     0    1    0    0
     0    0    1    0
     0    0    0    1
```

TABLE 2.2   SOME BUILT-IN FUNCTIONS FOR CREATING MATRICES.

Function	Returns
diag	matrix with specified diagonal entries; or extracts the diagonal entries of a matrix
eye	identity matrix
ones	matrix filled with ones
rand	matrix filled with random numbers
zeros	matrix filled with zeros
length	the number of elements in a vector
linspace	row vector of linearly spaced elements
logspace	row vector of logarithmically spaced elements
size	the number of rows and columns in a matrix

If two parameters are supplied to the eye function, the first is the number of rows, and the second is the number of columns in the matrix to be created. The diagonal with $i = j$, where i is the row index and j is the column index, is filled with ones:

```
>> D = eye(3,5)
D =
    1    0    0    0    0
    0    1    0    0    0
    0    0    1    0    0
```

The diag function either creates a matrix with specified values on a diagonal or it extracts the diagonal entries. To create a diagonal matrix with diag, the input argument must be a vector. The vector can be created explicitly, as in

```
>> v = [1 2 3];
>> A = diag(v)
A =
    1    0    0
    0    2    0
    0    0    3
```

or it can be specified directly in the input argument, as in

```
>> B = diag([1 2 1 2])
B =
    1    0    0    0
    0    2    0    0
    0    0    1    0
    0    0    0    2
```

To extract the diagonal entries of an existing matrix, the same diag function is used, but with the input being a matrix instead of a vector:

```
>> w = diag(B)
w =
    1
    2
    1
    2
```

The input-dependent behavior of the diag function is an important feature shared by many MATLAB functions. To someone just learning MATLAB, the ability of a single function to perform very different—yet related—tasks can be confusing. Once this concept becomes familiar, however, it becomes a significant advantage, because it reduces the sheer number of functions that need to be remembered.

The ones and zeros functions are very similar: ones creates a matrix filled with ones, and zeros creates a matrix filled with zeros. Both of these functions take two input arguments. The first argument is the number of rows in the matrix, and the second argument is the number of columns:

```
>> D = ones(3,3)
D =
    1    1    1
    1    1    1
    1    1    1
```

Of course, the matrix need not be square:

```
>> E = ones(2,4)
E =
    1    1    1    1
    1    1    1    1
```

Indeed, ones and zeros can be used to create row and column vectors:

```
>> s = ones(1,4)
s =
    1    1    1    1

>> t = zeros(3,1)
t =
    0
    0
    0
```

The linspace function creates row vectors with equally spaced elements. It has the two forms

```
linspace(startValue,endValue)
```

and

```
linspace(startValue,endValue,numPoints)
```

where $startValue$ and $endValue$ are the starting and ending values in the sequence of elements and $numPoints$ is the number of elements to be created. For example, we might have

```
>> u = linspace(0.0,0.25,5)
u =
         0    0.0625    0.1250    0.1875    0.2500
```

In the two-parameter form, $numPoints$ takes the default value of 100.

In its standard form, the `linspace` function creates row vectors. To create a column vector instead, simply append the transpose operator, as in

```
>> v = linspace(0,9,4)'
v =
     0
     3
     6
     9
```

The `logspace` function is similar to the `linspace` function, except that it creates elements that are logarithmically equally spaced. The statement

```
logspace(startValue,endValue,numPoints)
```

creates *numPoints* elements between $10^{startValue}$ and $10^{endValue}$, as in the following expression:

```
>> w = logspace(1,4,4)
w =
        10       100      1000     10000
```

If the third argument is omitted, 50 elements are created between $10^{startValue}$ and $10^{endValue}$.

Example 2.1: A Table of Trigonometric Function Values

The MATLAB statements that follow create vectors containing the values of trigonometric functions. These vectors are then combined to form the columns of a matrix so that the values may be displayed in tabular form:

```
>> x = linspace(0,2*pi,6);
>> s = sin(x);
>> c = cos(x);
>> t = tan(x);
>> [x' s' c' t']
ans =
         0        0    1.0000        0
    1.2566   0.9511    0.3090    3.0777
    2.5133   0.5878   -0.8090   -0.7265
    3.7699  -0.5878   -0.8090    0.7265
    5.0265  -0.9511    0.3090   -3.0777
    6.2832        0    1.0000   -0.0000
```

The expression [x' s' c' t'] creates a matrix whose columns are the transpose of the x, s, c, and t vectors. What happens if the transpose operations are omitted? Can you create a table in which the first row contains the values of x and the second through fourth rows contain the values of s, c, and t, respectively?

2.2.2 Subscript Notation for Matrix Elements

Elements of a matrix can be referred to with a Fortran-like subscript notation. If v is a row or column vector, v(k) selects the kth element. If A is a matrix, A(m,n) selects the element in the mth row and nth column, as in

```
>> A = [1 2 3; 4 5 6; 7 8 9];
>> A(3,2)
ans =
     8
```

In extracting values from a matrix, the use of subscripts outside the current matrix dimensions results in an error:

```
>> A = [1 2 3; 4 5 6; 7 8 9];
>> A(1,4)
??? Index exceeds matrix dimensions.
```

Subscript notation may be used to assign matrix elements:

```
>> A = [1 2 3; 4 5 6; 7 8 9];
>> A(1,1) = 2
A =
     2     2     3
     4     5     6
     7     8     9
```

Unlike attempting to extract an element outside the index range of a matrix, an *assignment* operation can legally refer to row and column indices that do not currently constitute a part of the matrix. If an assignment uses an index that exceeds the current matrix dimension, MATLAB simply increases the size of the matrix to accommodate the new element(s).

```
>> D = eye(3,5)
D =
     1     0     0     0     0
     0     1     0     0     0
     0     0     1     0     0

>> D(4,2) = 2
D =
     1     0     0     0     0
     0     1     0     0     0
     0     0     1     0     0
     0     2     0     0     0
```

Matrices that automatically grow to fit the need are a powerful feature that takes the tedium and complexity out of some linear-algebra tasks. Like many of MATLAB's elegant features, however, this one can also hide pernicious bugs. (See, for example, Exercise 18.)

The `length` and `size` functions are used to determine the number of elements in vectors and matrices. These functions are helpful when one is working with matrices of unknown or variable size, especially when writing loops. (See § 3.4.5–3.4.6.) For example, the following statements create a vector and replace its last element with zero:

```
>> x = 0:5    % define an sample vector
x =
    0   1   2   3   4   5

>> n = length(x)
n =
    6

>> x(n) = 0
x =
    0    1    2    3    4    0
```

The `size` command returns two values and has the syntax

```
[nrows,ncols] = size(matrix)
```

where *nrows* and *ncols* are the number of rows and columns, respectively, in *matrix*. Note that the return parameters must be separated by a comma and enclosed in square brackets. Here are some examples of using the `size` function:

```
>> A = eye(3,5);
>> [nr,nc] = size(A)
nr =
    3
nc =
    5

>> B = zeros(size(A))
B =
    0    0    0    0    0
    0    0    0    0    0
    0    0    0    0    0
```

The second example shows that the output of the `size` function can be the argument of another command. This type of expression is often used to initialize a matrix so that it has the same shape as another matrix. In this example, of course, the definition of the B matrix could be obtained with `B = zeros(nr,nc)`, where `nr` and `nc` are assigned with `[nr,nc] = size(A)`.

2.2.3 Colon Notation

MATLAB has a very powerful and highly compact syntax referred to as colon notation. This notation can be used either to create vectors or, combined with subscript notation (the previous section), to extract ranges of matrix elements. Although colon notation is very terse and a bit tricky to master, it can be used to great advantage.

Two forms of colon notation may be used to create vectors:

```
vector = startValue:endValue
vector = startValue:increment:endValue
```

Here, *startValue* and *endValue* are the endpoints of the interval, *increment* is the spacing between points in the interval, and *vector* is the result. Consider these examples:

```
>> s = 1:5
s =
     1     2     3     4     5

>> t = 0:0.1:0.5
t =
     0    0.1000    0.2000    0.3000    0.4000    0.5000
```

The second example shows that *startValue*, *increment*, and *endValue* need not be integers. As with the `linspace` function, colon expressions create row vectors by default. To create a column vector instead, enclose the expression in parentheses and append the transpose operator:

```
>> u = (1:5)'
u =
     1
     2
     3
     4
     5
```

The parentheses are necessary because the transpose operator has higher precedence than the colon.[4] For example,

---

[4]See § 3.4.2 on page 107 for a discussion of operator precedence rules.

```
>> v = 1:5'
v =
     1    2    3    4    5
```

results in a row vector because the transpose operator is applied to the scalar 5 before the vector is created.

A colon can be used as a wild card to refer to an entire row or column:

```
>> A = [1 2 3; 4 5 6; 7 8 9];
>> A(:,1)
ans =
     1
     4
     7

>> A(2,:)
ans =
     4    5    6
```

Alternatively, a range of values can be selected by using a colon expression in place of a simple subscript:

```
>> A = [1 2 3; 4 5 6; 7 8 9];
>> A(2:3,1)
ans =
     4
     7

>> A(1:2,2:3)
ans =
     2    3
     5    6
```

Colon notation can also be used in assignment operations. The following statements create a matrix of ones and then assign new values to the first row:

```
>> B = ones(3,4);
>> B(1,:) = [2 4 6 8]
B =
     2    4    6    8
     1    1    1    1
     1    1    1    1
```

The second statement can be further contracted with colon notation:

```
>> B(1,:) = 2:2:8
```

In some situations, one needs to retrieve the last value, the second to last value, etc., in a matrix or vector. One way to do this is as follows:

```
>> x = ...          %  define the x vector
>> s = x(end);      %  last element in x
>> t = x(end-1);    %  second-to-last element in x, etc.
```

In this context, the end keyword may be used instead of defining a variable to be equal to the length of the vector. For example, we might have

```
>> x = rand(1,5)
x =
    0.7621    0.4565    0.0185    0.8214    0.4447

>> x(end)
ans =
    0.4447

>> x(end-1)
ans =
    0.8214
```

The end keyword extends to matrices in an obvious way:

```
>> A = [1 2 3; 4 5 6; 7 8 9];   %  define a matrix
>> B = A(2:end,1:end-1)         %  extract lower left corner
B =
    4    5
    7    8
```

2.2.4 Deleting Elements from Vectors and Matrices

Individual elements or groups of elements can be deleted from vectors and matrices by assigning those elements to the null matrix, [ ]. If the x vector has been previously defined, all of its elements are removed by the assignment x = [ ]. Selected elements of the x vector are removed with appropriate subscripts, as in,

```
>> x = 1:5;         %  Create a sample x vector
>> x(3) = []        %  and delete the third element
x =
    1    2    4    5
```

Ranges of vector elements can be deleted with colon notation:

```
>> x = 1:5;
>> x(1:3) = []                         %  Delete the first 3 elements
x =
     4     5


>> x = 1:10;
>> x(1:2:9) = []                       %  Delete odd elements
x =
     2     4     6     8    10


>> x = 1:10;
>> x(length(x)-3:length(x)) = []   %  Delete last 4 elements
x =
     1     2     3     4     5     6
```

The preceding statement can be shortened by the use of the end keyword:

```
>> x = ...
>> x = (end-3,end) = []
```

Deletion operations on matrices must involve entire rows or columns:

```
>> A = [1 2 3; 4 5 6; 7 8 9];        %  Sample matrix
>> A(:,1) = []
A =
     2     3
     5     6
     8     9


>> A = [1 2 3; 4 5 6; 7 8 9];
>> A(3,3) = []
???  Indexed empty matrix assignment is not allowed.
```

The $(3,3)$ element cannot be deleted, because matrices must retain their rectangular shape.

2.2.5 Mathematical Operations with Matrices

The basic arithmetic operations of addition, subtraction and multiplication may be applied directly to matrix variables, provided that the particular operation is legal under the rules of linear algebra. For example, it is permissible to add and subtract two row vectors of equal length:

```
>> u = [10 9 8];    %  u and v are row vectors
>> v = [1 2 3];
>> u+v              %  sum is element by element
ans =

    11    11    11

>> u-v              %  difference is element by element
ans =

    9    7    5
```

The * operator performs the appropriate matrix-matrix, matrix-vector, inner, and outer product, depending on the operands. (The matrix-matrix, matrix-vector, and inner product operations are briefly discussed here; for a more detailed exposition, see Chapter 7.) Given any two compatible matrix variables A and B, the MATLAB expression A*B evaluates the product of A and B as defined by the rules of linear algebra. The following are examples of matrix-matrix and matrix-vector products:

```
>> A = ones(2,3);    B = [1 2; 3 4; 5 6];
>> A*B
ans =
    9    12
    9    12


>> C = diag(1:3); D = ones(3,3);
>> C*D
ans =
    1    1    1
    2    2    2
    3    3    3


>> x = [1; 0; 1];
>> A*x
ans =
    2
    2

>> C*x
ans =
    1
    0
    3
```

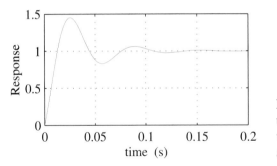

Figure 2.2 Response of an underdamped second-order system with $\omega_n = 104$, $\zeta = 0.3$, and $u_0 = 1$.

The next step is to evaluate the response formula. In a language like C or Fortran, this would require a loop to evaluate x at each value of t. In MATLAB, the computation can be done in one line without a loop:

```
>> x = u0*(1 - exp(-zeta*omegan*t) .* (cos(omegad*t) - gam*sin(omegad*t)) );
```

The array operator, `.*`, is required because the subexpressions `exp(-zeta*omegan*t)` and `cos(omegad*t)` - `gam*sin(omegad*t)` both produce row vectors with 100 elements. The array operator performs an element-by-element multiplication of these vectors before the result is assigned to the x vector. What happens when a simple `*` operator is used?

A plot of the x-versus-t curve created with MATLAB is shown in Figure 2.2. The commands for creating this plot are described in § 2.5.

2.2.6 Reshaping Matrices

Occasionally, data stored in a matrix need to be reorganized without being mathematically transformed. For example, to make a calculation more convenient, it may be desirable to convert a matrix to a vector. If the visual image of a matrix is a rectangle, then converting a matrix to a vector involves changing the shape of the matrix from a squarish rectangle to a long, skinny rectangle. The reshape function is used to perform this operation. In other situations, a trick with colon notation is more elegant.

The reshape function has three input arguments, as in

```
outputMatrix = reshape(inputMatrix,newRows,newColumns)
```

where *inputMatrix* is the matrix to be reshaped and *newRows* and *newColumns* are, respectively, the number of rows and columns in *outputMatrix* created from the elements in *inputMatrix*. The product of *newRows* and *newColumns* must equal the total number of elements in *inputMatrix*. A partially filled last column is not allowed. The following statements illustrate the `reshape` function:

```
>> A = [1 5 9; 2 6 10; 3 7 11; 4 8 12]
A =
      1     5     9
      2     6    10
      3     7    11
      4     8    12

>> B = reshape(A,2,6)
B =
      1     3     5     7     9    11
      2     4     6     8    10    12

>> s = reshape(A,1,12)
s =
      1    2    3    4    5    6    7    8    9    10    11    12
```

The elements in the A matrix are chosen to highlight how the `reshape` function reorganizes the input matrix *by columns*.

Since a row or column vector is also a matrix, the `reshape` function can be used to create rectangular matrices from vectors:

```
>> t = 1:6;
>> C = reshape(t,2,3)
C =
      1     3     5
      2     4     6
```

It is also possible to change the shape of a matrix in place (i.e., without copying it to another matrix):

```
>> D = [ 1 2 3; 1 2 3; 1 2 3 ]
D =
      1     2     3
      1     2     3
      1     2     3

>> D = reshape(D,1,9)
D =
      1    1    1    2    2    2    3    3    3
```

The colon operator can be used to reshape any matrix into a column vector. The operation has the rather unusual syntax

```
columnVector = matrix(:)
```

where the output is always a column vector and the `matrix` on the right-hand side can have any number of rows or columns:

```
>> E = [1 4; 2 5; 3 6]
E =
        1        4
        2        5
        3        6

>> v = E(:)
v =
        1
        2
        3
        4
        5
        6
```

It is not a great restriction that this colon notation trick produces only column vectors. If a row vector is needed, simply append the transpose operator:

```
>> E = [1 4; 2 5; 3 6];
>> w = E(:)'
w =
        1     2     3     4     5     6
```

As with `reshape`, the colon notation trick can be applied to a vector in place:

```
>> y = 1:5;
>> y = y(:)
y =
        1
        2
        3
        4
        5
```

Reshaping with colon notation is very useful when the input to a procedure must be a column vector or must be a row vector. The transpose operator merely flips a row vector to a column vector and vice versa. In contrast, the colon operation `x(:)` always produces a column vector.

The reshaping operations take advantage of the built-in vectorization capabilities of MATLAB. As a result, reshaping operations are much more efficient than the algorithmically equivalent procedure of copying elements one at a time to another matrix of the desired shape.

.3 ADDITIONAL TYPES OF VARIABLES

For most numerical problem solving, MATLAB variables will take on either numeric or string values. Strings are used primarily in labeling plots or in referring to the names of user-defined functions. Numeric values may be either real or complex. This section describes built-in features of MATLAB that support working with complex numbers and strings. A set of functions for manipulating polynomials is described as well.

User-defined MATLAB variables are *objects* that contain several distinct pieces of data. Part of the object contains the numeric or string data that we think of as being stored in the variable. Another part holds the size of the object (i.e., the number of rows and columns in the matrix). In addition, each object contains a list of attributes used internally by MATLAB. One such attribute is a flag indicating whether imaginary data are stored in the object. Users need not worry about these hidden attributes; they are part of the machinery that accounts for the ease of working with MATLAB variables.

2.3.1 Complex Numbers

Complex arithmetic is fully integrated into MATLAB. All variables may be considered to be complex, and the +, −, *, and / operators automatically perform appropriate manipulations of the real and imaginary parts of scalar, vector, and matrix variables. The unit imaginary numbers $i = j = \sqrt{-1}$ are preassigned to the variables i and j. Using i and j in assignment operations allows the creation of complex-valued variables in a natural and obvious way:

```
>> x = 1 + 2*i        %   or, if you prefer,   x = 1 + 2*j
x =
   1.0000 + 2.0000i

>> y = 1 - 2*i
y =
   1.0000 - 2.0000i

>> z = x*y
z =
     5
```

In the preceding statements, a j could be used instead of an i. Regardless of the symbol (i or j) used to represent the unit imaginary number as input, MATLAB always uses an i to *display* imaginary values:

```
>> x = 1 + 2*j
x =
   1.0000 + 2.0000i
```

TABLE 2.3   BUILT-IN FUNCTIONS FOR WORKING WITH COMPLEX NUMBERS.

Function	Operation
abs	Compute the magnitude of a number [i.e., abs(z) is equivalent to sqrt(real(z)^2 + imag(z)^2)]
angle	Angle of complex number in Euler notation
conj	Complex conjugate of a number
imag	Extract the imaginary part of a complex number
real	Extract the real part of a complex number

In assigning complex values, constant scalar multiples of i or j can be indicated with or without the ∗ operator. In other words,

```
>> x = 1 + 2*i
```

and

```
>> x = 1 + 2i
```

are equivalent. Omission of the ∗ is allowed as long as the unit imaginary values i or j are at the end of a subexpression. In other words, the assignment x = 1 + i2 is not allowed. The shorthand notation also does not work with variables, since the notation is ambiguous:

```
>> w = 2;
>> x = 1 + wi
??? Undefined function or variable wi.
```

Note that i and j are just ordinary MATLAB variables that have been preassigned the value $\sqrt{-1}$. If either of these variables is *re*assigned, then the output of the preceding statements will be different. Consider the following calculation:

```
>> i = 5;    t = 8;    u = sqrt(t-i)
u =
    1.7321
```

The assignment i = 5 replaces any previous values stored in the variable named i, so that t-i results in the value 3, not $8 - \sqrt{-1}$. The potential for confusion is easily resolved by following a commonsense rule:

> **When using complex numbers, reserve either i or j for the value of $\sqrt{-1}$.**

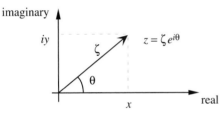

Figure 2.3   Euler notation for complex numbers.

In other programming languages, the i and j symbols are often used as array subscripts. This is also legal in MATLAB, but doing so requires the reassignment of i or j:

```
>> A = [1 2; 3 4];   i = 2;   A(i,i) = 1
A =
      1      2
      3      1
```

Complex numbers can be used in any calculation, as long as the existence of an imaginary part makes sense. Table 2.3 lists built-in functions that are useful for manipulating complex numbers. The exp function supports the use of complex numbers in Euler's notation, $z = \zeta e^{i\theta}$, where ζ is the magnitude and θ is the angle in the polar representation of z. Figure 2.3 shows a complex number represented with Euler notation and Cartesian coordinates in the complex plane. The statements to describe a complex number with $\zeta = 5$ and $\theta = \pi/3$, for example, are

```
>> zeta = 5;   theta = pi/3;   z = zeta*exp(i*theta)
z =
   2.5000 + 4.3301i

>> abs(z)
ans =
      5

>> angle(z)*180/pi
ans =
   60.0000
```

Of course, z could be entered in Cartesian coordinates instead of Euler notation. The real, imag, conj, abs, and angle functions simplify the conversion between these representations.

Multiplication and division operations automatically manage the combinations of complex and real parts:

```
>> s = 3*exp(i*pi/3);   t = 3*exp(i*2*pi/3);
>> s-t
ans =
   3.0000

>> s+t
ans =
   0.0000 + 5.1962i

>> s*t
ans =
   -9.0000 + 0.0000i

>> s/t
ans =
   0.5000 - 0.8660i
```

The preceding calculations have counterparts involving matrices with complex elements:

```
>> A = [1 2; 3 4] + i*[1 2; 3 4]
A =
   1.0000 + 1.0000i 2.0000 + 2.0000i
   3.0000 + 3.0000i 4.0000 + 4.0000i

>> B = abs(A)
B =
   1.4142   2.8284
   4.2426   5.6569

>> C = A*A'
C =
   10      22
   22      50

>> D = A'*A
D =
   20      28
   28      40
```

2.3.2 Strings

Strings are matrices with character elements. The normal rules of assignment and creation of variables apply. The simplest way to create a string is to use it on the left side of an equals sign where the expression on the right side of the equals sign evaluates to a string. String constants are enclosed in single quotes, as in

```
>> first = 'John';
>> last  = 'Coltrane';
>> name  = [first,' ',last]
name =
John Coltrane
```

The first two lines define two string variables. The third line creates a new string variable from three other strings. This type of assignment is the most straightforward way to concatenate strings. Substrings can be extracted with index and colon notation:

```
>> sentence = 'The red ball is on the table';
>> subject = sentence(9:12)
subject =
ball
```

Although strings are often used as row vectors, column vectors are also allowed:

```
>> color = sentence(5:8)'
color =
r
e
d
```

Since the transpose operator and the string delimiter are the same character (the single quote), creating a string column vector with a direct assignment requires enclosing the string literal in parentheses:

```
>> newColor = ('blue')'
newColor =
b
l
u
e
```

String matrices can also be created:

```
>> fruit = ['apples ';'oranges';'kiwis  ']    % notice extra blanks
fruit =
apples
oranges
kiwis
```

As with numeric matrices, all rows of a string matrix must have the same length. When the `fruit` variable is created, "apples" and "kiwis" are padded with spaces so that these strings have the same length as "oranges." The `str2mat` function allows for more convenient creation of string matrices by automatically padding the input strings to the same length. Each input string to `str2mat` is put on a separate row of the output matrix. The preceding assignment statement can thus be replaced with

```
>> fruit = str2mat('apples','oranges','kiwis')
fruit =
apples
oranges
kiwis
```

In creating plots (see § 2.5.2) or creating a printout in a program (see § 3.3.2), it is sometimes desirable to construct a string from numerical data. This is achieved with either the `num2str` or the `sprintf` function. The `num2str` function converts a number to a string with a simple syntax. The `sprintf` function has a more complicated syntax that allows precise control over the number-to-string conversion. A typical use of `num2str` involves building a larger string matrix from smaller components, for example,

```
>> root3 = ['The square root of 3 is ',num2str(sqrt(3))]
root3 =
The square root of 3 is 1.732
```

Note that `num2str(sqrt(3))` returns a string value, so it is not enclosed in quotes. The `num2str` function has an optional second argument used to specify the precision of the display:

```
>> root3 = ['The square root of 3 is ',num2str(sqrt(3),10)]
root3 =
The square root of 3 is 1.732050808
```

The `sprintf` function allows specification of the number of digits in the display, as in

```
>> root3 = sprintf('The square root of 3 is %9.7f',(sqrt(3)))
root3 =
The square root of 3 is 1.7320508
```

or the use of the exponential format:

```
>> root3 = sprintf('The square root of 3 is %11.5e',(sqrt(3)))
root3 =
The square root of 3 is 1.73205e+00
```

The format string of `sprintf` is constructed from the same components as the format string of `fprintf` discussed in § 3.3.2. (For additional information, consult *Using* MATLAB [73].)

2.3.3 Polynomials

MATLAB provides a number of built-in functions that operate on polynomials. A MATLAB polynomial is just a vector of real or complex coefficients, and as such, it is not a distinct data type. Functions for polynomial computations manipulate these vectors of coefficients. The ordinary arithmetic operators (+, -, *) or array operators (.*, ./, .^) may be applied to vectors of polynomial coefficients, but the results are obtained via the rules of linear algebra and MATLAB operator precedence.

A polynomial of degree n is represented by the vector of coefficients when the polynomial is written in *descending* powers of x:

$$P_n(x) = c_1 x^n + c_2 x^{n-1} + \cdots + c_n x + c_{n+1}. \qquad (2.1)$$

The polynomial $x^3 - 2x + 12$, for example, is specified by [1 0 -2 12]. Given a polynomial defined by its coefficients, the `polyval` function evaluates the polynomial at a given x. Thus, to evaluate $x^3 - 2x + 12$ at $x = -1.5$, enter

```
>> c = [1  0  -2  12];
>> polyval(c,1.5)
ans =
   12.3750
```

TABLE 2.4   BUILT-IN FUNCTIONS FOR MANIPULATING POLYNOMIALS. UNLESS OTHERWISE SPECIFIED, THE "POLYNOMIAL" INPUT TO AND OUTPUT FROM THESE FUNCTIONS IS A VECTOR OF COEFFICIENTS THAT DEFINE A POLYNOMIAL IN DESCENDING POWERS OF THE INDEPENDENT VARIABLE.

Function	Description
conv	Compute the polynomial resulting from the product of two polynomials.
deconv	Compute the polynomial resulting from the division of two polynomials.
poly	Create a polynomial having specified roots.
polyder	Compute the polynomial resulting from differentiating a polynomial.
polyval	Evaluate a polynomial $P_n(x)$ at a particular x.
polyvalm	Evaluate a polynomial expression for a square matrix A. Powers of A are evaluated as matrix-matrix products.
polyfit	Compute coefficients of the polynomial $y = P_n(x)$, of degree n, that is the least squares fit of a set of (x, y) data. (See also Chapter 9.)
residue	Compute the partial fraction expansion of the ratio of two polynomials, or, given vectors containing the residues, poles, and direct coefficients, compute the corresponding ratio of polynomials.
roots	Find the n roots of a polynomial of degree n. (See also Chapter 6.)

The two preceding statements can also be combined [i.e., `polyval([1 0 -2 12],` `1.5)`]. If the x input is a vector instead of a scalar, `polyval` returns a vector containing the values of the polynomials evaluated at each x_i:

```
>> c = [1  0  -2  12];
>> x = 1:5;
>> polyval(c,x)
ans =
    11    16    33    68    127
```

Table 2.4 lists the built-in functions for manipulating polynomials in MATLAB version 5.

2.4 MANAGING THE INTERACTIVE ENVIRONMENT

During a MATLAB session, it may be desirable to save some or all of the variables to disk for later use, or load a previously saved set of variables, or clear all or some of the variables from memory. These tasks involve the manipulation of variables in the MATLAB *workspace*.

2.4.1 The MATLAB Workspace

When a variable is defined by a user command, the MATLAB memory manager allocates a chunk of the computer's random access memory (RAM) for the data and the other items necessary to fully describe the variable object. Once a variable is defined, it becomes part of the MATLAB *workspace*. The workspace can be thought of as a list of all variables defined at any one time in a MATLAB session. To see how this works, start up MATLAB and type in the following statements:

```
>> clear
>> a = 5;  b = 2;  c = 1;
>> d(1) = sqrt(b^2 - 4*a*c);    d(2) = -d(1);
>> who
Your variables are:

a          b          c          d
```

The `who` command lists the variables defined in the workspace and the memory used by those variables. The `whos` (who plus "size") command provides more detailed information:

```
>> whos

   Name      Size          Bytes  Class

    a        1x1               8  double array
    b        1x1               8  double array
    c        1x1               8  double array
    d        1x2              32  double array (complex)

Grand total is 5 elements using 56 bytes
```

This table gives the matrix dimension of each variable ("1 × 1" for scalar variables), the number of bytes occupied by the entire matrix variable, and the "class" of the variable. The class defines how the information contained in the variable is stored and accessed in memory, as well as the kinds of operations that are allowed for the variable. The built-in class types are double, sparse, struct, cell, and char. MATLAB also allows user-defined classes. To implement fundamental numerical methods, we only need to use variables in the double class, which is used to store numeric values. The char class will occasionally be used to manipulate character strings, with the primary applications being the creation of formatted output or the labeling of plots. Consult *Using* MATLAB [73] for information on the other classes of variables.

As more variables are defined, they are added to the workspace. The workspace grows until a clear command is issued or until the MATLAB session is ended. Keeping track of variables in the workspace is especially important when one is working with the script files described in § 3.1. When large matrices are used in an interactive session, it may be advantageous to clear some unused variables to free up memory used in the workspace. In that case, the whos command can be used to determine the variables occupying the most memory. Those variables can then be selectively deleted with the clear command, provided, of course, that they are no longer needed. For example, to delete the a and d variables from the preceding sample session, type

```
>> clear a d
```

2.4.2 Working with Data from External Files

Results from a MATLAB session can be saved to disk and reloaded in another MATLAB session, or they may be exported for use with other programs. Data obtained from experimental measurements or saved from other programs can be imported into MATLAB for further analysis. The simplest and least flexible export and import commands are, respectively, save and load. The advantage of using save and load is that the data can be exported or imported in a single step and the user need not be concerned with the details of the input and output (I/O). More powerful functions, though not difficult to use, require the user to perform a few additional steps and to specify explicitly how the data are converted to or from the file.

The save **and** load **Commands**   The save command writes variables defined in the active session to a file. Simple forms of save are as follows

```
save fileName
save fileName variable1 variable2 ...
save fileName variable1 variable2 ...   -ascii
```

In each case, the name of the destination file must be specified. If no list of variables is given, then all variables defined in the workspace are written to the file. The result of the first two forms of the save command is the creation of a binary "mat" file. The mat file format contains the names of the variables and their size, as well as the data stored in the matrix elements. For example,

```
>> clear
>> x = 0:5;    y=5*x;
>> save xyfile
```

creates the file xyfile.mat containing the x and y variables.[7] The save command has an equivalent "function form,"

```
save('fileName','var1','var2', ... )
```

where *fileName* is the name of the mat file to be created and *var1, var2, ...* are the *names* of variables to be stored in the mat file. Using the function form of save, we could create the xyfile.mat file with

```
>> x = 0:5;    y=5*x;
>> save('xyfile','x','y')
```

Note that the input parameters are 'x' and 'y' (i.e., the *names* of the variables).
    The "-ascii" form of the save command creates a plain text file that can be opened with a text editor. For example,

```
>> x = 0:5;    y=5*x;
>> XY = [x' y'];
>> save xyvals.txt  XY  -ascii
```

---

[7]If the clear command had not been issued, any additional variables in the workspace would also be saved to the xyfile.mat file.

creates the plain text file containing

```
0.0000000e+00    0.0000000e+00
1.0000000e+00    5.0000000e+00
2.0000000e+00    1.0000000e+01
3.0000000e+00    1.5000000e+01
4.0000000e+00    2.0000000e+01
5.0000000e+00    2.5000000e+01
```

In the preceding example, the XY matrix needs to be created explicitly, because the MATLAB interpreter can not parse the ' character or square brackets [ ] in the save command. The ascii form of the save command only writes the matrix element values to the file. The names of the variables, their size, and other workspace information are written only when the binary mat format is used. In general, use the non-ascii form of the save command to create a mat file when the variables are to be read into MATLAB at a later date. Use the ascii form when the data are to be imported by another program, such as a spreadsheet or word processor.

The load command is the companion to save for reading data into MATLAB. There are two forms of the load command:

```
load fileName
load fileName matrixVariable
```

The action of the load command depends on the contents of the file being read. The first form, in which only the file name is specified, must be used to load a binary mat file. If *fileName* is a binary mat file, then the variables stored to the mat file are re-created in the current workspace. The second form can be used if the file contains only columns of numbers that correspond to a matrix. If *fileName* is an ascii file containing columns of numbers, then *matrixVariable* is created, and all the data stored in the file are read into the columns of *matrixVariable*.

The syntax of the function form of load is

```
D = load('fileName')
```

where *fileName* is either a mat file or a plain text file containing columns of data. If *fileName* is a plain text file, it can have an extension such as .dat or .txt. If *fileName* is a mat file, the *D* variable created by D = load('*fileName*') is a MATLAB structure. If *fileName* is a plain text file, the *D* variable will be a matrix containing all of the data in fileName. The fileName parameter can also be a path specification, such as

```
>> D = load('C:\myData\someFile.dat');     % DOS/Windows file system
or
>> D = load('~/myData/someFile.dat');      % Unix file system
```

Example 2.3: Loading Matrices from mat Files

Consider the following MATLAB session:

```
>> clear
>> x = linspace(0,2*pi);   y = cos(x);   z = sin(x);
>> save trigvar
```

The result is the creation of the `trigvar.mat` file in the current working directory. Enter pwd at the command line to see the name of the current working directory, and enter dir or ls at the command line to list the names of files in the current working directory.

The `trigvar.mat` file contains the data in the x, y, and z variables, along with the association of the data to the named x, y, and z variables. At some later time, perhaps in the same MATLAB session or perhaps after quitting and restarting MATLAB, the following statements restore the x, y, and z variables from `trigvar.mat`:

```
>> clear        %  clear all variables from workspace (not necessary)
>> whos         %  Now the workspace is empty

>> load trigvar  %  Read contents of trigvar.mat into the workspace
>> whos

   Name      Size        Bytes  Class

   x        1x100          800  double array
   y        1x100          800  double array
   z        1x100          800  double array

Grand total is 300 elements using 2400 bytes
```

Although y and z were defined using a mathematical expression involving x, the data in the `trigvar.mat` file does not reflect that fact. Indeed, the mathematical relationships between variables are never stored in the workspace.

The x, y, and z variables could also be imported with the function form of load:

```
>> load('trigvar')
```

Example 2.4: Loading Data from Plain Text Files

An important application of the load command is reading data from a plain text file for analysis and plotting. For the load command to be successful, the file must contain only numbers organized in columns of equal length. There can be no text, such as column headings.

The `pdxTemp.dat` file in the data directory of the NMM toolbox contains historic average temperature data for Portland, Oregon. The data are organized into four columns, with each row corresponding to a month. To see the contents of `pdxTemp.dat` enter the following statement in the command window

```
>> type pdxTemp.dat
```

If you get a "file not found" error message then the NMM toolbox has not been properly installed on your computer. Refer to the install.m and ReadMe.m files accompanying the NMM Toolbox. The first column in pdxTemp.dat is the month (1 through 12), the second through fourth columns are, respectively, the average high temperature, the average low temperature, and the average temperature for the month. The average high temperature, for example, is the average of all the highest daily temperatures recorded in the month. All temperatures are in degrees Fahrenheit.

The following statements load the data from pdxTemp.dat into MATLAB variables (the comments to the right of the statements provide further elaboration):

```
>> D = load('pdxTemp.dat')      %  Data are stored in D matrix
>> month = D(:,1);              %  Copy first column of pdxTemp to month
>> T = D(:,2:4)                 %  Copy columns 2 through 4 of pdxTemp to T
T =
    45.3600   33.8400   39.6000
    50.8700   35.9800   43.4300
    56.0500   38.5500   47.3000
    60.4900   41.3600   50.9200
    67.1700   46.9200   57.0500
    73.8200   52.8000   63.3100
    79.7200   56.4300   68.0700
    80.1400   56.7900   68.4700
    74.5400   51.8300   63.1800
    64.0800   44.9500   54.5200
    52.6600   39.5400   46.1000
    45.5900   34.7500   40.1700
```

Now that the temperature data are loaded into the T matrix, some simple calculations can be performed. The highest of the monthly high temperatures is

```
>> Thigh_max = max(T(:,1))
Thigh_max =
   80.1400
```

and the lowest of the monthly lows is

```
>> Tlow_min = min(T(:,2))
Tlow_min =
   33.8400
```

The annual average temperature is

```
>> Tave_ave = mean(T(:,3))      %  Find the average of the monthly averages
Tave_ave =
   53.5100
```

The preceding session creates the following variables:

```
>> whos
  Name              Size          Bytes  Class

  pdxTemp           12x4            384  double array
  T                 12x3            288  double array
  Tave_ave          1x1              8  double array
  Thigh_max         1x1              8  double array
  Tlow_min          1x1              8  double array
  month             12x1             96  double array

Grand total is 99 elements using 792 bytes
```

Note that the data are originally stored in the pdxTemp matrix, and this matrix persists after the data are copied to the month and T variables.

The Search Path   When you enter statements like

```
>> x = 2;
>> y = someFunction(x)
```

MATLAB searches through a relatively small number of predefined directories on your computer for the m-file function[8] named someFunction. The list of predefined directories in which MATLAB expects to find m-files and data are called the search path, or, more simply, the path. If an m-file (e.g., someFunction) is not in the search path, MATLAB cannot find the function, so it prints an error message:

```
??? Undefined function or variable 'someFunction'.
```

Similarly, attempting to load data from a file that is not in the search path results in an error:

```
>> load theFile
??? Error using ==> load
theFile.mat: File not found.
```

Although the search path is predefined, it can be changed. Usually, the search path is expanded so that MATLAB looks in additional directories. Customizing the search path allows you to organize your personal MATLAB files into separate directories according to the project or application for the files.

---

[8]m-file functions are described in detail in Chapter 3. For now, all you need to know is that m-files are used to define subprograms that act like the built-in functions in MATLAB. In fact, most of the built-in functions in MATLAB are m-files.

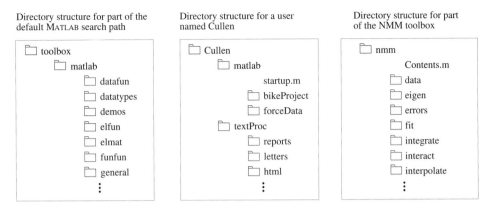

Directory structure for part of the default MATLAB search path

Directory structure for a user named Cullen

Directory structure for part of the NMM toolbox

Figure 2.4   Partial listing of the directory structures for the built-in MATLAB toolbox, a user named Cullen, and the NMM toolbox.

Consider a user named Cullen who stores his files in a subdirectory of a file server. This same computer (or another computer on the network) will have the MATLAB application and (perhaps) a copy of the NMM toolbox. The storage of files into directories is represented schematically in Figure 2.4. All three directory trees in the figure may reside on the same computer, but Cullen will, in general, only be able to modify files in subdirectories of his home directory. When MATLAB is installed, the search path includes the `toolbox` directory. For all users at this site to have access to the NMM toolbox, the system administrator for the file server will need to include the `nmm` directory tree (at the far right of Figure 2.4) to the MATLAB search path. This is achieved by editing the `pathdef.m` file in the `local` directory in the MATLAB home directory. Alternatively, Cullen could install the NMM toolbox in his `matlab` directory and then include that directory in the search path.

For Cullen to include his directories in the search path, he can use the built-in `path` and `addpath` functions. These functions only modify the path for the current session, however. The techniques for telling MATLAB to add specific directories to the search path for each session vary slightly according to the operating system of the computer that is running MATLAB. If Cullen is using a Unix computer, he will need to modify the `startup.m` file, which is located in the `matlab` subdirectory of his home directory. If Cullen is using a Windows computer or a Macintosh, he can use the *path browser* to modify the default path for his sessions. Consult *Using* MATLAB [73] for a complete description of the path-setting options for your particular operating system.

Low-Level Input/Output Functions   `load` and `save` can be thought of as high-level I/O functions. The user issues a single statement that automatically manages the details necessary to transfer data to or from a disk. The cost of this simplicity is a loss of control over the details. For example, the load command can import data stored in mat format or numerical data arranged in columns. This is not helpful, however, if the data are saved in a plain text file organized in columns with text column headings.[9] To read and write data with greater control over the file format, MATLAB provides several low-level I/O functions. Here, we present a limited introduction to these functions, with the goal of showing how to read data from a text file with column headings. When working with these low-level I/O functions, the user must also be aware of peculiarities of the operating system. Consult *Using* MATLAB [73] for more information.

The fopen function establishes a connection between a file and a *file identifier*. The general form of fopen is

```
fid = fopen(fileName,permission)
```

where *fileName* is the name of the file to open (or create), *permission* is a string indicating the kinds of file operations that are to be allowed, and *fid* is the *file identifier*. The most commonly used file permissions are described in Table 2.5. The *fid* returned by fopen is a numeric value that will be a positive integer if the file was successfully opened or -1 if there was an error. The value of *fid* is then used in other file I/O operations. After a file has been used for input or output, it is a good idea to close the link to the file with the fclose to prevent accidental corruption of the file. A typical use of fopen is

```
>> fp = fopen('myFile.dat','rt');   % open text file myFile.dat for input
>> ...                              % read data from myFile.dat
>> fclose(fp)                       % close the file
```

Example 2.5 on page 61 provides another sample usage.

TABLE 2.5   FILE PERMISSIONS COMMONLY USED WITH THE fopen FUNCTION. TYPE "help fopen" FOR MORE INFORMATION.

Permission	File operations
'r'	Open a file for reading.
'w'	Open for writing. Create the file if it does not already exist. *Overwrite* the file if it already exists.
'a'	Open for appending. Create the file if it does not already exist. *Append* data to the end the file if it already exists.

Note: Computers running Windows or VMS require 'rt' and 'wt' permissions to read and write plain text files.

[9]One can, of course, open the data file with a text editor and delete the column headings, but this defeats the purpose of using the headings in the first place.

Once a file is opened with `fopen`, its contents can be read with the `fgetl` and `fscanf` functions. The `fgetl` function reads one line of text from a plain text file. The syntax of `fgetl` is

```
line = fgetl(fid)
```

where *line* is a string variable containing the line of text. Different computer operating systems use different conventions for separating the lines of text in a plain text file. The end of a line is indicated by a special character sequence. The end-of-line character(s) is not included in the *line* string returned by `fgetl`. If the end-of-line sequence is needed (in most cases it is not used), then the `fgets` function should be used. (See *Using* MATLAB [73].)

The `fscanf` function reads data from a file into a single MATLAB variable. C programmers should be aware of important differences in syntax between the MATLAB `fscanf` and the C `fscanf` functions. The general form of the `fscanf` function is

```
x = fscanf(fid,format)
x = fscanf(fid,format,size)
```

where *fid* is a file identifier returned by `fopen` and *format* is a string that indicates how the data are to be interpreted as they are converted to the return variable *x*. (Format conversion strings are listed in Table 3.2 on page 104.) For reading numerical values, the `%f` format string is appropriate, as demonstrated in Example 2.5.

The optional *size* parameter for `fscanf` is used to indicate the extent of the data to be read from the file. If *size* is a scalar n, then the `fscanf` function attempts to read n values from the file using the format specification in *format*. If *size* is a two-element row vector `[m n]`, then the variable returned from `fscanf` is a matrix with m rows and n columns. The use of the corresponding `fprintf` function to write data to a plain text file is described in § 3.3.2 beginning on page 102.

Example 2.5: Loading Data from Plain Text Files with Column Headings

Often, data files contain text headings along with numeric data. The built-in `load` command cannot read data from such a file until the text headings are removed with a text editor. But removing text headings is undesirable, since they provide documentation for the data. Instead of deleting the column headings, one can use the low-level I/O functions `fopen`, `fgetl`, and `fscanf` to read the headings and the numerical data in the file.

To read a file containing both text and data, the structure of the file must be known in advance. In particular, one must know how many lines of text are contained in the file and where those text lines are located relative to the data. The `fgetl` function is used to read the text lines, and the fscanf function is used to read the numeric data. One fgetl function can read only one line of text at a time, whereas multiple lines of numeric data can be read with a single fscanf function.

In Example 2.4, temperature data from the pdxTemp.dat file are read into MATLAB variables with the load command. The same data are contained in the pdxThead.dat file, with the exception that the first line has the column headings "month," "high," "low," and "ave." The following statements read the temperature data from pdxThead.dat:

```
>> fid = fopen('pdxThead.dat','rt');   % Open pdxThead.dat for reading
>> headings = fgetl(fid)               % Read line containing column headings
headings =
month  high    low     ave

>> d = fscanf(fid,'%f');               % Read all data into the d vector
>> fclose(fid)                         % Close the file
>> d = reshape(d,[4 12])'              % Convert to a 12-by-4 matrix,
                                       % note transpose
data =
     1.0000   45.3600   33.8400   39.6000
     2.0000   50.8700   35.9800   43.4300
     3.0000   56.0500   38.5500   47.3000
     4.0000   60.4900   41.3600   50.9200
     5.0000   67.1700   46.9200   57.0500
     6.0000   73.8200   52.8000   63.3100
     7.0000   79.7200   56.4300   68.0700
     8.0000   80.1400   56.7900   68.4700
     9.0000   74.5400   51.8300   63.1800
    10.0000   64.0800   44.9500   54.5200
    11.0000   52.6600   39.5400   46.1000
    12.0000   45.5900   34.7500   40.1700

>> m = d(:,1);          %  copy month data into the m vector
>> T = d(:,2:4);        %  copy temperature data into the T matrix
```

Alternatively, the same effect could be obtained with the statements

```
>> fid = fopen('pdxThead.dat','r');
>> headings = fgetl(fid);
>> d = fscanf(fid,'%f',[4 12])';    %  Read 48 numeric values and store in
                                    %  a 12-by-4 matrix, note transpose
>> fclose(fid)
>> m = d(:,1);      T = d(:,2:4);
```

(See the loadColData function in the util directory of the NMM toolbox for a more general solution to the problem of reading data from files with text headings.)

.5 PLOTTING IN MATLAB

MATLAB can plot numerical data stored in vectors or matrices. The data can be obtained by evaluating an analytical function, or the data can be read from a file. Basic line-plotting functions are used to create a single curve $y = f(x)$ or multiple curves $y_1 = f(x_1)$, $y_2 = f(x_2)$, etc., on a single plot. Two-dimensional data of the form $z = f(x, y)$ are displayed with a contour or surface plot. Three-dimensional objects (i.e., physical objects like chairs, tables, gears and people) can be rendered as shaded surface plots. Each of these types of plot can also be animated by displaying a sequence of images in rapid succession.

Examples of creating basic line, contour, and three-dimensional plots are presented in this section. Additional plotting functions are considered in the end-of-chapter exercises. Readers interested in more sophisticated graphics should consult *Using* MATLAB *Graphics*, [74], and [51].

2.5.1 Line Plots

Line plots are used to display the variation of one variable—the dependent variable—as a function of another variable—the independent variable. Suppose that the vectors x and y contain data evaluated from some function $y = f(x)$. To create a line plot of y versus x, enter the statements

```
>> x = ...        %  create x and y data
>> y = ...
>> plot(x,y)
```

By default, the plot function connects the data with a solid line. To put open circles at each point instead, use

```
plot(x,y,'o')
```

Figure 2.5 contains two examples of simple line plots. Other line and symbol types are available. The general form of the plot function for a single data set is

```
plot(xdata,ydata,symbol)
```

where *symbol* is a string constructed from the characters in Table 2.6. Both the color and symbol (or line) type can be combined so that, for example,

```
plot(x,y,'yo')
```

puts yellow circles at the data points,

```
plot(x,y,'r--')
```

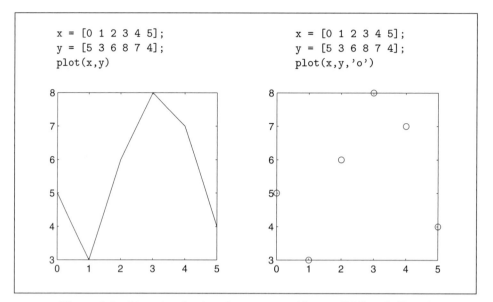

Figure 2.5 Line plots having data connected by a solid line (left) and with symbols only (right).

TABLE 2.6 COLORS, SYMBOLS, AND LINE TYPE SPECIFIERS USED WITH THE `plot` FUNCTION IN MATLAB VERSION 5.

Color		Symbol		Line	
y	yellow	.	point	–	solid
m	magenta	o	circle	:	dotted
c	cyan	x	x-mark	–.	dash dotted
r	red	+	plus	– –	dashed
g	green	*	star		
b	blue	s	square		
w	white	d	diamond		
k	black	v	triangle (down)		
		^	triangle (up)		
		<	triangle (left)		
		>	triangle (right)		
		p	pentagram		
		h	hexagram		

connects the data with with red dashed lines, and

```
plot(x,y,'k+--')
```

plots individual data points with black plus signs and connects the points with a black dashed line.

The same function can be used to place multiple curves on the same plot. For example, to display three curves defined by the vector pairs (x1, y1), (x2, y2), and (x3, y3), use

```
plot(x1,y1,x2,y2,x3,y3)
```

To control the symbols used with each curve, specify the symbol type with a string argument, as in

```
plot(x1,y1,s1,x2,y2,s2,x3,y3,s3)
```

where s1, s2, and s3 are strings constructed from the characters in Table 2.6.

Log-log and semilog plots are created with the `loglog`, `semilogx`, and `semilogy` functions that take the same arguments as the `plot` function. Figure 2.6

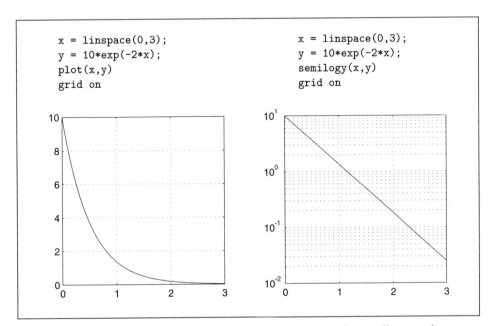

Figure 2.6   Plot of an exponentially decaying function on linear and semilog axes.

gives an example of using `semilogy` to plot an exponential decay. To highlight the difference between the linear and logarithmic scaling of the *y*-axis, the grid is made visible with the `grid` function described subsequently.

2.5.2 Annotating Plots

Axis labels, legends, and other annotations greatly enhance the amount and quality of information conveyed by a plot. These elements are added with the functions listed in Table 2.7.

The `xlabel`, `ylabel`, and `title` functions add text strings to the *x*- and *y*-axes and to the top of the plot, respectively. These functions take a single text string as an argument. Placement of the labels is handled automatically.

The `legend` function places a legend on the plot to identify curves drawn with different symbol and line types. The syntax of `legend` is

```
legend(label1,label2,label3,...)
legend(label1,label2,label3,...,position)
```

where *label1*, *label2*, ... , are strings to be associated with the symbol and line types used in a preceding call to the `plot` (or equivalent) function. The optional *position* parameter determines where in the plot the legend is created. By default, MATLAB tries to locate the legend so that it interferes the least with the lines and symbols used to represent the data.

Suppose, for example, that a plot is to be created from some analytical or experimental data describing the position *x*, velocity *v*, and acceleration *a* of an object and that each of these quantities varies with time. The following statements create a plot of the data and a corresponding legend:

TABLE 2.7 ANNOTATION FUNCTIONS.

Annotation function	Operation(s) performed
axis	Prescribe the minimum and maximum values on the *x*- and *y*-axes.
grid	Draw grid lines corresponding to the major ticks on the *x*- and *y*-axes.
gtext	Add text to a location indicated interactively with mouse input.
legend	Identify symbols and line types used when multiple curves are drawn on the same plot.
text	Add text at a specified (x, y) location.
title	Add a title above the plot.
xlabel	Label the *x*-axis with a text string.
ylabel	Label the *y*-axis with a text string.

```
>> t = ...        % define time data
>> x = ...        % position
>> v = ...        % velocity
>> a = ...        % acceleration
>> plot(t,x,'-',t,v,'*',t,a,'o')
>> xlabel('time  (seconds)')
>> legend('position','velocity','acceleration')
```

The order of the labels in the `legend` function must be consistent with the order of
the data sets in the `plot` function.

Example 2.6: Use of Annotation Functions

In Example 2.4, temperature data from the Portland airport were loaded from a text file
and analyzed. The following statements plot that same data (the `xlabel`, `ylabel`, `title`,
`title`, `axis`, and `legend` functions are used to annotate the plot, which is shown in Figure 2.7):

```
load pdxTemp.dat;      %  Read data into pdxTemp matrix
m = pdxTemp(:,1);      %  Copy first column into m (month) vector
t = pdxTemp(:,2:4);    %  and remaining columns into t (temperature) matrix

%  Create the plot with different symbols for each data set
plot(m,t(:,1),'ro',m,t(:,2),'k+',m,t(:,3),'b-');
```

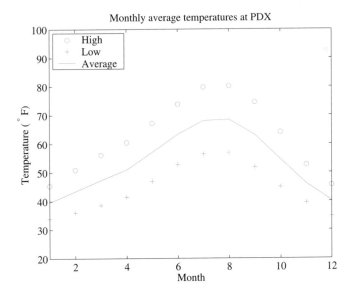

Figure 2.7   Demonstration of annotation functions on a plot of average
monthly temperature variations at the airport in Portland, Oregon.

```
xlabel('Month');                        %  Add axis labels and plot title
ylabel('Temperature ({}^\circ F)');
title('Monthly average temperature for Portland International Airport');
axis([1 12 20 100]);
legend('High','Low','Average',2);       %  Create the legend
```

The degrees symbol in the *y*-axis label is obtained with the TEX string {}^\circ. Refer to
Using MATLAB *Graphics* for information on using TEX strings in annotations [74].

2.5.3 Subplots

Often, it is desirable to place more than one plot in a single figure window. This is
achieved with the subplot function, which is always called with three arguments,
as in

```
subplot(nrows,ncols,thisPlot)
```

where *nrows* and *ncols* define a visual matrix of plots to be arranged in a single
figure window and *thisPlot* indicates the number of the subplot that is being
currently drawn. *thisPlot* is an integer that counts across rows and then columns.
For a given arrangement of subplots in a figure window, the *nrows* and *ncols*
arguments do not change. Just before each plot in the matrix is drawn, the subplot
function is issued with the appropriate value of *thisPlot*. Figure 2.8 shows four

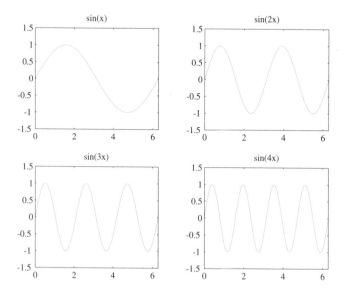

Figure 2.8   Four subplots in a figure window.

subplots created with the following statements:

```
>> x = linspace(0,2*pi);
>> subplot(2,2,1);
>> plot(x,sin(x));       axis([0 2*pi -1.5 1.5]);   title('sin(x)');

>> subplot(2,2,2);
>> plot(x,sin(2*x));     axis([0 2*pi -1.5 1.5]);   title('sin(2x)');

>> subplot(2,2,3);
>> plot(x,sin(3*x));     axis([0 2*pi -1.5 1.5]);   title('sin(3x)');

>> subplot(2,2,4);
>> plot(x,sin(4*x));     axis([0 2*pi -1.5 1.5]);   title('sin(4x)');
```

2.5.4 Surface Plots

A scalar function of two independent variables, $z = f(x, y)$, defines a surface in three-dimensional space. This surface may be represented graphically in a number of ways. The mesh, meshc, surf, surfc, and surfl functions create surface plots with different appearances. The mesh and meshc functions render the surface as a wire mesh. The surf, surfc, and surfl functions render the surface as a collection of small facets filled with color according to different lighting and shading schemes. The meshc and surfc functions combine their respective surface rendering with a contour plot on a $z = $ constant plane beneath the surface. In their most basic forms, the mesh and surf functions take the same input parameters. Only the surf function will be discussed in detail here.

Before attempting to the use the surface plot functions, it makes sense to try the excellent built-in plotting demos available with the

```
>> graf2d2
>> graf3d
```

functions. The adage that pictures are more valuable than words certainly applies to three-dimensional graphics and to the plotting demos provided by the MathWorks.

The surf function may be called in the following ways:

```
surf(Zdata)
surf(xvec,yvec,Zdata)
surf(Xmat,Ymat,Zdata)
```

The function $z = f(x, y)$ is stored in the Zdata matrix and is defined on a grid specified either by the xvec and yvec *vectors* or the Xmat and Ymat *matrices*. If the grid is defined with the vectors xvec and yvec, the surface function $z = f(x, y)$

corresponds to

```
Zdata(i,j) = f(xvec(i),yvec(j))
```

which requires that the grid be rectangular. Arbitrary grids may be specified with the grid matrices *Xmat* and *Ymat*, in which case the surface function corresponds to

```
Zdata(i,j) = f(Xmat(i,j),Ymat(i,j))
```

When no grid is specified [i.e., when `surf(Zdata)` is used] the grid is assumed to be defined by `xgrid = 1:m` and `ygrid = 1:n`, where `[m,n] = size(Zdata)`.

The `surf` and `mesh` functions can be used to plot data from external files or from an analytical function evaluated in MATLAB. In evaluating analytical functions, the `meshgrid` function is often a handy way to generate the (x, y) data used to evaluate $z = f(x, y)$. The statement

```
[X,Y] = meshgrid(xg,yg)
```

creates the $m \times n$ matrices X and Y

$$X = \begin{bmatrix} xg_1 & xg_2 & \cdots & xg_n \\ xg_1 & xg_2 & \cdots & xg_n \\ \vdots & \vdots & & \vdots \\ xg_1 & xg_2 & \cdots & xg_n \end{bmatrix} \qquad Y = \begin{bmatrix} yg_1 & yg_1 & \cdots & yg_1 \\ yg_2 & yg_2 & \cdots & yg_2 \\ \vdots & \vdots & & \vdots \\ yg_m & yg_m & \cdots & yg_m \end{bmatrix}$$

where xg and yg are *vectors* defining grid lines perpendicular to the x- and y-axes, respectively. The use of `meshgrid` and `surf` functions to create a surface plot is illustrated in the following examples.

Example 2.7: Surface Plot of an Analytical Function

Consider the quadratic function

$$z = 2 - x^2 - y^2 \qquad (2.2)$$

defined over the region $-5 \le x \le 5, -5 \le y \le 5$. Creating a surface plot of $z = f(x, y)$ requires (1) definition of the (x, y) grid, (2) evaluation of z at the grid nodes, and (3) construction of the surface with the appropriate `surf` or `mesh` function. The following statements create the surface plot shown in Figure 2.9:

```
>> xg = linspace(-5,5,20);    %  x grid vector (used for y also)
>> [X,Y] = meshgrid(xg,xg);   %  Grid matrices on a square
>> Z = 2 - X.^2 - Y.^2;       %  Vectorized evaluation of Z = f(X,Y)
>> surf(X,Y,Z)                %  Create the surface plot
>> xlabel('x');  ylabel('y'); %  Add axis labels
```

Alternative types of surface plots are explored in Exercise 32.

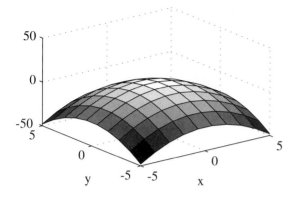

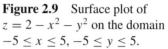

Figure 2.9   Surface plot of $z = 2 - x^2 - y^2$ on the domain $-5 \le x \le 5, -5 \le y \le 5$.

Example 2.8: Demonstration of Surface Plot Types

The following statements illustrate four different surface plot types for the same $z = 2 - x^2 - y^2$ function:

```
>> x = linspace(-5,5,20);       %  x grid vector (used for y also)
>> [X,Y] = meshgrid(x,x);       %  Grid matrices on a square
>> Z = 2 - (X.^2 + Y.^2);       %  Vectorized evaluation of Z = f(X,Y)

>> subplot(2,2,1);  mesh(x,x,Z);      title('mesh plot');
>> subplot(2,2,2);  surf(x,x,Z);      title('surf plot');
>> subplot(2,2,3);  surfc(x,x,Z);     title('surfc plot');
>> subplot(2,2,4);  surfl(x,x,Z);     title('surfl plot');
```

The result is shown in Figure 2.10. More elaborate examples of surface plots are available with the built-in `graf2d2` and `graf3d` demonstration functions.

Viewing Angles and Color Maps   The viewing angle of the surface plot can be changed with the `view` function

```
view(azimuth,elevation)
```

where `azimuth` and `elevation` are angles measured between the line of sight of the observer and the origin of the (x, y, z) coordinate system in which the surface is rendered. These angles are shown in Figure 2.11. The azimuth α is measured in the (x, y)-plane between the projection of the viewer's line of sight and the x-axis. The elevation γ is measured in the plane containing the line-of-sight vector and the z-axis. After a surface plot is rendered, the `view` function changes the perspective on the rendered surface without altering the data that define the surface.

The default viewer perspective is equivalent to

```
>> view(-37.5,15)
```

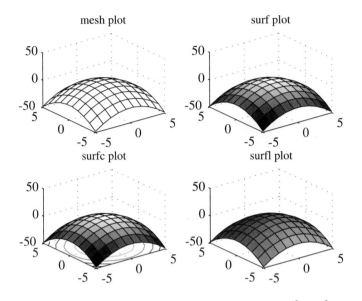

Figure 2.10   Four types of surface plots for $z = 2 - x^2 - y^2$ on the domain $-5 \le x \le 5$, $-5 \le y \le 5$.

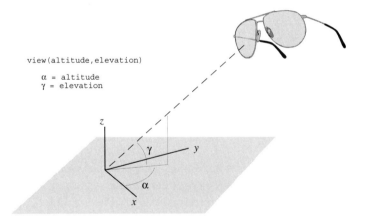

Figure 2.11   The viewing angle for three-dimensional plots is defined by the azimuth α and the elevation γ.

After creating the surface plot in Example 2.7, experiment with the following statements:

```
>> view(-10,15)
>> view(30,15)
>> view(30,0)
>> view(30,45)
>> view(30,60)
>> view(30,90)
```

In addition to changing the viewing perspective, the appearance of the surface can be altered by changing the resolution of the grid, by changing the color map, or by changing the shading. For an analytical function such as Equation (2.2), the number of x and y grid lines can be arbitrarily increased at the expense of time needed to render the image. Increasing the resolution will cause the surface to appear smoother as the planar facets that approximate the surface get smaller.

The color map is a table used to associate a color value with each element of the Z matrix passed to the surf function. MATLAB has predefined color maps referred to by string names such as 'bone', 'cool', 'gray', 'hot, and 'jet'. For example, the statement

```
>> colormap('hot')
```

sets the color map so that numerical values on a surface plot are represented with a color spectrum from dark red to bright red to yellow and then white. (See *Using* MATLAB *Graphics* [74], or enter "help graph3D" at the command line for more details.) As with changing viewing angle with the view function, altering the color map changes the appearance of the surface without affecting the data that define the surface.

The shading of a surface can be chosen with one of the following statements:

```
>> shading('flat')
>> shading('faceted')
>> shading('interp')
```

The default shading is "flat," which results in assigning a uniform color to each of the small planar surfaces used to render the $z = f(x, y)$ surface. The "faceted" shading scheme draws a line around each of the planes created to approximate the surface. This has the effect of accentuating the planes that are a normal part of the default rendering. The "interp" shading scheme renders each small plane with a continuous color variation. This makes the surface appear more smooth without increasing the number of planes with which the surface is constructed.

The graf3d demo allows interactive exploration of the surface-rendering scheme, the color-map specification, and the shading scheme.

2.5.5 Contour Plots

A contour plot shows the "level lines" of the function $z = f(x, y)$ (i.e., the curves for which $z = $ constant). A conventional contour plot is a two-dimensional projection of the level lines onto the (x, y)-plane. Whereas surface plots give an intuitive and visually striking display of the $z = f(x, y)$ data, contour plots can convey more quantitative information. Topographical maps are a common form of contour plot containing large amounts of precise information used for navigation on land. The contour lines on a topographical map are lines of constant elevation above sea level. An experienced map reader can look at a topographical map and see the surface elevations implied by the contour lines.

The contour function has several forms:

```
contour(Zdata)
contour(Zdata,ncont)
contour(Zdata,cvals)
contour(Xgrid,Ygrid,Zdata)
contour(Xgrid,Ygrid,Zdata,ncont)
contour(Xgrid,Ygrid,Zdata,cvals)
```

The function $z = f(x, y)$ is stored in the Zdata matrix, and is defined on the grid in Xgrid and Ygrid. As with the surf function, the grid may be specified by vectors or matrices. The number of contour lines is specified by ncont. Alternatively, one can specify a vector, cvals, containing the precise values of z at which the contour lines should be drawn. (Additional variations on the contour are described in on-line help and in the MATLAB *Language Reference Manual* [75].)

Example 2.9: Contour Plot of an Analytical Function

A contour plot of the surface defined by Equation (2.2) contains the same information as the surface plot in Figure 2.9. The following statements create the contour plot shown in Figure 2.12.

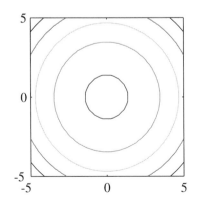

Figure 2.12 Contour plot of $z = 2 - x^2 - y^2$ on the domain $-5 \le x \le 5, -5 \le y \le 5$.

```
>> xg = linspace(-5,5,20);     %  Grid vector
>> [X,Y] = meshgrid(xg,xg);    %  Create matrices of X and Y values
>> Z = 2 - X.^2 - Y.^2;        %  Vectorized evaluation of Z = f(X,Y)
>> contour(X,Y,Z)              %  Create the contour plot
>> axis('square')             %  True aspect ratio for axis
```

The contours are circles, since $z = $ constant implies that $x^2 + y^2 = $ constant. Alternative methods of creating the contour plot are explored in Exercise 34.

Example 2.10: Visualization of Source–Sink Pair

The Laplace equation

$$\frac{\partial^2 \varphi}{\partial x^2} + \frac{\partial^2 \varphi}{\partial y^2} = 0$$

governs potential fields that have applications in electrostatics, magnetism, and ideal fluid flow. Elementary solutions to the Laplace equation may be superposed to construct more general solutions. One of the elementary building blocks is a source–sink pair, as depicted in Figure 2.13. The potential for a source–sink pair is

$$\varphi = \frac{\Gamma}{2\pi} \left[\ln R_{\text{si}} - \ln R_{\text{so}} \right],$$

where Γ is the strength of the source and sink, R_{si} is the distance from a point (x, y) to the sink, and R_{so} is the distance from a point to the source. Of course,

$$R_{\text{si}} = \sqrt{(x + a)^2 + y^2} \quad \text{and} \quad R_{\text{so}} = \sqrt{(x - a)^2 + y^2}.$$

The parameter a locates the source and sink symmetrically on either side of the origin. The following statements create the surface plot and contour plot representation of the $\varphi(x, y)$

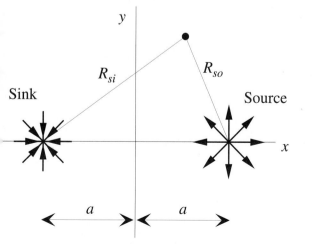

Figure 2.13   Source–sink pair located in the (x, y)-plane.

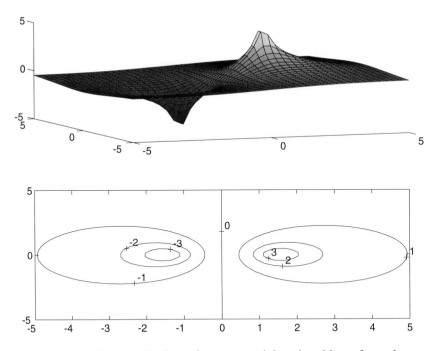

Figure 2.14 Visualization of a source–sink pair with surface plot (above) and labeled contour plot (below).

function shown in Figure 2.14:

```
>> ngrid = 40;                          %  Number of grid lines
>> xg = linspace(-5,5,ngrid);           %  Vector of both x and y grid locations
>> [X,Y] = meshgrid(xg,xg);             %  Prepare for vectorized R calculations
>>
>> gam = 10;                            %  Strength of the source and sink
>> a = 1.5;                             %  Distance from origin to source-sink
>> Rsi = sqrt( (X+a).^2 + Y.^2 );           %  Distance from sink
>> Rso = sqrt( (X-a).^2 + Y.^2 );           %  Distance from source
>> phi = (gam/(2*pi))*(log(Rsi) - log(Rso)); %  Potential function

>> subplot(2,1,1)                       %  First subplot for surface plot
>> surf(X,Y,phi)                        %  Create surface plot
>> view(-20,15)                         %  Adjust the viewing angle

>> subplot(2,1,2)                       %  Second surface plot for contours
>> levels = -3:3;                       %  Contour levels to be drawn
>> cs = contour(xg,xg,phi,levels);      %  Create contours
>> clabel(cs,levels);                   %  and label them
```

2.6 SUMMARY

This chapter presented the primary operations of interactive MATLAB computing. The many functions of MATLAB are best learned by experimentation. For more information about the advanced use of MATLAB functions, see *Using* MATLAB [73], the MATLAB *Language Reference Manual* [75], and reference books such as [34] and [51].

All of the interactive functions discussed in this chapter can be called from user-written MATLAB programs, which are the subject of the next chapter.

EXERCISES

Note: Many exercises require the use of built-in functions that are not described in this chapter. The intention is for you to learn about these new functions through the on-line help or the manuals and then apply the functions to the problem presented.

The number in parentheses at the beginning of each exercise indicates the degree of skill and amount of effort necessary to complete the exercise. (See § 1.4 on page 10 for a description of the rating system.)

OLUTION

1. (1) Use the `lookfor` command to search for functions associated with the string "max." From the list of functions returned, use the `help` facility to determine the function that finds the maximum of all entries in a matrix. Apply this function to find the largest entry in the following matrices:

$$A = \begin{bmatrix} 1 & -5 & -2 \\ 3 & 4 & -9 \\ -7 & 2 & 6 \end{bmatrix}; \quad B = \begin{bmatrix} \sin(1) & \sin(-5) & \sin(-2) \\ \sin(3) & \sin(4) & \sin(-9) \\ \sin(-7) & \sin(2) & \sin(6) \end{bmatrix}.$$

2. (1 each) Evaluate the following quantities by using built-in MATLAB functions:
   (a) $\cosh(5)$
   (b) $\sinh(-2)$
   (c) $(e^5 + e^{-5})/2$
   (d) $\mathrm{erf}(1.2)$, where $\mathrm{erf}(x) = \frac{2}{\sqrt{\pi}} \int_0^x e^{-\eta^2} \, d\eta$ is the error function
   (e) $\beta(1, 2)$, where $\beta(m, n) = \int_0^1 x^{m-1}(1 - x)^{n-1} \, dx$
   (f) $\beta(0.4, 0.7)$
   (g) $J_0(2)$, where $J_\nu(x)$ is the zeroth-order Bessel function of the first kind.
   (h) $Y_0(2)$, where $Y_\nu(x)$ is the zeroth-order Bessel function of the second kind.

3. (2) Use colon notation to create vectors identical to those obtained with the statements that follow. Use multiple statements where necessary. Use MATLAB's built-in `norm` function to test whether two vectors are equal *without* printing the elements. (See § 7.1.2 for a discussion of vector norms.)
   (a) `x = linspace(0,10,5)`
   (b) `x = linspace(-5,5)`

(c) `x = logspace(1,3,3)`
(d) `x = logspace(1,3,5)`

4. (1+) Repeat the preceding problem, but create column vectors instead of row vectors.

SOLUTION **5.** (1+) Use the `linspace` function to create vectors identical to those obtained with the statements that follow. Use multiple statements where necessary. (Use MATLAB's built-in `norm` function to test whether two vectors are equal *without* printing the elements.)

(a) `x = 0:10`
(b) `x = 0:0.2:10`
(c) `x = -12:12`
(d) `x = 10:-1:1`

6. (1+) Repeat the preceding problem, but create column vectors instead of row vectors.

7. (1+) Use the `logspace` function to write a one-line expression that creates the vector $x = [250, 2500, 25000, 250000]$.

8. (1+) Create a sequence of MATLAB expressions that perform the calculations in Example 2.1 on page 30. Create the `x`, `s`, `c` and `t` vectors so that the expression `[x s c t]` displays the table of trigonometric function values. Can you achieve this goal using only one transpose operation? Can you achieve it using no transpose operations?

SOLUTION **9.** (2−) Given the row vector $x = \begin{bmatrix} 10 & 9 & 8 & 7 \end{bmatrix}$ and column vector

$$y = \begin{bmatrix} 1 \\ 2 \\ 3 \\ 4 \end{bmatrix},$$

write at least two different ways to compute the *row vector* z defined by $z_i = x_i - y_i$. Your answers should take only one assignment operation. Do not, for example, explicitly write out equations for all of the elements of z.

10. (1) Write the MATLAB statements to manually enter the matrix

$$A = \begin{bmatrix} 1 & 2 & 3 \\ 4 & 5 & 6 \\ 7 & 8 & 9 \end{bmatrix}, \quad \text{and then obtain the matrix} \quad B = \begin{bmatrix} 7 & 8 & 9 \\ 4 & 5 & 6 \\ 1 & 2 & 3 \end{bmatrix}$$

from A. Do not enter the B matrix manually. (*Hint*: Use "`lookfor flip`.")

11. (1) A matrix can be treated as a collection of row or column vectors. Given the row vectors $u = (1, 2, 3)$ and $v = (4, 5, 6)$, write the (single) statement to create the 2×3 matrix A having u as its first row vector and v as its second row vector.

12. (1) Given the matrix

$$C = \begin{bmatrix} 11 & 5 \\ 2 & 1 \\ 18 & 7 \end{bmatrix},$$

write the two statements to create $s = (11, 2, 18)^T$ and $t = (5, 1, 7)^T$ by extracting the columns of C.

13. (1) Use the `diag` function and colon notation to create the following matrices

(a) $\begin{bmatrix} 1 & 0 & 0 & 0 \\ 0 & 2 & 0 & 0 \\ 0 & 0 & 3 & 0 \\ 0 & 0 & 0 & 4 \end{bmatrix}$ (b) $\begin{bmatrix} 4 & 0 & 0 & 0 \\ 0 & 3 & 0 & 0 \\ 0 & 0 & 2 & 0 \\ 0 & 0 & 0 & 1 \end{bmatrix}$ (c) $\begin{bmatrix} 1 & 0 & 0 & 0 \\ 0 & 7 & 0 & 0 \\ 0 & 0 & 13 & 0 \\ 0 & 0 & 0 & 19 \end{bmatrix}$

Your assignment statement should not involve any zeros.

14. (1+) Use the `diag` function to create the symmetric, $n \times n$, tridiagonal matrix

$$D = \begin{bmatrix} 2 & -1 & 0 & 0 \\ -1 & 2 & -1 & 0 \\ 0 & -1 & 2 & -1 \\ 0 & 0 & -1 & 2 \end{bmatrix}.$$

(*Hint*: The two-parameter form of `diag` will be helpful.)

OLUTION **15.** (1) Use the `eye` and `fliplr` functions to create the matrix

$$E = \begin{bmatrix} 0 & 0 & 1 \\ 0 & 1 & 0 \\ 1 & 0 & 0 \end{bmatrix}.$$

Does the same trick work with `flipud`?

16. (2+) Write a one-line expression to create the following matrix:

$$\begin{bmatrix} 1 & 0 & 0 & 0 & 1 \\ -1 & 1 & 0 & 0 & 1 \\ -1 & -1 & 1 & 0 & 1 \\ -1 & -1 & -1 & 1 & 1 \\ -1 & -1 & -1 & -1 & 1 \end{bmatrix}$$

(*Hint*: One solution uses matrix addition and the built-in `tril`, `ones`, `eye`, and `zeros` commands.)

17. (1) Use the `reshape` function and colon notation to create the following matrices

(a) $\begin{bmatrix} 2 & 8 & 14 & 20 \\ 4 & 10 & 16 & 22 \\ 6 & 12 & 18 & 24 \end{bmatrix}$ (b) $\begin{bmatrix} -5 & -3 & -1 & 1 & 3 & 5 \\ -4 & -2 & 0 & 2 & 4 & 6 \end{bmatrix}$

Your assignment statement should first create a vector with colon notation and then reshape that vector to produce the desired matrix. This can be done in a single statement, if desired.

18. (2−) Consider the following sequence of statements:

```
>> A = ones(3,2);   B = 2*ones(2,3);   A*B;
>> A(2,3) = 2;
>> A*B
??? Error using ==> *
Inner matrix dimensions must agree.
```

Why is the first evaluation of A*B allowable, but not the second evaluation? Which statement created the problem? Assuming that this error was caused by a typo, suggest a correction.

19. (2) Explain the error in the following calculation involving the array operator .*:

```
>> u = 0:3;   v = (3:-1:0)';
>> w = u.*v
??? Error using ==> .*
Matrix dimensions must agree.
```

Why should the inner dimensions matter when a matrix product is not being computed? Suggest a way to create a column vector w such that w(i) = u(i)*v(i) *without* using a loop.

20. (2) For each of the following matrices

$$C = \begin{bmatrix} (9+2) & (-2-2) \\ (3-1) & (1+1) \\ (-3+4) & (7+4) \end{bmatrix} \qquad D = \begin{bmatrix} (9-2^2) & (-2-2^2) \\ (3-1) & (1-1) \\ (-3-4^2) & (7-4^2) \end{bmatrix}$$

$$E = \begin{bmatrix} \frac{9}{2} & \frac{-2}{-2} \\ \frac{3}{-1} & \frac{1}{1} \\ \frac{-3}{4} & \frac{7}{4} \end{bmatrix}$$

(a) Find the value of the element in each column that has the largest absolute value.

(b) Find the value of the element in the entire matrix that has the largest absolute value.

(c) Find the value of the element in the entire matrix that has the smallest absolute value.

Note that the elements of C, D, and E are easily computed by first defining two other matrices:

$$A = \begin{bmatrix} 9 & -2 \\ 3 & 1 \\ -3 & 7 \end{bmatrix} \qquad B = \begin{bmatrix} 2 & -2 \\ -1 & 1 \\ 4 & 4 \end{bmatrix}$$

21. (1+) Write the MATLAB statements to create a table of $y = \text{erf}(\alpha x)$ for $0 \le x \le 5$ and $\alpha = 0.1, 0.3, 0.5, 0.7, 0.9, 1.1$. Use on-line help to find out more about the built-in erf function. Arrange the table so that rows correspond to x values and columns correspond to α values. Choose 10 x values to keep the table short.

22. (2) Why are the error messages different for the `A(k,k)` and `A(i,i)` expressions in the following sequence of statements?

```
>> clear all
>> A = ones(3,3);
>> A(k,k)
??? Undefined function or variable 'k'.

>> A(i,i)
???  Index exceeds matrix dimensions.
```

23. (1) Use hand calculations to verify the complex-arithmetic expressions in the examples involving the `s` and `t` variables on page 48.

OLUTION **24.** (1) Plot $\sin\theta$ versus θ for 60 points in the interval $0 \le \theta \le 2\pi$. Connect the points with a dashed line *and* label the points with open circles. (*Hint*: Users of MATLAB version 4 will need to plot the data twice in order to combine the symbol and line plots.)

OLUTION **25.** (1+) Create a plot of the response of a second-order system with $\zeta = 0$, $\zeta = 0.3$, and $\zeta = 0.9$. Use the formula in Example 2.2, and combine the response curves for all three ζ values on the same plot. Label the axes and identify the curves with a legend.

26. (2+) Write the MATLAB statements to plot $\tan\theta$ versus θ for $-\pi \le \theta \le \pi$. What happens at $\theta = \pm\pi/2$ if all the data are stored in just two vectors (i.e., `theta` and `tanTheta`)? Remedy the situation by dividing the data into three separate arrays and plotting all three sets on the same axes.

27. (1+) Write the MATLAB statements to create a plot of $y = \mathrm{erf}(\alpha x)$ for $0 \le x \le 5$ and $\alpha = 0.1, 0.3, 0.5, 0.7, 0.9, 1.1$. Use on-line help to find out more about the built-in `erf` function. Arrange the plot so that x is on the horizontal axis, and different curves correspond to α values. Choose 100 x values to make the plotted curves look smooth.

28. (1+) Plot the variation of air and water viscosity with temperature from the data that follow. Which function, `plot`, `semilogy`, or `loglog`, creates the "best" plot? Why? The data are stored in the `airvisc.dat` and `H2Ovisc.dat` files in the `data` directory of the NMM toolbox.

T °C	μ_{air} kg/(m·s)	T °C	μ_{H_2O} kg/(m·s)
0	1.720×10^{-5}	2	1.652×10^{-3}
20	1.817×10^{-5}	22	9.590×10^{-4}
40	1.911×10^{-5}	42	6.310×10^{-4}
60	2.002×10^{-5}	62	4.530×10^{-4}
80	2.091×10^{-5}	87	3.240×10^{-4}
100	2.177×10^{-5}	107	2.600×10^{-4}
127	2.294×10^{-5}	127	2.170×10^{-4}
177	2.493×10^{-5}	177	1.520×10^{-4}
227	2.701×10^{-5}	227	1.180×10^{-4}

29. (2) A theoretical model of an athlete in a sprint race is (see W.G. Pritchard, *Mathematical Models of Running*, SIAM Review, Vol. 35, No. 3, pp. 359–379, September 1993)

$$x(t) = a\tau \left[t - \tau(1 - e^{-t/\tau}) \right],$$

where x is the distance traveled in time t, and a and τ are constants for a given runner and distance of the race. Measured values of $x(t)$ for Carl Lewis and Ben Johnson in the 100-meter final at the 1987 World Championships in Rome are given in the following table:

x (m)	0	10	20	30	40	50	60	70	80	90	100
Lewis time (s)	0	1.94	2.96	3.91	4.78	5.64	6.50	7.36	8.22	9.07	9.93
Johnson time (s)	0	1.84	2.86	3.80	4.67	5.53	6.38	7.23	8.10	8.96	9.83

A curve fit to the Lewis data gives $\tau = 0.739$ s and $a = 14.4$ m/s^2. Plot the measured times for Lewis and Johnson versus the theoretical model of Carl Lewis on the same graph. Use a solid line for the theoretical model, and use symbols with no line for the measured data. To make the theoretical curve look smooth at small times, choose a small time increment, say, 0.2 s. Label the axes and add a legend to the plot. The data are available in the `sprint.dat` file in the `data` directory of the NMM toolbox.

SOLUTION **30.** (2) Data in the table that follows were obtained from an experiment in which the theoretical model is $y = 5x \exp(-3x)$. The x_m and y_m values were measured, and the δ_y values were obtained from an uncertainty analysis. Use the built-in `errorbar` function to create a plot of the experimental data with error bars. Use the `hold on` and `plot` functions to overlay a plot of the measured data with the theoretical model. The data are stored in the `xydy.dat` file in the `data` directory of the NMM toolbox.

x_m	0.010	0.223	0.507	0.740	1.010	1.220	1.530	1.742	2.100
y_m	0.102	0.620	0.582	0.409	0.312	0.187	0.122	0.081	0.009
δ_y	0.0053	0.0490	0.0671	0.0080	0.0383	0.0067	0.0417	0.0687	0.0589

31. (2+) Given the sequence of MATLAB statements that follow on the left, what additional *statements* are necessary to create the plot shown on the right? *Do not* create

```
x = [2  3  4  5  6  7];
y = [7  6  6  3  2  3];
z = 5*sin(x);
```

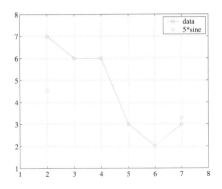

any additional data. Do not worry about the fonts or font sizes in the legend or on the axes. Do not use the interactive plot-editing tools in MATLAB version 5.3 or later.

32. (1) Using the statements in Example 2.7 on page 70 as a guide, create surface plots with the following statements instead of surf(X,Y,Z):

   (a) mesh(X,Y,Z)

   (b) meshc(X,Y,Z)

   (c) surf(X,Y,Z); shading('interp');

   (d) surfc(X,Y,Z); shading('flat');

   (e) surfl(X,Y,Z);

   (f) surfl(X,Y,Z); colormap('bone')

33. (2+) Surface plots do not need to be defined on a rectangular grid. Create a surface plot of $z = 2 + x^2 + y^2$ defined on the domain bounded by the circle $x^2 + y^2 = 5$. The trick is to evaluate the function at points inside the circle. MATLAB's plotting routines will do the hard work. First define the r and θ vectors with

```
>> r = linspace(0,5,20);
>> theta = linspace(0,2*pi,10)
```

Then evaluate the X and Y *matrices* with outer products

$$X_{i,j} = r_i \cos(\Theta_j) \qquad \text{and} \qquad Y_{i,j} = r_i \sin(\Theta_j).$$

The surface function $Z = f(X, Y)$ is evaluated just as in Example 2.7. Contrast the resulting plot from that obtained when X and Y result from

```
>> x = linspace(-5,5,20);
>> [X,Y] = meshgrid(x,x);
```

34. (1) Using the statements in Example 2.9 on page 74 as a guide, create contour plots with the following statements instead of contour(X,Y,Z):

(a) `minz = min(min(Z));   maxz = max(max(Z));`
    `intervals = linspace(minz,maxz,25);`
    `contour(X,Y,Z,intervals);`
(b) `[c,h] = contour(X,Y,Z); clabel(c,h); colorbar('vert')`
(c) `contourf(X,Y,Z)`
(d) `contour3(X,Y,Z)`
(e) `meshc(X,Y,Z)`
(f) `surfc(X,Y,Z)`

3

MATLAB Programming

This chapter covers the structure and syntax of MATLAB programs. New functions used in programming are introduced. Numerous examples are provided. The material presented here assumes that you are already familiar with basic MATLAB functions and working with the command window as described in the preceding chapter.

There are many similarities between MATLAB and other high-level languages. The syntax is similar to Fortran, with some ideas borrowed from C. MATLAB has loop and conditional execution constructs. Subprogram modules act like Fortran subroutines and C functions in that data are passed between modules via input and output parameters. Variables that are not input and output parameters are local to the subprogram. One subprogram can call other subprograms.

Several important features of MATLAB differentiate it from other high-level languages. MATLAB programs are tightly integrated into an interactive environment. MATLAB programs are interpreted, not compiled. All MATLAB variables are sophisticated data structures that manifest themselves to the user as matrices. MATLAB automatically manages dynamic memory allocation for matrices, which affords convenience and flexibility in the development of algorithms. MATLAB provides highly optimized, built-in routines for multiplying, adding, and subtracting matrices, along with solving linear systems and computing eigenvalues.

Topics Covered in This Chapter

1. **Script m-files**
   Script files are useful for automating simple tasks. Script files have no input and output parameters, and they share variables with the command workspace. The creation and limitations of scripts are discussed.

2. **Function m-files**
   Function m-files are programs with input and output parameters. The syntax of function m-files is described.

3. **Input and Output**
   Functions for requesting user input and for creating text output are presented.

4. **Flow Control**
   Conditional statements using `if` constructs, `for` and `while` loops, and related concepts are demonstrated.

5. **Vectorization**
   The use of vectorized statements instead of explicit `for` loops is described. Built-in commands for vectorized search and replacement operations are demonstrated.

6. **Deus ex Machina**
   Special constructs used to solve more complicated programming problems are presented.

Figure 3.1   Primary topics discussed in Chapter 3.

Figure 3.1 summarizes the organization of the chapter. Readers wishing to write their own programs need to be familiar with nearly all the material presented here. The last two sections, "Vectorization" and "Deus ex Machina," can be skimmed on a first reading of the chapter and used as reference for later chapters. Readers who only want to know how to *run* programs will need to understand the use of scripts and functions as described in the first two sections.

3.1 SCRIPT m-FILES

There are two different kinds of MATLAB programs: scripts and functions. Our discussion of programming begins with scripts and then moves on to functions. Scripts are just sequences of interactive statements stored in a file. Typing the *name* of the script at the command prompt has the same effect as typing the contents of the script file at the command prompt. Script m-files have no input or output parameters; hence, they are most useful for those tasks that never change.

Example 3.1: A Script to Define Engineering Constants

Each engineering discipline has a set of physical constants and conversion factors that are commonly used in design calculations. If these constants are defined in a script m-file, they can be quickly referred to during MATLAB calculations. The myCon script in Listing 3.1 is an example of such a script. The myCon script can be found in the program directory of the NMM toolbox. You probably want to modify it to suit your own discipline.

Run the myCon script by typing its name at the command prompt:

```
>> myCon
```

Nothing appears to happen! The statements in the myCon script are executed without any printing to the command window. Once myCon is executed, however, all of the variables defined in the script are added to the workspace. (See § 3.1.2.) After executing myCon, it is easy, for example, to compute the number of (US) gallons in 25 liters:

```
>> 25*galPerLiter
ans =
     6.6043
```

```
% myCon    Defines useful constants in the workspace
%          This must be a script, not a function m-file, in order to add
%          variables defined here to the workspace

% --- fundamental constants
Avagadro = 6.024e23;         %  number of molecules in a mole
cLight = 2.998e8;            %  Speed of light;  m/s
gravity = 9.807;             %  acceleration of gravity,  m/s^2
hPlank = 6.625e-34;          %  Plank's "h" constant;  J*s/molecule
kBoltzmann = 1.380e-23;      %  Boltzmann's constant;  J/K/molecule
Rgas = 8315;                 %  Universal gas constant;  J/kmol/K

% --- unit conversions
galPerMeter3 = 264.17;              %  number of US gallons in a cubic meter
galPerLiter = galPerMeter3/1000;    %  number of US gallons in a liter
inchPerMeter = 1/25.4e-2;           %  number of inches in a meter
inchPerGal = 231;                   %  number of cubic inches in a gallon
lbPerkg = 2.2046;                   %  number of pounds (mass) per kilogram
psiPerPascal = 14.696/101325;       %  number of PSI per Pascal
```

Listing 3.1   A MATLAB script to define physical constants used in engineering analysis.

It may be hard to remember the names of the constants defined in myCon. One easy way to recall the variables is simply to list the contents of the script to the command window:

```
>> type myCon      (Prints the myCon function in the command window)
```

3.1.1 Creating m-Files

MATLAB scripts and functions must be stored in plain text files that end with the extension ".m." These files, not surprisingly, are called m-files. A plain text file contains only the alphanumeric characters found on a typewriter keyboard. None of the special formatting characters included by default in files created by word processors are allowed. Most word processors provide the option of saving the file as plain text. (Look for a "Save As..." option in the "File" menu.) A word-processor is overkill for creating m-files, however, and it is usually more convenient to use a simple text editor or a programmer's editor. On Unix or Linux systems, the emacs or vi editors are commonly used to create m-files.

The Windows version of MATLAB 5 includes a text editor that uses color to highlight language constructs and comments. This syntax coloring provides a significant advantage in editing and debugging. To open a file with the built-in editor, select "Open ... " from the "File" menu. To create a new m-file, select "New ... " from the "File" menu. Consult *Using* MATLAB [73] for information about creating and editing m-files on your particular computing platform.

Example 3.2: A Script to Find Take-Out Food

Suppose that you often do your programming late at night and you sometimes need to get a snack. Suppose also that you are fortunate enough to have several good take-out restaurants in your neighborhood. The problem is that you can never remember their phone numbers. The script file takeout in Listing 3.2 is a solution to this problem. The script defines a series of string variables that contain the telephone numbers of (fictitious) take-out restaurants. Once the script is defined, you can just type takeout at the MATLAB

```
% takeout  Script to display restaurant telephone numbers.
mandarin_cove = '221-8343'
pizza_express = '335-7616'
bernstein_deli = '239-4772'
big_burger = '629-4085'
burrito_barn = '881-8844'
tofu_palace = '310-7900'
```

Listing 3.2   A MATLAB script to display phone numbers of take-out restaurants.

prompt instead of looking up the telephone numbers in the phone book. Before you use the script, though, you will need to create `takeout.m` file and store it in the MATLAB path (Cf. §2.4.2.)

To create this script, select "New" from the MATLAB "File" menu, and type the contents of Listing 3.2 into the editor window.[1] The first line begins with the % character. This is a comment statement that is ignored by MATLAB. Comment statements are described in § 3.1.3. When entering the telephone number, be sure to enclose the numbers in plain single quotes (not the "fancy" left (') and right (') single-quote characters). Save the file with the name `takeout.m` in your working directory.

Once the `takeout.m` file is in the MATLAB path, type `takeout` at the command prompt. The result should be (with extra spaces between lines removed here for compactness)

```
>> takeout

mandarin_cove =
221-8343
pizza_express =
335-7616
bernstein_deli =
239-4772
big_burger =
629-4085
burrito_barn =
881-8844
tofu_palace =
310-7900
```

Variations on the `takeout` script are explored in the end-of-chapter exercises.

Example 3.3: A Script to Plot Functions

Although it is easy to create and annotate plots in MATLAB, sometimes the process involves a little fiddling to get the plot exactly the way you want it. This example shows how a script file (or function m-file) can help in the development of a publication-quality plot. First, the statements used to create a simple version of the plot are stored in a script m-file. Then, by means of successive refinements to the script file, the plot is elaborated. Each time the statements in the script file are changed, the script is rerun, and the plot is re-created.

The basic lesson is that a script (or function) m-file can be used to refine a calculation through trial and error. Because the MATLAB statements are stored in a file, it is easy to start the computations from scratch. To keep the presentation as straightforward as possible, the plot is of familiar trigonometric quantities. The same procedure is applicable to more complicated analytical functions, or to experimental data stored in a text file.

---

[1] You probably want to substitute the names and telephone numbers of your favorite take-out restaurants.

Suppose that we wish to plot $\sin\theta$, $\cos\theta$, and $\sin\theta\,\cos\theta$ for $0 \le \theta \le 2\pi$. In keeping with our strategy of "keep it simple and then refine," open a plain text file[2] and enter the following statements:

```
t = linspace(0,2*pi);
y1 = sin(t);
y2 = cos(t);
y3 = y1.*y2;      % notice the array operator, .*
plot(t,y1,'-',t,y2,'.',t,y3,'--');
```

Save this file as "`trigplot.m`," switch to the MATLAB command window, and enter

```
>> trigplot
```

Assuming that the `trigplot` script contains no typographical errors, the result is that in the top of Figure 3.2. Inspecting the plot, we see that the axes are not labeled and that the $\cos\theta$ curve is not attractive when rendered as dots. To rectify these problems, we change the `plot` statment and add some annotation statements. (We keep the statements defining t, y1, y2, and y3, replace the `plot` statement, and add the `axis` and `legend` statements.)

```
plot(t,y1,'-',t,y2,':',t,y3,'--');
axis([0 2*pi -1.5  1.5])
legend('sin(t)','cos(t)','sin(t)*cos(t)');
```

Now we enter the following statements in the command window:

```
>> close all;  trigplot
```

The `close all` statement closes all open figure windows, forcing MATLAB to open a new figure window when the `plot` statement is encountered. This guarantees that any statements affecting the figure window will be operating without any influence from preceding runs of the script.

Finally, we use TEX notation to display "θ" instead of t, we change the font of the axis labels to Times, and we add a title, also in Times font, with

```
legend('sin(\theta)','cos(\theta)','sin(\theta)*cos(\theta)')
xlabel('\theta (radians)','FontName','Times','FontSize',14)
title('Plot of simple trigonometric functions','FontName','Times',
      'FontSize',12)
```

Then we re-create the plot once more with

```
>> close all;  trigplot
```

---

[2]On Windows computers, select "*New*→m-file" from the *File* menu. On Unix or Linux computers, open a plain text file with a text editor.

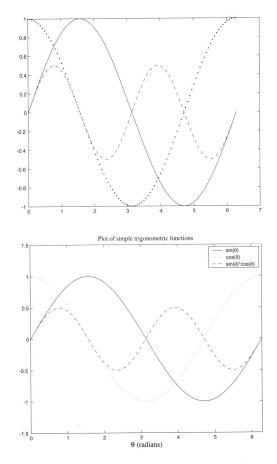

Figure 3.2   Plots created at the beginning and end of developing the `trigplot` script.

The result should be the plot in the bottom half of Figure 3.2. The final version of the `trigplot` script is shown in Listing 3.3.

The important idea in this example is that a script (or function) m-file can be used to incrementally develop a solution. One need not have fully and completely concieved the computing task before starting to write and execute the m-file. Of course, the extreme version of this idea—unplanned flailing in the editor window—is counterproductive. Chapter 4 presents a simple strategy for developing MATLAB programming solutions in a structured and incremental process of refinement.

3.1.2 Script Side Effects

All variables used in a script are added to the workspace. (Cf. § 2.4.1 on page 52.) Variables existing in the workspace will be replaced by any variables of the same

```
% trigplot Script to plot sin(x), cos(x), and sin(x)*cos(x)

x = linspace(0,2*pi);     %  generate data
y1 = sin(x);
y2 = cos(x);
y3 = y1.*y2;              %  y3 = sin(x)*cos(x)

plot(t,y1,'-',t,y2,':',t,y3,'--');
axis([0 2*pi -1.5  1.5])
legend('sin(\theta)','cos(\theta)','sin(\theta)*cos(\theta)')
xlabel('\theta (radians)','FontName','Times','FontSize',14)
title('Plot of simple trigonometric functions',...
      'FontName','Times','FontSize',12)
```

Listing 3.3   Script for plotting data created by editing the script file created in Example 3.3.

name that are defined in the script. This is referred to as a *side effect*[3] of running the script.

The `trigplot` script from the preceding example will be used to show the side effect of running a script. With the `trigplot.m` file in the MATLAB path, enter the following statements in the command window.

```
>> clear
>> who                   (no variable names are displayed)
>> trigplot              (creates x, y1, y2, and y3 in the workspace)
>> who
```

Your variables are:

```
x          y1        y2        y3
```

The `clear` command clears all variables from the MATLAB workspace. The first `who` command shows that, immediately after the `clear` command is executed, there are no variables in the workspace. When the `trigplot` script is executed, the desired plot is created, *and* the x, y1, y2, and y3 variables are added to the workspace, as indicated by the second `who` command.

---

[3] Any action other than transforming the input of a function to the output of the function is a side effect. Practically speaking, a side effect occurs when a program unit changes a variable that is not first created by and then destroyed by that program unit. A common example of a side effect is when a subprogram changes a global variable. Allowing some side effects can give the programmer much greater flexibility. On the other hand, reckless disregard for side effects will surely cause programming errors, often of a kind that is very hard to track down and eliminate.

Suppose that `trigplot` is used as part of a sequence of calculations. If any of the x, y1, y2, or y3 variables were already defined, running the script replaces the content of those workspace variables with data created in `trigplot`. Perhaps this replacement is desirable, as it would be if calculations involving the newly updated x and y1, y2, or y3 vectors were performed following the use of the script. Adding variables to the workspace is the point of the `myCon` script in Example 3.1. On the other hand, running `trigplot` gives no warning that x, y1, y2, and y3 have been replaced. It is possible that subsequent analysis involving these variable names could result in errors because the data stored in those variables have been changed by the script.

Because script files have side effects, it is recommended that function m-files be used almost exclusively for numerical analysis. Function m-files are just as easy to create as scripts, and they are safer and much more flexible.

3.1.3 Comment Statements

The script files in the preceding examples contain comment statements to describe the code. Comment statements consist of any characters between a % and the end of the line. Short comments can appear on the same line as executable statements. Comments that stretch over several lines must have a % at the beginning of each line.

The comment character can be used to turn programming statements on and off. This is convenient during debugging, or to save the steps of an alternative, but unused, procedure for later reference. To deactivate a programming statement, simply insert the comment character (%) into the beginning of the program line in the script or function m-file.

3.2 FUNCTION m-FILES

Function m-files are MATLAB subprograms analogous to Fortran subroutines or C functions. User-defined MATLAB functions work just like the built-in functions. In fact, most of the MATLAB functions are function m-files.[4] Functions are modules of code that communicate with the command window and other functions via a predefined list of input and output parameters. Global variables can also be used to exchange data between modules, as described in § 3.6.2. All other variables defined in the function are local to that function. A local variable can be used only inside the function in which it is defined.

Functions allow the development of modular, reusable, and structured solutions to programming tasks. Routines can be made flexible with input and out-

---

[4]Have a look in the `matlab` directory inside the `toolbox` directory where the MATLAB program is stored.

put parameters. Organizing code into modules helps to manage the debugging and maintenance for a large programming project as described in Chapter 4. For these reasons, function m-files are recommended over scripts for most numerical work.

3.2.1 Function Syntax

The first line of a function m-file has the form

```
function [outputParameterList] = functionName(inputParameterList)
```

where *inputParameterList* and *outputParameterList* are comma-separated lists of variables used to pass data into and out of the function. Unlike subprograms in most other programming languages, MATLAB functions have two parameter lists, one for input and one for output. This syntax reinforces the idea that MATLAB operates on one set of data—the input—and returns another separate set of data—the output.

The first word on the first line of the function definition must always be "function." Following that, the (optional) output parameters are enclosed in square brackets, [ ]. If the function has no output parameter list, the square brackets and the equals sign are also omitted. If there is only one variable in the output parameter list, then the square brackets are optional. Examples of these different forms of function definitions are given in § 3.2.2.

The "functionName" is a character string that is used to call the function. The function name *must also be* the same as the file name (without the ".m") in which the function is stored. In other words, the function "foo" must be stored in the file "foo.m." Following the file name is the (optional) *inputParameterList* enclosed in parentheses. Both the input and output parameter lists consist of valid MATLAB variable names. The variables may be any MATLAB data type, such as vectors, matrices, strings, structs, or cell arrays.

3.2.2 Input and Output Parameters

Listing 3.4 contains a sequence of functions to demonstrate the use of input and output parameters. The calculations performed by these functions are of no particular significance. The functions are contained in three separate m-files: twosum.m, threesum.m, and addmult.m.

The twosum function in Listing 3.4 has two input arguments and no output arguments. The function adds the two input values and prints the result to the screen. The result is not stored in another variable. This is a valid MATLAB operation and is similar to defining the variables x and y in the command window and then typing x + y. The twosum function is provided in the program directory of the NMM tool-

twosum.m

```
function twosum(x,y)
% twosum   Add two matrices and print the result
x+y
```

threesum.m

```
function s = threesum(x,y,z)
% threesum   Add three variable and returns the result
s = x+y+z;
```

addmult.m

```
function [s,p] = addmult(x,y)
% addmult   Compute sum and product of two matrices
s = x+y;
p = x*y;
```

Listing 3.4   Three functions demonstrating the use of input and output parameters. The functions are contained in three separate m-files: twosum.m, threesum.m, and addmult.m.

box. The following interactive statements are starting points for experimentation with the twosum function (Try them!):

```
>> twosum(2,2)
>> x = [1 2];  y = [3 4];   twosum(x,y)
>> twosum(x,y')
>> A = [1 2; 3 4];  B = [5 6; 7 8];  twosum(A,B)
>> twosum('one','two')
```

Does the function work as expected? How does MATLAB compute the sum of two string values, 'one' and 'two'?

Now try

```
>> clear
>> twosum(2,3)
>> disp([x y])
>> who
```

The clear command erases all user-defined variables from the workspace. The twosum(2,3) statement adds 2 and 3, and prints the result to the screen. While the twosum function is executing, the x and y variables belonging to twosum are created and set equal to the input arguments, 2 and 3. When the function terminates, x and y are destroyed (i.e., the memory allocated to these variables is freed). This

simple example demonstrates the powerful idea of local[5] variables. Since x and y are local to the twosum function, they are distinct from any other variables called x and y defined in the workspace. (Compare this behavior with that demonstrated in § 3.1.2 on page 91.)

At the risk of beating the point into the ground, try the following statements:

```
>> clear
>> x = 4; y = -2;          (x and y are defined in the workspace)
>> twosum(1,2)            (local x and y are created and used in the twosum)
>> disp([x y])           (displays workspace variables, not twosum variables)
>> who
```

The threesum function in Listing 3.4 has a single output argument and three input arguments. Once threesum.m is in the MATLAB path, you can type

```
>> a = threesum(1,2,3)
a =
     6
```

The output of threesum does not need to be assigned to another variable as, for example, in

```
>> threesum(4,5,6)
ans =
    15
```

And, of course, the result can be assigned to a variable without printing to the screen by adding a semicolon to the end of the command line:

```
>> b = threesum(7,8,9);
```

The addmult function in Listing 3.4 demonstrates how multiple output parameters are passed out of a function. Remember that the input parameters are always enclosed in parentheses and that multiple output parameters are always enclosed in square brackets. Once the addmult.m file is defined and included in the MATLAB path, it can be called like this:

---

[5]At this point, a computer scientist would introduce the notion of *scope* and explain that the scope of x and y is limited to the function in which they are defined. In contrast to variables in function m-files, all variables used in *script* m-files have the same scope as variables defined and used in the command window.

```
>> [a,b] = addmult(3,2)
a =
    5
b =
    6
```

Unlike functions with single output parameters, failing to assign the output parameters of `addmult` does not make sense; for example,

```
>> addmult(3,2)
```

produces

```
ans =
    5
```

MATLAB cannot be tricked by assigning the two return values to a vector. That is,

```
>> v = addmult(3,2)
v =
    5
```

The preceding experiments demonstrate that *the number of output parameters used when a function is called must match the number of output parameters that the function is expected to return.*[6]

Example 3.4: A Function m-file to Plot Data

A common application of MATLAB programming is in the analysis of experimental data. Suppose you have a plain text file containing (x, y) data pairs from a data acquisition system. Using the `load` command, it is easy to assign the x and y data to MATLAB variables and create the plot. This task becomes tedious, however, when it needs to be repeated for many different data files. It is easy to write an m-file function to automate the loading and plotting of the data.

The `plotData` function in Listing 3.5 uses the built-in `load` function to import data and then create a simple plot. There are four executable statements in `plotData`. The first is a call to the `load` function. After the data matrix is returned from `load`, the first two columns are copied into the x and y variables, and the (x, y) data are plotted. The function listing includes several lines of comment statements at the top. These describe the function and its input and output parameters using a format discussed in §4.1.4 beginning on page 157.

The `xy.dat` file in the data directory of the NMM toolbox contains two columns of data. To plot the data in `xy.dat`, enter

---

[6]This restriction can be relaxed by using the `nargout` utility to build a function that detects the number of output parameters with which the function was invoked. Defining functions with variable numbers of output arguments is discussed in § 3.6.1.

```
function plotData(fname)
% plotData   Plot (x,y) data from columns of an external file
%
% Synopsis:  plotData(fname)
%
% Input:     fname = (string) name, including extension, of the
%                    file containing data to be plotted
%
% Output:    A plot in a separate figure window

data = load(fname);   %  load contents of file into data matrix
x = data(:,1);        %  x and y are in first two columns of data
y = data(:,2);
plot(x,y,'o');
```

Listing 3.5   The plotData function plots data from a plain text file.

```
>> plotData('xy.dat')
```

Note that xy.dat must be enclosed in single quotes, because plotData and load expect a string variable as input. (See Exercises 26 through 27 for variations on the plotData function.)

3.2.3 Primary and Secondary Functions

In MATLAB versions 4 and earlier, each m-file must contain exactly one function. Version 5.x allows multiple functions per *function* m-file. The first function in the m-file is called the *primary function*. All other functions are called *subfunctions*. Only the primary function can be called from the command window or functions in other m-files. Subfunctions in a given m-file can call other subfunctions in that m-file.

Using subfunctions has several advantages. Grouping related functions in a single file reduces the sheer number of m-files that need to be managed. Since subfunctions may be called only by the primary function in an m-file, the same subfunction name can be used with different primary functions. Subfunctions can be used to encapsulate large blocks of code, thereby allowing the primary function to be more compact, making it easier to read and debug. This can be a significant advantage if the subfunction encapsulates a block of code that is used in several places in the primary function.

Example 3.5: Area and Perimeter of an *n*-sided Regular Polygon

The total area a and the total perimeter p of an n-sided regular polygon are given by the following formulas:

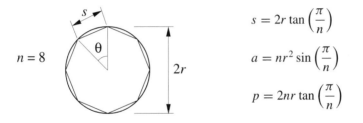

$$s = 2r \tan\left(\frac{\pi}{n}\right)$$

$$a = nr^2 \sin\left(\frac{\pi}{n}\right)$$

$$p = 2nr \tan\left(\frac{\pi}{n}\right)$$

The `polyGeom` function in Listing 3.6 demonstrates the use of a primary function that calls separate subfunctions to compute a and p. (Clearly, the computation of a and p could be easily and more compactly implemented in two lines of MATLAB code, instead of using a subfunction call.) The `area` and `perimeter` subfunctions cannot be called from the command window. This is an advantage, because the names "area" and "perimeter" are rather generic and might be confused with similar codes performing area and perimeter calculations for different geometrical objects.

```
function [a,p] = polyGeom(s,n)
% polyGeom  Compute area and perimeter of a regular polygon
%
% Synopsis:  [a,p] = polyGeom(s,n)
%
% Input:   s = length of one side of the polygon
%          n = number of sides of the polygon
%
% Output:  a = total area of the polygon
%          p = total perimeter of the polygon

r = s/(2*tan(pi/n));   %  "radius" of the polygon
a = area(r,n);
p = perimeter(r,n);

% ============= subfunction "area"
function a = area(r,n)
% area  Compute area of an n-sided polygon of radius r
a = n*r^2*sin(pi/n);

% ============= subfunction "perimeter"
function p = perimeter(r,n)
% perimeter  Compute perimeter of an n-sided polygon of radius r
p = n*2*r*tan(pi/n);
```

Listing 3.6   Demonstrate use of primary functions and subfunctions. The `polyGeom` function computes area and perimeter of a n-sided polygon.

3.3 INPUT AND OUTPUT

The natural way to get data into and out of a function is via the input and output parameter lists. In some situations, alternative input and output mechanisms are advantageous. It may be desirable, for example, to prompt the user for some additional inputs while the function is executing. In other cases, a formatted table of results will be more meaningful than an unlabeled matrix of numerical values. This section describes built-in functions that support these input and output tasks. (Input and output to files are described in § 2.4.2 beginning on page 59.)

3.3.1 Prompting for User Input

The input function prints a message to the screen and waits for the user to enter a response from the keyboard. Here is a simple example;

```
>> x = input('Enter a value for x');
```

The argument of the input function is the prompt string to be displayed. By default, the input function returns a numerical value. To obtain a string input, a second parameter, 's', must be provided, as in

```
>> yourName = input('enter your name ','s');
```

The input function can easily be overused. Consider the modified form of the threesum function in Listing 3.7. Though well meaning, the author of inputAbuse is sure to annoy anyone who will use this function more than once or twice. Relying on the input function as a substitute for input parameters is like putting speed bumps in the path of a competent MATLAB user. To experience this abuse, try the inputAbuse function on several sets of data, and then repeat the analysis with the threesum function. Most users prefer input parameters to unnec-

```
function s = inputAbuse
% inputAbuse  Use annoying input messages to compute sum of three variables
%             Compare this function with threesum

x = input('Enter the first variable to be added ');
y = input('Enter the second variable to be added ');
z = input('Enter the third variable to be added ');
s = x+y+z;
```

Listing 3.7   A variation on the threesum function demonstrating how to abuse the input function.

essary prompting, especially with functions that are to be used as part of a larger and automated analysis. It is far better to provide on-line help to document the input parameters (see § 4.1.4), and let the user supply data via the input parameter list. In general, it is best to use `input` sparingly or not at all.

3.3.2 Text Output

There are two functions for text output: `disp` and `fprintf`. The `disp` function is suitable for simple printing tasks. The `fprintf` function provides fine control over the displayed information, as well as the capability of directing the output to a file. MATLAB also offers a variety of graphical and binary file output options. (Plotting options are described in Chapter 2; see the MATLAB *Language Reference Manual* [75] for information on binary file output.)

The `disp` Function   The `disp` function takes only one argument, which may be either a string matrix or a numerical matrix. To display a simple text message, enclose it in single quotes:

```
>> disp('My favorite color is red')
```

Often, one wants to display a text message along with the value of a program variable. Since `disp` requires only one argument, the message *and* the variable must be combined into a single string. Consider the following code:

```
>> yourName = input('enter your name ','s');
>> disp(['Your name is ',yourName]);
```

The argument of `disp` in this example is the string row vector, `['Your name is ',yourName]`. The comma causes the string `'Your name is '` to be concatenated with the contents of the variable `yourName`.

Displaying a message along with the value of a numeric variable requires the numeric variable to be converted to a string with the `num2str` function:

```
>> x = ...                        %  Assign a value to x
>> outstring = ['x = ',num2str(x)];   %  A string containing the value of x
>> disp(outstring)
```

Explicit creation of the `outstring` variable can be avoided by assembling the output string directly in the argument of `disp`, as in

```
>> disp(['x = ',num2str(x)])
```

The `disp` function can be used to print a table of numbers stored in a matrix or a group of column vectors. Since `disp` can take only one input argument, the columns of the table must be combined into a single matrix, as in the following statements:

```
>> x = 0:pi/5:2*pi;        %  x is a row vector
>> y = sin(x);             %  and so is y
>> disp([x' y']);          %  Transpose x and y and then combine
```

Alternatively x can be created as a column vector:

```
>> x = (0:pi/5:2*pi)';     %  x is a now a column vector
>> y = sin(x);             %  and so is y
>> disp([x y]);            %  no transpose is needed before combining
```

The `format` **Command**   The `format` command controls the display of numerical values in the command window. It is issued once to set the display mode, and stays in effect until the next `format` command is issued. Here are some examples:

```
>> format short;  disp(pi)
      3.1416
>> format long;  disp(pi)
        3.14159265358979
```

Table 3.1 summarizes the effect of the `format` command on the display of numerical values. The `format` command affects the display of numerical values with `disp` and any values printed from expressions that do not end in a semicolon. The `fprintf` function is not affected by the `format` command.

The `fprintf` **Function**   The MATLAB `fprintf` function is similar to the `fprintf` function in the C programming language. It provides versatile control over the printed output, at the expense of a slightly more complicated syntax. The

TABLE 3.1   EFFECT OF THE BASIC `format`
COMMANDS ON THE STATEMENT, `disp(x)`
WHEN x = 1.23456789.

x = 1.23456789; disp(x);	
`format` statement	Output
`format short`	1.2345
`format long`	1.23456789000000
`format short e`	1.2345e+00
`format +`	+
`format bank`	1.23

`fprintf` function has the common forms

```
fprintf(format)
fprintf(format,variables)
fprintf(fid,format,variables)
```

where *format* is a text string indicating how the output is to be formatted, *variables* is a comma-separated list of variables to be written using the information in *format*, and *fid* is a *file identifier* for the file to which the output is sent. The value of *fid* is set with the `fopen` function as described shortly.

The first version of `fprintf` is used to print a simple text message—for example,

```
>> fprintf('Warning:  x is negative\n');
```

The text message is enclosed in single quotes and is terminated with (an optional) \n, the *newline* string. (C programmers, be warned: The format string in the `fprintf` function is contained in single, not double, quotes.) Without \n, the message would be printed, and the command prompt would appear at the end of "negative." Multiple newline strings can be included in the format string to advance the output. It is also possible to break a text message into several `fprintf` functions while inserting newlines as desired.

The second form of the `fprintf` function,

```
fprintf(format,variables)
```

provides formatted output of internal variables. The following example shows how to print the value of a string variable and a scalar numerical value to the screen:

```
>> name = 'Elvis';   age = str2num(datestr(now,10))-1935;
>> fprintf('%s is %d years old\n',name,age);
Elvis is 65 years old
```

The format string contains format codes and optional characters used to construct a string to be displayed. The format code indicates how a variable is to be converted as it is assembled into the output string. The %s format code is used to display a value as a string, and the %d format code is used to display a numerical value as an integer. These codes specify a conversion operation between the internal (binary) representation of a variable and the ASCII characters printed to the output destination. Table 3.2 presents a summary of format codes in their most basic form. More control over the appearance of the output is possible by adding specifiers for the width of the field and (in the case of numerical variables) the number of digits to be displayed to the right of the decimal point. To prescribe the

TABLE 3.2 SUMMARY OF FORMAT CODES FOR USE WITH `fprintf` AND `fscanf`.

Code	Conversion instruction
%s	format as a string
%d	format with no fractional part (integer format)
%f	format as a floating-point value
%e	format as a floating-point value in scientific notation
%g	format in the most compact form of either %f or %e
\n	insert newline in output string
\t	insert tab in output string

field width (i.e., the total number of digits in the output) include an integer between the % and the s, d, f, e, or g in the output specifier. The number of decimal places displayed for floating-point values is controlled by adding a decimal point and a second numerical value between the % and the f or e. The use of field width and precision specifiers in the format code is demonstrated in Table 3.3.

The third form of the `fprintf` function,

`fprintf(fid,format,variables)`

allows the formatted output to be written to a file. To write to or read from a file, a link must be established between the file and the current MATLAB session. The `fid` parameter is a MATLAB variable assigned by the `fopen` function and used in subsequent `fprintf` functions to refer to the file. (The `fopen` function is described in § 2.4.2 on page 59.) The following statements open a file called `myfile.dat` and write the contents of a vector to it:

```
x = ...                           %  define contents of x vector
fout = fopen('myfile.dat','wt');  %  open myfile.dat for output
fprintf(fout,'    k       x(k)\n');
for k=1:length(x)
   fprintf(fout,'%4d      %5.2f\n',k,x(k));
end
fclose(fout)                      %  close myfile.dat
```

TABLE 3.3 EFFECT OF FORMATTING CODES ON VALUES DISPLAYED BY `fprintf`.

Value	%8.4f	%12.3e	%10g	%8d
2	2.0000	2.000e+00	2	2
sqrt(2)	1.4142	1.414e+00	1.41421	1.414214e+00
sqrt(2e-11)	0.0000	4.472e-06	4.47214e-06	4.472136e-06
sqrt(2e11)	447213.5955	4.472e+05	447214	4.472136e+05

The for ... end loop construct is used to sweep through all elements in the x vector. See § 3.4.5 beginning on page 110 for a description of loops in MATLAB; see also *Using* MATLAB [73] or the on-line help for more information on the fscanf, fopen, and fclose functions.

4 FLOW CONTROL

All but the simplest of algorithms require the conditional execution of program blocks. Many algorithms also require repeated evaluation of the same formulas, or application of the same formula to a large number of similar data. The conditional execution of a group of statements is supported with if ... else ... and related constructs. Repeated evaluation is managed with for ... end loops and while ... end constructs. All of these either explicitly or implicitly require some means of testing whether a condition is true or false.

This section begins with a discussion of the relational and logical operators necessary to establish a conditional test. The if ... else ... constructs are discussed next. Following that, looping with the for ... end and while ... end structures is described. The section concludes with documentation of the break and return statements.

3.4.1 Relational Operators

The statement, "is A equal to B?" involves a comparison between the arguments "A" and "B" with the relational operator "is equal to." The arguments "A" and "B" can in turn be complicated relational expressions. Table 3.4 lists the relational operators in MATLAB.

Relation operators can appear in assignment statements:

```
>> a = 2;  b = 4;
>> aIsSmaller = a < b
aIsSmaller =
     1

>> bIsSmaller = b < a
bIsSmaller =
     0
```

The result of a relational operation is either true or false. The numerical equivalent of "true" is any nonzero number, and the numerical equivalent of "false" is zero. In many computer languages, there is a *Boolean* data type used to store true and false values. In MATLAB, the result of relational operations can be assigned

TABLE 3.4 RELATIONAL AND LOGICAL OPERATORS IN MATLAB. THE DISTINCTION BETWEEN THE RELATIONAL AND LOGICAL TYPES IS IMPORTANT IN EVALUATING THE PRECEDENCE OF OPERATORS. (SEE § 3.4.2).

Operator	Type	Meaning	Number of Arguments
<	relational	is less than	two
<=	relational	is less than or equal to	two
>	relational	is greater than	two
>=	relational	is greater than or equal to	two
==	relational	is equal to	two
~=	relational	is not equal to	two
&	logical	and	two
|	logical	or	two
~	logical	not	one

to a matrix variable. The `aIsSmaller` and `bIsSmaller` variables in the preceding example are scalars (1×1 matrices) and may be used in any subsequent numerical expression. Logical operations can be performed by combining relational expressions with the "and," "or," and "not" operators:

```
>> bothTrue = aIsSmaller & bIsSmaller
bothTrue =
     0

>> eitherTrue = aIsSmaller | bIsSmaller
eitherTrue =
     1

>> ~eitherTrue
ans =
     0
```

Relational operations can also be performed on matrices of the same shape, as in

```
>> x = 1:5;   y = 5:-1:1;
>> z = x>y
z =
     0     0     0     1     1
```

The result is a vector of ones and zeros ("true" and "false" values). Such a vector can be used in compact expressions for extracting elements from a matrix, as discussed in § 3.5.3.

3.4.2 Operator Precedence

There is an unambiguous set of rules governing the order in which relational and arithmetic operations are evaluated. For example, the MATLAB expression

```
>> x = 2 + 3^2/4
```

is equivalent to

$$x = 2 + \frac{3^2}{4}, \qquad \text{not} \qquad x = 2 + 3^{2/4},$$

because the exponentiation operator has higher *precedence* than the division operator. Operators with higher precedence are evaluated first. Operators of equal precedence are evaluated as they appear in order from left to right.

The precedence rules are grouped into three categories:

1. arithmetic operators   highest precedence
2. relational operators   ↓
3. logical operators   lowest precedence

Arithmetic operators have a higher precedence than relational operators, which have a higher precedence than logical operators. Thus, in the expression

```
>> y = 3>8-2 | sqrt(15)>4
```

the 8−2 is evaluated before the result is compared with 3, giving a value of "false." Next, the `sqrt(15)>4` is evaluated, giving the result "false." Finally the logical "or" is applied, giving a "false" value, which is assigned to y.

Within the set of arithmetic operators, there is a hierarchy of precedence rules, summarized in Table 3.5. The default rules of operator precedence can be overridden with parentheses. In general, it is good practice to make the intent of an expression obvious by placing parentheses that may not strictly be necessary. The precedence rules are well defined, so that the computer can unambiguously evaluate an expression. Anything that makes the code easier for *humans* will help prevent programming errors. As an example, consider the following two equivalent expressions:

```
x = s.^2/t/3*sin(pi/4*n)          x = ( (s.^2)/(3*t) ) * sin(n*pi/4)
```

Extra parentheses and spaces in the expression on the right remove any ambiguity in how the formula is to be evaluated.

TABLE 3.5 PRECEDENCE OF ARITHMETIC OPERATORS. HORIZONTAL LINES SEPARATE GROUPS OF OPERATORS WITH EQUAL PRECEDENCE. AN OPERATOR GROUP HAS PRECEDENCE OVER OTHER GROUPS THAT APPEAR BELOW IT IN THE TABLE. WITHIN A GROUP, PRECEDENCE IS ESTABLISHED BY THE LEFT-TO-RIGHT ORDER IN WHICH THE OPERATORS APPEAR IN AN EXPRESSION.

Operator	Description
.'	Element-by-element transpose (complex conjugate transpose)
.^	Element-by-element exponentiation
'	Matrix transpose (complex conjugate transpose)
^	Matrix power
+	Unary plus
–	Unary minus (negation)
.*	Element-by-element multiplication
./	Element-by-element right division
.\	Element-by-element left division
*	Matrix multiplication
/	Matrix right division
\	Matrix left division
+	Addition
–	Subtraction
:	Colon operator

3.4.3 if ... else ...

Relational operations are usually combined with an `if ... else` structure to selectively execute blocks of code. The general format is

```
if expression
    block of statements
end
```

Statements in the "block of statements" are executed only if the "expression" is true. Indentation is not required, although it is strongly recommended to make the code easier to read. Here is an example of a simple "if" construct:

```
if a < 0
   disp('a is negative');
end
```

Note that semicolons are not needed for the `if` and `end`, because these partial statements do not evaluate an expression. Short `if ... else` constructs can be combined on one line:

```
if a < 0,  disp('a is negative'); end
```

Here, a comma is required at the end of "if a < 0" to make the statement unambiguous to the MATLAB interpreter.

The if ... elseif ... end construct is used to select one of two mutually exclusive choices:

```
if x >= y
   c = x^2 - y;
elseif y/x > 0.0
   c = log(y/x);
end
```

The elseif block is evaluated only if the first condition is false *and* the second condition is true. If, for example, $x = -2$ and $y = 5$, both of the preceding tests will be false, and the variable c will never be assigned. This may or may not be the intention of the person writing the code. An alternative is to use if ... else ... end, which guarantees that one of the blocks is executed:

```
if x >= y
   c = x^2 - y;
elseif y/x > 0.0
   c = log(y/x);
else
   fprintf('WARNING: either x and y are both negative or x<y\n');
   fprintf('x = %f    y= %f\n',x,y);
end
```

Notice that if the last choice is determined by an else, it will catch all cases that did not match the conditions for the preceding tests. In general, it is good practice to include such a default condition in complex logical tests.

3.4.4 Case Selection with switch Structure

The switch structure is an alternative to a long sequence of elseif blocks in an if ... else ... structure. The syntax of a switch structure is

```
switch  expression
  case value1
    block of statements
  case value2
    block of statements
      ⋮
  otherwise
    block of statements
end
```

```
x = ...                          %  create a vector
sumx = 0;                        %  initialize the sum
for k = 1:length(x)
   sumx = sumx + x(k);
end
```

The expression k=1:length(x) creates a row vector 1:length(x) with unit increments and having the same number of elements as x. The loop is repeated once for each column of the 1:length(x) vector, while the value of k is assigned to the elements of 1:length(x).

Loops with arbitrary indexing can be created by constructing appropriate vectors in the for statement. A loop with an index incremented by two is

```
for k = 1:2:n
   ...
end
```

A loop with an index that counts down is possible, such as

```
for k = n:-1:1
   ...
end
```

as is a loop with noninteger increments:

```
for x = 0:pi/15:pi
   disp(sin(x));
end
```

The MATLAB for ... end syntax is more subtle than the equivalent construct in most other programming languages. The number of times the loop is executed is determined by the number of *columns* in the right-hand side of the vector expression in the for statement. Thus, the loop beginning for x=0:pi/15:pi is executed 16 times, because length(0:pi/15:pi) = 16. Furthermore, the index variable does not need to be a scalar. Consider the following example, which computes the average values in the columns of a matrix:

```
A = [1 2 3; 4 5 6; 7 8 9; 10 11 12];    %  Create a matrix
for v = A                                %  Loop over columns of A
   disp(mean(v));                        %  Print average of current column
end
```

The loop is executed three times, because A has three columns. Each time through the loop, v is assigned to one of the columns of A. It is a good idea to study the preceding statements carefully. Consider, for example, what would happen if the line `for v=A` were replaced with `for v=A'`.

Example 3.7: Horner's Rule

The fourth-order polynomial

$$p_4(x) = b_1 + b_2 x + b_3 x^2 + b_4 x^3 + b_5 x^4 = \sum_{i=1}^{5} b_i x^{i-1}$$

can be evaluated with

$$p = b(1) + b(2)*x + b(3)*x^2 + b(4)*x^3 + b(5)*x^4; \qquad (3.1)$$

assuming that the b_i coefficients are stored in the b vector. Although this statement is straightforward (and algebraically correct), it is not a good implementation of polynomial evaluation. A better implementation, one that uses fewer calculations, is *Horner's rule*, which is also called *nested multiplication*:

$$p = b(1) + x*(b(2) + x*(b(3) + x*(b(4) + x*b(5)))); \qquad (3.2)$$

Equation (3.1) requires 10 multiplications and 4 additions, whereas Equation (3.2) requires 4 multiplications and 4 additions. Because it involves fewer floating-point calculations, Horner's rule is both more efficient and less susceptible to round-off error. (Cf. Chapter 5.)

Storing the polynomial coefficients in an array allows Horner's rule to be implemented with a `for` loop:

```
n = ... ;        %  the polynomial is of order n-1
x = ... ;        %  evaluate the polynomial at this value
p = b(n);
for k=n-1:-1:1
    p = p*x + b(k);
end
```

Occasionally, a polynomial and its derivative(s) are simultaneously required. Since

$$p_n(x) = \sum_{i=1}^{n+1} b_i x^{i-1} \implies \frac{dp_n}{dx} = \sum_{i=2}^{n+1} b_i (i-1) x^{i-2},$$

a single loop can compute both $p_n(x)$ and $dp_n/dx|_x$. (See Exercise 20.) Although Horner's rule is more efficient than using powers of x to evaluate the polynomial, the built-in `polyval` function should be used for routine polynomial evaluation in MATLAB. (See § 2.3.3 and Exercise 21.)

Note that the built-in functions for manipulating polynomials define a polynomial in *descending* powers of x. (See § 2.3.3 on page 51.) The idea of nested multiplication can be applied to polynomials defined in ascending or descending powers of x.

3.4.6 `while` **loops**

The general format of a `while` loop is

```
while expression
    block of statements
end
```

Indentation of the block of statements enclosed by the `while` ... end is strongly recommended. The body of the loop is executed as long as `expression` evaluates to "true."

A `while` loop is useful when, in contrast to a `for` loop, the calculations are to be repeated an undetermined number of times. Such calculations are typical of iterative procedures in which an initial guess is refined until some condition is met. Here is a simple (and rather useless) loop:

```
x = 1;
while x > 0.01
    x = x/2;
end
disp(x)
```

The first time the `while` statement is encountered, the value of x is obviously greater than 0.01, so the body of the loop is executed. The loop is repeated until the test returns a value of "false." It is always possible (see, e.g., Exercise 6) to use a `for` loop instead of a `while` loop.

Example 3.8: Newton Iterations for Computing $\sqrt{x}$

A formula using Newton's method to compute the square root of x is

$$r_k = \frac{1}{2}\left(r_{k-1} + \frac{x}{r_{k-1}}\right), \tag{3.3}$$

where r_k is the kth approximation to $\sqrt{x}$. The calculations begin with an initial guess, usually $r_0 = x$, and proceed until two subsequent approximations to the root are so close together that the difference between them is negligible. One implementation of this algorithm is

```
delta = ...               %  set convergence tolerance
r = ...                   %  initialize r and rold
rold = ...
while abs(rold-r) > delta
    rold = r;             %  save old value for convergence test
    r = 0.5*(rold + x/rold);  %  update the guess at the root
end
```

where delta is an appropriately chosen convergence tolerance. (See also § 5.2.4.) The while loop is preferable to a for loop in this situation, because the number of iterations required to reach convergence is not known at the start of the loop. Usually, it is a good idea to put an upper limit on the number of iterations performed by a while loop. A safer version of the square-root calculations would be

```
delta = ...                   %  set convergence tolerance
r = ...                       %  initialize r and rold
rold = ...
it = 0;                       %  intialize iteration counter
maxit = 25;                   %  maximum number of iterations
while abs(rold-r) > delta & it<maxit
   rold = r;                  %  save old value for convergence test
   r = 0.5*(rold + x/rold);   %  update the guess at the root
   it = it + 1;               %  increment the iteration counter
end
```

The logical test in the while statement requires both conditions to be true for the loop body to be executed.

3.4.7 The break Command

In a repetitive calculation involving a while ... end construct, there should be some sort of escape mechanism to prevent an infinite loop. This can often be achieved by setting an upper limit on the number of iterations. For example, the following loop iteratively updates x until the change in the value of x from one iteration to the next is less than a tolerance:

```
iter = 0;            %  iteration counter
tol = ...            %  convergence tolerance
xold = ...           %  initial values
x = ...
while iter<maxit
   xold = x;                     %  save for convergence check
   x = ...                       %  update x
   iter = iter + 1
   if abs((x-xold)/xold)<tol     %  Test for convergence.  If true,
     break;                      %  jump to first statement after
   end                          %  the enclosing while...end
end
```

When a break command is encountered, the enclosing while loop is immediately terminated, and execution continues at the first statement after the loop. The break command can also be used inside a for ... end loop. (Cf. Exercise 6.) Note that the break statement in

```
function k = demoBreak(n)
% demoBreak  Show how "break" command causes exit from a while loop
%            Search a random vector to find index of first element
%            greater than 0.8.
%
% Synopsis:  k = demoBreak(n)
%
% Input:     n = size of random vector to be generated
%
% Output:    k = first (smallest) index in x such that x(k)>0.8
x = rand(1,n);
k = 1;
while k<=n
   if x(k)>0.8
     break
   end
   k = k + 1;
end
fprintf('x(k)=%f   for k = %d   n = %d\n',x(k),k,n);

%  What happens if loop terminates without finding x(k)>0.8 ?
```

Listing 3.9 Simple function to demonstrate use of the break command.

```
while ...
   if ...
      break;
   end
end
```

refers, *not* to the if ... end block, but to the while ... end structure that *encloses* the if ... end block.

Example 3.9: Using the break Command

The demoBreak function in Listing 3.9 is a contrived program to demonstrate the use of the break command. A vector of length n is created with elements that are random numbers with magnitude between 0 and 1. (See "help rand".) The loop is used to examine each element of the vector. The function returns the index of the first element greater than 0.8. For example, three possible outcomes are

```
>> demoBreak(5)        %  your results are likely to differ
ans =
    3
```

```
>> demoBreak(35)
ans =
     1

>> demoBreak(35)
ans =
     7
```

Notice that the `break` command refers, not to the `if ... end` construct, but rather, to the `while ... end` construct. When a value of `x(k)>0` is encountered, execution is transferred to the `fprintf` statement immediately after the `while ... end`.

The `demoBreak` function contains a bug, as suggested by the comment statement in the last line of the function. Fixing the bug is the objective of Exercise 40.

3.4.8 The `return` Command

Whereas the `break` command causes the enclosing loop to terminate, the `return` command causes the currently executing function (m-file) to terminate. When a `return` command is encountered, the values of all currently defined output parameters are passed back to the calling function, or to the workspace if the function was called from the command line. Figure 3.3 illustrates the difference between the `break` and `return` statements.

Example 3.10: Using the `return` Command

The `demoReturn` function in Listing 3.10 is a variation of the preceding example. Instead of exiting the loop with the `break` command, a `return` command is used to exit the function entirely. Note that the `demoReturn` function contains the same bug as the `demoBreak` function.

```
function k = demoBreak(n)                    function k = demoReturn(n)

...                                          ...

while k<=n                                   while k<=n
   if x(k)>0.8                                  if x(k)>0.8
      break;                                       return;              return to calling
   end                                          end                    function
   k = k + 1;                                   k = k + 1;
end                                          end

        jump to end of enclosing
        "while ... end" block
```

Figure 3.3   Visual representation of difference between the `break` and `return` statements.

```
function k = demoReturn(n)
% demoReturn  Show how "return" command causes exit from a function
%             Search a random vector to find index of first element
%             greater than 0.8.
%
% Synopsis:  k = demoReturn(n)
%
% Input:     n = size of random vector to be generated
%
% Output:    k = first (smallest) index in x such that x(k)>0.8
x = rand(1,n);
k = 1;

while k<=n
   if x(k)>0.8
     return
   end
   k = k + 1;
end              %  What happens if loop terminates without finding x(k)>0.8 ?
```

Listing 3.10 Simple function to demonstrate use of the `return` command.

Additional examples of the `return` statement can be found in the `demoArgs` function on page 130 and the `H2Odensity` function on page 132.

3.5 VECTORIZATION

Vectorization is the transformation of code that operates on scalars to code that operates on vectors. This transformation is most obvious when the original scalar code is expressed with `for` or `while` loop structures that traverse the elements of a matrix or vector. Vectorization does not change the number of arithmetic operations necessary to produce a computed result; it merely changes how efficiently those operations are performed by MATLAB. Vectorized statements are executed much more quickly than the equivalent scalar statements, because vectorized statements are executed with optimized binary code in the MATLAB kernel, not with interpreted scalar code in an m-file.

Vectorization was introduced in § 2.2.5 as a means of writing compact statements that operate on all elements of a matrix or vector. In this section, we show how vectorization can be used to improve the performance of MATLAB code.

3.5.1 Using Vector Operations instead of Loops

Using `while` and `for` loop constructs, one can write MATLAB programs that are direct translations of Fortran or C. These programs, though syntactically correct, can be inefficient when the loops contain many scalar operations. Consider a loop to evaluate $y = \sin(3x)$ for $0 \le x \le 2\pi$

```
dx = pi/30;
nx = 1 + 2*pi/dx;
for i = 1:nx
   x(i) = (i-1)*dx;
   y(i) = sin(3*x(i));
end
```

The preceding code consists of perfectly legal MATLAB statements, but it is an inefficient way to create the x and y vectors. The primary cause of inefficiency is the interpreted evaluation of x(i) and y(i) one element at a time. A secondary cause is that, each time through the loop, MATLAB must expand the x and y vectors to accommodate one new element. (Memory allocation issues are discussed in § 3.5.2.)

The preferred way to create the same two x and y vectors is

```
x = 0:pi/30:2*pi
y = sin(3*x);
```

Not only is the loop eliminated, but (given a familiarity with colon notation) the *intent* of the code is easier to grasp.

Copy Operations   The most efficient way to copy elements of a matrix (or vector) to another matrix is to avoid using a loop. This is achieved with vectorized copy operations utilizing colon notation. The technique will be demonstrated with examples.

Consider the goal of copying a column of one matrix into a column of another matrix having the same number of rows. For example, start with the A and B matrices

```
>> A = [1 2 3; 4 5 6; 7 8 9];
>> B = ones(size(A));
```

and copy the first column of A into the first column of B. The scalar and vectorized forms of the copy operations are as follows:

Scalar Code	**Vector Code**
`for i=1:3`	
`    B(i,1) = A(i,1);`	`B(:,1) = A(:,1);`
`end`	

Copy operations can involve any combination of rows and columns, as long as the same number of elements is specified in both the source and target matrices and as long as the subscript ranges in the two matrices are valid. For example, part of the last column of the A matrix just defined can be copied into (part of) the first row of the B matrix. The equivalent scalar and vector versions of such a copy operation are as follows:

Scalar Code	**Vector Code**
`for j=2:3`	
`    B(1,j) = A(j,3);`	`B(1,2:3) = A(2:3,3)'`
`end`	

Vectorized copy operations using colon notation can make for cryptic code. Since it is always a good idea to make code easier to read, comment statements should be provided to explain vectorized copy operations.

3.5.2 Preallocating Memory for Vectors and Matrices

Although MATLAB will automatically increase the size of a matrix (or vector) to accommodate new elements, it is usually a good idea to preallocate memory for the matrix. This is especially important when elements of the matrix are assigned one at a time inside a loop. Preallocation involves creating a matrix (or vector) with one vectorized statement before any of the matrix elements are referenced individually. The ones and zeros functions are typically used to preallocate memory.

Suppose that the s vector was not defined before the following loop is executed:

```
y = ...       %  some computation to define y
for j=1:length(y)
   if y(j)>0
     s(j) = sqrt(y(j));
   else
     s(j) = 0;
   end
end
```

The loop contains legal MATLAB statements, but it is inefficient because s is repeatedly enlarged to handle more elements. Preallocating memory for s involves inserting s = zeros(size(y)) before the beginning of the for loop:

```
y = ...        %  some computation to define y
s = zeros(size(y));
for j=1:length(y)
   if y(j)>0
     s(j) = sqrt(y(j));
   end
end
```

The advantage of preallocation of memory is that the time taken to allocate memory for a matrix is incurred only once *and* the matrix elements are stored in a contiguous block in the MATLAB memory space. Notice that preallocation, in this example, has also eliminated the need for the s(j) = 0 assignment inside the body of the loop. This contributes a further gain in efficiency.

3.5.3 Vectorized Indexing and Logical Functions

MATLAB's use of matrices as a fundamental data structure allows for compact expressions that do not appear in other programming languages. An important application of matrix syntax is the use of a vector or matrix as an *index* to the elements of another matrix. This is known as *array indexing*. A related, but different, technique is *logical indexing*, in which a matrix of ones and zeros is used as a mask to select elements from another matrix. Both array indexing and logical indexing allow operations to be performed on entire matrices, thereby eliminating the need to write explicit loops. The result is compact code that executes faster. A disadvantage is that the use of array indexing and logic indexing can result in rather cryptic code that is hard to decipher by inexperienced MATLAB programmers.

Array Indexing   Consider the following statements:

```
>> x = 10:10:50             %  Define a row vector
>> y = [5 3 1 2 4];         %  Another vector with same shape as x
>> z = x(y)                 %  Use y as index into x
z =
    50    30    10    20    40
```

The effect of x(y) is to use the elements of y as indices of x. The z = x(y) statement is the vectorized equivalent of the following scalar loop:

```
for i=1:length(y)
  z(i) = x(y(i));
end
```

The loop form makes it apparent that, to avoid indexing errors, (1) the elements of y must have values between 1 and length(x), and, (2) length(y) $\leq$ length(x). Here are two examples of the kinds of errors that can occur:

```
>> y(1) = 6
y =
      6    3    1    2    4

>> x(y)
???  Index exceeds matrix dimensions.

>> y(1) = -2;
>> x(y)

Warning: Subscript indices must be integer values.
??? Index into matrix is negative or zero.  See release notes on changes to
logical indices.
```

The rules for array indexing are summarized in Figure 3.4.

Logical Operations and Logical Indexing   A logical operation returns a one or zero (true or false) as the result of evaluating a relational expression or executing a logical function. Two simple examples are

```
>> y = pi<sqrt(10)
y =
      1
```

and

```
>> r = isreal(sqrt(-2))
r =
      0
```

Rules for the array or logical indexing operation C = A(B):

1. The total number of elements in B must not be greater than the total number of elements in A.

2. When A and B are both matrices (as opposed to vectors), the order of extracting element is determined as if A and B were first converted to column vectors. In other words, C = A(B) is equivalent to

   X = A(:); Y = B(:); C = X(Y);

3. *For array indexing*, values of elements in B must be valid indices of A.

4. *For logical indexing* elements in B must be only ones or zeros.

Figure 3.4   Rules for array and logical indexing.

TABLE 3.6   A SAMPLE OF BUILT-IN LOGICAL FUNCTIONS.

Function	Description	Returns
all(X)	true if all elements of X are nonzero	Scalar
any(X)	true for each column of X that has nonzero elements	Scalar if X is a vector; row vector if X is a matrix
isreal(X)	true if X has only real elements (no imaginary elements)	Scalar
isstudent	true if running version of MATLAB is the student edition	Scalar
isempty(X)	true if X is a null matrix, []	Scalar
isnumeric(X)	true if X is numeric (as opposed to string, cell, or struct)	Scalar
isnan(X)	true for each element of X that is a NAN	Matrix of same shape as X
isfinite(X)	true for each element of X that is less than Inf	Matrix of same shape as X

Table 3.6 gives a small sample of MATLAB's built-in logical functions. Note that the shape of the value returned by logical functions varies. Some functions, such as isreal, always return scalars, whereas other functions, such as isnan, return matrices having the same shape as the input matrix. The any function has the peculiar behavior of returning a row vector if the input is a matrix and returning a scalar if the input is a vector or a scalar.

As indicated in § 3.4.1, relational operators can be used to create logical results. When a relational operator is applied to two or more compatible matrices, the result is a matrix of ones and zeros. For example,[8] consider the code

```
>> A = rand(3,3)
A =
    0.9501    0.4860    0.4565
    0.2311    0.8913    0.0185
    0.6068    0.7621    0.8214

>> F = A>0.5        %  Note: results depend on elements of A = rand(3,3)
F =
    1    0    0
    0    1    0
    1    1    1
```

The expression F = A>0.5 is equivalent to the following scalar code:

[8]The particular pattern of ones and zeros in F will vary each time rand is called.

```
[m,n] = size(A);
F = zeros(m,n);
for i=1:m
  for j=1:n
    if A(i,j)>0.5
      F(i,j) = 1;
    end
  end
end
```

In most respects F, is an ordinary MATLAB matrix. F is special, however, in that its elements are *only* ones and zeros. This allows F to be used for *logical indexing* of the elements of A. Logical indexing utilizes an index matrix (or vector) to extract elements from another matrix. (Call it the source matrix.) The index matrix must contain only ones and zeros, and it must not have more elements than the source matrix it is used to index. Given A and F as just defined, A(F) uses F to perform logical indexing on A:

```
>> b = A(F)          %  Note: results depend on elements of A = rand(3,3)
b =
    0.9501
    0.6068
    0.8913
    0.7621
    0.8214
```

The A(F) expression uses F as a mask to select the (i,j)th elements of A corresponding to F(i,j) = 1. The assignment b = A(F) is equivalent to the scalar code

```
[m,n] = size(A);
k = 0;
for i=1:m
  for j=1:n
    if F(i,j) == 1
      k = k + 1;
      b(k) = A(i,j);
    end
  end
end
```

If the goal is to extract those elements of A meeting the criteria A(i,j)>0.5, then the F matrix does not need to be created. Instead, we can simply write

```
>> b = A(A>0.5)
```

The rules for logical indexing are summarized in Figure 3.4. These are the same rules for array indexing, *except* that index values of zero are allowed.

The find **Function**   The built-in find function is useful in many logical and array indexing applications. The find function takes a logical matrix expression and returns a set of one-dimensional array indices for the elements in the input argument that satisfy the condition. The syntax of the find function is

```
indexVector = find(findCondition)
```

The *findCondition* subexpression should produce a matrix of ones and zeros. The *indexVector* is a vector containing *only those indexes* for which *findCondition* is true. If *findCondition* produces a matrix, the result of find is a vector of the positions of the nonzeros in *findCondition* when *findCondition* is reshaped as a column vector, as in

```
>> A = rand(3,3)
A =
      0.9501      0.4860      0.4565
      0.2311      0.8913      0.0185
      0.6068      0.7621      0.8214

>> A>0.5
ans =
      1      0      0
      0      1      0
      1      1      1
>> find(A>0.5)
ans =
      1
      3
      5
      6
      9
```

Given A = rand(3,3), it is useful to contrast the following two expressions:

```
>> b = A(A>0.5)              >> i = find(A>0.5)
b =                          i =
    0.9501                       1
    0.6068                       3
    0.8913                       5
    0.7621                       6
    0.8214                       9
```

On the left, A(A>0.5) returns the *values* of the elements in A that meet the condition A(i)>0.5. On the right, find(A>0.5) returns the *indices* that meet the condition A(i)>0.5. Thus, A(find(A>0.5)) is equivalent to A(A>0.5).

The `max(find(x<=xhat))` expression provides the correct index in the x vector, unless xhat is exactly equal to the last element in x. As an example, examine the result of these statements:

```
>> x = 0:5;    xhat = 5;
>> i = max( find(x<=xhat) )
i =
     6
```

When `i=length(x)`, the expression `x(i+1)` in Equation (3.4) causes an index error. This is a problem, for example, in a linear interpolation that requires the values of `x(i)` and `x(i+1)`. The solution is to provide a second test to make sure that the value of i is less than `length(x)`. The complete search operation is contained in the two lines

```
>> i = max( find(x<=xhat) );        %  Find largest i such that x(i)<= xhat
>> if i==length(x), i = i-1;   end  %  Fix case where i=length(x)
```

or, alternatively,

```
>> i = max( find(x<=xhat) );        %  Find largest i such that x(i)<= xhat
>> i = min( i, length(x)-1 );       %  Fix case where i=length(x)
```

Other implementations for a vectorized incremental search also are possible.

3.6 DEUS EX MACHINA

As more capabilities are added to a computer program, the logic to handle special cases can sometimes become quite contorted. Dealing with many exceptions, for example, can lead to a tangled set of `if ... end` statements. Often, these situations must be resolved with a major redesign of the code. In other cases, an elegant solution can be achieved with the programming equivalent of a *deus ex machina*.[9] Four such devices in MATLAB are the provision for variable input and output parameters, global variables, the `feval` function, and in-line function objects. These are specialized tools for resolving particular programming problems.

---

[9]In Greek tragedies, the hero is manipulated by the gods. Occasionally, when the plot has developed into an impossible situation, a god descends into the world of humans and directly intervenes to aid the hero. More generally, a literary device used to intervene in an unresolvable dilemma is referred to as a *"deus ex machina,"* literally, "a god from a machine." In Greek tragedies, the *deus ex machina* is a god lowered into the scene by a crane.

3.6.1 Variable Number of Input and Output Parameters

Function m-files can be made very flexible and easy to use if the number of input and output parameters can be changed according to the needs of the user or the calling program. Many of the functions in the standard toolbox use this capability.

As an example, consider the built-in `plot` function, which can be called in a number of ways:

```
plot(x,y);
plot(x,y,'+');
plot(x1,y1,x2,y2);
plot(x1,y1,'+',x2,y2,'ro');
```

Without the ability to use variable input parameters, either the MATLAB toolbox would have to contain a large number of very similar `plot` functions to accommodate all of the special cases, or the `plot` function would require a long list of options for even the most simple plots. Using the `plot` function is much easier with variable numbers of input parameters.

Optional input and output parameters are made possible by two special variables, `nargin` and `nargout`, that are automatically defined for each function m-file. The value of `nargin` is the number of input parameters (arguments) with which the function was called. The value of `nargout` is the number of output parameters that are expected to be returned. The values of `nargin` and `nargout` can be different each time the function is called, so to support this capability, the function must have logic to decide how to process the input and how to package the output.

Supporting variable numbers of input–output parameters can involve extensive code logic, especially when different types of variables (i.e., string or numeric) are present in the input list. As an example, consider the logic necessary to support the kinds of inputs that are acceptable to the built-in `plot` function.

Example 3.13: Demonstration of Variable Input and Output Parameters

The `demoArgs` function in Listing 3.11 demonstrates how `nargin` and `nargout` can be used to provide variable numbers of input and output parameters. As is typical when `nargin` is used, the optional input parameters are processed at the beginning of the function.

`demoArgs` is just a shell of a function. It prints the number of input parameters and computes the sum and product of the inputs. The number of output parameters on the call to `demoArgs` determines which of the computed values are returned to the calling routine.

When optional input and output parameters are used, the function definition (in the first line of the m-file) must specify *all* of the possible input and output parameters. The values of `nargin` and `nargout` determine which of these parameters are significant for a particular execution of the function. The variable output parameters are defined only if the

```
function [out1,out2] = demoArgs(in1,in2,in3)
% demoArgs  Variable numbers of input and output parameters
%
% Synopsis:  demoArgs
%            demoArgs(in1)
%            demoArgs(in1,in2)
%            demoArgs(in1,in2,in3)
%            out1 = demoArgs(in1,in2,in3)
%            [out1,out2] = demoArgs(in1,in2,in3)
%
% Input:    in1,in2,in3 = optional dummy input arguments
%
% Output:   out1, out2 = optional dummy input arguments
%           If input arguments are provided, out1 is the sum
%           of the inputs, and out2 is the product of the inputs

if nargin == 0                          % process optional inputs
  disp('no input arguments');  return;
elseif nargin == 1
  disp('one input argument');
  sumin = in1;  prodin = in1;
elseif nargin == 2
  disp('two input arguments');
  sumin = in1+in2;  prodin = in1*in2;
elseif nargin == 3
  disp('three input arguments');
  sumin = in1+in2+in3;  prodin = in1*in2*in3;
else
  error('Too many inputs to demoArgs');
end

if nargout==0                           % process optional outputs
  return;
elseif nargout==1
  out1 = sumin;
else
  out1 = sumin;  out2 = prodin;
end
```

Listing 3.11 The demoArgs function, designed to illustrate the use of variable numbers of input and output parameters.

user is expecting them to be returned. Thus, in demoArgs, the sum of the input values is computed and stored in sumin. The result is copied to out1 *only if* nargout is greater than or equal to one.

Example 3.14: Evaluating a Curve Fit for the Density of Liquid Water

One particularly handy use of variable input parameters is to provide a set of default values for use with a function. This use is demonstrated by the H2Odensity function in Listing 3.12.

Given tabulated values of $\rho(T)$ and procedures described in Chapter 9, one can create a curve fit of the form

$$\rho = c_1 T^3 + c_2 T^2 + c_3 T + c_4,$$

where ρ is the density of water, T is the temperature, and the c_i are constant coefficients. The values of the c_i depend on the units of ρ and T, along with the range of T values used to obtain the curve fit. A convenient implementation of the preceding formula in a MATLAB function allows for different systems of units, in addition to the option of not requiring a temperature input if the density at standard ambient conditions is desired. This flexibility is not hard to provide with variable input arguments.

The H2Odensity function can be called in one of three ways:

```
rho = H2Odensity
rho = H2Odensity(T)
rho = H2Odensity(T,units)
```

The optional input parameters are T, the temperature at which the density is evaluated, and units, a string indicating the system of units used for T and the output value, rho.

With no input parameters, H2Odensity computes the density of liquid water at 20°C in SI units:

```
>> r = H2Odensity
r =
  998.2000
```

With one input, the density is evaluated at a temperature other than 20°C

```
>> r = H2Odensity(31)
r =
  995.3755
```

With two inputs, the temperature can be specified in degrees Fahrenheit, which causes the density to be returned in lbm/ft³:

```
>> r = H2Odensity(68,'f')
r =
   62.3139
```

Note that if the British units are used, both the T and units parameters must be specified.

```
function  rho = H2Odensity(T,units)
% H2Odensity  Density of saturated liquid water
%
% Synopsis:   rho = H2Odensity
%             rho = H2Odensity(T)
%             rho = H2Odensity(T,units)
%
% Input:   T    = (optional) temperature at which density is evaluated
%                   Default: T = 20C. If units='F' then T is degrees F
%          units = (optional) units for input temperature, Default = 'C'
%                   units = 'C' for Celsius, units = 'F' for Fahrenheit
%
% Output:  rho = density, kg/m^3 if units = 'C', or lbm/ft^3 if units = 'F'

% Notes:   Use 4th order polynomial curve fit of data in Table B.2
%          (Appendix B) of "Fundamentals of Fluid Mechanics",
%          B.R. Munson, et al., 2nd edition, 1994, Wiley and Sons, NY

if nargin<1
  rho = 998.2;  return;    %  Density at 20 C w/out evaluating curve fit
elseif nargin==1
  units='C';               %  Default units are C
end

% --- Convert to degrees C, if necessary
if upper(units)=='F'
  Tin = (T-32)*5/9;        %  Convert F to C; don't change input variable
elseif upper(units) == 'C'
  Tin = T;
else
  error(sprintf('units = ''%s'' not allowed in H2Odensity',units));
end

% --- Make sure temperature is within range of curve fit
if Tin<0 | Tin>100
  error(sprintf('T = %f (C) is out of range for density curve fits',Tin));
end

% --- Curve fit coefficients
c = [ 1.543908249780381441e-05  -5.878005395030049852e-03 ...
      1.788447211945859774e-02   1.000009926781338436e+03];

rho = polyval(c,Tin);    % Evaluate polynomial curve fit
if upper(units)=='F'
  rho = rho*6.243e-2;    % Convert kg/m^3 to lbm/ft^3
end
```

Listing 3.12   The H2Odensity function takes advantage of variable input parameters to supply default values and to allow flexibility in the type of input.

3.6.2 Global Variables

Global variables provide a way to bypass the input and output parameter lists of functions. Programming with global variables can solve advanced coding problems, *but* global variables *should not* be used when the standard input and output parameter lists can do the same job. Global variables are sometimes abused by lazy programmers, who, in a fit of false economy, do not bother using input and output parameters to communicate directly with a function m-file. This usually leads to a complicated web of m-files that are linked in mysterious ways. Reading a collection of m-files that share global variables requires a simultaneous understanding of *all* the m-files. In contrast, restricting communication between functions to the input and output parameter lists allows the reader to conceptualize each m-file as a stand-alone module. There are some situations, however, in which using global variables can lead to an elegant programming solution.

When global variables are *not* used, the variables in the workspace (see § 2.4.1 on page 52) are distinct from variables used within functions called from the workspace or in other functions. This situation is depicted by the upper half of Figure 3.5. The *values* of x, y, and s defined in the command window, are copied to the internal variables a, b, and c of localFun.

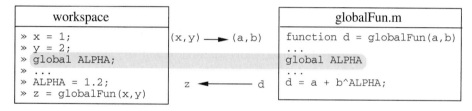

Figure 3.5   Bypassing input–output parameters with global variables.

The value of c inside `localFun` is computed and then copied back to the z variable in the command window. The x, y, s, and z variables in this example exist only in the workspace, whereas the a, b, c, and d variables belong to a separate memory space that exists only while `localFun` is executing.

Global variables provide direct access to the variables defined in the workspace or in other functions. An example is shown in the lower half of Figure 3.5. As before, x and y are defined in the command window, and copies are sent as input to `globalFun`. Another variable, ALPHA, is defined and declared global with

```
global  ALPHA
```

In this book, the names of global variables are always uppercase, to make these variables prominent. Multiple global variables can be declared in a single statement, as in

```
global  ALPHA SIGMA ZETA
```

Note that the variables in the global declaration are separated by spaces, and that there is no semicolon at the end of the line.

As shown in Figure 3.5, the global variable must be declared as global in both the workspace and the function needing access to that variable. Furthermore, the variable name must be identical in both places. In this example, there is no need to make ALPHA a global variable. The value of ALPHA could and *should* be passed to `globalFun` as an input parameter.

It is not necessary to involve the workspace in the sharing of global variables: Two functions can share global variables in the same way that global variables are shared between the workspace and a function.

3.6.3 The `feval` Function

There are several numerical algorithms for which the user must supply a utility routine to evaluate a problem-specific function. For example, to compute the numerical approximation to

$$I = \int_a^b f(x)\, dx,$$

the $f(x)$ function must be evaluated at arbitrary points in the interval $a \le x \le b$. A general-purpose routine for numerically approximating the integral should be able to work with any reasonable $f(x)$. This poses a problem, because the input to the computational procedure is not a value—say, the value stored in x—but is instead the *name* of the routine (name of the m-file) that evaluates $f(x)$ for any x. In MATLAB, the solution to this programming problem is the `feval` function.

The syntax of the `feval` function is

```
feval(fun,p1,p2, ... )
```

The first parameter, `fun`, is a string giving the name of the function to be called. The remaining parameters, `p1`, `p2`, ... , are passed to the function referred to by `fun`. The following two statements, for example, are equivalent:

```
>> feval('sin',pi/2);
ans =
    1
```

```
>> sin(pi/2);
ans =
    1
```

There is no need, of course, to use the `feval` function to evaluate the sine of an angle; the preceding example merely demonstrates that there is an equivalence between the direct evaluation of a function and the indirect evaluation of that function with `feval`. In practice, the `feval` function is used only when the name of an m-file is to be passed as an input parameter to another m-file.

Example 3.15: Average of Sampled Function

Suppose that it is necessary to evaluate the sum of discrete values of an arbitrary function at n equally spaced points in an interval $a \leq x \leq b$. Let s be the sum

$$s = \sum_{i=1}^{n} f(x_i),$$

where

$$x_i = a + (i-1)h, \qquad h = \frac{b-a}{n-1}.$$

It would be easy to write the code to perform this task for a particular function, say, $\sin(x)$. A completely separate function could then be written to evaluate the sum of $\cos(x)$. The `feval` function allows a more general solution, as implemented by the `fsum` function in Listing 3.13. The first input to `fsum` is the *name* of the function, which must be a string. For example, to use `fsum` to compute the sum of the sin and cos functions at five points in the interval $0 \leq \theta \leq \pi$, enter the following statements:

```
>> fsum('sin',0,pi,5)
ans =
    2.4142
```

```
>> fsum('cos',0,pi,5)
ans =
    0
```

```
function s = fsum(fun,a,b,n)
% fsum  Computes sum of f(x) values at n points in  a <= x <= b
%
% Synopsis:   s = fsum(fun,a,b,n)
%
% Input:   fun = (string) name of the function, f(x), to be evaluated
%          a,b = endpoints of the interval
%          n   = number of points in the interval
%
% Output:  s = sum of f(x) at n discrete points in the interval

x = linspace(a,b,n);     %  create points in the interval
y = feval(fun,x);        %  evaluate function at sample points
s = sum(y);              %  compute the sum
```

Listing 3.13   The fsum function to evaluate the sum of any function in a user-defined interval.

The first argument in the fsum statements must be enclosed in single quotes so that fsum will interpret it as a string. The fsum function can be used with arbitrary functions. To do so, the function must be embodied in an m-file that can accept a vector as input and return a vector of function values as output. As an example, the sincos function in Listing 3.14 evaluates the product $\sin(x)\cos(x)$. Once the sincos.m file is created and located in the MATLAB path, the statement

```
>> fsum('sincos',0,pi,15)
ans =
   3.3307e-16
```

evaluates the sum of $\sin(x)\cos(x)$ at 15 points on the interval $0 \le x \le \pi$.

```
function y = sincos(x)
% sincos  Evaluates sin(x)*cos(x) for any input x
%
% Synopsis:  y = sincos(x)
%
% Input:     x = angle in radians, or vector of angles in radians
%
% Output:    y = value of sin(x)*cos(x) for each element in x

y = sin(x).*cos(x);
```

Listing 3.14   The sincos used to demonstrate the fsum function in Listing 3.13.

3.6.4 Inline Function Objects

Support for object-oriented programming was added in version 5 of MATLAB. Object-oriented programming uses a variety of techniques to associate behaviors (actions) with *objects*, which are an abstract extension of the variables we have been using to store numbers. Objects can be created to store many types of entities: numbers, strings, matrices, functions, other objects, and combinations of these entities. For each object, the programmer defines a number of *methods*, which are extensions of the functions we have been using to manipulate variables. Object-oriented programming is a very powerful paradigm for organizing computing tasks. It also is more subtle and requires a greater level of skill to use successfully. For our basic numerical analysis tasks, we do not need to use object-oriented programming, although, for complex program development, it may be useful.

One object-oriented feature that is handy for numerical tasks is the *inline function object*. Inline functions are easy to define and use, and they eliminate the need for creating short m-file functions that are used to evaluate simple formulas. An inline function object is an object that holds a MATLAB expression to be evaluated. Usually, the expression contains one or more variables that act like the input parameters in an m-file function. Consider the following MATLAB session:

```
>> scfun = inline('sin(x).*cos(x)')
scfun =
     Inline function:
     scfun(x) = sin(x).*cos(x)
```

The `scfun = inline('sin(x).*cos(x)')` statement creates an inline function object called `scfun`. The immediate response to this statement is

```
Inline function:
scfun(x) = sin(x).*cos(x)
```

indicating that MATLAB has assumed x to be an input variable to the `scfun` function object. Variables in `inline` function objects are determined automatically by the MATLAB parser. See `help inline` for more information on how these variables are detected.

Once `scfun` is defined, it can be used like any other m-file function. In other words, the `scfun` inline function can be used instead of the `sincos` function in Listing 3.14:

```
>> scfun(5)-sin(5)*cos(5)
ans =
     0

>> scfun(0:pi/4:pi)
ans =
          0    0.5000         0   -0.5000          0
```

Inline function objects are different from m-file functions in some important ways. An inline function is created in the MATLAB workspace, and it exists only in the current session:

```
>> whos
  Name          Size            Bytes  Class

   ans           1x5                40  double array
   scfun         1x1               844  inline object

Grand total is 52 elements using 884 bytes
```

Once an inline function object is assigned to a MATLAB variable, it may be passed as a parameter to another function. For example,

```
>> fsum(scfun,0,pi,15)
ans =
   3.3307e-16
```

passes the scfun object to the fsum function described in Example 3.15. Note that there are no single quotes around scfun, in contrast to the statement

```
>> fsum('sincos',0,pi,15)
ans =
   3.3307e-16
```

which produces the same numerical result.

Inline function objects can be created within an m-file function, and that feature will be exploited throughout this book. Listing 3.15 shows how this is accomplished.

```
function s = demoXcosx(n)
% demoXcosx   Use an inline function object with the fsum function
%
% Synopsis:   s = demoXcosx
%
% Input:      n = number of points at which x*cos(x) is evaluated
%                 in the interval 0 <= x <= 2*pi
%
% Output:     s = sum of x*cos(x) at n points

xcosx = inline('x.*cos(x)');
s = fsum(xcosx,0,3*pi,n);
```

Listing 3.15   The demoXcosx shows how an inline function object can be defined and used within a convention m-file function.

.7 SUMMARY

This chapter deals with the creation of program modules in MATLAB. Both script m-files and function m-files are discussed. Since functions are more useful for structured programming, function m-files are recommended over scripts for nearly every programming task.

A primary goal of the chapter is to describe and demonstrate MATLAB language constructs. Examples are provided in snippets of code and in m-files. Table 3.7 lists the functions and script m-files developed in this chapter. Unlike m-files in subsequent chapters, the m-files in Table 3.7 are not general-purpose routines intended to be incorporated into other programming projects. Rather, the m-files developed in this chapter are designed to illustrate specific programming techniques.

Further Reading

The primary source of documentation for MATLAB programming is the set of manuals for the current version of MATLAB. The on-line documentation via the help and helpwin commands provides concise summaries of each function. Every MATLAB license comes with printed manuals, as well as Portable Document For-

TABLE 3.7   NMM TOOLBOX FUNCTIONS USED TO INTRODUCE PROGRAMMING CONCEPTS.

Function	Page	Description
addmult	95	Computes the sum and product of two matrices
demoArgs	130	Demonstrates the use of variable numbers of input and output parameters
demoBreak	116	Demonstrates the use of the break statement.
demoReturn	118	Demonstrates the use of the return statement.
demoXcosx	138	Demonstrates how an in-line function object can be defined and used within a conventional m-file function.
fsum	136	Computes sum of $f(x)$ values at n points in $a \le x \le b$
H2Odensity	132	Computes the density of saturated liquid water
inputAbuse	100	Computes the sum of three variables, but only after demanding that the user enter each value one at a time. An example of how *not* to use the input function. Compare this function with threesum.
myCon	87	Defines useful constants in the workspace.
plotData	98	Plots data from a plain text file.
polyGeom	99	Demonstrates the use of primary functions and subfunctions.
sincos	136	Evaluates $\sin(x)\cos(x)$ for any input x
takeout	88	Script to display restaurant telephone numbers.
threesum	95	Adds three matrices and returns the result
trigplot	92	Script to plot $\sin(x)$, $\cos(x)$, and $\sin(x)\cos(x)$
twosum	95	Adds two matrices and prints the result

mat (PDF) versions of more comprehensive references. Readers wishing another detailed source of information on advanced MATLAB commands should consult Hanselman and Littlefield [34].

EXERCISES

The number in parentheses at the beginning of each exercise indicates the degree of skill and amount of effort necessary to complete the exercise. (See § 1.4 on page 10 for a description of the rating system.)

1. (1) Modify the myCon script so that it includes constants and conversion factors appropriate to your discipline.

2. (1−) Modify the twosum function in Listing 3.4 so that it returns the result in a variable s. Suppress printing of the result inside of twosum.

SOLUTION
3. (1+) Transform the takeout script in Listing 3.2 to a function. Add a single input argument called kind that allows you to select a type of food from your list of favorite take-out restaurants. Inside the body of the function, set up a multiple-choice if ... elseif ... end block to match the kind string with the predefined restaurant types. Make sure that there is a default choice—either a restaurant type or an error message—if kind does not match any of the available restaurant types. (*Hint*: use the strcmp function to compare to strings for equality.)

4. (1+) Refine the takeout function created in the preceding problem. Instead of requiring an exact match between kind and the restaurant types, compare only the first *n* characters, where *n* is just long enough to distinguish restaurant types. In addition, create a new internal variable, lowerkind, that has the same characters as kind, but all in lowercase. Test lowerkind against the lowercase restaurant types. This strategy will make the comparisons used to match restaurant types case insensitive.

SOLUTION
5. (1) Write a newtsqrt function to compute the square root of a number, using Newton's algorithm. Your function should encapsulate the code on page 115.

6. (1+) Write a newtsqrt function to compute the square root of a number with Newton's algorithm and using a for ... end construct instead of a while ... end. How do you cause the for loop to terminate when the convergence criterion is met *before* the maximum number of iterations is performed?

SOLUTION
7. (1) Elvis Presley was born January 8, 1935, and died on August 16, 1977. Write an elvisAge function that returns Elvis's age in years, assuming that he were alive today. (The fragment of code on page 103 may be of some help.)

8. (2) Extend the elvisAge function developed in the preceding problem so that an optional input argument, onDate, can be provided for testing. The modified elvisAge function should return Elvis's age in years on onDate, where onDate is a MATLAB date number. (See help datenum.) Your program should correctly compute Elvis's age on the following test dates

  (**a**) When he died on August 16, 1977.
      (Test statement should be elvisAge(datenum(1977,8,16)).)

(b) One day before his first birthday, January 7, 1936

(c) On his first birthday, January 8, 1936

(*Hint*: one solution to this programming assignment uses the built-in `datevec` function.) *Answers*: a. 42 years, b. 0 years, c. 1 year.

9. (2) Extend the `elvisAge` function developed in the preceding problem to provide an optional return of the months and days since Elvis was born. Calls to the modified `elvisAge` function should return the following values:

```
>> y = elvisAge(datenum(1977,8,16))
y =
      42


>> [y,m] = elvisAge(datenum(1977,8,16))
y =
      42
m =
       7


>> [y,m,d] = elvisAge(datenum(1977,8,16))
y =
      42
m =
       7
d =
       8
```

OLUTION 10. (2) Write a function called `mydiag` that mimics the behavior of the built-in `diag` function. At a minimum, the `mydiag` function should return a diagonal matrix if the input is a vector and return the diagonal entries of a matrix if the input is a matrix. (*Hint*: The `size` function will be helpful.)

11. (2) Create an m-file function called `sequint` that returns a matrix having elements that are a sequence of integers arranged by columns. The function should have two inputs, *m* the number of rows, and *n* the number of columns. The statements `sequint(2,3)` and `sequint(4,4)` should produce the matrices

$$
\begin{bmatrix} 1 & 3 & 5 \\ 2 & 4 & 6 \end{bmatrix}
\qquad
\begin{bmatrix} 1 & 5 & 9 & 13 \\ 2 & 6 & 10 & 14 \\ 3 & 7 & 11 & 15 \\ 4 & 8 & 12 & 16 \end{bmatrix}
$$

(*Hint:* Create a vector of integers in sequence then convert the vector to a matrix.)

12. (2−) Write two function m-files, `FtoC` and `CtoF`, to convert temperatures from degrees Fahrenheit to degrees Celsius and from degrees Celsius to degrees Fahrenheit. Each function should have one input parameter and one output parameter. Test your functions with

```
>> FtoC( CtoF(100) )
>> CtoF( FtoC(32) )
>> FtoC(0:10:100)
>> CtoF(0:10:100)
```

along with any other tests you think are appropriate.

13. (2) Given a MATLAB vector x of arbitrary length, write a sequence of statements to print x =, followed by the values of the elements in x, all on the same line. For example, if x is created with x = 0:0.25:2, your code should produce

```
x =    0.00  0.25  0.50  0.75  1.00  1.25  1.50  1.75  2.00
```

Without any alteration to the code, it should also produce

```
x =    0.00  0.25  0.50  0.75  1.00
```

given x = 0:0.25:1 as input. (*Hint*: Spreading the printing operation over more than one fprintf will be helpful.)

14. (2) Write a function that uses the built-in diag function to create the symmetric, $n \times n$, tridiagonal matrix

$$D = \begin{bmatrix} c & d & 0 & 0 & \cdots & 0 \\ d & c & d & 0 & & \\ 0 & d & c & d & & 0 \\ & 0 & \ddots & \ddots & \ddots & \\ & & & & d & c \end{bmatrix},$$

where c and d are scalars. A function definition of the form function A = tridiag(c,d,n), where n is the dimension of the matrix, will be helpful. (*Hint*: The two-parameter form of diag will also be helpful.)

15. (3) Expand the previous function to allow c and d to be vectors instead of scalars. In other words, create the matrix

$$D = \begin{bmatrix} c_1 & d_1 & 0 & 0 & \cdots & 0 \\ d_1 & c_2 & d_2 & 0 & & \\ 0 & d_2 & c_3 & d_3 & & 0 \\ & 0 & \ddots & \ddots & \ddots & \\ & & & & d_{n-1} & c_n \end{bmatrix}$$

if c and d are vectors, or create the matrix from the preceding problem if c and d are scalars. Note that D is symmetric, i.e., $D = D^T$. (*Hint*: Check the size of c and d to see if these input values are vectors or scalars.)

SOLUTION **16.** (1) Write the MATLAB statements that use a loop and the fprintf function to produce the following table (the format of the numerical values should agree exactly with those printed in the table).

theta	sin(theta)	cos(theta)
0	0.0000	1.0000
60	0.8660	0.5000
120	0.8660	-0.5000
180	-0.0000	-1.0000
240	-0.8660	-0.5000
300	-0.8660	0.5000
360	0.0000	1.0000

17. (1) Write the MATLAB statements that use a loop and the `fprintf` function to produce the following output:

(**a**) `1^2 = 1`
      `2^2 = 4`
      `3^2 = 9`
      `4^2 = 16`
      `5^2 = 25`

(**b**) `(0.10)^2 =    0.0100`
      `(0.20)^2 =    0.0400`
      `(0.30)^2 =    0.0900`
      `(0.40)^2 =    0.1600`
      `(0.50)^2 =    0.2500`

18. (1+) Write a `horner` function that uses Horner's rule to evaluate a polynomial of arbitrary degree. (Cf. Example 3.7 on page 113). Use the function definition

```
function p = horner(b,x)
```

where b is a vector of coefficients that define the polynomial. The return value p is the value of the polynomial at x. Test your function with b = `[1 2 -1 0]` at x = 1, 2, 3, 4, 5.

19. (2+) Extend the function developed in Exercise 18 so that it returns a vector of polynomial values if the input x is a vector.

20. (2+) Extend the function developed in Exercise 19 so that it can be called in two ways, viz.,

```
p = horner(b,x)
```

and

```
[p,pp] = horner(b,x)
```

where p is the value of the polynomial at x and pp (p prime, $p' = dp/dx$) is the value of the first derivative of $p(x)$ evaluated at x. Make sure that your function returns p and pp as vectors if x is a vector.

21. (1+) How does the built-in `polyval` function evaluate a scalar polynomial? What sort of sound does it make while doing so? (*Hint*: Read the source code of `polyval`.)

SOLUTION **22.** (2+) Write a function to plot the displacement of a cantilevered beam under a uniform load. In addition to creating the plot, the function should return the maximum deflection and angle between the horizontal and the surface of the beam at its tip. The formulas for the displacement y and tip angle θ are

$$y = -\frac{wx^2}{24EI}(6L^2 - 4Lx + x^2) \qquad \text{and} \qquad \theta = \frac{1}{6}\frac{wL^3}{EI},$$

where w is the load per unit length, E is Young's modulus for the beam, I is the moment of inertia of the beam, and L is the length of the beam. Test your function with $E = 30$ Mpsi, $I = 0.163$ in^4, $L = 10$ in, $w = 100$ lb$_f$/in.

23. (2+) Write a function to plot the displacement of a cantilevered beam under a point load. In addition to creating the plot, the function should return the maximum deflection and the angle between the horizontal and the surface of the beam at its tip. The geometry of the beam is shown in the following diagram:

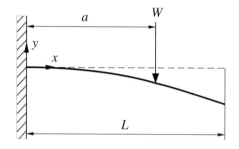

The formulas for the displacement y and tip angle θ are

$$y = -\frac{Wx^2}{6EI}(3a - x), \qquad \text{for} \quad 0 \le x \le a,$$

$$y = -\frac{Wa^2}{6EI}(3x - a), \qquad \text{for} \quad a \le x \le L,$$

and

$$\theta = \frac{Wa^2}{2EI},$$

where W is the point load, E is Young's modulus for the beam, I is the moment of inertia of the beam, and L is the length of the beam. Test your function with $E = 30$ Mpsi, $I = 0.163$ in^4, $L = 10$ in, $a = 3$ in, and $W = 1,000$ lb$_f$.

24. (2+) The location and value of the maximum displacement of a simply supported beam under a concentrated load are, respectively,

$$x_{\max} = \sqrt{a(a + 2b)/3} \quad \text{and} \quad y_{\max} = -\frac{Wab}{27EIL}(a + 2b)\sqrt{3a(a + 2b)},$$

where W is the load, E is Young's modulus for the beam, I is the moment of inertia of the beam, and $L = a + b$ is the length of the beam. If $a < b$, then $x_{max} = L - \sqrt{b(b + 2a/3)}$ and the roles of a and b in the formula for y_{max} are reversed.

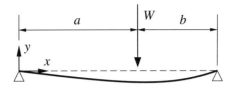

Write a function that returns x_{max} and y_{max}, given values of W, a, b, E and I. For $E = 30$ Mpsi, $I = 0.163$ in^4, $L = 10$ in, and $W = 1000$ lb$_f$, plot x_{max} and y_{max} as a function of a/L for $0 \le a/L \le 1$. To make the variations of x_{max} and y_{max} distinct, use the built-in `plotyy` function, or make two separate plot windows.

25. (2) The data in `xy.dat` were produced by adding noise to $t = \pi(\sin(x) + \cos(x))$, for $0 \le x \le 5\pi/2$, (i.e., $y = t +$ noise). Create a modified `plotData` function that plots the (x, y) and (x, t) data sets, along with a horizontal line through $\bar{y}$, the average value of y. The (x, y) data should be plotted with open circles, the (x, t) data should be plotted with a solid line, and the $\bar{y}$ value should be indicated with a dashed line. Use the `legend` function to label the three curves.

26. (1) Modify the plotData function so that it works with a data file having the x values in the first row and the y values in the second row. Use the `xtyt.dat` data in the data directory of the NMM toolbox to test your function. The modified `plotData` function should produce the same plot with `xtyt.dat` that the original `plotData` function produces with the `xy.dat` file.

27. (2) Modify the `plotData` function so that it reads and plots files with an arbitrary number of y data columns. The file would look like

$$x \quad y_1 \quad y_2 \quad \cdots \;,$$
$$\vdots \quad \vdots \quad \vdots \quad \vdots$$

where $y_1, y_2, \ldots$, are a family of curves sharing the same abscissas (x values). Your function should work without any modification for both the `xy2.dat` and `xy4.dat` data files in the data directory of the NMM toolbox. (*Hint*: The `hold on` command will be helpful.)

28. (3) The `corvRain.dat` file in the data directory of the NMM toolbox contains monthly precipitation data for Corvallis, Oregon, from 1890 to 1994. The data are organized into columns, where the first column lists the year and the next 12 columns give the precipitation, in hundredths of an inch for each month. Write a MATLAB function to compute and plot the *yearly total* precipitation in inches (not hundredths of an inch) from 1890 to 1994. The function should also print the average, the highest, and the lowest annual precipitation for that period. The `loadColData` function in the `utils` directory of the NMM toolbox will be helpful in reading the data without having to delete the column headings. Can you compute the yearly total precipitation without using any loops?

29. (2) Extend the solution to the preceding exercise by computing and printing the average rainfall for each month from the `CorvRain.dat` data file. In addition, compute and print the total amount of rainfall for each month over the period from 1890 to 1994. Report the averages and totals in inches, not hundredths of an inch.

30. (1+) Evaluate the following expressions by hand, and then test your results with MATLAB:

   (a) 5 | 4
   (b) ~3
   (c) x = log10(25*2^2)
   (d) y = 5+2 & ~pi<eps
   (e)   **i.** s = (x>y) & (x>4)
           ii. t = ~(x|y)
          iii. u = x((x>y) & (x>4))
           given x = [0 5 3 7] and y = [0 2 8 7].
   (f) A = reshape(1:8,2,4); B = A(5*ones(2,2))
   (g) A = reshape(1:8,4,2); B = A(5*ones(2,2))

SOLUTION **31.** (2−) Write a function called `maxi` to return the index of the most positive element in a vector. In other words `imax = maxi(v)` returns `imax` such that $v(imax) \geq v(i)$ for all `i`.

32. (2) Write a version of `maxi` from the preceding problem that uses only one line of MATLAB code. (*Hint*: Use the built-in `find` command.)

33. (2−) Write a function called `maxai` to return the index of the element with greatest absolute value. In other words, `imax = maxai(v)` returns `imax` such that $abs(v(imax)) \geq abs(v(i))$ for all `i`.

34. (2) Write a version of `maxai` from the preceding problem that uses only one line of MATLAB code. (*Hint*: Use the built-in `find` command.)

35. (2) Given the x vector

```
>> x = [21 22 23 24];
```

and B matrix

```
>> B = ones(3,3);
```

write the one-line vectorized copy operation that has the same effect as the following scalar loop:

```
k = 0;
for i=2:3
  for j=1:2
     k = k + 1;
     B(i,j) = x(k);
  end
end
```

(*Hint*: The built-in `reshape` function will be helpful.)

36. (2+) The snippet of code on page 121 at the end of § 3.5.2 computes

$$s_j = \begin{cases} \sqrt{y_j}, & \text{if } y_j > 0 \\ 0, & \text{otherwise} \end{cases}.$$

Write a vectorized (no loop) version of this code. (*Hint*: Preallocate s and use the `find` function.

37. (2+) Write another solution to the preceding problem using logical indexing on the left and right sides of a single expression after s is preallocated.

38. (2) Write an `indexCheck` function with the definition

```
function ok = indexCheck(A,B)
```

in order to verify, according to the rules in Figure 3.4, that `A(B)` is a valid array indexing or logical indexing expression. If `A(B)` is not valid, return ok = 0 and print an appropriate error message. If `A(B)` is valid, return ok = 0.

39. (3) Write the code for the `evenChecker` function that meets the description of the following prologue:

```
function A = evenChecker(m,n)
% evenChecker  Create a checkerboard matrix of ones and zeros
%
% Syntax:  A = evenChecker(m,n)
%
% Input:   m,n = number of rows and columns in matrix
%
% Output:  A = an m-by-n matrix having ones in all elements with even
%              values of i+j and zeros in all elements with odd values
%              of i+j, where i and j are the row and column indices,
%              respectively
```

40. (2) Describe the bug in the `demoBreak` function in Listing 3.9 on page 116, and then fix it. The fixed version should still use a `break` function.

41. (2) Describe the bug in the `demoReturn` function in Listing 3.10 on page 118 and then fix it. The fixed version should still use a `return` function.

42. (1+) Use an `inline` function object and the `fsum` function (cf. Listing 3.13 on page 136) to evaluate $s = \sum_{i=1}^{n} \tan(x)\cos(x)$ for $x = \texttt{linspace(0, 2 * pi, n)}$, and $n = 5, 10, 25, 50$.

SOLUTION **43.** (2+) Write an m-file function to compute the heat transfer coefficient for a cylinder in cross flow. The heat transfer coefficient h is defined in terms of the dimensionless Nusselt number Nu $= hd/k$, where d is the diameter of the cylinder and k is the thermal conductivity of the fluid. The Nusselt number is correlated with the Reynolds number Re and Prandtl number Pr by

$$\text{Nu} = C\text{Re}^m\text{Pr}^{1/3}, \qquad \text{where} \qquad \text{Re} = \frac{\rho V d}{\mu} \quad \text{and Pr} = \frac{\mu c_p}{k},$$

in which ρ, μ, and c_p are, respectively, the density, dynamic viscosity, and specific heat of the fluid and V is the velocity of the fluid approaching the cylinder. The parameters C and m depend on Re according to the following table:

Re range	C	m
0.4–4	0.989	0.330
4–40	0.911	0.385
40–4000	0.683	0.466
4000–40,000	0.193	0.618
40,000–400,000	0.027	0.805

For the first line of your m-file, use

```
function h = cylhtc(d,v)
```

where d is the diameter of the cylinder and v is the velocity of the fluid. Use the properties of air at one atmosphere and 20°C:

$$\rho = 1.204 \text{ kg/m}^3, \quad \mu = 1.82 \times 10^{-5} \text{ N} \cdot \text{s/m}^2, \quad c_p = 1,007 \text{ J/(kg K)},$$

$$k = 26.3 \times 10^{-3} \text{ W/(m°C)}.$$

44. (2+) Explain what happens to the function `demoArgs` defined in Figure 3.11 on page 130 when the statements

```
sumin = in1+in2+in3;
prodin = in1*in2*in3;
```

are moved to the line after the first end statement (after line 33). (*Hint:* Make this change, and then enter `demoArgs(1,3)` in the command window.)

45. (2) Extend the `H2Odensity` function in Listing 3.12 on page 132 so that it returns a second, *optional* string argument, `units`. The return argument should not have the same name as the internal "`units`" variable.

46. (2+) Extend the cylhtc function from Problem 43 so that it takes an optional third input argument, fluid. In other words, the first line of the m-file should now read

```
function h = cylhtc(d,v,fluid)
```

so that a user can call this function with any of these statements:

```
>> h = cylhtc(d,v)
>> h = cylhtc(d,v,'air')
>> h = cylhtc(d,v,'water')
```

Use the nargin facility to detect whether two or three input arguments are passed to cylhtc. The "fluid" argument should be a string variable that must equal either "air" or "water." (Use the strcmp to test for the equality of two strings.) The value of fluid determines whether the properties of air or water are used in the calculation of Nu, Re, and Pr.

47. (3) Using the H2Odensity function in Listing 3.12 as a guide, construct an airProps function that returns values for the density (ρ), viscosity (μ), specific heat at constant pressure (c_p), and thermal conductivity (k), of air as a function of temperature and pressure. The function definition statement should be

```
function [rho,cp,mu,k] = airProps(T,p,units)
```

Where T is the temperature, p is the pressure, and units is a string indicating the system of units. Values for T, p, and units should be optional. Your function should be callable in the following ways:

```
[rho,cp,mu,k] = airProps
[rho,cp,mu,k] = airProps(T)
[rho,cp,mu,k] = airProps(T,p)
[rho,cp,mu,k] = airProps(T,p,units)
```

with reasonable default values for T, p, and units provided. Use the following equations to compute the density and the thermophysical properties:

$$\rho = \frac{p}{RT} \qquad\qquad c_p = \sum_{i=1}^{n} c_{cp,i} T^{n-i+1}$$

$$\mu = \sum_{i-1}^{n} c_{\mu,i} T^{n-i+1} \qquad k = \sum_{i=1}^{n} c_{k,i} T^{n-i+1}$$

where p is the absolute pressure of the air, $R = 287.0$ J/kg/K is the ideal gas constant for air, T is the *absolute* temperature in kelvins ($T(K) = 273.15 + T(°C)$), and $c_{cp,i}$, $c_{\mu,i}$, and $c_{k,i}$ are constants in the following table

i	$c_{cp,i}$	$c_{\mu,i}$	$c_{k,i}$
1	$-2.455322455 \times 10^{-7}$	$2.156954157 \times 10^{-14}$	$-2.486402486 \times 10^{-12}$
2	$6.701631702 \times 10^{-4}$	$-5.332634033 \times 10^{-11}$	$-2.871794872 \times 10^{-8}$
3	$-2.992579643 \times 10^{-1}$	$7.477905983 \times 10^{-8}$	$9.629059829 \times 10^{-5}$
4	$1.042503030 \times 10^{3}$	$2.527878788e \times 10^{-7}$	$2.060606061 \times 10^{-5}$

These polynomial curve fit coefficients were obtained from data in the range $100 \leq T \leq 600K$. Make sure you check that the input value of T lies in this range.

4

Organizing and Debugging
MATLAB Programs

The preceding chapters describe the basic components of MATLAB. The chapters that follow describe tools for solving a variety of computational problems. This chapter provides two additional components of applied numerical computation: techniques for organizing the development of numerical solutions and techniques for systematically removing programming errors from MATLAB code.

Figure 4.1 summaries the contents of the chapter. The first two sections contain suggestions for organizing a MATLAB program to solve practical numerical problems. The structure of the code within a single m-file, as well as the division of computational tasks among separate m-files, is considered. The recommendations for organizing MATLAB code are demonstrated through a series of interconnected examples in the analysis of a large data set.

The use of well-organized code can help minimize the occurrence of errors. Furthermore, the use of good code structure and defensive strategies will isolate any errors that might otherwise propagate between code modules. Inevitably, errors will occur, however. Programming errors are called *bugs*, and the process of finding and removing them is called *debugging*. The last half of the chapter offers suggestions on how to debug MATLAB code.

The material on organizing code should be immediately useful to a reader proceeding sequentially through the chapters of this book. The information on de-

Topics Covered in This Chapter

1. Organizing and Documenting m-files

A standard structure for individual m-files is provided. General techniques for documenting m-files are discussed, and the function prologue used in the NMM Toolbox is described.

2. Organizing a Numerical Solution

Design of numerical analysis codes using stepwise refinement is described. The method is applied to a project of modest complexity through a series of interconnected examples.

3. Debugging

Strategies to make debugging code more efficient are discussed. Some of MATLAB's elementary debugging tools are introduced.

Figure 4.1   Primary topics discussed in Chapter 4.

bugging in the last third of the chapter may take on greater significance and utility as more significant programming projects are tackled. It may be beneficial, therefore, to skim through the debugging sections now and then refer back to them as necessary.

4.1 ORGANIZING AND DOCUMENTING M-FILES

My experience is that the amount of time needed to write a program and make it work usually exceeds (and often by a large factor) the amount of time spent running it. Most of the development time is spent debugging. My experience also shows that good organization of code makes debugging easier, so it is natural that organizing code and debugging it are considered together. Good organization and debugging techniques apply to simple, as well as complex, numerical analysis projects. Instead of attempting to quickly write and then immediately use code, I suggest that you first *design* the code, then write it, and before using it on some important problem, *test* it. This methodical approach is likely to save time in the end.

Careful code design takes time. It is easy to assume that any activity, such as design, that delays the actual writing of the code will necessarily add to the overall time to finish the numerical calculations. In fact, good design shortens the time to write and debug code. In addition, good design helps insure that the code achieves the original objectives, including producing a "correct" result. There are several techniques for designing code. The method called *stepwise refinement* is presented in § 4.2.1. Remember that a design method is a tool, not a doctrine. Learning how and when to use it will help you become more proficient at developing numerical solutions. Be prepared to consider other techniques.

Given these admonitions, it may seem hypocritical that the design phase is not presented for the overwhelming majority of numerical methods presented in this book. The reason for this omission is that working through a systematic design for each algorithm would be impractical. It would make the book much longer than it already is, and it would force the reader to wade through pages of material just to get to the final implementation of a particular method.

Another reason for omitting the design of the numerical methods presented here is that these methods are very well understood. The methods themselves have been successfully utilized in many programs, and the behavior of the methods have been studied by many mathematicians. There will be few, if any, surprises in how these methods perform on the problems for which they were developed. It is in the *application* of numerical methods that the recommendations for organizing code presented in this chapter will be most beneficial.

4.1.1 Use of a Consistent Style

Most people who write programs with any regularity develop habitual ways of writing code. Comment statements, for example, may begin with a series of dashes, or the body of an if . . . end construct are indented two spaces, three spaces, or one tab. These habits constitute a programming style, which, at the very least, give the code a visual familiarity. The matter of style should not be dismissed lightly. Using regular patterns helps to write correct code that it easy to read and understand. Debugging code is easier when it is visually, as well as structurally, organized.

Figure 4.2 represents the structure of a typical m-file function appearing in this book. The functions always have a prologue, as described in § 4.1.4. Following the prologue, the first executable statements process any optional input parameters (see § 3.6.1) and check the ranges of the input variables as part of a defensive

```
function y = myFunction(x)
```

Prologue

Process optional input arguments and verify input values

Primary computational task

Prepare optional output arguments

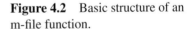

Figure 4.2   Basic structure of an m-file function.

programming strategy. (See § 4.3.1.) The central part of the function performs the primary computational task. At the end of the function, the optional output parameters are assigned.

The structure summarized in Figure 4.2 is simple and obvious, since the flow of execution within an m-file is sequential. Organizing code into separate modules is discussed in § 4.2.

4.1.2 Visual Blocking and Whitespace

An important aspect of programming style is visual consistency. Similar constructs should appear the same in all parts of a program. In particular, block constructs, such as `for` loops, `while` loops, and `if...end` structures should be indented.

The use of indentation is demonstrated in the code that follows, where the same set of statements are written with and without indentation. In this example the computations are not as significant as the visual structure of the code.

```
n = length(x)
if mean(x)<0
  y(1) = 0;   y(n) = 0;
  for k=2:n-1
    y(k) = x(k+1)-x(k-1);
  end
else
  y(1) = x(1);   y(n) = x(n);
  for k=2:n-1
    y(k) = 0.5*(x(k+1)+x(k-1));
  end
end
```

```
n = length(x)
if mean(x)<0
y(1) = 0;   y(n) = 0;
for k=2:n-1
y(k) = x(k+1)-x(k-1);
end
else
y(1) = x(1);   y(n) = x(n);
for k=2:n-1
y(k) = 0.5*(x(k+1)+x(k-1));
end
end
```

Visual blocking makes the code on the left easier to comprehend than the code on the right. The human mind makes logical assumptions from the visual cues given by the indentations. This is an advantage, because the nested indentation is consistent with the hierarchy of logic in the code.

Use of indentation does not improve poorly written code. Indentation is merely a means of conveying the logical structure of the code to the reader. Furthermore, indentation has no effect on how the MATLAB interpreter parses the code.

The indentation of code blocks is an example of the use of *whitespace*. In the design of a book, whitespace is an area of a page that is not covered by the microscopic dots of ink that constitute the text or figures. Whitespace includes the margins, the space between paragraphs, the indentation at the beginning of a paragraph, and even the spaces between words. You can more easily see the whitespace if you squint and let your eyes become unfocused while looking at this page. The whitespace organizes the page into blocks that provide cues to the reader.

As with page layout in a book, whitespace in a computer program gives visual clues about the content. Indenting block constructs is one use of whitespace to create visual order. Whitespace is also helpful between variables and within nested parenthesis. Here, for example, are four ways to write a single line of MATLAB code:

```
y(k)=0.5*(x(k+1)+x(k-1));
                              % or
y(k) = 0.5*(x(k+1)+x(k-1));
                              % or
y(k) = 0.5*( x(k+1) + x(k-1) );
                              % or
y(k) = 0.5 * ( x(k+1) + x(k-1) );
```

The amount of whitespace is a matter of personal preference. More whitespace is not always better. Sometimes, too much space in one line is a distraction, especially if the line becomes too wide to fit into the editor window. The most important thing is to become conscious of the use of whitespace and to use it to your advantage in organizing your code.

Many of the functions in this book could be made more readable by increasing the amount of whitespace in their listings. The recommendations just given were not followed whenever it meant that a function listing would not fit on a single page. It seems that, for the purpose of including code in a textbook, some compromise is appropriate in order to save paper and to allow the reader to view an entire m-file without having to flip pages.[1]

4.1.3 Meaningful Variable Names

Descriptive variable names aid in reading code. This makes debugging easier, especially if the bug is discovered well after the code is written. MATLAB provides considerable flexibility in the creation of variable names, so there is no need to rely only on generic variables, such as x and y, when more descriptive variable names will aid in code documentation. On the other hand, variable names that are too long are cumbersome.

Consider the task of calculating the inner and outer radii of a pipe, given the inner diameter and the wall thickness. Presented next are calculations demonstrating two possible choices for the variable names. Before reading any of the code, cover up the statements on the right with your hand. Carefully study the code on the left before lifting you hand and reading the code on the right.

---

[1] Kernighan and Plauger [47] recommend that code modules be limited in length to one printed page. Modules that are longer than a page should be divided into two or more modules that perform parts of the tasks that constitute the original module. This advice is better considered as a guide than a rigid rule. If a module is so long that it spans multiple pages, it is a good candidate for subdivision.

```
d = 5;                          d_in = 5;
t = 0.02;                       thick = 0.02;
r = d/2;                        r_in = d_in/2;
r2 = r + t;                     r_out = r_in + thick;
```

Although both sets of statements are correct, the statements on the right are unambiguous. In the calculations on the left, it is not immediately obvious that d is the inner diameter and r is the inner radius. The potential for confusion increases the possibility of introducing a bug in the calculation.

4.1.4 Documentation

Documentation is critical for any code that is not going to be used and immediately discarded. Documentation takes the form of comment statements that describe the input and output parameters of a function, as well as the steps performed in the analysis. Writing documentation should be considered an inseparable part of writing the code. In particular, the documentation should be written simultaneously with the code itself, not some time after the code is in use. Attempting to reuse code from a program that lacks documentation requires rediscovering the logic and mathematics incorporated in the code. Good documentation speeds up the process of understanding code, it helps to prevent errors in applying the code, and it aids in making revisions that extend the code's capabilities.

Documentation can take two primary forms: either as an external, written report defining the theory and operation of a program, or as an internal description of the statements and input–output variables used by the program. The internal documentation is contained in comment statements that coexist with the lines of executable code.

Comment Statements   MATLAB comment statements begin with the % character and extend to the end of the line containing the % character. Comment statements are ignored by the interpreter when the program module is executed.

Comment statements can be preceded whitespace to identify major blocks of code. Examples of this are the comments on lines 25, 34, and 39 of the H2Odensity function in Listing 4.4 on page 175. Short comment statements can be included on the same line as MATLAB statements, as shown in the last three lines of fsum function in Listing 3.13 on page 136.

Again, comment statements should be written at the same time as the code itself is being written. That makes the documentation a continual process, rather than a chore to be completed after the code is running. It also improves the likelihood, though it hardly guarantees, that the comment statements are an accurate reflection of what the code is doing. Another benefit is that the process of writing comments provides additional opportunity to reflect on the outcome of the statements. Mistakes in code can be discovered if the code does not do what the comment statements say it should.

Kernighan and Plauger provide good advice on the development of code documentation [47]. Their summary recommendations are repeated here:

1. If a program is incorrect, it matters little what the documentation says.
2. If documentation does not agree with the code, it is not worth much.
3. Consequently, code must largely document itself. If it cannot, rewrite the code rather than increase the supplementary documentation. Good code needs fewer comments than bad code does.
4. Comments should provide additional information that is not readily obtainable from the code itself. Comments should never parrot the code.
5. Mnemonic variable names and labels, and a layout that emphasizes logical structure, help make a program self-documenting.

Function Prologues   Comment statements at the top of a function are called the prologue. For many simple functions, the prologue may take more lines than the MATLAB statements that perform the calculations. This is not a problem, since the goal is to enhance the usability of a function by providing good documentation of its behavior. The extra disk space consumed by comment statements is inconsequential. The goal, however, is not to maximize the number of comment statements!

The purpose of the prologue is to document the function for someone reading the m-file source code *and* to support MATLAB's `help` and `lookfor` commands. Recall that if a user enters

```
>> help funName
```

at the command prompt, MATLAB will print the comment statements at the beginning of the *funName.m* file. Specifically, the comment statements between the function definition and the first blank line are printed. To support on-line help, there must be no blank line immediately following the function definition or within the body of the prologue.

All of the substantial functions developed in this book have a prologue with a Summary, a Synopsis, and descriptions of the input and output parameters. The exception is in simple programs, often containing just one or two lines of code, that evaluate a simple formula. In these cases, a the prologue is a one-line Summary.

Figure 4.3 is an annotated version of the prologue for the `H2Odensity` function. (See also Listing 4.4 on page 175). The purpose of each major element of the prologue is described next. It is helpful to compare the following verbal descriptions with the comment statements in Figure 4.3:

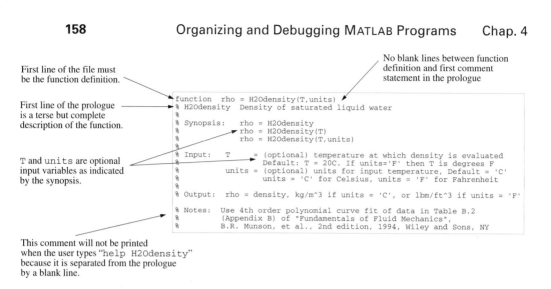

First line of the file must be the function definition.

No blank lines between function definition and first comment statement in the prologue

First line of the prologue is a terse but complete description of the function.

T and units are optional input variables as indicated by the synopsis.

```
function  rho = H2Odensity(T,units)
% H2Odensity  Density of saturated liquid water
%
% Synopsis:    rho = H2Odensity
%              rho = H2Odensity(T)
%              rho = H2Odensity(T,units)
%
% Input:    T    = (optional) temperature at which density is evaluated
%                    Default: T = 20C. If units='F' then T is degrees F
%           units = (optional) units for input temperature, Default = 'C'
%                    units = 'C' for Celsius, units = 'F' for Fahrenheit
%
% Output:  rho = density, kg/m^3 if units = 'C', or lbm/ft^3 if units = 'F'
%
% Notes:   Use 4th order polynomial curve fit of data in Table B.2
%          (Appendix B) of "Fundamentals of Fluid Mechanics",
%          B.R. Munson, et al., 2nd edition, 1994, Wiley and Sons, NY
```

This comment will not be printed when the user types "help H2Odensity" because it is separated from the prologue by a blank line.

Figure 4.3   Layout of a typical m-file prologue used in this book.

Summary: The first line immediately following the function definition gives the program name and a one-line description of what the function does. Additional description may be provided on subsequent lines, but the first line is critical to support the built-in `lookfor` command.

When the user types "`lookfor findString`", MATLAB searches the *first line* of all m-files in its path for *findString*. Whenever *findString* is found, the line containing that string is printed to the command window. A carefully written summary line is important, therefore, if the function is to properly advertise itself via the `lookfor` command. The summary line needs to be descriptive, and it should contain key words that a user is likely to associate with the function. It is also important that the name of the m-file, which is also the name of the function, be included on the first line. If the first comment line in the prologue does not contain the function name, a user of the `lookfor` function will have difficulty finding the m-file or using on-line help to get more information about it. See the demonstration of the `lookfor` function on page 24 for an example of how this is helpful.

Synopsis: The synopsis is a listing of the various ways in which the function can be called. If there are no optional input or output arguments, then the synopsis has only one line.

Input: Each input variable is described. Optional input variables are labeled as such, and the default values for optional inputs are given.

Output: Each output variable is described. If no variables are returned, a brief description of any information printed to the screen or plotted in a figure window is provided.

If the prologue is to be useful, it must provide an accurate description of how the function works. This requires that the comment statements be updated whenever changes are made to the input or output parameters or when the algorithm in the function is changed.

4.2 ORGANIZING A NUMERICAL SOLUTION

Some numerical tasks can be implemented interactively in MATLAB with little planning. Depending on one's proficiency with MATLAB and one's familiarity with the analysis to be performed, it may be possible to quickly enter a few statements and obtain the necessary results. For this type of analysis, the scope, as well as the details, of the task can be simultaneously comprehended by the fortunate user. When the task becomes more complex—because of the difficulty in the analysis or the sheer number of steps involved—it is beneficial to design the code before it is written.

The approach advocated here involves four basic steps. First, plan the solution before implementing it on the computer. A simple *stepwise refinement* strategy is recommended, whereby major steps in the process are identified and then subdivided into increasingly smaller steps until all of the small steps have solutions that are obvious (or nearly so). The second step is to use the results of stepwise refinement to guide the definition of separate program modules that perform one task or a small number of closely related tasks. These first two steps constitute the design phase of creating the numerical solution. The third step is to translate the module definitions into working MATLAB code. If the first two steps are effective, then writing the MATLAB functions to implement the tasks is relatively straightforward. The fourth step is testing. Before a numerical method is applied to a problem for which the solution is unknown—the reason for developing the method in the first place—it should be tested.

The following example presents a problem of modest complexity. The solution to this problem is implemented in subsequent examples.

Example 4.1: Analysis of Glen Canyon Dam Data

The Glen Canyon Dam on the Colorado River is managed to maximize power production. The flow rate of water through the power-generating turbines is adjusted to match the electricity demand, which can change dramatically during the course of a single hour. The canyons and beaches downstream of the dam are seriously affected by fluctuations in flow rate. To guard against damage to the downstream environment, it is necessary to monitor and report the flow rate of water through the dam.

Data for the dam flow rate are available on an hourly basis for an entire year. The assignment is to plot the hourly flow data and to compute and plot the daily and weekly flow rates. Given the volumetric hourly flow rate, $Q(t)$, the daily total flow rate for the ith day of the year is

$$Q_{d,i} = \frac{1}{24} \int_{t_i}^{t_i+23} Q(t)\, dt, \tag{4.1}$$

where t is the time in hours. Similarly, the average flow rate in the jth week is

$$Q_{w,j} = \frac{1}{167} \int_{t_j}^{t_j+166} Q(t)\, dt, \tag{4.2}$$

where $167 = 7 \times 24$ is the number of hours in a week.

This assignment is not conceptually difficult, yet completing it will require several steps and the evaluations of the integrals for $Q_{d,i}$ and $Q_{w,i}$. The planning, implementation, and testing of a solution is the subject of a sequence of examples throughout this chapter.

4.2.1 Stepwise Refinement

Given an abstract, verbal description of a computing task, such as that presented in the preceding example, it is usually necessary to develop a sequence of smaller tasks that can be implemented sequentially. *Stepwise refinement* is a software design strategy by which a large task is decomposed into a series of smaller tasks. Each of the smaller tasks is decomposed further until one is left with a number of relatively simple tasks that have obvious solutions. The same procedure is also called *top-down* design or *divide and conquer*.

Not all programming projects are immediately amenable to stepwise refinement. If the primary objective is unknown or poorly defined, more comprehensive software planning tools will be needed. Only when a specific task, or *action item*, is agreed upon can one begin to plan the implementation with stepwise refinement.

Consider the assignment: *Plot a sine wave from 0 to 2π*. This simple task is executed as a sequence of three smaller steps:

1. Generate a vector x with elements between 0 and 2π.
2. Evaluate $y_i = \sin(x_i)$.
3. Plot y_i versus x_i.

Creating the three subtasks from a single task is an example of one level of stepwise refinement. Each of these subtasks can be directly implemented in MATLAB, so no further refinement is necessary. The translation to MATLAB is summarized in the following table.[2]

---

[2]Statements like `plot(0:pi/50:2*pi,sin(0:pi/50:2*pi))` or `fplot('sin', [0 2*pi])` merely combine the three steps into a single line.

Task	$\longrightarrow$	MATLAB statement
1. Generate vector x with elements between 0 and 2π.		`x = linspace(0,2*pi);`
2. Evaluate $y_i = \sin(x_i)$.		`y = sin(x);`
3. Plot y_i versus x_i.		`plot(x,y);`

More complicated tasks require multiple levels of stepwise refinement, starting at the highest or most abstract level of the problem definition. Note that stepwise refinement is performed with pencil and paper before starting to write any code. Working at a conceptual level provides an opportunity to develop the overall logic of the analysis before committing time to writing and debugging the program.

Example 4.2: Stepwise Refinement for Analysis of Glen Canyon Dam Data

Example 4.1 on page 159 describes an analysis project for flow data from the Glen Canyon Dam. In this Example, stepwise refinement is used to create a sequence of simple tasks that meet the overall objective of the analysis. Stepwise refinement begins with the most general statement of the problem:

> Plot the flow data.

This trivial statement provides motivation for the next level of refinement. A more detailed list of tasks follows by answering the question, "What do I need to do to plot the flow data?" Stepwise refinement proceeds by adding only the obvious steps at each stage of refinement. To plot the flow data, we need to

- Read flow data from a file.
- Plot the hourly flow rate versus time.
- Plot the daily flow rate versus time.
- Plot the weekly flow rate versus time.

Before the daily and weekly flow rates can be plotted, they must be computed from the hourly data. Making these tasks explicit and reorganizing the list gives four major tasks:

   I. Read data from a file into MATLAB variables.
  II. Compute the daily total flow rate.
 III. Compute the weekly average flow rate.
  IV. Plot the hourly, daily, and weekly flow rate data.

Each of these tasks can be further subdivided. Reading the data into a file (task I) requires

  a. load the data into a MATLAB matrix.
  b. copy the data matrix into a vector of times and a vector of flow rates.

Making similar recursive divisions of the primary tasks gives the following set of tasks for the entire analysis:

   I. Read data from file into MATLAB variables:
      a. Load the data into a MATLAB matrix.
      b. Copy the data matrix into a vector of times and a vector of flow rates.
   II. Compute the daily average flow rate:
      a. Determine the total number of days in the data set.
      b. Integrate the flow rate with respect to time over each day.
      c. Divide by the total time in each day.
   III. Compute the weekly average flow rate:
      a. Determine the total number of weeks in the data set.
      b. Integrate the flow rate with respect to time over each week.
      c. Divide by the total time in each week.
   IV. Plot the hourly, daily, and weekly flow rate data.

These tasks are translated into MATLAB code in Example 4.3.

4.2.2 Implementation: One Program, Multiple m-files

It is wise to divide a long and complicated numerical calculation into separate code modules, with each module dedicated to a specific task. For MATLAB programs, a module is a function m-file. Script m-files are not useful for modular programming, because they cause side effects (see page 91) and they lack input and output parameters.

The advantage of dividing a larger project into modules is that each module can be developed and tested independently. In addition, general-purpose modules can be reused in other projects, thereby minimizing the duplication of code. Furthermore, if a shared module is improved (e.g., if its efficiency is increased), then the benefits are immediately available to other projects using that shared module.

The stepwise refinement technique described in the preceding section transforms a large task into smaller tasks that are more easily understood and implemented. The resulting list of tasks provides a starting point for dividing an analysis into modules. Each module may perform one or more tasks, however, so some judgment is needed in how finely the code should be subdivided. Breaking an analysis into modules is not an end in itself. The goal is not to maximize the number of m-files, but rather to provide a useful arrangement of smaller tasks for the purpose of realizing a larger objective. Programming experience helps when deciding how to compartmentalize an analysis.

Once coding begins, the programmer's understanding of the problem will evolve, and the task decomposition obtained from a stepwise refinement may turn out to be less than optimal. The modules may need to be completely redesigned, or it may be necessary to add more stages the stepwise refinement. Modular programming is beneficial in either case, because modules can be changed or rearranged much more easily than a monolithic code.

Since modules are isolated blocks of code, the programmer needs to provide input and output parameters to allow communication with other program modules. The task assigned to a module dictates which inputs are needed and which outputs are returned. Specifying input and output parameters is part of the process of module definition that occurs before the coding begins.

Taking the preceding issues into account, I recommend the following steps to subdivide programming tasks into code modules:

0. Obtain the task decomposition from stepwise refinement. (Given.)

1. Assign groups of related tasks to individual modules.

2. List input and output parameters necessary for each module to complete its task(s).

3. Review the module design for potential improvements. Repeat steps 1 and 2 as necessary.

For a substantial programming project, the preceding steps may need to be iterated several times until a workable program design emerges. It is much more efficient to make such design changes in the planning process than after the code is written.

Example 4.3: Implementation of Glen Canyon Dam Analysis

Example 4.2 on page 161 resulted in a detailed list of tasks for analyzing the Glen Canyon Dam data. Now those tasks will be translated into a MATLAB program.

Step 1: Assign Related Tasks to Modules: An obvious first choice for organizing the code is to assign one module to each of the major tasks in the outline. This task decomposition is represented by the following diagram:

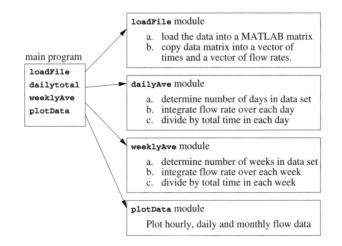

Each module is represented by a box containing a list of tasks. The visual appearance is not important. In practice, one would be working with pencil and paper, and the boxes might correspond to separate sheets of paper or 3×5 note cards.

The main, or driver, module defines the structure of the analysis at the highest level. As depicted above, the main module consists primarily of calls to lower level modules. The loadFile, dailyAve, weeklyAve, and plotData modules do all of the work.

The preceding module definitions form a preliminary draft of the analysis plan. Now is a good time to look for any potential for improving the structure of the code. In particular, any subtasks that are duplicated in separate modules provide opportunities for simplification. Common subtasks can be put into a separate shared module.

In the current example the dailyAve and weeklyAve modules both require the integration of flow data. The trapzDat function in Listing 11.3 on page 611 integrates discrete $y = f(x)$ data with the trapezoidal rule. The details of the trapezoidal rule are not important at this point. As long as the module performs according to specification, we will (temporarily!) treat the module as an input–output system (a "black box"). Using trapzDat function to perform the integration tasks results in the following module diagram:

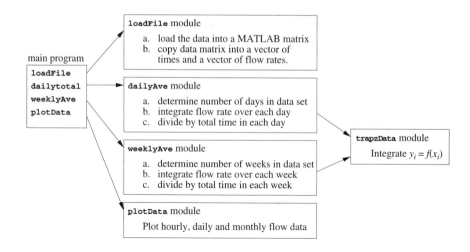

The decomposition step is now complete. No additional simplifications are apparent. Additional information from the next step may suggest further changes in the module definitions.

Step 2: List Input and Output Parameters for Each Module: The module diagrams are now extended by including the input and output parameters of each module. At this level of module refinement, the inputs and outputs are identified by English words. This is merely a convenience in documenting the module behavior. Later, after the module design is complete, the input and output parameters are given valid MATLAB variable names. The following diagrams show the input and output parameters of each of the major modules:

```
loadFile module
input: file name
output: hour vector, hourly flow vector
tasks:
    a.  load the data into a MATLAB matrix
    b.  copy data matrix into a vector of
        times and a vector of flow rates.
```

```
plotData module
input: hour, hourly flow, day, daily flow,
       week, weekly flow
output: plot of flow rates
tasks:
    Plot hourly, daily and monthly flow data
```

```
dailyAve module
input: hour vector, hourly flow vector
output: day vector, daily total vector
tasks:
    a.  determine number of days in data set
    b.  daily flow = trapzdat(hourly flow)
    c.  daily ave = daily flow/24
```

```
weeklyAve module
input: hour vector, hourly flow vector
output: week vector, weekly flow vector
tasks:
    a.  determine number of weeks in data set
    b.  weekly flow = trapzdat(hourly flow)
    c.  weekly ave = weekly flow/hours per week
```

Step 3: Review and Revise Module Designs: The four modules described in the preceding step can be translated into a working set of m-files. An inspection of the input and output parameters indicates that these modules can be improved. Some of the improvements are described here before the modules are implemented as MATLAB code. Other improvements are left as exercises for the reader. Each module will be considered in turn. To save space, only the function prologues for the modules are printed in the text. The full source code for the functions is provided in the NMM toolbox.

The loadFile ***Module.***   The final version of the loadFile module differs from the description in step 2. In fact, the loadFile code does not need to be written, because the built-in load function can be used to read the hourly flow rate from the data file. Using the function (as opposed to command) form of the load function, data from the gc87.dat file can be read into a two-column matrix with

```
D = load('gc87.dat');
```

It would be convenient[3] in the subsequent analysis to store the hour and flow rate in separate vectors. This can be accomplished by copying the data from D into (say) h and f:

```
h = D(:,1); f = D(:,2);
```

After creating h and f the D matrix is redundant and consuming memory. If memory is a constraint, this step could be avoided, and D(:,1) and D(:,2) could be used instead of creating separate h and f vectors. Additional memory savings can be obtained by noticing that the hour data in gc87.dat are all integers. Thus, the h vector would not need to be stored. Whenever a vector of hours is needed, it could be created on the fly with the statement (1:length(f))'. Exploiting this fact might allow small savings in memory

---

[3]though not strictly necessary

now, but it will cause the code to fail if it is used on a data file containing noninteger hourly data. Rather than make the code specific to the gc87.dat file, the h vector will be retained. The final version of the code for the loadFile module is

```
D = load(fname);              % Read data from file into D matrix
h = D(:,1);   f = D(:,2);     % Copy data into hour and flow rate vectors
D = [];                       % Free memory used by D matrix
```

The last step of freeing memory by deleting D is probably not necessary, but is included in case an unexpected large data file is encountered.

Up to now, the loadFile module has be described as if it were to be coded into a separate m-file function. That is a reasonable and workable solution. Since the functionality of the loadFile module is obtained in three MATLAB statements, we will just include this code in the main program.

The dailyAve **and** weeklyAve **Modules**   The daily average and weekly average flow rates are computed with very similar formulas, the only difference being the duration of the time interval over which the average is defined. (Compare Equation (4.1) with Equation (4.2).) Because of this close similarity, it would be good to combine these modules into one function having the duration of the averaging interval as an input parameter. This consolidation is left to the reader (See Exercise 8.) The less elegant solution of using separate dailyAve and weeklyAve functions is supplied here. The dailyAve and weeklyAve prologues are given in Listing 4.1.

The trapzDat **Module**   The integrals in Equations (4.1) and (4.2) are evaluated with the trapezoid rule for discrete data. The computations are implemented in the trapzDat function, which is described more completely in § 11.2.1. The inputs to trapzDat are vectors of x and $f(x)$ data, and the output is $\int f(x)\,dx$.

The average flow rate for a day or week is defined with only part of the hourly time and flow data. The trapzDat function, however, computes the integral using all the input data supplied to it. This requires that only limited ranges of the time and flow data be given as input to trapzDat. The following excerpts from dailyAve show how this is done:

```
function [d,fave] = dailyAve(t,f)
...  % function prologue

n = length(f);    % Number of points in input data
... % additional statements to manage data sets with uneven number of hours

for i=1:24:n
  k = k + 1;
  dayAve(k) = trapzDat(t(i:i+23),f(i:i+23));   % integrate flow*dt
end
dayAve = dayAve/24;
```

```
function [days,dayAve] = dailyAve(dtime,flow)
% dailyAve    Compute average daily flow from hourly flow data
%
% Synopsis:   [days,dayAve] = dailyTotal(dtime,flow)
%
% Input:      dtime = time in days from the begining of the year.
%                     Fractional values correspond to hours during the day
%             flow  = flow rate (cfs)
%
% Output:     days    = vector of integer days from beginning of the year
%             dayAve = total flow rate for each day of the year
```

```
function [week,flowAve] = weeklyAve(dtime,flow)
% weeklyAve   Compute average weekly flow from hourly flow data
%
% Synopsis:   [weektot,flowAve] = weeklyTotal(dtime,flow)
%
% Input:      dtime = time in days from the begining of the year.
%                     Fractional values correspond to hours during the day
%             flow  = flow rate (cfs)
%
% Output:     week    = vector of integer weeks from beginning of the year
%             flowAve = average flow rate for each week of the year
```

Listing 4.1 Prologues for the dailyAve and weeklyAve functions used in the analysis of Glen Canyon Dam flow data.

The t(i:i+23) and f(i:i+23) subexpressions select 24 element sequences from the t and f vectors. These segments implicitly define the limits for the integration performed by trapzDat.

The plotData **Module**   The preliminary design has the plotting performed in a separate plotData module. This requires that all of the flow rate data be transferred from the main program to the plotting module. Since creating a plot is quite easy in MATLAB, the choice made here is to avoid the passing of data to another function by incorporating the plotting statements in the main program. In other words, the tasks originally assigned to the plotData module are absorbed into the riverReport (the main) m-file.

The riverReport **Main Program**   The main program for the river flow analysis is the riverReport function in Listing 4.2. The riverReport function has one input, the name of the file containing the data to be analyzed. By making the file name a variable, the same code can be used on data from any year.

The riverReport function calls load with the name of the data file. It then copies the columns of the single matrix returned by load into two vectors, h and f, for the hour

```
function riverReport(fname)
% riverReport  Compute and plot summary of river flow data
%
% Synopsis:  riverReport(fname)
%
% Input:     fname = (string) name of file containing flow data
%
% Output:    Printed summary statistics and plots of flow data vs. time

% --- Read data into working vectors
D = load(fname);            %  Read data from file into D matrix
h = D(:,1);   f = D(:,2);   %  Copy data into hour and flow rate vectors
D = [];                     %  Free memory used by D matrix

% --- Compute daily total and weekly average flow rates
[day,flowPerDay]   = dailyAve(h,f);
[week,flowPerWeek] = weeklyAve(h,f);

% --- Plot flow rates
subplot(2,1,1)
plot(h,f,'b.','markerSize',2);
xlabel('day of the year');  ylabel('Hourly Flow rate,  CFS');
title(sprintf('Flow data from %s',fname));

midweek = 7*week - 3.5;     %  vector of days in the middle of the week
subplot(2,1,2)
plot(day,flowPerDay,'r-',midweek,flowPerWeek,'ko');
xlabel('day of the year');  ylabel('Flow rate,  CFS');
legend('daily','weekly');
```

Listing 4.2   The riverReport function controls the overall data reduction process and makes the summary plots.

and the hourly flow rate, respectively. The memory used by the data matrix is then freed
by assigning a null matrix ([]) to the data variable. The daily and weekly averaged flow
rate is computed by the dailyAve and weeklyAve functions. The results are then plotted.
A typical run of the riverReport function is obtained with the statement

```
>> riverReport('gc87.dat')
```

which produces the plots in Figure 4.4. Obtaining the plots is not proof that the
riverReport and support functions are working properly. In fact, there is at least one bug
in these calculations. (See Exercise 6.)

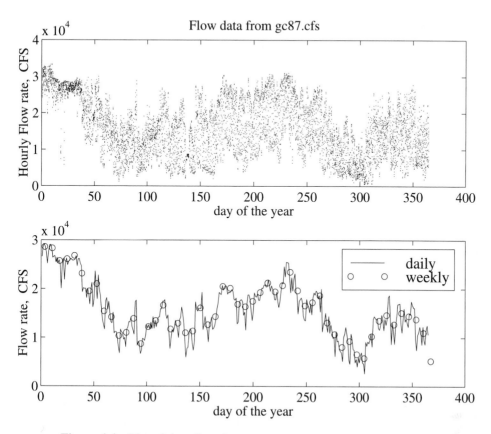

Figure 4.4   Plot of river flow data.

4.2.3 Testing

It is important to verify that m-files are working correctly before they are used to produce results that inform other decisions. If a program that computes the stress in a machine component contains an error, then the component may fail during operation. Alternatively, the component may be so overdesigned that the cost of the machine will be unnecessarily high. In other situations, erroneous computational results may cause injury to people or property. For these reasons, the output from *any* computer program should be regarded with healthy skepticism.

The best check on any calculation, be it manual or automatic, is by an independent test. Physical experiments with prototypes are a common means of verifying a design. Since experimentation is usually expensive, it still makes sense to test programs that perform numerical computations before they are used in making design decisions.

Modular programming provides a good framework for program testing. Individual modules can be tested separately and in combination. Typically, one writes a specialized diagnostic program to call a module with inputs that produce known results. If the expected results are not produced, then the details of the module must be examined. Additional and more specialized diagnostic programs may have to be devised. Interactive debuggers are also useful at this phase of program development. Once the errors in the module have been found and fixed, it makes sense to retain the diagnostic program(s) for future use. If improvements to the module are made, the diagnostic program can be run again, and obvious bugs can be eliminated before the module is incorporated into a more complicated analysis.

Sometimes, it makes sense to include diagnostic calculations into the module itself. Once the module is running to specification, the diagnostics can be "turned off" by enclosing them in an `if . . . end` construct or changing the diagnostic statements into comments. One of the simplest forms of diagnostics is the printing of results at each step of an iterative procedure. Such a printout is usually not necessary when the method is working well, but it is often useful to be able to turn the printing on and off when the method is being applied to a new problem. A simple flag in the input parameter list can be used to turn the printing on and off. See, for example, the `verbose` flag in the `bisect` function on page 260, or the `newton` function on page 266.

When creating diagnostic programs, it is helpful to use test problems that have exact analytical answers. Examples of such test programs are the demo functions used throughout this text to show how a particular numerical method works. See, for example, the demoNewton function on page 264, the demoEuler function on page 685, or the demoTrap function on page 608. The following example provides an additional demonstration of the use of diagnostic programs:

Example 4.4: Testing the `trapzDat` Function

The `trapzDat` function applies the trapezoid rule to integrate a discrete set of data. For a continuous function $f(x)$, the trapezoid rule is

$$I = \int_a^b f(x)\,dx = \frac{h}{2} \sum_{i=2}^{n} (f_i + f_{i-1}) + \mathcal{O}(h^2),$$

where h is the spacing between evaluations of f on the x-axis

$$h = \frac{b - a}{n - 1}$$

and n is the number of points in the data set. If the x_i are not uniformly spaced, then

$$I \approx \frac{1}{2} \sum_{i=2}^{n} (f_i + f_{i-1})(x_i - x_{i-1}).$$

The `trapzDat` function in Listing 11.3 on page 611 evaluates the preceding formula for a given set of $(x_i, f(x_i))$ pairs. A discussion of `trapzDat` is provided in § 11.2.1. The purpose of this example is to show how the calculations in `trapzDat` can be verified. Checking the correctness of a computational module does not require knowing anything about the internal details of the module. The testing should be based on the description of the function and its input and output parameters given in the code documentation.

A simple test of the `trapzDat` function is to evaluate the integral of a known function $f(x)$. A problem with such a test is that the trapezoid rule has a nonzero truncation error. Thus, there will be a difference between the exact integral and the result obtained with trapezoid rule, even if there are no errors in the program. If, however, a piecewise-constant function is integrated with the trapezoid rule, the truncation error is zero.[4] The following statements, for example, show that `trapzDat` produces the correct result for $f(x) = 1$:

```
>> x = linspace(0,1);
>> f = ones(size(x));   %  constant f(x)
>> s = trapzDat(x,f)
s =
      1
```

The prologue of `trapzDat` claims that the input data can be arbitrarily spaced. The preceding test uses uniformly spaced data. The `trapzDatTest` function in Listing 4.3 uses three variations on the integral of a constant function to test whether `trapzDat` correctly handles nonuniformly spaced x data. The first test is to integrate $f(x) = \pi$ for an even number of data pairs. The second test evaluates the integral for an odd number of data pairs. The third test computes $\int_0^1 \pi \, dx$ for randomly spaced x values. The results of the tests are shown later.

Another test of the `trapzDat` function is to determine whether the truncation error depends on h, as predicted by a theoretical analysis. The basis of the test is discussed in § 5.3.2 beginning on page 226, and in Example 11.6 on page 607. For any two evaluations of the integral with different h, the error E in the integral should give

$$\alpha = \frac{\log\left(\dfrac{E(x, h_2)}{E(x, h_1)}\right)}{\log\left(\dfrac{h_2}{h_1}\right)},$$

where $\alpha = 2$ for the trapezoid rule. The `trapzDatTest` function uses the trapezoid rule to compute $\int_a^b \sin x \, dx$ for $a = -5\pi/7$, $b = 3\pi/5$, and a sequence of decreasing h values. The strange values of a and b are chosen to include negative values of x and to avoid the possibility that a simple value of the integral would be obtained. For each h, the numerically computed value of the integral and the exact value are subtracted to obtain the absolute truncation error. Then, α is computed from subsequent h values. Running `trapzDatTest` gives

---

[4]The trapezoid rule produces the exact result for an $f(x)$ that is a piecewise polynomial of degree ≤ 1. A piecewise constant is chosen for convenience.

```
function trapzDatTest
% trapzDatTest   Verify trapzDat function for different types of input
%
% Synopsis:   trapzDatTest
%
% Input:      none
%
% Output:     Print out of test results

% --- Integral of a constant
fprintf('Integrate a constant function\n');
x = linspace(-5,7,8);        %  Test 1:  even number of intervals
f = pi*ones(size(x));        %  constant function
s = trapzDat(x,f);
err = s - pi*(max(x)-min(x));
fprintf('\tEven interval test:    s = %8.4f   error = %10.3e\n',s,err);


x = linspace(-5,7,9);        %  Test 2:  odd number of intervals
f = pi*ones(size(x));        %  constant function
s = trapzDat(x,f);
err = s - pi*(max(x)-min(x));
fprintf('\tOdd interval test:     s = %8.4f   error = %10.3e\n',s,err);


x = sort(rand(5,1)-0.2);     %  Test 3:  randomly spaced x data
f = pi*ones(size(x));
s = trapzDat(x,f);
err = s - pi*(max(x)-min(x));
fprintf('\tRandom spacing test:   s = %8.4f   error = %10.3e\n',s,err);


% --- Truncation error test
fprintf('\nTruncation error test\n');
fprintf('   n       integral           error         alpha\n');
xmin = -5*pi/7;   xmax =  3*pi/5;  % oddball starting and stoping points
hold = -5;        errold = 0;      % initialize test for first try

for n = [10  17  25  100  315  2001  4522]
  x = linspace(xmin,xmax,n);
  f = sin(x);
  s = trapzDat(x,f);
  err = s - (cos(x(1)) - cos(x(n)));
  fprintf('%5d  %15.12f  %12.3e',n,s,err);
  h = (xmax-xmin)/(n-1);
  if hold<0
    fprintf('\n');             %  first iteration, skip test
  else
    fprintf('  %9.5f\n',log(err/errold)/log(h/hold));
  end
  hold = h;  errold = err;    %  prepare for next iteration
end
```

Listing 4.3 The `trapzDatTest` function tests the `trapzDat` function.

```
>> trapzDatTest
Integrate a constant function
Even interval test:    s =   37.6991   error =   0.000e+00
Odd interval test:     s =   37.6991   error = -7.105e-15
Random spacing test:   s =    1.6643   error =   0.000e+00

Truncation error test
    n       integral           error         alpha
   10   -0.308937718819     5.535e-03
   17   -0.312725683473     1.747e-03     2.00419
   25   -0.313696787292     7.760e-04     2.00152
  100   -0.314427222335     4.559e-05     2.00033
  315   -0.314468276181     4.531e-06     2.00002
 2001   -0.314472695792     1.117e-07     2.00000
 4522   -0.314472785626     2.186e-08     2.00000
```

The first three tests show that trapzDat obtains the exact value (to within roundoff) of the integral of a constant function. The last test shows that as the number of points n in the interval is increased, the measured value of alpha approaches a value of 2, as it should. The result of the four tests in trapzDatTest give us confidence that the trapzDat function is a correct implementation of the trapezoid rule.

4.3 DEBUGGING

Searching for and removing bugs is an inevitable part of programming. Bugs are caused by a number of factors from outright programming blunders to the improper application of a numerical method. When a program is first written, it is likely to contain bugs that lead to *fatal errors*, which cause MATLAB to stop execution. Consider the multiply function

```
function z = multiply(x,y)
% multiply   Compute product of two arguments
z = x*y;
```

This function contains no errors, and the statement

```
>> multiply(2,3)
ans =
     6
```

works as expected. The following statements produce a fatal error.

```
>> x = 1:4;   y = 1:4;
>> multiply(x,y)
??? Error using ==> *
Inner matrix dimensions must agree.
```

Line	Code description
2–13	The prologue provides complete and concise documentation of the input and output variables and the syntax of the function call.
26–32	The `if...` structure that checks `units` provides a default `else...` `error` trap. If the `elseif` statement on line 28 were replaced with an `else`, then any value of `units` other than `'F'` would result in calculation in °C. The error trap prevents the user from erroneously, assuming that some other unsupported system of units (e.g., `'R'` for degrees Rankine or `'K'` for kelvins).
26, 28, 44	The `units` variable is converted to uppercase for all comparisons. This allows a user to enter lower case "f" to indicate °F.
27,29	In converting from Fahrenheit to Celsius, the input variable `T` is not overwritten. A new variable `Tin` is created instead.
35–37	The value of `Tin` is tested to make sure it falls in the range of the curve fit. If not, a meaningful error message is given, and execution is stopped.

4.3.2 Debugging Tools

Version 5 of MATLAB includes an interactive debugger that is a huge asset to programmers. Because the debugger works slightly differently on each computer platform, it will not be described here. It is well worth the effort to work through the
interactive debugging tutorial in *Using* MATLAB [73]. Debugging is also facilitated
by several MATLAB commands. Only four simple commands will be discussed
here.

The `type` and `dbtype` Commands   Whenever MATLAB encounters a
fatal error, it gives the name of the routine that caused the error, along with an
error message. If the function that caused the error was called by another function,
the name of the calling function and the line number of the call is given. The
call hierarchy is then traced back through all functions until the instigating user
statement is reached.

Upon receiving an error message, the first step is to identify the conditions
leading up to the error. The most basic way of doing this is to view the statements
of the m-file that caused the error. The contents of any m-file can be listed in the
command window by typing

```
type filename
```

where `filename` is the name of an m-file (without the `.m` extension) in the current
path. Executing the `type` command produces the entire listing of an m-file. It is
often helpful to use the `dbtype` command to list just a few lines near the cause of
the error message. The `dbtype` command has the two forms

```
dbtype filename
```

which prints the entire contents of a file along with line numbers, and

```
dbtype filename start:stop
```

which lists line number *start* through line number *stop*.

The error Function   The error function (not to be confused with erf) allows rudimentary error handling to be added to a m-file function. The syntax is

```
error(message)
```

where *message* is a character string to be printed to the screen when the error function is executed. The error function is incorporated into an m-file, and not executed from the command line. A typical usage is

```
if error condition test
  error(message)
end
```

where *error condition test* is a logical expression that attempts to detect the symptoms of a bug. When the error function is executed, MATLAB lists the name of the function containing the call to error and prints the *message*. In addition, the names of any functions that called the one containing the error are printed. MATLAB then halts execution of the program and returns control to the command window.

Use of the error function is shown in the trivial noneg function, which is listed here:

```
function y = noneg(x)
% noneg  Returns x if x>0, otherwise prints an error message and stops
if x<0
  error('x is negative');
end
y = x;
```

Running noneg with an negative input value gives, for example,

```
>> y = noneg(3-5)
??? Error using ==> noneg
x is negative
```

The error message can be made more meaningful by including numerical values related to the error. This requires building a text string as the argument to the error function. Here an some alternative expressions that could be substituted into the noneg function:

```
message = ['x = ',num2str(x),' cannot be negative'];
error(message);
```
                                                                         % or
```
error(['x = ',num2str(x),' cannot be negative']);
```
                                                                             % or
```
error(sprintf('x = %f cannot be negative',x));
```

Incorporating the last version into the old noneg function gives

```
function y = noneg2(x)
% noneg2  Returns x if x>0, otherwise prints an error message and stops.
%         The error message contains the value of x.
if x<0
  error(sprintf('x = %f cannot be negative',x));
end
y = x;
```

The pause **Command**   The pause command temporarily suspends the execution of an m-file. This is a useful way to print a warning message without necessarily aborting an analysis. When a pause statement is encountered, MATLAB stops execution and changes the cursor to a large "P" to indicate that the program has paused. At this point, the user can terminate the analysis by pressing control-C or allow the execution to continue by pressing the return key. The pause(n) command causes MATLAB to suspend execution for *n* seconds *without* waiting for the user to respond to the pause.

    Here is the nonegp function, which uses a pause instead of aborting the execution when the input value is negative:

```
function y = nonegp(x)
% nonegp  Returns x if x>0, otherwise prints a message and pauses
if x<0
  disp('x is negative, press return to proceed');
  pause;
end
y = x;
```

Try the command nonegp(-1), for example, to experience the effect of a pause.

The keyboard **Command**   The keyboard command suspends execution of an m-file and gives control over to the user. The keyboard command is much more powerful than the pause command, because it gives the user access to the internal variables of the function (m-file) containing the keyboard command.

    The keyboard command is usually inserted in an m-file that has a known bug. When a keyboard command is encountered, the prompt in the command window changes from >> to K>>. At the K>> prompt, any of the local variables in the m-file can be printed in an effort to determine the cause of the error. Normally, these local variables are not shared by the MATLAB command window. Execution of the m-file is resumed when the user enters the `return` at the MATLAB prompt. The use of the `keyboard` command is demonstrated in the next example.

The interactive debugger enables the interruption of an m-file without literally inserting a `keyboard` command. When MATLAB encounters a breakpoint set by the interactive debugger, the user can query variables local to the function.

Example 4.6: Using the `keyboard` Command

The `quadroot` function in Listing 4.5 computes the two roots of a second-order polynomial with the improved formula described in § 6.7 on page 279. Suppose that a bug in some other function (not shown here) was caused when `quadroot` returned complex roots. One way to investigate the problem is to put a `keyboard` command inside the `quadroot` function. This would allow, for example, the coefficients of the quadratic formula to be examined. The purpose here is to demonstrate the `keyboard` command, not to imply that there is a bug in `quadroot`.

```
function r = quadroot(a,b,c)
% quadroot    Roots of quadratic equation and demo of keyboard command
%
% Synopsis:   r = quadroot(a,b,c)
%
% Input:      a,b,c = coefficients of  a*x^2 + b*x + c = 0
%
% Output:     r = column vector containing the real or complex roots

% See Chapter 4, Unavoidable Errors in Computing, for a discussion
% of the formula for r(1) and r(2)
d = b^2 - 4*a*c;
if d<0
  fprintf('Warning in function QUADROOT:\n');
  fprintf('\tNegative discriminant\n\tType "return" to continue\n');
  keyboard;
end
q = -0.5*( b + sign(b)*sqrt(b^2 - 4*a*c) );

r = [q/a; c/q];  % store roots in a column vector
```

Listing 4.5   The quadroot function is designed to illustrate the use of the keyboard command

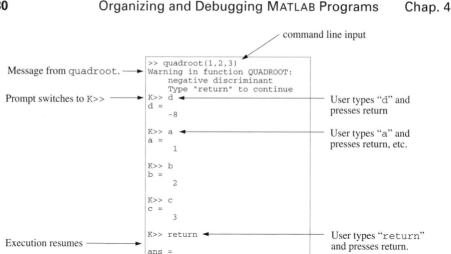

command line input

Message from quadroot. →

Prompt switches to K>> →

Execution resumes →

```
>> quadroot(1,2,3)
Warning in function QUADROOT:
    negative discriminant
    Type "return" to continue
K>> d
d =
      -8

K>> a
a =
       1

K>> b
b =
       2

K>> c
c =
       3

K>> return

ans =
   -1.0000- 1.4142i
   -1.0000+ 1.4142i
```

User types "d" and
presses return

User types "a" and
presses return, etc.

User types "return"
and presses return.

Figure 4.5   Example of responses to the keyboard command appearing in the quadroot function from Listing 4.5. This session is initiated by typing quadroot(1,2,3) in the command window.

Figure 4.5 lists a sample MATLAB session showing how the quadroot function responds to the occurrence of complex roots. The session is initiated by entering

```
>> quadroot(1,2,3)
```

The "user types" messages on the right-hand side of Figure 4.5 are statements that you enter in the command window. Notice that after execution is resumed the quadroot function computes the two complex roots correctly.

4.4 SUMMARY

Recommendations for organizing MATLAB codes are presented in this chapter. The use of modular code that is well documented enables a programmer to develop complicated programs with less overall effort. Well structured code also aids in debugging. The techniques recommended here are demonstrated by an example. The m-files used in this chapter are listed in Table 4.1.

Further Reading

One of the best ways to learn about writing code is to read the code written by experienced programmers. Even if the code is well written, it usually takes time to read it carefully. MATLAB users have a wealth of high-quality code provided in

TABLE 4.1 NMM TOOLBOX FUNCTIONS USED TO INTRODUCE PROGRAM ORGANIZATION AND DEBUGGING.

Function	Page	Description
dailyAve	167	Compute average daily flow rate from hourly flow data
H20density	175	Density of saturated liquid water
multiply	173	Compute product of two arguments
noneg	177	Returns x if $x > 0$; otherwise prints an error message and stops
noneg2	178	Returns x if $x > 0$; otherwise prints an error message and stops The error message contains the value of x.
nonegp	178	Returns x if $x > 0$; otherwise prints a message and pauses
quadroot	179	Roots of quadratic equation and demo of keyboard command
riverReport	168	Compute and plot summary of river flow data.
trapzDatTest	172	Reduce a number by factors of two until it is set to zero
weeklyAve	167	Compute average weekly flow rate from hourly flow data.

the standard MATLAB toolbox. Although this code is sparsely documented, it provides many excellent examples on how to subdivide large computational tasks into smaller more manageable modules. The standard toolbox codes are complicated by their generality, so it is helpful to read the code by assuming that the inputs are simple; that is, choose the fewest number of input and output parameters.

I have attempted to make the m-files in the NMM Toolbox examples of well-written code. A careful reader will certainly find opportunities for improving those m-files. In some cases, there are too many statements crammed on a single line. This is to get the code to fit onto a single page of this book. In other cases, the comment statements are terse or even missing! So why not go ahead and improve those codes? I encourage you to do so. As you edit the codes, ask yourself: Are the changes mere ornamentation? Or am I increasing the readability, maintainability, or usability of the code? I recommend that you first make a copy of the mfile in question, so that you may easily revert to to the original.

Kernighan and Plauger provide good advice on how to write organized code that is easy to read and maintain [47]. Their examples, given in Fortran and PL/1, may be directly translated to MATLAB code. Kernighan and Pike use examples from C, C++, and Java to discuss good programming style and debugging strategies, along with other good software development practices [46].

EXERCISES

The number in parentheses at the beginning of each exercise indicates the degree of skill and amount of effort necessary to complete the exercise. See § 1.4 on page 10 for a description of the rating system.

1. (1+) For each of the following MATLAB statements, make a list of all functions that are called to produce the value of y.

(a) `y = bessel(1,3.2);`

(b) `y = besselk(2,5);`

Hint: Read the source code of the functions by entering "`type bessel`" at the command prompt.

SOLUTION **2.** (2) Use stepwise refinement to describe all of the steps necessary to compute the average and standard deviation of the elements in a vector x. Implement these tasks in an m-file, and test your solution. Do not use the built-in `mean` and `std` functions. Rather, develop your solution from the equations for the average and standard deviation of a finite sample.

3. (3) Semiconductor devices are mass produced on wafers of Silicon that can hold more than a hundred devices each. As a wafer moves through production, random failures can occur during any one of the many stages of processing. When the wafer is completely processed, each device on the wafer is tested, and the wafer is cut into individual devices, or *chips*. Chips passing the final test are attached to a lead frame and encapsulated in a package that is eventually assembled into a circuit board. The ratio of successful chips to the total number of chips is called the yield of the process.

    The `chip.dat` file in the `data` directory of the NMM toolbox contains data for a production run of a semiconductor device. The first column is the serial number of the chip, and the second column is the chip's speed limit in megahertz (MHz). The speed limit is the highest clock speed at which a chip can reliably run. Entries in the second column equal to `NaN` indicate that the chip completely failed the speed test.

    Use stepwise refinement to create a program (that may consist of multiple m-file functions) to determine the gross yield and the number of chips in the data set that qualified at 250, 300, 350, 400, and 450 MHz.

4. (3−) Starting with the solution to the preceding problem, add a printed report that lists the serial numbers of the chips that qualify in each frequency bin.

5. (3) File `traffic.dat` contains traffic metering data from a city street. The file contains a single column with the time (in decimal hours) at which a vehicle passes the metering site. Use stepwise refinement to create a program that prints the traffic passing the meter for each hour of the day.

6. (3) There is an error in the calculation of the average weekly flow data in Example 4.3. Since 365 is not a multiple of 7, the last week of the year will not be seven days long. When a year does not contain an even number of weeks, the averaging process in the `weeklyAve` function is incorrect. The effect of this error is evident in the last weekly flow rate data point in Figure 4.4. Fix this bug.

7. (3−) For the river report program in Example 4.3, create a new `dailyMinMax` function that determines the high and low flow rate for each day of the year.

8. (3) The code modules developed in Example 4.3 can be further simplified by eliminating redundancies in the `dailyAve` and `weeklyAve` modules. Computation of the daily average and weekly average are specific variations on the more general problem of computing an average over a fixed time interval. Without writing any MATLAB code, design a module that would compute the daily average or weekly average, depending on the input variables. Your design should include a complete description of the tasks performed by the module, along with its input and output parameters. Note that there are several ways to implement this idea. It may be simpler to move some of the logic up to a higher level module instead of combining all the functionality of dailyAve and weeklyAve into one module.

9. (3) Implement and test the module you designed in the preceding problem. Is your function immune from the bug described in Exercise 6?

10. (3) The indent script contains the code on page 154 and a few extra lines. Running indent with the following statements reveals that there is a subtle bug in the script.

```
>> nx = 6;
>> indent
>> nx = 4;
>> indent
```

Find the bug, describe it in words, and create a corrected version of indent.m.

11. (2) The built-in interp1 function performs interpolation of one-dimensional data (i.e., $y = f(x)$). When the point at which the interpolant is to be evaluated is out of range of the tabulated data, interp1 returns a NaN value without any warning to the user. For example,

```
>> interp1([1 2 3 4 5],[9 8 7 6 5],11,'linear')
ans =
   NaN
```

Write a safeInterp function that uses interp1 for linear interpolation, while also implementing the following defensive programming tactics:

i) Check for NaN as a return values of interp1. (Can you write this for the case when xi and yi are vectors?)

ii) If a NaN (or more than one NaN) is found, test for range errors (i.e., xi > max(xtable) or xi < min(xtable)).

iii) Print a warning message to the user if range errors are found.

iv) Assign yi value(s) to the ytable value corresponding to y value at min(xtable) or max(xtable), depending on the the type of range violation.

PART 2
Numerical Techniques

5

Unavoidable Errors in Computing

There are many causes for malfunction in computer systems. Sometimes, the hardware (e.g., the disk drive) fails. Other times, critical data—everything from serial numbers and billing amounts to operating instructions—are entered incorrectly, causing a program to *reliably* perform the *wrong* task. Still other failures are caused when the program being used—from a word processor to the control system for a nuclear power plant—contains a logic error, resulting in unexpected behavior, corrupted data, or a system crash.

An error in software is called a *bug*[1], and the operation of removing bugs is called *debugging*. A software bug causes deterministic errors in program execution. Given the same initial data, a specific sequence of actions results in the same erroneous outcome. The more complex the software is, the more effort is required

---

[1]Usage of the term *bug* to describe a computer malfunction is first attributed to Grace Hopper, who was working on the Mark II computer. (See, e.g., Kahaner et al. [43, p.35].) The Mark II, as was typical of computers before the transister was invented, had logic circuits consisting of vacuum tubes and electromechanical relays. On one occassion, when the Mark II was producing incorrect results, Ms. Hopper traced the problem to a moth that had crawled between two exposed contacts of a relay. This killed the insect and caused a short in the logic circuit. Ms. Hopper removed the moth, pasted it into her laboratory notebook, and wrote that the malfunction was caused by a "bug" in the computer.

to test for and remove the bugs. Software bugs may appear to be random in some situations, because the symptoms of the error may depend on the state of the computer, specifically the data in memory, when the error occurs.

Software that performs mathematical calculations is as susceptible to bugs as any other type of software. There are, however, two additional types of errors that are particular to numerical computation: *roundoff error* and *truncation error*. Unlike programming bugs, roundoff and truncation errors are unavoidable. Roundoff occurs in a computer calculation whenever digits to the right of the decimal point are discarded. The digits are lost because there is a limit on the memory available for storing any one numerical value. Truncation error is introduced whenever a numerical computation uses formulas involving discrete values as an approximation to a continuous mathematical function. A goal of numerical analysis is to find ways to solve a given problem such that it is impervious to roundoff and such that the truncation error is below a user-prescribed tolerance.[2] Concern for roundoff and truncation errors must be included in the design of robust numerical algorithms. This chapter provides a background for the consideration of roundoff and truncation errors in the programs presented through the remainder of this book.

Uncertainty in the input data is yet another type of error affecting the results of numerical computations. Uncertainty is introduced from errors in input data, for example, when the data are from experimental measurements or in the rounding of input data when they are first stored in computer memory. The significance of uncertainty in the inputs is determined by the *condition* of the numerical computation. A well-conditioned numerical computation will be relatively insensitive to perturbations in the input, whereas a poorly conditioned, or *ill-conditioned*, computation will lead to results that are highly suspect (at best) or totally worthless. Because the impact of conditioning is specific to each numerical method, it will be discussed as particular methods are described in later chapters.

Perhaps it is odd to some readers to start out a discussion of numerical methods with such a depressing topic as unavoidable errors. Why should we begin with a consideration of what goes wrong before even presenting any useful algorithms? This decision is more significant than choosing between good news or bad news first. By examining the source of unavoidable numerical errors, the foundation is established for many algorithmic decisions taken to minimize the impact of these errors. It is difficult to appreciate the design of good algorithms without a fundamental understanding of the errors that are inherent in numerical calculations.

Figure 5.1 summarizes the key topics covered in this chapter.

---

[2]Trefethen argues that numerical analysts have incorrectly defined their activity as the study of numerical errors [76]. The purpose of this book is to present the implementation, not the analysis, of numerical methods. Though concern for errors will arise throughout the book, it is not the primary focus.

Topics Covered in This Chapter

1. **Digital Representation of Numbers**

   Storage of numerical values in digital format introduces limitations on the range and precision of real numbers. **Floating-point numbers**, the digital incarnation of real numbers, and the basic format for storage of numerical values in MATLAB are defined in this section.

2. **Finite Precision Arithmetic**

   Digital storage of numbers introduces **roundoff errors** in arithmetic operations. The size of roundoff is characterized by **machine precision**. This section provides recommendations on how to manage the effect of roundoff in comparison operations, especially for **convergence criteria** of iterative calculations.

3. **Truncation Error of Algorithms**

   Truncation error is introduced when a continuous function is approximated with a simpler arithmetic formula involving only discrete values. **Order notation** expresses the order of magnitude influence of key parameters that control the size of the truncation error. This section covers the basic idea of truncation error in preparation for the consideration of truncation error in the remainder of the book.

Figure 5.1   Primary topics discussed in Chapter 5.

Example 5.1: Spontaneous Generation of Digits

As motivation for studying floating-point arithmetic, consider the following simple calculations in MATLAB.[3]

```
>> format long e        % display all of the significant digits
>> 2.6 + 0.2
ans =
     2.800000000000000e+00

>> ans + 0.2
ans =
     3.000000000000000e+00

>> ans + 0.2
ans =
     3.200000000000001e+00
```

[3]Mark Reichelt posted this example to the comp.soft-sys.matlab newsgroup on 6 December 1993.

Repeated addition of the perfectly reasonable fraction 0.2 results in the creation of an erroneous digit. Although the error is in the least significant digit, one wonders why and how it was created in the first place. To add to the mystery, consider what happens when 0.6 is added repeatedly.

```
>> 2.6 + 0.6
ans =
      3.200000000000000e+00

>>ans + 0.6
ans =
      3.800000000000000e+00

>>ans + 0.6
ans =
      4.400000000000000e+00

>>ans + 0.6
ans =
    5
```

Not only is there no apparent loss of precision, but MATLAB displays the final result as "5", an integer. This behavior is caused by the finite arithmetic used in numerical computations.

Example 5.2: The Pentium™ FDIV Bug

The most famous recent example of a bug in numerical calculations occurred in early generations of the Intel Pentium™ microprocessor. This bug was discovered by Thomas Nicely, a mathematician doing research on prime numbers. Nicely noticed an abnormally large roundoff error in the quotient of certain combinations of integers. After testing his programs on a variety of computers, he began to suspect that the error was in the hardware, not the software.

Nicely's program exposed an error that occurred when the microprocessor executed a FDIV instruction with special combinations of operands. The so-called FDIV bug was caused by missing entries in a table that are part of the permanent, on-chip memory of the Pentium™. For certain combinations of operands, a division that should be accurate to 16 digits was only accurate to 7 digits.

Only a few operands caused incorrect division results. Since a numerical computer simulation can involve billions of operations for a single computed result, one could never guarantee that calculations with a buggy Pentium™ chip were free of significant errors. When an erroneous division occurred, the roundoff errors that normally behave in predictable ways would suddenly increase by several orders of magnitude. Though it initially downplayed the significance of the bug, Intel eventually offered to replace defective chips. For a concise history of the discovery, documentation, and interim patches for the bug, see Moler [54]. A mathematical analysis of the bug is given by Edelman [20].

.1 DIGITAL REPRESENTATION OF NUMBERS

For practical reasons, computers use only a fixed number of digits to represent a number. As a result, the numerical values stored in a computer are said to have finite precision. Limiting precision has the desirable effects of increasing the speed of numerical calculations and reducing the memory required to store numbers. It has the undesirable effect of introducing *roundoff*, the error caused by discarding the least significant digits of a calculation. To understand the source of roundoff, one needs to consider the fundamental way in which numbers are stored in computers.

5.1.1 Bits, Bytes, and Words

Nearly all modern computers manipulate binary numbers (i.e., the number system using base 2). Table 5.1 shows some examples of base-10 and base-2 numbers. Bits, bytes, and words are binary numbers with different numbers of digits.

A bit is a binary digit (i.e., a 1 or a 0). A byte is a group of eight bits. The numbers in the last column of Table 5.1 are bytes. A word is the smallest addressable unit of memory for a particular computer. The word size of a computer depends on the operating system and the underlying computer architecture. Computer experts talk about "64-bit microprocessors" and "32-bit operating systems". These are references to the word size of the computer hardware and the word size used by the operating system, respectively. The word size affects the speed and capabilities of a computer, but for the immediate discussion, words are less important than bits and bytes.

There are three basic types of numbers: integers, real numbers, and complex numbers. A number from any one of these sets can be uniquely identified by a symbol, such as 14, π, and $2 + 3i$. When calculations are performed on a computer, the numerical values represented by the symbols must be stored in computer memory. This requires a translation between the *symbolic* format used when we

TABLE 5.1   EXAMPLES OF BASE 10 AND BINARY (BASE 2) NUMBERS AND THE CONVERSION BETWEEN THEM.

Base 10	Conversion	Base 2
1	$1 =$ 2^0	0000 0001
2	$2 =$ 2^1	0000 0010
4	$4 =$ 2^2	0000 0100
8	$8 =$ 2^3	0000 1000
9	$8 + 1 =$ $2^3 + 2^0$	0000 1001
10	$8 + 2 =$ $2^3 + 2^1$	0000 1010
27	$16 + 8 + 2 + 1 = 2^4 + 2^3 + 2^1 + 2^0$	0001 1011

one byte

manipulate numbers with pencil and paper to a *numeric* format represented by a sequence of bits. The translation is constrained by the number of bytes available to store each type of number. Corresponding to the integers of exact mathematics are the integers computers use, which have a limited range of values. Corresponding to the real numbers are the *floating-point* numbers computers use, which have a limited range and a limited number of decimal digits. Complex numbers are treated as pairs of floating-point numbers, so apart from the rules for complex arithmetic, complex numbers used by computers have the same constraints as floating-point numbers.

5.1.2 Integers

Integers stored in computers are usually[4] represented by a fixed number of binary digits. This section is a brief exploration of how memory is allocated to each integer. Since MATLAB does not use integer variables, the current discussion is merely a prelude to the description of floating-point numbers.

Consider how the decimal value 25 is represented as a binary number. To convert from base 10 to base 2, first express the decimal value as a sum of decimal powers of 2. Then, assign the appropriate bit to each decimal power of 2. Thus,

$$25 = 16 + 8 + 1 = 2^4 + 2^3 + 2^0 = (11001)_2.$$

The notation $(bbbb)_2$ is used to designate a base-2 number in situations where it could be confused for a base 10 number. The b is a bit value (i.e., 1 or 0). Conversion from base 10 to base 2 is automated by the built-in dec2bin function:

```
>> dec2bin(25)
ans =
11001
```

The four-digit decimal number 25 requires 5 bits. Since not all of the bits are turned on, those same 5 bits can represent larger numbers. The largest 5-bit number has a binary representation of $(11111)_2$. Converting $(11111)_2$ to its decimal equivalent gives (see also the bin2dec function)

$$(11111)_2 = 2^4 + 2^3 + 2^2 + 2^1 + 2^0 = 31,$$

which is the same as $2^5 - 1$. The -1 arises because the number 2^5 actually needs 6 bits to be represented in base 2. The least significant (rightmost) bit corresponds to 2^0. The decimal equivalent of the most significant (leftmost) bit in any binary number of n bits corresponds to 2^{n-1}.

---

[4]Though software for manipulating numbers of arbitrary range is readily available, most *numerical* computations are performed with integers and floating-point numbers of fixed range and precision.

Most computers reserve either 16 bits (2 bytes) or 32-bits (4 bytes) for integer values. These two lengths are sometimes called integers and long integers, respectively. Once the type of integer, either "regular" or long is chosen, all integers using that type require the same amount of computer memory. For example, when the value 123 is assigned to a 16-bit integer variable, all 16 bits are reserved in the computer memory, even though only 7 bits are needed to represent 123. The reason for this apparent wastage is that computer hardware can be more simple and efficient if it only handles numbers with a predetermined number of bits.

The absolute upper limit on the largest unsigned integer that can be stored as a 16-bit binary number, is $2^{16} - 1 = 65535$. To accommodate negative integers, computer scientists invented *two's-complement* notation, which allows positive and negative integers to be stored without wasting a bit for the sign. This notation allows 16 bits to represent all the integers in the range $[-32768, 32767]$. The range is not symmetric, because zero is included as one of the values.

Fortunately the computer takes care of the details of decimal-to-binary conversion. As computer users, we only need to remember that because integers are represented by a finite number of bits, there are upper and lower limits to the range of integers that can be readily used in any calculation. Similar range limitations also apply to floating-point numbers.

5.1.3 Floating-point Numbers

Floating-point numbers are the digital representations of numerical values that have nonzero fractional parts. In this section, the binary representation of floating-point numbers is related to the range and precision limits on floating-point values.

Binary Representation   Because binary numbers do not have an inherent fractional part, floating-point numbers cannot be represented with the same storage scheme as integers. Floating-point numbers are instead stored in a binary equivalent of scientific notation.

There are many equivalent ways to write a given number in scientific notation, for example,

$$123.456 = 123.456 \times 10^0 = 1.23456 \times 10^2 = 123456 \times 10^{-3} = \ldots,$$

the difference being in the placement of the decimal point of the *mantissa*, the number multiplying the power of 10. For our purposes, it is sufficient to use the convention that the first digit to the left of the decimal point will always be zero and the first digit to the right of the decimal point will never be zero.[5] Here are some examples of how floating-point values are represented with this convention:

---

[5]Refer to Goldberg for an extensive discussion of the IEEE Floating-Point Standard [29]. Moler describes how MATLAB uses the IEEE Standard [55].

Value	Normalized notation
37.5	0.3750×10^2
−812.5	-0.8125×10^3
0.005781	0.5781×10^{-2}

Each of these values can be written as

$$\pm (0.d_1 d_2 \dots d_n) \times 10^s, \tag{5.1}$$

where the d_i are the decimal digits of the mantissa and s is the exponent. Computers store floating-point values in base 2. The base-2 equivalent of Equation (5.1) is written as

$$\pm p \times 2^t = \pm (b_1 b_2 \dots b_m) \times 2^t,$$

where p is the binary equivalent of the mantissa and t is the binary equivalent of the exponent.

Floating-point numbers are stored as 32-bit values for *single precision* or as 64-bit values for *double precision*. The precision dictates how many digits are reserved for each floating-point value and how the digits are allocated between the mantissa and exponent. A single-precision floating-point number has 23 bits allocated to the mantissa and 8 bits allocated to the exponent. A 64-bit (double-precision) floating-point number uses 53 bits for the mantissa including a sign bit, and 11 bits for the exponent including a sign bit. The base-2 equivalent of a double-precision value looks like the following:

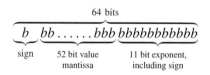

The finite representation of floating-point numbers has two important consequences: The range (magnitude) of floating-point numbers is limited, and the floating-point number line is not continuous. These limits are discussed in the next few sections.

Range Limits   The magnitude of a floating-point value is constrained by the number of bits allocated to the storage of the exponent. Double-precision exponents use 11 bits. The sign takes one bit, leaving 10 bits for the magnitude of the exponent in double precision. The magnitude of the largest 10-bit base-2 number is $2^{10} - 1 = 1023$. Thus, the largest magnitude of the base-10 number expressible in double precision is roughly

$$2^{1023} \sim 9 \times 10^{307}.$$

TABLE 5.2   SUMMARY OF APPROXIMATE MAGNITUDE RANGES FOR SINGLE- AND DOUBLE-PRECISION DATA TYPES ON COMPUTERS USING 32-BIT MICROPROCESSORS. THE COMMON MATLAB VARIABLES WE CONSIDER IN THIS TEXT ARE OF DOUBLE PRECISION. MATLAB'S COMPLEX VALUES HAVE DOUBLE-PRECISION REAL AND DOUBLE-PRECISION IMAGINARY PARTS.

Fortran data type	Range
integer	$-32768 \leq I \leq 32767$
single precision	$-3.40 \times 10^{38} \leq x \leq -1.18 \times 10^{-38}$ 0 $1.18 \times 10^{-38} \leq x \leq 3.40 \times 10^{38}$
double precision	$-1.80 \times 10^{308} \leq x \leq -2.23 \times 10^{-308}$ 0 $2.23 \times 10^{-308} \leq x \leq 1.80 \times 10^{308}$
complex	$a + ib$, where $i \equiv \sqrt{-1}$ and a and b are single-precision values

Table 5.2 uses Fortran data types to summarize the range limits on integers and floating-point numbers for a typical personal computer. In C, the `float` data type corresponds to Fortran single precision, and `double` corresponds to Fortran double precision. C has no built-in complex data type.

MATLAB version 5 and later allows numeric variables to be created as eight-bit integers or double-precision floating point values. The eight-bit integer is used in specialized applications, such as image processing. For our purposes, we assume that all numeric MATLAB variables correspond to Fortran double precision. If a MATLAB variable has a complex value, both the real and complex parts are stored as double-precision values.

The limitations of 64-bit (double-precision) floating-point values are also depicted graphically in Figure 5.2. Numbers with magnitudes greater than roughly 10^{+308} do not exist on the number line of 64-bit floating-point values. Any MATLAB calculation resulting in a magnitude greater than $\sim 10^{+308}$ causes an *overflow* error. In addition to the upper limits on the magnitude, there are also limits on the smallest magnitude floating-point numbers. Any MATLAB calculation that results in a magnitude smaller than $\sim 10^{-308}$, and not exactly equal to zero, cannot be represented by a 64-bit number. Thus, there are no double-precision numbers between zero and roughly $\pm 10^{-308}$. This hole in the number line is the range where *underflow* errors occur.

The built-in MATLAB variables `realmin` and `realmax` correspond to the underflow and overflow limits, respectively. The overflow limit is `realmax`, the

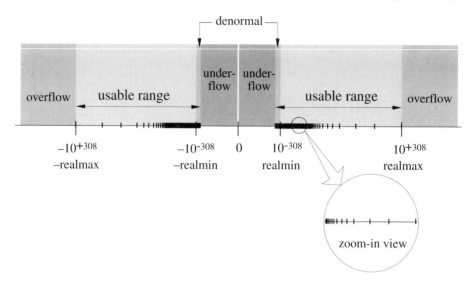

Figure 5.2   Discrete approximation to the real number line.

floating-point number having a binary representation with all of its usable bits turned on. Without any more bits, it is impossible to store a number larger than `realmax`. A number greater than `realmax` is assigned the special value `Inf`.

```
>> 10*realmax
ans =
     ∞
```

At the other end of the spectrum is `realmin`, the smallest floating-point number that can be stored without a loss of precision. It is possible to store a floating-point number smaller than `realmin` if bits that are normally associated with the mantissa are used by the exponent. Such a number is called a *denormal*, because it is not stored in the normalized format used for other values on the floating-point number line. The denormal values are depicted by the narrow bands between ±`realmin` and the underflow areas in Figure 5.2. When a calculation results in a value smaller than `realmin`, there are two types of outcomes. If the result is slightly less than `realmin`, the number is stored as a denormal:

```
>> format long e
>> realmin/10
ans =
     2.225073858507203e-309
```

In MATLAB, the denormals are used just like other valid floating-point values, but they are corrupted, because they have fewer significant digits than normal floating-point values. The use of denormals allows for gradual underflow. The other possible outcome occurs when a computed result is significantly less than `realmin`, i.e., if the value is too small to be stored as a denormal. In that case the result is stored as exactly zero.

```
>> format long e
>> realmin/1e16
ans =
    0
```

The use of denormals and the zeroing of results that would otherwise lie in the underflow range provide a failsafe mechanism. One cannot easily guarantee that an algorithm will never encounter the conditions that lead to underflow, but at least if underflow does occur, the MATLAB calculations will not crash.

Precision Limits   The precision of a floating-point number is determined by the number of bits used to store its mantissa. MATLAB variables are double precision, meaning that they have 53 bits allocated to their mantissa. Using the normalized notation of Equation (5.1), a floating-point mantissa always has a value greater than or equal to 0.1 and less than 1.0. Storing mantissas in a computer involves representing these fractional values in base 2.

The "natural" way to store the decimal digits of the mantissa in base 2 is to use multiples of powers of $1/2$. The mantissa of a number is computed from its bit pattern by

$$f = \sum_{k=1}^{m} b_k 2^{-k}, \tag{5.2}$$

where b_k is the bit corresponding to the kth power of $1/2$, and m is the number of bits allocated to the mantissa. For example, the binary mantissa $(011)_2$ is equivalent to

$$0 \times \left(\frac{1}{2}\right)^1 + 1 \times \left(\frac{1}{2}\right)^2 + 1 \times \left(\frac{1}{2}\right)^3 = 0.375.$$

No decimal point is needed in the bit pattern, because the powers of $1/2$ automatically generate the necessary fractional part. As with integers, the most significant bit is on the left, and the least significant bit is on the right.

Converting the binary representation of a mantissa to its floating-point equivalent is accomplished by directly evaluating Equation (5.2). The reverse conversion is not too difficult. Let r_k be the cumulative remainder of the mantissa after $\sum_{j=1}^{k} b_k 2^{-k}$ has been subtracted, viz.

sufficient, however, to guarantee that all floating-point operations involving integer operands will yield exact results.

To see the effects of roundoff in a simple calculation, one need only to force the computer to store the intermediate results. A variation on the following sequence of calculations is suggested by Moler [55]:

```
>> format long e
>> a = 4/3                      % Store double precision approx of 4/3
a =
    1.333333333333333e+00
>> b = a-1                      % Remove most significant digit
b =
    3.333333333333333e-01
>> c = 1 - 3*b                  % 3*b = 1 in exact math
c =
    2.220446049250313e-16
```

The assignment b = a - 1 causes the digits of the mantissa in a - 1 to shift to the left. This introduces a zero, as the least significant bit of b. As a result, the value of 3*b is one least significant bit less than 1.

In the next section, a quantitative measure of the size of roundoff errors is introduced. Before that, the following examples demonstrate how roundoff errors can lead to significant inaccuracies, even in simple calculations:

Example 5.3: Roundoff Errors in the Quadratic Formula

The commonly used quadratic formula is susceptible to roundoff, especially when coefficients of the quadratic have large differences in magnitude and when the formula is evaluated with a limited number of decimal digits. This example shows how these errors occur. A better quadratic formula, one that is less commonly used, is presented. The better formula is less susceptible to roundoff even when computations are performed with a limited number of decimal digits.

The classic formula for the roots of $ax^2 + bx + c = 0$ is

$$x = \frac{-b \pm \sqrt{b^2 - 4ac}}{2a}. \tag{5.3}$$

Due to roundoff error, the roots given by this equation may not be precise. Consider the equation

$$x^2 - 54.32\,x + 0.1 = 0, \tag{5.4}$$

which has the exact (to eleven digits) roots

$$x_1 = 54.318158995, \qquad x_2 = 0.0018410049576.$$

For this equation, $b^2 = 2950.7 \gg 4ac = 0.4$. To illustrate the effect of roundoff, evaluate x_1 and x_2 with Equation (5.3) using four-digit floating-point arithmetic. In other words, after each floating-point operation, round the result to four significant digits. The discriminant is, to four digits,

$$\sqrt{b^2 - 4ac} = \sqrt{(-54.32)^2 - 0.4000} = \sqrt{2951 - 0.4000} = \sqrt{2951} = 54.32.$$

Use $x_{1,4}$ to designate the first root computed with four-digit arithmetic:

$$x_{1,4} = \frac{-b + \sqrt{b^2 - 4ac}}{2a} = \frac{+54.32 + 54.32}{2.000} = \frac{108.6}{2.000} = 54.30.$$

This value of x_1 is in error by 0.04 percent. Not bad, considering the number of digits used in the computation. Using four-digit arithmetic the second root, $x_{2,4}$, is

$$x_{2,4} = \frac{-b - \sqrt{b^2 - 4ac}}{2a} = \frac{+54.32 - 54.32}{2.000} \tag{i}$$

$$= \frac{0.000}{2.000} \tag{ii}$$

$$= 0, \tag{iii}$$

which is in error by 100 percent! The poor approximation to $x_{2,4}$ is caused by roundoff in the calculation of $\sqrt{b^2 - 4ac}$, which leads to the subtraction of two equal numbers in line (i). If more digits had been carried in the computation of $\sqrt{b^2 - 4ac}$, the value of $-b - \sqrt{b^2 - 4ac}$ would not be zero. Carrying more digits in each step will improve the overall result (see Exercise 7), but it can not completely eliminate the inherent inaccuracy of subtracting two nearly equal numbers with finite precision arithmetic.

An algorithmic solution to the inaccurate calculation of $x_{2,4}$ is to rewrite Equation (5.3) in a form that is less susceptible to roundoff. Begin by rationalizing the numerators of the expressions for the two roots:

$$x_1 = \frac{-b + \sqrt{b^2 - 4ac}}{2a} \left(\frac{-b - \sqrt{b^2 - 4ac}}{-b - \sqrt{b^2 - 4ac}} \right) = \frac{2c}{-b - \sqrt{b^2 - 4ac}}, \tag{5.5}$$

$$x_2 = \frac{-b - \sqrt{b^2 - 4ac}}{2a} \left(\frac{-b + \sqrt{b^2 - 4ac}}{-b + \sqrt{b^2 - 4ac}} \right) = \frac{2c}{-b + \sqrt{b^2 - 4ac}} \tag{5.6}$$

Now, use Equation (5.6) to compute the troublesome second root with four digit arithmetic (recall that to four digits, $\sqrt{b^2 - 4ac} = 54.32$):

$$x_{2,4} = \frac{2c}{-b + \sqrt{b^2 - 4ac}} = \frac{0.2000}{+54.32 + 54.32} = \frac{0.2000}{108.6} = 0.001842.$$

The result is in error by only 0.05 percent.

Note that the two formulations for $x_{2,4}$ are algebraically equivalent. The difference in the computed result is due to roundoff alone. Although Equation (5.6) is not completely immune to roundoff, for the given values of a, b, and c, Equation (5.6) will not produce the catastrophic cancellation errors that caused problems for the formula it replaced.

So should we abandon the classic quadratic formula and use Equations (5.5) and (5.6) instead? The answer is no! Evaluating $x_{1,4}$ with Equation (5.5) leads to a cancellation that is truly catastrophic:

$$x_{1,4} = \frac{2c}{-b - \sqrt{b^2 - 4ac}} = \frac{0.2000}{+54.32 - 54.32} = \frac{0.2000}{0} = \infty.$$

So, should we use $x_{1,4}$ from the classic quadratic formula and $x_{2,4}$ from the modified formula in Equation (5.6)? The answer is still no. The appropriate formula depends on the sign of the b coefficient in the original quadratic. The ultimate solution is to use a formula that takes the sign of b into account in a way that prevents catastrophic cancellation.

The recommended procedure for computing the roots of a quadratic equation is as follows. Given the values of a, b, and c in $ax^2 + bx + c = 0$, first evaluate

$$q \equiv -\frac{1}{2} \left[b + \text{sign}(b)\sqrt{b^2 - 4ac} \right], \tag{5.7}$$

where

$$\text{sign}(b) = \begin{cases} 1, & \text{if } b \geq 0, \\ -1, & \text{otherwise.} \end{cases}$$

Then, the roots to the quadratic equation are

$$x_1 = \frac{q}{a}, \qquad x_2 = \frac{c}{q}. \tag{5.8}$$

The preceding formula and a corresponding formula for cubic equations are found in [1, 61]. The verification of the superior roundoff properties of Equations (5.7) and (5.8) is the objective of Exercise 8.

It may seem paranoid to worry about the corruption due to roundoff, since real computers use more than four digits. Indeed, one of the easiest ways to reduce the effect of roundoff is to use double-precision arithmetic instead of single precision. For many numerical problems, especially those involving large systems of linear equations, even double precision cannot compensate for an algorithm that is susceptible to roundoff. The solution is to use algorithms that are *designed* to minimize the effect of roundoff.

Example 5.4: Large Roundoff Errors in a Simple Formula

The base of the natural logarithm can be computed from

$$e = e^1 = \lim_{n \to \infty} \left(1 + \frac{1}{n} \right)^n.$$

Computational substep	
$1 + 1/n$	Rou... For... larg... to 1
$(1 + 1/n)^n$	The... amp...

It is important to note
operations. While it is true
and multiplications can hav
possible that catastrophic er

5.2.1 Machine Precisi

Two numbers that are ve
tinguished on the *floating*
significant bit of their m:
increases, for example, b
ability of resolve differen
in floating-point arithmet
epsilon, which is usually
  Machine precision
least significant bit of the

1.0

Equation (5.9) makes no
saying that for exact aritl
use floating-point arithm
of numerical algorithms
over ε_m as a quantifier of
  Figure 5.3 provides
bers $1 - \varepsilon_m$ and $1 + \varepsilon_m$ are
$|\delta| < \varepsilon_m$ is added to 1, tl
and is rounded to 1. The

[7]There is a subtle differ
bit of the mantissa" and Equa
of the rounding errors due to
discussion of the subtleties.

```
function epprox
% epprox   Demonstrate catastrophic cancellation in evaluation of
%            e = exp(1) = lim_{n->infinity} (1 + 1/n)^n
%
% Synopsis:  y = epprox
%
% Input:     none
%
% Output:    Table comparing exp(1) and f(n) = (1 + 1/n)^n as n -> infinity
%
% Ref:  N.J. Higham, Accuracy and Stability of Numerical Algorithms,
%        1996, SIAM, section 1.11

e = exp(1);
fprintf('\n    n             f(n)            error\n');
for n=logspace(0,16,9)
    f = (1+1/n)^n;
    fprintf('%9.1e  %14.10f  %14.10f\n',n,f,abs(f-e));
end
```

Listing 5.2   The epprox function demonstrates truncation errors in an approximation of e^1.

The limit implies that the accuracy of the computed value of e will increase indefinitely as n is increased. While this limiting behavior is true in exact arithmetic, Higham points out that the preceding formula is sensitive to rounding errors for modest values of n [36]. The epprox function in Listing 5.2 evaluates $f(n) = (1 + 1/n)^n$ for a range of n and compares $f(n)$ to the value of exp(1). Running epprox produces the following result:

```
>> epprox
    n             f(n)            error
 1.0e+00    2.0000000000    0.7182818285
 1.0e+02    2.7048138294    0.0134679990
 1.0e+04    2.7181459268    0.0001359016
 1.0e+06    2.7182804691    0.0000013594
 1.0e+08    2.7182817983    0.0000000301
 1.0e+10    2.7182820532    0.0000002248
 1.0e+12    2.7185234960    0.0002416676
 1.0e+14    2.7161100341    0.0021717944
 1.0e+16    1.0000000000    1.7182818285
```

Notice that the error decreases to a minimum at $n = 10^8$ and then *increases* with increasing n.

  There are two roundoff errors in the evaluation of $(1 + 1/n)^n$. One error is relatively minor, and the other is catastrophic. The minor error is due to the inability to exactly rep-

resent $1/n$ witl
of $1/10$ in the 1

The error in te
value of 10^{-n}.

The mor
even when $1/n$
computation of
the position of
now be demon

When tw
tion to the sum
significant digi
x and y are de
Writing the sur

$$E_{\text{rel}}(\hat{\alpha}) = \frac{|\hat{\alpha} - \alpha|}{|\alpha|}.$$

This is useful as long as α is not zero. In the preceding formulas, the value of α is assumed to be known. Extension to the case where α is the unknown limit of an iterative sequence is considered after the following example.

Example 5.5: Errors in Balancing a Checkbook

In computer calculations, it is usually a good idea to report both relative and absolute errors. The computation of relative errors is always complicated, however, by the question: *Relative to what?*

Suppose that while balancing your checkbook, you discover an error of $100 in the deposit of a paycheck. Your pay stub indicates that you earned $350 last week, and you are certain that the entire paycheck was deposited in your account. Your bank statement, however, indicates a deposit of only $250. The absolute and relative errors in the bank deposit are

$$E_{\text{abs}} = \$100, \qquad E_{\text{rel}} = \frac{100}{350} = 0.286.$$

Suppose further that during the same week, and at the same bank, Gill Bates, the CEO of Megasoft Corporation deposited her weekly $35,000 paycheck. Mysteriously, only $34,900 is credited to her account—another $100 error in the bank's favor. For Gill, the absolute and relative errors are

$$E_{\text{abs}} = \$100, \qquad E_{\text{rel}} = \frac{100}{35000} = 0.00286.$$

Though the absolute errors are the same for both transactions, the relative errors reflect the reality that the loss of $100 is more significant for you than it is for Bates. Here the significance is measured relative to the size of the paycheck, not the buying power of the lost funds. For instance, you both could buy the same number of cups of coffee, music CDs, or shoelaces with the $100.

It is likely that having discovered a loss of such (relative) magnitude, you would invest the effort necessary to correct the error. On the other hand, Ms. Bates would likely not notice, or if she did, she might compute that since she earns $875 per hour, it may not be worth her time to call the bank to report and correct the error.[9] In other words, a relative error of 0.286 is unacceptable to you, whereas a relative error of 0.00286 might indicate that the approximate deposit is "close enough" for Ms. Bates.

This contrived example demonstrates that it is important to put the significance of errors in perspective. In many situations, the perspective depends on what is trying to be achieved. For the bank, with perhaps $3.5 million in deposits during the week, the $200 in errors may not cause any alarms. On the other hand, a concerned banking executive might

In this particul
sum. The num
order of magni

In the ev
Although the c
computed witl
the sum. Wher
from epprox,
to 1 produces
the next sectio

The erro

Comput
subs

$1/$

---

[9]Then again, perhaps she is CEO because she does not tolerate accounting errors, no matter how small.

decide that deposit errors should be measured relative to the individual deposits, not the gross deposits for the bank.

5.2.4 Convergence of Iterative Sequences

Iteration is a common component of numerical algorithms. In the most abstract form, an iteration generates a sequence of scalar values x_k, $k = 1, 2, 3, \ldots$. The sequence converges to a limit ξ if

$$|x_k - \xi| < \delta, \qquad \text{for all } k > N,$$

where δ is a small number called the convergence tolerance. In this case, we say that the sequence has converged to within the tolerance δ after N iterations. The problem with this statement of convergence is that, in general, the limit ξ is not known unless (for a convergent iteration) the value of k is allowed to approach infinity. In a practical calculation, it is important to be able to detect convergence as soon as the tolerance is met, not after $k \to \infty$. At convergence, one is, in essence, declaring that x_k is "close enough" to the *unknown* value of ξ.

Fortunately, the preceding condition of convergence is equivalent to (see, e.g., [70, § 5.2])

$$|x_\ell - x_k| < \delta, \qquad \text{for all } \ell, k > N.$$

In practice, the test is expressed as

$$|x_{k+1} - x_k| < \delta, \qquad \text{when } k > N.$$

The number of iterations N to reach convergence depends on the value of δ. In general, as δ decreases, N will increase. In other words, it takes more work to achieve convergence to a tighter tolerance.

Example 5.6: Iterative Computation of the Square Root

The `newtsqrt` function in Listing 5.3 uses an iterative procedure based on Newton's method to compute the square root of a number. Given a guess r_k at the square root of x, the next guess is $r_{k+1} = (1/2)(r_k + x/r_k)$. The iterations continue until $r_{k+1} \approx r_k$. The convergence test in Listing 5.3 is incomplete. The goal of this example is to explore the use of different expressions to replace the "NOT_CONVERGED" string in the `while` statement. (*Note*: The code in Listing 5.3 is stored in the `newtsqrtBlank` function in the NMM Toolbox. There is no `newtsqrt` function in the NMM Toolbox. In the end of chapter exercises you are asked to create various versions of `newstsqrt` by editing the code in `newtsqrtBlank.m`.)

The `testsqrt` function in Listing 5.4 calls `newtsqrt` with a series of input values and compares the accuracy of the `newtsqrt` function with the built-in `sqrt` function. You can use the `testsqrt` funtion after you have created a `newtsqrt` function.

```
function r = newtsqrt(x,delta,maxit)
% newtsqrt   Use Newton's method to compute the square root of a number
%
% Synopsis:  r = newtsqrt(x,delta,maxit)
%
% Input:   x     = number for which the square root is desired
%          delta = (optional) convergence tolerance.  Default: delta = 5e-9
%          maxit = (optional) maximum number of iterations.  Default: maxit = 25
%
% Output:    r = square root of x to within delta/2

if x<0,  error('Negative input to newtsqrt not allowed');   end
if x==0,      r=x;  return;    end
if nargin<2,  delta = 5e-9;    end
if nargin<3,  maxit=25;        end

r = x/2;  rold = x;   %  Initialize, make sure convergence test fails on
                      %  first try
it = 0;
while NOT_CONVERGED & it<maxit    %  Convergence test
   rold = r;                      %  Save old value for next convergence test
   r = 0.5*(rold + x/rold);       %  Update the guess
   it = it + 1;
end
```

Listing 5.3   The `newtsqrtBlank` code contains everything but the convergence test for iterative computation of $\sqrt{x}$.

The following code fragments are bad implementations of the convergence test:

```
while r~=rold & it<maxit           %  Bad test #1


while (r-rold)>delta & it<maxit    %  Bad test #2
```

The first test requires that `r` and `rold` agree exactly. This condition will only be met if the bit pattern stored in `r` is identical to the bit pattern stored in `rold`. This implies that the sequence of computations leading to `r` and `rold` have produced values that are within ε_m of each other. The second test is met whenever `r` is greater than `rold`, not when `r` and `rold` are close in value. The obvious improvement to the preceding test is

```
while abs(r-rold)>delta & it<maxit    % absolute difference
```

When the preceding absolute difference convergence criterion is used in `newtsqrt`, the output of `testsqrt` is

```
function testSqrt
% testSqrt   Test the newtsqrt function for a range of inputs

xtest = [4  0.04  4e-4  4e-6  4e-8  4e-10  4e-12];   % arguments to test

fprintf('\n Absolute Convergence Criterion\n');
fprintf('    x            sqrt(x)   newtsqrt(x)     error        relerr\n');

for x=xtest              %  repeat for each column in xtest
   r = sqrt(x);
   rn = newtsqrt(x);
   err = abs(rn - r);
   relerr = err/r;
   fprintf('%10.3e  %10.3e  %10.3e  %10.3e  %10.3e\n',x,r,rn,err,relerr)
end
```

Listing 5.4   The testsqrt function uses a sequence of input values
to test the newtsqrt function. (*Note*: the newtsqrt function is not
part of the NMM Toolbox. To run testsqrt you need to open the
newtsqrtBlank.m file, make appropriate changes to the convergence
test, and save the resulting function as newtsqrt.)

```
>> testsqrt      %  absolute difference convergence criterion

     x         sqrt(x)    newtsqrt(x)     error        relerr
  4.000e+00   2.000e+00   2.000e+00   0.000e+00   0.000e+00
  4.000e-02   2.000e-01   2.000e-01   0.000e+00   0.000e+00
  4.000e-04   2.000e-02   2.000e-02   0.000e+00   0.000e+00
  4.000e-06   2.000e-03   2.000e-03   2.342e-17   1.171e-14
  4.000e-08   2.000e-04   2.000e-04   1.649e-15   8.246e-12
  4.000e-10   2.000e-05   2.000e-10   2.000e-05   1.000e+00
  4.000e-12   2.000e-06   2.000e-12   2.000e-06   1.000e+00
```

The absolute difference convergence criterion does not work for small arguments of the
newtsqrt function. For example, when $x = 4 \times 10^{-10}$, the absolute error tolerance is met
when the relative error is 100 percent. The reliability of the newtSqrt function is improved
by using the *relative difference* in the convergence test:

```
while abs((r-rold)/rold)>delta & it<maxit       % relative difference
```

When the relative difference convergence criterion is used in newtsqrt, the output of
testsqrt is

```
>> testsqrt      %  relative difference convergence criterion
```

x	sqrt(x)	newtsqrt(x)	error	relerr
4.000e+00	2.000e+00	2.000e+00	0.000e+00	0.000e+00
4.000e-02	2.000e-01	2.000e-01	0.000e+00	0.000e+00
4.000e-04	2.000e-02	2.000e-02	0.000e+00	0.000e+00
4.000e-06	2.000e-03	2.000e-03	0.000e+00	0.000e+00
4.000e-08	2.000e-04	2.000e-04	2.711e-20	1.355e-16
4.000e-10	2.000e-05	2.000e-05	3.388e-21	1.694e-16
4.000e-12	2.000e-06	2.000e-06	0.000e+00	0.000e+00

The relative difference criterion scales the change in r with the previous value of r. As long as rold $\neq 0$, this test provides for a convergence tolerance that is independent of the scale of the input argument.

5.2.5 Relative and Absolute Convergence Criteria

The preceding example demonstrated the behavior of two convergence criteria,

$$|x_k - x_{k-1}| < \Delta_a, \qquad \left| \frac{x_k - x_{k-1}}{x_{k-1}} \right| < \delta_r, \qquad (5.12)$$

where Δ_a and δ_r are absolute and relative convergence tolerances, respectively. The relative convergence criterion is usually preferable, since it does not change if the problem is suitably scaled. A 0.5-kg error, for example, in computing the mass of a person weighing 60 kg is 0.83 percent. This relative error value does not change if the persons mass is reported in pounds, tons, or metric tonnes.

The relative difference convergence criterion δ_r can be interpreted as the largest acceptable uncertainty in the least significant digit of the computed result. Accordingly, relative convergence tolerances are usually specified as 5×10^{-p}, where an uncertainty in the $(p - 1)$th digit of the result is acceptable. A value of $\delta_r = 5 \times 10^{-4}$, for example, implies that the difference between r and rold is desired to be smaller than the third digit of rold. The factor of 5 in the tolerance acknowledges the uncertainty in rounding a value up or down. Rounding 1.234567 to two digits gives 1.2, since $3 < 5$, whereas rounding 1.234567 to six digits gives 1.23457, since $6 > 5$.

The absolute convergence criterion is advantageous whenever the limit of the iterative sequence is near zero. An alternative convergence criterion is obtained by combining the absolute and relative tolerances:

$$|x_k - x_{k-1}| < \max [\Delta_a, \; \delta_r |x_{k-1}|]. \qquad (5.13)$$

With the combined criterion, the iterations continue until the *largest* tolerance is met.

Although appropriate values for Δ_a and δ_r will vary from problem to problem, ε_m is the lower bound for both criteria. Using Equation (5.12) or Equation (5.13) with $\Delta_a < \varepsilon_m$ or $\delta_r < \varepsilon_m$ may result in an infinite loop. Due to roundoff errors, the difference between x_k and x_{k-1} may never become less than ε_m even for a sequence that converges in exact arithmetic. When no problem-specific information is available (e.g., when writing a general-purpose routine, tolerance values of $5\varepsilon_m$, $100\varepsilon_m$, or larger are likely to far exceed the requirements of most engineering applications).

5.3 TRUNCATION ERROR OF ALGORITHMS

Truncation error results from approximating continuous mathematical expressions with discrete, algebraic formulas. Unlike roundoff, which is controlled by the hardware and the computer language being used, truncation error is under the control of the programmer or user. Truncation error can be reduced by selecting more accurate discrete approximations. It cannot be eliminated entirely.

Truncation-error analysis is specific to each numerical method. Throughout this book, the truncation-error behavior of particular numerical methods will be described. In this section, infinite series are used to demonstrate the concept of truncation errors. In the next section, truncation error will be related to the Taylor series expansion of a function.

Consider the series representation of e^x:

$$e^x = 1 + x + \frac{x^2}{2!} + \frac{x^3}{3!} + \cdots . \tag{5.14}$$

It is not possible, and not necessary, to literally add an infinite number of terms in the calculation of e^x. At some point, higher order terms may be neglected, because they do not make a significant contribution to the sum. The difference between the true value of e^x and the value computed with a finite number of terms is the truncation error. The word *truncation* suggests the cause of the error, namely, that the series has been truncated. The truncation error in Equation (5.14) also depends on the argument of the e^x function. For $x \ll 1$, the numerator of successive terms rapidly decays. For large x, many terms will be needed before the factorial term in the denominator overcomes the power term in the numerator.

The number of terms required to get an accurate value of e^x is independent of the number of digits used in calculating each term. In other words, roundoff and truncation error are independent, as demonstrated in Example 5.8.

Example 5.7: Evaluating the Series for sin(x)

The sine function is defined as the infinite series

$$\sin(x) = x - \frac{x^3}{3!} + \frac{x^5}{5!} - \frac{x^7}{7!} + \cdots .$$

```
function ssum = sinser(x,tol,nmax)
% sinser   Evaluate the series representation of the sine function
%
% Synopsis: ssum = sinser(x)
%           ssum = sinser(x,tol)
%           ssum = sinser(x,tol,nmax)
%
% Input:    x   = argument of the sine function, i.e., compute sin(x)
%           tol = (optional) tolerance on accumulated sum. Default:  tol = 5e-9
%                 Series is terminated when abs(T_k/S_k) < delta.   T_k is the
%                 kth term and S_k is the sum after the kth term is added.
%           nmax = (optional) maximum number of terms. Default: n = 15
%
% Output:   ssum = value of series sum after nterms or tolerance is met

if nargin<2,  tol = 5e-9;  end
if nargin<3,  nmax = 15;   end

term = x;  ssum = term;         %  Initialize series
fprintf('Series approximation to sin(%f)\n\n  k       term         ssum\n',x);
fprintf('%3d  %11.3e  %12.8f\n',1,term,ssum);

for k=3:2:(2*nmax-1)
  term = -term * x*x/(k*(k-1));                % Next term in the series
  ssum = ssum + term;
  fprintf('%3d  %11.3e  %12.8f\n',k,term,ssum);
  if abs(term/ssum)<tol, break;  end           % True at convergence
end
fprintf('\nTruncation error after %d terms is %g\n\n',(k+1)/2,abs(ssum-sin(x)));
```

Listing 5.5   The sinser function uses a truncated series to evaluate sin(x).

Although the terms get smaller as the order increases, the magnitude of the numerator and denominator can grow quite large. An efficient and robust implementation of the series uses recursion to avoid overflow in the evaluation of individual terms. If T_k is the kth term ($k = \{1, 3, 5, \ldots\}$) then

$$T_k = \frac{x^2}{k(k-1)} T_{k-2}.$$

This formula not only prevents overflow and loss of precision, it also results in much more efficient computation, since the numerator and denominator of each term are not evaluated *ab initio*.

The sinser function in Listing 5.5 uses the recursive formula and the termination criterion

$$\left| \frac{T_k}{S_k} \right| < \delta,$$

where S_k is the sum after k terms. The choice of termination criterion is the subject of Exercise 22. A typical run of the `sinser` function produces the following result:

```
>> sinser(pi/6);
Series approximation to sin(0.523599)

 k       term          ssum
 1     5.236e-01    0.52359878
 3    -2.392e-02    0.49967418
 5     3.280e-04    0.50000213
 7    -2.141e-06    0.49999999
 9     8.151e-09    0.50000000
11    -2.032e-11    0.50000000

Truncation error after 6 terms is  3.56e-14
```

By changing values of the (optional) `tol` and `nmax` parameters of `sinser`, the behavior of the truncation error can be studied. The truncation error is also strongly dependent on the argument of the sine function. It is instructive, for example, to run `sinser` to evaluate $\sin(x)$ for $x = \pi/6, 5\pi/6, 11\pi/6, 17\pi/6$. How could the `sinser` function be modified to avoid the undesirable behavior demonstrated by this sequence of arguments?

Example 5.8: Roundoff and Truncation Errors in the Series for e^x

The series expansion for e^x is given by Equation (5.14). Let T_k be the kth term in the series and S_k be the value of the sum after k terms:

$$T_k = \frac{x^k}{k!}, \qquad S_k = 1 + \sum_{j=1}^{k} T_k.$$

If the sum on the right-hand side is truncated after k terms, the absolute error in the series approximation is

$$E_{\text{abs},k} = \left| S_k - e^x \right|.$$

The `expSeriesPlot` function in Listing 5.6 evaluates the sum and plots $E_{\text{abs},k}$ as a function of k. The terms are evaluated recursively, as described in Example 5.7. The plot in Figure 5.4 shows the absolute error for $\exp(-10)$ evaluated with

```
>> expSeriesPlot(-10,5e-12,60)
```

With $|x| \gg 1$, the absolute error first increases because the numerator terms grow more rapidly than the factorial terms in the denominator. For $x = -10$, the factorial in the

```
function ssum = expSeriesPlot(x,tol,n)
% expSeriesPlot  Evaluate and plot series representation of exp(x)
%
% Synopsis:  ssum = expSeriesPlot(x)
%            ssum = expSeriesPlot(x,tol)
%            ssum = expSeriesPlot(x,tol,n)
%
% Input:  x   = argument of the exp function, i.e., compute exp(x)
%         tol = (optional) tolerance on accumulated sum. Default: tol = 5e-9
%               Series is terminated when T_k/S_k < delta, where T_k is the
%               kth term and S_k is the sum after the kth term is added.
%         n   = (optional) maximum number of terms. Default: n = 15
%
% Output:  ssum = value of series sum after n or tolerance is met

if nargin < 2,  tol = 5e-9;  end
if nargin < 3,  n = 15;      end

term = 1;  ssum = term;  Eabs(1) = abs(ssum-exp(x));   % Initialize
fprintf('Series approximation to exp(%f)\n\n',x);
fprintf('  k       term          ssum          Eabs\n');
fprintf('%3d  %11.3e  %11.3e  %11.3e\n',1,x,ssum,Eabs(1));

for k=2:n
  term = term*x/(k-1);                     % Next term in the series
  ssum = ssum + term;
  Eabs(k) = abs(ssum-exp(x));
  fprintf('%3d  %11.3e  %11.3e  %11.3e\n',k,term,ssum,Eabs(k));
  if abs(term/ssum)<tol, break;  end   % True at convergence
end

semilogy(1:k,Eabs,'-');
xlabel('Number of terms');   ylabel('Absolute Error');
fprintf('\nTruncation error after %d terms is %11.3e\n\n',k,Eabs(k));
```

Listing 5.6 Function to evaluate the series for e^x and plot the absolute error as a function of the number of terms in the sum.

denominator begins to control the size of the terms for $k > 10$. As k increases further, $E_{abs,k}$ decreases, due to a decrease in the truncation error.

Eventually, roundoff prevents any change in S_k. As $T_{k+1} \to 0$, the statement

```
ssum = ssum + term
```

produces no change in ssum. For $x = -10$ this occurs at $k \sim 48$. At this point, the truncation error, $|S_k - e^x|$ is not zero. Rather, $|T_{k+1}/S_k| < \varepsilon_m$. This is an example of the

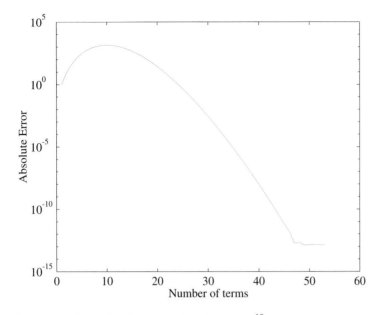

Figure 5.4   Plot of series approximations to e^{-10}.

independence of truncation error and roundoff error. For $k < 48$, the error in evaluating the series is controlled by truncation error. For $k > 48$, roundoff error prevents any reduction in truncation error.

5.3.1 Taylor Series

Taylor series approximations are used to derive and analyze the behavior of numerical methods. In this section, basic properties of the Taylor series are defined. Examples are given to show how Taylor series analysis can be used to describe the truncation error in numerical computations.

For a sufficiently differentiable function $f(x)$ on the interval $x \in [a, b]$, let $P_n(x)$ be defined as follows [9]:

$$P_n(x) = \tag{5.15}$$

$$f(x_0) + (x - x_0)\frac{df}{dx}\bigg|_{x=x_0} + \frac{(x - x_0)^2}{2}\frac{d^2 f}{dx^2}\bigg|_{x=x_0} + \cdots + \frac{(x - x_0)^n}{n!}\frac{d^n f}{dx^n}\bigg|_{x=x_0}.$$

Then, there exists $\xi(x)$ with $x_0 \leq \xi(x) \leq x$ such that

$$f(x) = P_n(x) + R_n(x) \tag{5.16}$$

and

$$R_n(x) = \frac{(x - x_0)^{(n+1)}}{(n + 1)!} \frac{d^{(n+1)} f}{dx^{(n+1)}}\bigg|_{x=\xi}. \tag{5.17}$$

The polynomial $P_n(x)$ is called the nth order Taylor series approximation to $f(x)$. $R_n(x)$ is the remainder, or *truncation error*, when $P_n(x)$ is used to approximate $f(x)$.

The definition of $R_n(x)$ in Equation (5.17) suggests that the value of truncation error can be computed, but this is not possible in general, because the value of ξ is not knowable. This is not a serious drawback, because in choosing an algorithm, it is more important to know the general behavior of the truncation error than its exact value.

In practice, the derivative term in Equation (5.17) is treated as an unknown constant, and the focus is shifted to the $(x - x_0)^{(n+1)}/(n + 1)!$ coefficient. Usually, we define $h = x - x_0$, and typically $h \ll 1$. Under these conditions, $h^{n+1}/(n + 1)! \to 0$ rapidly as n increases. As long as the derivatives of f are bounded, $R_n \to 0$ as n increases. It is then up to the programmer, analyst, or user (depending on the situation) to select a value of n so that the truncation error is within an acceptable tolerance.

Example 5.9: Taylor Series Approximations to $1/(1 - x)$

Consider the function

$$f(x) = \frac{1}{1 - x}. \tag{5.18}$$

The Taylor Series approximations to $f(x)$ of order 1, 2 and 3 are

$$P_1(x) = \frac{1}{1 - x_0} + \frac{x - x_0}{(1 - x_0)^2}, \tag{5.19}$$

$$P_2(x) = \frac{1}{1 - x_0} + \frac{x - x_0}{(1 - x_0)^2} + \frac{(x - x_0)^2}{(1 - x_0)^3}, \tag{5.20}$$

$$P_3(x) = \frac{1}{1 - x_0} + \frac{x - x_0}{(1 - x_0)^2} + \frac{(x - x_0)^2}{(1 - x_0)^3} + \frac{(x - x_0)^3}{(1 - x_0)^4}, \tag{5.21}$$

respectively, where x_0 is the point about which the Taylor series expansion is made. The demoTaylor function in Listing 5.7 evaluates and plots these approximations in a user-specified neighborhood. The function and its approximations in the interval $1.2 \leq x \leq 2$ are shown in Figure 5.5. To obtain this figure, use

```
>> demoTaylor(1.6,0.8)
```

```
function demoTaylor(x0,dx)
% demoTaylor  Taylor Series approximations for f(x) = 1/(1-x)
%
% Synopsis:  demoTaylor
%            demoTaylor(x0,dx)
%
% Input:  x0 = (optional) point about which the Taylor Series expansion is
%              made.  Default:  x0 = 1.6;
%         dx = (optional) size of neighborhood over which the expansion
%              is evaluated.  Default:  dx = 0.8
%
% Output:  a plot of f(x) and its Taylor Series approximations

if nargin<2,  x0 = 1.6;  dx = 0.8;  end

x = linspace(x0-dx/2,x0+dx/2,20);    %  x-values at which f(x) is evaluated
fx = 1./(1-x);                       %  Exact f(x); notice the array operator

h = x - x0;                  %  Avoid recomputing intermediate values,
t = 1/(1-x0);                %  h and t
p1x = t*ones(size(x)) + h*t^2;   %  First order Taylor polynomial
p2x = p1x + (h.^2)*t^3;      %  Second order "  "  "
p3x = p2x + (h.^3)*t^4;      %  Third

plot(x,fx,'-',x,p1x,'o-',x,p2x,'^-',x,p3x,'s-');
legend('exact   ','P_1(x)','P_2(x)','P_3(x)',4);
xlabel('x');    ylabel('Approximations to f(x) = 1/(1-x)');
```

Listing 5.7   The demoTaylor function evaluates and plots Taylor Series approximations to $f(x) = 1/(1 - x)$.

All of the Taylor polynomials agree with $f(x)$ near $x_0 = 1.6$. The higher order polynomials agree over a larger range of x.

Note that Equations (5.20) and (5.21) offer no computational savings over the original function (5.18). The purpose of this example is to demonstrate how to compute the Taylor series approximation to a function. Figure 5.5 shows that as more terms are retained in the Taylor series, the series approximation more closely approximates the original function.

5.3.2 Order Notation

Order-of-magnitude estimates are an important complement to precise numerical values. So-called *rules of thumb* or *back-of-the-envelope calculations* use order-of-magnitude estimates and simple arithmetic to obtain results that are correct to usu-

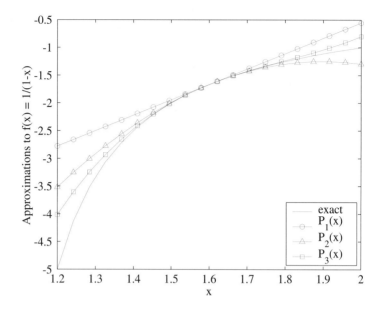

Figure 5.5   Plot of Taylor series approximations to $f(x) = 1/(1 - x)$.

ally one decimal place. Such estimates are very helpful in assessing the feasibility of a design or a calculation procedure. The ability to work with order-of-magnitude estimates is the mark of an experienced engineer or analyst.

Simple Order-of-magnitude Estimates   Consider, for example the computer memory necessary to perform a calculation with a large matrix. A square $n \times n$ matrix requires storage for n^2 floating-point numbers. In MATLAB, each element of the matrix uses eight bytes of memory. Thus, a 100×100 matrix requires at least $8 \times 100^2 = 8 \times 10^4 = 0.08$ megabytes (MB) of memory, which should not pose any problems. The "at least" qualification reflects the need for defining additional quantities (e.g., vectors used in the matrix calculations) that will also need computer memory for storage. Continuing the memory estimate, one easily finds that a 1000×1000 matrix requires 8 MB and that a 10000×10000 matrix needs 800 MB. Given this information, one can very quickly assess whether the available computing resources allow the calculation to be performed. The advantage of such estimates is that the results are quickly obtained and no programming or detailed analysis is necessary. Note that the memory requirements are not the only limitations on the feasibility of a calculation involving matrices. The execution time for a particular algorithm is also strongly dependent on the size of the matrix. For many important calculations involving matrices, the computational cost increases with n^3. (See Chapter 8 for details.)

Order notation is used to facilitate order-of-magnitude calculations. It is used to express the order-of-magnitude of the dominant term in a mathematical formula. The order-of-magnitude of a quantity is indicated with a capital letter "$\mathcal{O}$," or "big-oh" notation. For example, the memory required to store an $n \times n$ matrix in MATLAB is $8n^2$, or $\mathcal{O}(n^2)$, which is read either as "big-oh n squared" or "of order n squared". In most cases, multiplying constants, such as the factor of 8 in the preceding memory estimate, are dropped in the order-of-magnitude estimate. Although constant factors affect the numerical result obtained from the order-of-magnitude estimate, the factors are the same in two instances of the same calculation. In the memory requirement estimate, for example, one concludes that a 1000×1000 matrix takes 100 times as much memory as a 100×100 matrix, a result that is independent of the factor of 8.

When an order-of-magnitude estimate of a quantity is needed, only the dominant terms in an expression are retained. For example, the Taylor series formulas in Equations (5.16) and (5.17) are more compactly written as

$$f(x) = P_n(x) + \mathcal{O}\left(\frac{(x - x_0)^{(n+1)}}{(n + 1)!} \right),$$

or, more simply,

$$f(x) = P_n(x) + \mathcal{O}(h^{n+1}), \tag{5.22}$$

where $h = x - x_0$. The $1/(n + 1)!$ factor has been dropped, because for small h, the h^{n+1} term approaches zero much faster as n increases than $1/(n + 1)!$. In other words, since h^{n+1} has a much stronger influence on the order-of-magnitude of $(h^{n+1})/(n + 1)!$, only it is retained in the order-of-magnitude estimate.

Order notation also provides flexibility in writing mathematical expressions. Equation (5.22) does not say that h^{n+1} is added to $P_n(x)$ in order to make the equality hold. Rather, it is just a reminder that $f(x)$ and $P_n(x)$ differ by some small quantity that is of order h^{n+1} and, furthermore, that the difference between $f(x)$ and $P_n(x)$ decreases as n increases.

Example 5.10: Order of Series Approximations to e^x

The infinite series representation of e^x is

$$e^x = 1 + x + \frac{x^2}{2!} + \cdots + \frac{x^n}{n!} + \cdots .$$

If $x < 1$, each successive term in the series is smaller than the previous term. Terminating the series after a finite number of terms results in discarding higher order corrections. For example, the approximations

Further Reading

Many introductory texts on numerical analysis give a detailed discussion of the rounding behavior of floating-point arithmetic. Burden and Faires [9] and Cheney and Kincaid [10] provide a good starting point for the analysis of algorithms in the presence of rounding errors. Stewart [68] and Gill et al. [28] give a good overview of floating-point arithmetic and its consequences for practical computation. A more mathematical approach to the same material is provided by Stoer and Bulirsch [70], and Isaacson and Keller [40]. Goldberg [29] carefully describes the details of floating-point arithmetic with an emphasis on role of computing hardware. Higham [36] provides comprehensive coverage of the analysis of roundoff in numerical linear algebra.

EXERCISES

The number in parenthesis at the beginning of each exercise indicates the degree of skill and amount of effort necessary to complete the exercise. See § 1.4 on page 10 for a description of the rating system.

1. (1) Write the base 2 equivalents of the integers $1, 2, \ldots, 8$.

2. (1) Manually convert the following numbers to base 2: 5, 21, 35, 64. Check your conversion with the built-in dec2bin function.

<u>SOLUTION</u>   3. (1) Convert the following numbers to normalized floating-point values with eight-bit mantissas: 0.4, 0.5, 1.5.

4. (3) Translate Algorithm 5.1 on page 198 into a MATLAB function that computes the bit pattern of a floating-point mantissa. Store the bit pattern in a string vector. The remainder r can be stored in a scalar that is overwritten for each k. Why does the built in dec2bin function not work for this algorithm? Test your function by converting the values used in the preceding exercise.

5. (1) On page 196 an example of overflow was created by evaluating realmax*10. Why doesn't realmax + 1 generate overflow?

6. (3) Why is the upper limit of the loop in the halfDiff function set to 1075? Are there some input values for the halfDiff function that will not result in $\delta = 0$ after 1075 steps? (*Hint*: Consider the analysis in § 6.3.1.)

7. (1) Manually evaluate the two roots from Example 5.3 using five-digit arithmetic in the classic quadratic formula. Repeat the calculations using six-digit arithmetic. What are the relative errors in the two roots for each case?

8. (1) Manually evaluate the two roots from Example 5.3 using four-digit arithmetic in Equations (5.7) and (5.8). What are the relative errors in the two roots for each case?

<u>SOLUTION</u>   9. (3−) Modify the epprox function in Listing 5.2 on page 207 so that vectors of n and abs(f-e) are saved inside the loop. (*Hint*: Create the nn and err vectors, but

```
function lintest
% lintest   Compare schemes for generating

fprintf('  n      norm(y1-y)      norm(y2-y)
for n=[4 5 6 9 10 20 50 100]
  y  = linspace(0,1,n);
  y1 = linsp1(0,1,n);       y2 = linsp2(0,1,
  e1 = norm(y1-y,'inf');   e2 = norm(y2-y,'
   fprintf('%4d  %12g  %12g  %12g\n',n,e1,e
end
```

Running the `lintest` function gives

```
>> lintest
   n      norm(y1-y)      norm(y2-y)      no:
   4          0               0           1.1:
   5          0               0
   6      1.11022e-16     1.11022e-16
   9          0               0
  10      2.22045e-16     1.11022e-16     1.11
  20      4.44089e-16     1.11022e-16     1.11
  50      7.77156e-16     1.11022e-16     1.11
 100      1.9984e-15      1.11022e-16     1.11
```

Obviously, `linsp1`, `linsp2`, and `linsp3` give diff
does $\|y1 - y\|_\infty$ increase for $n > 10$? Why are $\|y2$
than $\varepsilon_m/2$ for all values of n in the experiments?
beginning on page 301 for background information

18. (2) Make the necessary changes to the `newtsqrt` fu
the results in Example 5.6. This might best be acco
`newtsqrta` and `newtsqrtr` that implement the ab
respectively. As a diagnostic, print the number of it
vergence for each argument of `newtsqrt`.

19. (2+) Implement the combined tolerance $|x_k - x_{k-}$
`newtsqrt` function in Listing 5.3. Note that Δ_a a
to your `newtsqrt` function. As a diagnostic, print
sary to achieve convergence for each argument of n
Example 5.6, what are good default values for Δ_a a
gence behavior significantly different than the result
absolute tolerance helpful for this algorithm?

20. (2+) The convergence criteria in Equation (5.12) are
but the convergence criteria in Example 5.6 are writt

```
while abs((r-rold)/rold)>delta & it<maxit
```

Is this an error? Should the `while` statement have a

do not modify the loop index n.) Remove (i.e., comment out) the `fprintf` statements, and increase the resolution of the loop by changing the `for` statement to `for
n=logspace(1,16,400)`. Plot the variation of the absolute error with n. Do not con-
nect the points with line segments. Rather, use a symbol, such as '+' for each point.
Explain the behavior of the error for $n > 10^7$.

10. (1+) Approximately what is the difference between `realmax` and the first double-
precision floating-point number less than `realmax`. In other words, what is the distance between the two rightmost vertical tick marks on the number line in Figure 5.2?

11. (2+) Beginning with the MATLAB code on page 210, write a function m-file to compute ε_m. The code on page 210 will give an ε_m value that is slightly different from the
built-in variable eps. Make sure your function returns a value exactly equal to eps.
What modification is necessary? Explain.

12. (2+) Using the m-file developed as the solution to Exercise 11, replace the line
`epsilon = epsilon/2` with `epsilon = epsilon/10`. What value does this modified routine return as ε_m? Why is it important to divide by 2 instead of 10 when
searching for ε_m? (*Hint*: How does division by 2 or 10 affect the bit pattern?)

13. (2+) Modify the m-file you obtained as the solution to exercise 11 so that it takes a
single input argument x_0. Use x_0 as the reference value for computing a relative ε_m. In
other words, find $\widehat{\varepsilon}_m$ such that $x_0 + \delta = x_0$ whenever $\delta < \widehat{\varepsilon}_m$. Evaluate $\widehat{\varepsilon}_m$ for the two
sequences of x_0 values $x_0 = \{1, 10, 100, 1000\}$ and $x_0 = \{1, 2, 4, 8\}$. Explain why the
value of $\widehat{\varepsilon}_m$ increases in different proportions for the two series of x_0 values.

14. (1) Let $c(x) = 1 - x^2/2! + x^4/4!$ and $s(x) = x - x^3/3! + x^5/5!$ be approximations
to $\cos(x)$ and $\sin(x)$, respectively. What are the relative and absolute errors in using
these formulas for $x = -2, -1, 0, 1, 2$ degrees?

15. (2+) Use $\sinh(x) = \frac{1}{2}(e^x - e^{-x})$ to evaluate $\sinh(x)$ for $x = \text{logspace}(-12, 12, 100)$.
Plot the absolute and relative error obtained by using this formula instead of the built-
in `sinh` function (which we can assume to give the correct value of $\sinh(x)$). What is
the cause of error for small x?

16. (2+) The built-in `linspace` function generates a vector of n equally spaced elements
with the statement

```
y = [d1+(0:n-2)*(d2-d1)/(n-1) d2]
```

Describe, in words, the calculations implied by the expression on the right-hand side
of the equals sign. Why is this not written as

```
y = [d1+(0:n-1)*(d2-d1)/(n-1)]
```

instead? (*Hint*: enter `type linspace` at the command prompt to get a complete listing
of the built-in function.)

17. (3−) Listing 5.10 contains three functions `linsp1`, `linsp2`, `linsp3`, which are alternative version of the built-in `linspace` function. These functions are experimentally
compared with the `lintest` function:

```
function x = linsp1(x1,x2,n)
% linsp1  Generate a vector of equally s
%
% Synopsis:  x = linsp1(x1,x2)
%            x = linsp1(x1,x2,n)
%
% Input:     x1, x2 = lower and upper l
%            n = (optional) number of el
%
% Output:    x = vector of n equally spa
if nargin<3,  n=100;   end
dx = (x2-x1)/(n-1);
x(1) = x1;
for k=2:n
  x(k) = x(k-1) + dx;
end
```

```
function x = linsp2(x1,x2,n)
% linsp2  Generate a vector of equally sp
%
% Synopsis:  x = linsp2(x1,x2)
%            x = linsp2(x1,x2,n)
%
% Input:     x1, x2 = lower and upper li
%            n = (optional) number of ele
%
% Output:    x = vector of n equally space
if nargin<3,  n=100;   end
dx = (x2-x1)/(n-1);
x(1) = x1;
for k=2:n
  x(k) = x1 + (k-1)*dx;
end
```

```
function x = linsp3(x1,x2,n)
% linsp2  Generate a vector of equally spa
%
% Synopsis:  x = linsp3(x1,x2)
%            x = linsp3(x1,x2,n)
%
% Input:     x1, x2 = lower and upper lim
%            n = (optional) number of elem
%
% Output:    x = vector of n equally spaced
if nargin<3,  n=100;   end
dx = (x2-x1)/(n-1);
x = x1:dx:x2;
```

Listing 5.10   Inferior alternatives

21. (2+) Use the `sinser` function in Listing 5.5 and a fixed value of the convergence tolerance, `tol = 5e-9`, to explore the sensitivity of the convergence rate to the value of x in $\sin(x)$. In particular, make a plot of the number of terms to reach convergence n, versus x for 10 points in the interval $0 \le x \le 8\pi$. You will need to modify the `sinser` function so that it returns a value of n. You will also need to specify a minimum of 50 terms in the series to see a trend in n versus x.

22. (2+) Modify the `sinser` function in Listing 5.5 so that the termination criterion is

$$\frac{T_k}{T_{k-2}} < \delta,$$

where T_k is the current term being added to the sum S_k. Is there a significant difference between this convergence criterion and the original criterion? Compare the number of terms necessary for convergence when the same value of δ is used for your function and the original `sinser`. Which convergence criterion do you recommend?

SOLUTION 23. (2+) Use the `sinser` function in Listing 5.5 to evaluate $\sin(x)$, for $x = \pi/6, 5\pi/6, 11\pi/6$, and $17\pi/6$. Use the periodicity of the sine function to modify the `sinser` function to avoid the undesirable behavior demonstrated by this sequence of arguments. (*Hint*: The modification does not involve any change in the statements inside the `for...end` loop.)

24. (2+) Using the `sinser` function in Listing 5.5 as a guide, write a function to evaluate the series representation of $\ln(1 + x)$. Use your function to compute $\ln(1 + x)$, for $x = 0.01, 0.1, 0.9$, and 1.0.

25. (3+) With a Web browser, go to netlib at `www.netlib.org` and browse the fn directory. Download a routine for the evaluation of $\sin(x)$ or $\cos(x)$. Read the source code and write a report describing how these library routines evaluate $\sin(x)$ (or $\cos(x)$). How many Fortran functions are used?

26. (3+) Euler's constant γ is obtained as a limit:

$$\gamma = \lim_{n \to \infty} \gamma_n, \qquad \text{where} \qquad \gamma_n = \left[1 + \frac{1}{2} + \frac{1}{3} + \frac{1}{4} + \cdots + \frac{1}{n} - \ln n \right].$$

γ appears in analytical expressions for special mathematical functions, such as exponential integrals and some Bessel functions. Since $\gamma_n \to$ constant as $n \to \infty$, consider the use of $\gamma_n - \gamma_{n+1}$ as a convergence tolerance. From the definition of γ_n, develop an expression for $\gamma_n - \gamma_{n+1}$ as a function of n, and use this expression to estimate how many terms are necessary to obtain $\gamma_n - \gamma_{n+1} < 5 \times 10^{-5}$? Note that solving for n in terms of $\gamma_n - \gamma_{n+1}$ is not possible, so a graphical solution is sufficient for obtaining the estimate. Write an m-file function that evaluates γ. When $\gamma_n - \gamma_{n+1}$ is used as a convergence criterion, is it a good estimate of the truncation error?

SOLUTION 27. (1) Derive the Taylor series expansions $P_1(x)$, $P_2(x)$, and $P_3(x)$ in Example 5.9 on page 222.

28. (2) Using the `demoTaylor` function in Listing 5.7 as a model, derive and plot the Taylor series expansions $P_1(x)$, $P_2(x)$, and $P_3(x)$ for $f(x) = \ln(x)$ in the neighborhood of $x_0 = 1$.

29. (1+) Use the series expansion for $\sin(x)$ to show that the truncation error for the Archimedes algorithm in Example 5.11 is $E(d, n) = \mathcal{O}(1/n^2)$.

30. (3−) Modify the `logspace` statement in the `fidiff` function in Listing 5.9 (page 230) so that a vector of 400 logarithmically spaced points are created in the interval $10^{-12} \leq h \leq 1$. Run your modified `fidiff` function for $x = 1$, and explain the behavior of the error for $h < 10^{-7}$. It will also be helpful to comment out the `fprintf` statements or put them inside an `if`...`end` construct.

$$\boxed{\quad \underline{\qquad} \ \text{\huge 6} \ \underline{\qquad} \\[2em] \textit{Finding the Roots of f(x) = 0} \quad}$$

In many practical situations, equations appear that cannot be manipulated and solved analytically. Other times, though an analytical solution is possible, it may be tedious and time consuming. An important example of this class of problems is finding the values of x that satisfy $f(x) = 0$. These x values are called zeros, or roots, of the equation. Any function of one variable can be put into this form. Figure 6.1 provides an outline summary of the material covered in this chapter. Extending root finding techniques to systems of nonlinear equations is described in Chapter 8.

Example 6.1: Designing a Picnic Table Leg

Consider the design of the picnic table shown in the photograph in Figure 6.2. The relevant dimensions of the legs are identified in Figure 6.3. The overall layout of the table is determined by the width w and height h of the leg assembly. The choice of leg material determines b. For aesthetic and practical reasons, the h and the w of the table and the b dimension of the material are chosen first: then, all remaining dimensions of the legs are calculated. To manufacture the legs the dimensions, a, c, d_1, and d_2 must be known.

From the geometry in Figure 6.3,

$$h = 2d_2 \sin\theta, \quad w = 2d_2 \cos\theta + b_2, \quad \text{and} \quad b = b_2 \sin\theta. \tag{6.1}$$

Topics Covered in This Chapter

1. Preliminaries

This section discusses aspects of the root finding problem that are common to all numerical root finding methods. When a root is suspected to lie in the range $x_{\text{left}} \leq x \leq x_{\text{right}}$, the pair $(x_{\text{left}}, x_{\text{right}})$ is referred to as a **bracket** for the root. A MATLAB routine for finding and plotting brackets is developed.

2. Fixed-Point Iteration

Fixed-point iteration involves evaluating a formula that takes a guess at a root as input, and returns an updated guess at the root as output. The success of fixed-point iteration depends on the choice of formula that is iterated.

3. Bisection

Given an initial bracket for a root, the systematic halving of the bracket around the root is called the **bisection method**. Though it does so slowly, bisection *always* converges.

4. Newton's Method

Using an initial guess at the root and the slope of $f(x)$, **Newton's Method** uses extrapolation to estimate where $f(x)$ crosses the x-axis. When it converges, Newton's method does so quickly, but it can diverge if $f'(x) = 0$ is encountered during the iterations to find the root.

5. The Secant Method

Instead of evaluating $f'(x)$ analytically, the **secant method** approximates $f'(x)$ from the value of $f(x)$ at two previous guesses at the root. The secant method is nearly as fast as Newton's method, but it, too, can fail near $f'(x) = 0$.

6. Hybrid Methods

By combining the features of more than one basic root finding methods, a **hybrid method** can achieve both fast *and* reliable convergence to a root. The built-in `fzero` function is a highly recommended, hybrid root finding procedure.

7. Roots of Polynomials

Finding the roots of polynomials involves unique numerical challenges. The `roots` function finds all the roots of a polynomial by solving a related **eigenvalue problem**. The formulation of the eigenvalue problem and the use of `roots` are discussed in this section.

Figure 6.1   Primary topics discussed in Chapter 6.

Figure 6.2 A picnic table. When width of the leg material and the over-all height and width of the table are chosen, the remaining dimensions of the leg can be determined from a root-finding procedure.

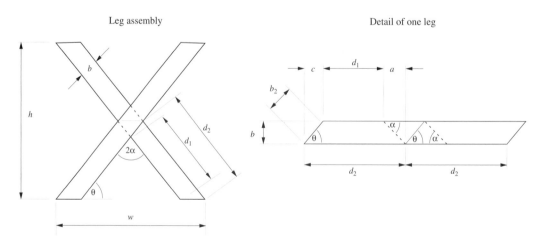

Figure 6.3 Dimensions of picnic table legs.

Combining the preceding equations to eliminate d_2 yields

$$w \sin \theta = h \cos \theta + b \tag{6.2}$$

Solving Equation (6.2) for θ allows us to calculate d_2 from the first of Equations (6.1). If $b = 0$, then $h/w = \tan \theta$, as expected. The other primary dimension is d_1, which can be computed from

$$d_1 = d_2 - a - c,$$

where

$$a = \frac{b}{\tan \alpha}, \quad c = \frac{b}{\tan \theta}, \quad \text{and} \quad \alpha = \frac{\pi}{2} - \theta.$$

Though it may not be obvious, an analytical solution to Equation (6.2) exists. (See Problem 1.) When faced with this kind of equation, one can either invest time in finding the analytical solution or use one of the numerical methods presented in this chapter to find values of θ for given values of w, b, and h.

.1 PRELIMINARIES

This section provides a prelude to methods for finding roots. Some of the tradeoffs in choosing a root-finding method are discussed, and an overview of the numerical process of root-finding is given. The method of bracketing for finding initial guesses at roots is described.

6.1.1 General Considerations

The choice root finding method depends somewhat on the problem at hand. The following are some things to consider:

- Is this a special function that will be evaluated often? If so, some analytical study and possibly some algebraic manipulation of the function will be a good idea. It may be possible to devise a custom iterative scheme that requires very little computer code [2].
- How much precision is needed? Engineering calculations often require only a few significant figures. A simple root finding procedure may be adequate.
- How fast and robust must the method be? If the root finding is embedded in another program that automatically changes the parameters of $f(x)$, it is important that the root finding routine be robust. A robust procedure is relatively immune to the initial guess, and it converges quickly without being overly sensitive to the behavior of $f(x)$ in the expected parameter space.

- Is the function a polynomial? There are special procedures for finding the roots of polynomials. These should be used instead of the general procedures, such as bisection, Newton's method, or the secant method.

- Does the function have singularities? Some root finding procedures will converge to a singularity, as well as converge to a root. This must be guarded against.

6.1.2 The Basic Root-finding Procedure

Figure 6.4 depicts some $f(x)$ with two roots, x_1 and x_2, in the given range of x. The graph of the function makes the roots obvious, and for this reason, it is always a good idea to plot the function when the roots of $f(x)$ are to be found. In addition to providing an initial guess at the roots, the plot may reveal pathological behavior of $f(x)$ that may cause the root-finding procedure to fail.

After the plot of $f(x)$ has been inspected, and an initial guess at the root has been obtained, the numerical root finding procedure is applied to refine the initial guess. The result is a sequence of values that, if all goes well, get progressively closer to the root. If x_k is the estimate to the root on the kth iteration, then the iterations converge if $\lim_{k\to\infty} x_k = \xi$, where ξ is the root. For practical reasons, it is desirable that the root finder converge in as few steps as possible. Full automation of the root finding algorithm also requires a way to determine when to stop the iterations.

After a root has been found with an automatic root-finding procedure, it is a good idea to substitute the root back into the function to see whether $f(x) \approx 0$. This will verify that the suspected root is not a singularity, and it will indicate how closely the alleged root satisfies the original equation.

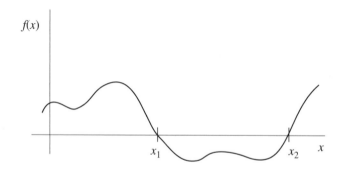

Figure 6.4　Roots of a generic scalar function $f(x) = 0$.

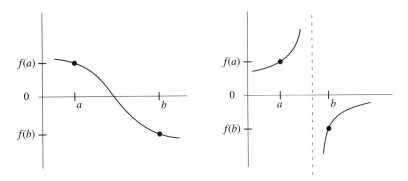

Figure 6.5   Testing for a change in sign of $f(x)$ will bracket either a root or a singularity.

6.1.3 Bracketing

Bracketing is a procedure to perform a coarse level search for roots over a large interval on the x-axis. The result is the identification of a set of subintervals that are likely to contain roots. Recursive refinement of the subintervals by another bracketing sweep is possible, but it is very inefficient and not recommended. Bracketing answers the question, "Where might the roots be?" The methods described in later sections of the chapter then answer the question, "Given a starting guess, what is the value of the root?"

Bracketing begins with subdividing a large interval into a number of smaller subintervals. The sign of the function at the ends of each subinterval is examined to determine whether the function crosses the x-axis—an indication that there is likely a root in the subinterval. The plot in the left half of Figure 6.5 shows a function crossing the x-axis between two points $x = a$ and $x = b$. A root is bracketed in the interval $[a, b]$ if $f(a)$ and $f(b)$ have opposite sign. As shown in the right half of Figure 6.5, a sign change can also occur at a singularity of $f(x)$.

The bracketing algorithm is

Algorithm 6.1   Bracketing

given: $f(x)$, $x_{\min}$, $x_{\max}$, n

$dx = (x_{\max} - x_{\min})/n$ (size of bracket interval)
$a = x_{\min}$ (initialize left side of test bracket)
$i = 0$ (initialize counter)

while $i < n$
    $i \leftarrow i + 1$
    $b = a + dx$

it is a user-defined function. (See Example 6.3.) The `xmin` and `xmax` parameters define the range over which the test intervals are created. An optional fourth parameter `nx` allows specification of the number of test intervals. The default value of `nx` is 20. The output `Xb` is a two column matrix of brackets. Each row contains the left and right brackets for a suspected root.

In a typical root-finding procedure, bracketing of roots occurs on intervals that are relatively coarse. The next step is to refine the estimate of the root. This is done with the methods discussed in subsequent sections.

Example 6.2: Bracketing the Roots of sin(x)

The roots of $\sin(x)$ occur at integer multiples of π. This provides an easy test for `brackPlot`. Applying `brackPlot` to $\sin(x) = 0$ on the interval $-4\pi \leq x \leq 4\pi$ results in the plot shown in Figure 6.6 and the following text output:

```
>> brackPlot('sin',-4*pi,4*pi)
ans =
   -12.5664   -11.2436
    -9.9208    -8.5980
    -7.2753    -5.9525
    -3.3069    -1.9842
    -0.6614     0.6614
     1.9842     3.3069
     5.9525     7.2753
     8.5980     9.9208
    11.2436    12.5664
```

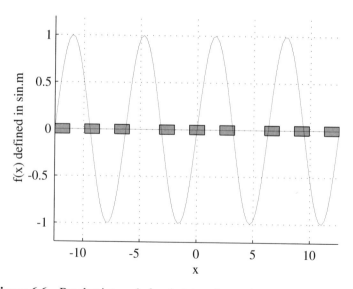

Figure 6.6   Bracket intervals for $\sin(x) = 0$ on $-4\pi \leq x \leq 4\pi$ created by the `brackPlot` function.

Notice that the brackets are not centered around the roots. The bracketing algorithm only guarantees that the function changes sign in the bracket; it gives no information about how close the the zero-crossing is to the left and right ends of the bracket.

Example 6.3: Bracketing the Roots of a User-Defined *f*(*x*)

The `brackPlot` function can be applied to any $f(x)$ that can be coded into a MATLAB function. Often, the $f(x)$ can be evaluated by a single MATLAB statement, though this is not a requirement. The m-file that evaluates $y = f(x)$ must accept a vector of x values and return a vector of y values. This usually requires the use of array operators (`.*`, `./`, and `.^`) in the MATLAB expressions to evaluate $f(x)$.

Consider the function

$$f(x) = x - x^{1/3} - 2 = 0, \qquad (6.3)$$

which has a single real root near $x = 3.5$. The `fx3` function in Listing 6.2 evaluates Equation (6.3). The array operator in the expression `x.^(1/3)` allows the function to process

```
function f = fx3(x)
% fx3    Evaluates f(x) = x - x^(1/3) - 2
f = x - x.^(1/3) - 2;
```

Listing 6.2   MATLAB function `fx3` to evaluate the left hand side of Equation (6.3).

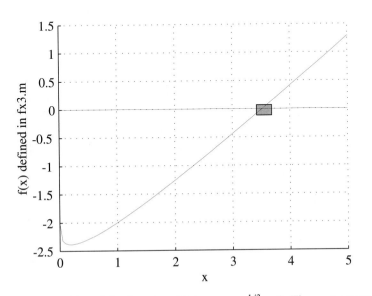

Figure 6.7   Plot of the function $f(x) = x - x^{1/3} - 2$. The root occurs at approximately $x = 3.5$.

an input vector, as well as a scalar. Using `brackPlot` to find brackets for Equation (6.3) gives the following text output and the plot shown in Figure 6.7:

```
>> brackPlot('fx3',0,5)
ans =
     3.4000    3.6000
```

6.2 FIXED-POINT ITERATION

Fixed-point iteration is the name given to both a simple root-finding procedure and a theoretical framework for the analysis of root-finding methods. As a simple root-finding procedure, fixed-point iteration is often used in hand calculations. To solve $f(x) = 0$, isolate one of the terms involving x, so that the equation can be written as

$$x_{\text{new}} = g(x_{\text{old}}).$$

The $g(x)$ is referred to as the *iteration function*. Given a formula for $g(x)$, the following algorithm performs fixed-point iteration to find the roots of $f(x) = 0$:

Algorithm 6.2   Fixed-Point Iteration

initialize: $x_0 = \ldots$
for $k = 1, 2, \ldots$
   $x_k = g(x_{k-1})$
   if converged, stop
end

The "if converged, stop" step is intentionally vague. Convergence criteria for root-finding algorithms are discussed in § 6.3.2. Note that only two of the x iterates need to be stored: Instead of creating a vector of x values, two variables, such as `xnew` and `xold`, might be used, with the value of `xold` replaced by the value of `xnew` at the end of each iteration.

    The fixed-point algorithm gets its name from its behavior at convergence: Recycling the output as input does not change the output. If the sequence x_1, $x_2, \ldots$, generated by the iteration function $x_k = g(x_{k-1})$ converges to ξ (i.e., if $\lim_{k\to\infty} x_k = \xi$), then ξ is said to be a *fixed point* of $g(x)$. To find the roots of $f(x) = 0$, it is possible to construct an arbitrary number of $g(x)$ having different convergence (or divergence!) behaviors. The choice of the $g(x)$ function is crucial to the success of fixed-point iteration, as demonstrated in the next two examples.

Example 6.4: Fixed-Point Iteration for $x - x^{1/3} - 2 = 0$

As demonstrated in Example 6.3, the function

$$f(x) = x - x^{1/3} - 2 = 0$$

is well behaved and has a root near $x = 3.5$. Two obvious candidates for fixed-point iteration functions are obtained by isolating the first and second x in the equation for $f(x)$:

$$g_1(x) = x^{1/3} + 2, \quad \text{and} \quad g_2(x) = (x - 2)^3.$$

Yet another iteration function is

$$g_3(x) = \frac{6 + 2x^{1/3}}{3 - x^{-2/3}},$$

though $g_3(x)$ is not obtained with an algebraic rearrangement of $f(x)$. The following table shows what happens when these $g(x)$ functions are iterated for an initial guess of $x_0 = 3$:

k	$g_1(x_{k-1})$	$g_2(x_{k-1})$	$g_3(x_{k-1})$
0	3	3	3
1	3.4422495703	1	3.5266442931
2	3.5098974493	−1	3.5213801474
3	3.5197243050	−27	3.5213797068
4	3.5211412691	−24389	3.5213797068
5	3.5213453678	-1.451×10^{13}	3.5213797068
6	3.5213747615	-3.055×10^{39}	3.5213797068
7	3.5213789946	-2.852×10^{118}	3.5213797068
8	3.5213796042	∞	3.5213797068
9	3.5213796920	∞	3.5213797068

The $g_1(x)$ iteration function converges, while the $g_2(x)$ iteration function diverges. Even with an initial guess of $x = 3.5213797$, $g_2(x)$ will diverge. The $g_3(x)$ iteration function converges to 11 digits in only 3 iterations, whereas after 9 iterations, $g_1(x)$ produces only 7 correct digits.

Example 6.5: Fixed-Point Iteration for $x - 12x^{1/3} + 12 = 0$

Fixed-point iteration is easily applied to

$$f(x) = x - 12x^{1/3} + 12, \tag{6.4}$$

which has the same form as Equation (6.3), but with different coefficients. Figure 6.8 shows that Equation (6.4) has two roots, one near $x = 1.5$ and one near $x = 21$. Three iteration functions for Equation (6.4) are

$$g_1(x) = 12x^{1/3} - 12, \quad g_2(x) = \left(\frac{x + 12}{12}\right)^3, \quad g_3(x) = \frac{8x^{1/3} - 12}{1 - 4x^{-2/3}}.$$

9	3.51953125	3.52148438	3.52343750	8.959e-05
10	3.51953125	3.52050781	3.52148438	-7.463e-04
11	3.52050781	3.52099609	3.52148438	-3.284e-04
12	3.52099609	3.52124023	3.52148438	-1.194e-04
13	3.52124023	3.52136230	3.52148438	-1.490e-05
14	3.52136230	3.52142334	3.52148438	3.735e-05
15	3.52136230	3.52139282	3.52142334	1.123e-05

```
ans =
     3.5214
```

The iterations show that bisection slowly closes in on the root. Although the bracket interval is reduced by half during each iteration, the value of f(xmid) is *not* reduced monotonically. For example, the value of xmid at k = 10 is a worse approximation to the root than the value of xmid at k = 9. A similar situation occurs between iteration 13 and iteration 14. The bisection algorithm guarantees that the bracket size is reduced by half and that the root is always bracketed. It does not optimize the location of the next guess at the root.

6.3.1 Analysis of the Bisection Method

It is easy to analyze the performance of the bisection method. Let δ_n be the size of the bracketing interval at the nth stage of bisection. Then, $\delta_0 = b - a$ is the initial bracketing interval, and

$$\delta_1 = \frac{1}{2}\delta_0,$$

$$\delta_2 = \frac{1}{2}\delta_1 = \frac{1}{4}\delta_0,$$

$$\vdots$$

$$\delta_n = \left(\frac{1}{2}\right)^n \delta_0. \tag{6.5}$$

The size of the bracket interval measures the error in the location of the root. Since the bracket size is reduced by a constant factor at each step, the convergence rate (i.e., the reduction in the error) is said to be linear. The relative reduction in bracket size after n bisections is

$$\frac{\delta_n}{\delta_0} = \left(\frac{1}{2}\right)^n = 2^{-n}. \tag{6.6}$$

Solving this equation for n gives the number of bisections required to obtain a desired reduction in bracket size, namely,

TABLE 6.1   REDUCTION OF BRACKET SIZE
AND INCREASE IN COMPUTATIONAL EFFORT
AS A FUNCTION OF THE NUMBER OF
BISECTIONS.

n	$\dfrac{\delta_n}{\delta_0}$	function evaluations
5	3.1×10^{-2}	7
10	9.8×10^{-4}	12
20	9.5×10^{-7}	22
30	9.3×10^{-10}	32
40	9.1×10^{-13}	42
50	8.9×10^{-16}	52

$$ n = \log_2 \left(\frac{\delta_n}{\delta_0} \right). $$

Values of δ_n/δ_0 for some representative values of n are given in Table 6.1. Also listed is the number of times that the function $f(x)$ has to be evaluated. After the initial bracket is established, the function needs to be evaluated just once per iteration.

6.3.2 Convergence Criteria

Automatic root-finding procedures iteratively refine an initial estimate for the root. The root is (almost) never known exactly, since it is extremely unlikely that a numerical procedure will find the precise value of x that makes $f(x)$ exactly zero in floating-point arithmetic. The algorithm must decide how close to the root the guess should be before stopping the search.

Figure 6.10 shows a function crossing the x-axis. Two criteria can be applied in testing for convergence. The first criterion is to test the magnitude by which the estimate of the root changes from iteration to iteration. This requires the user to

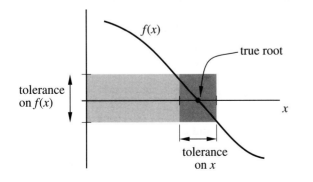

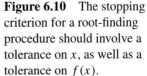

Figure 6.10   The stopping criterion for a root-finding procedure should involve a tolerance on x, as well as a tolerance on $f(x)$.

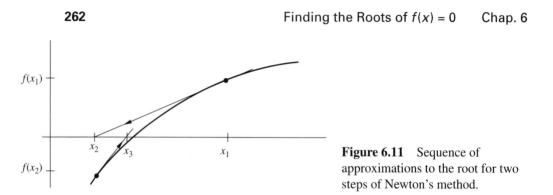

Figure 6.11 Sequence of approximations to the root for two steps of Newton's method.

where Δx is the distance from x_k to the place where the approximation is desired. Substituting $\Delta x = x_{k+1} - x_k$ into Equation (6.11) and retaining only the first term in the series expansion gives

$$f(x_{k+1}) \approx f(x_k) + (x_{k+1} - x_k) f'(x_k),$$

where

$$f'(x_k) = \left. \frac{df}{dx} \right|_{x_k} .$$

The goal of the calculations is to find the value of x that makes $f(x) = 0$. Setting $f(x_{k+1}) = 0$ and solving for x_{k+1} yields

$$x_{k+1} = x_k - \frac{f(x_k)}{f'(x_k)}. \tag{6.12}$$

Given a value of x_k and an analytical representation for the function, the right-hand side of Equation (6.12) is readily computable. A root-finding algorithm using Newton's method is compact, because there is no logic associated with the maintenance of a bracket interval. The algorithm is as follows:

Algorithm 6.4   Newton's Method for Scalar Equations

initialize: $x_1 = \dots$
for $k = 2, 3, \dots$
    $x_k = x_{k-1} - f(x_{k-1})/f'(x_{k-1})$
    if converged, stop
end

Unlike the bisection method, Newton's method does not search for roots within a limited range of the x-axis. As a result, the iterations for the root can wander far from the initial guess. In the worst case the iterations may diverge and cause a

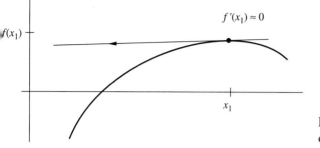

$f'(x_1) \approx 0$

x_1

Figure 6.12   Pathological failure of Newton's method.

floating-point exception.[1] If the first derivative of $f(x)$ vanishes, then the procedure for computing x_{k+1} fails, as depicted in Figure 6.12. Even though a good initial guess to the root is available, Newton's method may diverge if the first derivative of the function approaches zero near the current estimate of the root. When it does converge, Newton's method converges in far fewer iterations than the bisection method.

Newton's method is a form of fixed-point iteration. The iteration function is

$$g(x) = x - \frac{f(x)}{f'(x)}.$$

This is the basis of the $g_3(x)$ formulas in Examples 6.4 and 6.5.

Example 6.7: Apply Newton's Method to $x - x^{1/3} - 2 = 0$

The demoNewton function in Listing 6.5 uses Newton's method to find the root of Equation (6.3). The $f(x)$ and $f'(x)$ from Equation (6.3) are coded directly into demoNewton. A more flexible implementation of Newton's method is presented in the next section.

Running demoNewton for an initial guess of $x = 3$ gives the following results:

```
>> demoNewton(3)
   k         f(x)            dfdx           x(k+1)
   0     -4.422e-01       8.398e-01     3.526644293139033
   1      4.507e-03       8.561e-01     3.521380147397328
   2      3.771e-07       8.560e-01     3.521379706804571
   3      2.665e-15       8.560e-01     3.521379706804568
   4      0.000e+00       8.560e-01     3.521379706804568

ans =
      3.5214
```

[1] A calculation resulting in a NaN or Inf .

```
function x = demoNewton(x0,n)
% demoNewton   Use Newton's method to find the root of f(x) = x - x^(1/3) - 2
%
% Synopsis:  x = demoNewton(x0)
%            x = demoNewton(x0,n)
%
% Input:   x0 = initial guess
%          n = (optional) number of iterations, Default: n = 5
%
% Output   x = estimate of the root

if nargin<2, n=5; end      %  Default number of iterations
x = x0;                    %  Initial guess

fprintf('  k         f(x)            dfdx              x(k+1)\n');
for k=1:n
  f = x - x.^(1/3) - 2;
  dfdx = 1 - (1/3)*x.^(-2/3);
  x = x - f/dfdx;
  fprintf('%3d  %12.3e  %12.3e   %18.15f\n',k-1,f,dfdx,x);
end
```

Listing 6.5   The demoNewton function finds the root of $x - x^{1/3} - 2 = 0$ using a fixed number of Newton iterations.

      The Newton steps converge very quickly. After 3 iterations the root estimate is known to 16 digits and gives $f(x) = 0$ to machine precision. Compare this with the bisection iterations (see page 254), which, after 15 iterations, give only the first five digits of the root.

6.4.1 Convergence of Newton's Method

If $f(x)$, $f'(x)$, and $f''(x)$ are continuous and if $f'(x)$ and $f''(x)$ are nonzero in a neighborhood of the root, then it is possible to obtain an analytical expression describing the rapid convergence of Newton's Method. (See, for example, [10, 66, 68] for a proof.)

      Let ξ be the exact root of $f(x)$. If the initial guess x_0 is sufficiently close to the root (i.e., if $|x_0 - \xi| \leq \rho$ for some positive ρ), then $|x_k - \xi| \leq \rho$ for all subsequent iterations using Equation (6.12), and

$$|x_{k+1} - \xi| \leq C(\rho) |x_k - \xi|^2,$$

where $C(\rho)$ is a factor independent of k. This expression shows that the error, $e_{k+1} = x_{k+1} - \xi$, is the square of the error at the preceding iteration, and because of this, Newton's method is said to have a *quadratic* convergence. Contrast this with the linear convergence rate of bisection. (See Equation (6.5).)

The quadratic convergence of Newton's method comes with restrictions. First of all, Newton's method is not guaranteed to converge unless $|x_0 - \xi| \leq \rho$, where, in general both ξ (of course) and ρ are not known. In other words, Newton's method converges if the initial guess is close enough to the root, but neither the root nor a measure of "close enough" can be prescribed ahead of time. Second, if the root is repeated, then $f'(\xi) = 0$, and the convergence formula just given does not apply. At repeated roots, the convergence of Newton's method is only linear, not quadratic.

For well-behaved functions, the rapid convergence of Newton's method can be exploited. For general-purpose root finding, a more robust solution is desirable. One way to improve the convergence behavior is to use a hybrid method that combines bisection and Newton's method. (See § 6.6.)

6.4.2 A General Implementation of Newton's Method

The preceding example demonstrated how Newton's method can be applied to a specific $f(x)$. That approach requires rewriting the root-finding code whenever it is to be applied to another function. The `newton` function shown in Listing 6.6 implements Newton's method for an arbitrary $f(x)$. The `newton` function can be invoked in one of four ways:

```
r = newton(fun,x0)
r = newton(fun,x0,xtol)
r = newton(fun,x0,xtol,ftol)
r = newton(fun,x0,xtol,ftol,verbose)
```

The first parameter `fun` is the name of the function that evaluates $f(x)$ and $f'(x)$ for any given x. The initial guess is supplied in the second parameter, `x0`. *Absolute* tolerances on the changes in x and changes in $f(x)$ are specified with `xtol` and `ftol`, respectively. The `verbose` flag is used to control whether a printout of the iterations is provided. The output is `r`, the estimate of the root.

Checking for convergence is complicated, because there is no initial bracket to provide an easy reference for a relative convergence tolerance. The simple implementation in Listing 6.6 requires that the user supply absolute tolerances for x and $f(x)$. Contrast this with the relative tolerances used in the `bisect` function in Listing 6.4 on page 260.

The first argument of `newton` is the name of the user-supplied function that evaluates $f(x)$ and $f'(x)$. The details of creating such a function are demonstrated in Example 6.8.

The choice of whether to use a hand-coded function or the more general `newton` function is a matter of preference and expediency. It makes sense to reuse

```
function r = newton(fun,x0,xtol,ftol,verbose)
% newton    Newton's method to find a root of the scalar equation f(x) = 0
%
% Synopsis:  r = newton(fun,x0)
%            r = newton(fun,x0,xtol)
%            r = newton(fun,x0,xtol,ftol)
%            r = newton(fun,x0,xtol,ftol,verbose)
%
% Input:  fun    = (string) name of mfile that returns f(x) and f'(x).
%         x0     = initial guess
%         xtol   = (optional) absolute tolerance on x.   Default: xtol=5*eps
%         ftol   = (optional) absolute tolerance on f(x). Default: ftol=5*eps
%         verbose = (optional) flag.  Default: verbose=0, no printing.
%
% Output:  r = the root of the function

if nargin < 3,  xtol = 5*eps;  end
if nargin < 4,  ftol = 5*eps;  end
if nargin < 5,  verbose = 0;   end
xeps = max(xtol,5*eps);  feps = max(ftol,5*eps);  % Smallest tols are 5*eps

if verbose
  fprintf('\nNewton iterations for %s.m\n',fun);
  fprintf('  k       f(x)           dfdx         x(k+1)\n');
end

x = x0;  k = 0;  maxit = 15;    % Initial guess, current and max iterations
while k <= maxit
  k = k + 1;
  [f,dfdx] = feval(fun,x);      %  Returns f( x(k-1) ) and f'( x(k-1) )
  dx = f/dfdx;
  x = x - dx;
  if verbose, fprintf('%3d %12.3e %12.3e %18.14f\n',k,f,dfdx,x);  end

  if ( abs(f) < feps ) | ( abs(dx) < xeps ),  r = x;  return;  end
end
warning(sprintf('root not found within tolerance after %d iterations\n',k));
```

Listing 6.6 MATLAB function newton to find roots by Newton's
method.

the general newton function, since it has been debugged and will correctly perform
Newton iterations with any user-supplied function. Moreover, the convergence tolerances are implemented in a flexible and fairly general way. On the other hand,
the Newton iteration formula is so compact that it may make sense to combine the
evaluation of $f(x)$ and $f'(x)$ with the overall Newton algorithm. Such a custom-

```
function [f,dfdx] = fx3n(x)
% fx3n   Evaluate f(x) = x - x^(1/3) - 2 and dfdx for Newton algorithm
f    = x - x.^(1/3) - 2;
dfdx = 1 - (1/3)*x.^(-2/3);
```

> **Listing 6.7**   MATLAB function fx3n evaluates $f(x)$ and $f'(x)$ for
> $f(x) = x - x^{1/3} - 2$. Values are returned in a row vector to be compatible with the newton function.

made Newton iteration has the advantage that all of the code is contained in one file.

Example 6.8: Using the newton Function

Using newton to find the root of Equation (6.3) requires a function m-file to evaluate $f(x)$ and $f'(x)$. The fx3n function in Listing 6.7 performs the required calculations and returns $f(x)$ and $f'(x)$ in the f and dfdx variables.

Here is the result of applying newton to fx3n with an initial guess of 3.

```
>> newton('fx3n',3,5e-16,5e-16,1)

Newton iterations for fx3n.m
 k      f(x)          dfdx          x(k+1)
 1   -4.422e-01    8.398e-01    3.52664429313903
 2    4.507e-03    8.561e-01    3.52138014739733
 3    3.771e-07    8.560e-01    3.52137970680457
 4    2.665e-15    8.560e-01    3.52137970680457
 5    0.000e+00    8.560e-01    3.52137970680457

ans =
    3.5214
```

The verbose flag is set to true, so that the convergence history is printed. The xtol and ftol parameters are set to unnecessarily small values to allow comparison with the results of the demoNewton example.

As expected, these results are identical to the ones arrived at with the demoNewton function in Example 6.7.

Example 6.9: Picnic Table Leg Design with Newton's Method

Solving the picnic table problem (see Example 6.1 on page 240) with Newton's method requires the same steps as the preceding example: Write an m-file that evaluates $f(\theta)$ and $f'(\theta)$ and pass the name of this m-file, along with an initial guess, to the newton function. The equations to be coded in the auxiliary m-file are derived from Equation (6.2):

$$f(\theta) = w \sin\theta - h \cos\theta - b, \qquad f'(\theta) = w \cos\theta + h \sin\theta.$$

In implementing the m-file to evaluate $f(\theta)$ and $f'(\theta)$, a decision must be made on how to assign the values to the w, h, and b parameters. The newton function only knows about the independent variable (θ for this problem) and the value of the function and its first derivative. There is no provision for communicating additional parameters through newton to the function that evaluates $f(\theta)$ and $f'(\theta)$ function. (A variation on newton that does this is discussed at the end of the example.)

A simple solution is to hard code specific values of w, b, and h into the auxiliary m-file. Obviously, this requires rewriting the auxiliary m-file whenever w, h, and b are changed. Another approach is to abandon the use of the generic newton function and write a custom Newton routine for this specific problem. This custom routine would evaluate $f(\theta)$ and $f'(\theta)$ in the same m-file routine that manages the Newton iterations. (See Example 6.7 and Problem 20.) A third approach—the one taken here—is to use global variables to bypass newton in the setting of w, h, and b in the auxiliary m-file. For a review of global variables in MATLAB, refer to § 3.6.2 on page 133.

Listing 6.8 contains the tablen (main) program and the legsn (auxiliary) program for determining the table dimensions. The leg parameters w, h, and b are communicated to legsn via the global variables WLENGTH, HLENGTH, and BLENGTH. The global variables are given distinctive names (instead of w, h, and b) and written in all capital letters to prevent name clashes with other global variables. In addition, these variables are copied from the input parameters of newton in adherence with the convention that one should avoid changing input variables to a MATLAB function. The relationship between the global variables and the functions that share them are shown in Figure 6.13.

Running tablen gives the following results:

```
>> tablen(28,27,3.5);
theta =    49.1 degrees    d1 =    10.782    d2 =    17.855
```

The use of global variables can be eliminated if the newton function is rewritten to allow additional parameters to be passed through to the user-defined $f(x)$ function. Curious readers can study the newtonNG, tablenNG, and legsNG m-files included in the NMM toolbox. The newtonNG function uses the varargin utility to pass the w, h, and b parameters on to legsNG function. Refer to Example 6.11 to see how this technique works with the built-in fzero function.

6.5 THE SECANT METHOD

The secant method is similar to Newton's method in that it uses information about the slope of the function near the current approximation to the root. Rather than evaluate an analytical formula for $f'(x)$, the secant method uses the last two guesses at the root to estimate the slope. Given the values of x_k, $f(x_k)$, x_{k-1}, and $f(x_{k-1})$, the first derivative of $f(x)$ can be approximated as

$$f'(x_k) \approx \frac{f(x_k) - f(x_{k-1})}{x_k - x_{k-1}}.$$

```
function tablen(w,h,b,t0)
% tablen  Use Newton's method to find dimensions of picnic table legs
%
% Synopsis:  tablen(w,b,h)
%            tablen(w,b,h,t0)
%
% Input:    w,h = width and height of the table legs
%           b   = width of the material used to make the legs
%           t0  = (optional) initial guess at theta.  Default: t0 = pi/4 (rad)
%
% Output:   Print out table dimensions

global WLENGTH HLENGTH BLENGTH          %  Define global variables
WLENGTH = w;  HLENGTH = h;  BLENGTH = b;  %  Global copies of input variables

if nargin<3
   error('All three dimensions, w, h, b, must be specified');
elseif nargin<4
   t0 = pi/4;       % default initial guess
end

theta = newton('legsn',t0);      %  Root-finding is done in newton

%  --- Compute other dimensions once theta is known
alpha = pi/2 - theta;     a  = BLENGTH/tan(alpha);     c = BLENGTH/tan(theta);
d2 = HLENGTH/(2*sin(theta));     d1 = d2 - a - c;
fprintf('theta = %6.1f degrees    d1 = %8.3f    d2 = %8.3f\n',theta*180/pi,d1,d2);
```

```
function [f,dfdt] = legsn(theta)
% legsn  Evaluate f(theta) and fprime(theta) for the picnic leg problem.
%        Used with the Newton's method.
%
% Synopsis:  [f,dfdt] = legsn(theta)
%
% Input:     theta = angle of table leg in radians
%            WLENGTH HLENGTH and BLENGTH are global variables giving
%                 table dimensions
%
% Output:    f    = value of f(theta). As theta approaches a root,
%                 f(theta) approaches zero.
%            dfdt = fprime(theta), ie. df/dtheta
global  WLENGTH  HLENGTH  BLENGTH

f    = WLENGTH*sin(theta) - HLENGTH*cos(theta) - BLENGTH;
dfdt = WLENGTH*cos(theta) + HLENGTH*sin(theta);
```

Listing 6.8 The table and legsn functions used to design picnic table
legs. Root-finding is performed by the newton function in Listing 6.6.

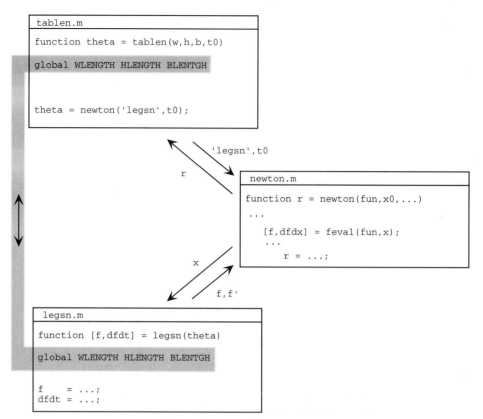

Figure 6.13   Using global variables to communicate between main and auxiliary functions while bypassing `newton`.

Substituting this expression into Equation (6.12) gives

$$x_{k+1} = x_k - f(x_k) \left[\frac{(x_k - x_{k-1})}{f(x_k) - f(x_{k-1})} \right]. \tag{6.13}$$

Like the bisection method, the secant method needs two initial approximations at the root. These can be bracket values or values from two iterations of the some other root-finding procedure. Unlike the bisection method, however, the secant method does not restrict its search for the root to the initial bracket. The secant method continually updates the values used as approximations to the root, regardless of whether these values lie inside or outside of the bracket formed by the first two root estimates.

The secant algorithm is

Algorithm 6.5   Secant

initialize: $x_1 = \ldots, x_2 = \ldots$
for $k = 2, 3 \ldots$
$\quad x_{k+1} = x_k - f(x_k)(x_k - x_{k-1})/(f(x_k) - f(x_{k-1}))$
$\quad$ if converged, stop
end

A representative sequence of iterations is shown schematically in Figure 6.14. Assume that x_1 and x_2 are obtained by bracketing. The third estimate of the root, x_3, is within the bracket, but the next estimate, x_4, is outside the bracket.

It is tempting to algebraically rearrange Equation (6.13) as

$$x_{k+1} = \frac{f(x_k)x_{k-1} - f(x_{k-1})x_k}{f(x_k) - f(x_{k-1})}, \tag{6.14}$$

but this is not recommended. Although Equations (6.13) and (6.14) are equivalent in exact arithmetic, Equation (6.13) is better suited for numerical computation. The difference between Equation (6.13) and (6.14) becomes apparent as the iterations approach convergence. Ideally,

$$\frac{x_k - x_{k-1}}{f(x_k) - f(x_{k-1})} \longrightarrow \frac{1}{f'(\xi)} \quad \text{as} \quad x_k \longrightarrow \xi,$$

where ξ is the root. It is quite possible, however, that due to roundoff errors, the numerical value of $f(x_k) - f(x_{k-1})$ might be zero. Even if it is not zero, the difference between $f(x_k)$ and $f(x_{k-1})$ will suffer a loss of precision as the values of $f(x_k)$ and $f(x_{k-1})$ become closer. This loss of precision leads to *catastrophic cancellation*, because the small error in the denominator becomes a large error when $(x_k - x_{k-1})/f(x_k) - f(x_{k-1})$ is evaluated.

Both Equation (6.13) and Equation (6.14) can have catastrophic cancellation, due to roundoff in the computation of $f(x_k) - f(x_{k-1})$. In Equation (6.14), the

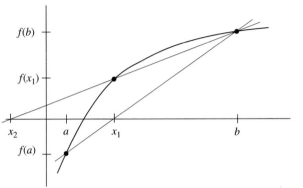

Figure 6.14   Sequence of approximations to a root generated by the secant method.

$(b, f(b))$ and $(c, f(c))$. Inverse quadratic interpolation involves finding the point x_{quad} where the *quadratic* crosses the x-axis. If the three points are not distinct (i.e., if $a \approx b$ or $b \approx c$), then the secant method is used to find x_{lin}, the point where a linear interpolant crosses the x-axis. If x_{quad} and x_{lin} do not lie in the original bracket interval, then a bisection step is taken.

The algorithm in `fzero` is more sophisticated than the description just given. Care is taken to avoid unnecessary calculations and to minimize the effects of roundoff. Readers interested in the details should consult [8, 24, 61] in addition to reading the code in `fzero.m`. A Fortran implementation of `fzero` is described by Forsythe et al. [24]. A C version is provided by Press et al. [61]. The algorithm was first developed by van Wijngaarden and Dekker and then improved and popularized by Brent [8].

The syntax of the `fzero` function has changed with the evolution of MATLAB from version 4.0 through version 5.3. Here we describe the syntax for version 5.3. Users of older versions will have to consult the documentation, especially for the use of options that control the execution of `fzero`.

The (version 5.3) `fzero` function may be called in a number of ways. Three of the more basic uses of `fzero` are as follows:[2]

```
r = fzero(fun,x0)
r = fzero(fun,x0,options)
r = fzero(fun,x0,options,arg1,arg2, ... )
```

Here `fun` is the name of the m-file that evaluates $f(x)$, and $x0$ is the initial guess at the root. The $x0$ parameter can be supplied as a scalar value or as a vector with two elements. If $x0$ is a scalar, `fzero` begins a preliminary search phase in which it attempts to find a bracket for the root. Once a bracket is found, `fzero` proceeds with the main algorithm. If $x0$ is a two-element vector, the two elements must be a bracket on a suspected root. In other words, evaluating $f(x)$ at $x0(1)$ and $x0(2)$ should produce values of f with opposite sign.

The initial guess for `fzero` can be supplied by visual inspection of the $f(x)$ function. This step can be automated with the `brackPlot` function. For example, the following statements find the root of Equation (6.3) (see also Listing 6.2 on page 249):

```
>> xb = brackPlot('fx3',0,5);
>> fzero('fx3',xb)
ans =
    3.5214
```

---

[2]Enter `help fzero` for a complete list of input and output possibilities.

The *options* parameter is a special data structure created by the optimset function. Use of *options* is described in the next paragraph. The additional parameters *arg1*, *arg2*, ... , are not used by fzero. Instead, these are passed on to the function specified by fun. These *pass-through* parameters provide a way of specifying (potentially variable) coefficients in $f(x)$ without using global variables. Example 6.11 shows how this is done.

The use of *options* is a new feature of MATLAB version 5.3. Earlier versions allowed only two options: the convergence tolerance and a flag to control printing while fzero is running. The optimset function is a utility that allows individual options to be set for a variety of optimization functions. Some of the optimization functions (e.g., fzero and fmins) are part of the standard MATLAB toolbox. Others are part of the Optimization Toolbox, which must be purchased separately from the MathWorks. Because optimset is an interface to a large number of functions, a casual user may easily be overwhelmed by the documentation provided by help optimset. Only a few parameters set by optimset are useful when working with fzero.

To specify optional parameters that control fzero, one first uses optimset to create an *options* data structure. The *options* data structure is then passed as the third argument of fzero. A typical usage would be

```
>> x0 = ...
>> options = optimset( ... )
>> x = fzero('myFun',x0,options)
```

The syntax of the optimset function is

```
options = optimset('parameterName',parameterValue, ... )
```

where *parameterName* is the name of the option to be set and *parameterValue* is the value to be assigned to the option described by *parameterName*. The only numerical option is the convergence tolerance. This value is adjusted with

```
>> options = optimset('TolX',delta)
```

where *delta* is a positive, scalar value. The default value of *delta* is eps $= 2.2 \times 10^{-16}$.

The 'Display' parameter controls the amount of information printed during fzero iterations. 'Display' can be set to one of 'iter', 'off', or 'final'. If 'Display' is set to 'final' (the default value), a message indicating the initial bracket interval and the final value of the root is printed to the screen. If 'Display' is set to 'iter', the results of each major step in the solution process are reported to the command window. If 'Display' is set to 'off', fzero does its work without printing any messages.

The following statements use the `optimset` and `fzero` function to find a zero-crossing of $\sin(x)$ while printing the intermediate results of the iterations:

```
>> options = optimset('Display','iter');
>> r = fzero('sin',[pi/4 3*pi/2],options)
```

```
Func-count       x            f(x)          Procedure
    1        0.785398      0.707107          initial
    2        4.71239            -1           initial
    3        2.41201       0.666558          interpolation
    4         3.5622       -0.408315         bisection
    5        3.12527       0.0163175         interpolation
    6        3.14206      -0.000471667       interpolation
    7        3.14159       2.03284e-008      interpolation
    8        3.14159      -7.65714e-016      interpolation
    9        3.14159       5.66554e-016      interpolation
Zero found in the interval: [0.7854, 4.7124].
r =
    3.1416
```

Note that the output of the `optimset` function can be assigned to any MATLAB variable; that is, it need not be called `options`. The explicit creation of an `options` variable can be omitted entirely by including the call to `optimset` in the parameter list of `fzero`. To repeat the preceding computations while suppressing all output, one could enter

```
>> r = fzero('sin',[pi/4 3*pi/2],optimset('Display','off'))
r =
    3.1416
```

Both the `'Display'` and `'TolX'` parameters can be set simultaneously. For example, to repeat the root-finding one more time with a (much) looser convergence tolerance, enter the following at the command line:

```
>> options = optimset('Display','iter','TolX',0.05);
>> r = fzero('sin',[pi/4 3*pi/2],options)
```

```
Func-count       x            f(x)          Procedure
    1        0.785398      0.707107          initial
    2        4.71239            -1           initial
    3        2.41201       0.666558          interpolation
    4         3.5622       -0.408315         bisection
    5        3.12527       0.0163175         interpolation
Zero found in the interval: [0.7854, 4.7124].
r =
    3.1253
```

These five steps are identical to the first five steps produced with the default parameters. Adjusting the convergence tolerance only makes a difference when the calculations are stopped, not the path toward convergence.

For general-purpose root finding, `fzero` is recommended over the other techniques presented earlier in this chapter. If the function and its derivatives are easy to evaluate and are well behaved, then Newton's method may converge faster than `fzero`. For simple functions, the difference in computing time is negligible, unless roots are to be found many, many times.

Example 6.11: Use `fzero` to Solve Picnic Table Design Problem

In this example, the `fzero` function is used to solve Equation (6.2) for the angle that defines the dimensions of a picnic table leg. The basic solution requires only a small variation from the code presented in Example 6.9. In addition, a feature of `fzero` is demonstrated that eliminates the need to use global variables. Issues relating to the use of global variables are discussed in Example 6.9.

Specifying the dimensions of a picnic table leg requires finding the value of θ that satisfies

$$f(\theta) = w \sin\theta - h \cos\theta - b = 0,$$

where w, h, and b are, respectively, the width and height of the table and the width of leg material, respectively. (See Figure 6.3 on page 242.) The `fzero` function is used to find θ given values for w, h, and b. To make the numerical solution as flexible as possible, the w, h, and b parameters are not hard coded into the m-file that defines $f(\theta)$. Rather, values of these parameters are passed through `fzero` to the $f(\theta)$ m-file.

As just described, a call to `fzero` of the form

```
r = fzero(fun,x0,options,arg1,arg2, ... )
```

passes *arg1*, *arg2*, ... on to the m-file specified by the *fun* parameter. This feature is used by the `tablez` and `legz` functions in Listing 6.9. The main program, `tablez`, calls `fzero` with

```
theta = fzero('legz',t0,[],0,w,h,b);
```

or

```
theta = fzero('legz',t0,optimset('Display','off'),w,h,b);
```

depending on which version of MATLAB is detected at runtime. The pass-through parameters come at the end of the parameter list, so that values must be supplied for the optional control parameters (*tol* and *trace* in version 5.2 and earlier; *optimset* in version 5.3 and later). In the version 5.2 syntax, supplying a null matrix [] for the third parameters instructs `fzero` to use the default tolerances.

```
function tablez(w,h,b,t0)
% tablez  Use fzero to find dimensions of picnic table legs
%
% Synopsis:  tablez(w,b,h)
%            tablez(w,b,h,t0)
%
% Input:    w = width of the table legs
%           h = height of the table legs
%           b = width of the stock used to make the legs
%           t0 = (optional) initial guess at theta (in radians)
%                Default:  t0 = pi/4
%
% Output:   Print out of table dimensions

if nargin<3
   error('All three dimensions, w, h, b, must be specified');
elseif nargin<4
   t0 = pi/4;        % default initial guess
end

[v,d] = version;
vnum = str2num(v(1:3));   % vnum is version number in d.d format
if vnum<5.3
  % "old" fzero syntax
  theta = fzero('legz',t0,[],0,w,h,b);    %  w,h,b are passed through to legz
else
  % optimset('Display','off') stops printing *and* avoids warning from parser
  theta = fzero('legz',t0,optimset('Display','off'),w,h,b);
end

%  --- Compute other dimensions once theta is known
alpha = pi/2 - theta;    a  = b/tan(alpha);       c = b/tan(theta);
d2 = h/(2*sin(theta));   d1 = d2 - a - c;
fprintf('theta = %6.1f degrees    d1 = %8.3f    d2 = %8.3f\n',theta*180/pi,d1,d2);
```

```
function f = legz(theta,w,h,b)
% legz  Evaluate f(theta) for picnic leg geometry.  Use pass-through
%       parameters in fzero to send w, h, and b values to this function
f = w*sin(theta) - h*cos(theta) - b;
```

Listing 6.9 The `tablez` and `legsz` functions used to design picnic table legs. Root finding is performed by the built-in `fzero` function.

The pass-through parameters become additional inputs to the m-file function specified by the first parameter to `fzero`. Accordingly, the $f(x)$ m-file must have the correct number of input parameters to accept the pass-through values from `fzero`. The function definition for `legz` is

The c

```
function f = legz(theta,w,h,b)
```

Running `tablez` gives the same results as `tablen` in Example 6.9:

```
>> tablez(28,27,3.5);
theta =    49.1 degrees    d1 =    10.782    d2 =    17.855
```

The e

6.7 ROOTS OF POLYNOMIALS

Equat
in Eq

phisti   The routines discussed up to this point can be applied to polynomials, because a
probl   polynomial in x can always be put in the form $f(x) = 0$. These methods have
probl   difficulty, however, when multiple roots, closely spaced roots, or complex roots
does a   are encountered. To find the roots of a polynomial, it is better to use specialized
an ele   numerical algorithms that are desgned to deal with these complications.
probl   Figure 6.17 shows plots of three quadratic polynomials:

in Fig

$$f_1(x) = x^2 - 3x + 2, \quad f_2(x) = x^2 - 10x + 25, \quad f_3(x) = x^2 - 17x + 72.5.$$

>> ro
ans = $f_1(x)$ has two distinct, real roots, $f_2(x)$ has repeated real roots, and $f_3(x)$ has
            complex roots.

>> ro
ans =

>> ro
ans =
8.
8.

Exam

Consi
the bu
(4/3).
it is p

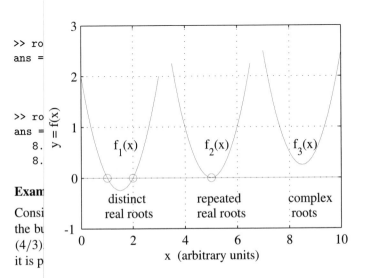

Figure 6.17 Polynomials with distinct real roots, repeated real roots, and complex roots.

buoyancy force

$$\rho g V_s = \rho_w g V_w, \qquad \text{or,} \qquad s V_s = V_w, \tag{6.17}$$

where ρ is the density of the sphere material, g is the acceleration of gravity, ρ_w is the density of water, and $s = \rho/\rho_w$ is the specific gravity of the sphere material. As depicted in the left-hand side of Figure 6.18, when $0 \leq s < 0.5$, the sphere floats with its center above the surface of the water. If $0.5 < s < 1$, the sphere floats with its center below the surface of the water.

The spherical sections of dimension h shown in Figure 6.18 have a volume

$$V_h = \frac{\pi}{3} \left(3rh^2 - h^3 \right).$$

If $s < 0.5$ then $V_w = V_h$ and Equation (6.17) can be rearranged as

$$h^3 - 3rh^2 + 4sr^3 = 0. \tag{6.18}$$

Given values of r and s, the values of h that satisfy Equation (6.18) can be obtained with the roots function:

```
>> r = 1;    s = 0.25;         %  (arbitrary) radius and specific gravity
>> p = [1  -3*r   0  4*s*r^3 ];  %  polynomial coefficients
>> h = roots(p)
h =
     2.8794
     0.6527
    -0.5321
```

Only $h = 0.6527$ makes sense for $s < 0.5$ and $r = 1$. Note that in the definition of p, the coefficient of the h term must appear as a zero. It can not be simply omitted.

As with any root-finding procedure, the values returned by the roots function should be verified by substitution back into the polynomial. This is easily accomplished with the

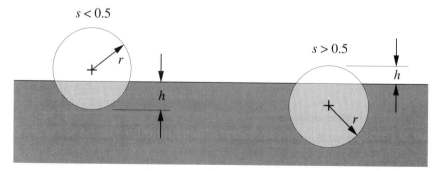

Figure 6.18 Solid spheres floating in water. The depth to which a sphere floats is determined by its specific gravity $s = \rho/\rho_w$.

polyval function. In the preceding statements, the coefficients of the polynomial are defined by the vector p, and the roots are returned in the vector h. Evaluating the polynomial at the suspected roots gives

```
>> polyval(p,h)
ans =
   1.0e-13 *
   0.1077
   0.0056
  -0.0022
```

Unlike the other root finding routines presented in this chapter, there is no way to adjust the tolerance on the values returned by the roots function.

6.8 SUMMARY

This chapter describes several routines for finding the roots (zeros) of a scalar function written as $f(x) = 0$. Table 6.2 lists the MATLAB functions developed in this chapter.

For nonpolynomial $f(x)$, fixed-point iteration, bisection, Newton's method, and the secant method are applicable. It is a good idea to verify that the roots

TABLE 6.2 FUNCTIONS FOR ROOT FINDING DEVELOPED IN THIS CHAPTER. FUNCTIONS WITH N.A. (NOT APPLICABLE) FOR A PAGE NUMBER ARE NOT LISTED IN THE TEXT, BUT ARE INCLUDED IN THE NMM TOOLBOX.

Function	page	Description
bisect	260	General-purpose bisection routine to find a root of $f(x) = 0$.
brackPlot	247	Find and plot brackets for roots of a function.
demoBisect	255	Use bisection to find the root of $x - x^{1/3} - 2$.
demoNewton	264	Use Newton's method to find the root of $f(x) = x - x^{1/3} - 2$.
fx3	249	Evaluate the function $f(x) = x - x^{1/3} - 2$.
fx3n	267	Evaluate $f(x) = x - x^{1/3} - 2$ and df/dx for Newton's method.
legsn	269	Evaluate $f(\theta)$ and $f'(\theta)$ for the picnic table problem. Used with the Newton's method only.
legsnNG	N.A.	Evaluate $f(\theta)$ and $f'(\theta)$ for the picnic table problem. Used with Newton's method and tablenNG.
legz	278	Evaluate $f(\theta)$ for the picnic table problem.
newton	266	General-purpose Newton's method to find a root of $f(x) = 0$.
newtonNG	N.A.	General-purpose Newton's method to find a root of $f(x) = 0$. Extra parameters for $f(x)$ are passed through newtonNG without needing to use global variables.
tablen	269	Use Newton's method to find dimensions of picnic table legs.
tablenNG	N.A.	Use Newton's method to find dimensions of picnic table legs. Avoids global variables by using newtonNG and legsnNG.
tablez	278	Use fzero to find dimensions of picnic table legs.

returned from these procedure produce $f(x) \approx 0$. In particular, the bracketing and bisection methods cannot distinguish a root from a singularity of $f(x) = 0$. In the general case, when an initial guess for the root is unknown, bracketing is a useful technique for identifying intervals on the x-axis that are likely to contain a root. The `brackPlot` function described in § 6.1.3 provides a convenient way to plot a user-defined $f(x)$ over an interval on the x-axis, and to obtain brackets in that interval.

The built-in `fzero` function is highly recommended. `fzero` combines the reliability of bisection with the efficiency of the secant method and inverse quadratic interpolation. To find the roots of $f(x) = 0$ with `fzero`, a user must provide an m-file function to evaluate $f(x)$ for any x. Since the same routine is required as input for `brackPlot`, there is little extra user effort to create a plot of the function and automatically generate initial guesses with `brackPlot` before these guesses are passed on to `fzero`.

A distinction is made between an arbitrary $f(x)$ and the special case where $f(x)$ is polynomial in x. The most effective routines for finding the roots of polynomials are designed especially for that task. Of the techniques for finding roots of a polynomial only the companion matrix method is described in this chapter. The characteristic polynomial of the companion matrix is identical to the polynomial for which the roots are sought. The root-finding problem is thereby converted into an eigenvalue problem, which is readily solved with highly optimized built-in MATLAB routines. The complexity and sophistication of this procedure is hidden by the `roots` function, which returns all of the real and complex roots of a polynomial.

Further Reading

Root finding is covered in most texts on numerical analysis. A Fortran implementation of `fzero` is provided by Forsythe et al. [24]. Fortran and C implementations of the same algorithm are given by Press et al. [61].

EXERCISES

The number in parenthesis at the beginning of each exercise indicates the degree of skill and amount of effort necessary to complete the exercise. See § 1.4 on page 10 for a description of the rating system.

1. (1) Show that the analytical solution to Equation (6.2) is

$$\cos\theta = \frac{1}{(h^2 + w^2)}\left(-bh + \sqrt{b^2h^2 + (h^2 + w^2)(w^2 - b^2)}\right).$$

(*Hint:* Square both sides of Equation (6.2) and substitute $\sin^2\theta = 1 - \cos^2\theta$.)

OLUTION   **2.** (2) The function $f(x) = \sin(x^2) + x^2 - 2x - 0.09$ has four roots in the interval $-1 \le x \le 3$. Given the m-file `fx.m`, which contains

```
function f = fx(x)
f = sin(x.^2) + x.^2 - 2*x - 0.09;
```

the statement

```
>> brackPlot('fx',-1,3)
```

produces only two brackets. Is this result due to a bug in `brackPlot` or `fx`? What needs to be changed so that all four roots are found? Demonstrate that your solution works.

3. (1) Apply the `brackPlot` function to each of the following equations. How many roots are in the designated interval?
 (a) $\cos(x) = x$ for $-2\pi \le x \le 2\pi$.
 (b) $\cos(5x) = x$ for $-2\pi \le x \le 2\pi$.
 (c) $\tan(x) = 0$ for $-2\pi \le x \le 2\pi$.
 (d) $\sin(1/x) = 0$ for $\pi/50 \le x \le \pi/3$.

4. (1) Write a `bracket` function by removing the plotting code from the `brackPlot` function. Test the `bracket` function with the equations in Exercise 3.

5. (2) In Algorithm 6.1, why is the test for the while loop "while $i < n$" instead of "while $a < b$"?

6. (1) Given the function $\cos(x) = x$, derive two fixed point iteration formulas. Which one converges for an initial guess of $x_0 = 0.5$ radians?

7. (1) Verify that the behavior of the iteration functions in Example 6.4 is consistent with the convergence criterion $|g'(x) < 1|$ for fixed-point iteration.

8. (1+) Consider the Colebrook equation for the friction factor in fully developed pipe flow

$$\frac{1}{\sqrt{f}} = -2\log_{10}\left(\frac{\epsilon/D}{3.7} + \frac{2.51}{Re_D\sqrt{f}}\right),$$

where f is the Darcy friction factor, ϵ/D is the relative roughness of the pipe material, and Re_D is the Reynolds number based on pipe diameter D. In the simplest kind of pipe flow analysis, the values of ϵ/D and Re_D are known, and f is to be determined. Derive the following alternative fixed point iteration formulas:

$$f_{new} = \left[2\log_{10}\left(\frac{\epsilon/D}{3.7} + \frac{2.51}{Re_D\sqrt{f_{old}}}\right)\right]^{-2}$$

and

$$f_{new} = \left[\frac{Re_D}{2.51}\left(10^{1/(2\sqrt{f_{old}})} - \frac{\epsilon/D}{3.7}\right)\right]^{-2}.$$

Write two separate function m-files to implement these iteration formulas. Use these m-files to find f for $\epsilon/D = 0.02$, Re $= 10^5$ and an initial guess of $f = 0.01$. Report the number of iterations to reach convergence for each formulation.

9. (1) Use the `bisect` function to find the roots of each equation in Exercise 3. How do you know you have found all of the roots?

10. (1+) Find the roots of $f(x) = (2/x - x)\cos x + 0.0119$ on the interval [0.5, 5].

SOLUTION 11. (1+) Use the `bisect` function to evaluate the root of the Colebrook equation (see Exercise 8) for $\epsilon/D = 0.02$ and Re $= 10^5$. *Do not modify* `bisect.m`. This requires that you write an appropriate function m-file to evaluate the Colebrook equation.

12. (2) Write an `autoRoot` function that contains the code on page 261 for automated search and refinement of roots. The inputs should be the name of the m-file that evaluates $f(x)$, and the limits (`xmin` and `xmax`) in the interval in which the roots are suspected to exist. Provide an optional fourth input, `nx`, to specify the number of subinterval used to search for brackets in `brackPlot`. Test your `autoRoot` function by finding the four roots of $f(x) = \sin(x^2) + x^2 - 2x - 0.09$ in the interval $-1 \le x \le 3$.

SOLUTION 13. (1) Derive the $g_3(x)$ functions in Example 6.4 and Example 6.5. (*Hint*: What is the fixed-point formula for Newton's method?)

14. (1) Derive an iterative formula for finding the roots of $\cos(x) = x$ with Newton's method. Starting with an initial guess of $x = 5$ radians, determine the estimate of the root after five iterations. How many iterations are needed to get $f(x) < 5 \times 10^{-10}$ for initial guesses $x_0 = \pi$, $x_0 = 3\pi/2$, and $x_0 = 2\pi$?

15. (1) Use the iterative formula for Newton's method to derive the formula for evaluating $\sqrt{x}$ in Equation (3.3) on page 114. (*Hint*: Define $f(r) = r^2 - x$, where x is the number for which the square root is to be evaluated.)

16. (2) Use the `newton` function to find the four roots of $f(x) = \sin(x^2) + x^2 - 2x - 0.09$ in the interval $-1 \le x \le 3$. Report the value of the initial guess used to find each root.

SOLUTION 17. (2+) K. Wark and D. E. Richards (*Thermodynamics*, 6th ed., 1999, McGraw-Hill, Boston, Example 14-2, pp. 768–769) compute the equilibrium composition of a mixture of carbon monoxide and oxygen gas at one atmosphere. Determining the final composition requires solving

$$3.06 = \frac{(1-x)(3+x)^{1/2}}{x(1+x)^{1/2}}$$

for x. Obtain a fixed-point iteration formula for finding the roots of this equation. Implement your formula in a MATLAB function and use your function to find x. If your formula does not converge, develop one that does.

18. (2) Develop the m-file(s) that use the `bisect` function to solve the equation in Exercise 17.

19. (2) Develop the m-file(s) that use the `newton` function to solve the equation in Exercise 17. Report on the behavior of the iterations for initial guesses of $x = 0.3$ and $x = 1$.

20. (1+) Write a *single* m-file that uses Newton's method to solve the picnic table design problem for any input values of w, h, and b.

21. (1+) David Peters (*SIAM Review*, vol. 39, no. 1, pp. 118–122, March 1997) obtains the following equation for the optimum damping ratio of a spring–mass–damper system designed to minimize the transmitted force when an impact is applied to the mass:

$$\cos\left[4\zeta\sqrt{1-\zeta^2}\right] = -1 + 8\zeta^2 - 8\zeta^4$$

Write the m-file(s) necessary to obtain the value of ζ that satisfies this equation. What is the value of ζ?

22. (1+) Fins are used to enhance the cooling of an object. Fins are manufactured in a wide variety of shapes and sizes, and for a mass-produced product, it may be beneficial to optimize the shape of the fin. Typically, the optimization seeks to find the dimensions of the fin that achieve a maximum thermal efficiency at a minimum of cost. The cost is usually expressed as the mass of the material. Optimization of a single cylindrical fin requires finding the value of β that satisfies $10\beta = 3\sinh(2\beta)$. (See A.D. Kraus, and A. Bar-Cohen, *Design and Analysis of Heat Sinks*, 1995, Wiley, NY, p. 250.) Find the value of $\beta > 0$ that optimizes the cylindrical fin.

23. (2+) Heat sinks are often attached to electronic devices to increase the cooling efficiency and thereby lower the temperature of the device. One common configuration of these heat sinks is an array of so-called pin fins, as depicted in the accompanying sketch. Given the overall dimensions L, H, and W of the array, it is desirable to know the optimal spacing and size of the fins. Adrian Bejan ("Geometric optimization of cooling techniques" pp. 1–45 in *Air Cooling Technology for Electronic Equipment*, S.J. Kim and J.S. Woo, eds., 1996, CRC Press) presents the formula for the optimal spacing (S_{opt}) as

$$\frac{S_{opt}}{D} \frac{2 + S_{opt}/D}{\left(1 + S_{opt}/D\right)^{2/3}} = 2.75 \left(\frac{H}{D}\right)^{1/3} \mathrm{Ra}^{-1/4}$$

where D is the diameter of the fins and Ra is the Rayleigh number, a dimensionless indicator of the strength of the natural convection responsible for cooling the fins. Write a function m-file to compute the optimal spacing given D, H, and Ra. Use your function to plot S_{opt} for $H/D = 5, 10, 15, 20$ over the range $300 \le \mathrm{Ra} \le 10000$.

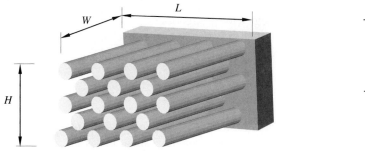

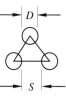

spacing detail

<u>SOLUTION</u> **24.** (2+) Create a modified `newton` function (say, `newtonb`) that takes a bracket interval as input instead of a single initial guess. From the bracket limits take one bisection step to determine x_0, the initial guess for Newton iterations. Use the bracket limits to develop relative tolerances on x and $f(x)$ as in the `bisect` function in Listing 6.4.

25. (3) Write a utility routine called `newtBrack` that takes a single step of Newton's method and checks whether the new guess at the root lies within a bracket. The function should have a definition resembling

```
function [ok,xnewt] = newtBrack(a,b,x,f,fprime)
```

where a and b are the bracket values, x is the current guess at the root, and f and fprime are the values of $f(x)$ and $f'(x)$ at x. The value of xnewt is the new guess at the root using a Newton step. The value of ok is either one or zero depending on whether xnewt is in the interval $a \le x \le b$. Insert a call to `newtBrack` in the `newtonb` function developed in the solution to the preceding Exercise. The modified `newtonb` function should continue with normal Newton iterations, but print a warning message if ok is "false." This code is part of a larger programming project, which is completed in the next Exercise.

26. (3+) Using the `newtBrack` and `newtonb` functions developed in the two preceding Exercises, write a `newtsafe` routine that takes a Newton step only if that step would result in a root inside the original bracket. If the root from Newton's method falls outside the original bracket, print a warning message and take a bisection step instead. (Note that it is possible to write the `newtbrak` function in two lines. In that case, it makes sense to just incorporate those lines into the `newtSafe` function.) Test your `newtSafe` function by using it to solve for x in the $f(x)$ defined in Exercise 17 when the initial bracket is [0.3, 1.2].

<u>SOLUTION</u> **27.** (3−) Implement the secant method using Algorithm 6.5 and Equation (6.13). Test your program by re-creating the results in Example 6.10. What happens if 10 iterations are performed? Replace the formula in Equation (6.13) with

$$x_{k+1} = x_k - f(x_k) \left[\frac{(x_k - x_{k-1})}{f(x_k) - f(x_{k-1}) + \varepsilon} \right],$$

where ε is a small number on the order of ε_m. How *and why* does this change the results?

28. (3−) Implement the secant method using Algorithm 6.5 and Equation (6.14). Test your program by re-creating the results in Example 6.10. What happens if 10 iterations are performed? Replace the formula in Equation (6.13) with

$$x_{k+1} = \frac{f(x_k)x_{k-1} - f(x_{k-1})x_k}{f(x_k) - f(x_{k-1}) + \varepsilon},$$

where ε is a small number on the order of ε_m. How does this compare to the results of Exercise 27? Which formulation has better numerical properties?

29. (3) The prologue for a MATLAB implementation of the secant method is

```
function r = secant(fun,xb,xtol,ftol,verbose)
% secant  Secant method for finding roots of scalar f(x) = 0
%
% Synopsis:  r = secant(fun,xb)
%            r = secant(fun,xb,xtol)
%            r = secant(fun,xb,xtol,ftol)
%            r = secant(fun,xb,xtol,ftol,verbose)
%
% Input: fun     = (string) name of function for which roots are sought
%        xb      = vector of bracket endpoints. xleft = xb(1), xright = xb(2)
%        xtol    = (optional) relative x tolerance.   Default:  xtol=5*eps
%        ftol    = (optional) relative f(x) tolerance. Default:  ftol=5*eps
%        verbose = (optional) print switch. Default: verbose=0, no printing
%
% Output:  r = the root of the function
```

Complete the code for this function using Algorithm 6.5 and the modification suggested in Exercise 27. Verify that your implementation works by finding the root of Equation 6.3 using the fx3 function. The fx3 function and the shell of the secant function are in the rootfind directory of the NMM Toolbox.

30. (2+) Line 81 of the fzero function (MATLAB version 5) uses the test

```
if (fa > 0) == (fb > 0)
```

to determine whether the function changes sign on the interval $a \le x \le b$. Why is this used instead of if fa*fb<0? Why is this used instead of sign(fa)==sign(fb)? (*Hint*: What is sign(0)?)

31. (1+) Write a m-file function that takes ϵ/D and Re as inputs and returns the value of f that satisfies the Colebrook equation. (See Exercise 8.) Use fzero and do not use global variables. An initial guess at the root can be obtained from

$$f = \left\{ 1.8 \log_{10} \left[\frac{6.9}{\mathrm{Re}} + \left(\frac{\epsilon/D}{3.7} \right)^{1.11} \right] \right\}^{-2}$$

which is an approximate formula for the f that satisfies the Colebrook equation. Find f for the following combinations of ϵ/D and Re
(a) $\epsilon/D = 0$, $\mathrm{Re} = 5000$
(b) $\epsilon/D = 0.0001$, $\mathrm{Re} = 3 \times 10^5$
(c) $\epsilon/D = 0.0001$, $\mathrm{Re} = 5 \times 10^7$
(d) $\epsilon/D = 0.03$, $\mathrm{Re} = 1 \times 10^4$
(e) $\epsilon/D = 0.01$, $\mathrm{Re} = 3 \times 10^5$

32. (1+) At low values of Re the friction factor for flow in a pipe is

$$f = \frac{64}{\text{Re}} \qquad \text{for Re} \leq 3000, \quad \text{any } \epsilon/D$$

Extend the solution to the preceding Exercise to include the case of low Re (also called *laminar*) flow. Test your modified code for the cases

(a) Re = 1000
(b) Re = 2000
(c) Re = 3001
(d) $\epsilon/D = 0.001$, Re = 3001

SOLUTION **33.** (3−) Write an m-file function to compute h, the depth to which a sphere of radius r, and specific gravity s, floats. (See Example 6.12 on page 281.) The inputs are r and s, and the output is h. Only compute h when $s < 0.5$. The $s \geq 0.5$ case is dealt with in the following Exercise. If $s \geq 0.5$ is input, have your function print an error message and stop. (The built-in `error` function will be useful.) Your function needs to include logic to select the correct root from the list of values returned by the built-in `roots` function.

34. (3−) Derive an equation similar to Equation 6.18 that applies to the case of $s > 0.5$. Use this equation to expand the function developed in the preceding exercise to cover all s in the range $0 < s < 1$. Test the input values of s to select the appropriate formula for defining the cubic polynomial in h. To avoid complications, test for the special values of $s = 0$, $s = 0.5$, and $s = 1$ using *exact equality tests*. Physical reasoning should allow you to deduce the value of h for $s = 0.5$ without needing to solve for the roots of the polynomial. As an additional defensive programming strategy, test the input for $s < 0$ and $s > 1$.

35. (2−) Use the m-file function developed in the solution to the preceding problem to plot h versus s, for `s = linspace(0.0001,0.9999,50)`.

36. (2+) The equation $x \tan(x) = c$, where c is a known parameter, has two roots in the range $0 \leq x \leq 2\pi$. Plot the variation of the two roots as a function of c in the range $0.1 \leq c \leq 10$. What are the two roots for $c = 0$? Does $c = 0$ cause any trouble for your root finder?

37. (3+) The following sketch depicts a sphere of diameter d falling through the air:

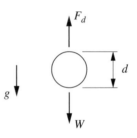

After its release, the sphere accelerates until it reaches a terminal velocity. The terminal velocity is obtained when the drag force F_d balances the weight $w = mg$ of the sphere:

$$F_d = mg. \tag{6.19}$$

The mass of the sphere is m, and g is the acceleration of gravity. The drag force can be computed from

$$F_d = c_d \frac{1}{2} \rho v^2 A, \tag{6.20}$$

where c_d is an empirical *drag coefficient*, ρ is the density of the fluid (air in this case), v is the velocity of the sphere, and $A = (\pi d^2)/4$ is the *frontal* area of the sphere. F.M. White (*Viscous Fluid Flow*, 2d ed., 1991, McGraw-Hill, p. 182) gives the following curve fit to experimental data on the aerodynamic drag of spheres:

$$c_d = \frac{24}{\text{Re}} + \frac{6}{1 + \sqrt{\text{Re}}} + 0.4 \qquad 0 \le \text{Re} \le 2 \times 10^5 \tag{6.21}$$

$\text{Re} = (\rho v d)/\mu$ is the *Reynolds number* and μ is the dynamic viscosity of the fluid (air). Substitute Equations (6.21) and (6.20) into Equation (6.19) to obtain an expression relating the terminal velocity to the weight. Leave the expression for c_d in terms of Re (even though you will need to substitute v into Re to compute evaluate the formula). Arrange the resulting formula so that it is in the form $f(x) = 0$.

Using the `tablez` function as a model (see Example 6.11 on page 277), develop a two-m-file solution to find the terminal velocity of any sphere falling through air. One m-file (the driver) accepts the user inputs of m and d from the command line. The other m-file evaluates the $f(x)$ function for the root finding procedure. How do values of m, d, ρ, and μ get into the $f(x)$ m-file? Avoid using global variables. Use your m-file functions to find the terminal velocity for the following situations:

(a) $m = 2$ gm, $d = 2$ cm.
(b) $m = 2$ kg, $d = 15$ cm.
(c) $m = 200$ kg, $d = 1$ m.

Is Equation (6.21) valid for each combination of m and d?

38. (3+) Equation (6.21) from Exercise 37 is valid for only a limited range of Re. At $\text{Re} \sim 10^5$, the value of c_d drops precipitously in what is known as drag crisis. The exact Re for drag crisis depends on whether the sphere is smooth or rough, with rough spheres experiencing drag crisis at lower Re. Golf balls are rough, so they will experience drag crisis, and hence lower aerodynamic drag, at lower velocities.

The `sphereCd.dat` file in the `data` directory of the NMM Toolbox contains $c_d = f(\text{Re})$ data in the range $2 \times 10^4 \le \text{Re} \le 3.99 \times 10^6$ for smooth spheres. The data comes from R.D. Mehta, "Aerodynamics of Sport Balls", in *Annual Review of Fluid Mechanics*, M. Van Dyke (ed.), vol. 17, pp. 151–189, 1985, Annual Reviews, Inc. Write an m-file function (call it `sphereCd`, say) that returns an appropriate c_d given any Re. For $0 \le \text{Re} \le 2 \times 10^4$ use Equation (6.21). For $2 \times 10^4 \le \text{Re} \le 3.99 \times 10^6$, use linear interpolation on the data in sphereCd.dat. (The built-in interp1 function will be helpful.) For Re $>$ 3.99 $\times$ 10^6, assume that c_d is constant at its value for Re $=$ 3.99 $\times$ 10^6.

Use your sphereCd function instead of Equation (6.21) to recalculate the terminal velocities in Exercise 37. How do the terminal velocities for the three spheres compare with those obtained when only Equation (6.21) is used?

7

A Review of Linear Algebra

Linear algebra deals with the systematic manipulation of matrices and vectors. Two of its most common applications are solving systems of linear equations and computing the eigenvalues of a matrix. Other applications include computer graphics, time integration of dynamic systems, statistical analysis, curve fitting, and optimization. Regardless of how linear algebra is used, its utility depends on the rigorous rules that define how matrices and vectors are manipulated. This chapter deals with those rules. The solution of systems of equations is deferred to Chapter 8.

Figure 7.1 summarizes the material covered in this chapter. The first three sections, which deal with vectors, matrices, and the mathematical properties of vectors and matrices, are of primary importance and should be read in preparation for Chapter 8. The section on special matrices should be initially browsed and referred to again as necessary.

The focus of this chapter is primarily on the fundamentals of linear algebra, not on the description of MATLAB functions and programs. Once the mathematics of manipulating matrices and vectors are firmly understood, working with MAT-LAB matrices will be natural. This is not to suggest that this chapter should be read without exercising MATLAB skills. The name "MATLAB" originated as an abbreviation for "Matrix Laboratory." MATLAB is a good environment for learning linear algebra, because it is easy to verify one's understanding of matrix operations by

linear combination $\alpha u + \beta v = w$:

$$\alpha \begin{bmatrix} u_1 \\ u_2 \\ \vdots \\ u_m \end{bmatrix} + \beta \begin{bmatrix} v_1 \\ v_2 \\ \vdots \\ v_m \end{bmatrix} = \begin{bmatrix} \alpha u_1 + \beta v_1 \\ \alpha u_2 + \beta v_2 \\ \vdots \\ \alpha u_m + \beta v_m \end{bmatrix} = \begin{bmatrix} w_1 \\ w_2 \\ \vdots \\ w_m \end{bmatrix}$$

Vector addition is a special case of a linear combination where the scalar multipliers all have the value 1. Linear combinations may be formed from any group of vectors having the same "shape." Row vectors cannot be combined with column vectors, column vectors that have two elements cannot be combined with those that have four elements.

As a concrete example, the vector $w = [4, 2]^T$ can be produced by the linear combination

$$w = \begin{bmatrix} 4 \\ 2 \end{bmatrix} = 4 \begin{bmatrix} 1 \\ 0 \end{bmatrix} + 2 \begin{bmatrix} 0 \\ 1 \end{bmatrix}.$$

Other equally valid ways of constructing $w = [4, 2]^T$ are

$$w = 6 \begin{bmatrix} 1 \\ 0 \end{bmatrix} - 2 \begin{bmatrix} 1 \\ -1 \end{bmatrix}, \quad w = \begin{bmatrix} 2 \\ 4 \end{bmatrix} - 2 \begin{bmatrix} -1 \\ 1 \end{bmatrix},$$

and

$$w = 2 \begin{bmatrix} 4 \\ 2 \end{bmatrix} - 4 \begin{bmatrix} 1 \\ 0 \end{bmatrix} - 2 \begin{bmatrix} 0 \\ 1 \end{bmatrix}.$$

In Figure 7.2, these vectors are represented by arrows. The tails of the arrows are all at the origin $(x, y) = (0, 0)$. The tips of the arrows are at the (x, y)-coordinates equal to the first and second elements in the vectors.

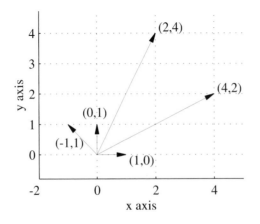

Figure 7.2   Vectors in $\mathbf{R}^2$.

Vector Inner Product   The *inner product*, or *dot product*, is an operation between two vectors that have the same number of elements. The result of the inner product is a scalar, not another vector. Let x be an n-element *row* vector, y be n-element *column* vector, and σ be a scalar. The inner product of x and y is

$$\sigma = x \cdot y \quad \Longleftrightarrow \quad \sigma = \sum_{i=1}^{n} x_i y_i, \qquad \begin{array}{l} x \text{ is a row vector} \\ y \text{ is a column vector} \end{array}$$

Designating an inner product by placing a dot between the two vectors is common and convenient, but a more precise notation is needed. According to the rules of linear algebra, an inner product cannot be computed between two row vectors or two column vectors. *Inner products can only be carried out in one configuration: a row vector on the left multiplying a column vector on the right.* If x is a four-element row vector and y is a four-element column vector, then

$$[x_1 \quad x_2 \quad x_3 \quad x_4] \begin{bmatrix} y_1 \\ y_2 \\ y_3 \\ y_4 \end{bmatrix} = x_1 y_1 + x_2 y_2 + x_3 y_3 + x_4 y_4.$$

It is possible to compute the inner product of two column vectors *if* the vector on the left is first transposed into a row vector. Thus, for two n-element column vectors u and v, the inner product is

$$\sigma = u^T v \quad \Longleftrightarrow \quad \sigma = \sum_{i=1}^{n} u_i v_i, \qquad u \text{ and } v \text{ are column vectors}$$

If s and t are two n-element row vectors, the symbolic representation is $\sigma = st^T$. The inner product is commutative, so that (for two column vectors)

$$u^T v = v^T u.$$

In summary, the "dot notation" implies that the vectors are of equal length and that the appropriate transpose is taken. For hand calculation or for programming in Fortran or C, the transpose notation for the inner product is just a mathematical formalism. The calculation is simply performed by summing the products of corresponding elements. In MATLAB, the distinction between row and column vectors is significant.

The multiplication operator ($*$) is used to compute the inner product of two vectors in MATLAB. If the vectors are either both row or both column vectors, then one of the two will have to be transposed. Failure to use compatible vector types will result in an error. Consider the following examples:

```
>> u = (0:3)';
>> v = (3:-1:0)';
>> s = u*v
??? Error using ==> *
Inner matrix dimensions must agree.

>> s = u'*v
s =
     4
>> t = v'*u
t =
     4
```

The transpose operator is so typographically small that it is easy to overlook. MAT-LAB will remind you, however, if it is missing.

The dot command computes the inner product of two vectors without regard to whether they are compatible row and column vectors. Curious readers should enter "type dot" at the command line to see how this is done.

Example 7.1: Inner Product in an Invoice Calculation

Inner products appear in computations that superficially have no obvious connection with linear algebra. Consider the operations necessary to calculate the total cost of the following invoice:

Item	Quantity	Description	unit cost	item cost
1	2	box of pencils	1.75	3.50
2	2	box of pens	2.25	4.50
3	3	notebooks	1.50	4.50
4	2	erasers	0.25	0.50
5	1	three ring binders	2.75	2.75
			total	15.75

The following statements show that the invoice total can be computed either by the sum of the item costs or as the inner product of the quantity and the unit cost:

```
>> quantity = [2 2 3 2 1]';
>> unitCost = [1.75 2.25 1.50 0.25 2.75]';
>> itemCost = quantity.*unitCost;      %  array op., not inner product
>> total = quantity'*unitCost          %  inner product
total =

   15.7500

>> check = sum(itemCost) - total
check =
     0
```

Recall from Chapter 2 that the *array operator* (. *) involves element-by-element multiplication of two vectors with the result being another vector.

Vector Outer Product   There is another type of vector–vector multiplication called the *outer* product, which results in a matrix, not a scalar. Outer products do not have their own symbol like the "dot" in the dot product. The outer product of two *column* vectors u and v is written as

$$A = uv^T \quad \Longleftrightarrow \quad a_{i,j} = u_i v_j. \tag{7.1}$$

In symbolic form, the outer product of two 4×1 vectors is written as

$$uv^T = \begin{bmatrix} u_1 \\ u_2 \\ u_3 \\ u_4 \end{bmatrix} \begin{bmatrix} v_1 & v_2 & v_3 & v_4 \end{bmatrix} = \begin{bmatrix} u_1 v_1 & u_1 v_2 & u_1 v_3 & u_1 v_4 \\ u_2 v_1 & u_2 v_2 & u_2 v_3 & u_2 v_4 \\ u_3 v_1 & u_3 v_2 & u_3 v_3 & u_3 v_4 \\ u_4 v_1 & u_4 v_2 & u_4 v_3 & u_4 v_4 \end{bmatrix}. \tag{7.2}$$

Equations (7.1) and (7.2) show that the rows of A differ only by scalar multipliers and that the columns of A differ only by scalar multipliers. The matrix produced by an outer product is, therefore, *singular*. Specifically, an outer product produces a rank one matrix. The subject of matrix rank is taken up in § 7.3.4 beginning on page 341.

Here is what an outer product computation looks like in MATLAB:

```
>> u = (0:4)';     % column vector u = [0 1 2 3 4]'
>> v = (4:-1:0)';  % column vector v = [4 3 2 1 0]'
>> A = u*v'        % outer product creates a matrix
A =
     0     0     0     0     0
     4     3     2     1     0
     8     6     4     2     0
    12     9     6     3     0
    16    12     8     4     0
```

The outer product obeys the rule for matrix multiplication (see § 7.2.2) where the left vector is an $m \times 1$ matrix and the right vector is a $1 \times n$ matrix.

7.1.2 Vector Norms

A vector with two elements is two-dimensional, and a vector with n elements is n-dimensional. There are many situations where we need to compare the size of two vectors having the same dimension. In this context, the size of a vector is its magnitude, or length, not its dimension. Using this concept of size, a unit vector— no matter what its dimension—has magnitude 1, and the zero vector (a vector with all elements equal to zero) has magnitude zero. One would say that unit vectors are larger than zero vectors. How can this notion of magnitude be extended to arbitrary n-element vectors?

To begin to answer this question, consider the more familiar problem of comparing the magnitude of two scalars with the absolute value function. The magnitude of α is larger than the magnitude of β if

$$|\alpha| > |\beta|,$$

where α and β are scalars. Analogous to the absolute value function for scalars, a *vector norm* defines a mathematical function for the evaluation and comparison of vector magnitudes. As the absolute value operator measures the size of a scalar (whether positive or negative), a norm measures the size of a vector, regardless of the sign of its elements. Thus, for two *vectors* x and y the magnitude of x is larger than the magnitude of y if

$$\|x\| > \|y\|,$$

where $\|x\|$ is read "the norm of x."

The obvious way to compare the size of two- and three-dimensional vectors is by their geometric lengths. Consider the sketches of vectors in two-dimensional space depicted in Figure 7.3. Let ℓ designate the lengths of those vectors:

$$\ell_a = \sqrt{4^2 + 2^2} = \sqrt{20}, \qquad \ell_b = \sqrt{2^2 + 4^2} = \sqrt{20}, \qquad \ell_c = \sqrt{2^2 + 1^2} = \sqrt{5}.$$

Extending this length calculation to a vector x with n elements gives the so-called L_2, or *Euclidean*, norm defined as

$$\|x\|_2 = \left(x_1^2 + x_2^2 + \cdots + x_n^2\right)^{1/2} = \left(\sum_{i=1}^{n} x_i^2\right)^{1/2}. \tag{7.3}$$

The name comes from the obvious connection with vector lengths in two- and three-dimensional Euclidean geometry. The subscript on $\|x\|_2$ indicates the type of

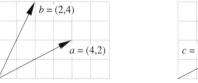
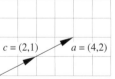

Two unequal vectors having   Two vectors of different length
the same length.   pointing in the same direction.

Figure 7.3   Comparing the lengths of two-dimensional vectors lying in the plane of the page.

norm—in this case L_2. The L_2 norm can also be expressed in terms of the inner product:

$$\|x\|_2 = \sqrt{x^T x}.$$

Three vector norms are common and useful, and all are members of the family of so-called p norms defined by

$$\|x\|_p = \left(|x_1|^p + |x_2|^p + \cdots + |x_n|^p\right)^{1/p}. \tag{7.4}$$

The L_2 norm is one of the p norms. The L_1 norm ($p = 1$) of a vector is

$$\|x\|_1 = |x_1| + |x_2| + \cdots + |x_n| = \sum_{i=1}^{n} |x_i|, \tag{7.5}$$

and the L_∞ norm ($p = \infty$) or *max norm* of a vector is

$$\|x\|_\infty = \max\left(|x_1|, |x_2|, \ldots, |x_n|\right) = \max_i \left(|x_i|\right). \tag{7.6}$$

The built-in norm function computes p-norms of vectors. If only one argument is passed to norm, the L_2 norm is returned:

```
>> u = -2:2;
>> norm(u)
ans =
      3.1623
```

A second argument is used to specify the value of p,

```
>> norm(u,2)
ans =
      3.1623

>> norm(u,1)
ans =
   6

>> norm(u,Inf)
ans =
   2
```

In the last example, the internal MATLAB constant Inf is used to select the L_∞ norm.

Example 7.2: Are two vectors (nearly) equal?

Two scalars α and β are, in a practical sense, equal if $\alpha \neq 0$ and

$$\frac{|\alpha - \beta|}{|\alpha|} < \delta,$$

where δ is some small tolerance. (See § 5.2.3 beginning on page 211.) Vector norms provide an analogous way to test for the equality of two vectors y and z:

$$\frac{\|y - z\|}{\|z\|} < \delta. \tag{7.7}$$

To demonstrate this use of vector norms, consider two ways to compute a vector of values of the tangent function:

```
>> x = linspace(0,2*pi);    %  vector of angles
>> y = sin(x)./cos(x);      %  use array operator to compute tan(x)
>> z = tan(x);
```

The y and z vectors could be compared by plotting them against x with plot(x,y, 'o',x,z,'-'). The plot (not shown here) reveals that to the unaided eye, these vectors are the same. A quantitative comparison is available by evaluating a norm of $y - z$. If y and z are exactly equal, then $\|y - z\| = 0$. Exact equality is unlikely, however, due to small details in the calculations of y and z, and due to roundoff in the computation of y-z. A practical test of equality is obtained by applying Equation (7.7) (note that any of the p-norms can be used in the test):

```
>> norm(y-z,1)/norm(z,1)        %  relative error in the L1 norm
ans =
   7.3821e-17

>> norm(y-z,2)/norm(z,2)        %  relative error in the L2 norm
ans =
   1.0998e-16

>> norm(y-z,inf)/norm(z,inf)    %  relative error in the infinity norm
ans =
   1.1275e-16
```

These tests lead to the conclusion that, although y and z are not identical, they are, for all practical purposes, indistinguishable.

Example 7.3: Convergence of a Vector Sequence

An important application of norms is in determining the convergence of a sequence of vectors. In the iterative solution of large systems of equations, for example, it is important to know whether the trial solution is improving as the iterations proceed. The idea of testing vector convergence is demonstrated here with a simple, and somewhat contrived, example.

It is well known that the geometric series

$$\sum_{k=0}^{\infty} \sigma^n = 1 + \sigma + \sigma^2 + \dots$$

converges for the scalar σ whenever $|\sigma| < 1$. Now, consider the effect of applying a geometric series to each element of a vector x. To avoid ambiguity, define the symbol $[x]^k$ as the operation of raising each element of x to the kth power. In other words, $[x]^k$ is equivalent to the MATLAB array operation x.^k.

It is possible that some elements of x have magnitude greater than one and that others have magnitude less than one. Does the vector magnitude approach zero as the power increases? Intuitively, we surmise that as k increases, the value of the largest element in x raised to the kth power will be significantly larger than any of the other elements raised to the kth power. If the largest element is greater in magnitude than unity, then the magnitude of $[x]^k$ will also increase. Convergence of the geometric vector sequence, therefore, requires that all elements must be less than one. Is this borne out by numerical experiment?

The vectorSequence function shown in Listing 7.1 evaluates the L_1, L_2, and L_∞ norms of the vectors in the sequence $[x]^k$, for $k = 1, 2, \dots n$. Optional inputs to vectorSequence are x, the vector used to start the sequence, and n, the maximum number of iterations. The default vector, x = [1/2 1/4 1/8 1/16], converges rapidly, as demonstrated by the following output:

```
>> vectorSequence
    k     norm(x^k,1)     norm(x^k,2)     norm(x^k,Inf)
    0     4.000e+00       2.000e+00       1.000e+00
    1     9.375e-01       5.762e-01       5.000e-01
    2     3.320e-01       2.582e-01       2.500e-01
   ...       ...             ...             ...
    9     1.957e-03       1.953e-03       1.953e-03
   10     9.775e-04       9.766e-04       9.766e-04
```

The L_∞ norm in the last column is just the geometric sequence 0.5^k, where 0.5 is the largest element in x. The L_1 and L_2 norms of x^k approach the value of L_∞ as k increases. As deduced above, the largest element of x controls the rate at which $\|[x]^k\| \to 0$.

If the input vector has one or more elements with magnitude close to 1 the convergence of the sequence is slower. For example,

```
>> vectorSequence([0.3 0.5 0.7 0.9])
    k     norm(x^k,1)     norm(x^k,2)     norm(x^k,Inf)
    0     4.000e+00       2.000e+00       1.000e+00
    1     2.400e+00       1.281e+00       9.000e-01
    2     1.640e+00       9.833e-01       8.100e-01
```

```
function vectorSequence(x,n)
% vectorSequence  Behavior of a vector sequence x.^k in different p-norms
%
% Synopsis:  vectorSequence
%            vectorSequence(x)
%            vectorSequence(x,n)
%
% Input:     x = (optional) vector used in sequence x.^k
%                   Default:  x = [1/2  1/4  1/8  1/16];
%                n = (optional) maximum number of iterations; Default: n = 10
%
% Output:    Plot of norm(x.^k,p) for k = 1,2,...,n and p = 1, 2, Inf

if nargin<1,  x = [1/2  1/4  1/8  1/16];  end
if nargin<2,  n = 10;                     end

fprintf('   k    norm(x^k,1)    norm(x^k,2)    norm(x^k,Inf)\n');
for k=0:n
  y = x.^k;
  norm1 = norm(y,1);  norm2 = norm(y);  normi = norm(y,inf);
  fprintf('%4d %12.3e   %12.3e   %12.3e\n',k,norm1,norm2,normi);
  semilogy(k,norm1,'d',k,norm2,'o',k,normi,'+');
  hold on
end
hold off
xlabel('iteration, k');  ylabel('norms of x^k');
legend('1 norm','2 norm','\infty norm');
```

Listing 7.1   The `vectorSequence` function uses vector norms to investigate the convergence of $[x]^k$, for $k = 1, 2, \ldots$, where x is a vector.

```
  ...       ...            ...            ...
   9     4.297e-01      3.895e-01      3.874e-01
  10     3.779e-01      3.498e-01      3.487e-01
```

Figure 7.4 is a plot of the norms of the $[x]^k$ sequence for x = [1/2 1/4 1/8 1/16] and x = [0.3 0.5 0.7 0.9]. The plots show that both vectors converge in all three norms. The convergence rate for x = [0.3 0.5 0.7 0.9] is much slower. In addition, the convergence rate in the L_2 norm appears to be bounded by the convergence rate in the L_1 norm from above and the L_∞ norm from below.

Mathematical Properties of Vector Norms   Vector norms are mathematical functions having the following properties:

$$\|x\| > 0 \text{ for all } x \neq 0,$$

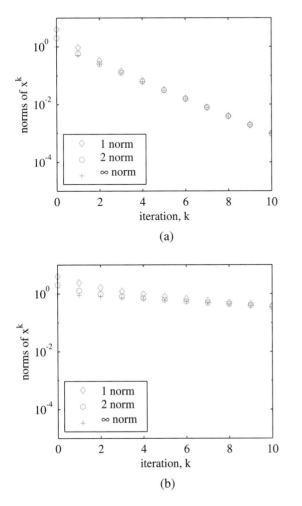

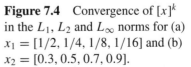

Figure 7.4 Convergence of $[x]^k$ in the L_1, L_2 and L_∞ norms for (a) $x_1 = [1/2, 1/4, 1/8, 1/16]$ and (b) $x_2 = [0.3, 0.5, 0.7, 0.9]$.

$\|\alpha x\| = |\alpha| \, \|x\|$ for any scalar α,

$\|x + y\| \le \|x\| + \|y\|$ for any two vectors x and y.

The last condition is the so-called *triangle inequality*, which is depicted in Figure 7.5.

In Example 7.3, the L_1, L_2, and L_∞ norms were consistent in measuring the convergence of the vector sequence $[x]^k$. This property is sometimes called *norm equivalence*, and it means that for sequences of vectors having real elements, we can choose a convenient p-norm to measure convergence. When the p-norms are used to measure the magnitude of n-dimensional vectors of real numbers, the following conditions hold (see, for example, [32]):

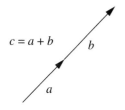

$c = a + b$

$\|c\|_2 = \|a\|_2 + \|b\|_2$

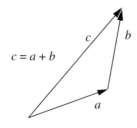

$c = a + b$

$\|c\|_2 < \|a\|_2 + \|b\|_2$

Figure 7.5   Graphical depiction of the triangle inequality for two-dimensional vectors.

$$\|x\|_2 \leq \|x\|_1 \leq \sqrt{n}\|x\|_2,$$

$$\|x\|_\infty \leq \|x\|_2 \leq \sqrt{n}\|x\|_\infty,$$

$$\|x\|_\infty \leq \|x\|_1 \leq n\|x\|_\infty.$$

This is consistent with the experimental results in Figure 7.4, which show that $\|x\|_\infty \leq \|x\|_2 \leq \|x\|_1$. For most calculations, we will use the L_2 norm. If computational efficiency is of primary importance the L_∞ norm is used.

7.1.3 Orthogonal Vectors

The vector inner product has a geometric interpretation. The angle θ between two nonzero column vectors can be computed from

$$\cos\theta = \frac{u^T v}{\|u\|_2 \|v\|_2}. \tag{7.8}$$

The measurement of arbitrary angles between vectors is much less interesting and useful than the detection of one special angle, namely, 90 degrees. Vectors in two- or three-dimensional space are said to be perpendicular, or *orthogonal*, when the angle between them is 90 degrees. The term orthogonal is applied to higher dimensions, where a physical interpretation of right angles is problematic.

What does it mean that two vectors are orthogonal? From Equation (7.8), $\theta = \pi/2$ requires that $u^T v = 0$. Since Equation (7.8) applies to vectors of arbitrary magnitude, it follows that two vectors are orthogonal if and only if their inner product is zero.

Orthonormal Vectors   Orthonormal vectors are *unit* vectors that are orthogonal. A unit vector has magnitude of one regardless of its dimension. Any vector can be converted to a unit vector by dividing by its L_2 norm; that is,

$$\hat{u} = \frac{u}{\|u\|_2}$$

is a unit vector in the direction of u. Since

$$\|u\|_2 = \sqrt{u^T u},$$

it follows that $u^T u = 1$ if u is a unit vector.

.2 MATRICES

A matrix is a rectangular array of real or complex numbers. The A matrix with m rows and n columns is written as

$$A = \begin{bmatrix} a_{11} & a_{12} & \cdots & a_{1n} \\ a_{21} & a_{22} & & a_{2n} \\ \vdots & & & \vdots \\ a_{m1} & & \cdots & a_{mn} \end{bmatrix}.$$

Uppercase roman letters designate an entire matrix. The elements of a matrix are written as lowercase letters with individual elements referred to by double-subscript notation. The first subscript indicates the row, and the second subscript indicates the column. The dimension of the matrix is specified by its total number of rows and columns.

In MATLAB, the only difference between a matrix and a vector is the number of rows and columns each contains. A MATLAB scalar is a matrix with one row and one column. Though matrix variables can have any valid MATLAB variable name, for clarity and consistency in the following examples, uppercase letters are used for matrix variables, and lowercase letters are used for vector and scalar variables. (Cf. Table 7.1 on page 295).

7.2.1 The Rows and Columns of a Matrix Are Vectors

A matrix can be viewed as a collection of row or column vectors. Many operations can be compactly written and efficiently implemented on a column or row basis. The following statements construct a matrix A from three row vectors:

```
>> u = 1:4;    v = 5:8;    w = 9:12;
>> A = [u; v; w]
A =
      1     2     3     4
      5     6     7     8
      9    10    11    12
```

The transpose of these same three vectors can be used to create another matrix B by columns:

```
>> B = [u'  v'  w']
B =
     1      5      9
     2      6     10
     3      7     11
     4      8     12
```

Remember that spaces are used to separate the columns of a MATLAB matrix and that semicolons are used to separate rows.

Treating a matrix as a collection of vectors provides a convenient method for extracting its rows and columns using colon notation. (See also § 2.2.3.) For example, the first row and the second column of the matrix B (just defined) are extracted with the following code:

```
>> B(1,:)
ans =
     1      5      9

>> B(:,2)
ans =
     5
     6
     7
     8
```

Colon notation can be used to select submatrices that are not complete rows or columns. A submatrix of one matrix variable can be assigned to another matrix variable, as in these examples (with B as just defined):

```
>> C = B(2:3,1:2)
C =
     2      6
     3      7

>> D = B(3:4,:)
D =
     3      7     11
     4      8     12
```

7.2.2 Matrix Operations

In this section, rules for operations involving matrices are described. Element-by-element computational formulas are given, along with a mathematical interpretation of the significance of the operations. Although it is important to understand the element-by-element formulas, greater insight is obtained by concentrating on

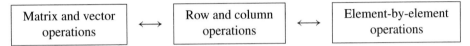

Figure 7.6 Levels of abstraction in expressing operations involving matrices and vectors. The power of linear algebra is in its ability to express higher level concepts (on the left) that are implemented with precise rules (on the right). The bridge between the high-level ideas and the low-level details is through row and column operations.

row- and column-level operations, especially for the matrix–matrix and matrix–vector products. Once these row- and column-level operations are understood, the lower level formulas can easily be reconstructed. Figure 7.6 summarizes the relationship between the high-level descriptions of matrix operations and the low-level implementation involving element-by-element manipulations.

Addition and Subtraction   Let A, B, C, and D be $m \times n$ matrices. Addition or subtraction involves element-by-element addition or subtraction:

$$C = A + B \iff c_{i,j} = a_{i,j} + b_{i,j} \quad i = 1, \dots, m; \quad j = 1, \dots, n,$$

$$D = A - B \iff d_{i,j} = a_{i,j} - b_{i,j} \quad i = 1, \dots, m; \quad j = 1, \dots, n.$$

MATLAB expressions involving matrix addition and subtraction operations look just like scalar addition and subtraction:

```
>> A = [1 2; 3 4];    B = [5 4; 3 2];
>> C = A+B
C =
     6     6
     6     6

>> D = A-B
D =
    -4    -2
     0     2
```

Multiplication By a Scalar   Let A and B be $m \times n$ matrices, and let σ be a scalar. Evaluating the product σA involves multiplying each element of A by σ:

$$B = \sigma A \iff b_{i,j} = \sigma a_{i,j} \quad i = 1, \dots, m; \quad j = 1, \dots, n.$$

Multiplying a matrix by a scalar in MATLAB is straightforward:

```
>> A = [1 2; 3 4];   s = 3;
>> s*A
ans =
     3     6
     9    12

>> A*s
ans =
     3     6
     9    12
```

As the preceding calculations demonstrate, multiplication of a scalar and a matrix is commutative.

Matrix Transpose   The vector transpose converts a row vector into a column vector and vice versa. When applied to a matrix, the transpose operator converts each row into a column. On an element-by-element basis, the transpose has the effect of interchanging row and column indices of a matrix:

$$B = A^T \Longleftrightarrow b_{i,j} = a_{j,i} \quad i = 1, \dots, m; \quad j = 1, \dots, n.$$

For a square matrix, the effect is to exchange elements that are in symmetric positions relative to the diagonal.

The MATLAB transpose operator for matrices is the apostrophe, the same as for vectors. The following is simple transpose operation in MATLAB:

```
>> A = [0 0 0; 0 0 0; 1 2 3; 0 0 0]
A =
     0     0     0
     0     0     0
     1     2     3
     0     0     0

>> B = A'
B =
     0     0     1     0
     0     0     2     0
     0     0     3     0
```

If $A = A^T$, then A is called a *symmetric* matrix.

When dealing with complex matrices (i.e., a matrix with elements that are complex values), the transpose is not used. The corresponding operation is called the *conjugate transpose*, the *adjoint*, or the *hermitian conjugate*, and it involves reflecting the elements about the diagonal *and* computing the complex conjugate

of the elements. If A is a complex matrix, the conjugate transpose is denoted[1] A^H.
For a 3×2 matrix, this looks like:

$$
A = \begin{bmatrix} a_{11} & a_{12} \\ a_{21} & a_{22} \\ a_{31} & a_{32} \end{bmatrix}
\quad\Longrightarrow\quad
A^H = \begin{bmatrix} \bar{a}_{11} & \bar{a}_{21} & \bar{a}_{31} \\ \bar{a}_{12} & \bar{a}_{22} & \bar{a}_{32} \end{bmatrix},
$$

where $\bar{a}_{ij}$ is the complex conjugate of a_{ij}. In MATLAB, the apostrophe operator
also returns the conjugate transpose of a matrix, as in

```
>> C = sqrt( [1 -4; 9 16; -25 36] )
C =
   1.0000                0 + 2.0000i
   3.0000           4.0000
        0 + 5.0000i   6.0000

>> D = C'
D =
   1.0000           3.0000                0 - 5.0000i
        0 - 2.0000i   4.0000           6.0000
```

Matrix–Vector Product: The Column View   Multiplication of matrices and vectors is an essential operation in numerical linear algebra. The product
of the matrix A and the column vector x can be interpreted as either a linear combination of the columns of A or as a series of inner products involving the rows of
A and (the one column of) x. The view of Ax being a combination of the columns
of A is presented first.

Consider linear combinations involving the set of n column vectors $\{a_{(1)}, a_{(2)},$
$\ldots, a_{(n)}\}$. As before, the parenthesis around the subscript is a reminder that $a_{(1)}$ is
the first vector in the set, not the first element of a vector a. For a given set of
coefficients x_j, $j = 1, \ldots, n$; a linear combination of the $a_{(j)}$ results in another
vector b:

$$
x_1 a_{(1)} + x_2 a_{(2)} + \cdots + x_n a_{(n)} = b, \qquad \text{or} \qquad \sum_{j=1}^{n} a_{(j)} x_j = b. \tag{7.9}
$$

Each $a_{(j)}$ has m components, and m need not be equal to n, the number of vectors in
the linear combination. Two subscripts on a are needed to write out all the terms in
the sum: a_{ij} denotes the ith element (ith row) of vector $a_{(j)}$. With this convention,
Equation (7.9) is written as

---

[1]In some books, A^* is used.

$$
x_1 \begin{bmatrix} a_{11} \\ a_{21} \\ \vdots \\ a_{m1} \end{bmatrix} + x_2 \begin{bmatrix} a_{12} \\ a_{22} \\ \vdots \\ a_{m2} \end{bmatrix} + \cdots + x_n \begin{bmatrix} a_{1n} \\ a_{2n} \\ \vdots \\ a_{mn} \end{bmatrix} = \begin{bmatrix} b_1 \\ b_2 \\ \vdots \\ b_m \end{bmatrix}.
$$

The number of elements m in b must equal the number of elements in each $a_{(j)}$, and the number of x_j coefficients n must equal the number of $a_{(j)}$ vectors. The preceding equation can be written more compactly if the $a_{(j)}$ column vectors are combined to form a matrix:

$$
\begin{bmatrix} \Big| & \Big| & & \Big| \\ a_{(1)} & a_{(2)} & \cdots & a_{(n)} \\ \Big| & \Big| & & \Big| \end{bmatrix} \begin{bmatrix} x_1 \\ x_2 \\ \vdots \\ x_n \end{bmatrix} = \begin{bmatrix} \\ b \\ \\ \end{bmatrix}
$$

This shows that the x_j coefficients of the linear combination are the elements of a vector. Writing out the terms in the matrix and right-hand side vector gives

$$
\begin{bmatrix} a_{11} & a_{12} & \cdots & a_{1n} \\ a_{21} & a_{22} & \cdots & a_{2n} \\ \vdots & \vdots & & \vdots \\ a_{m1} & a_{m2} & \cdots & a_{mn} \end{bmatrix} \begin{bmatrix} x_1 \\ x_2 \\ \vdots \\ x_n \end{bmatrix} = \begin{bmatrix} b_1 \\ b_2 \\ \vdots \\ b_m \end{bmatrix}.
$$

To save space and to eliminate the tedious copying of subscripts, this equation is written as

$$
Ax = b,
$$

where the columns of A are the set of vectors in the linear combination. The preceding manipulations show that

> **The matrix–vector product $b = Ax$ produces a vector b from a linear combination of the column vectors in A.**

There are other equally valid interpretations of Ax, which are explored in subsequent sections of this chapter.

To translate the column-oriented operations into a sequence of computer operations, we need a detailed formula for matrix–vector multiplication. This is achieved by making the row indices explicit in Equation (7.9). The vectors in Equation (7.9) are $a_{(j)}$ and b. The ith row of each $a_{(j)}$ contributes to the ith row of b, and thus

$$b = Ax \iff b_i = \sum_{j=1}^{n} a_{ij}x_j, \quad \text{where } x \text{ and } b \text{ are column vectors.} \quad (7.10)$$

Equation (7.10) is the rule for matrix–vector multiplication (i.e., *right* multiplication of an $n \times 1$ column vector x by an $m \times n$ matrix A). For this formula to work, the number of columns in A must equal the number of rows in x. The dimensions of the compatible matrix and vector for a matrix–vector product are

$$[m \times n] \cdot [n \times 1] = [m \times 1].$$

The *inner* dimensions n of A and x, must be equal, and the size of vector b is determined by the outer dimensions, m and 1, of the quantities on the left side of the equals sign. Translating the preceding formulas into an algorithm for computing the matrix–vector product yields

Algorithm 7.1   Matrix–Vector Multiplication by Columns

initialize: $b = \texttt{zeros}(n, 1)$
for $j = 1, \ldots, n$
  for $i = 1, \ldots, m$
    $b(i) = A(i, j)x(j) + b(i)$
  end
end

The MATLAB $*$ operator automatically performs Algorithm 7.1 for compatible matrices and vectors. For example,

```
>> A = [1:4;  5:8;  9:12];
A =
     1     2     3     4
     5     6     7     8
     9    10    11    12


>> x = (0.1:0.1:0.4)'
x =
    0.1000
    0.2000
    0.3000
    0.4000
```

```
>> b = A*x
b =
    3.0000
    7.0000
   11.0000
```

The column-level operations can also be made explicit with the use of colon nota-tion. Given A and x defined by the preceding statements,

```
>> b = x(1)*A(:,1) + x(2)*A(:,2) + x(3)*A(:,3) + x(4)*A(:,4)
b =
    3.0000
    7.0000
   11.0000
```

which agrees with the result of A*x, as it must.

Section 7.3.2 provides additional use and interpretation of the column view of matrix–vector multiplication. Example 7.5 on page 319 shows how the matrix–vector product can also be viewed as a coordinate transformation.

Example 7.4: The Matrix–Vector View of Linear Combinations of Vectors

In § 7.1.1 beginning on page 297, linear combinations of vectors are used to create other vectors. For example,

$$w = \begin{bmatrix} 4 \\ 2 \end{bmatrix} = 4 \begin{bmatrix} 1 \\ 0 \end{bmatrix} + 2 \begin{bmatrix} 0 \\ 1 \end{bmatrix}.$$

In § 7.2.2, the matrix–vector product is interpreted as a linear combination of the column vectors that form the matrix. If the two vectors on the far right side of the preceding equa-tion are used as the columns of a matrix, the w vector can be created with

$$\begin{bmatrix} 1 & 0 \\ 0 & 1 \end{bmatrix} \begin{bmatrix} 4 \\ 2 \end{bmatrix} = \begin{bmatrix} 4 \\ 2 \end{bmatrix}.$$

Similarly, the linear combination

$$w = 2 \begin{bmatrix} 4 \\ 2 \end{bmatrix} - 4 \begin{bmatrix} 1 \\ 0 \end{bmatrix} - 2 \begin{bmatrix} 0 \\ 1 \end{bmatrix}$$

is equivalent to

$$\begin{bmatrix} 4 & 1 & 0 \\ 2 & 0 & 1 \end{bmatrix} \begin{bmatrix} 2 \\ -4 \\ -2 \end{bmatrix} = \begin{bmatrix} 4 \\ 2 \end{bmatrix}.$$

The reader is encouraged to verify these calculations by evaluating the matrix–vector prod-ucts.

Matrix–Vector Product: The Row View   The column view of matrix–vector multiplication is consistent with the interpretation of a matrix as a collection of column vectors. An alternative view of the matrix–vector product is obtained by considering a matrix as a collection of row vectors. In the row view, a matrix–vector product is a series of inner products between the rows of the matrix and the vector. Both the column view and the row view produce the same result. The column view provides deeper insight into the mathematics of matrix–vector operations. The row view is more convenient for hand calculations.

Consider the following matrix–vector product written out as a linear combination of matrix columns:

$$
\begin{bmatrix} 5 & 0 & 0 & -1 \\ -3 & 4 & -7 & 1 \\ 1 & 2 & 3 & 6 \end{bmatrix} \begin{bmatrix} 4 \\ 2 \\ -3 \\ -1 \end{bmatrix} = 4 \begin{bmatrix} 5 \\ -3 \\ 1 \end{bmatrix} + 2 \begin{bmatrix} 0 \\ 4 \\ 2 \end{bmatrix} - 3 \begin{bmatrix} 0 \\ -7 \\ 3 \end{bmatrix} - 1 \begin{bmatrix} -1 \\ 1 \\ 6 \end{bmatrix}
$$

$$
= \begin{bmatrix} (5)(4) & + & (0)(2) & + & (0)(-3) & + & (-1)(-1) \\ (-3)(4) & + & (4)(2) & + & (-7)(-3) & + & (1)(-1) \\ (1)(4) & + & (2)(2) & + & (3)(-3) & + & (6)(-1) \end{bmatrix} = \begin{bmatrix} 21 \\ 16 \\ -7 \end{bmatrix}
$$

Here the order of multiplication of the elements have been reversed in the first vector on the second line. The preceding calculation reveals that each element in the result vector is an inner product between a row of the matrix and the vector $[4, \ 2, \ -3, \ -1]^T$ on the left-hand side. For example,

$$
\begin{bmatrix} 5 & 0 & 0 & -1 \end{bmatrix} \begin{bmatrix} 4 \\ 2 \\ -3 \\ -1 \end{bmatrix} = (5)(4) + (0)(2) + (0)(-3) + (-1)(-1) = 21.
$$

Using this row view of matrix–vector multiplication, we see that the product of an arbitrary 3×4 matrix A with a 4×1 vector x looks like

$$
\begin{bmatrix} \underline{\quad a'_{(1)} \quad} \\ \underline{\quad a'_{(2)} \quad} \\ a'_{(3)} \end{bmatrix} \begin{bmatrix} x_1 \\ x_2 \\ x_3 \\ x_4 \end{bmatrix} = \begin{bmatrix} a'_{(1)} \cdot x \\ a'_{(2)} \cdot x \\ a'_{(3)} \cdot x \end{bmatrix} = \begin{bmatrix} b_1 \\ b_2 \\ b_3 \end{bmatrix},
$$

where $a'_{(1)}, a'_{(2)},$ and $a'_{(3)},$ are the row vectors constituting the A matrix. The primes are used to distinguish $a'_{(i)}$, the ith row of A, from $a_{(i)}$, the ith column of A. In summary,

```
function  v = rotvec(u,alpha,beta,zeta)
% rotvec  Rotates a three dimensional vector
%
% Synopsis:  v = rotvec(u,alpha,beta,zeta)
%
% Input:    u     = initial vector
%           alpha = angle, in degrees, of rotation about the x-axis
%           beta  = angle, in degrees, of rotation about the y-axis
%           zeta  = angle, in degrees, of rotation about the z-axis
%
% Output:   v = final vector, i.e. result of rotating u through
%               the angles alpha, beta and zeta

a = alpha*pi/180;  b = beta*pi/180;  z = zeta*pi/180;  % convert to radians

% --- set up rotation matrices
Rx = [ 1  0  0; 0  cos(a)  -sin(a); 0  sin(a)  cos(a)];
Ry = [ cos(b)  0  sin(b); 0  1  0; -sin(b)  0  cos(b) ];
Rz = [ cos(z) -sin(z)  0;  sin(z)  cos(z)  0; 0  0  1 ];

v = Rz*Ry*Rx*u;            % apply the rotation
```

Listing 7.2 The rotvec function for rotating vectors in three-dimensional space.

the y–z plane, a rotation about the x-axis leaves the result v in the y–z plane. This simple case will not hold for arbitrary rotations or different initial positions.

The rotvec function in Listing 7.2 performs the vector rotation operations. The three rotation matrices are applied in series:

$$s = R_x u, \quad t = R_y s, \quad v = R_z t.$$

This is equivalent to computing the total transformation matrix $T = R_z R_y R_x$ and applying it to u:

$$v = Tu = R_z R_y R_x u$$

The following statements exercise the rotvec function:

```
>> v = rotvec([1; 0; 0],0,0,90)
v =
        0
        1
        0
```

```
>> v = rotvec([1; 0; 0],0,180,0)
v =
    -1
     0
     0

>> v = rotvec([1; 1; 1],45,45,45)
v =
    1.2071
    1.2071
    0.2929
```

Note that rotation of a vector does not change its length:

```
>> u = [-2 3 1]';
>> v = rotvec(u,25,-145,202);
>> norm(v)/norm(u)
ans =
    1
```

Vector–Matrix Product: The Row View   Up to this point, the product of a matrix and a vector has involved multiplying a matrix with a column vector. Visually, the matrix is on the left, and the column vector is on the right. A related operation is the multiplication of a row vector into a matrix from the left. To emphasize the distinction, the terms "vector–matrix" and "matrix–vector" multiplication are used in this chapter. These products can be represented schematically as

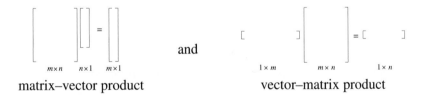

matrix–vector product   vector–matrix product

Elsewhere in this book, you will need to infer the proper operation by the vector and matrix in use.

As with matrix–vector multiplication, there are both column and row views of vector–matrix multiplication, and both views are discussed here. The patterns should start to seem familiar. To shorten the presentation, row and column operations are treated as building-block operations. You should, of course, be able to fill in the details of each computational step. One view of the vector–matrix product is that it forms a vector from a linear combination of the rows of a matrix. Let $\{a'_{(1)}, a'_{(2)}, \ldots, a'_{(m)}\}$ be a set of row vectors each with n-elements. The linear combination

$$u_1 a'_{(1)} + u_2 a'_{(2)} + \ldots u_m a'_{(m)} = v \tag{7.11}$$

produces another n-element row vector v. If the $a'_{(i)}$ vectors are assembled into a matrix, then the u_i coefficients are the elements of a row vector u. The linear combination in Equation (7.11) is equivalent to the vector–matrix product

$$
\begin{bmatrix} u_1 & u_2 & \cdots & u_m \end{bmatrix}
\begin{bmatrix}
a'_{(1)} \\
\hline
a'_{(2)} \\
\hline
\vdots \\
\hline
a'_{(m)}
\end{bmatrix}
= \begin{bmatrix} v_1 & v_2 & \cdots & v_n \end{bmatrix},
$$

or

$$uA = v.$$

For this product to work, the number of columns in u must equal the number of rows in A. Vector v has the same number of columns as matrix A. The dimensions of the compatible vector and matrix for a vector–matrix product are

$$[1 \times m] \cdot [m \times n] = [1 \times n].$$

The inner dimension m must be the same for the vector and the matrix.

Using double-subscript matrix notation to identify a_{ij} as the jth element of the row vector $a'_{(i)}$ allows the vector–matrix product to be written as

$$
\begin{bmatrix} u_1 & u_2 & \cdots & u_m \end{bmatrix}
\begin{bmatrix}
a_{11} & a_{12} & \cdots & a_{1n} \\
a_{21} & a_{22} & & a_{2n} \\
\vdots & & & \vdots \\
\vdots & & & \vdots \\
a_{m1} & & \cdots & a_{mn}
\end{bmatrix}
= \begin{bmatrix} v_1 & v_2 & \cdots & v_n \end{bmatrix}.
$$

The computational formula for the vector–matrix product is

$$uA = v \iff v_j = \sum_{i=1}^{m} u_i a_{ij}, \qquad u \text{ and } v \text{ are row vectors} \tag{7.12}$$

Translating this formula into an algorithm gives

Algorithm 7.3   Vector–Matrix Multiplication by Rows

initialize: $v = \texttt{zeros}(1, n)$
for $i = 1, \ldots, m$
  for $j = 1, \ldots, n$
    $v(j) = u(i)A(i, j) + v(j)$
  end
end

The MATLAB $*$ operator computes the vector–matrix product. Consider, for example, the product of the vector u and the matrix A:

```
>> u = [-3  2  -1]
u =
    -3    2   -1

>> A = [3 2 -4 0; 0 3 -1 2; -3 7 3 -1]
A =
    3    2   -4    0
    0    3   -1    2
   -3    7    3   -1

>> v = u*A
v =
   -6   -7    7    5
```

Explicit calculation with Algorithm 7.3 is easy:

```
>> v = u(1)*A(1,:) + u(2)*A(2,:) + u(3)*A(3,:)
v =
   -6   -7    7    5
```

Vector–Matrix Product: The Column View   The operations in the vector–matrix product can be performed in an order that focuses on the columns of A. The result is that the vector–matrix product $uA = v$ forms the elements of vector v as a series of inner products between u and the columns of A.

Using u and A defined in the preceding MATLAB example and expressing $uA = v$ as a linear combination of the rows of A gives

$$uA = v = -3\begin{bmatrix} 3 & 2 & -4 & 0 \end{bmatrix} + 2\begin{bmatrix} 0 & 3 & -1 & 2 \end{bmatrix} - 1\begin{bmatrix} -3 & 7 & 3 & -1 \end{bmatrix}.$$

The operations contributing to v_1 are

$$v_1 = (-3)(3) + (2)(0) + (-1)(-3) = u \cdot a_{(1)}.$$

Thus, each element of v is obtained from the inner product of u with the corresponding column of A. Multiplication of an arbitrary 1×3 vector into an arbitrary 3×4 matrix looks like

$$\begin{bmatrix} u_1 & u_2 & u_3 \end{bmatrix} \begin{bmatrix} a_{(1)} & a_{(2)} & a_{(3)} & a_{(4)} \end{bmatrix} = \begin{bmatrix} u \cdot a_{(1)} & u \cdot a_{(2)} & u \cdot a_{(3)} & u \cdot a_{(4)} \end{bmatrix},$$

where $u \cdot a_{(j)}$ is the inner product of u and the jth column of A. Using MATLAB to evaluate the column view algorithm gives

```
>> v = [u*A(:,1)  u*A(:,2)  u*A(:,3)  u*A(:,4)]
v =
     -6     -7     7     5
```

The algorithm for computing the vector–matrix product by columns is:

Algorithm 7.4   Vector–Matrix Multiplication by Columns

initialize: $v = \texttt{zeros}(1, n)$
for $j = 1, \dots, n$
  for $i = 1, \dots, m$
    $v(j) = u(i)A(i, j) + v(j)$
  end
end

Summary of Products Between Matrices and Vectors   The preceding sections have described in detail two operations: the matrix–vector product and the vector–matrix product. Each operation can be organized by columns or rows of the matrix. The organization does not affect the outcome.[2] One organization provides for a better conceptual understanding by expressing the product as a linear combination of the vectors that constitute the matrix. The complimentary organization is more amenable to hand calculation. Figure 7.7 summarizes these operations and the ways in which they might be organized.

If A is a matrix and u and x are compatible vectors, then the preferred way to compute the vector–matrix and matrix–vector product in MATLAB is simply

```
v = u*A;    % vector-matrix product
y = A*x;    % matrix-vector product
```

---

[2]The *speed* of the computation depends on the ordering of the loops. The optimum order is determined by how the matrix is stored in memory, software optimization, and the memory architecture of the computer.(See [32].)

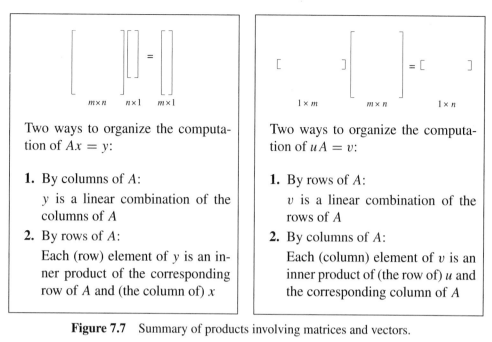

Two ways to organize the computation of $Ax = y$:

1. By columns of A:

   y is a linear combination of the columns of A

2. By rows of A:

   Each (row) element of y is an inner product of the corresponding row of A and (the column of) x

Two ways to organize the computation of $uA = v$:

1. By rows of A:

   v is a linear combination of the rows of A

2. By columns of A:

   Each (column) element of v is an inner product of (the row of) u and the corresponding column of A

Figure 7.7   Summary of products involving matrices and vectors.

The MATLAB interpreter detects the number of rows and columns in each operand and produces the appropriate result.

Matrix–Matrix Product: The Column View   The product of two matrices is another matrix. The rule for evaluating the product is a direct extension of the column and row operations used in matrix–vector and vector–matrix products. The purpose of developing alternative algorithms is to highlight important aspects of the matrix–matrix product that extend far beyond the mechanical computation of element values. To avoid getting lost in the details, keep in mind the following three ideas as you read through this section:

- The column view provides mathematical insight.
- The row view is easiest to perform with hand calculations.
- The MATLAB $*$ operator takes care of the details.

It is unwise to rely only on the MATLAB $*$ operator and ignore the details of the multiplication algorithms. First of all, the compatibility requirement on the matrices to be multiplied follows directly from the algorithms for the multiplication. The second reason for learning the algorithms is that not all important matrix computations are numerical. It is very likely that you will need to be able to perform the *symbolic* multiplication of matrices. Whether or not a package for symbolic ma-

By rearranging the order of the loops (see, for example, [32]), it is possible to create six different algorithms for the matrix–matrix product that are mathematically equivalent. Next, we consider the organization of the calculations that focuses on the row view of the matrix A.

Matrix–Matrix Product: The Row View   Figure 7.8 shows the jth column of $C = AB$ being produced by a matrix–vector product of A with the jth column of B. If the elements of $c_{(j)}$ are computed with Algorithm 7.2, which calculates the matrix–vector product by the row view, then the matrix–matrix product is obtained as a series of inner products between the rows of A and the columns of B. This view of the matrix–matrix product is shown in Figure 7.9. The calculations depicted in the figure produce a single entry in the C matrix. Computing all elements of C requires a double loop over the rows of A and the columns of B. The result is the next algorithm.

Algorithm 7.6   Matrix–Matrix Multiplication by Inner Products

initialize: $C = \texttt{zeros}(m, n)$
for $i = 1, \ldots, m$
   for $j = 1, \ldots, n$
     for $k = 1, \ldots, r$
      $C(i, j) = A(i, k)B(k, j) + C(i, j)$
     end
   end
end

Algorithm 7.6 has exactly the same number of flops as Algorithm 7.5. Superficially, all that has been changed is the order of the two outer loops. The order of calculations in this new algorithm makes it convenient for hand computations.

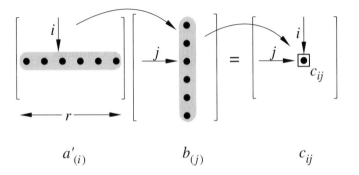

Figure 7.9   Graphical representation of Algorithm 7.6 for computing the product $AB = C$ of an $m \times r$ matrix A with an $r \times n$ matrix B.

Summary of Matrix–Matrix Multiplication   For compatible A and B matrices, the computations for producing $C = AB$ can be achieved with different algorithms. The essential difference between these algorithms is the order in which the products and sums in Equation (7.14) are performed. The order of loops that optimizes performance depends on the computer hardware, the underlying data structure used to store the matrix, and any special structure to the nonzero entries in the matrix. The designers of MATLAB have put much effort into optimizing its performance, so one can use simple expressions such as

```
>> C = A*B;
```

and be reasonably certain that an efficient calculation of the matrix–matrix product is being performed.

For the product AB to work, the number of columns in A must equal the number of rows in B. The dimensions of compatible matrices in a matrix–matrix product are

$$[m \times r] \cdot [r \times n] = [m \times n].$$

This is consistent with the compatibility requirements for a matrix–vector product,

$$[m \times n] \cdot [n \times 1] = [m \times 1],$$

a vector–matrix product,

$$[1 \times m] \cdot [m \times n] = [1 \times n],$$

a vector inner product,

$$[1 \times n] \cdot [n \times 1] = [1 \times 1], \quad \text{(a scalar)}$$

and a vector outer product,

$$[m \times 1] \cdot [1 \times n] = [m \times n].$$

The preceding compatibility conditions may be summarized as follows:

> **Any product involving matrices and vectors requires that the operands have equal inner dimensions.**

This unity of compatibility requirements allows MATLAB to use only one data type—a matrix—to store and manipulate matrices, vectors, and scalars.

It is important to remember that the order of the multiplication is significant. Reversing the order of AB requires that A and B be square and have the same dimensions. Even if A and B are square matrices of the same dimensions, however, the order of multiplication matters. In other words, for arbitrary (but compatible) matrices,

$$AB \neq BA,$$

Example 7.6: Row and Column Scaling

Matrix multiplication can be viewed as a transformation operation. The equation $C = DA$ transforms A to a new matrix C by multiplication with D. This example deals with two simple transformations: the multiplicative scaling of the rows of a matrix and the multiplicative scaling of the columns of a matrix.

Consider the case where D is a diagonal matrix, (i.e., $d_{i,j} = 0$ for all $i \neq j$). Due to the zeros in the nondiagonal elements of D, the product DA has the effect of multiplying all elements in a row of A by the corresponding diagonal element of D. Multiplication by D on the left scales the row elements of A, and multiplication by D on the right scales the column elements of A. To see how row scaling works, simply write out the terms of the product DA according to Equation (7.14):

$$C = DA \iff c_{i,j} = \sum_{k=1}^{r} d_{i,k}\, a_{k,j}$$

The product inside the sum has only one nonzero term

$$c_{i,j} = d_{i,i}\, a_{i,j} \quad \text{since } d_{i,k} = 0 \text{ for all } i \neq k.$$

The same multiplier, $d_{i,i}$, applies to all j, so DA is a row scaling. Column scaling is obtained by right multiplication with D:

$$C = AD \iff c_{i,j} = \sum_{k=1}^{r} a_{i,k}\, d_{k,j} = a_{i,j}\, d_{j,j}.$$

Here, the $d_{j,j}$ multipliers are applied to all i (i.e., all elements in a column), and hence AD is a column scaling of A.

Row and column scaling are demonstrated with the following MATLAB statements:

```
>> A = ones(3,3);
>> D = diag([1 2 3]);
>> C1 = D*A
C1 =
        1       1       1
        2       2       2
        3       3       3
```

```
>> C2 = A*D
C2 =
       1       2       3
       1       2       3
       1       2       3
```

It is usually not necessary or desirable to literally carry out the matrix multiplication implied by row and column scaling. For large matrices, the DA calculation is very inefficient, given the intended outcome. Matrix D consists of relatively few nonzero entries, so most of the operations in the matrix multiplication are trivial: multiplication by zero and addition of the resulting zero to an accumulating sum. D is a simple example of a *sparse* matrix. (See Appendix B.)

The expression DA, where D is diagonal, is an example of how linear algebra notation is used to concisely represent the *outcome* of an algorithm without necessarily providing the actual prescription for its implementation. It is mathematically more efficient (i.e., takes fewer symbols), to write $C = DA$ than to write out "multiply each row of A by the corresponding element in the vector d." On the other hand, the efficient numerical implementation of the scaling would indeed use "multiply each row of A by the corresponding element in the vector d," and *not* "perform the matrix multiplication DA." The compact symbolic notation, in this case, is a shorthand for an algorithm that would have the same effect as evaluating the product DA. (See Exercises 20–22.)

7.2.3 Operation Counts for Matrix and Vector Operations

Since vectors and matrices can be arbitrarily large, it is important to be aware of the effort needed to perform basic operations. The easiest way to measure computational effort is to count the number of *floating-point operations*, or *flops*, in an algorithm. A flop is an addition, subtraction, multiplication or division.[3] As a rough model of computational speed, we assume that each flop takes the same amount of time. Thus, algorithms that have higher flop counts usually take longer to run than algorithms with lower flop counts.

Consider the inner product of two column vectors u and v with five elements:

$$\sigma = u^T v = u_1 v_1 + u_2 v_2 + u_3 v_3 + u_4 v_4 + u_5 v_5.$$

The computation of $u^T v$ appears to take five multiplications and four additions, or nine total flops. One more flop is hidden when the inner product is written in the preceding mathematical form. The implementation of the inner product calculation

---

[3]Some numerical analysts (e.g., [12]) consider one flop to be the equivalent of a multiplication *and* an addition. The reasoning is that most linear algebra operations involve calculations like $s = t + x_i y_i$, where the addition and multiplication usually appear together. According to that convention, an inner product requires n, not $2n$, flops. The convention used is not as important, as long as it is applied consistently. In this book, multiplication and addition are counted separately, which is the convention used by the MATLAB `flops` function.

in a computer would look like

```
s = 0;
for k=1:length(u)
    s = s + u(k)*v(k);
end
```

which requires ten flops if u and v each have five elements. The extra flop comes from the addition of the u(1)*v(1) to s on the first trip through the loop. An inner product of two vectors of length n, therefore, takes $2n$ flops.

The flops function reports the number of flops performed by a sequence of calculations.[4] The flops count is reset with flops(0); otherwise, the flops function returns the number of flops since the start of the MATLAB session. The following statements verify the flop count for an inner product:

```
>> x = rand(25,1);   y = rand(25,1);
>> flops(0)
>> s = x'*y
s =
    7.4562

>> flops
ans =
    50
```

From Figure 7.9 and Equation (7.14), it is apparent that the elements of $C = AB$ can be formed by inner products of the rows of A and the columns of B. The product of an $m \times r$ matrix and an $r \times n$ matrix involves mn inner products of length r, for a total of $2mnr$ flops. If the two matrices are square (i.e., $m = r = n$), then the matrix–matrix product takes $2n^3$, or $\mathcal{O}(n^3)$, flops.

The notation $\mathcal{O}(n^3)$ is read "of order n cubed." In discussing the number of flops required by matrix operations, one is usually only concerned with a single significant digit in the work estimate. Greater precision is not justified, because the actual execution time can be greatly influenced by implementation details in the software and the design of the computer hardware. The order of magnitude notation conveys this lack of precision. Furthermore, the goal of counting flops is to

---

[4]MATLAB version 6, which was in development as this book went to press, will not support the flops function for many built-in computations involving matrices and vectors. The loss of accurate flops reporting is a consequence of using LAPACK routines for matrix and vector operations. The LAPACK routines are the successor to LINPACK and EISPACK, which have been at the core of MATLAB since its inception. LAPACK routines are more computational efficient and robust, and are based on the hierarchical Basic Linear Algebra Subroutine (BLAS) libraries. Since the BLAS routines do not count flops, the new version of MATLAB will not be able to report the work of computations involving the BLAS, and hence the LAPACK library. See C. Moler, "MATLAB Incorporates LAPACK," MATLAB *News and Notes*, Winter 2000, The MathWorks, Natick, MA.

TABLE 7.2 FLOP COUNTS FOR VECTOR AND MATRIX PRODUCTS.

Operation	flops	Comments
inner product, $x^T y$	$\mathcal{O}(n)$	x and y are $n \times 1$
outer product, xy^T	$\mathcal{O}(n^2)$	x and y are $n \times 1$
matrix–vector product, Ax	$\mathcal{O}(n^2)$	A is $n \times n$ and x is $n \times 1$
matrix–matrix product, AB	$\mathcal{O}(n^3)$	A and B are $n \times n$

establish how the performance of a operation depends on the size of the operands. For example, compared with the vector inner product, which takes $\mathcal{O}(n)$ flops, the matrix–matrix product, which takes $\mathcal{O}(n^3)$ flops, requires *significantly* more work as n increases. Table 7.2 summarizes the flop counts for the matrix and vector products described in this chapter.

7.2.4 Matrix Norms

A matrix norm associates a scalar with a matrix. As with vector norms, this scalar is a measure of the magnitude the elements in the matrix. An obvious way to define matrix norms is to simply apply the formulas for vector norms to the elements of the matrix. This idea assumes that it is meaningful to reshape a matrix into vector (e.g. changing an $m \times n$ matrix to an $mn \times 1$ vector) in order to measure its size. (See, for example, [76, Chapter 3] or [38, § 5.6].) One matrix norm, called the *Frobenius norm*, uses that strategy

$$\|A\|_F = \left[\sum_{i=1}^{m} \sum_{j=1}^{n} |a_{ij}|^2 \right]^{1/2}. \tag{7.15}$$

For the purpose of analyzing matrix–vector operations, a different type of matrix norm is useful. The so-called *induced matrix norms* use a vector norm to define a related matrix norm.

The significance of induced matrix norms is apparent when matrices are considered to be linear transformation operators. The statement

$$y = Ax$$

indicates that the matrix A transforms the column vector x into the column vector y. The output y results from a rotation and stretching (or shrinking) of the input x. Now, let x be taken from the set of all unit vectors (i.e., all $\|x\|_2 = 1$). The set of y vectors that results from computing Ax for each of the unit vectors x is determined by the inherent characteristics of A. In particular, the largest of all the L_2 norms of all of the y vectors will indicate the degree to which A can stretch a vector. This idea is the basis for defining the L_2 norm of a matrix:

$$\|A\|_2 = \max_{\|x\|_2=1} \|Ax\|_2. \tag{7.16}$$

Computing the L_2 norm of a matrix is not as easy as computing the L_2 norm of a vector. Since there are infinitely many unit vectors, it is not feasible to compute $\|A\|_2$ by directly evaluating Equation (7.16). It turns out that $\|A\|_2$ is equal to the square root of the largest eigenvalue of $A^T A$ [32, 38]. For this reason, it is often called the *spectral norm* of the matrix.

Fortunately there are two induced matrix norms that are easy to compute. These are the 1 and ∞ norms

$$\|A\|_1 = \max_{1 \le j \le n} \sum_{i=1}^{m} |a_{ij}| \qquad \text{(column sum norm)}$$

$$\|A\|_\infty = \max_{1 \le i \le m} \sum_{j=1}^{n} |a_{ij}| \qquad \text{(row sum norm)}$$

The MATLAB norm function computes the 1, 2, ∞, and Frobenius norms of a matrix. The syntax is identical to the norm function for vectors, so it will not be discussed further.

All matrix norms have the following mathematical properties:

$\|A\| > 0$ for all $A \ne 0$,

$\|\alpha A\| = |\alpha| \|A\|$ for any scalar α,

$\|A + B\| \le \|A\| + \|B\|$ for any two matrices A and B.

In addition, matrix norms are required to be consistent

$\|AB\| \le \|A\| \|B\|$ for any two matrices A and B.

$\|Ax\| \le \|A\| \|x\|$ for any matrix A and any vector x.

The second consistency requirement is a special case of the first consistency requirement, since a column vector is a matrix with one column.

7.3 MATHEMATICAL PROPERTIES OF VECTORS AND MATRICES

This section briefly summarizes the important mathematical properties of matrices and vectors. The concepts of linear independence, vector spaces, and the vector spaces associated with the columns and rows of a matrix are introduced. This material provides a foundation for understanding the solution to the linear system of equations defined by $Ax = b$, where A is a matrix and x and b are column vectors. It will be helpful to refer back the material presented here while reading Chapter 8.

To make the presentation as concrete as possible, vectors used in examples will have only two or three elements. This makes it possible to visualize the vectors in physical space. Remember that all the results presented here extend to vectors with any number of elements.

7.3.1 Linear Independence

Consider the two vectors

$$u = \begin{bmatrix} 1 \\ 1 \\ 1 \end{bmatrix} \quad \text{and} \quad v = -2u = \begin{bmatrix} -2 \\ -2 \\ -2 \end{bmatrix}.$$

Because these two vectors lie along the same line, they are not really independent. Either of the vectors defines a direction, and all vectors in that direction differ only by a scalar multiplier. Now consider two vectors that do not lie on the same line, say,

$$v = \begin{bmatrix} -2 \\ -2 \\ -2 \end{bmatrix} \quad \text{and} \quad w = \begin{bmatrix} 0 \\ 0 \\ 1 \end{bmatrix}.$$

These vectors define a plane. Any other vector x that lies in the plane can be created from a linear combination of v and w (i.e., $x = \alpha v + \beta w$, where α and β are scalars). Although v and w are distinct, x is *linearly dependent* on v and w. This notion of dependence can be extended to arbitrary numbers of vectors.

Consider a set of n column vectors $\{v_{(1)}, v_{(2)}, \ldots, v_{(n)}\}$ each with m elements. Remember that the notation $v_{(i)}$ indicates the ith *vector* in the set, not the ith element of some vector v. The set as a whole is said to be linearly independent if it is impossible to create any one of the $v_{(i)}$ from a linear combination of the other $v_{(j)}$ in the set. More precisely, the set of vectors is linearly independent if the sum

$$\alpha_1 v_{(1)} + \alpha_2 v_{(2)} + \cdots + \alpha_n v_{(n)} = 0 \tag{7.17}$$

only holds when *all* of the scalar coefficients α_i are zero. Conversely, the set of vectors is linearly dependent if at least one of the α_i is nonzero in Equation (7.17).

Linear independence is easy to see for vectors that are orthogonal. For example, the vectors

$$\begin{bmatrix} 4 \\ 0 \\ 0 \\ 0 \end{bmatrix}, \quad \begin{bmatrix} 0 \\ -3 \\ 0 \\ 0 \end{bmatrix}, \quad \text{and} \quad \begin{bmatrix} 0 \\ 0 \\ 1 \\ 0 \end{bmatrix}$$

are linearly independent. Vectors need not be orthogonal to be linearly independent, however. As an example, the following set of vectors is linearly independent:

$$
\begin{bmatrix} 1 \\ -2 \\ 1 \end{bmatrix}, \quad \begin{bmatrix} 1 \\ 0 \\ 4 \end{bmatrix}, \quad \text{and} \quad \begin{bmatrix} 2 \\ -1 \\ 0 \end{bmatrix}. \tag{7.18}
$$

Equation (7.17) defines the criteria for linear independence of a set of vectors. If the set of vectors $\{v_{(1)}, v_{(2)}, \ldots, v_{(n)}\}$ is organized as the columns of a matrix, Equation (7.17) is equivalent to a matrix–vector product:

$$
\begin{bmatrix} & | & | & & | \\ v_{(1)} & v_{(2)} & \cdots & v_{(n)} \\ & | & | & & | \end{bmatrix} \begin{bmatrix} \alpha_1 \\ \alpha_2 \\ \vdots \\ \alpha_n \end{bmatrix} = \begin{bmatrix} 0 \\ 0 \\ \vdots \\ 0 \end{bmatrix}. \tag{7.19}
$$

This provides a concise way of expressing the condition of linear independence for the columns of a matrix.

> **The columns of the $m \times n$ matrix A are linearly independent if and only if $x = (0, 0, \ldots, 0)^T$ is the only n-element column vector that satisfies $Ax = 0$.**

To determine whether the columns of A are linearly independent, solve $Ax = 0$ using the methods presented in Chapter 8. If the solution fails, then the columns of A are not linearly independent. An alternative procedure is to use the `rank` function described in § 7.3.4.

7.3.2 Vector Spaces

A vector is rarely considered in isolation. An elementary way to group vectors is by the number of elements they contain. For example, when dealing with three-dimensional physical space, we use vectors with three elements, where each element is associated with one of the (x, y, z)-coordinate directions. Vectors with three elements belong to a group that is separate from vectors having 2, 4, 15, or 3000 elements. Vectors from these distinct groups cannot be mixed.

A *vector space* is a group of vectors having the same number of elements *and* obeying the rules of addition and multiplication defined for that space. (See, for example, Strang [71, 72].) Specifically, a vector space is a group of vectors that is *closed* for all linear combinations of vectors in the space. For any two scalars α and β and any two vectors u and v in the space, the linear combination $w = \alpha u + \beta v$

must also be in the space. In other words, a closed space contains all possible linear combinations of vectors in that space.

The set of all vectors having three components that are real numbers is the vector space designated $\mathbf{R}^3$. The "3" indicates the number of elements (components), and the $\mathbf{R}$ indicates that the elements are real numbers. $\mathbf{C}^3$ is the corresponding set of vectors having three elements that are complex numbers.

The vector spaces $\mathbf{R}^1$, $\mathbf{R}^2$, and $\mathbf{R}^3$ have direct geometric interpretations. The elements of vectors in $\mathbf{R}^1$ define all the coordinates along a line (the real axis). The elements of vectors in $\mathbf{R}^2$ define the coordinates in a plane. The vectors displayed in Figure 7.2 on page 298, for example, are contained in $\mathbf{R}^2$. The vector space $\mathbf{R}^n$ consists of all vectors with n-elements that are real numbers. By convention, $\mathbf{R}^n$ designates the space of n-element *column* vectors.

Subspaces   A *subspace* is a vector space that is contained within another vector space. In general, a subspace of $\mathbf{R}^n$ is a subset of $\mathbf{R}^n$ that is also a vector space. A subspace must, therefore, also be closed for all linear combinations in the subspace.

Consider vectors in $\mathbf{R}^3$. If the tail of each vector is located at the origin $[0, 0, 0]^T$, then the elements of the vectors can be interpreted as the (x, y, z)-coordinates of the vector tips. Figure 7.10 depicts the three vectors

$$u = \begin{bmatrix} 1 \\ 2 \\ 0 \end{bmatrix}, \qquad v = \begin{bmatrix} -2 \\ 1 \\ 3 \end{bmatrix}, \qquad \text{and} \qquad w = \begin{bmatrix} 3 \\ 1 \\ -3 \end{bmatrix}.$$

Although u, v, and w have three elements, they all lie in the same plane. We say that u, v, and w exist in a subspace of $\mathbf{R}^3$.

Span of a Subspace   A set of vectors $\{v_{(1)}, v_{(2)}, \ldots, v_{(n)}\}$ can be used as building blocks to create an arbitrary number of other vectors via linear combinations. If a vector w can be created by the linear combination

$$\beta_1 v_{(1)} + \beta_2 v_{(2)} + \cdots + \beta_n v_{(n)} = w,$$

where β_i are scalars, then w is said to be in the *subspace* that is *spanned* by $\{v_{(1)}, v_{(2)}, \ldots, v_{(n)}\}$. If the $v_{(i)}$ are members of $\mathbf{R}^m$, then the subspace spanned by the $v_{(i)}$ is a subspace of $\mathbf{R}^m$. If $n \geq m$, it is possible, though not guaranteed, that the $v_{(i)}$ could span $\mathbf{R}^m$.

Vectors that span a subspace need not be linearly independent. All that is necessary is that the vectors can be used in linear combinations to construct all other vectors in the subspace.

Basis and Dimension of a Subspace   A *basis* of a subspace is a set of linearly independent vectors that spans the space. Since a basis set is linearly

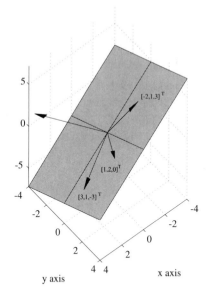

Figure 7.10 Three-element vectors in a subspace of $\mathbf{R}^3$. The fourth, unlabeled vector is the normal to the plane.

independent, it must also contain the smallest number of vectors that spans the subspace. The number of vectors in the basis set is called the *dimension* of the subspace. A basis for $\mathbf{R}^n$ has exactly n linearly independent vectors. Any set of n linearly independent vectors with n elements forms a basis for $\mathbf{R}^n$.

The terms basis and dimension are applied to subspaces and to entire spaces like $\mathbf{R}^n$. Thus, we say that the three vectors in Figure 7.10 span a two-dimensional subspace of $\mathbf{R}^3$, and those three vectors also form a basis for that subspace. Although those vectors span a two-dimensional subspace, they are not members of $\mathbf{R}^2$, because they have three components, not two.

Mutually orthogonal vectors, such as

$$a = \begin{bmatrix} 1 \\ 0 \\ 0 \end{bmatrix}, \qquad b = \begin{bmatrix} 0 \\ 1 \\ 0 \end{bmatrix}, \quad \text{and} \quad c = \begin{bmatrix} 0 \\ 0 \\ 1 \end{bmatrix}, \qquad (7.20)$$

are convenient basis vectors. Basis vectors need not be orthogonal, however. For example, the set

$$r = \begin{bmatrix} 4 \\ 0 \\ 2 \\ -3 \end{bmatrix}, \quad s = \begin{bmatrix} 1 \\ 3 \\ 1 \\ 1 \end{bmatrix}, \quad t = \begin{bmatrix} 2 \\ 1 \\ 7 \\ 2 \end{bmatrix}, \quad \text{and} \quad u = \begin{bmatrix} 4 \\ -2 \\ -1 \\ 5 \end{bmatrix} \qquad (7.21)$$

is a basis for $\mathbf{R}^4$.

7.3.3 Subspaces Associated with Matrices

There are four subspaces associated with any matrix. These are the column space, the row space, the null space, and the left null space. We will briefly discuss the column space and null space. (See Strang [71, 72] for a more complete exposition.)

The Column Space   Recall that the matrix–vector product $y = Ax$ can be interpreted as creating a new vector y from a linear combination of the columns of A. The columns of A, therefore, form the basis of a subspace called the *column space* or *range* of A. Different y vectors in the space are obtained by altering the coefficients in the linear combination (i.e., by altering the elements of x). On the other hand, if y does not lie in the column space of A, then no x exists that will give y as the product Ax.

If A is an $m \times n$ matrix, the column space will have a dimension less than or equal to m. Since the length of the columns in A is m, these vectors lie in a subspace of $\mathbf{R}^m$. The dimension of the column space is equal to the number of linearly independent columns in A. Since there are n columns in A, the maximum dimension of the column space can not exceed n. If $n > m$, then the columns in A must be linearly *dependent*.

The matrix

$$A = \begin{bmatrix} 1 & 2 & 0 \\ -3 & -2 & -4 \\ -2 & 0 & 2 \end{bmatrix} \tag{7.22}$$

consists of three columns that are linearly independent. Thus, the column space of A has dimension three, and the columns of A span $\mathbf{R}^3$.

The matrix

$$B = \begin{bmatrix} 1 & -2 & 3 \\ 2 & 1 & 1 \\ 0 & 3 & -3 \end{bmatrix} \tag{7.23}$$

has only two linearly independent columns (the third column is obtained by subtracting the second column from the first column), so the column space of B has dimension two. If the columns of B are represented by arrows in three-dimensional physical space, these arrows all lie in a plane, as shown in Figure 7.10.

Null Space   The null space of A, designated null(A), is the set of all vectors that satisfy $Ax = 0$. There is always at least one vector in null(A): It is $x = 0$. If A is an $m \times n$ matrix, the null space of A is a subspace of $\mathbf{R}^n$ (not $\mathbf{R}^m$). For all the elements of $y = Ax$ to be zero, Algorithm 7.2 (the row-oriented matrix–vector product) implies that any vector satisfying $Ax = 0$ must be orthogonal to the *rows* of A.

As examples, consider the null spaces for the matrices defined by Equations (7.22) and (7.23). The A matrix defined in Equation (7.22) has three linearly independent columns. From Equation (7.19), we know that the only solution to $Ax = 0$ is $x = 0$. The null space of A, therefore, contains only the zero vector. The B matrix defined in Equation (7.23) has only two linearly independent columns. One solution to $Bx = 0$ is $x = [1, -1, -1]^T$, which is easily verified by direct substitution. Any scalar multiple of this vector is also a solution to $Bx = 0$. The null space of B is the line passing through $[0, 0, 0]^T$ and $[1, -1, -1]^T$. This is the norml to the plane defined by the *row* vectors of B. (See Example 7.7.)

The built-in `null` function computes the null space of a matrix. It has two forms

```
Z = null(A)
Z = null(A,'r')
```

For a given input matrix `A`, the `null(A)` function returns an orthonormal basis for the null space of `A` in the columns of `Z`. The orthonormal basis is obtained with the *Singular Value Decomposition* algorithm. The second variation of the `null` function, `Z = null(A,'r')`, produces a basis for the null space of `A` in the columns of `Z`, such that the elements of `Z` are ratios of integers (i.e., rational numbers). The algorithm used by `null(A,'r')` is described by Strang [72, § 3.2]. The `null(A)` form produces more reliable numerical values for the elements of `Z`, whereas the `null(A,'r')` form produces a matrix `Z` that is easier to visualize when matrix `A` has just a few rows and columns.

Example 7.7: null(A) Is Orthogonal to the Row Space of A.

As the columns of a matrix span its column space, the rows span the *row space* of the matrix. Vectors in the null space of a matrix A satisfy $Ax = 0$, which means that these vectors are orthogonal to the row space of A. That is how the normal vector to the plane in Figure 7.10 is created.

Let B be the matrix defined in Equation (7.23):

```
>> B = [1  -2  3;  2  1  1;  0  3  -3];
```

Figure 7.10 shows that the columns of B lie in a plane. The vector

```
>> Z = null(B)
Z =
    0.5774
   -0.5774
   -0.5774
```

is in the null space of B, but it is *not* orthogonal to the columns of B. For example,

```
>> B(:,1)'*Z
ans =
   -0.5774
```

To find the subspace that is orthogonal to the column space of B, compute the null space of B^T. Vectors in null(B^T) are orthogonal to the rows of B^T, which are the columns of B. For example, consider

```
>> Zr = null(B','r')
Zr =
    1.2000
   -0.6000
    1.0000
```

This is the normal to the plane in Figure 7.10.

7.3.4 Matrix Rank

The *rank* of a matrix is the number of linearly independent column vectors in the matrix. The rank of a matrix, therefore, is equal to the dimension of its column space. It is also true that the rank is equal to the number of linearly independent row vectors in the matrix. Thus, the rank is also equal to the dimension of the row space of the matrix.

An $m \times n$ matrix will, in general, have a rank r, where r is an integer $r \leq \min\{m, n\}$. If $r = \min\{m, n\}$, then the matrix is said to be *full rank*. If $r < \min\{m, n\}$, then the matrix is said to be *rank deficient*. For simple matrices, the rank can be determined by inspection. Here are some matrices that are obviously rank deficient[5]

$$A = \begin{bmatrix} 1 & 1 \\ 2 & 2 \end{bmatrix}, \qquad B = \begin{bmatrix} 1 & 0 & 1 \\ 2 & 1 & 0 \\ 3 & 1 & 1 \end{bmatrix}.$$

In principle, the rank of a matrix can be determined by using elementary row operations (Gaussian elimination) to reduce the matrix to upper triangular form U. Strang [72, § 3.2] describes this procedure in detail. After reducing the matrix to triangular form, we find that the rank is the number of columns with nonzero values on the diagonal of U. In practice, especially for large matrices, roundoff errors during the row operations may cause a loss of accuracy in this method of rank computation. (See [28, § 5.8] for a more comprehensive discussion.)

---

[5]*Hint*: for the matrix B, add two times the second column to the third column, or add the first and second rows.

The built-in `rank` function uses *Singular Value Decomposition* to estimate the rank of a matrix:

```
>> rank([1 2; 1 2])
ans =
    1

>> rank([1 0 1; 2 1 0; 3 1 1])
ans =
    2
```

See Gill et al. [28, § 5.8] and Golub and Van Loan [32, § 5.5.8] for a discussion of the computational algorithm. Curious readers should study the short source code of the `rank` function to see how this computation can be elegantly performed with MATLAB.

7.3.5 Matrix Determinant

For each square (i.e, $n \times n$) matrix, there is a unique scalar value called the determinant, which is given the symbol $\det(A)$. When A is written as a rectangular array of elements, the determinant is designated by replacing the curved or square brackets by vertical bars. If, for example, A is a 2×2 matrix, then

$$\det(A) = \begin{vmatrix} a_{11} & a_{12} \\ a_{21} & a_{22} \end{vmatrix} = a_{11}a_{22} - a_{12}a_{21}. \qquad (7.24)$$

For larger matrices, the determinant may be evaluated through a recursive series of increasingly small determinants that end with the formula for the 2×2 matrix. This procedure is described shortly.

The determinant has important properties that make it useful for theoretical analysis. In general, however, the determinant is not useful in numerical computations. It is expensive to compute and for matrices of modest dimension, the value of the determinant can be so large that it causes overflow.

For hand calculation, the determinant of a matrix can be written as a recursive sum of matrix elements multiplied by their respective minors. A minor is the determinant of the submatrix associated with a single element of the original matrix. The submatrix is formed by removing the row and column containing the element in question. The general rule for calculating a matrix determinant by row minors can be condensed to

$$\det(A) = \sum_{j=1}^{n} a_{ij}(-1)^{i+j} M_{ij}, \quad \text{for any } \textit{one } i, \qquad (7.25)$$

where the *minor*, M_{ij}, is the determinant of the $(n-1) \times (n-1)$ matrix formed by deleting row i and column j from A. In applying the preceding formula for

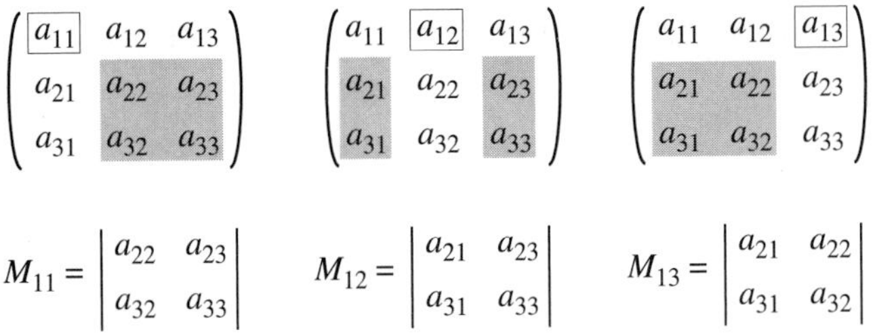

$$\begin{pmatrix} \boxed{a_{11}} & a_{12} & a_{13} \\ a_{21} & a_{22} & a_{23} \\ a_{31} & a_{32} & a_{33} \end{pmatrix} \qquad \begin{pmatrix} a_{11} & \boxed{a_{12}} & a_{13} \\ a_{21} & a_{22} & a_{23} \\ a_{31} & a_{32} & a_{33} \end{pmatrix} \qquad \begin{pmatrix} a_{11} & a_{12} & \boxed{a_{13}} \\ a_{21} & a_{22} & a_{23} \\ a_{31} & a_{32} & a_{33} \end{pmatrix}$$

$$M_{11} = \begin{vmatrix} a_{22} & a_{23} \\ a_{32} & a_{33} \end{vmatrix} \qquad M_{12} = \begin{vmatrix} a_{21} & a_{23} \\ a_{31} & a_{33} \end{vmatrix} \qquad M_{13} = \begin{vmatrix} a_{21} & a_{22} \\ a_{31} & a_{32} \end{vmatrix}$$

Figure 7.11   The minors $M_{1,j}$ of the first row of a 3×3 matrix are formed by taking the determinant of the shaded submatrices.

$\det(A)$, the sum is over all columns in a single row. The corresponding expression for calculating a matrix determinant by column minors is

$$\det(A) = \sum_{i=1}^{n} a_{ij}(-1)^{i+j} M_{ij}, \quad \text{for any } \textit{one } j. \tag{7.26}$$

As an example, the three minors associated with the first row of a 3×3 matrix are represented schematically in Figure 7.11. The formula for the determinant of a 3×3 matrix obtained by expanding along minors of the first row is

$$\begin{vmatrix} a_{11} & a_{12} & a_{13} \\ a_{21} & a_{22} & a_{23} \\ a_{31} & a_{32} & a_{33} \end{vmatrix} = a_{11}(-1)^{1+1} \begin{vmatrix} a_{22} & a_{23} \\ a_{32} & a_{33} \end{vmatrix} + a_{12}(-1)^{1+2} \begin{vmatrix} a_{21} & a_{23} \\ a_{31} & a_{33} \end{vmatrix}$$

$$+ a_{13}(-1)^{1+3} \begin{vmatrix} a_{21} & a_{22} \\ a_{31} & a_{32} \end{vmatrix}$$

$$= a_{11}M_{11} - a_{12}M_{12} + a_{13}M_{13}. \tag{7.27}$$

The numerical value of this expression is evaluated by applying Equation (7.24) to M_{11}, M_{12}, and M_{13}. For larger matrices, the expansion by minors formulas (Equations (7.25) and (7.26)) are applied recursively until the resulting expression only contains determinants of 2×2 matrices.

Expansion by minors is not a viable computational formula for anything but the smallest of matrices. To see why, consider how the computational effort grows as this formula used for larger matrices. Let $fp(n)$ be the number of flops to compute the determinant of an $n \times n$ matrix with an expansion by minors. From Equations (7.24), (7.27), and, (7.25), the flop counts are

$$fp(2) = 3,$$

$$fp(3) = 3[fp(2) + 2] = 15,$$

$$fp(4) = 4[fp(3) + 2] = 4\{3[fp(2) + 2] + 2\},$$

$$\vdots$$

$$fp(n) = n[fp(n-1) + 2] \sim O(n!).$$

For large n, the computational effort is prohibitive!

The formal solution[6] of the linear system $Ax = b$ can be expressed by Cramer's Rule: The ith element of the solution vector is

$$x_i = \frac{\det(A_i)}{\det(A)}, \tag{7.28}$$

where A_i is the matrix formed by replacing the ith column of A with the right-hand-side vector b. Using Cramer's Rule to solve for x requires the evaluation of $n + 1$ determinants of $n \times n$ matrices. For even modest values of n, say, $n > 5$, this procedure is inefficient. The practical inefficiency is masked by the compactness of Equation (7.28).

If Cramer's Rule and its many evaluations of $\det(A)$ are not useful for solving systems of equations, it would appear that $\det(A)$ at least has diagnostic value. From Equation (7.28), one concludes that the solution does not exist if $\det(A) = 0$. While it is true that $\det(A) \neq 0$ guarantees that the solution to the matrix equation $Ax = b$ exists, computing $\det(A)$, even with the most efficient algorithm, is as costly as trying to solve the system in the first place. Thus, checking the magnitude of $\det(A)$ before attempting to solve $Ax = b$ doubles the effort necessary to solve the system.

The matrix determinant *can* be computed efficiently for some matrices that have advantageous patterns of zeros. Consider the 4×4 diagonal matrix. Application of Equation (7.25) gives

$$\begin{vmatrix} d_1 & 0 & 0 & 0 \\ 0 & d_2 & 0 & 0 \\ 0 & 0 & d_3 & 0 \\ 0 & 0 & 0 & d_4 \end{vmatrix} = d_1 d_2 d_3 d_4. \tag{7.29}$$

This convenient simplification also applies to triangular matrices. An upper triangular matrix has nonzero elements only on and above the main diagonal ($j \geq i$, where j is the column index and i is the row index). A lower triangular matrix has nonzero elements only on and below the main diagonal ($i \geq j$). For example, the determinant of a 4×4 upper triangular matrix is

[6]Solution of linear systems is covered in Chapter 8.

$$\begin{vmatrix} a_{11} & a_{12} & a_{13} & a_{14} \\ 0 & a_{22} & a_{23} & a_{24} \\ 0 & 0 & a_{33} & a_{34} \\ 0 & 0 & 0 & a_{44} \end{vmatrix} = a_{11}a_{22}a_{33}a_{44}. \tag{7.30}$$

In general, if A is an $n \times n$ upper triangular or lower triangular matrix, then

$$\det(A) = a_{11}a_{22}\ldots a_{nn} \qquad \text{(triangular } A \text{ only).}$$

The relative efficiency of computing determinants of triangular matrices can be applied to an arbitrary square matrix by first *factoring* the matrix into the product of two triangular matrices. The so-called LU decomposition (see § 8.4.1 on page 410) of A gives a lower triangular matrix L and an upper triangular matrix U such that[7]

$$A = LU.$$

Given any two square matrices B and C, the determinant of the product BC is the product of the determinants, $\det(BC) = \det(B)\det(C)$. (See, for example, [12, 78].) Thus, if $A = LU$, then

$$\det(A) = \det(L)\det(U) = (\ell_{11}\ell_{22}\ldots\ell_{nn})(u_{11}u_{22}\ldots u_{nn}).$$

The LU factorization of A takes $\mathcal{O}(n^3)$ flops. Once L and U are found, computing $\det(L)$ and $\det(U)$ takes only $2n$ flops, which is negligible compared with n^3. Thus, computing the determinant of A by first computing its LU factorization requires $\mathcal{O}(n^3)$ flops. This procedure is significantly more efficient than the expansion by minors for all but the smallest matrices. The built-in MATLAB function det computes the determinant of a square matrix from the determinants of its L and U factors.

Given this more efficient procedure, it still does not make sense to use determinants as part of practical numerical algorithms. The preferred technique for solving a linear system of equations utilizes the same LU factorization needed to compute the determinant. If the system of equations is singular (i.e., if $\det(A) = 0$), then the algorithm for computing L and U will encounter a division by zero and fail. In this case, the information implied by $\det(A) = 0$ is supplied before the computation of $\det(A)$ can be completed.

Yet another problem with computing $\det(A)$ is the potential for overflow, since the magnitude of the determinant can become can be quite large. Consider, for example, the determinant of a 128×128 triangular matrix having diagonal coefficients with magnitude of order 1000. Such a matrix could hardly be considered

---

[7]Note that computing L and U is *not* a simple matter of extracting the upper and lower triangular parts of A.

large by modern computing standards. The determinant of this matrix has an order of magnitude of $1000^{128} = 10^{384}$, which is larger than `realmax`, the largest
floating-point number that can be represented in double precision. Even though
the determinant of this matrix is well defined in this case, it can not be computed
without resorting to a special procedure.

The determinant is another example of how an idea from linear algebra may
be written one way with mathematical notation, but implemented with very different steps in a computer program. (For more discussion on the limitations of
determinants, see, for example, [28, § 3.6] and [68, Chapter 10].)

7.4 SPECIAL MATRICES

Although a matrix can be any two-dimensional array of numbers, there are smaller,
but very important, classes of matrices having special characteristics that can be exploited in linear algebra operations. The same rules apply, of course, but something
in the matrix structure allows a simplification in the calculations. This section provides a survey of the commonly occurring "special" matrices and the MATLAB
commands used to create them.

7.4.1 Diagonal Matrices

If i is the row index and j is the column index for matrix elements, a diagonal
matrix has zeros for all elements with $i \neq j$. An $n \times n$ diagonal matrix, therefore,
has only n nonzero entries. This makes it convenient to represent a diagonal matrix
by an n-dimensional vector consisting of its diagonal elements. The mathematical
notation is

$$C = \operatorname{diag}(c_1, c_2, \dots, c_n) = \begin{bmatrix} c_1 & 0 & \cdots & 0 \\ 0 & c_2 & & 0 \\ \vdots & & \ddots & \vdots \\ 0 & 0 & \cdots & c_n \end{bmatrix}.$$

The MATLAB `diag` function is used to either create a diagonal matrix from a vector
or and extract the diagonal entries of a matrix. If the input argument of the `diag`
function is a vector, MATLAB uses the vector to create a diagonal matrix:

```
>> x = [1 -5  2  6];
>> A = diag(x)
A =
     1     0     0     0
     0    -5     0     0
     0     0     2     0
     0     0     0     6
```

If the input argument of the diag function is a matrix, the result is a vector of the diagonal elements:

```
>> B = [1 -5  2; 6  12  -4; 0  7  9];
>> y = diag(B);
y =
     1
    12
     9
```

Multiplying a matrix A by a diagonal matrix has the effect of scaling the rows or columns of A. (See Example 7.6, page 330.)

7.4.2 The Identity Matrix

In scalar arithmetic, the expression $\alpha \times 1$ leaves α unchanged. In linear algebra, the expression AI leaves the A matrix unchanged. I is an *identity matrix*. An identity matrix is a diagonal matrix with ones on the main diagonal.

Identity matrices are square; that is, they have the same number of rows and columns. For $AI = A$ to hold, the compatibility rules for matrix multiplication require that the number of rows in I must equal the number of columns in A. The size of an identity matrix, therefore, is determined by context. Sometimes, the number of rows (and columns) in an identity matrix is indicated by attaching a single subscript to the I. The 4×4 identity matrix, for example, may be written as

$$I_4 = \begin{bmatrix} 1 & 0 & 0 & 0 \\ 0 & 1 & 0 & 0 \\ 0 & 0 & 1 & 0 \\ 0 & 0 & 0 & 1 \end{bmatrix}.$$

The use of a single subscript to denote the size of an identity matrix is an exception to matrix nomenclature convention.

Identity matrices are created with the eye function, which can take either one or two input arguments.

```
I = eye(n)
I = eye(m,n)
```

In the single input form, n specifies the number of rows and columns in a square identity matrix. In the second form, m specifies the number of rows, and n specifies the number of columns in a rectangular, identity-like matrix with ones on the main diagonal.

```
>> Q'*Q
ans =
   1.0000        0        0        0
        0   1.0000        0        0
        0        0   1.0000        0
        0        0        0   1.0000
```

7.4.8 Permutation Matrices

A permutation matrix, usually given the symbol P, is a matrix obtained by permuting the rows of an identity matrix. The product $B = PA$, where P is a permutation matrix and A is another matrix of compatible dimension, results in a matrix B equal to A, except for the interchange of two rows. For example, the 3×3 matrix

$$P = \begin{bmatrix} 1 & 0 & 0 \\ 0 & 0 & 1 \\ 0 & 1 & 0 \end{bmatrix}$$

exchanges the second and third rows of another $3 \times n$ matrix when P multiplies that matrix on the left, as shown by the following code:

```
>> A = [1 2 3 4; 5 6 7 8; 9 10 11 12];  P = [1 0 0; 0 0 1; 0 1 0];
>> B = P*A
B =
     1     2     3     4
     9    10    11    12
     5     6     7     8
```

When this P multiplies an $m \times 3$ matrix on the right, it swaps the corresponding columns:

```
>> C = A';
>> D = C*P
D =
     1     9     5
     2    10     6
     3    11     7
     4    12     8
```

Permutation matrices are easy to construct. To swap rows r and s of any matrix, start with an identity matrix of the same size and exchange rows r and s in the identity matrix. The result is the desired permutation matrix. Note that permutation matrices are also orthogonal.

In a mathematical formula, multiplication by a permutation matrix is an elegant way to indicate a row or column swap. In a computer program, however, a permutation matrix is rarely constructed and then applied to a matrix. It is inefficient to use memory to create P in the first place and then perform many multiplication and additions involving zeros in the evaluation of PA. If the two rows of a matrix must be swapped, the following MATLAB statements will do the job for any size A:

```
>> i1 = ...;   i2 = ...;    % Indices of rows to swap
>> tmp = A(i1,:);           % Save row i1 in the tmp vector
>> A(i1,:) = A(i2,:);       % Copy row i2 into row i1
>> A(i2,:) = tmp;           % move old contents of row i1 into row i2
```

If several rows of a matrix need to be exchanged and the overhead of constructing and applying a permutation matrix is to be avoided, a permutation *vector* can be used. A permutation vector provides the row indices in a MATLAB assignment operation. Consider the following example:

```
>> A = [1 1 1; 2 2 2; 3 3 3; 4 4 4; 5 5 5];
>> p = [2 5 3 1 4]';     % length (p) must equal number of rows in A
>> B = A(p,:)            % Copy rows of A into B according to order in p
B =
        2       2       2
        5       5       5
        3       3       3
        1       1       1
        4       4       4
```

The A(p,:) expression is an example of MATLAB *array indexing*, which is discussed in § 3.5.3 beginning on page 121. Given a permutation vector p, the corresponding permutation matrix can be created with

```
>> [m,n] = size(A);    % A is target matrix to have it's rows swapped
>> P = eye(m,m);       % P is square
>> P = P(p,:);         % permute the rows of the identity matrix
```

The use of permutation matrices is another example of how matrix and vector operations are used as a compact mathematical description, but not a direct prescription, for a computer implementation.

7.5 SUMMARY

This chapter is a review of linear algebra and the MATLAB functions necessary to affect basic operations on vectors and matrices. Much information has been presented here. Working with linear algebra requires, at the very least, an ability to execute computations with vectors and matrices. Upon completion of this chapter, you should be able to perform the following basic calculations *by hand*:

- addition and subtraction of two vectors or matrices
- vector inner product
- vector outer product
- L_1, L_2 and L_∞ norms of a vector
- L_1 and L_∞ norms of a matrix
- matrix–vector, vector–matrix, and matrix–matrix products

As a prerequisite to performing these calculations, you must understand the compatibility requirements for the vectors and matrices used in each operation. These are summarized in Tables 7.4 and 7.5. You should also, of course, know how to perform these calculations in MATLAB.

It is important to see operations involving matrices and vectors as more than computational formulas involving scalar elements. The key idea is to treat the columns of a matrix as vectors. This is especially true of the matrix–vector and matrix–matrix products. One of the central ideas to carry into the next chapter is that the equation $Ax = b$ involves the construction of the b vector from the columns of the A matrix.

In addition to the purely computational aspects, it is also important to see the mathematical ideas that underly linear algebra. In particular, one should be comfortable with the following ideas:

- use of norms to measure the "size" of vectors and matrices
- linear independence of a set of vectors
- the difference between the dimension of a space spanned by a set of vectors and the number of vectors in the set
- the column space and null space of a matrix

The few new MATLAB functions developed in this chapter are summarized in Table 7.3. These functions do not embody numerical methods. Rather, they are used

TABLE 7.3 FUNCTIONS FOR LINEAR ALGEBRA REVIEW DEVELOPED IN THIS CHAPTER. FUNCTIONS WITH N.A. (NOT APPLICABLE) FOR A PAGE NUMBER ARE NOT LISTED IN THE TEXT, BUT ARE INCLUDED IN THE NMM TOOLBOX.

Function	page	Description
vectorSequence	306	Demonstrate vector norms
rotvec	320	Rotate vectors in three-dimensional space
tridiag	N.A.	Create a full tridiagonal matrix

TABLE 7.4   SUMMARY OF RESTRICTIONS ON BASIC OPERATIONS INVOLVING TWO VECTORS.

Operation	Example	Conditions	Result
addition	x+y	x and y must either both be row vectors or both be column vectors. The length (number of columns or number of rows) of these vectors must be the same.	a vector with the same number of rows or columns as x and y
subtraction	x−y	Same as addition.	same as addition
inner product	x*y	x is a row vector, and y is a column vector. The number of columns in x must equal the number of rows in y.	a scalar
outer product	x*y	x is a column vector, and y is a row vector. The number of rows in x must equal the number of columns in y.	a matrix

TABLE 7.5   SUMMARY OF RESTRICTIONS ON BASIC OPERATIONS INVOLVING TWO MATRICES.

Operation	Example	Conditions	Result
addition	A+B	A and B must both be $m \times n$ matrices where m is the number of rows and n is the number of columns.	An $m \times n$ matrix.
subtraction	A−B	same as addition	same as addition
multiplication	A*B	The inner dimensions of A and B must be the same; that is, if A is an $m \times r$ matrix, then B must be an $r \times n$ matrix.	If A is $m \times r$ and B is $r \times n$, then C $= A * B$ is $m \times n$.

used to demonstrate ideas or, in the case of `tridiag`, used to automate the creation of a special matrix. The essential features of MATLAB presented in this chapter are the * and : symbols.[8] Mastery of the types and significance of the various matrix and vector products provides a solid foundation for work with linear algebra. The MATLAB * operator is used for all vector and matrix products. Only legal * operations are allowed by the MATLAB interpreter. The appropriate output type— scalar, vector, or matrix—is automatically created. This great power and flexibility allows one to write compact statements that involve many detailed calculations.

The other potent MATLAB symbol, :, is a great asset when dealing with row and column operations in matrices. Use of : to refer to rows and columns should not be viewed as a programming trick. Rather, the : is a way to express matrix operations in their most natural form.

---

[8]The \ operator is added in the next chapter.

Further Reading

There are numerous books dedicated entirely to linear algebra. Many of these also provide examples with MATLAB code. MATLAB colon notation has been adopted by many numerical analysts as a standard way to indicate row and column operations on matrices.

Strang [71, 72] provides an excellent introduction to linear algebra that is motivated by concrete examples and intuitive arguments. Gill et al. [28, Chapter 1] give a compact summary of the mathematical rules and then link this material to the solution of linear systems and optimization. Datta [12] and Watkins [78] cover linear algebra at an intermediate level and with reference to practical applications. Trefethen and Bau [76] use a format of forty lectures to present linear algebra at an intermediate-to-advanced level, with the focus on developing a deep mathematical intuition. Demmel [15] develops the implementation ideas behind state-of-the-art numerical linear algebra, providing a good complement to [76]. The classic contemporary reference on the subject is the book by Golub and Van Loan [32], though this is not easy reading for those unfamiliar with the subject. Stewart [69] gives a thorough treatment of LU and QR factorizations at an advanced level. Many other books are available.

The works cited here provide substantial resources for the reader seeking to expand his or her understanding of linear algebra. Many books (e.g., [12, 72]) provide MATLAB code to augment the development of the material. Others (e.g., [32, 69, 76]) use MATLAB notation extensively.

EXERCISES

The number in parenthesis at the beginning of each exercise indicates the degree of skill and amount of effort necessary to complete the exercise. See § 1.4 on page 10 for a description of the rating system.

1. (1) Write the MATLAB statements to create the following:
   (a) a row vector $t = [0, \pi/4, \pi/2, 3\pi/4, \pi]$.
   (b) a row vector $u = [0, \pi/100, 2\pi/100, \ldots 99\pi/100, \pi]$.
   (c) a column vector $v = [\sin(0) - \cos(0), \sin(\pi/100) - \cos(\pi/100), \ldots \sin(\pi) - \cos(\pi)]^T$.

2. (1) Let x and y be n-element column vectors, u and v be m-element row vectors, A be an $m \times n$ matrix, and B be an $n \times k$ matrix. For each of the expressions in the accompanying table identify the result as being either a scalar, vector, or matrix, or illegal. If the result is a vector or matrix, specify the number of rows and columns in the result. If the expression is legal for only certain combinations of m, n, and k, identify those conditions.

Expression	Result	Expression	Result
$x - y$		uAy	
$x - u$		AB	
$x^T y$		BA	
xy^T		$A^T A$	
yv		$A^T Ax$	
$x^T A$		$I - xy^T$	
uA		$xy^T A$	
$x^T Ax$		$(Ax)^T y$	

3. (1) Manually compute $C = AB$ for

$$A = \begin{bmatrix} 1 & 1 \\ 2 & 3 \end{bmatrix}, \qquad B = \begin{bmatrix} 3 & -1 \\ -2 & 1 \end{bmatrix}.$$

What is the relationship between A and B?

4. (1) Given the matrices A and B and the vector v

$$A = \begin{bmatrix} 2 & -1 & 0 \\ -1 & 2 & -1 \\ 0 & -1 & 2 \end{bmatrix}, \qquad B = \begin{bmatrix} 3/4 & 1/2 & 1/4 \\ 1/2 & 1 & 1/2 \\ 1/4 & 1/2 & 3/4 \end{bmatrix}, \qquad v = \begin{bmatrix} 3 \\ 6 \\ 3 \end{bmatrix},$$

perform the following calculations *by hand*, showing all your work:

(a) Av

(b) $v^T A$

(c) $v^T A v$

(d) AB.

Is there any special relationship between A and B?

5. (1) Perform the following computations by hand. Show the details of the calculations and identify the algorithm used.

(a) AB, where

$$A = \begin{bmatrix} 4 & -3 \\ 2 & -1 \end{bmatrix}, \qquad B = \begin{bmatrix} 5 & 3 \\ 1 & -2 \end{bmatrix}.$$

(b) AB, where

$$A = \begin{bmatrix} 5 & 1 & 4 & 0 \\ -3 & 0 & 3 & -5 \end{bmatrix}, \qquad B = \begin{bmatrix} 3 & 4 \\ -1 & 0 \\ 0 & -3 \\ 3 & -1 \end{bmatrix}.$$

(c) BA, where A and B are the same as in part (b).

33. (2+) Use Algorithm 7.5 and Figure 7.8 to prove that $AI = A$.

34. (2−) Carry out an expansion by minors to prove Equation (7.29).

35. (2−) Carry out an expansion by minors to prove Equation (7.30).

36. (2) Use the prod function to write a one-line expression for computing det(A) when A is tridiagonal or diagonal. How does the number of flops of this approach compare with that of the det function for tridiagonal and diagonal matrices?

37. (2+) In § 7.3.5, it is argued that computation of the determinant of A = triu(1000* ones(128,128)); will cause overflow. Explain the output of det(A) for this matrix. Is this a correct result? Does this matrix have an inverse?

38. (2+) Write a function that determines whether a matrix is strictly diagonally dominant. (Cf. Equation (7.32).) The input to the function should be a matrix, and the output should be one (true) if the matrix is strictly diagonally dominant and zero (false) if it is not. Test your function with the $(-1, 2, -1)$ tridiagonal matrix.

39. (3−) Given the matrices

$$A = \begin{bmatrix} \cos(\theta) & \sin(\theta) \\ -\sin(\theta) & \cos(\theta) \end{bmatrix}, \quad \text{and} \quad B = \begin{bmatrix} \cos(\theta) & \sin(\theta) \\ \sin(\theta) & -\cos(\theta) \end{bmatrix},$$

(a) compute (by hand) $A^T A$ and $B^T B$. What kind of matrices are A and B?

(b) for $\theta = \pi/4$ and $u = [1, 0]$, $u = [1, 1]$, $u = [0, 1]$, compute Au and Bu. What is the geometrical significance of these products? (*Hint:* Draw these vectors in the (x, y)-plane with tails at $(0, 0)$ and tips at (u_1, u_2). Add the line through $(0, 0)$ and $(x, y) = (\cos(\theta/2), \sin(\theta/2))$.) The myArrow function in the util directory of the NMM toolbox can help automate the drawing.

40. (2) Prove (by direct calculation) that the r, s, t, and u vectors defined in § 7.4.7 are both orthogonal and normal.

41. (2) If Q is orthonormal, Qx preserves the L_2 norm of x:

$$\|Qx\|_2 = \left[(Qx)^T(Qx)\right]^{1/2} = \left[(x^T Q^T)(Qx)\right]^{1/2} = \left[x^T(Q^T Q)x\right]^{1/2}$$
$$= \left[x^T x\right]^{1/2} = \|x\|_2.$$

Use MATLAB statements to experimentally verify that matrix Q defined in § 7.4.7 preserves the L_2 norm of four random x vectors.

8

Solving Systems of Equations

Solving systems of equations is one of the most widely automated computing tasks. This chapter focuses on setting up a system of equations, using the built-in capabilities of MATLAB to solve the system, and developing an understanding of the numerical complications that affect the reliability of the computed result. Figure 8.1 is an outline of the organization of the chapter. At the very least, you should study the first three sections: "Basic Concepts" through "Limitations on Numerical Solutions to $Ax = b$." The section entitled "Factorization Methods" provides a more detailed view into the computations used by MATLAB's built-in backslash operator. The final section on nonlinear systems should be studied as interest and time allows.

Example 8.1: A Model of a Pump Curve

Centrifugal pumps are common devices used to move liquid through piping systems. Figure 8.2 shows a typical *pump curve*, which relates the flow rate, q to the pressure head h. Different pump designs have different pump curves. In general, the flow rate a pump can deliver decreases as the opposing pressure head increases, although the shape of the curve varies with the physical design characteristics of the pump. In Figure 8.2, the pump curve shows an initial increase in head with flow rate near $q = 0$. This is observed for some types of pumps.

Topics Covered in This Chapter

1. **Basic Concepts**
   The matrix formulation of a system of linear systems is described, and the conditions necessary for obtaining a solution are identified.

2. **Gaussian Elimination**
   Solution to a system of n equations in n unknowns via **Gaussian elimination** is described. Manual calculations and the use of MATLAB's **backslash** operator for solving $n \times n$ systems are demonstrated.

3. **Limitations on Numerical Solutions to** $Ax = b$
   Guidelines and limitations for use of library routines in the solution of $Ax = b$ are presented. The characteristics of **ill conditioned** systems are defined. The computational effort to obtain a solution is discussed.

4. **Factorization Methods**
   The modern approach to solving linear systems involves factorization of the coefficient matrix. This section describes the **LU** and **Cholesky factorizations** and how these are used in MATLAB. At the end of this section, a more complete account of the algorithms used by the **backslash** operator is given.

5. **Nonlinear Systems of Equations**
   The formulation and solution of nonlinear systems of equations via **successive substitution** and **Newton's method** are discussed. A general implementation of Newton's method for solving nonlinear systems is provided.

Figure 8.1　Primary topics discussed in Chapter 8.

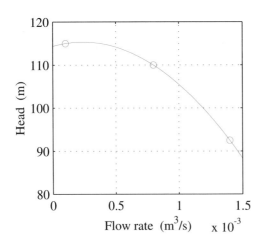

Figure 8.2　Typical performance curve for a centrifugal pump.

Selecting a pump for a particular piping system involves finding the intersection of the pump curve, $h_{pump}(q)$, with the *system curve*, $h_{sys}(q)$, which describes how the pressure drop in the system increases as the flow rate through the system increases. Pump manufacturers supply pump curves in graphical or tabular form. To automate design calculations, it is advantageous to have a formula for the pump curve. The $h(q)$ curve shown in Figure 8.2 appears to be roughly parabolic, so it is reasonable to seek a relationship of the form

$$h = c_1 q^2 + c_2 q + c_3.$$

Three convenient (q, h) data points are $(1 \times 10^{-4}, 115)$, $(8 \times 10^{-4}, 110)$, and $(1.4 \times 10^{-3}, 92.5)$. These points are shown as open circles in Figure 8.2. Substituting the (q, h) pairs into the preceding equation results in three equations for the unknown c_i:

$$
\begin{aligned}
115 &= \quad 1 \times 10^{-8}\, c_1 + \quad 1 \times 10^{-4}\, c_2 + c_3, \\
110 &= \quad 64 \times 10^{-8}\, c_1 + \quad 8 \times 10^{-4}\, c_2 + c_3, \\
92.5 &= 196 \times 10^{-8}\, c_1 + 14 \times 10^{-4}\, c_2 + c_3,
\end{aligned}
$$

which can be written in matrix form as

$$
\begin{bmatrix}
1 \times 10^{-8} & 1 \times 10^{-4} & 1 \\
64 \times 10^{-8} & 8 \times 10^{-4} & 1 \\
196 \times 10^{-8} & 14 \times 10^{-4} & 1
\end{bmatrix}
\begin{bmatrix} c_1 \\ c_2 \\ c_3 \end{bmatrix}
=
\begin{bmatrix} 115 \\ 110 \\ 92.5 \end{bmatrix}.
$$

Using more compact symbolic notation the matrix equation is $Ax = b$, where

$$
A = \begin{bmatrix}
1 \times 10^{-8} & 1 \times 10^{-4} & 1 \\
64 \times 10^{-8} & 8 \times 10^{-4} & 1 \\
196 \times 10^{-8} & 14 \times 10^{-4} & 1
\end{bmatrix}, \qquad
x = \begin{bmatrix} c_1 \\ c_2 \\ c_3 \end{bmatrix}, \qquad
b = \begin{bmatrix} 115 \\ 110 \\ 92.5 \end{bmatrix}.
$$

Once the equations are put into matrix form, the system is easily solved with the MATLAB functions presented in this chapter.

8.1 BASIC CONCEPTS

Before using a computer to automate the solution of linear systems, it is important to understand basic principles involved. In this section, the matrix formulation of a system of equations is introduced, and the requirements for obtaining a meaningful solution are described.

8.1.1 Matrix Formulation

To solve a system of linear equations with a numerical algorithm, the equations are first put into a standard form. In this chapter, the generic system of equations is written

$$Ax = b, \tag{8.1}$$

Identify Unknowns   In the analysis of this system, the power dissipation of the transistor Q_c and the ambient temperature T_a are known. The resistances can be computed from knowledge of the material properties, physical dimensions, and empirical correlations for heat flows in different physical configurations. (See, for example, F.P. Incropera, and D.P. Dewitt, *Fundamentals of Heat and Mass Transfer*, 4th edition, 1996, John Wiley & Sons, New York.) Thus, Q_c, T_a, and all the R_i are known. The unknowns are Q_1, Q_2, Q_3, Q_4, T_c, T_p, and T_w. Corresponding to Equation (8.1), we have

$$x = \begin{bmatrix} Q_1, & Q_2, & Q_3, & Q_4, & T_c, & T_p, & T_w \end{bmatrix}^T .$$

Since there are seven equations in seven unknowns, we have a reasonable expectation that a solution for the unknowns in x can be found.

Isolate the Unknowns   The preceding set of equations can be rearranged as

$$R_1 Q_1 - T_c + T_p = 0,$$

$$R_2 Q_2 - T_p + T_w = 0,$$

$$R_3 Q_3 - T_c = -T_a,$$

$$R_4 Q_4 - T_p = -T_a,$$

$$R_5 Q_2 - T_w = -T_a,$$

$$Q_1 + Q_3 = Q_c,$$

$$Q_1 - Q_2 - Q_4 = 0.$$

Note that the unknown elements of x appear on the left-hand side of each equation and that the known values appear either as multipliers of the unkowns or as values on the right-hand side of each equation.

Write in Matrix Form   The matrix form of the preceding system of equations is

$$\begin{bmatrix} R_1 & 0 & 0 & 0 & -1 & 1 & 0 \\ 0 & R_2 & 0 & 0 & 0 & -1 & 1 \\ 0 & 0 & R_3 & 0 & -1 & 0 & 0 \\ 0 & 0 & 0 & R_4 & 0 & -1 & 0 \\ 0 & R_5 & 0 & 0 & 0 & 0 & -1 \\ 1 & 0 & 1 & 0 & 0 & 0 & 0 \\ 1 & -1 & 0 & -1 & 0 & 0 & 0 \end{bmatrix} \begin{bmatrix} Q_1 \\ Q_2 \\ Q_3 \\ Q_4 \\ T_c \\ T_p \\ T_w \end{bmatrix} = \begin{bmatrix} 0 \\ 0 \\ -T_a \\ -T_a \\ -T_a \\ Q_c \\ 0 \end{bmatrix} . \qquad (8.2)$$

Given values of T_a, Q_c, and the R_i, we can compute the heat flows and temperatures by solving this system of seven equations in seven unknowns.

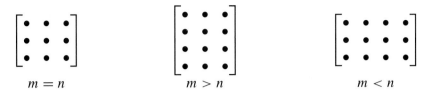

$$m = n \qquad\qquad\qquad m > n \qquad\qquad\qquad m < n$$

| Solving $Ax = b$ for n unknowns related by n equations | Overdetermined systems (e.g., least-squares problems) | Underdetermined systems (e.g., optimization) |

Figure 8.4   Shapes and applications of matrices with m rows and n columns. Each • represents an element of the matrix.

8.1.2 Requirements for a Solution

The nature of the solution to Equation (8.1) depends on the shape of A, whether or not b is in the column space of A, and whether or not the columns of A are linearly independent. Refer to § 7.3 beginning on page 334 for a discussion of the background material underlying the ideas presented here.

In general, a matrix will have m rows and n columns. Each row of the matrix corresponds to the left-hand side of a linear equation, and each column corresponds to an element in x. The matrix equation $Ax = b$, where A is $m \times n$, describes a system of m equations in n unknowns. Figure 8.4 depicts three types of matrix shapes based on the relative values of m and n. A common situation (many people consider this the only situation) involving linear systems of equation is when there are n equations in n unknowns. When $m > n$, there are more equations than unknowns, and the system is said to be overdetermined. Overdetermined systems are usually solved by the method of least squares. A common application is to fit a set of m (x, y) data pairs to an equation involving n coefficients. (See Chapter 9.) When $m < n$, there are fewer equations than unknowns, and the system is said to be underdetermined. An underdetermined system may have no solution or an infinite number of solutions. A typical application of underdetermined systems is numerical optimization. (See [28, 72].)

Consistency   The elements of the vector x in Equation (8.1) are the coefficients in the linear combination of the columns of A that yield the vector b; that is,

$$Ax = b \iff x_1 \begin{bmatrix} a_{11} \\ a_{21} \\ \vdots \\ a_{m1} \end{bmatrix} + x_2 \begin{bmatrix} a_{12} \\ a_{22} \\ \vdots \\ a_{m2} \end{bmatrix} + \cdots + x_n \begin{bmatrix} a_{1n} \\ a_{2n} \\ \vdots \\ a_{mn} \end{bmatrix} = \begin{bmatrix} b_1 \\ b_2 \\ \vdots \\ b_m \end{bmatrix}. \qquad (8.3)$$

The existence of a solution x to Equation (8.1) requires that the linear combination in Equation (8.3) be possible. Using the language of vector spaces (cf. § 7.3.2), a solution to Equation (8.1) exists only if b lies in the column space of A. Such a system (both A and b) is said to be *consistent*.[1] If b does not lie in the column space of A, then no combination of the column vectors of A exists that will yield vector b. Such a system is said to be *inconsistent*. Inconsistent systems have practical applications, as is demonstrated in Example 8.3 and throughout Chapter 9. When A is $n \times n$, the requirement of consistency is guaranteed if A is nonsingular, as defined below.

Consistency of A and b can be concisely expressed by forming the *augmented matrix* $\tilde{A}$ from the columns of A and the vector b:

$$\tilde{A} = \left[\begin{array}{cccccc|c} a_{11} & a_{12} & a_{13} & \cdots & a_{1n} & b_1 \\ a_{21} & a_{22} & a_{23} & \cdots & a_{2n} & b_2 \\ a_{31} & a_{32} & a_{33} & & a_{3n} & b_3 \\ \vdots & \vdots & & \ddots & \vdots & \vdots \\ a_{m1} & a_{m2} & a_{m3} & \cdots & a_{mn} & b_m \end{array}\right].$$

A and b are consistent if and only if $\tilde{A}$ and A have the same rank. When $\tilde{A}$ and A have the same rank, the column vectors of $\tilde{A}$ are linearly dependent, and the b vector lies in the subspace spanned by the columns of A.

Example 8.3: An Inconsistent System from Data Fitting.

Suppose that an experiment yielded the following measurements for $y = f(x)$:

x	1	2	3
y	2	1	0.5

These data are plotted in Figure 8.5. The plot reveals that the three data points are nearly, but not exactly, collinear. A practical *model* for the experimental results might be

$$y = \alpha x + \beta,$$

which is the equation of a line. Substituting the data into the model equation and writing the resulting three equations in matrix form gives

$$\begin{bmatrix} 1 & 1 \\ 2 & 1 \\ 3 & 1 \end{bmatrix} \begin{bmatrix} \alpha \\ \beta \end{bmatrix} = \begin{bmatrix} 2 \\ 1 \\ 0.5 \end{bmatrix}.$$

The columns of the matrix are linearly independent, but there are more equations than unknowns. Is it possible to find an exact solution to this system? The answer is determined by whether the coefficient matrix and right-hand-side vector are consistent.

---

[1] Some authors (e.g., [28]) use the term *compatible*.

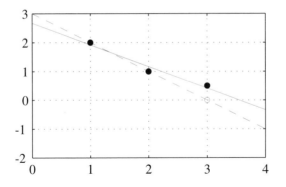

Figure 8.5   An inconsistent system arising from fitting three data points (solid circles) to a line. The system is inconsistent, because the three noncolinear points cannot be described by a linear function of two parameters. A least-squares solution (solid line) to the inconsistent system provides a compromise. If the value of y_3 is changed from 0.5 (solid circle) to 0.0 (open circle), the three data points lie along the dashed line. The points on the dashed line correspond to a consistent system involving three equations and two unknowns.

```
>> A = [1 1; 2 1; 3 1];   b = [2; 1; 0.5];
>> rank(A)
ans =
     2

>> rank([A b])
ans =
     3
```

Since rank(A) < rank([$A\ b$]), the b vector does not lie in the column space of A. An exact solution for α and β, therefore, is not possible. This is also evident from the plot in Figure 8.5. Since the data do not lie along a line, it is impossible to find a single pair of slope and intercept values that satisfy the model equation for all three data points. It is possible to find a least-squares solution for α and β such that the line comes close to passing through the given data. Least-squares solutions are described in Chapter 9.

Now consider the results of a second experiment in which the measured y value for the third data point turns out to be zero instead of 0.5, and all other measured values of x and y are the same as in the first experiment. The system of equations for α and β becomes

$$\begin{bmatrix} 1 & 1 \\ 2 & 1 \\ 3 & 1 \end{bmatrix} \begin{bmatrix} \alpha \\ \beta \end{bmatrix} = \begin{bmatrix} 2 \\ 1 \\ 0 \end{bmatrix}.$$

The consistency test shows that this system does have an exact solution:

without a separate numerical procedure for computing A^{-1}. The formal solution, therefore, is a mathematical statement, not a method for solving the system of equations.

Even if A^{-1} is available (or a routine exists for computing it), solving $Ax = b$ by evaluating $x = A^{-1}b$ is considered poor practice. It takes fewer floating-point operations to solve $Ax = b$ by Gaussian elimination than to compute A^{-1} and *then* multiply it with b. Using Gaussian elimination not only saves computer time (which will not be important for small systems), it produces a result with less roundoff error, since fewer operations are involved. Equation (8.4) is best thought of as a shorthand for "solve $Ax = b$ for x" with an appropriate method. The matrix inverse, like the determinant (see § 7.3.5) and rank(A), is more of a conceptual device than a computational tool.

The existence of A^{-1} (whether or not it is actually computed) is important in determining whether an exact solution to $Ax = b$ can be found. If A^{-1} exists, then A is said to be *invertible*, or *nonsingular*. If A^{-1} does not exist, then A is said to be *noninvertible*, or *singular*.

Summary   The characteristics of the solution to Equation (8.1) are determined by the consistency of the system and rank(A). Consistency determines whether a solution is possible. The rank of A determines whether a solution, if it exists, is unique. For the system $Ax = b$, where A is $m \times n$, the implications of consistency and rank are as follows:

- If rank(A) $= n$ and the system is *consistent*, a unique solution exists.
- If rank(A) $= n$ and the system is *inconsistent*, no solution exists.
- If rank(A) $< n$ and the system is consistent, an infinite number of solutions exist.

For an $n \times n$ system, rank(A) $= n$ automatically guarantees that the system is consistent. The following conditions are equivalent for a $n \times n$ matrix, A:

- The columns of A are linearly independent.
- The rows of A are linearly independent.
- rank(A) $= n$.
- det(A) $\neq 0$.
- A^{-1} exists.
- The solution to $Ax = b$ exists and is unique.

Example 8.4: Geometric Interpretation of Singularity

Consider the intersection of two lines in the (x, y)-plane. The equations of these lines form a 2×2 system of equations. A specific example (in slope-intercept form) is the system

$$y = -2x + 6,$$

$$y = \frac{1}{2}x + 1.$$

Since the slopes are different, the lines intersect at one point. Rewriting the equations in $Ax = b$ form gives

$$\begin{bmatrix} 2 & 1 \\ -1/2 & 1 \end{bmatrix} \begin{bmatrix} x_1 \\ x_2 \end{bmatrix} = \begin{bmatrix} 6 \\ 1 \end{bmatrix}, \tag{8.5}$$

where $x_1 = x$ and $x_2 = y$. The solution to this system is the vector $(x_1, x_2)^T = (2, 2)^T$, which contains the coordinates of the intersection of the two lines. The intersection is the solution, because it is the only point (vector of values) that satisfies both equations.

A 2×2 system allows easy geometric interpretation of the existence, nonexistence, or multiplicity of a solution. Different situations are demonstrated by changing elements in the coefficient matrix and right-hand-side vector of Equation (8.5). The possible outcomes are depicted in Figure 8.6. The upper left corner of Figure 8.6 shows the solution to Equation (8.5). The two lines intersect at a distinct point, so that the solution is clearly defined. The system is consistent, and the A matrix is nonsingular.

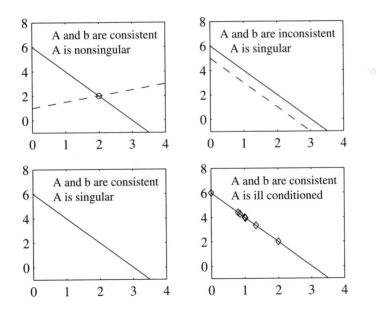

Figure 8.6   Solution scenarios for a 2×2 system of equations. In the upper left plot, the unique solution is indicated by the open circle at the intersection of the two lines. In the lower right plot, multiple solutions are indicated by diamonds. Each diamond corresponds to a different value of δ in Equation (8.6).

The upper right corner of Figure 8.6 shows the two lines defined by the system

$$\begin{bmatrix} 2 & 1 \\ 2 & 1 \end{bmatrix} \begin{bmatrix} x_1 \\ x_2 \end{bmatrix} = \begin{bmatrix} 6 \\ 5 \end{bmatrix}.$$

The lines are parallel, so there is no solution to the system. The rows of the coefficient matrix are linearly dependent, and the matrix is singular. The column space of the coefficient matrix is the line $x_2 = x_1$. The system is inconsistent, because the right-hand-side vector $[6, 5]^T$ does not lie on that line.

A singular coefficient matrix leads to an infinite number of solutions if the system (*A and b*) is consistent. For a 2×2 system this situation corresponds to coincident lines, as demonstrated by the plot in the lower left corner of Figure 8.6. The matrix form of the equations for this case is

$$\begin{bmatrix} 2 & 1 \\ 2 & 1 \end{bmatrix} \begin{bmatrix} x_1 \\ x_2 \end{bmatrix} = \begin{bmatrix} 6 \\ 6 \end{bmatrix}.$$

Note that it is easy to create the vector $[6, 6]^T$ from linear combinations of the columns of the coefficient matrix.

Finally, consider the effect of perturbations to element a_{21} of the preceding coefficient matrix and element b_2 of the right-hand-side vector:

$$\begin{bmatrix} 2 & 1 \\ 2 + \delta & 1 \end{bmatrix} \begin{bmatrix} x_1 \\ x_2 \end{bmatrix} = \begin{bmatrix} 6 \\ 6 + \delta \end{bmatrix}. \tag{8.6}$$

The solutions obtained from the vector of δ values, where $\delta = \texttt{logspace}(-16, -8)$, are shown in the lower right plot of Figure 8.6. The solutions, each one corresponding to a different value of δ and indicated by a diamond, fall along the line $x_2 = -2x_1 + 6$. Although the perturbations are small relative to the absolute values of a_{21} and b_2, the changes in the solution are quite large. This is characteristic behavior of an *ill conditioned* matrix: Small changes in inputs (the coefficient matrix and right-hand-side vector) can cause large changes in the result (the solution vector) for an ill conditioned system. The matter of conditioning is taken up in § 8.3.2. Variations on this ill conditioned system are explored in Exercise 15.

Example 8.5: Model of a Wheatstone Bridge

A Wheatstone bridge is an electrical circuit used to amplify and measure the signal from a transducer. One of the many configurations of wheatstone bridges is shown in Figure 8.7. An applied voltage V_{in} creates current flows through the resistor network. Resistor R_2 is part of a transducer circuit (not shown), so that the value of R_2 changes in response to some environmental conditions (e.g., temperature or strain). By choosing the values of the other resistors in the bridge, it is possible to make voltage measurements V_{out} that are sensitive to changes in the value of R_2.

An analysis of the bridge circuit yields a system of linear equations. The steps identified in § 8.1.1 will be used to obtain these equations in matrix form. Following these steps initially leads to a singular coefficient matrix. The reason for the singular matrix is explained, and the remedy is identified.

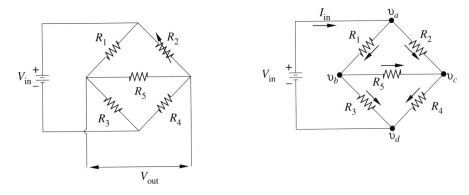

Figure 8.7   Circuit diagram (left), and nodal voltage definitions (right)
for a Wheatstone bridge.

Write Equations in Natural Form   The bridge can be analyzed by applying
Kirchhoff's voltage law (the sum of voltages around a loop is zero) and Kirchhoff's current
law (the sum of currents into a node is zero). In the right-hand-side of Figure 8.7, each
node of the circuit is labeled with a voltage. Between each node is an arrow indicating an
assumed direction of current flow.[3] The current flowing through each of the five resistors
is

$$i_1 = \frac{v_a - v_b}{R_1}, \quad i_2 = \frac{v_a - v_c}{R_2}, \quad i_3 = \frac{v_b - v_d}{R_3}, \quad i_4 = \frac{v_c - v_d}{R_4}, \quad i_5 = \frac{v_b - v_c}{R_5}.$$

Applying Kirchhoff's current law for the current flowing into each of the four nodes v_a,
v_b, v_c, and v_d gives

$$I_{in} - \frac{v_a - v_b}{R_1} - \frac{v_a - v_c}{R_2} = 0, \tag{8.7}$$

$$\frac{v_a - v_b}{R_1} - \frac{v_b - v_c}{R_5} - \frac{v_b - v_d}{R_3} = 0, \tag{8.8}$$

$$\frac{v_a - v_c}{R_2} + \frac{v_b - v_c}{R_5} - \frac{v_c - v_d}{R_4} = 0, \tag{8.9}$$

$$\frac{v_b - v_d}{R_3} + \frac{v_c - v_d}{R_4} - I_{in} = 0. \tag{8.10}$$

Identify Unknowns   The unknowns in this system are the four nodal voltages
v_a, v_b, v_c, and v_d and the supply current I_{in}. Since there are only four equations for the five
unknowns, more information about the circuit system needs to be applied.

---

[3]The assigned directions of current flows in Figure 8.7 do not have to be the actual direction of
the current flow. A direction is assumed, and the basic physical law is applied, based on the assumed
direction. If the actual direction of current flow is opposite to the assumed direction, the solution to
the system of equations will give a negative current.

The unknown I_{in} can be eliminated by adding Equations (8.7) and (8.10) to get

$$\frac{v_b - v_d}{R_3} + \frac{v_c - v_d}{R_4} - \frac{v_a - v_b}{R_1} - \frac{v_a - v_c}{R_2} = 0. \tag{8.11}$$

An additional equation is obtained by noting that the difference between v_a and v_d is determined by the supply V_{in}:

$$v_a = v_d + V_{\text{in}}. \tag{8.12}$$

Substituting Equation (8.12) into Equations (8.11), (8.8), and (8.9) gives

$$\frac{v_b - v_d}{R_3} + \frac{v_c - v_d}{R_4} - \frac{v_d + V_{\text{in}} - v_b}{R_1} - \frac{v_d + V_{\text{in}} - v_c}{R_2} = 0, \tag{8.13}$$

$$\frac{v_d + V_{\text{in}} - v_b}{R_1} - \frac{v_b - v_c}{R_5} - \frac{v_b - v_d}{R_3} = 0, \tag{8.14}$$

$$\frac{v_d + V_{\text{in}} - v_c}{R_2} + \frac{v_b - v_c}{R_5} - \frac{v_c - v_d}{R_4} = 0. \tag{8.15}$$

This is a system of three equations for the three unknowns (v_b, v_c, and v_d). The vector of unknowns is $x = (v_b, v_c, v_d)^T$.

Isolate the Unknowns   Rearranging Equations (8.13)–(8.15) to isolate v_b, v_c, and v_d produces

$$\left[\frac{1}{R_1} + \frac{1}{R_3} + \frac{1}{R_5}\right] v_b - \frac{1}{R_5} v_c - \left[\frac{1}{R_1} + \frac{1}{R_3}\right] v_d = \frac{1}{R_1} V_{\text{in}}, \tag{8.16}$$

$$-\frac{1}{R_5} v_b + \left[\frac{1}{R_2} + \frac{1}{R_4} + \frac{1}{R_5}\right] v_c - \left[\frac{1}{R_2} + \frac{1}{R_4}\right] v_d = \frac{1}{R_2} V_{\text{in}}, \tag{8.17}$$

$$\left[\frac{1}{R_1} + \frac{1}{R_3}\right] v_b + \left[\frac{1}{R_2} + \frac{1}{R_4}\right] v_c - \left[\frac{1}{R_1} + \frac{1}{R_2} + \frac{1}{R_3} + \frac{1}{R_4}\right] v_d = \left[\frac{1}{R_1} + \frac{1}{R_2}\right] V_{\text{in}}. \tag{8.18}$$

Write in Matrix Form   The matrix form of the preceding equation is

$$\begin{bmatrix} \left[\frac{1}{R_1} + \frac{1}{R_3} + \frac{1}{R_5}\right] & -\frac{1}{R_5} & -\left[\frac{1}{R_1} + \frac{1}{R_3}\right] \\ -\frac{1}{R_5} & \left[\frac{1}{R_2} + \frac{1}{R_4} + \frac{1}{R_5}\right] & -\left[\frac{1}{R_2} + \frac{1}{R_4}\right] \\ \left[\frac{1}{R_1} + \frac{1}{R_3}\right] & \left[\frac{1}{R_2} + \frac{1}{R_4}\right] & -\left[\frac{1}{R_1} + \frac{1}{R_2} + \frac{1}{R_3} + \frac{1}{R_4}\right] \end{bmatrix} \begin{bmatrix} v_b \\ v_c \\ v_d \end{bmatrix} = \begin{bmatrix} \frac{1}{R_1} \\ \frac{1}{R_2} \\ \frac{1}{R_1} + \frac{1}{R_2} \end{bmatrix} V_{\text{in}}.$$

This equation does not have a unique solution, because the 3×3 matrix on the left-hand side is singular. The third column can be obtained by adding together the first two columns, and the third row is equal to the sum of the first two rows. The singularity is *not* due to an error in the formulation. Rather, it is the direct consequence of a physical fact. The absolute level of v_b, v_c, and v_d can be adjusted by an arbitrary additive constant, and the bridge will still function. In practice, the floating potential of the bridge will likely cause data acquisition problems that can be solved by attaching a ground cable to a convenient point on the bridge circuit. If the ground cable is attached at node v_d, then the potential at v_d is zero. Mathematically, we can set v_d to zero by eliminating the third column and third row of the matrix to get

$$
\begin{bmatrix} \left[\frac{1}{R_1} + \frac{1}{R_3} + \frac{1}{R_5} \right] & -\frac{1}{R_5} \\ -\frac{1}{R_5} & \left[\frac{1}{R_2} + \frac{1}{R_4} + \frac{1}{R_5} \right] \end{bmatrix} \begin{bmatrix} v_b \\ v_c \end{bmatrix} = \begin{bmatrix} \frac{1}{R_1} \\ \frac{1}{R_2} \end{bmatrix} V_{\text{in}}. \tag{8.19}
$$

This system is explored further in Exercises 24 through 26 at the end of the chapter.

The important point of this example is that the system of equations arising from the physical model may turn out to be singular. In such a situation, some additional information about the physical problem must be applied.

8.2 GAUSSIAN ELIMINATION

Gaussian[4] elimination with backward substitution is a fundamental procedure for solving systems of linear equations. Gaussian elimination is usually applied to square (i.e., $n \times n$) matrices, although Strang [71, 72] shows how elimination can be used to reveal the properties of rectangular ($m \times n$) matrices. Unless explicitly noted otherwise, *all coefficient matrices will be square for the rest of this chapter.*

The solution of a linear system of equations with Gaussian elimination is achieved in two phases. The first phase—elimination—uses row operations to convert a matrix into an equivalent upper triangular matrix. Elimination takes the most of the effort, and it is the phase most susceptible to corruption by roundoff errors. The second phase obtains the solution to the upper triangular system by backward substitution. Before dealing with the more complicated process of elimination, we will look at why it is advantageous to convert a system to triangular form in the first place.

8.2.1 Solving Diagonal Systems

Diagonal systems are trivial to solve because they essentially state the solution. For example, the system $Ax = b$, where

---

[4]The procedure is attributed to Carl Friedrick Gauss (1777–1855), one of the most influential mathematicians of all time. Gauss developed elimination as a way to study the precision of the least-squares problem for data fitting. See Stewart [67] for a brief history of Gauss's least-squares work and the elimination procedure he developed.

$$\tilde{A}_{(2)} = \left[\begin{array}{ccc|c} -3 & 2 & -1 & -1 \\ 0 & -2 & 5 & -9 \\ 0 & 0 & -2 & 2 \end{array}\right].$$

Note that this second elimination step does not destroy the zeros recently created in the first column. The coefficient matrix is now in triangular form. The solution to the system is obtained by backward substitution:

$$x_3 = \frac{2}{-2} = -1, \quad x_2 = \frac{1}{-2}(-9 - 5x_3) = 2, \quad x_1 = \frac{1}{-3}(-1 - 2x_2 + x_3) = 2.$$

Cartoon Version To develop an elimination algorithm for arbitrary square matrices, the row operations used in the preceding examples need to be expressed with the (i, j) indices of elements in an augmented matrix. Before trying to write down the formula for row-by-row elimination, consider the visual pattern that is created during execution of the (as yet unspecified) algorithm. Figure 8.8 shows a cartoon version of the elimination process for a 4×4 system of equations. The elements of the augmented matrix in the figure are designated with x's. This is a notational convenience; the elements have arbitrary, but not necessarily equal, values.

At each stage of elimination, a *pivot row* in the augmented system is used to eliminate the first nonzero element in the rows below it. The element on the main diagonal of the pivot row is called the *pivot element*, or simply the *pivot*. In

$$\begin{bmatrix} \boxed{x} & x & x & x & x \\ 0 & x' & x' & x' & x' \\ x & x & x & x & x \\ x & x & x & x & x \end{bmatrix} \longrightarrow \begin{bmatrix} \boxed{x} & x & x & x & x \\ 0 & x' & x' & x' & x' \\ 0 & x' & x' & x' & x' \\ x & x & x & x & x \end{bmatrix} \longrightarrow \begin{bmatrix} \boxed{x} & x & x & x & x \\ 0 & x' & x' & x' & x' \\ 0 & x' & x' & x' & x' \\ 0 & x' & x' & x' & x' \end{bmatrix}$$

$$\begin{bmatrix} x & x & x & x & x \\ 0 & \boxed{x'} & x' & x' & x' \\ 0 & 0 & x'' & x'' & x'' \\ 0 & x' & x' & x' & x' \end{bmatrix} \longrightarrow \begin{bmatrix} x & x & x & x & x \\ 0 & \boxed{x'} & x' & x' & x' \\ 0 & 0 & x'' & x'' & x'' \\ 0 & 0 & x'' & x'' & x'' \end{bmatrix}$$

$$\begin{bmatrix} x & x & x & x & x \\ 0 & x' & x' & x' & x' \\ 0 & 0 & \boxed{x''} & x'' & x'' \\ 0 & 0 & 0 & x''' & x''' \end{bmatrix}$$

Figure 8.8 Cartoon version of Gaussian elimination for a 4×4 system of equations. Nonzero elements of the augmented system are denoted by x, but the different x values are necessarily not equal. Primes indicate the number of times an element has been modified. The boxed element is the *pivot* at each stage of elimination.

Figure 8.8, the pivot element at each stage of elimination is enclosed in a box. The operations that introduce a zero in the column under the pivot element also change all other elements in the row containing the newly created zero. These changes are indicated by primes. Elements in lower rows (greater i index) are modified more than elements in higher rows, and, hence, at the end of elimination, these elements have a larger number of primes.

The Algorithm   The features of elimination identified in the preceding sections can now be put together into a computational algorithm. From the hand-calculated version, we have the idea that multiples of the pivot row are subtracted from other rows. From the cartoon version, we have a visual representation of the order of the calculations.

We develop the algorithm using the stepwise refinement strategy described in Chapter 4. Stepwise refinement begins with a short (one-sentence) verbal description of the task to be performed. This high-level description is then divided into a sequence of smaller tasks. Each of the smaller tasks is recursively divided until only simple tasks with straightforward implementations remain. To develop Gaussian elimination, we will use a variation on this idea. At each level of refinement, a new, nested loop structure is revealed. Using stepwise refinement allows the loop indices for each stage of the calculations to be clearly exposed. The highest-level description of the elimination process is

Convert an augmented matrix to upper triangular form.

Since the augmented matrix has n rows and $n + 1$ columns, the end result will be a rectangular version of a triangular matrix, namely, the first n columns are triangular.

The augmented matrix is converted to rectangular form by row operations. A scalar multiple of the pivot row is used to eliminate elements below the pivot element. The first row is used to zero the elements in rows 2 through n of the first column. The second row is used to zero elements in rows 3 through n of the second column, and so on. A high-level algorithmic statement of these row operations is

```
for i = 1 ... n − 1
    use pivot row i to zero elements in column i, for rows i + 1 to n
end
```

Elimination is complete when row $n - 1$ is used to zero the element in row n, column $n - 1$. Thus, row n is not used as a pivot row, and the outer loop is from $i = 1$ to $i = n - 1$.

$$\begin{bmatrix} 2 & 4 & -2 & -2 & -4 \\ 0 & 3 & 5 & -4 & 5 \\ 0 & 3 & 5 & -5 & 1 \\ 0 & 0 & 5 & -2 & 7 \end{bmatrix}.$$

To continue with the elimination, subtract (1 times) row 2 from row 3:

$$\begin{bmatrix} 2 & 4 & -2 & -2 & -4 \\ 0 & 3 & 5 & -4 & 5 \\ 0 & 0 & 0 & -1 & -4 \\ 0 & 0 & 5 & -2 & 7 \end{bmatrix}.$$

Another zero appears in the pivot position. Remedy this by swapping row 3 and row 4:

$$\begin{bmatrix} 2 & 4 & -2 & -2 & -4 \\ 0 & 3 & 5 & -4 & 5 \\ 0 & 0 & 5 & -2 & 7 \\ 0 & 0 & 0 & -1 & -4 \end{bmatrix}. \tag{8.22}$$

The system is now in triangular form and ready for backward substitution.

Row and Column Interchanges   We have shown that row interchanges can be used to avoid a zero pivot element. Column exchanges can also be performed, and both row *and* column exchanges can be performed. Any exchange must be done in a way that preserves the solution to the original system of equations. Row interchanges correspond to writing the original set of equations in a different order. Column interchanges correspond to reordering the unknowns in the solution vector.

To see how a column exchange is implemented, consider the situation for a 4×4 matrix. As shown in the following matrix, assume the first row has been used to eliminate all elements in the first column below a_{11}:

$$\begin{bmatrix} a_{11} & a_{12} & a_{13} & a_{14} \\ 0 & a'_{22} & a'_{23} & a'_{24} \\ 0 & a'_{32} & a'_{33} & a'_{34} \\ 0 & a'_{42} & a'_{43} & a'_{44} \end{bmatrix} \begin{bmatrix} x_1 \\ x_2 \\ x_3 \\ x_4 \end{bmatrix} \begin{bmatrix} b_1 \\ b'_2 \\ b'_3 \\ b'_4 \end{bmatrix}.$$

Suppose that in the process of eliminating a_{21}, we find that the value of a'_{22} turns out to be zero, or at least small enough that pivoting would be a good idea. Assume that a'_{24} is the most desirable pivot, so that an exchange between columns two and four is to be performed. The elements affected by this column exchange are shown in boxes:

$$\begin{bmatrix} a_{11} & a_{12} & a_{13} & a_{14} \\ 0 & a'_{22} & a'_{23} & a'_{24} \\ 0 & a'_{32} & a'_{33} & a'_{34} \\ 0 & a'_{42} & a'_{43} & a'_{44} \end{bmatrix} \begin{bmatrix} x_1 \\ x_2 \\ x_3 \\ x_4 \end{bmatrix} = \begin{bmatrix} b_1 \\ b'_2 \\ b'_3 \\ b'_4 \end{bmatrix}.$$

After the column exchange, the system of equations becomes

$$\begin{bmatrix} a_{11} & a_{14} & a_{13} & a_{12} \\ 0 & a'_{24} & a'_{23} & a'_{22} \\ 0 & a'_{34} & a'_{33} & a'_{32} \\ 0 & a'_{44} & a'_{43} & a'_{42} \end{bmatrix} \begin{bmatrix} x_1 \\ x_4 \\ x_3 \\ x_2 \end{bmatrix} \begin{bmatrix} b_1 \\ b'_2 \\ b'_3 \\ b'_4 \end{bmatrix}.$$

The columns of A and the entries in x are rearranged, while b is unaffected.

Column exchanges are more complicated to program than row exchanges. For most matrices that arise in practical physical problems, the row exchanges are sufficient to guarantee a successful forward elimination procedure. When both row exchanges and column exchanges are used, the strategy is known as *full pivoting*, or *complete pivoting*.

In the preceding examples, pivoting occurred when a pivot value equaled zero. Robust Gaussian elimination algorithms use a more aggressive pivoting strategy. Rather than waiting to encounter a pivot element that is exactly zero, it is always better to replace the pivot row with the row having the largest element in the pivot column. Example 8.6 shows why this is a good idea. Using this strategy the augmented matrix in Equation (8.21) will have a row exchange *before* the first elimination step. The first and third rows of the matrix are swapped to give

$$\tilde{A} = \begin{bmatrix} -3 & -3 & 8 & -2 & 7 \\ 1 & 2 & 4 & -3 & 5 \\ 2 & 4 & -2 & -2 & -4 \\ -1 & 1 & 6 & -3 & 7 \end{bmatrix}.$$

Elimination with the first row yields

$$\tilde{A} = \begin{bmatrix} -3 & -3 & 8 & -2 & 7 \\ 0 & 1 & 6\frac{2}{3} & -3\frac{2}{3} & 7\frac{1}{3} \\ 0 & 2 & 3\frac{1}{3} & -3\frac{1}{3} & \frac{2}{3} \\ 0 & 2 & 3\frac{1}{3} & -2\frac{1}{3} & 4\frac{2}{3} \end{bmatrix}.$$

Next, although the $\tilde{a}_{22}$ element is nonzero, the second and third rows are exchanged:

$$\tilde{A} = \begin{bmatrix} -3 & -3 & 8 & -2 & 7 \\ 0 & 2 & 3\frac{1}{3} & -3\frac{1}{3} & \frac{2}{3} \\ 0 & 1 & 6\frac{2}{3} & -3\frac{2}{3} & 7\frac{1}{3} \\ 0 & 2 & 3\frac{1}{3} & -2\frac{1}{3} & 4\frac{2}{3} \end{bmatrix}.$$

Continuing elimination with the second row as pivot gives

$$\tilde{A} = \begin{bmatrix} -3 & -3 & 8 & -2 & 7 \\ 0 & 2 & 3\frac{1}{3} & -3\frac{1}{3} & \frac{2}{3} \\ 0 & 0 & 5 & -2 & 7 \\ 0 & 0 & 0 & 1 & 4 \end{bmatrix}.$$

Use of the second row pivot fortuitously zeros the $\tilde{a}_{43}$ element, so no further elimination is necessary. Although the triangular system has different coefficients than Equation (8.22), the solution is the same.

Example 8.6: The Effect of Small Pivots

The preceding section demonstrates that a zero pivot element causes elimination to fail. This example shows that small pivots, not just zero pivots, cause errors when finite-precision arithmetic is used in elimination. The calculations presented here are from Gill et al. [28].

Consider solution to the system $Ax = b$ defined by the augmented matrix

$$\tilde{A} = \begin{bmatrix} 0.0001 & 0.5 & 0.5 \\ 0.4 & -0.3 & 0.1 \end{bmatrix}.$$

To make the effect of finite-precision obvious, each stage of the elimination and backward substitution is performed in four-digit arithmetic. The exact solution rounded to four significant figures is $x = [0.9999, 0.9998]^T$.

Since $\tilde{a}_{11} \neq 0$, it appears that no pivoting is necessary. To eliminate $\tilde{a}_{21}$, subtract $0.4/0.0001 = 4000$ times the first row from the second row. Note that there is no loss of precision in computing this multiplier. Using four-digit arithmetic, we see that the nonzero elements in the second row become

$$\tilde{a}_{22} = -0.3 - (4000)(0.5) = -2000, \qquad \tilde{a}_{23} = 0.1 - (4000)(0.5) = -2000,$$

so the augmented system is

$$\tilde{A} = \begin{bmatrix} 0.0001 & 0.5 & 0.5 \\ 0 & -2000 & -2000 \end{bmatrix}.$$

Backward substitution using four-digit arithmetic gives

$$x_2 = \frac{-2000}{-2000} = 1, \qquad x_1 = \frac{1}{0.0001}(0.5 - (0.5)(1)) = 0,$$

which is far from the exact solution.

The most significant contribution to the error occurs during the calculation of $\tilde{a}_{22}$ and $\tilde{a}_{23}$. The small pivot value, $\tilde{a}_{11} = 0.0001$, causes the multiplier to be large and the subtraction with four-digit arithmetic to loose *all* significant digits from the elements in the second row. The loss of precision in the elimination phase results in a system that has the same exact solution as a different augmented system:

$$\tilde{A}^* = \begin{bmatrix} 0.0001 & 0.5 & | & 0.5 \\ 0.4 & 0 & | & 0 \end{bmatrix}.$$

Systems $\tilde{A}$ and $\tilde{A}^*$ are very different, despite the small ($\sim 5 \times 10^{-5}$) perturbations in $\tilde{A}$ introduced during the elimination process. This situation can be remedied by using a row exchange to replace the small pivot.

Repeat the elimination calculations in four-digit arithmetic after using a row exchange to replace the 0.0001 pivot. The row exchange gives the augmented matrix

$$\tilde{A} = \begin{bmatrix} 0.4 & -0.3 & | & 0.1 \\ 0.0001 & 0.5 & | & 0.5 \end{bmatrix}.$$

To eliminate $\tilde{a}_{21}$, subtract $0.0001/0.4 = 2.500 \times 10^{-4}$ times the first row from the second row. Carrying out the four-digit arithmetic, we find that the nonzero elements in the second row become

$$\tilde{a}_{22} = 0.5 - (2.500 \times 10^{-4})(-0.3) = 0.5 - 7.5 \times 10^{-5} = 0.5000,$$

$$\tilde{a}_{23} = 0.5 - (2.500 \times 10^{-4})(0.1) = 0.5 - 7.5 \times 10^{-5} = 0.5000,$$

so that

$$\tilde{A} = \begin{bmatrix} 0.4 & -0.3 & | & 0.1 \\ 0.0 & 0.5 & | & 0.5 \end{bmatrix}.$$

Continuing with four-digit arithmetic for the backward substitution we get

$$x_2 = \frac{0.5}{0.5} = 1,$$

$$x_1 = \frac{1}{0.4}(0.1 + (0.3)(1)) = 1,$$

which is very close to the exact solution.

This example gives empirical evidence that smaller roundoff errors during elimination will occur if row exchanges are used *at each step* to select the largest available pivot.

In practice, Gaussian elimination codes use this strategy rather than pivoting only in the case where a pivot element is identically zero.

See Watkins [78, § 2.6] for an informal and lucid discussion of how small pivots systematically corrupt the elements of the triangular factors of A during elimination.

Implementation　　The following algorithm includes the pivoting strategy just outlined.

Algorithm 8.5　Gaussian Elimination with Partial Pivoting

Input: A, b
form $\tilde{A} = [A \quad b]$
for $i = 1 \ldots n - 1$
　find i_p such that $\max(|\tilde{a}_{i_p i}|) \geq \max(|\tilde{a}_{ki}|)$ for $k = i \ldots n$
　exchange row i_p with row i
　for $k = i + 1 \ldots n$
　　for $j = i \ldots n + 1$
　　　$\tilde{a}_{k,j} = \tilde{a}_{k,j} - (\tilde{a}_{k,i}/\tilde{a}_{i,i})\tilde{a}_{i,j}$
　　end
　end
end

The GEPivShow function in Listing 8.2 implements Algorithm 8.5. The pivot selection and row-exchange operations are performed by three compact MATLAB statements that need some explanation. The search for a good pivot is performed with the two-parameter form of the built-in max function:

```
[pivot,p] = max(abs(Ab(i:n,i)));
```

This returns the element with the largest absolute value (`pivot`) and the index of that element in the *column vector* `Ab(i:n,i)`. If the maximum absolute value is on the diagonal of the augmented matrix, then p = 1. The statement ip = p + i - 1 computes the true row index of the desired pivot value. The rows are swapped with the statement

```
Ab([i ip],:) = Ab([ip i],:);
```

After the pivot is selected and the rows are swapped, the algorithm continues exactly as in GEshow.

```
function x = GEPivShow(A,b,ptol)
% GEPivShow  Show steps in Gauss elimination with partial pivoting and
%            back substitution
%
% Synopsis:  x = GEPivShow(A,b)
%            x = GEPivShow(A,b,ptol)
%
% Input:     A,b = coefficient matrix and right hand side vector
%            ptol = (optional) tolerance for detection of zero pivot
%                   Default:  ptol = 50*eps
%
% Output:    x = solution vector, if solution exists

if nargin<3, ptol = 50*eps;  end
[m,n] = size(A);
if m~=n,  error('A matrix needs to be square');  end
nb = n+1;   Ab = [A b];    % Augmented system
fprintf('\nBegin forward elmination with Augmented system:\n');  disp(Ab);

% --- Elimination
for i = 1:n-1                        %  loop over pivot row
  [pivot,p] = max(abs(Ab(i:n,i)));   %  value and index of largest pivot
  ip = p + i - 1;                    %  p is index in subvector i:n
  if ip~=i                          %  ip is true row index of desired pivot
    fprintf('\nSwap rows %d and %d;  new pivot = %g\n',i,ip,Ab(ip,i));
    Ab([i ip],:) = Ab([ip i],:);    %  perform the swap
  end
  pivot = Ab(i,i);
  if abs(pivot)<ptol, error('zero pivot encountered after row exchange');  end
  for k = i+1:n            %  k = index of next row to be eliminated
    Ab(k,i:nb) = Ab(k,i:nb) - (Ab(k,i)/pivot)*Ab(i,i:nb);
  end
  fprintf('\nAfter elimination in column %d with pivot = %f\n',i,pivot);
  disp(Ab);
end

% --- Back substitution
x = zeros(n,1);             %  preallocate memory for and initialize x
x(n) = Ab(n,nb)/Ab(n,n);
for i=n-1:-1:1
  x(i) = (Ab(i,nb) - Ab(i,i+1:n)*x(i+1:n))/Ab(i,i);
end
```

Listing 8.2   The GEPivShow function solves a system with Gaussian elimination with partial pivoting and prints the results of each step of elimination.

except for the roundoff errors committed when the elements of A and b are first computed and stored in memory, the solution to $Ax = b$ is performed in exact arithmetic.

Consider, for example, a 2×2 system with $b = [1, 2/3]^T$. Since $2/3$ cannot be represented exactly as a base-2 floating-point value, the assignment

```
>> b = [ 1; 2/3 ]
b =
    1.0000
    0.6667
```

introduces a roundoff error in the value of b_2. One expects that the *exact* solutions to

$$Ax = \begin{bmatrix} 1 \\ 2/3 \end{bmatrix} \quad \text{and} \quad Ax = \begin{bmatrix} 1 \\ 0.6667 \end{bmatrix}$$

will be different. If A is *well-conditioned* the difference between the solutions will be negligible, whereas if A is *ill conditioned*, the difference will be large. By examining the influence of perturbations to A and b on the solution to $Ax = b$, the meanings of ill conditioned and well-conditioned can be made more precise. First consider perturbations to b.

Let A be a nonsingular matrix, and let δb be a vector that contains elements that are small compared with the elements in b. Let $x + \delta x_b$ be the *exact* solution to the perturbed system

$$A(x + \delta x_b) = b + \delta b. \tag{8.24}$$

The subscript b on δx_b is a reminder that the changes to x result from perturbations in b. Since x is the solution to $Ax = b$, subtract Ax from the left-hand side and b from the right-hand side of the preceding equation to get $A \, \delta x_b = \delta b$, or

$$\delta x_b = A^{-1} \delta b. \tag{8.25}$$

Intuitively, it seems that if δb is "small," or, more precisely, if

$$\frac{\|\delta b\|}{\|b\|} \ll 1,$$

then one would hope that

$$\frac{\|\delta x_b\|}{\|x\|} \ll 1.$$

As we shall soon see, a small $\|\delta x_b\|/\|x\|$ is not guaranteed.

Taking a suitable[8] norm of Equation (8.25) gives $\|\delta x_b\| = \|A^{-1}\,\delta b\|$. Applying the consistency requirement of matrix norms (cf. § 7.2.4) gives

$$\|\delta x_b\| \leq \|A^{-1}\|\|\delta b\|. \tag{8.26}$$

Similarly, $Ax = b$ gives $\|b\| = \|Ax\|$, and

$$\|b\| \leq \|A\|\|x\|. \tag{8.27}$$

Equations (8.26) and (8.27) involve scalars and thus can be manipulated with simple algebra. A simple rearrangement of Equation (8.27) yields

$$\frac{1}{\|x\|} \leq \frac{\|A\|}{\|b\|}. \tag{8.28}$$

Multiplying this equation by Equation (8.26) gives

$$\frac{\|\delta x_b\|}{\|x\|} \leq \|A\|\|A^{-1}\|\frac{\|\delta b\|}{\|b\|}. \tag{8.29}$$

This important result shows that a small $\|\delta b\|/\|b\|$ causes a small $\|\delta x_b\|/\|x\|$ *only if* the product $\|A\|\|A^{-1}\|$ is $\mathcal{O}(1)$. An ill conditioned A has $\|A\|\|A^{-1}\| \gg 1$.

Now, perform a similar analysis for the response of the solution to a perturbation δA of A. In this case, δA is a matrix having the same shape as A and for which $\|\delta A\|/\|A\|$ is small. Assume that both A and $A + \delta A$ are nonsingular and that $x + \delta x_A$ is the exact solution to

$$(A + \delta A)(x + \delta x_A) = b. \tag{8.30}$$

The preceding equation is linear, so

$$Ax + A\delta x_A + \delta A(x + \delta x_A) = b.$$

Canceling Ax on the left-hand side with b on the right-hand side and rearranging term gives

$$\delta x_A = -A^{-1}\delta A(x + \delta x_A).$$

Taking a suitable norm and applying the consistency requirement gives

$$\|\delta x_A\| = \|A^{-1}\delta A(x + \delta x_A)\|$$
$$\leq \|A^{-1}\|\ \|\delta A(x + \delta x_A)\|$$
$$\leq \|A^{-1}\|\ \|\delta A\|\ \|(x + \delta x_A)\|.$$

---

[8] Any p-norm, for example, will do.

A final rearrangement yields

$$\frac{\|\delta x_A\|}{\|x + \delta x_A\|} \le \|A\| \|A^{-1}\| \frac{\|\delta A\|}{\|A\|}. \tag{8.31}$$

For a given x, allowing δx_A to vary between zero and infinity shows that

$$0 \le \frac{\|\delta x_A\|}{\|x + \delta x_A\|} \le 1.$$

Thus, the left-hand side of Equation (8.31) indicates that δA will cause a small perturbation to x *only if* the factor $\|A\| \|A^{-1}\|$ is $\mathcal{O}(1)$.

A similar analysis allowing simultaneous perturbations to both A and b gives (see, for example, Datta [12] for a derivation)

$$\frac{\|\delta x\|}{\|x + \delta x\|} \le \frac{\|A\| \|A^{-1}\|}{1 - \|A\| \|A^{-1}\| \frac{\|\delta A\|}{\|A\|}} \left[\frac{\|\delta A\|}{\|A\|} + \frac{\|\delta b\|}{\|b\|} \right]. \tag{8.32}$$

Once again, the factor $\|A\| \|A^{-1}\|$ decides the sensitivity of the solution to perturbations in A and b.

Condition Number for Linear Systems   Analysis in the preceding section shows that the *condition number* defined as

$$\kappa(A) \equiv \|A\| \|A^{-1}\| \tag{8.33}$$

indicates the sensitivity of the solution to perturbations in A and b. The condition number can be measured with any p-norm. Typically, the 2-norm is used, although efficient routines for estimating the condition number are based on the 1-norm. The condition number is always in the range

$$1 \le \kappa(A) \le \infty,$$

regardless of the p-norm. The lower limit is attained for identity matrices (see Exercise 30), and $\kappa(A) = \infty$ if A is singular. As $\kappa(A) \to \infty$, the matrix becomes increasingly ill conditioned.

The solution to $Ax = b$ exists only if A is nonsingular, and *in exact arithmetic*, the distinction between singular and nonsingular is unambiguous. In contrast, in floating-point arithmetic, singularity is a matter of degree: the condition number is a measure of how close a matrix is to being *numerically* singular. The case of $\kappa(A) = \infty$ corresponds to a matrix that is singular in exact arithmetic.

Equations (8.29), (8.31), and (8.32) show that the solution grows increasingly sensitive to perturbations as $\kappa(A)$ increases. These perturbations may be introduced when the elements of A and b are stored in memory. A small change in any one of the coefficients might lead to a large change in the computed solution if $\kappa(A)$ is large. A more precise definition of "large" is deferred until § 8.3.5.

Readers should note that condition numbers can be derived for any numerical computation. The central idea is that a condition number reflects the sensitivity of the computation to perturbations in the input data. Another key idea is that the condition number is associated with a problem to be solved, not with the algorithm used in the solution. The numerical solution produced by *any algorithm* will be sensitive to the inputs if the problem is ill conditioned.

Example 8.8: Conditioning of a Simple Matrix

Consider the matrix used at the end of Example 8.4

$$A = \begin{bmatrix} 2 & 1 \\ 2+\delta & 1 \end{bmatrix},$$

where δ is a small parameter. If $\delta = 0$, then A is singular. (Why?) It is easy to verify that

$$A^{-1} = \frac{1}{\delta} \begin{bmatrix} -1 & 1 \\ 2+\delta & -2 \end{bmatrix}$$

and

$$\|A\|_1 = 4 + \delta, \qquad \|A^{-1}\|_1 = \frac{3}{\delta} + 1,$$

so that

$$\kappa_1(A) = \frac{12}{\delta} + 7 + \delta.$$

Therefore, as $\delta \to 0$, $\kappa_1(A) \to \infty$.

Example 8.9: A Well-Conditioned System and an Ill-Conditioned System

This example demonstrates how the solutions of well-conditioned and ill-conditioned systems of equations respond to perturbations in the right-hand-side vector. The condition number of the matrices is computed with the built-in cond command, which is described in § 8.3.6.

First, consider a 2×2 system of equations with the well-conditioned coefficient matrix

```
>> A = [1 1; 2 3]
A =
      1    1
      2    3

>> cond(A)
ans =
   14.9330
```

The solution to $Ax = b$ with $b = [1, 2]^T$ is $x = [1, 0]^T$. Since $b = [1, 2]^T$ is the same as the first column of A, the solution can be expressed as

$$\begin{bmatrix} 1 \\ 2 \end{bmatrix} = 1 \begin{bmatrix} 1 \\ 2 \end{bmatrix} + 0 \begin{bmatrix} 1 \\ 3 \end{bmatrix},$$

and solving the system with the MATLAB \ operator gives the expected result:

```
>> b = [1; 2]
>> x = A\b
x =
     1
     0
```

When the right-hand-side vector of this well-conditioned system is slightly perturbed, the solution also changes slightly,

```
>> bp = [1.001; 2];
>> xp = A\bp
xp =
     1.0030
    -0.0020
```

Since the perturbed b is not exactly aligned with the first column of A, component x_2 of the solution must be nonzero. A 0.1% change in b_1 results in a 0.3% change in x_1, and the absolute change in x_2 is comparable to the absolute change in x_1.

Now consider solution to $Cx = b$, where C is the ill conditioned 2×2 matrix

```
>> C = [1 1; 2 2+100*eps]
C =
     1     1
     2     2

>> cond(C)
ans =
     4.5422e+14
```

Again, b is exactly equal to the first column of C, so even though the C matrix is ill conditioned the exact solution is still $x = [1, 0]^T$. Although $\kappa(C)$ is large, MATLAB obtains the exact solution:

```
>> b = [1; 2]
>> x = C\b
x =
     1
     0
```

```
>> x - [1; 0]
ans =
      0
      0
```

A small perturbation to b will result in a large change in the computed solution, because C is ill conditioned. Consider $b' = [1 + \delta, 2]^T$ where $\delta = 0.01$.

```
>> bp = [1.001;   2];
>> xp = C\bp
xp =
   1.0e+10 *
      9.0072
     -9.0072
```

Note that the two components of the solution to the perturbed system differ by ~ 1:

```
>> xp(1)+xp(2)
ans =
      1.0010
```

The linear combination

$$\begin{bmatrix} 1.001 \\ 2 \end{bmatrix} = x_1 \begin{bmatrix} 1 \\ 2 \end{bmatrix} + x_2 \begin{bmatrix} 1 \\ 2 + 100\varepsilon_m \end{bmatrix}$$

requires values of x_1 and x_2 that are very large and that very nearly cancel each other.

8.3.3 Computational Stability

The preceding section shows that an ill-conditioned system is sensitive to perturbations in the inputs. The perturbations may be caused by measurement errors if the elements of A and b are from an experiment, or the perturbations may be due to roundoff when the numerical approximations to the coefficients are evaluated and stored in memory. Sensitivity to perturbations in the inputs is a characteristic of the problem being solved, not of the algorithm used to obtain the solution. This bears restating. *The conditioning of the system is independent of the algorithm used to solve the problem.*

Having identified the properties of the problem that limit the attainable accuracy of a numerical solution, it is time to focus on the solution algorithm. In particular, are some algorithms for solving $Ax = b$ better than others? Rigorous answers to this question quantify the degree to which a solution algorithm amplifies errors present in the input data or introduced as roundoff during the elimination and backward substitution phases. A "bad" solution algorithm will unacceptably amplify roundoff errors. A "good" solution algorithm also amplifies roundoff errors, but at a rate that gives a solution error not much larger, in an order-of-magnitude sense, than the uncertainty of the inputs. This property of *not* amplifying errors is called *stability*.

Gaussian elimination with partial pivoting followed by backward substitution is stable for solving $Ax = b$ in the following sense. The algorithm produces the *exact* solution to

$$(A + E)\hat{x} = b, \qquad \text{where} \qquad \|E\|_\infty \leq n^3 g\, \varepsilon_m \|A\|_\infty \qquad (8.34)$$

and n is the number of rows (and columns) in A, g is the *growth factor*, and ε_m is machine precision. (See, for example, [32] for a proof.) The growth factor measures the increase in magnitude of the matrix elements as A is converted to triangular form. Equation (8.34) is a theoretical bound on the error. For the matrices that are encountered in practical problems, this error bound is far too pessimistic.[9] Although Equation (8.34) indicates that large errors are potentially possible, the results attained in practice have much smaller errors. For routine use of Gaussian elimination with partial pivoting and backward substitution, one can ignore g and the factor of n^3, so that a *practical*, as opposed to provable, error bound is

$$\boxed{(A + E)\hat{x} = b, \qquad \text{where} \qquad \|E\|_\infty \leq \varepsilon_m \|A\|_\infty.} \qquad (8.35)$$

What does this mean?

The $(A + E)\hat{x} = b$ part of (8.35) states that Gaussian elimination with partial pivoting and backward substitution obtains the exact solution to a problem that differs from the original problem. The $\|E\|_\infty \leq \varepsilon_m \|A\|_\infty$ part of (8.35) says that difference between these two problems is very small. To borrow a phrase from Trefethen and Bau [76, p. 104], *Gaussian elimination with partial pivoting and backward substitution "gives exactly the right answer to nearly the right question."* An algorithm that gives the exact answer to a problem that is near to the original problem is said to be *backward stable*. Note that this is only an indirect statement on the accuracy of the numerical solution. Further quantification of the accuracy is provided in the next section.

Gaussian elimination *without* pivoting is *not* backward stable for all coefficient matrices. Matrices that are symmetric and positive definite, however, can be accurately solved using Gaussian elimination without pivoting.

A stable algorithm is only guaranteed to produce a good result for well-conditioned problems. The results of perturbation analysis summarized by Equations (8.29), (8.31), and (8.32) indicate that one cannot guarantee the accuracy of a solution to an ill-conditioned problem. Recall that these perturbation results were obtained by assuming that no roundoff errors occurred during the solution.

---

[9]If this bound represented the practically attained accuracy, Gaussian elimination with partial pivoting and backward substitution would be useless!

8.3.4 The Residual

Let $\hat{x}$ designate the numerical solution to $Ax = b$. Due to ill conditioning and to roundoff during Gaussian elimination and back substitution, $\hat{x}$ will differ from x. The *residual* vector

$$r = b - A\hat{x} \qquad (8.36)$$

is a measure of how well the original equations are satisfied. From the definition of r, it would seem that if $\hat{x}$ is close to the exact solution, then $\|r\|$ should be close to zero. Unfortunately, an accurate $\hat{x}$ is not guaranteed by a small $\|r\|$. It is not hard to show (see Exercise 36) that

$$\frac{\|\hat{x} - x\|}{\|\hat{x}\|} \le \kappa(A)\frac{\|r\|}{\|b\|}, \qquad (8.37)$$

where $\kappa(A)$ is the condition number of A defined by Equation (8.33). As usual, any of the p-norms can be used in Equation (8.37).

The left-hand side of Equation (8.37) is the relative error in the solution. The right-hand side also gives a strong hint about what constitutes meaningful reference for determining the size of r. Since b is known, $\|b\|$ can be easily computed. Momentarily ignoring the $\kappa(A)$ factor in Equation (8.37) suggests that if $\|r\|/\|b\| \ll 1$, then the computed solution $\hat{x}$ is not far from the exact solution x. The presence of $\kappa(A)$ means that small $\|r\|$ does not guarantee a small $\|\hat{x} - x\|$. *A small residual indicates a successful solution only if the coefficient matrix is well-conditioned.* If $\kappa(A)$ is large, the $\hat{x}$ returned by Gaussian elimination and backward substitution is not guaranteed to be anywhere near the true solution to $Ax = b$.

8.3.5 Rules of Thumb

The analysis of §§ 8.3.2–8.3.4 leads to the following rules of thumb:

> ➤ Applying Gaussian elimination with partial pivoting and backward substitution to $Ax = b$ yields a numerical solution $\hat{x}$ such that the residual vector $r = b - A\hat{x}$ is small *even if* the $\kappa(A)$ is large.
> ➤ If A and b are stored to machine precision ε_m, the numerical solution to $Ax = b$ by any variant of Gaussian elimination is correct to d digits, where
>
> $$d = |\log_{10}(\varepsilon_m)| - \log_{10}(\kappa(A)). \qquad (8.38)$$

The realization of small residuals follows from Equation (8.35). Rearranging Equation (8.35) and taking norms gives $\|A\hat{x} - b\| = \|E\hat{x}\|$. Thus,

$$\|r\| \le \|E\|\|\hat{x}\| \le \varepsilon_m \|A\|\|\hat{x}\|, \qquad \text{or} \qquad \frac{\|r\|}{\|A\|\|\hat{x}\|} \le \varepsilon_m.$$

Since this result is independent of $\kappa(A)$, applying Gaussian elimination, partial pivoting, and backward substitution returns a numerical solution that has a small residual, even though the solution may not be accurate. The role of $\kappa(A)$ in influencing the accuracy is evident from Equation (8.37).

Equation (8.38) is a consequence of Equation (8.32), which, in terms of $\kappa(A)$, is

$$\frac{\|\delta x\|}{\|x + \delta x\|} \le \frac{\kappa(A)}{1 - \kappa(A)\frac{\|\delta A\|}{\|A\|}} \left[\frac{\|\delta A\|}{\|A\|} + \frac{\|\delta b\|}{\|b\|} \right].$$

If the perturbations to A and b are caused by roundoff in the storage of the coefficients (i.e., $\|\delta A\| = \varepsilon_m \|A\|$ and $\|\delta b\| = \varepsilon_m \|b\|$), and $\kappa(A)\varepsilon_m \ll 1$, then

$$1 - \kappa(A)\frac{\|\delta A\|}{\|A\|} \approx 1,$$

and

$$\frac{\|\delta x\|}{\|x + \delta x\|} \approx \kappa(A)\varepsilon_m.$$

Setting $10^{-d} = \kappa(A)\varepsilon_m$ gives Equation (8.38).

Equation (8.38) provides a basis for establishing the meaning of a large condition number. A useful solution to a system of equations will need several correct digits. For computations with MATLAB, $\varepsilon_m \sim 10^{-16}$, so to obtain a result with approximately six correct digits, the condition number of the coefficient matrix must be less than 10^{10}. One would still consider $\kappa(A) = 10^{10}$ to be a large condition number. (See Exercise 35.)

8.3.6 Computing $\kappa(A)$

Exact evaluation of the condition number is computationally expensive. Calculation of $\kappa(A)$ from Equation (8.33) requires A^{-1}, which takes $\mathcal{O}(n^3)$ flops to compute from A. If A^{-1} is available, using the 1 or ∞ matrix norms to compute $\kappa(A)$ reduces the flop count for the final evaluation of $\|A\|\|A^{-1}\|$. The 2-norm condition number $\kappa_2(A)$ is usually calculated with SVD algorithm, because

$$\kappa_2(A) = \frac{\max(\sigma_i)}{\min(\sigma_i)},$$

where σ_i are the singular values of A. (See Gill et al. [28, § 3.6.2] for a derivation of this result.) Computing the SVD of an $n \times n$ matrix takes $\mathcal{O}(n^3)$ flops, so evaluating $\kappa_2(A)$ is also expensive. Since solving a system takes $\mathcal{O}(n^3)$ flops, adding an evaluation of $\kappa(A)$ roughly doubles the work. Thus, one can expect to double the execution time of solving $Ax = b$ if an evaluation of $\kappa(A)$ is also desired. For small matrices,[10] the cost of calculating $\kappa(A)$ is not prohibitive.

In general, $\kappa(A)$ is a diagnostic, not an end in itself. As a diagnostic, the exact value of $\kappa(A)$ is much less important than its order of magnitude. It is often advantageous, therefore, to use an *estimate* of $\kappa(A)$ that is more efficient to compute than the exact value of $\kappa(A)$. Algorithms to estimate $\kappa(A)$ that use $\mathcal{O}(n^2)$ flops instead of $\mathcal{O}(n^3)$ flops (as required by the calculation of A^{-1}) have been developed. The two most widely used condition number estimators are provided by the built in MATLAB functions condest and rcond. The older routine, rcond, estimates the value of $1/\kappa_1(A)$. condest uses a different algorithm to estimate $\kappa_1(A)$ directly.

If A is stored as a dense[11] matrix, use of the \ operator automatically involves a call to rcond to check the condition of the coefficient matrix. A warning message is printed if the value returned by rcond is smaller than a tolerance. For example,

```
>> A = [1 0; 0 eps]      %  a very ill conditioned matrix
A =
    1.0000         0
         0    0.0000

>> A\[1; 1]

Warning: Matrix is close to singular or badly scaled.
         Results may be inaccurate. RCOND = 2.220446e-16.
ans =
    1.0e+15 *
    0.0000
    4.5036
```

Note that since rcond estimates $1/\kappa_1(A)$ a *small* return value indicates an ill-conditioned matrix. When the \ operator is used with a sparse coefficient matrix, an automatic condition number estimation is not provided. If the coefficient matrix is sparse, condest must be used instead of rcond.[12]

Though the rcond and condest condition number estimators are widely used and trusted, it is possible to devise matrices for which the estimated con-

---

[10] Say, $n \leq 500$, to pick an arbitrary definition of small systems in the year 2000.

[11] See Appendix B for the definitions of dense and sparse storage. MATLAB matrices created in the usual way with the A = [...] syntax are stored in dense format.

[12] The algorithm used by rcond can, in principle, be applied to sparse matrices, but it is not implemented in the MATLAB \ operator.

dition number is far from the true condition number. These counterexamples are rare and do not arise in the solution of most practical problems. (See Higham [36, Chapter 14] for a comprehensive introduction to condition number estimation.)

8.4 FACTORIZATION METHODS

Gaussian elimination involves a transformation of the augmented coefficient matrix $\tilde{A} = [A, b]$ to triangular form. The steps in the elimination phase are equivalent to factoring A into a product of a lower triangular matrix L and an upper triangular matrix U. The explicit calculation of L and U is called the LU *factorization* or LU *decomposition* of A. If A is symmetric and positive definite, the Cholesky factorization, which is more efficient than the LU factorization, may be used instead. In this section, the LU and Cholesky factorizations are presented. The \ operator automatically uses the LU or Cholesky factorizations if these apply to the coefficient matrix. (See § 8.4.3.)

Table 8.2 lists four important matrix factorizations. The QR factorization is discussed in § 9.2.3. The SVD is briefly described in Appendix A.

8.4.1 LU Factorization

The LU factorization is presented in four subsections: *Motivation*, *Derivation*, *Implementing Row Exchanges*, and *The* `lu` *Function*. On a first reading the *Derivation* and *Implementing Row Exchanges* subsections can be skimmed. The first and last subsections should be read carefully.

Motivation   The LU factorization of a matrix A involves finding the lower triangular matrix L and the upper triangular matrix U such that

$$A = LU. \tag{8.39}$$

TABLE 8.2   COMMONLY USED MATRIX FACTORIZATIONS. ALL OF THESE FACTORIZATIONS ARE PROVIDED BY BUILT IN MATLAB FUNCTIONS. (SEE `lu`, `chol`, `qr`, AND `svd`.)

Factorization	Name	Restrictions and Properties
$A = LU$	LU	A is square, and nonsingular. L is lower triangular, and U is upper triangular.
$A = C^T C$	Cholesky	A is symmetric and positive definite. C is upper triangular.
$A = QR$	QR	A is $m \times n$. Q is orthogonal and R is upper triangular.
$A = USV^T$	Singular Value Decomposition (SVD)	A is $m \times n$ and may be rank deficient. U is $m \times n$ and orthogonal, S is $n \times n$ and diagonal, and V is $n \times n$ and orthogonal.

The factorization alone does not solve $Ax = b$. Recall that Gaussian elimination only transforms an augmented coefficient matrix to triangular form. It is the backward substitution phase that obtains the solution. Similarly the factorization of A into L and U sets up the solution $Ax = b$ via two triangular solves.

Since $A = LU$, the system $Ax = b$ is equivalent to

$$(LU)x = b. \tag{8.40}$$

The product on the left-hand side can be regrouped (since matrix multiplication is associative) as $L(Ux) = b$. The Ux subexpression produces a column vector—call it y—having the same number of rows as x and b. With $y = Ux$, Equation (8.40) becomes

$$Ly = b.$$

Since L is triangular, the solution $y = L^{-1}b$ is easily obtained with a forward substitution (not by explicitly computing L^{-1}). Given y, we then have the system

$$Ux = b,$$

which is easily solved for x with a backward substitution. Putting these pieces together gives an algorithm for solving $Ax = b$.

Algorithm 8.6   Solve $Ax = b$ with LU factorization

Factor A into L and U
Solve $Ly = b$ for y use forward substitution
Solve $Ux = y$ for x use backward substitution

The factorization step takes $\mathcal{O}(n^3)$ flops. The first two steps (factor A and solve $Ly = b$) are equivalent to performing Gaussian elimination on the augmented coefficient matrix. Thus, solving the system with LU factorization takes as much work as solving it with Gaussian elimination. If the same coefficient matrix is used in systems with different right-hand-sides, however, LU factorization and backward substitution are much more efficient, because the LU factorization (step 1) needs to be performed only once. The computational work of backward substitution is negligible compared with the work of computing the LU factorization.

Derivation   The algorithm for computing the LU factorization of a matrix can be derived in different ways. Here, we use an intuitive approach (see also Stewart [68] and Strang [72]) based on multiplication of A with elimination matrices. Gill et al. [28] provide a concise description of alternative derivations.

Consider the 3×3 system of equations defined by

$$A = \begin{bmatrix} -3 & 2 & -1 \\ 6 & -6 & 7 \\ 3 & -4 & 4 \end{bmatrix}, \qquad b = \begin{bmatrix} -1 \\ -7 \\ -6 \end{bmatrix}.$$

This is the same system of equations used in the step-by-step exposition of Gaussian elimination beginning on page 383. It is instructive to compare those computations with the computations presented next.

Without worrying, for the moment, how these matrices are created, define two *elimination matrices* $M_{(1)}$ and $M_{(2)}$

$$M_{(1)} = \begin{bmatrix} 1 & 0 & 0 \\ 2 & 1 & 0 \\ 1 & 0 & 1 \end{bmatrix}, \qquad M_{(2)} = \begin{bmatrix} 1 & 0 & 0 \\ 0 & 1 & 0 \\ 0 & -1 & 1 \end{bmatrix},$$

and evaluate the following matrix–vector products:

$$A_{(1)} = M_{(1)} A = \begin{bmatrix} -3 & 2 & -1 \\ 0 & -2 & 5 \\ 0 & -2 & 3 \end{bmatrix},$$

$$A_{(2)} = M_{(2)} A_{(1)} = M_{(2)} M_{(1)} A = \begin{bmatrix} -3 & 2 & -1 \\ 0 & -2 & 5 \\ 0 & 0 & -2 \end{bmatrix}.$$

Observe that $A_{(1)}$ is the same matrix obtained by elimination with the first row of A. Note also that $A_{(2)}$ is the same matrix obtained by elimination with the second row of $A_{(1)}$. The end result, $A_{(2)}$, is the triangular matrix obtained from Gaussian elimination on A. Multiplication by $M_{(1)}$ and $M_{(2)}$ (in that order!), therefore, is equivalent to performing Gaussian elimination. The expression $M_{(1)} A = A_{(1)}$ is the matrix algebra equivalent of the calculations necessary to zero the elements below the main diagonal in the first column of A. Elements below the main diagonal in the second column are eliminated with $M_{(2)} A_{(1)} = A_{(2)}$. Note that $M_{(2)}$ multiplies $A_{(1)}$, not A. The order of multiplication by the $M_{(i)}$ is important, because the order of operations in Gaussian elimination matters.

The connection between the $M_{(i)}$ and Gaussian elimination is no accident. Recall that the formula for eliminating the elements in a row is (cf. Equation (8.20))

$$a_{kj} \leftarrow a_{kj} - m_{kj} a_{ij}, \qquad j = 1, \dots, n,$$

where

$$m_{ki} = \frac{a_{ki}}{a_{ii}}, \qquad j = 1, \dots, n \qquad (8.41)$$

is the multiplier selected to eliminate element a_{ki} when the pivot row (row i) is subtracted from row k. Equation (8.41) defines the negative of the subdiagonal elements in the $M_{(i)}$ matrices; that is,

$$M_{(1)} = \begin{bmatrix} 1 & 0 & 0 \\ -m_{21} & 1 & 0 \\ -m_{31} & 0 & 1 \end{bmatrix}, \qquad M_{(2)} = \begin{bmatrix} 1 & 0 & 0 \\ 0 & 1 & 0 \\ 0 & -m_{32} & 1 \end{bmatrix}. \tag{8.42}$$

The preceding operations for the 3×3 matrix generalize to $n \times n$ matrices. A square matrix is transformed to triangular form by a sequence of multiplications with elimination matrices[13]

$$M_{(n-1)} \ldots M_{(2)} M_{(1)} A = U, \tag{8.43}$$

where U is upper triangular and $M_{(i)}$ is the elimination matrix corresponding to pivot row i

$$M_{(i)} = \begin{bmatrix} 1 & 0 & 0 & \cdots & & & & \\ 0 & 1 & 0 & & & & & \\ \vdots & & \ddots & & & & & \\ & 0 & & 1 & 0 & & & \\ & & & -m_{i+1,i} & 1 & & & \\ & & & -m_{i+2,i} & 0 & 1 & & \\ & & & \vdots & & & \ddots & \\ & & & -m_{n,i} & & & 0 & 1 \end{bmatrix}.$$

The transformation in Equation (8.43) is the goal of Gaussian elimination. The connection to the LU factorization becomes apparent when Equation (8.43) is unraveled, so that A is once again alone on the left-hand side. Multiply both sides of Equation (8.43) by the inverses of the $M_{(i)}$ to get

$$M_{(n-2)} \ldots M_{(2)} M_{(1)} A = M_{(n-1)}^{-1} U$$

$$\ldots M_{(2)} M_{(1)} A = M_{(n-2)}^{-1} M_{(n-1)}^{-1} U$$

$$\vdots$$

$$A = M_{(1)}^{-1} M_{(2)}^{-1} \ldots M_{(n-2)}^{-1} M_{(n-1)}^{-1} U. \tag{8.44}$$

Comparing this last result with Equation (8.39) reveals that

$$L = M_{(1)}^{-1} M_{(2)}^{-1} \ldots M_{(n-2)}^{-1} M_{(n-1)}^{-1}. \tag{8.45}$$

---

[13] A is assumed to be nonsingular. Pivoting can be included with the multiplication by $M_{(1)}$ as described later.

Algorithm 8.8   LU Factorization in Place

given A

```
for i = 1 ... n - 1              loop over pivot rows
  for k = i + 1 ... n           loop over column below the pivot
    a_ki = a_ki / a_ii          compute multiplier and store it in lower part of A
    for j = i + 1 ... n         loop over elements in row k
      a_kj = a_kj - a_ki a_ij
    end
  end
end
```

The `luNopiv` function in Listing 8.4 implements the in-place factorization of a matrix. As its name suggests, `luNopiv` does not perform the row exchanges required by partial pivoting. The last two lines of `luNopiv` explicitly create L and U from the in-place factorization of A. Creating copies of L and U is not necessary if the user of `luNopiv` is prepared to work with the in-place factorization. (See Exercise 40.) The modifications necessary for pivoting are described next.

Implementing Row Exchanges   As described in § 8.2.4, pivoting is required to avoid division by zero (or a very small number) during the elimination phase. The basic idea of pivoting in LU factorization is the same as it is for Gaussian elimination on the augmented coefficient matrix. The one important difference is that during the factorization phase, only the coefficient matrix is available. Any row exchanges during the factorization of A must be explicitly recorded so that they can be applied to b during the solution.

If one knew the order of the rows that would require no pivoting, then matrix A and vector b could be permuted before the elimination process begins. Mathematically, this is equivalent to solving

$$(PA)x = Pb, \tag{8.48}$$

where P is a permutation matrix. (Cf. § 7.4.8 on page 352). The solution to Equation (8.48) is the same as the solution to $Ax = b$. If row exchanges occur during the elimination, then the LU factorization algorithm produces the factorization of the permuted coefficient matrix

$$PA = LU, \tag{8.49}$$

where P, L, and U are the output and A is the input, that is,

$$A \xrightarrow[\text{LU factorization}]{} P, L, U.$$

```
function [L,U] = luNopiv(A,ptol)
% luNopiv  LU factorization without pivoting
%
% Synopsis:  [L,U] = luNopiv(A)
%            [L,U] = luNopiv(A,ptol)
%
% Input:     A   = coefficient matrix
%            ptol = (optional) tolerance for detection of zero pivot
%                     Default:  ptol = 50*eps
%
% Output:    L,U = lower triangular matrix, L, and upper triangular
%                  matrix, U, such that A = L*U

if nargin<3, ptol = 50*eps;  end    % Default tolerance for zero pivot
[m,n] = size(A);
if m~=n,  error('A matrix needs to be square');  end

for i = 1:n-1                       %  loop over pivot rows
  pivot = A(i,i);
  if abs(pivot)<ptol, error('zero pivot encountered');  end
  for k = i+1:n                               % row k is eliminated next
     A(k,i) = A(k,i)/pivot;                   % compute and store multiplier
     A(k,i+1:n) = A(k,i+1:n) - A(k,i)*A(i,i+1:n); % row ops to eliminate A(k,i)
  end
end

L = eye(size(A)) + tril(A,-1);  %  extract L and U
U = triu(A);
```

Listing 8.4   The `luNopiv` function factors a square nonsingular matrix into a unit lower triangular matrix L and an upper triangular matrix U. No pivoting is used.

After factorization, the P matrix must be applied to b (cf. Equation (8.48)) before L and U factors are used to solve for x.

The `luPiv` function in Listing 8.5 performs an in-place LU factorization with partial pivoting. The L and U factors are explicitly created after the factorization is complete. (See Exercise 40.) The row order resulting from partial pivoting is returned in a *permutation vector* pv instead of a permutation matrix P. The information in pv can be used to the same effect as multiplication by P. The following expressions are equivalent:

$$b \leftarrow Pb \quad \Longleftrightarrow \quad \mathrm{b = b(pv)}.$$

The expression `b(pv)` is an example of array indexing. (See § 3.5.3.)

```
function [L,U,pv] = luPiv(A,ptol)
% luPiv  LU factorization with partial pivoting
%
% Synopsis:  [L,U,pv] = luPiv(A)
%            [L,U,pv] = luPiv(A,ptol)
%
% Input:     A    = coefficient matrix
%            ptol = (optional) tolerance for detection of zero pivot
%                    Default:  ptol = 50*eps
%
% Output:    L,U = lower triangular matrix, L, and upper triangular
%                  matrix, U, such that A(pv,:) = L*U
%            pv  = index vector that records row exchanges used to select
%                  good pivots.  The row permutations performed during
%                  elimination can be applied to the right hand side vector
%                  with b(pv).  The L and U returned by luPiv are the
%                  factors of permuted matrix A(pv,:), which is equivalent
%                  to P*A where P is the permutation matrix created
%                  by the two statements P = eye(size(A));  P = P(pv,:).

if nargin<3, ptol = 50*eps;  end     % Default tolerance for zero pivot
[m,n] = size(A);
if m~=n,  error('A matrix needs to be square');  end
pv = (1:n)';

for i = 1:n-1                         % loop over pivot row
  [pivot,p] = max(abs(A(i:n,i)));     % value and index of largest pivot
  ip = p + i - 1;                     % p is index in subvector i:n
  if ip~=i                            % ip is true row index of desired pivot
    A([i ip],:) = A([ip i],:);        % swap the rows
    pv([i ip]) = pv([ip i]);          % record pivot order
  end
  pivot = A(i,i);
  if abs(pivot)<ptol, error('zero pivot encountered after row exchange');  end
  for k = i+1:n                              % row k is eliminated next
    A(k,i) = A(k,i)/pivot;                   % compute and store multiplier
    A(k,i+1:n) = A(k,i+1:n) - A(k,i)*A(i,i+1:n); % row ops to eliminate A(k,i)
  end
end

L = eye(size(A)) + tril(A,-1);  %  extract L and U
U = triu(A);
```

Listing 8.5 The luPiv function factors a square nonsingular matrix into a unit lower triangular matrix L and an upper triangular matrix U. Partial pivoting is used.

Here is an example of an application of the `luPiv` function:

```
>> A = [ 2 4 -2 -2; 1 2 4 -3; -3 -3 8 -2; -1 1 6 -3];
>> b = [-4; 5; 7; 7];
>> [L,U,pv] = luPiv(A)
L =
       1.0000         0         0         0
      -0.6667    1.0000         0         0
      -0.3333    0.5000    1.0000         0
       0.3333    1.0000    0.0000    1.0000
U =
      -3.0000   -3.0000    8.0000   -2.0000
            0    2.0000    3.3333   -3.3333
            0         0    5.0000   -2.0000
            0         0         0    1.0000
pv =
       3
       1
       2
       4
```

Given L, U, and pv, the triangular solution algorithms (Algorithm 8.2 and Algorithm 8.3) are used to implement the second and third steps of $Ax = b$ via Algorithm 8.6 to solve $Ax = b$. There is no need to develop m-file functions for these algorithms, however, because the built-in \ operator also solves triangular systems efficiently. The built-in \ operator contains preprocessing logic to determine whether the coefficient matrix is triangular. If \ detects a triangular matrix (or a permutation of a triangular matrix), then the appropriate triangular solution algorithm is used without performing elimination or factorization. Thus, given L, U, and pv created by the preceding statements,

```
>> y = L\b(pv)
y =
       7.0000
       0.6667
       7.0000
       4.0000

>> x = U\y
x =
       1.0000
       2.0000
       3.0000
       4.0000
```

completes the solution.

The `lu` Function   The built-in `lu` function performs the LU factorization with partial pivoting of a matrix. In all cases where an LU factorization is desired, the built-in `lu` function should be used instead of the `luNoPiv` and `luPiv` functions developed in the preceding sections. The `luNoPiv` and `luPiv` functions are intended to demonstrate how LU factorization can be implemented. The built-in `lu` function is a much more efficient implementation of the basic algorithm used in `luPiv`.

The `lu` function uses partial pivoting to produce the factorization in Equation (8.49). The permutation matrix P is treated explicitly or implicitly, depending on how `lu` is called. There are two forms of the `lu` function call.

```
[L⁽ᵖ⁾,U] = lu(A)
[L,U,P] = lu(A)
```

In the first form, the $L^{(p)}$ matrix is a permuted version of the lower triangular factor of A. From Equation (8.49), we obtain

$$A = P^{-1}LU = P^T LU = L^{(p)}U$$

where $L^{(p)} = P^T L$. (Why is $P^{-1} = P^T$?) The matrix $L^{(p)}$ is useful, because the \ operator can detect permuted triangular matrices. Given an expression of the form y = L\b, the \ operator discovers that L is a permuted triangular matrix. It extracts the permutation, applies it to b, and then uses forward substitution to solve for y. The following demonstrates how this implicit permutation of L is used with Algorithm 8.6:

```
>> A = [1 2 4; 1 3 9; 1 4 16];
>> b = [2; 4; 7];
>> [L,U] = lu(A)          % Factor A into L and U
L =
      1.0000          0          0
      1.0000     0.5000     1.0000
      1.0000     1.0000          0
U =
      1      2      4
      0      2     12
      0      0     -1

>> y = L\b                % Solve L*y = b
y =
      2.0000
      5.0000
     -0.5000
```

```
>> x = U\y                  % Solve U*x = y
x =
    1.0000
   -0.5000
    0.5000
```

It is important to remember that the y = L\b and x = U\y statements rely on the internal logic of the \ operator to detect triangular systems and use inexpensive triangular solves.

In the [L,U,P] = lu(A) form of the lu function, L is a strictly lower triangular matrix, and P is the (full) permutation matrix appearing in Equation (8.49). The U matrix is the same for both forms of the lu function. (Why?) Given L, U, and P from the lu function, we obtain the solution to $Ax = b$ through the last two-steps of Algorithm 8.6. Here is a MATLAB session demonstrating use of the lu function and explicit computation with P:

```
>> A = [1 2 4; 1 3 9; 1 4 16];   b = [2; 4; 7];
>> [L,U,P] = lu(A)
>> L
L =
    1.0000         0         0
    1.0000    1.0000         0
    1.0000    0.5000    1.0000

U =
    1     2     4
    0     2    12
    0     0    -1
P =
    1     0     0
    0     0     1
    0     1     0

>> y = L\(P*b)
y =
    2.0000
    5.0000
   -0.5000

>> x = U\y
x =
    1.0000
   -0.5000
    0.5000
```

As shown earlier, making matrix P explicit with the three-argument version of the lu function is not necessary. Note also that given L and U, we can obtain the

`C(1:i-1,i)'*C(1:i-1,j)`. Thus, *s* may be evaluated with

`s = A(i,j) - C(1:i-1,i)'*C(1:i-1,j)`

so that

`C(i,i) = sqrt(s)        % on-diagonal terms`

and

`C(i,j) = s/C(i,i)       % off-diagonal terms`

These observations are converted to MATLAB code in the Cholesky function in Listing 8.6.[16] The logic in Cholesky is complicated by two small details. First, the equation for $c_{1,1}$ involves no inner-product computation. This requires an exception to prevent a zero row index in the inner-product expression

`C(1:i-1,i)'*C(1:i-1,j)`

The second detail is the logic to prevent the evaluation of sqrt(s) when s is negative. Mathematically, s will be negative only if the A matrix is not symmetric and positive definite. Numerically, it may be possible to get a negative s if the matrix ill conditioned or is marginally positive definite. The if s<=0 test in the Cholesky function guards against either case.

The chol Function   The built-in chol function obtains the Cholesky factorization of a symmetric positive definite matrix. For routine computation the chol function should be used instead of the Cholesky function in Listing 8.6. Use of the chol function is demonstrated with an example. First define a matrix that is known from experience to be symmetric and positive definite:

```
>> A = [2 -1 0 0; -1 2 -1 0; 0 -1 2 -1; 0 0 -1 2]
A =
     2    -1     0     0
    -1     2    -1     0
     0    -1     2    -1
     0     0    -1     2
```

---

[16]This implementation of the Cholesky factorization is a variant of the cholDot function given by Van Loan [77].

```
function C = Cholesky(A)
% Cholesky  Cholesky factorization of a symmetric, positive definite matrix
%
% Synopsis:  C = Cholesky(A)
%
% Input:     A = symmetric positive definite matrix
%
% Output:    C = upper triangular matrix such that A = C'*C

[m,n] = size(A);
if m~=n,  error('A must be square');  end
C = zeros(n,n);

for i=1:n
  for j=i:n
    if j==1
      s = A(i,i);   % i=1, j=1 is special case
    else
      s = A(i,j) - C(1:i-1,i)'*C(1:i-1,j);
    end
    if j>i
      C(i,j) = s/C(i,i);
    else
      if s<=0, error('C is not positive definite to working precision'); end
      C(i,i) = sqrt(s);
    end
  end
end
```

Listing 8.6 Cholesky factorization of a symmetric, positive definite matrix.

Next, obtain the Cholesky factorization:

```
>> C = chol(A)
C =
    1.4142   -0.7071        0        0
         0    1.2247   -0.8165        0
         0         0    1.1547   -0.8660
         0         0         0    1.1180
```

Then, define a right-hand-side vector and compute the solution using the Cholesky factor:

```
>> b = [-1 0 0 -2]'
b =
    -1
     0
     0
    -2

>> y = C'\b
y =
   -0.7071
   -0.4082
   -0.2887
   -2.0125

>> x = C\y
x =
   -1.2000
   -1.4000
   -1.6000
   -1.8000
```

Using the statements C'*C - A and A\b, one can easily verify that the Cholesky factors were correctly computed and applied in the preceding example.

8.4.3 The Backslash Operator Reconsidered

The \ operator is shorthand for a sophisticated problem-solving strategy built into the MATLAB kernel. When the MATLAB interpreter encounters the expression A\b, it examines the contents of A and b and takes what it believes to be the best course of action. The following is a summary of the steps taken when the the \ operator is invoked (refer to *Using* MATLAB [73] for additional information):

1. MATLAB checks to see if matrix A is triangular or a permutation of a triangular matrix. If it is, the solution is obtained by the appropriate back substitution (forward for lower triangular, backward for upper triangular).

2. If A is square, MATLAB checks to see whether A is symmetric and whether it has positive diagonal elements. If both of these conditions are true, it attempts to perform the Cholesky factorization and associated triangular solves.

3. If A is square and fails the preceding tests, then the system is solved with LU factorization and back substitution.

4. If A is not square, a QR factorization of A is computed, and the least-squares solution to the system is obtained. (Refer to §9.2.3 for a discussion of how the QR factorization is applied to the least-squares problem.)

8.5 NONLINEAR SYSTEMS OF EQUATIONS

The system $Ax = b$ is nonlinear when either the coefficients in A or the elements in b depend on one or more of the x_i. For a linear system, the elements of A and b can be computed without any knowledge of x. For a nonlinear system, the elements of A or b (or both) are not known until the solution x is known.

Example 8.10: Intersection(s) of a Line and a Parabola

Consider a 2×2 system of equations that define a line and a parabola in the (x, y)-plane:

$$y = \alpha x + \beta,$$

$$y = x^2 + \sigma x + \tau,$$

where α, β, σ, and τ are parameters of the line and parabola. The intersection of these two curves, if it exists, is the solution to the system of equations. To put the preceding equations in the form of Equation (8.52), let $x_1 = x$ and $x_2 = y$. The system becomes

$$\alpha x_1 - x_2 = -\beta,$$

$$(x_1 + \sigma)x_1 - x_2 = -\tau,$$

which can be expressed in matrix notation as

$$\begin{bmatrix} \alpha & -1 \\ x_1 + \sigma & -1 \end{bmatrix} \begin{bmatrix} x_1 \\ x_2 \end{bmatrix} = \begin{bmatrix} -\beta \\ -\tau \end{bmatrix}. \tag{8.50}$$

For this problem, the nonlinearity occurs only in element a_{21} of the coefficient matrix. Solutions to Equation (8.50) are obtained in Examples 8.12 and 8.13.

Note that Equation (8.50) is not the only way to define and A and b for this system of equations. (See Exercise 44.)

8.5.1 Iterative Methods for Nonlinear Systems

The formal solution of a *linear* system is $x = A^{-1}b$. Since the right-hand side is independent of x, the solution to the linear system can be computed by so-called *direct methods*. Given a matrix and right-hand-side vector with known dimension, a direct method, such as Gaussian elimination with backward substitution, terminates with a known number of operations. (Cf. Table 8.1 on page 399). In this context, "direct" refers to the finite nature of the solution process. For a nonlinear system, the expression $x = A^{-1}(x) b(x)$ indicates that the right-hand side cannot be evaluated until x is known. The best one can do is to devise a method that gives a sequence of increasingly good guesses at the x that satisfies $A(x) x = b(x)$. This requires an *iterative method* as opposed to a direct method. Ideally, iterative methods produce solutions that get increasingly close to the true solution. The iterative process is terminated when the solution is "close enough." In principle, an infinite number of steps are required to obtain the exact solution with an iterative method.

A nonlinear system of equations can be written in the familiar form

$$Ax = b, \tag{8.51}$$

but now $A = A(x)$ and $b = b(x)$. Solution methods for nonlinear systems are generalizations of the root-finding methods (see Chapter 6) for solving scalar equations of the form $f(\xi) = 0$. When a system of nonlinear equations is to be solved, the ξ becomes a vector of unknowns, and solving $Ax = b$ is equivalent to finding the x that gives

$$f(x) = Ax - b = 0, \tag{8.52}$$

where $f(x)$ is a *vector valued* function of x. Alternatively, one can express the nonlinear problem in terms of the residual

$$r = b - Ax = -f(x). \tag{8.53}$$

An iterative method to solve Equation (8.51) can be written as

$$x^{(k+1)} = x^{(k)} + \Delta x^{(k)}, \qquad k = 1, 2, \ldots, \tag{8.54}$$

where the parentheses around the iteration counter k serve as a reminder that $x^{(k)}$ is *not* the kth power of x. Using this equation requires a procedure for computing the update vector $\Delta x^{(k)}$ from the *linearized* coefficient matrix and right-hand-side vector

$$A^{(k)} = A(x^{(k)}), \qquad b^{(k)} = b(x^{(k)}).$$

Before the update to $x^{(k)}$ is computed, the vector $f^{(k)} = f(x^{(k)})$, or

$$f^{(k)} = A^{(k)}x^{(k)} - b^{(k)}, \tag{8.55}$$

will not be zero unless $x^{(k)}$ is the solution to the nonlinear problem. Thus, convergence of the iterative algorithm is monitored by checking $\| f^{(k)} \|$. The logic of the iterative solution to Equation (8.51) is contained in Algorithm 8.10

Algorithm 8.10   Iterative Solution of Nonlinear Systems

initialize: $x = x^{(0)}$
for $k = 0, 1, 2, \ldots$
    $A^{(k)} = A(x^{(k)})$ Linearize A
    $b^{(k)} = b(x^{(k)})$ and b
    $f^{(k)} = A^{(k)}x^{(k)} - b^{(k)}$
    if $\| f^{(k)} \|$ is small enough, stop
    $\Delta x^{(k+1)} = \ldots$ Compute the update
    $x^{(k+1)} = x^{(k)} + \Delta x^{(k)}$
end

Two procedures for computing the update are given later.

In addition to the inability to solve Equation (8.51) in a finite number of steps, the nonlinearity of the system introduces other mathematical complexities. Most importantly the solution to Equation (8.51), or, equivalently, Equation (8.52), is not guaranteed to be unique. After applying a numerical technique to obtain a solution, one can never be sure that this solution is the only solution to the system.

Example 8.11: Types of Solutions

Example 8.10 develops the system of equations for the intersection of a line and quadratic curve. These equations have simple geometric interpretations that aid in describing the types of solutions that may exist. Figure 8.9 shows four possible outcomes for this system of equations. There may be zero, one, or two solutions, depending on the values of α, β, σ, and τ. For the curves in Figure 8.9, only α and β are changed.

8.5.2 Successive Substitution

Successive substitution is a simple iterative method for nonlinear systems. At each step, the linearized system $A^{(k)} x^{(k+1)} = b^{(k)}$ is solved for a new guess at the solution.

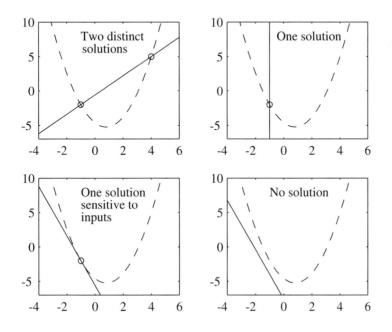

Figure 8.9   Solution scenarios for the system of nonlinear equations in Example 8.10.

3	-1.01961	-2.02745	3.79e-01
4	-0.99512	-1.99317	9.84e-02
5	-1.00122	-2.00171	2.44e-02
6	-0.99969	-1.99957	6.11e-03
7	-1.00008	-2.00011	1.53e-03
8	-0.99998	-1.99997	3.81e-04
9	-1.00000	-2.00001	9.54e-05
10	-1.00000	-2.00000	2.38e-05

If multiple solutions exist, successive substitution may favor one solution over other solutions. For example, if the initial guess is near the $(x, y) = (4, 5)$ solution, the successive substitution iterations still converge to the $(x, y) = (-1, -2)$ solution. This is the case for initial guesses of $x_0 = [5, 5]^T$ and $x_0 = [6, 6]^T$:

```
>> x = demoSSub(10,[5;5]);
```

k	x(1)	x(2)	norm(f)
1	2.00000	2.20000	7.53e+00
2	-4.00000	-6.20000	6.00e+00
⋮			
10	-1.00003	-2.00004	5.72e-04

```
>> x = demoSSub(10,[6;6]);
```

k	x(1)	x(2)	norm(f)
1	1.33333	1.26667	1.59e+01
2	-2.40000	-3.96000	6.22e+00
⋮			
10	-1.00002	-2.00002	3.34e-04

8.5.3 Newton's Method

Newton's method for a system of equations is analogous to Newton's method for a scalar equation. The solution to an $n \times n$ nonlinear system of equations is obtained when

$$f(x) = \begin{bmatrix} f_1(x_1, x_2, \dots, x_n)) \\ f_2(x_1, x_2, \dots, x_n)) \\ \vdots \\ f_n(x_1, x_2, \dots, x_n)) \end{bmatrix} = \begin{bmatrix} 0 \\ 0 \\ \vdots \\ 0 \end{bmatrix}.$$

As before, let $x^{(k)}$ be the guess at the solution for iteration k. Assuming that $\| f^{(k)} \|$ is not small enough, we seek an update vector $\Delta x^{(k)}$

$$x^{(k+1)} = x^{(k)} + \Delta x^{(k)} \quad \Longleftrightarrow \quad \begin{bmatrix} x_1^{(k+1)} \\ x_2^{(k+1)} \\ \vdots \\ x_n^{(k+1)} \end{bmatrix} = \begin{bmatrix} x_1^{(k)} \\ x_2^{(k)} \\ \vdots \\ x_n^{(k)} \end{bmatrix} + \begin{bmatrix} \Delta x_1^{(k)} \\ \Delta x_2^{(k)} \\ \vdots \\ \Delta x_n^{(k)} \end{bmatrix},$$

such that $f(x^{(k+1)}) = 0$. Using the multidimensional extension of Taylor's theorem to approximate the variation of $f(x)$ in the neighborhood of $x^{(k)}$ gives

$$f(x^{(k)} + \Delta x^{(k)}) = f(x^{(k)}) + f'(x^{(k)})\Delta x^{(k)} + \mathcal{O}\left(\|\Delta x^{(k)}\|^2\right), \qquad (8.56)$$

where $f'(x^{(k)})$ is the *Jacobian* of the system of equations:

$$f'(x) \equiv J(x) = \begin{bmatrix} \dfrac{\partial f_1}{\partial x_1} & \dfrac{\partial f_1}{\partial x_2} & \cdots & \dfrac{\partial f_1}{\partial x_n} \\[2ex] \dfrac{\partial f_2}{\partial x_1} & \dfrac{\partial f_2}{\partial x_2} & \cdots & \dfrac{\partial f_3}{\partial x_n} \\[2ex] \vdots & & \ddots & \\[2ex] \dfrac{\partial f_n}{\partial x_1} & \dfrac{\partial f_n}{\partial x_2} & \cdots & \dfrac{\partial f_n}{\partial x_n} \end{bmatrix}. \qquad (8.57)$$

Neglecting higher order terms and designating $J^{(k)}$ as the Jacobian evaluated at $x^{(k)}$, we can rearrange Equation (8.56) as

$$J^{(k)}\Delta x^{(k)} = -f(x^{(k)}) + f(x^{(k)} + \Delta x^{(k)}).$$

The goal of the Newton iterations is to make $f(x^{(k)} + \Delta x^{(k)}) = 0$, so setting that term to zero in the preceding equation gives

$$J^{(k)}\Delta x^{(k)} = -f(x^{(k)}). \qquad (8.58)$$

Equation (8.58) is a system of n *linear* equations in the n unknown $\Delta x^{(k)}$. Although the elements of J and f will, in general, depend on x, the system has been linearized by evaluating J and f at $x^{(k)}$. Each Newton iteration step involves evaluation of the vector $f^{(k)}$, the matrix $J^{(k)}$, and solution to Equation (8.58). Algorithm 8.12 is an implementation of Newton's method for a system of nonlinear equations.

Algorithm 8.12　Newton's Method for Systems

initialize: $x = x^{(0)}$
for $k = 0, 1, 2, \ldots$
$\quad f^{(k)} = A^{(k)} x^{(k)} - b^{(k)}$
$\quad$ if $\| f^{(k)} \|$ is small enough, stop
$\quad$ compute $J^{(k)}$
$\quad$ solve $J^{(k)} \Delta x^{(k)} = -f^{(k)}$
$\quad x^{(k+1)} = x^{(k)} + \Delta x^{(k)}$
end

As shown in Example 8.13, the evaluation of $f^{(k)}$ need not involve explicit computation of $A^{(k)}$.

Example 8.13: Solve a 2 × 2 System with Newton's Method

Example 8.12 demonstrated how to solve the 2×2 nonlinear system in Equation (8.50) with successive substitution. Here, we solve the same problem with Newton's method. First, define the f vector with

$$f = \begin{bmatrix} \alpha x_1 - x_2 + \beta \\ x_1^2 + \sigma x_1 - x_2 + \tau \end{bmatrix}$$

The terms in the Jacobian are

$$\frac{\partial f_1}{\partial x_1} = \alpha, \qquad\qquad \frac{\partial f_1}{\partial x_2} = -1,$$

$$\frac{\partial f_2}{\partial x_1} = 2x_1 + \sigma, \qquad\qquad \frac{\partial f_2}{\partial x_2} = -1.$$

Thus,

$$J = \begin{bmatrix} \alpha & -1 \\ (2x_1 + \sigma) & -1 \end{bmatrix}.$$

The demoNewtonSys function in Listing 8.8 implements Newton's method for solving this 2×2 system of equations. Running demoNewtonSys with the default input parameters gives

```
>> x = demoNewtonSys;

    k        x(1)        x(2)       norm(f)      norm(dx)
    0     0.00000     0.00000      4.64e+00      2.80e+00
    1    -1.33333    -2.46667      1.78e+00      5.40e-01
    2    -1.01961    -2.02745      9.84e-02      3.36e-02
    3    -1.00008    -2.00011      3.81e-04      1.31e-04
    4    -1.00000    -2.00000      5.82e-09      2.00e-09
    5    -1.00000    -2.00000
```

```
function x = demoNewtonSys(maxit,x0)
% demoNewtonSys    Solve a 2-by-2 nonlinear system by Newton's method
%                  The system is
%                             1.4*x1 - x2 = 0.6
%                        x1^2 - 1.6*x1 - x2 = 4.6
%
% Synopsis:  x = demoNewtonSys(maxit,x0)
%
% Input:   maxit = (optional) max number of iterations.  Default: maxit = 5
%          x0 = (optional) initial guess at solution.  Default:  x0 = [0; 0]
%
% Output:  x = estimate of solution after maxit iterations

if nargin<1,  maxit=5;          end
if nargin<2,  x0 = zeros(2,1);  end

% --- Coefficients for the case of two distinct solutions
alpha =  1.4;  bbeta = -0.6;  sigma = -1.6;  tau = -4.6;

x = x0;   f = zeros(size(x));

fprintf('\n   k       x(1)        x(2)       norm(f)      norm(dx)\n');
for k = 1:maxit
   f(1) = alpha*x(1) - x(2) + bbeta;
   f(2) = x(1)^2 + sigma*x(1) - x(2) + tau;
   J = [ alpha  -1; (2*x(1)+sigma)  -1 ];
   dx = -J\f;
   fprintf('%4d    %9.5f   %9.5f   %10.2e   %10.2e\n',...
            k-1,x(1),x(2),norm(f),norm(dx));
   x = x + dx;
end
fprintf('%4d    %9.5f    %9.5f\n',k,x(1),x(2));
```

Listing 8.8 The demoNewtonSys function uses Newton's method to
solve a system of two nonlinear equations.

In only 4 iterations, the solution obtained has a much smaller residual than that obtained
after 10 iterations with successive substitution. The alternative solution is also obtained in
just a few iterations given an appropriate initial guess:

```
>> x = demoNewtonSys(5,[5; 5]);
```

k	x(1)	x(2)	norm(f)	norm(dx)
0	5.00000	5.00000	7.53e+00	8.80e-01
1	4.14286	5.20000	7.35e-01	2.39e-01

2	4.00386	5.00541	1.93e-02	6.64e-03
3	4.00000	5.00000	1.49e-05	5.12e-06
4	4.00000	5.00000	8.86e-12	3.05e-12
5	4.00000	5.00000		

A General Implementation of Newton's Method   The demoNewton-Sys function shows how Newton's method may be used to solve two simultaneous nonlinear equations. A general implementation of Newton's method separates the solution algorithm from the evaluation of J and f. The newtonSys function in Listing 8.9 is such a general implementation. Careful readers will notice the strong similarity between newtonSys and the newton function for solution of scalar, nonlinear equations described in § 6.4 beginning on page 261.

The newtonSys function can be called with a number of optional input parameters. The simplest usage is

```
x = newtonSys('Jfun',x0)
```

where *Jfun* is the name of the m-file that evaluates J and f for the particular problem under consideration and *x0* is the intial guess at the solution. Example 8.14 shows how the optional input arguments to newtonSys can be used to solve a practical engineering problem.

The newtonSys function performs Newton iterations until one of two convergence criteria are met.

$$\|f\|_2 < \delta_f, \qquad \|\Delta x\|_2 < \delta_x$$

The progress of the Newton iterations can be monitored by setting the optional input parameter verbose to a nonzero value.

Example 8.14: Three-Reservoir Water Distribution Problem

Networks of pipelines are important in many aspects of our life. The water-supply system for our towns and cities is a pipe network. The piping for compressed air, chilled water, and process chemicals in a manufacturing plant are all pipe networks. The analysis of pipe networks leads to systems of nonlinear equations.

A simple example of a pipe network is the classic three-reservoir problem depicted in Figure 8.10. This system has many elements of larger pipe network problems. Three reservoirs are connected by three pipes that meet at a common junction. The pipes have different lengths and diameters, and the reservoirs are at different elevations. Given these physical parameters, we wish to know the flow rates through the pipes. Note that by adjusting the elevations of the reservoirs, it is possible to create flows of different magnitude and possibly of different direction.

Using mass and energy conservation, it is possible to develop a system of nonlinear equations that allow us to predict the flow rates. (See, for example, F.M. White, *Fluid*

```
function x = newtonSys(Jfun,x0,xtol,ftol,maxit,verbose,varargin)
% newtonSys  Newton's method for systems of nonlinear equations.
%
% Synopsis:  x = newtonSys(Jfun,x0)
%            x = newtonSys(Jfun,x0,xtol)
%            x = newtonSys(Jfun,x0,xtol,ftol)
%            x = newtonSys(Jfun,x0,xtol,ftol,verbose)
%            x = newtonSys(Jfun,x0,xtol,ftol,verbose,arg1,arg2,...)
%
% Input:   Jfun = (string) name of mfile that returns matrix J and vector f
%          x0   = initial guess at solution vector, x
%          xtol = (optional) tolerance on norm(x).  Default: xtol=5e-5
%          ftol = (optional) tolerance on norm(f).  Default: ftol=5e-5
%          verbose = (optional) flag.  Default: verbose=0, no printing.
%          arg1,arg2,... = (optional) optional arguments that are passed
%                       through to the mfile defined by the 'Jfun' argument
%
% Note:  Use [] to request default value of an optional input.  For example,
%        x = newtonSys('JFun',x0,[],[],[],arg1,arg2) passes arg1 and arg2 to
%        'JFun', while using the default values for xtol, ftol, and verbose
%
% Output:  x = solution vector;  x is returned after k iterations if tolerances
%              are met, or after maxit iterations if tolerances are not met.

if nargin < 3 | isempty(xtol),    xtol = 5e-5;  end
if nargin < 4 | isempty(ftol),    ftol = 5e-5;  end
if nargin < 5 | isempty(maxit),   maxit = 15;   end
if nargin < 5 | isempty(verbose), verbose = 0;  end
xeps = max(xtol,5*eps);  feps = max(ftol,5*eps);     % Smallest tols are 5*eps

if verbose, fprintf('\nNewton iterations\n  k      norm(f)       norm(dx)\n'); end

x = x0;  k = 0;         % Initial guess and current number of iterations
while k <= maxit
  k = k + 1;
  [J,f] = feval(Jfun,x,varargin{:});    %  Returns Jacobian matrix and f vector
  dx = J\f;
  x = x - dx;
  if verbose, fprintf('%3d %12.3e %12.3e\n',k,norm(f),norm(dx));  end
  if ( norm(f) < feps ) | ( norm(dx) < xeps ),  return;   end
end
warning(sprintf('Solution not found within tolerance after %d iterations\n',k));
```

Listing 8.9   The newtonSys function applies Newton's method to a user-defined systems of equations.

horizontal pipe ($z_1 - z_2$) with constant cross section ($V_1 = V_2$). The result is

$$\frac{p_1 - p_2}{\gamma} = cQ^2.$$

From experience, we know that if a fluid flows from station 1 to station 2 (i.e., $Q > 0$), then $p_1 > p_2$. If the flow is in the opposite direction (i.e., $Q < 0$), then $p_1 < p_2$. This sense can be restored to the energy equation if we use

$$\frac{p_1 - p_2}{\gamma} = -\text{sign}(Q)cQ^2.$$

Applying this modification to f gives

$$f = \begin{bmatrix} Q_1 + Q_2 - Q_3 \\ p_j/\gamma + c_1\text{sign}(Q_1)Q_1^2 + z_j - z_1 \\ p_j/\gamma + c_2\text{sign}(Q_2)Q_2^2 + z_j - z_2 \\ p_j/\gamma - c_3\text{sign}(Q_3)Q_3^2 + z_j - z_3 \end{bmatrix}. \tag{8.63}$$

The J defined in Equation (8.62) and the f defined in Equation (8.63) are coded in the JfReservoir function in Listing 8.11. The main program is demoThreeRes in Listing 8.10. demoThreeRes defines L, d, and z values for a particular set of reservoirs and connecting pipes. demoThreeRes then sets an initial guess and calls newtonSys to solve the system.

Running demoThreeRes with the default parameters gives

```
>> demoThreeRes

Newton iterations
  k      norm(f)        norm(dx)
  1    7.581e+01      1.400e+05
  2    3.734e+01      1.082e+05
  3    1.795e+02      4.277e+04
  4    4.333e+01      4.365e+04
  5    6.942e+00      1.929e+03
  6    4.972e-01      2.465e+02
  7    3.376e-03      1.865e+00
  8    1.586e-07      8.801e-05

Flow rates: Q1  = 1.19, Q2 = -0.32, Q3 = -0.86 m^3/s
Junction pressure     = 134841 Pa
Net flow rate into junction    = 0.000e+00 m^3/s
```

For the default elevations, $z_1 = 30$, $z_2 = 18$, $z_3 = 9$, and $z_j = 11$, water flows out of reservoir 1 and into reservoirs 2 and 3. Experimenting with different elevations of the reservoirs is encouraged. Does the model give expected results for demoThreeRes([12; 14; 16; 5]) and demoThreeRes([12; 12; 12; 15])?

```
function demoThreeRes(z,maxit)
% demoThreeRes  Solve the three reservoir problem with Newton's method
%
% Synopsis:  demoThreeRes(z,maxit)
%
% Input:  z = (optional) vector of four elements containing the elevation
%             of each of the three reservoirs (z(1:3)) and the elevation
%             of the junction, z(4).  Default:  z = [30; 18; 9; 11] (m).
%         maxit = (optional) max number of iterations.  Default: maxit = 5
%
% Output:  Solution is printed to command window

if nargin<1,  z = [30; 18; 9; 11];  end
if nargin<2,  maxit=15;             end

% --- Assign problem parameters
L = [3000; 600; 1000];            %  Lengths of pipes, (m)
d = [1; 0.45; 0.6];               %  diameters of pipes,  (m)
area = 0.25*pi*d.^2;              %  area of pipe sections
Kf = [0.015; 0.024; 0.020];       %  friction factor,  assumed constant
c = Kf.*(L./d)./(2*9.8*area.^2);  %  constant in head loss formula
q  = [1; 1; 1];                   %  intial guess at flow rates,  (m^3/s)
pj = 1e5;                         %  initial guess at junction pressure, (Pa)

% --- Solve the system and print results
x0 = [q; pj];                     %  initial guess at solution vector
x = newtonSys('JfReservoir',x0,[],[],maxit,1,z,c);

fprintf('\nFlows rates: Q1 = %5.2f, Q2 = %5.2f, Q3 = %5.2f m^3/s\n',x(1:3));
fprintf('Junction pressure = %8.0f Pa\n',x(4));
fprintf('Net flow rate into junction = %12.3e m^3/s\n',sum(x(1:3)));
```

Listing 8.10   The demoThreeRes function uses newtonSys to solve
the system of nonlinear equations that define the three-reservoir problem.

```
function [J,f] = JfReservoir(x,z,c)
% JFreservoir  Jacobian and f vector for three reservoir system
%
% Synopsis:  [J,f] = JFreservoir(x,z,c)
%
% Input: x = current guess at solution vector
%        z = vector of elevations of reservoirs and junction, (m)
%            z = [z1; z2; z3; zj]
%        c = constant in Darcy-Weisbach equation, c = f (L/d)(V^2/2/g)(1/A)
%            for each pipe.
%
% Output: J = Jacobian matrix for the system
%         f = right hand side vector for Newton iterations

gamw = 9790;                          %  specific weight of water, (N/m^3)
q = x(1:3);   pj = x(4);   zj = z(4); %  extract problem variables from x
f = zeros(4,1);   J = zeros(4,4);     %  Initialize

% ---- equation 1:  sum(q) = 0
f(1) = q(1) + q(2) + q(3);
J(1,1) = 1;   J(1,2) = 1;   J(1,3) = 1;

% ---- equation 2:  head loss in branch 1
f(2) = pj/gamw + sign(q(1))*c(1)*q(1)^2 + zj - z(1);
J(2,1) = sign(q(1))*2*c(1)*q(1);
J(2,4) = 1/gamw;

% --- equation 3:  head loss in branch 2
f(3) = pj/gamw + sign(q(2))*c(2)*q(2)^2 + zj - z(2);
J(3,2) = sign(q(2))*2*c(2)*q(2);
J(3,4) = 1/gamw;

% --- equation 4:  head loss in branch 3
f(4) = pj/gamw + sign(q(3))*c(3)*q(3)^2 + zj - z(3);
J(4,3) = sign(q(3))*2*c(3)*q(3);
J(4,4) = 1/gamw;
```

Listing 8.11   The JfReservoir function computes the Jacobian and right-hand-side vector for the three-reservoir problem.

.6 SUMMARY

A solution to the system $Ax = b$ exists if and only if A and b are consistent (i.e., if and only if b lies in the column space of A). Equivalently, A and b are consistent if $\text{rank}(A) = \text{rank}([A \; b])$. The solution to $Ax = b$ (if it exists) is unique if and only if $\text{rank}(A) = n$. Any system of n equations in n unknowns (i.e., A is $n \times n$) will be consistent if $\text{rank}(A) = n$. The solution to an $n \times n$ system, therefore, exists *and* is unique if and only if $\text{rank}(A) = n$.

If A is an $n \times n$ matrix with $\text{rank}(A) = n$, A is *nonsingular* and *invertible*. If A is invertible, then the inverse matrix A^{-1} exists, and the formal solution to $Ax = b$ is $x = A^{-1}b$. In general, one should not solve $Ax = b$ by first computing A^{-1} and then evaluating $A^{-1}b$. The mathematical statement $x = A^{-1}b$ should be interpreted as "solve $Ax = b$ with an appropriate numerical technique, such as Gaussian elimination with backward substitution."

Gaussian elimination with backward substitution is equivalent to finding the LU factorization of the coefficient matrix and applying triangular solutions with the L and U factors. If the coefficient matrix is symmetric and positive definite, the Cholesky factorization can be used. Solving a system with a Cholesky factorization reduces the number of floating-point operations by a factor of two.

The \ operator is the preferred way to solve linear systems of equations in MATLAB. The \ operator applies different methods depending on the shape and other properties of the coefficient matrix. Refer to § 8.4.3 for a summary of how the \ operator selects a solution method.

The numerical solution $\hat{x}$ of $Ax = b$ is different from the exact solution x because of roundoff errors in all stages of the solution process. Roundoff errors are initially introduced when A and b are stored in computer memory. More roundoff errors occur in the elimination (or factorization) of A, and during backward substitution to compute $\hat{x}$. The degree to which perturbations in A and b affect the numerical solution is determined by the value of the *condition number* $\kappa(A)$. A large value of $\kappa(A)$ indicates that A is close to being singular. When $\kappa(A)$ is large, A is said to be *ill conditioned*, and small perturbations in A and b can cause relatively large differences between $\hat{x}$ and x.

If $\kappa(A)$ is small, a stable algorithm like Gaussian elimination with partial pivoting will return a solution with a small residual, $r = b - A\hat{x}$. The number of correct significant digits in the $\hat{x}$ can be estimated from Equation (8.38). If $\kappa(A)$ is large, the solution returned by a computationally stable algorithm may have large errors even though the residuals are small.

Nonlinear systems of equations require an iterative solution because A or b or both depend on the solution x. At each iteration the computational effort is at least as much as solving a linear system of the same size. The successive substitution method and Newton's method are demonstrated in § 8.5. A general implementa-

TABLE 8.3   NMM TOOLBOX FUNCTIONS DEMONSTRATING SOLUTION METHODS FOR SYSTEM OF EQUATIONS. THESE MFILES ARE IN THE `LINALG` DIRECTORY OF THE NMM TOOLBOX.

Function	page	Description
Cholesky	425	Cholesky factorization of a symmetric, positive definite matrix
demoNewtonSys	435	Apply Newton's method to a nonlinear 2×2 system.
demoSSub	431	Apply successive substitution to a nonlinear 2×2 system.
demoThreeRes	441	Apply Newton's method to the system of four nonlinear equations arising from the three-reservoir problem.
GEPivShow	395	Solve a system with Gaussian elimination and print the result of each elimination step. Partial pivoting is used.
GEshow	388	Solve a system with Gaussian elimination and print the result of each elimination step. No pivoting is used.
JfReservoir	442	Function to evaluate the Jacobian matrix J and the vector f for the three-reservoir problem. See `demoThreeRes` and `newtonSys`.
pumpCurve	397	Solve the system of equations for a quadratic model of a centrifugal pump.
luNopiv	417	LU factorization without pivoting.
luPiv	418	LU factorization with partial pivoting.
newtonSys	437	General implementation of Newton's method for systems of nonlinear equations.

tion of the Newton's method for nonlinear systems is provided by the `newtonSys` function in the NMM Toolbox.

Table 8.3 lists the m-files developed in this chapter.

Further Reading

Strang [72] gives an excellent elementary description of computing the solution to $Ax = b$. In addition, he provides MATLAB functions to implement LU factorization and backward substitution. Strang's programs are easy to read, yet they reveal some of the details that are hidden in MATLAB's built-in `lu` function and backslash operator. Datta [12] and Van Loan [77] also provide MATLAB implementations of Gaussian elimination and LU factorization.

Stewart [68] gives a good introduction to the numerical solution of linear systems. His elegant presentation provides a bridge to more advanced references. Gill et al. [28] also provide a thorough and concise view of the solution to linear systems. Watkins [78] provides an excellent exposition of the computational aspects of solving linear systems. Kahaner et al. [43] describe the use of a Fortran software library to solve linear systems. This library is the basis of the codes used in MATLAB up to version 5.

For a comprehensive treatment of the solution to $Ax = b$, see Golub and Van Loan [32]. Several recent books also provide excellent treatment of numerical linear algebra at an advanced level. See Demmel [15] for a description of the state of the art in computational algorithms, Trefethen and Bau [76] for an elegant discussion of the mathematics behind the computations, and Higham [36] for a thorough discussion of roundoff errors in solving linear systems. Anderson et al. [4] document the LAPACK library, a state-of-the-art package of Fortran codes for solving linear systems. Version 6 of MATLAB incorporates LAPACK

Most elementary textbooks on numerical analysis provide a brief overview of Newton's method for nonlinear systems of equations. There are a variety of other methods, and here the problem of nonlinear systems of equations overlaps the problem of nonlinear optimization. Readers wishing an up-to-date, intermediate-level introduction to iterative methods for nonlinear systems should consult the book by Kelley [44], who provides MATLAB codes. For a discussion of nonlinear problems and optimization, see Dennis and Schanbel [16] and Kelley [45].

EXERCISES

The number in parenthesis at the beginning of each exercise indicates the degree of skill and amount of effort necessary to complete the exercise. See § 1.4 on page 10 for a description of the rating system.

1. (1) Convert the following set of equations for the unknowns a, b, and c to matrix form. Does a unique solution to the system exist? If so, what is it?

$$a = 4(b - c),$$

$$\frac{b - a}{2c} = 1,$$

$$a + b = c - 2.$$

2. (1) Convert the following set of equations for the unknowns a, b, and c to matrix form. Does a unique solution to the system exist? If so, what is it?

$$a = 4(b - c),$$

$$\frac{b - a}{2c} = 1,$$

$$a - b = 2(1 - c).$$

3. (1) Given $R_1 = 2\,°C/W$, $R_2 = 0.5\,°C/W$, $R_3 = 35\,°C/W$, $R_4 = 0.7\,°C/W$, $R_5 = 1\,°C/W$, determine whether Equation (8.2) on page 368 has a solution. If the solution exists, is it unique?

4. (2) In Example 8.2, a system of seven equations in seven unknowns is developed. In the last paragraph under "Write the equations in natural form" is a note about the substitution, $Q_5 = Q_2$. (See page 367.) Suppose that the equation $Q_2 = (T_w - T_a)/R_5$ was instead written as $Q_5 = (T_w - T_a)/R_5$. How many unkowns would there be in this new system? Identify the additional (trivial) equation necessary to define a system with the same number of equations as unknowns. Write the matrix form of this new system of equations. Using the numerical values from Exercise 3, determine whether this system has a solution. If the solution exists, is it unique?

5. (1) Manually evaluate $Q^T Q$ for

$$Q = \begin{bmatrix} 1/\sqrt{2} & 0 & -1/\sqrt{2} \\ 0 & 1 & 0 \\ 1/\sqrt{2} & 0 & 1/\sqrt{2} \end{bmatrix}.$$

Identify all special properties of Q.

SOLUTION **6.** (1+) Manually solve $QRx = b$ for x, where

$$Q = \begin{bmatrix} 1/\sqrt{2} & 0 & -1/\sqrt{2} \\ 0 & 1 & 0 \\ 1/\sqrt{2} & 0 & 1/\sqrt{2} \end{bmatrix}, \quad R = \sqrt{2} \begin{bmatrix} 1 & 1 & 1 \\ 0 & 1 & 1 \\ 0 & 0 & 1 \end{bmatrix}, \quad b = \begin{bmatrix} 2 \\ 2\sqrt{2} \\ 4 \end{bmatrix}.$$

(*Hint*: Take advantage of the properties of Q identified in the preceding problem.)

7. (1+) Manually solve $CDx = b$ for x, given that

$$C = \begin{bmatrix} 1 & 0 & 0 \\ 1/2 & 1 & 0 \\ 1/4 & 1/2 & 1 \end{bmatrix}, \quad D = \begin{bmatrix} 2 & 1 & 0 \\ 0 & 2 & 1 \\ 0 & 0 & 2 \end{bmatrix}, \quad b = \begin{bmatrix} 1 \\ 1 \\ 1 \end{bmatrix}.$$

(*Hint*: Study the structure of C and D before doing any algebra.)

8. (1+) Manually solve $CDEx = b$ for x, given that

$$C = \begin{bmatrix} 1 & 0 & 0 \\ 4 & 1 & 0 \\ 3 & 2 & 1 \end{bmatrix}, \quad D = \begin{bmatrix} 2 & 0 & 0 \\ 0 & 1 & 0 \\ 0 & 0 & 2 \end{bmatrix}, \quad E = \begin{bmatrix} 1 & 4 & 3 \\ 0 & 1 & 5 \\ 0 & 0 & 1 \end{bmatrix}, \quad b = \begin{bmatrix} 20 \\ 84 \\ 70 \end{bmatrix}.$$

(*Hint*: Study the structure of C, D, and E before doing any algebra.)

9. (1) On page 374 the "implications of consistency and rank" are listed as a series of bullets. Restate the text of the bullets by replacing all references to rank(A) with the appropriate description of the linear independence of the vectors that constitute A.

10. (2, each) Determine whether each of the given systems is consistent. For each consistent system, give a solution. Give more than one solution if multiple solutions are possible.

(a) $$\begin{bmatrix} 1 & 0 \\ 1 & 1 \end{bmatrix} \begin{bmatrix} x_1 \\ x_2 \end{bmatrix} = \begin{bmatrix} 2 \\ 1 \end{bmatrix}.$$
(b) $$\begin{bmatrix} 1 & 1 \\ 0 & 0 \end{bmatrix} \begin{bmatrix} x_1 \\ x_2 \end{bmatrix} = \begin{bmatrix} 2 \\ 1 \end{bmatrix}.$$

(c) $\begin{bmatrix} 1 & 1 \\ 0 & 0 \end{bmatrix}\begin{bmatrix} x_1 \\ x_2 \end{bmatrix} = \begin{bmatrix} 0 \\ 0 \end{bmatrix}.$

(d) $\begin{bmatrix} 1 & 0 \\ 0 & 0 \end{bmatrix}\begin{bmatrix} x_1 \\ x_2 \end{bmatrix} = \begin{bmatrix} 0 \\ 0 \end{bmatrix}.$

(e) $\begin{bmatrix} 1 & 1 \\ 1 & 0 \\ 0 & 1 \end{bmatrix}\begin{bmatrix} x_1 \\ x_2 \end{bmatrix} = \begin{bmatrix} 2 \\ 1 \\ 1 \end{bmatrix}.$

(f) $\begin{bmatrix} 1 & 1 \\ 1 & 0 \\ 0 & 1 \end{bmatrix}\begin{bmatrix} x_1 \\ x_2 \end{bmatrix} = \begin{bmatrix} 1 \\ -1 \\ -1 \end{bmatrix}.$

(g) $\begin{bmatrix} 1 & 2 & 0 & 2 \\ 0 & 1 & 3 & 4 \\ 1 & 0 & 1 & 2 \end{bmatrix}\begin{bmatrix} x_1 \\ x_2 \\ x_3 \\ x_4 \end{bmatrix} = \begin{bmatrix} 4 \\ 4 \\ 4 \end{bmatrix}.$

(h) $\begin{bmatrix} 1 & 2 & -3 & 1 \\ 0 & 1 & -2 & 1 \\ 1 & 0 & 1 & -1 \end{bmatrix}\begin{bmatrix} x_1 \\ x_2 \\ x_3 \\ x_4 \end{bmatrix} = \begin{bmatrix} -1 \\ 2 \\ 1 \end{bmatrix}.$

11. (2) By hand, use Gaussian elimination to solve the two systems of equations in Example 8.3. Write the augmented system for each of the two systems, and continue elimination using rows 1 and 2 to obtain a triangular (augmented) matrix. What is the last equation of each augmented system at the final step of elimination? How do these equations relate to a common-sense notion of consistency?

SOLUTION 12. (2+) Starting with the code in the GEshow function, develop a GErect function that performs Gaussian Elimination only (no backward substitution) for rectangular ($m \times n$) matrices. The GErect function should return $\tilde{A}$, the triangularized coefficient matrix, and $\tilde{b}$, the corresponding right-hand-side vector. Use the GErect function to solve Exercise 11.

13. (2) Use the GErect function developed in the preceding Exercise to apply Gaussian elimination to $Ax = b$ when A and b are defined as

$$A = \begin{bmatrix} 1 & 1 \\ 2 & 1 \\ 3 & 1 \end{bmatrix}, \qquad b = \begin{bmatrix} 2 \\ 1 \\ 0 \end{bmatrix}.$$

From the triangularized coefficient matrix, would you say that the system is consistant? (See also Example 8.3.)

14. (2) Use the \ operator to solve equation $Ax = b$, where A and b are defined as

$$A = \begin{bmatrix} 1 & 1 \\ 2 & 1 \\ 3 & 1 \end{bmatrix}, \qquad b = \begin{bmatrix} 2 \\ 1 \\ 0 \end{bmatrix}.$$

(See also Example 8.3.) Why are the values of x(1)+1 and x(2)-3 nonzero?

15. (2) Consider the singular system (cf. Example 8.4 on page 374)

$$\begin{bmatrix} 2 & 1 \\ 2 & 1 \end{bmatrix} \begin{bmatrix} x_1 \\ x_2 \end{bmatrix} = \begin{bmatrix} 6 \\ 6 \end{bmatrix}.$$

Find the four solutions obtained when the elements of A and b are perturbed as follows (use $\delta = 5 \times 10^{-9}$).

(a) $a_{21} = 2 + \delta$.

(b) $a_{22} = 1 + \delta$.

(c) $a_{11} = 2 + \delta$, $b_1 = 6 + \delta$.

(d) $a_{21} = 2 + \delta$, $b_2 = 6 + \delta$.

SOLUTION **16.** (2) Write an `lsolve` function to solve $Ax = b$ when A is a lower triangular matrix. Test your function by comparing solutions it obtains to with the solution obtained with the backslash operator.

17. (2) Write a `usolve` function to solve $Ax = b$ when A is a upper triangular matrix. Test your function by comparing the solutions it obtains to the solution obtained with the backslash operator.

18. (1) Using the resistance values in Exercise 3, $T_a = 25\,°C$, and $Q_c = 10\,W$, what are the temperatures and heat flows in the thermal network model of the IC package in Example 8.2?

19. (1+) Use MATLAB's built-in \ operator to solve the following system of equations:

$$x_1 + 2x_2 - x_4 = 9,$$
$$2x_1 + 3x_2 - x_3 = 9,$$
$$4x_2 + 2x_3 - 5x_4 = 26,$$
$$5x_1 + 5x_2 + 2x_3 - 4x_4 = 32.$$

20. (2) Write a `safeSolve` function with the definition

```
function x = safeSolve(A,b)
```

to provide an interface to the \ operator for solving $n \times n$ systems of equations. The `safeSolve` function should check the dimensions of A and b to make sure they are compatible, and thereby avoid unintended consequences of misapplying \. (In this context "compatible" does not refer to consistency of A and b or to the rank of A.) Print a meaningful error message if A and b are incompatible. If A and b are compatible evaluate x = A\b and return x. Verify that your function works by applying it to at least one compatible system, and two incompatible systems.

SOLUTION **21.** (3) The inverse of matrix A satisfies $AA^{-1} = I$. Using the column view of matrix–matrix multiplication (see Algorithm 7.5 on page 327) we see that the jth column of A^{-1} is the vector x such that $Ax = e_{(j)}$, where $e_{(j)}$ is the jth column of the identity matrix (e.g., $e_3 = [0, 0, 1, \ldots, 0]^T$). By solving $Ax = e_{(j)}$ for $j = 1, \ldots, n$ the columns of A^{-1} can be produced one at a time.

   (a) Write a function called `invByCol` that computes the inverse of an $n \times n$ matrix one column at a time. Use the backslash operator to solve for each column of A^{-1}.

   (b) Use the estimates in Table 8.1 to derive an order-of-magnitude estimate for how the flop count of `invByCol` depends on n for an $n \times n$ matrix.

   (c) Verify the estimate derived in part (b) by measuring the flop count of `invByCol` for matrices of increasing size. Use `A = rand(n,n)` for $n = 2, 4, 8, 16, 32, \ldots$, 128. Compare the flop count of `invByCol` with those of the built-in inv command. Note that the order-of-magnitude estimate will only hold as n becomes large. Users of MATLAB version 6 will not be able to use the `flops` function to measure the flops performed by `inv`. In that case, use the estimate that matrix inversion can be performed in $\mathcal{O}(n^3)$ flops.

22. (2) Write a `parabola` function to automatically set up and solve the system of equations for a parabola defined by $y = c_1 x^2 + c_2 x + c_3$. The function definition should be

```
function c = parabola(x,y)
```

The function should take two input vectors x and y, each of length three, that define three points through which the parabola passes. The function should return a vector of the three coefficients c_i.

Find the equation of the parabolas passing through each of the following sets of points. For each set of three points, use the c_i to create a vector of 100 points on the parabola, and plot these points along with the original three points to verify that the equation of the parabola has been obtained correctly.

   (a) $(-2, -1)$, $(0, 1)$, $(2, 2)$.

   (b) $(-2, -1)$, $(1, -1)$, $(2, 0)$.

   (c) $(-2, -2)$, $(-1, 1)$, $(2, -1)$.

   (d) $(-2, 2)$, $(0, 0)$, $(2, -2)$.

   (e) $(-2, 2)$, $(-1, -2)$, $(-1, 2)$.

23. (2) Consider the equation of a plane written as $a_1 x + a_2 y + a_3 = z$. Given three known points (x_1, y_1, z_1), (x_2, y_2, z_2), and (x_3, y_3, z_3), write the system of equations that determine a_1, a_2, and a_3. Write a `plane` function that returns the a_i given any three points. Test your function by finding the equation of the plane passing through $(1, 0, 0)$, $(0, 1, 0)$, and $(0, 0, 1)$. What are the values of z at $(x, y) = (0, 0.5)$, $(0.5, 0)$, $(0.25, 0.25)$, and $(0.5, 0.5)$?

24. (2) Using $R_1 = R_3 = R_4 = R_5 = 10\,k\Omega$ and $R_2 = 20\,k\Omega$, what is the rank of the 3×3 coefficient matrix in Example 8.5? Is the 3×3 system consistent for $V_{\text{in}} = 5\,V$? For the same resistance values, what is the rank of the 2×2 coefficient matrix in the system of equations for v_b and v_c? Given $V_{\text{in}} = 5\,V$, what are the values of v_a, v_b, v_c, and v_d?

25. (2+) An alternative way to resolve the singularity in the 3×3 coefficient matrix of Example 8.5 is to modify the elements of the matrix. Write a *trivial* equation involving v_b, v_c, and v_d that has the solution $v_d = 0$. Use this equation to replace the equation for v_d in the 3×3 system in Example 8.5. Solve the resulting 3×3 system to obtain the value of V_{out} for $R_1 = R_3 = R_4 = R_5 = 10\,k\Omega$, $R_2 = 20\,k\Omega$, and $V_{\text{in}} = 5\,V$.

26. (2) Plot $V_{out} = v_b - v_c$ versus R_2 in the range $1k\,\Omega \leq R_2 \leq 100k\,\Omega$ for the Wheatstone bridge in Example 8.5. Use $R_1 = R_3 = R_4 = R_5 = 10\,k\Omega$ and $V_{in} = 5\,V$. Can the computational work be reduced by factoring the coefficient matrix once and reusing it? (*Hint*: Automate the solution by writing a function to set up and solve the system for the resistance values input as a vector.)

27. (2−) Solve Equation (8.19) for $R_1 = R_3 = R_4 = R_5 = 10\,k\Omega$, $R_2 = 20\,k\Omega$ and $V_{in} = 5\,V$. What is the value of $V_{out} = v_b - v_c$?

28. (2) A paint company is trying to recycle unpopular paint colors by mixing them together to create more popular colors. All the paints in question are composed of four basic pigments. The following table lists the constituents of the four unpopular colors:

paint number	Percent of Pigments A	B	C	D
1	80	0	16	4
2	0	80	20	0
3	30	10	60	0
4	10	10	72	8

A more desirable color is 40% pigment A, 27% pigment B, 31% pigment C, and 2% pigment D. How much of each of the unpopular paints should be added to form one gallon of the popular color? (*Hint*: Let x_j be the fraction of a gallon of unpopular paint j that is to be combined to form the new paint. Then, the amount of pigment A in the new paint can be computed with $80x_1 + 30x_3 + 10x_4 = 40$.)

29. (2+) The accompanying sketch depicts an electrical circuit consisting of resistors and voltage sources. Requiring that the voltage drops around any loop sum to zero (Kirchhoff's voltage law) results in the following equations:

$$i_1 R_1 + v_1 + (i_1 - i_2)R_2 - v_3 = 0,$$

$$(i_2 - i_1)R_2 + i_2 R_3 + v_2 + i_2 R_4 + (i_2 - i_4)R_5 = 0,$$

$$i_3 R_6 + v_3 + (i_3 - i_4)R_8 + v_4 + i_3 R_7 = 0,$$

$$-v_4 + (i_4 - i_3)R_8 + (i_4 - i_2)R_5 + i_4 R_9 + v_5 = 0,$$

where i_k is the current around loop k.

(a) Rewrite these equations in the form $Ri = v$, where R is a matrix and i and v are vectors.

(b) Compute the current flowing through each loop given the resistors and voltage sources in the following tables:

resistor	1	2	3	4	5	6	7	8	9
R $(k\Omega)$	1	3.5	4	1.75	1	1	2	1.5	5

voltage source	1	2	3	4	5
v (V)	5	5	2.5	2	5

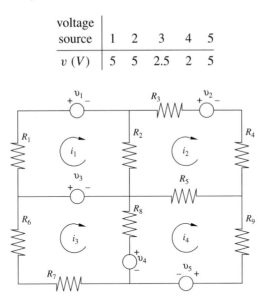

30. (2−) Derive an expression for the condition number $\kappa_1(D)$ for the arbitrary diagonal matrix

$$D = \mathrm{diag}(d_1, d_2, \ldots, d_n) = \begin{bmatrix} d_1 & & & \\ & d_2 & & \\ & & \ddots & \\ & & & d_n \end{bmatrix}.$$

Show that if the d_i are equal (i.e, $D = \alpha I$) for some scalar α, then $\kappa_1(D) = \alpha^2$. Finally, conclude that $\kappa_1(I) = 1$

31. (1+) Show that $\kappa(A) \geq 1$ for any A. (*Hint*: Start with $\|I\| = \|AA^{-1}\|$ and the final result of the preceding problem.)

32. (2) Modify the pumpCurve function from Example 8.1 to accept q and h vectors of arbitrary length as input. The degree of the interpolating polynomial does not need to be explicitly specified since it is determined by length(q)-1. (*Programming hints*: b = h(:), help vander.) In addition to computing the polynomial coefficients in your modified pumpCurve function, compute the condition number of matrix A. Use values from the following table to obtain the coefficients of the interpolating polynomials of degree 3 and 4.

q (m³/s)	0.0001	0.00025	0.0008	0.001	0.0014
h (m)	115	114.2	110	105.5	92.5

Use the first, second, third, and fifth points from the table to define the cubic polynomial interpolant. Report the polynomial coefficients and condition number of A

for both interpolants. How does the condition number change with the degree of the polynomial?

SOLUTION **33.** (3) Use the `pumpCurve` function developed in Exercise 32 to study the effect of perturbing the input data. Specifically, replace the second h value, $h = 114.2$, with $h = 114$, and re-evaluate the coefficients of the cubic interpolating polynomial. Let $\tilde{c}$ be the coefficients of the interpolating polynomial derived from the perturbed data, and let c be the coefficients of the polynomial derived from the original data. What is the relative difference, $(\tilde{c}_i - c_i)/c_i$, in each of the polynomial coefficients? Evaluate and plot $h(q)$ for the two cubic interpolating polynomials at 100 data points in the range $\min(q) \le q \le \max(q)$. What is the maximum difference in h for the interpolants derived from the original and the perturbed data? Discuss the practical significance of the effect perturbing the data on the values of c and the values of h obtained from the interpolant.

34. (3−) Repeat the computations in Exercise 33 after converting the q data to m^3/hour. Which of the results change? Which of the results are unaffected by the scaling? What are the merits of scaling the input data for this problem?

35. (2) Write a `condSurvey` function that computes and plots $\kappa_2(A)$ for matrices created with the built in `rand` function. For a sequence of increasing dimension (say n = [4 8 16 ... 128]), generate 10 random $n \times n$ matrices (10 for each n) and compute their condition number. Create a log–log plot of the variation of $\kappa(A)$ with n. What general trend is observed?

36. (2) Let x be the exact solution and $\hat{x}$ be the numerical solution to $Ax = b$. Define the residual by $r = b - A\hat{x}$, and derive Equation (8.37). (*Hint*: Show that $r = A(x - \hat{x})$, and use Equation (8.28).)

37. (2) In Example 8.9, two systems of the form

$$\begin{bmatrix} 1 & 1 \\ 2 & (2+\delta) \end{bmatrix} \begin{bmatrix} x_1 \\ x_2 \end{bmatrix} = \begin{bmatrix} 1 \\ 2 \end{bmatrix}, \qquad \begin{bmatrix} 1 & 1 \\ 2 & (2+\delta) \end{bmatrix} \begin{bmatrix} x_1 \\ x_2 \end{bmatrix} = \begin{bmatrix} 1.001 \\ 2 \end{bmatrix}$$

are solved with MATLAB's backslash operator. Use Gaussian elimination by hand to obtain the exact solutions to these systems. Does the backslash operator return the correct result when $\delta = 100\varepsilon_m$? Does the backslash operator return the correct result whe $\delta = \varepsilon_m/100$? Is the sensitivity of this system to perturbations of b dependent on whether the computations are performed in single or double precision?

38. (1) Verify that Equation (8.46) gives the inverses of

$$M_{(1)} = \begin{bmatrix} 1 & 0 & 0 \\ -m_{21} & 1 & 0 \\ -m_{31} & 0 & 1 \end{bmatrix} \quad \text{and} \quad M_{(2)} = \begin{bmatrix} 1 & 0 & 0 \\ 0 & 1 & 0 \\ 0 & -m_{32} & 1 \end{bmatrix}.$$

(*Hint*: Are the products equal to I?)

39. (2+) Starting with the `GEshow` function in Listing 8.1, write a `GEmultiplier` function that returns the matrix M such that MA is triangular. Your function should compute the M that gives

$$MA = \begin{bmatrix} -3 & 2 & -1 \\ 0 & -2 & 5 \\ 0 & 0 & -2 \end{bmatrix} \quad \text{when} \quad A = \begin{bmatrix} -3 & 2 & -1 \\ 6 & -6 & 7 \\ 3 & -4 & 4 \end{bmatrix}.$$

What is the M necessary to affect this transformation?

40. (3+) Develop the m-file functions necessary to solve $Ax = b$ with an in-place LU factorization of A. Specifically,

   (a) Create a modified version of `luPiv`, call it `luInPlace`, that returns the L and U factors of A in place of the original matrix A. The function definition line (first line of) `luInPlace` should be

   ```
   function [A,pv] = luInPlace(A,ptol)
   ```

   (b) Write a function called `luSolveInPlace` that solves $Ax = b$ and returns x given A and b as inputs. `luSolveInPlace` uses the factorization returned by `luInPlace` and solves the two triangular systems without explicitly creating L and U. The solve steps can be made compact by using the results of Exercises 16 and 17. Note that the `lsolve` function created in Exercise 16 will need to be modified so that multiplications and divisions by `L(i,i)` are replaced by implicit calculations involving ones.

   (c) Test your `luSolveInPlace` function by comparing the results it produces with the \ operator.

41. (2+) Explain the apparently inconsistent results of the following MATLAB statements:

   ```
   >> L = [1 0 0; 2 1 0; 3 1 1];
   >> U = [2 0 1; 0 2 1; 0 0 2];
   >> [L2,U2] = lu(L*U)
   ```

   Does this mean the LU factorization is not unique?

42. (3+) Given a Cholesky factorization $A = U^T U$, find the related symmetric factorization $A = LDL^T$, where L is lower triangular with ones on its diagonal, and D is a diagonal matrix. Write a MATLAB function called LDLT that returns the matrix L and a vector d containing the diagonal elements of D. Use `chol` to compute the Cholesky factorization inside LDLT. Test your function by factoring an $n \times n$ tridiagonal matrix with 2 on the diagonal and -1 on the sub and super diagonals. Use this test matrix as A in $Ax = b$, and solve for x when $b = [1, 0, \ldots, 0]^T$. (*Hint*: $A = U^T U = LDL^T = (LD^{1/2})(D^{1/2}L^T)$, where $D^{1/2}$ is the diagonal matrix such that $(D^{1/2})(D^{1/2}) = D$.) Also, note that $L^T = (D^{1/2})U$ is just a row scaling of U.

43. (3) Modify the LDLT function from the preceding exercise so that any row (or column) scaling operations do the minimum work by avoiding multiplication by zeros. Compare the flops of these two approaches.

44. (2+) Rewrite A and b for the system in Example 8.10 so that A is not dependent on x, but b is dependent on x. (*Hint*: Move all nonlinear terms to the right-hand side.) Create a modified version of `demoSsub` that solves the system with the new A and b.

Use your modified demoSsub to perform 15 successive substitution iterations with the sequence of initial guesses $x^{(0)} = [1, 1]^T, [2, 2]^T, \ldots [5, 5]^T$.

45. (3−) Modify the m-file function developed in Exercise 44 so that the coefficient matrix is factored with the lu function. Since A is constant, perform the LU factorization once outside the main loop. Use the built-in \ operator to perform triangular solves inside the main loop. Use the flops function to measure the effort saved by the LU factorization for 10 iterations. Develop an order-of-magnitude expression for the flop savings that can be realized using this strategy if matrix A is $n \times n$ and k successive substitution iterations are performed.

46. (2) Rewrite the demoNewtonSys function so that it uses the newtonSys function to solve the nonlinear system of equations in Example 8.13.

47. (4) For the circuit used in Exercise 29, find the value of R_5 such that $i_4 = -0.85\text{mA}$. There are different ways to solve this problem, but all are equivalent to a root-finding procedure:

- Manually iterate until i_4 is "close" to -0.85mA.
- Create a graphical solution using manually obtained data
- Embed the solution for the loop currents in a root-finding procedure. The function you wish to find the roots of is $f(R_5) = 0$. Each evaluation of $f(R_5)$ requires that the linear system be solved for the given guess at R_5. The returned value is the difference between the i_4 computed with the guess R_5 and the desired value of i_4.
- Solve the system with Newton's method.

9

Least-Squares Fitting of a Curve to Data

Curve fitting is the process of finding a relatively simple analytical function to approximate a set of data. The data are often from experimental measurements that may contain errors or have a limited number of significant digits. The approximating function contains parameters that are adjusted to give agreement with the data. The quality of the fit is most often measured by the summing the squares of differences between values of the approximating function and the given data. The *least-squares* principle asserts that the "best" fit is the one that minimizes this sum of squares.

The *linear* least-squares curve-fitting problem involves a set of *basis functions* $f_j(x)$, $j = 1, \ldots, n$, and undetermined fit coefficients c_j that define a fit function of the form

$$F(x) = c_1 f_1(x) + c_2 f_2(x) + \cdots + c_n f_n(x). \qquad (9.1)$$

For a given set of data pairs (x_i, y_i), $i = 1 \ldots m$, applying the least-squares principle provides a method for determining the c_j such that $F(x_j) \approx y_j$. In general, the number of data points m is larger than the number of undetermined coefficients n, so it is impossible to find the c_j that give $F(x_j) = y_j$ exactly.

For example, if $f_1(x) = x$ and $f_2(x) = 1$ (a constant), then

$$F(x) = c_1 x + c_2, \qquad (9.2)$$

455

and a straight line is fit to the data. The linear least-squares problem involves an $F(x)$ that is linearly dependent on the c_j, as in Equation (9.1). This does *not* require the $F(x)$ to be a linear function. For example, if $f_1(x) = x^2$, $f_2(x) = x$, and $f_3(x) = 1$, the approximation function $F(x)$ is a quadratic polynomial.

In the statistics literature, curve fitting is called *regression*. A thorough regression analysis involves an examination of the statistical properties of the input data and the fit function that results from solving the least-squares problem. Regression can also involve fitting procedures other than least-squares minimization. This chapter is concerned with the numerical aspects of specifying and solving the least-squares problem, not with a statistical analysis of data. A reader should have little trouble extending the m-files presented here to include statistical analysis. Refer to the "Further Reading" subsection of the end of the chapter summary for references that treat the statistical analysis of regression.

Figure 9.1 provides an overview of the chapter contents. We begin by developing the equations for fitting a line to data, as in Equation (9.2). The least-squares solution for the slope and intercept is implemented in an m-file function. The line-fitting procedure is then extended to functions that can be mathematically transformed into linear relationships. A common example of using transformations is in fitting data that exhibit an exponential decay. In this case, the *logarithm* of the output data (y) depends linearly on the input data (x).

Topics Covered in This Chapter

1. **Fitting Data to a Line**

   The least-squares problem is formulated for fitting data to a line. An m-file for performing the fit based on solution of the **normal equations** is developed. Use of linearizing transformations for some simple nonlinear-fitting problems is demonstrated.

2. **Fitting Data to Linear Combinations of Functions**

   The least-squares problem of fitting data to $y = F(x)$ where $F(x)$ is a linear combination of functions, is developed. M-files for performing the fit by solving the **normal equations** and by solving the overdetermined system via **QR factorization** are developed. Curve fitting to polynomials via the built-in `polyfit` function is covered.

3. **Multivariate Least Squares Fitting**

   The linear least-squares problem is extended to the case where the dependent variable y is a function of p independent parameters (i.e., $y = F(x_1, \ldots, x_p)$).

Figure 9.1 Primary topics discussed in Chapter 9.

After the procedure for least-squares fitting of a line is established, the general case of fitting a linear combination of arbitrary basis functions is developed. The coefficients of the least-squares fit may be obtained by solving the *normal equations* or by directly "solving" an overdetermined system with *QR factorization*. Both methods are developed in this chapter, and m-files are provided for curve-fitting with arbitrary combinations of basis functions. These m-files are useful for problems in which a mathematical model for the data is known in advance. When a model for the data is not known, it is common to use a polynomial for the fit function. In this case, the built-in `polyfit` function for polynomial curve-fitting is convenient. Use of the `polyfit` function is demonstrated with an example.

The final section of the chapter deals with the slightly more general problem of multivariate least-squares fitting. In this case, the dependent variable y is a function of more than one independent variable, $x_1, x_2, \ldots, x_p$.

Example 9.1: Time Constant for Discharge of a Capacitor

Figure 9.2(a) shows a simple experiment for measuring the voltage drop across a capacitor as it discharges. The switch is first moved to position 1, so that current from the battery charges the capacitor. At time $t = 0$, the switch is moved to position 2, so that current flows through the resistor, thereby discharging the capacitor. The time variation of the capacitor voltage is shown in Figure 9.2(b).

The variation of capacitor voltage with time is predicted by

$$V_c = V_{c,0} \exp\left(-\frac{t}{RC}\right).$$

If data for $V_c(t)$ are available, a least-squares fit can be used to find the value of the time constant $\tau = 1/(RC)$. A MATLAB implementation of this curve fit is provided in Example 9.5.

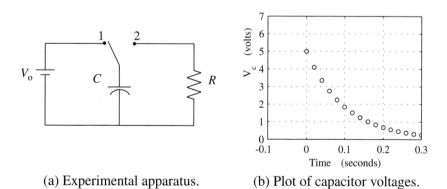

(a) Experimental apparatus.	(b) Plot of capacitor voltages.

Figure 9.2   Measuring the voltage across a discharging capacitor.

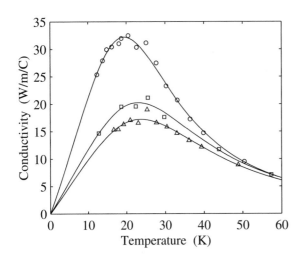

Figure 9.3   Measured values of the thermal conductivity of copper at low temperatures.

Example 9.2: Thermal Conductivity of Copper at Low Temperatures

Engineers developing very high-speed electronic circuits are attempting to take advantage of superconductivity at very low temperatures. By reducing the temperature, and thereby reducing electrical resistance of the semiconductor materials, the clock speed of the circuit can be increased. Getting the electrical signals into and out of the cryogenically cooled test circuit is one of the challenges of using this technology.

Heat transfer by conduction down the copper lead wires is a significant part of the heat load on the superconducting circuitry. To accurately model the flow of heat down the leads, the variation of thermal conductivity of copper with temperature must be taken into account. Figure 9.3 shows the results of thermal conductivity measurements for three different samples of copper used to make the leads. The data show that the conductivity k reaches a maximum and then decreases to zero as the temperature approaches absolute zero. A curve fit of $k(T)$ allows this experimental data to be used in the thermal design calculations. The thermal conductivity data used to create Figure 9.3 are stored in the cucon1.dat, cucon2.dat, and cucon3.dat files in the data directory of the NMM toolbox. The solid lines in Figure 9.3 are obtained from least-squares curve fits as described in Example 9.9 on page 481.

9.1 FITTING A LINE TO DATA

The simplest least-squares fitting problem involves finding the slope and intercept of the line that approximates a set of data. Solutions to this problem are ubiquitous—many hand-held calculators have built-in routines to do the job. The calculations necessary to obtain the slope and intercept are quite simple, and the eager reader may have already skipped ahead to the linefit function discussed in

§ 9.1.3 page 463. Although implementation of line fitting is easy, it is advantageous to carefully study the development of the equations that yield the fit coefficients. The same basic procedure, and the underlying principles, apply to the more interesting problem of fitting arbitrary linear combinations of functions.

Figure 9.4 shows a set of data that may be approximated by a line

$$y = F(x) = \alpha x + \beta \tag{9.3}$$

In Figure 9.4(a), lines with slightly different slopes and intercepts give plausible candidates for the best fit to the data. By adjusting α and β, it is possible to improve the fit for some data points at the expense of the fit for other data points. In general, it will be impossible to find a line that can approximate all the data equally well. Notice that the data in Figure 9.4 contain a point at $x \approx 4.5$ that is significantly below the lines that appear to fit most of the data. It is reasonable that a good choice for α and β will give a line that follows the trend of most of the data without passing too close to the outlier. A procedure for choosing α and β should somehow balance the quality of the fit for all data points.

Suppose that we measure the distance between the fit function and each data point and then combine these distances to obtain an overall measure of the goodness of the fit. Let r_i be the *vertical* distance between each data point and the line; that is,

$$r_i = y_i - F(x_i) = y_i - (\alpha x_i + \beta). \tag{9.4}$$

The symbol r is chosen because the r_i are residuals of the system of equations describing the fit. (See § 9.1.2.) The r_i are the vertical distances between the data

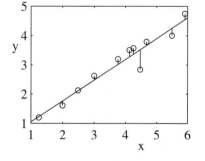

(a) Candidate lines for curve fits to some data. One data point near $x = 4.5$ appears to be an outlier.

(b) A least-squares fit minimizes the sum of squares of the $y_i - F(x_i)$ distances. This is the same data as in Figure 9.4a.

Figure 9.4   Least-squares fit of data to a line.

points and the fit function, as depicted in Figure 9.4(b). Since the r_i can be either positive or negative, we cannot simply add the r_i to obtain an aggregate measure of the fit. Two possible ways to combine the r_i are

$$\sum |r_i| \quad \text{and} \quad \sum r_i^2$$

The use of $\sum r_i^2$ to measure the quality of the fit has two significant advantages. First of all, it leads to a straightforward procedure for computing α and β (or, more generally, the c_j in Equation (9.1)). The second advantage is that, under appropriate restrictions on the (x_i, y_i) data, the values of α and β that minimize $\sum r_i^2$ are the most probable (in a statistical sense) values of α and β for the given (x_i, y_i). (See, for example, [19].)

Let ρ be the sum of the squares of the r_i:

$$\rho = \sum_{i=1}^{m} r_i^2 = \sum_{i=1}^{m} [y_i - (\alpha x_i + \beta)]^2. \tag{9.5}$$

Since the (x_i, y_i) data are given, only ρ, α, and β (all scalars) are unknown in Equation (9.5). Minimizing ρ with respect to α and β determines the line that obtains the *least-squares* fit of the data to the line. The "least" part refers to the process of minimization. The "squares" part refers to the quantity that is minimized, namely, $\rho = \sum r_i^2$. Applying the least-squares principle gives the equation of the line that corresponds to a minimum of the function $\rho(\alpha, \beta)$ defined by Equation (9.5). In the sections that follow, the equations for finding α and β are derived using two different approaches.

9.1.1 Minimizing the Residual

Our immediate goal is to develop a computational procedure for finding the values of α and β that minimize $\rho = \rho(\alpha, \beta)$. Necessary conditions for the minimum are

$$\left.\frac{\partial \rho}{\partial \alpha}\right|_{\beta=\text{constant}} = 0 \quad \text{and} \quad \left.\frac{\partial \rho}{\partial \beta}\right|_{\alpha=\text{constant}} = 0. \tag{9.6}$$

Carrying out the differentiation gives

$$\frac{\partial \rho}{\partial \alpha} = \sum_{i=1}^{m} \frac{\partial}{\partial \alpha} [y_i - (\alpha x_i + \beta)]^2 = \sum_{i=1}^{m} 2(-x_i)[y_i - (\alpha x_i + \beta)]$$

$$\frac{\partial \rho}{\partial \beta} = \sum_{i=1}^{m} \frac{\partial}{\partial \beta} [y_i - (\alpha x_i + \beta)]^2 = \sum_{i=1}^{m} 2(-1)[y_i - (\alpha x_i + \beta)]$$

Thus, Conditions (9.6) require that

$$0 = \sum_{i=1}^{m} x_i y_i - \alpha \sum_{i=1}^{m} x_i^2 - \beta \sum_{i=1}^{m} x_i$$

$$0 = \sum_{i=1}^{m} y_i - \alpha \sum_{i=1}^{m} x_i - \beta m$$

Rearranging terms gives

$$\left(\sum x_i^2 \right) \alpha + \left(\sum x_i \right) \beta = \sum x_i y_i \tag{9.7}$$

$$\left(\sum x_i \right) \alpha + m \beta = \sum y_i, \tag{9.8}$$

where the limits of the sum have been dropped for convenience. Equations (9.7) and (9.8) are the *normal equations* for the least-squares fit of data to a line. Manually solving this system for α and β yields

$$\alpha = \frac{\left(\sum x_i \right) \left(\sum y_i \right) - m \sum x_i y_i}{\left(\sum x_i \right)^2 - m \sum x_i^2}, \qquad \beta = \frac{\left(\sum x_i \right) \left(\sum x_i y_i \right) - \left(\sum x_i^2 \right) \left(\sum y_i \right)}{\left(\sum x_i \right)^2 - m \sum x_i^2}. \tag{9.9}$$

Equations (9.7) and (9.8) can also be written

$$\begin{bmatrix} \sum x_i^2 & \sum x_i \\ \sum x_i & m \end{bmatrix} \begin{bmatrix} \alpha \\ \beta \end{bmatrix} = \begin{bmatrix} \sum x_i y_i \\ \sum y_i \end{bmatrix}. \tag{9.10}$$

Before implementing an m-file to setup and solve Equation (9.10), we rederive this equation with an alternative approach.

9.1.2 An Overdetermined System of Equations

The preceding derivation uses a geometric motivation for finding the least-squares fit: The values of α and β are chosen to minimize the difference between the fit function and the data in the y-coordinate direction. The same curve fit can also be formulated directly as a system of m simultaneous linear equations in two parameters (α and β). Since there are fewer unknowns than equations, an exact solution is unlikely, and some additional constraints must be applied to obtain a solution.

Consider the case of fitting three data pairs (x_1, y_1), (x_2, y_2), and (x_3, y_3) to a line. It is possible, of course, to find the slope and intercept of a line that passes exactly through any *two* data pairs. For example, the line through the first and last data pairs has α and β that are the solution to

$$\begin{aligned} \alpha x_1 + \beta &= y_1, \\ \alpha x_3 + \beta &= y_3, \end{aligned} \quad \text{or} \quad \begin{bmatrix} x_1 & 1 \\ x_3 & 1 \end{bmatrix} \begin{bmatrix} \alpha \\ \beta \end{bmatrix} = \begin{bmatrix} y_1 \\ y_3 \end{bmatrix}.$$

This line, though a perfect fit through the first and last data pairs, does not minimize the value of ρ defined in Equation (9.5).

But why choose just the first and last points in the set? Instead, write down the equations of all the lines passing through each of the points. Doing so gives a system of equations with a nonsquare coefficient matrix

$$\begin{bmatrix} x_1 & 1 \\ x_2 & 1 \\ x_3 & 1 \end{bmatrix} \begin{bmatrix} \alpha \\ \beta \end{bmatrix} = \begin{bmatrix} y_1 \\ y_2 \\ y_3 \end{bmatrix}. \tag{9.11}$$

This equation is allowed by the rules of linear algebra, since the inner dimensions of the matrices on the left-hand side are compatible. (Cf. § 7.2.2 beginning on page 310).

The preceding development can be generalized to a set of m data pairs (x_i, y_i), $i = 1, \ldots, m$. If we write the m equations that express a linear dependence of y_i on x_i, we get

$$\begin{bmatrix} x_1 & 1 \\ x_2 & 1 \\ \vdots & \vdots \\ x_m & 1 \end{bmatrix} \begin{bmatrix} \alpha \\ \beta \end{bmatrix} = \begin{bmatrix} y_1 \\ y_2 \\ \vdots \\ y_m \end{bmatrix}.$$

This can be more compactly expressed as

$$Ac = y, \tag{9.12}$$

where

$$A = \begin{bmatrix} x_1 & 1 \\ x_2 & 1 \\ \vdots & \vdots \\ x_m & 1 \end{bmatrix}, \quad c = \begin{bmatrix} \alpha \\ \beta \end{bmatrix}, \quad y = \begin{bmatrix} y_1 \\ y_2 \\ \vdots \\ y_m \end{bmatrix}. \tag{9.13}$$

Equation (9.12) has an exact solution only if the y_i lie along a line defined by a particular choice of α and β. In the language of § 8.1.2, this means that an exact solution is possible only if y lies in the column space of A. Since an exact solution is unlikely, the residual vector

$$r = y - Ac \tag{9.14}$$

will be nonzero. The least-squares principle provides a compromise "solution" that gives the minimum value of $\|r\|_2$. Directly evaluating $\rho = \|r\|_2^2$ from Equation (9.14) gives

$$\rho = \|r\|_2^2 = r^T r = (y - Ac)^T (y - Ac)$$
$$= y^T y - y^T Ac - c^T A^T y + c^T A^T Ac$$
$$= y^T y - 2y^T Ac + c^T A^T Ac.$$

Minimizing ρ with respect to the vector of parameters, c, requires that $\partial \rho / \partial c = 0$. Evaluating the derivative using the rules of linear algebra gives

$$\frac{\partial \rho}{\partial c} = -2A^T y + 2A^T Ac.$$

For a minimum of ρ to exist, $-A^T y + A^T Ac = 0$, or

$$\boxed{(A^T A)c = A^T y.} \tag{9.15}$$

Equation (9.15) is the general form of the *normal equations* for least-squares curve-fitting. Direct computation. (See Exercise 5) reveals that Equation (9.15) is equivalent to Equation (9.10) for the line-fitting problem.

9.1.3 Implementation of Line Fitting

The preceding sections provide different views of least-squares fitting of data to a line. We now turn to the task of implementing the computations in an m-file. To fit data to a line, matrix A and vector y are defined as in Equation (9.13), and Equation (9.15) is solved for c. Alternatively (see Exercise 4), the slope and intercept of the line can be computed from Equations (9.9). We take the former approach here as it provides an example for the more general problem of least-squares fitting of arbitrary combinations of functions, as described later.

The linefit function in Listing 9.1 assembles matrix A and solves Equation (9.15). The linefit function can be called in one of two ways

```
c = linefit(x,y)
[c,R2] = linefit(x,y)
```

The inputs x and y are equal length vectors of data. The output c is a vector of length two containing the slope and intercept, respectively, of the least-squares line fit. The optional second parameter R2 is the R^2 statistic described in § 9.1.4. Example 9.3 shows how linefit is used.

Example 9.3: Fitting Four Data Points to a Line

Consider fitting the four points $(1,1)$, $(2, 2)$, $(4, 2)$, and $(5, 3)$ to a line. The linefit function does all the work once the (x, y) data are specified.

```
function [c,R2] = linefit(x,y)
% linefit    Least-squares fit of data to y = c(1)*x + c(2)
%
% Synopsis:   c    = linefit(x,y)
%            [c,R2] = linefit(x,y)
%
% Input:    x,y = vectors of independent and dependent variables
%
% Output:   c = vector of slope, c(1), and intercept, c(2) of least sq. line fit
%           R2 = (optional) coefficient of determination; 0 <= R2 <= 1
%               R2 close to 1 indicates a strong relationship between y and x
if length(y)~= length(x),  error('x and y are not compatible');  end

x = x(:);  y = y(:);    % Make sure that x and y are column vectors
A = [x ones(size(x))];  % m-by-n matrix of overdetermined system
c = (A'*A)\(A'*y);      % Solve normal equations
if nargout>1
  r = y - A*c;
  R2 = 1 - (norm(r)/norm(y-mean(y)))^2;
end
```

Listing 9.1   The `linefit` function returns the slope and intercept of the least-squares fit line for pairs of (x, y) data.

```
>> x = [1 2 4 5];   y = [1 2 2 3];
>> c = linefit(x,y)
c =
     0.4000
     0.8000
```

A qualitative check on the success of the fit is obtained by plotting the equation of the fit along with the original data. The following statements produce the plot shown in Figure 9.5:

```
>> xfit = [0 6];                  % Evaluate fit over this range of x
>> yfit = c(1)*xfit + c(2);       % Values of the fit function
>> plot(x,y,'o',xfit,yfit,'-')
>> grid on;
>> xlabel('x values');
>> ylabel('y data and fit function');
```

9.1.4 The R^2 Statistic

Visually inspecting the plot of a curve fit can give some indication of how well the fit approximates the given data. In this section, we discuss a quantitative indicator of the quality of the fit.

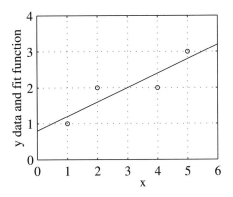

Figure 9.5   Least-squares fit of four data points to a line.

Let $\hat{y}$ be the value of y predicted by the fit equation at the known data points; that is,

$$\hat{y}_i = c_1 x_i + c_2. \tag{9.16}$$

From Equation (9.4), $r_i = y_i - \hat{y}_i$, and $\|r\|_2 = \sum_{i=1}^{m}(y_i - \hat{y}_i)^2$.

Now, instead of using a line to approximate the data, consider the simpler model of approximating the data by its mean. In other words approximate the data by $F(x) = \bar{y}$, where

$$\bar{y} = \frac{1}{m}\sum_{i=1}^{m} y_i.$$

Is this simpler model better than the line fit? A more useful way to rephrase that question is: How much does adding a second parameter, namely, the slope of the line, improve the approximation to the data? In an attempt to answer this question, we define the *coefficient of determination* as

$$R^2 = \frac{\sum(\hat{y}_i - \bar{y})^2}{\sum(y_i - \bar{y})^2}, \tag{9.17}$$

where both sums are for $i = 1, \ldots, m$. It is not too hard to show that

$$\sum(y_i - \bar{y})^2 = \sum(y_i - \hat{y}_i)^2 + \sum(\hat{y}_i - \bar{y})^2.$$

Substituting this result into Equation (9.17) gives

$$R^2 = 1 - \frac{\sum(y_i - \hat{y})^2}{\sum(y_i - \bar{y})^2} = 1 - \frac{\|r\|_2^2}{\sum(y_i - \bar{y})^2}. \tag{9.18}$$

This equivalent expression for R^2 shows the relationship of the apparent quality of the fit and the magnitude of the residual. The least-squares solution minimizes $\|r\|_2$, but as long as the fit function does not pass through each of the (x_i, y_i), $\|r\|_2 \neq 0$. If the square of the residual is small compared with $\sum(y_i - \bar{y})^2$, the the fit function passes near the data points, and the value of R^2 will be close to one.

Figure 9.6(a) shows a line fit to a set of data. The residuals of each data point are proportional to the vertical distances between the open circles and the least-squares line. In Figure 9.6(b), the same data are displayed along with a horizontal line through $\bar{y}$. The values of $y_i - \bar{y}$ are proportional to the lengths of the vertical lines in Figure 9.6(b). The line fit for this data has $R^2 = 0.934$, indicating that $\|r\|_2 \ll \sum(y_i - \bar{y})^2$ in Equation (9.18). This is consistent with the visual impression that the least-squares line (shown in Figure 9.6(a)) does a much better job of fitting the data than the line through $\bar{y}$ (shown in Figure 9.6(b)).

The numerator of Equation (9.17) is a measure of how much the fit function differs from the mean of the y data. If this number is very small compared with the denominator, then one might as well use a constant (i.e., $\bar{y}$), to approximate the data. The denominator of Equation (9.17) is a measure of how much the data differ from its mean. Since the fit function tends to average out differences, the numerator of Equation (9.17) cannot be greater than the denominator. Furthermore, since both the numerator and denominator are positive, we have $0 \leq R^2 \leq 1$.

The value of R^2 can be used as an indicator of the quality of the fit. Values of R^2 close to zero suggest that there is not a strong relationship between y and x. Values of R^2 close to one suggest that there is a strong relationship, but large R^2 *do not guarantee* that the apparent relationship is meaningful. (See Exercise 13.)

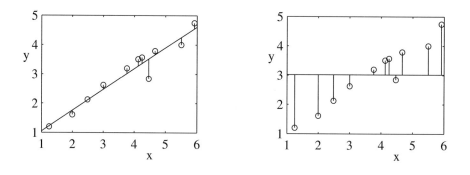

(a.) Distances used to compute
$$\|r\|^2 = \sum(y_i - \hat{y}_i)^2.$$

(b.) Distances used to compute $\sum(y_i - \bar{y})^2$. The horizontal line is through $\bar{y}$.

Figure 9.6   Graphical interpretation of quantities used to compute R^2.

R^2 is discussed again in § 9.2.2, and the reader is referred there for a discussion of the so-called *adjusted coefficient of determination*. The `linefit` function returns R^2 as an optional second argument.

Example 9.4: Bulk Modulus of Silicon Carbide versus Temperature

R. G. Munro[1] has published material property data for a form of sintered Silicon Carbide (SiC). An excerpt of this data is stored in the `SiC.dat` file in the `data` directory of the NMM Toolbox. The variation of bulk modulus versus temperature is given in the following table:

T (°C)	20	500	1000	1200	1400	1500
G (GPa)	203	197	191	188	186	184

The following MATLAB statements load the data from `SiC.dat` and obtain a least-squares fit of a line to the bulk modulus as a function of temperature:

```
>> [t,D,labels] = loadColData('SiC.dat',6,5);
>> g = D(:,1);
>> [c,R2] = linefit(t,g);
c =
   -0.0126
  203.3319
R2 =
    0.9985
```

Evaluating the fit function along with the original data gives the plot shown in Figure 9.7.

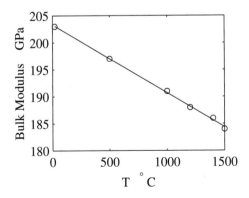

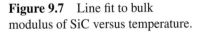

Figure 9.7   Line fit to bulk modulus of SiC versus temperature.

----

[1]"Material Properties of a Sintered alpha-SiC," *J. Physical Chem. Ref. Data*, vol. 26, pp. 1195–1203, 1997. (See also `www.nist.gov/srd/material.htm`.)

```
>> tfit = [ min(t) max(t)];
>> gfit = c(1)*tfit + c(2);
>> plot(t,g,'o',tfit,gfit,'-');
```

The relatively large value of R^2 is consistent with the plot, as both indicate that the line fits the data quite well.

9.1.5 Fitting Lines to Apparently Nonlinear Functions

There are several simple, nonlinear functions that may be transformed into linear functions. By applying a linearizing transformation, the linear least-squares method can be used to obtain a curve fit of the original, nonlinear function.

An important application of linearizing transformations is in fitting data that exhibit an exponential decay (or growth). Suppose that measurements from the electrical circuit in Example 9.1 are available. The data are expected to be described by

$$y = c_1 e^{c_2 x}, \tag{9.19}$$

where c_1 is the initial value of y and $-1/c_2$ is the time constant. Equation (9.19) is nonlinear in the parameters c_1 and c_2, so values of c_1 and c_2 cannot be directly computed with a *linear* least-squares procedure.

Taking the logarithm of both sides of Equation (9.19) yields

$$\ln y = \ln c_1 + c_2 x. \tag{9.20}$$

Introducing the variables

$$v = \ln y \quad \beta = \ln c_1, \quad \text{and} \quad \alpha = c_2 \tag{9.21}$$

transforms Equation (9.19) to

$$v = \alpha x + \beta,$$

which is linear in the parameters α and β. The steps to perform a linear least-squares fit to Equation (9.19) are:

1. Store the original (x, y) data in MATLAB variables.
2. Transform the data from (x, y) to (x, v).
3. Send the transformed data to a linear least-squares-fitting routine, which returns α and β.
4. Retrieve the original parameters $c_1 = e^\beta$ and $c_2 = \alpha$.

Table 9.1 provides a small sample of linearizing transformation useful for curve-fitting. Additional transformations are given in [50, 53].

TABLE 9.1 DATA TRANSFORMATIONS FOR USE WITH LINEAR LEAST-SQUARES FITTING.

Nonlinear Function of c_1 and c_2	Transformation to $v = \alpha u + \beta$	
$y = c_1 e^{c_2 x}$	$v = \ln y$	$u = x$
	$\beta = \ln c_1$	$\alpha = c_2$
$y = c_1 x^{c_2}$	$v = \ln y$	$u = \ln x$
	$\beta = \ln c_1$	$\alpha = c_2$
$y = c_1 x e^{c_2 x}$	$v = \ln(y/x)$	$u = x$
	$\beta = \ln c_1$	$\alpha = c_2$

Readers are warned that transforming data results in a minimization of residuals of the *transformed* data, not of the original data. For example, using the transformation in Equation (9.21) to fit data for an exponential decay results in values of c_1 and c_2 that minimize $\| \ln y - \ln y_{fit} \|_2$, not $\| y - y_{fit} \|_2$. Fitting the transformed data has the effect of giving less weight to small values of $y_{fit} - y$ than would be obtained by using a nonlinear least-squares procedure directly on Equation (9.19).

Example 9.5: Curve fit of Capacitor Discharge Data

The capacitor.dat file in the data directory of the NMM Toolbox contains voltage-versus-time data for the capacitor discharge experiment described in Example 9.1.

The following MATLAB statements obtain the least-squares fit of this data to Equation (9.20) with $y = v$ and $t = x$:

```
>> load capacitor.dat;
>> t = capacitor(:,1);        % copy data for convenience
>> v = capacitor(:,2);
>> ct = linefit(t,log(v));    % Line fit to transformed data
>> c = [exp(ct(2));  ct(1)]   % Extract parameters from transformation
c =
    5.0000
   -10.0000
```

The round numbers for c_1 and c_2 are due to the synthetic data in the capacitor.dat file. The voltage-versus-time data were generated by computing $v = 5e - 10t$. Fitting the transformed data has the effect of giving more weight to data points having values of $|y/y_{fit}|$ significantly different from one.

Example 9.6: Fitting Noisy Data to $y = 5xe^{-3x}$

In this example, the answer is known right from the start. To demonstrate a linearizing coordinate transformation, a known $g(x)$ is used to generate a set of (x, y) data. Artificial noise is then added to the y values to simulate measurement errors present in an experimental data set. A least-squares fit is performed on the noisy (x, y) data, allowing a comparison between the fit and the original $g(x)$ used to generate the data. By generating the data with

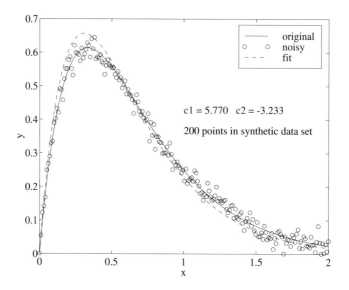

Figure 9.8 Fit of a synthetic data generated with $y = 5xe^{-3x}$ plus noise.

This example shows that the steps for least-squares fitting are straightforward. The results are seldom perfect, and a graphical inspection of the fit is strongly recommended. This is not to suggest that curve-fitting transformed data should be avoided. Rather, as with any calculation, it makes sense to double check the outcome. The extensive plotting capabilities of MATLAB makes visual inspection of calculations nearly effortless. It is wise to take advantage of this capability.

9.1.6 Summary of Fitting Data to a Line

The essential features of least-squares-fitting data to a line are:

1. m data pairs are given: (x_i, y_i), $i = 1, \ldots, m$.
2. The fit function $y = F(x) = c_1 x + c_2$ has $n = 2$ basis functions $f_1(x) = x$ and $f_2(x) = 1$.
3. Evaluating the fit function for each of the m data points gives an overdetermined system of equations

$$Ac = y,$$

where $c = [c_1, c_2]^T$, $y = [y_1, y_2, \ldots, y_m]^T$, and

$$A = \begin{bmatrix} f_1(x_1) & f_2(x_1) \\ f_1(x_2) & f_2(x_2) \\ \vdots & \vdots \\ f_1(x_m) & f_2(x_m) \end{bmatrix} = \begin{bmatrix} x_1 & 1 \\ x_2 & 1 \\ \vdots & \vdots \\ x_m & 1 \end{bmatrix}.$$

4. The least-squares principle defines the best fit as the values of c_1 and c_2 that minimize

$$\rho(c_1, c_2) = \|y - F(x)\|_2^2 = \|y - Ac\|_2^2.$$

5. Minimizing of $\rho(c_1, c_2)$ leads to the normal equations

$$(A^T A)c = A^T y,$$

where $(A^T A)$ is a 2×2 matrix and $A^T y$ is a two-element column vector.

6. Solving the normal equations gives the slope c_1 and intercept c_2 of the best fit line.

9.2 LEAST-SQUARES FIT TO A LINEAR COMBINATION OF FUNCTIONS

The least-squares fitting of data to a line is a specific example of a more general procedure. Consider the fitting function

$$y = F(x) = c_1 f_1(x) + c_2 f_2(x) + \cdots + c_n f_n(x), \tag{9.22}$$

where each of the *basis functions*, $f_j(x)$, $j = 1, \ldots, n$ is an arbitrary function independent of the coefficients c_j. The $f_j(x)$ functions need not be linear. The only requirement of linearity is that $F(x)$ must depend on a linear combination of the undetermined c_j parameters, and hence on a linear combination of the $f_j(x)$. The goal is to find values for the $c_1, \ldots, c_n$ that minimize the difference between the given data and the fit function.

To be more concrete, first consider the task of fitting m data points to three basis functions:

$$y = F(x) = c_1 f_1(x) + c_2 f_2(x) + c_3 f_3(x). \tag{9.23}$$

Assume for the moment that the c_i can be found so that the $F(x)$ passes exactly through all the data. (That is, suppose that the data "line up" so that the curve fit function acts like an interpolant.) Then, each of the following m equations would be satisfied exactly:

$$c_1 f_1(x_1) + c_2 f_2(x_1) + c_3 f_3(x_1) = y_1,$$
$$c_1 f_1(x_2) + c_2 f_2(x_2) + c_3 f_3(x_2) = y_2,$$

$$\vdots$$

$$c_1 f_1(x_m) + c_2 f_2(x_m) + c_3 f_3(x_m) = y_m.$$

This is equivalent to the overdetermined system

$$Ac = y, \tag{9.24}$$

where

$$A = \begin{bmatrix} f_1(x_1) & f_2(x_1) & f_3(x_1) \\ f_1(x_2) & f_2(x_2) & f_3(x_2) \\ \vdots & \vdots & \vdots \\ f_1(x_m) & f_2(x_m) & f_3(x_m) \end{bmatrix}, \quad c = \begin{bmatrix} c_1 \\ c_2 \\ c_3 \end{bmatrix}, \quad y = \begin{bmatrix} y_1 \\ y_2 \\ \vdots \\ y_m \end{bmatrix}. \tag{9.25}$$

To develop Equation (9.24), we momentarily assumed that the data fell along the curve given by Equation (9.23). In general, this will not be the case. Since there are more equations than free parameters ($m > n$), the exact solution to Equation (9.24) cannot be obtained. The least-squares method provides the compromise solution that minimizes $\rho = \|y - Ac\|_2^2$. As shown in §9.1.2, the minimum value of ρ is obtained by the vector c that satisfies the *normal equations*:

$$(A^T A)c = A^T y. \tag{9.26}$$

The definitions of A and c in Equation (9.25) apply only to the case of $n = 3$. In general, as indicated by Equation (9.22), there are n basis functions, so matrix A has n columns, and there are n elements in vector c:

$$A = \begin{bmatrix} f_1(x_1) & f_2(x_1) & \cdots & f_n(x_1) \\ f_1(x_2) & f_2(x_2) & \cdots & f_n(x_2) \\ \vdots & \vdots & & \vdots \\ f_1(x_m) & f_2(x_m) & \cdots & f_n(x_m) \end{bmatrix}, \quad c = \begin{bmatrix} c_1 \\ c_2 \\ \vdots \\ c_n \end{bmatrix}, \quad y = \begin{bmatrix} y_1 \\ y_2 \\ \vdots \\ y_m \end{bmatrix}. \tag{9.27}$$

The form of Equation (9.26) is unaffected by the number of basis functions.

9.2.1 Basis Functions

Equation (9.22) expresses the generic form of the fit function. The $F(x)$ function can be any combination of functions that are linear in the c_j. Thus, for example,

$$1, \ x, \ x^2, \ x^{2/3}, \ \sin x, \ e^x, \ xe^{4x}, \ \cos(\ln 25x)$$

are all valid basis functions. On the other hand,

$$\sin(c_1 x), \quad e^{c_3 x}, \quad x^{c_2}$$

are not valid basis functions as long as the c_j are the parameters of the fit.

The fit function for a cubic polynomial is

$$f(x) = c_1 x^3 + c_2 x^2 + c_3 x + c_4, \tag{9.28}$$

which has the basis functions

$$x^3, \quad x^2, \quad x, \quad 1.$$

The basis function "1" allows the fit function to have a constant term c_4. The polynomial in Equation (9.28) is written in decreasing powers of x, so that it corresponds to the format of the MATLAB toolbox functions `polyfit` and `polyval`, which are discussed in § 9.2.4.

9.2.2 Least-Squares Fit via Solution to the Normal Equations

The normal equations for least-squares fitting to a linear combination of basis functions have the same form as the normal equations for fitting data to a line. Only the definition of A and the number of undetermined coefficients change. To fit data to a linear combination of n basis functions, perform the following steps:

1. Choose the basis functions: $f_j(x)$, $j = 1, \ldots, n$.
2. Read in the data, (x_i, y_i), $i = 1, \ldots, m$.
3. Evaluate A in the first of Equations (9.27).
4. Solve Equation (9.26) for the vector of coefficients, c.

In the next example, the procedure for finding the least-squares fit of data to a nonlinear function is demonstrated with interactive MATLAB calculations. In the next section, an m-file function for automating these calculations is developed.

Example 9.7: Interactive Least-Squares Fitting

It is easy to solve least-squares fitting problems in just a few MATLAB statements. Consider the least-squares fit of (x, y) data to

$$y = \frac{c_1}{x} + c_2 x. \tag{9.29}$$

The data in the following table are available in the `xinvpx.dat` (x inverse plus x) file in the `data` directory of the NMM Toolbox:

x	0.955	1.380	1.854	2.093	2.674	3.006	3.255	3.940	4.060
y	5.722	4.812	4.727	4.850	5.011	5.253	5.617	6.282	6.255

The curve fit of the tabulated data to Equation (9.29) is obtained with the following statements:

```
>> load xinvpx.dat;       %  Read data from the "xinvpx.dat" file
>> x = xinvpx(:,1);       %  Copy data into the x and y vectors
>> y = xinvpx(:,2);       %     (a convenience, only)
>> A = [1./x  x];         %  Coefficient matrix of overdetermined system
>> c = (A'*A)\(A'*y)      %  Solve normal equations
c =
    4.2596
    1.3008
```

Note that the computation of A with $A = [1./x \quad x]$ works, because x is a column vector.

Next, consider the task of evaluating the curve fit at a set of x values other than those in the original data set. This is necessary, for example, to plot a smooth curve through the original data. Let x_f be a column vector of x values at which the fit is to be evaluated. Given the coefficients in the c vector, we can compute y_f with the following vectorized MATLAB statements:

```
>> xf = linspace(min(x),max(x));   %  100 points in range of original x data
>> yf = c(1)./xf + c(2)*xf;        %  Evaluate the fit function at xf
```

Since x_f is a column vector, we can also write the evaluation of $y_f = F(x_f)$ as

$$\begin{bmatrix} y_{f,1} \\ y_{f,2} \\ \vdots \\ y_{f,p} \end{bmatrix} = c_1 \begin{bmatrix} 1/x_{f,1} \\ 1/x_{f,2} \\ \vdots \\ 1/x_{f,p} \end{bmatrix} + c_2 \begin{bmatrix} x_{f,1} \\ x_{f,2} \\ \vdots \\ x_{f,p} \end{bmatrix}.$$

Using the column-oriented algorithm for the matrix–vector product (see Algorithm 7.1 on page 315), we can write the preceding expression as

$$y_f = A_f c,$$

where

$$A_f = \begin{bmatrix} 1/x_{f,1} & x_{f,1} \\ 1/x_{f,2} & x_{f,2} \\ \vdots & \vdots \\ 1/x_{f,p} & x_{f,p} \end{bmatrix}.$$

Thus, the fit function $y_f = F(x_f)$ can be evaluated and plotted with the following statements:

```
>> xf = linspace(min(x),max(x));   %  100 points in range of original x data
>> Af = [1./xf  xf];               %  Eval basis fcns at xf as columns of A
>> yf = Af*c;                      %  Evaluate the fit function at xf
>> plot(x,y,'o',xf,yf,'-');        %  Plot original data and fit function
```

The result is shown in Figure 9.9.

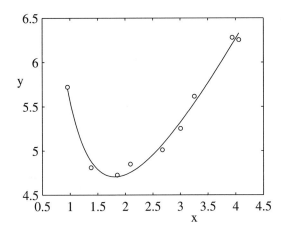

Figure 9.9 Plot of curve fit in Example 9.7.

A General Implementation   The procedure for performing the least-squares fit can be distilled to the following statements:

```
x = ...              %  Store x and y data in column vectors
y = ...
A = ...              %  Evaluate coefficient matrix of overdetermined system
c = (A'*A)\(A'*y)    %  Solve normal equations
```

Our current objective is to devise a general-purpose m-file function that will obtain the least-squares fit coefficients for any data set and any choice of basis functions. Clearly, the (x, y) data will be inputs to the general-purpose function. How are the basis functions specified? The basis functions are necessary to evaluate matrix A, which also depends on the data in x. The solution chosen here is to require the user to supply a routine to evaluate A given any column vector. Thus, rather than supplying matrix A as input, the user provides the *name* of the m-file that returns A for any x. This procedure is a bit indirect, considering that it takes only two lines of MATLAB code to set up and solve the normal equations. The advantage is that the specification of the problem to be solved and the procedure for solving it are separated. This allows the solution procedure to be updated in one place—for example, to add more sophisticated curve-fitting analysis.

The fitnorm function in Listing 9.4 on page 478 uses the ideas discussed in the preceding paragraph to perform a least-squares curve fit to an arbitrary set of basis functions. The fitnorm function can be called in one of the following three ways:

```
function [c,R2,rout] = fitnorm(x,y,basefun)
% fitnorm   Least-squares fit via solution to the normal equations
%           Given ordered pairs of data, (x_i,y_i), i=1,...,m, fitnorm
%           returns the vector of coefficients, c_1,...,c_n, such that
%               F(x) = c_1*f_1(x) + c_2*f_2(x) + ... + c_n*f_n(x)
%           minimizes the L2 norm of y_i - F(x_i).
%
% Synopsis:  c        = fitnorm(x,y,basefun)
%            [c,R2]    = fitnorm(x,y,basefun)
%            [c,R2,r]  = fitnorm(x,y,basefun)
%
% Input:    x,y      = vectors of data to be fit
%           basefun = (string) name of user-supplied m-file that computes
%                      matrix A.  The columns of A are the values of the
%                      basis functions evaluated at the x data points.
%
% Output:   c = vector of coefficients obtained from the fit
%           R2 = (optional) adjusted coefficient of determination; 0 <= R2 <= 1
%               R2 close to 1 indicates a strong relationship between y and x
%           r  = (optional) residuals of the fit

if length(y)~= length(x);  error('x and y are not compatible');  end

A = feval(basefun,x(:)); %  Coefficient matrix of overdetermined system
c = (A'*A)\(A'*y(:));     %  Solve normal equations, y(:) is always a column
if nargout>1
  r = y - A*c;            %  Residuals at data points used to obtain the fit
  [m,n] = size(A);
  R2 = 1 - (m-1)/(m-n-1)*(norm(r)/norm(y-mean(y)))^2;
  if nargout>2,  rout = r;  end
end
```

Listing 9.4 The fitnorm function solves the normal equations to obtain the linear least-squares fit of data to an arbitrary list of functions.

$$c = \text{fitnorm}(x,y,basefun)$$
$$[c,R2] = \text{fitnorm}(x,y,basefun)$$
$$[c,R2,r] = \text{fitnorm}(x,y,basefun)$$

where x and y are vectors of data to be fit and $basefun$ is the name of the user-defined m-file that evaluates A from the basis functions. The output parameters are c, the vector of coefficients of the basis functions in Equation (9.22), $R2$, the adjusted coefficient of determination (discussed below); and r, the residual vector, $r = y - Ac$.

The m-file referred to by $basefun$ takes a column vector x and returns the matrix

$$A = \begin{bmatrix} f_1(x_1) & f_2(x_1) & \cdots & f_n(x_1) \\ f_1(x_2) & f_2(x_2) & \cdots & f_n(x_2) \\ \vdots & \vdots & & \vdots \\ f_1(x_m) & f_2(x_m) & \cdots & f_n(x_m) \end{bmatrix}.$$

In fitnorm, the call to the *basefun* routine is made with the built-in feval function as follows:

```
A = feval(basefun,x(:));
```

The x(:) subexpression in the second argument of feval(...) makes sure that the vector passed to *basefun* is a column vector, even if the vector x passed to fitnorm is a row vector. Usually, the m-file that evaluates the basis functions is only one line of MATLAB code. As an example, consider the following function, which evaluates the matrix A in the curve fit problem from Example 9.7:

```
function A = xinvpxBasis(x)
% xinvpxBasis  Matrix with columns evaluated with 1/x and x
A = [1./x  x];
```

These statements need to be stored in a file named xinvpxBasis.m. The call to fitnorm is then

```
>> [c,r] = fitnorm(x,y,'xinvpxBasis');
```

Note that n, the number of basis functions, need not be explicitly defined in the *basefun* routine. In addition, the ".m" extension of the file name is not included in the string value of *basefun*.

For simple sets of basis functions, the routine that evaluates matrix A can be specified as an inline function object. This eliminates the need to create a separate m-file. The call to fitnorm with an inline function definition for xinvpxBasis is

```
>> Afun = inline('[1./x x]');
>> [c,r] = fitnorm(x,y,Afun);
```

Additional aspects of using an inline function object are discussed in Example 9.8. The normal equations are set up and solved in fitnorm by the statement

```
c = (A'*A)\(A'*y(:))
```

The y(:) subexpression guarantees that the y in $A^T y$ is a column vector. Use of the fitnorm function is demonstrated in Examples 9.8 and 9.9.

Since there are only four essential lines of code in the `fitnorm` function, it is reasonable to bypass the function call and perform the fit interactively. Alternatively, one could incorporate the critical lines of `fitnorm` into another routine that also evaluates the matrix A directly. The user is advised to follow whatever route makes sense for a particular application. Use of the `fitnorm` function is advantageous when the fit is to be performed with different data sets and different basis functions, as demonstrated in Example 9.9.

The R^2 Statistic for Arbitrary Fit Functions   The R^2 statistic defined in §9.1.4 on page 464 also applies to curve fits of arbitrary, linear combinations of functions. (Equations (9.17) and (9.18) make no explicit references to the basis functions.) When R^2 is computed for an arbitrary combination of basis functions, the $\hat{y}$ values are simply

$$\hat{y}_i = \sum_{j=1}^{n} c_j f_j(x_i) \tag{9.30}$$

(i.e., the fit function evaluated at the known (input) data).

Technically, it is appropriate to consider the *adjusted coefficient of determination* defined by

$$R^2_{\text{adjusted}} = 1 - \frac{m-1}{m-n-1} \frac{\sum(y_i - \hat{y})^2}{\sum(y_i - \bar{y})^2}, \tag{9.31}$$

where, consistent with usage throughout this chapter, m is the number of data points and n is the number of basis functions. The $(m-1)/(m-n-1)$ term accounts for the true number of degrees of freedom in determining R^2. For most curve-fitting problems, $(m-1)/(m-n-1) \approx 1$, because $m \gg n$. To allow for situtations in which m might not be much greater than n, the R^2_{adjusted} value is returned by `fitnorm` and `fitqr`.

It is important to remember that R^2 and R^2_{adjusted} are merely indicators of the quality of the fit. Values of R^2 or R^2_{adjusted} near one indicate the appearance of a relationship between the dependent variable y and the independent variable x. A large value of R^2 or R^2_{adjusted} does not guarantee that the fit is meaningful.

Example 9.8: Use of the `fitnorm` Function

The `fitnorm` function can be used to fit the data from Example 9.7. The basis functions of Equation (9.29) are evaluated in the `xinvpxBasis` m-file just described and available in the `fit` directory of the NMM Toolbox. The data to be fit is in the `xinvpx.dat` file in the `data` directory of the NMM Toolbox. The following interactive commands load the data and perform the fit.

```
>> load xinvpx.dat;        %   Contents of file stored in xinvpx matrix
>> x = xinvpx(:,1);        %   Copy 1st and 2nd columns into x and y
>> y = xinvpx(:,2);
>> [c,R2] = fitnorm(x,y,'xinvpxBasis')
c =
    4.2596
    1.3008

R2 =
    0.9817
```

To qualitatively inspect the fit, the original data are plotted along with the curve obtained by evaluating the fit function over the range of the x data. As in Example 9.7, the fit function is evaluated with a matrix–vector product:

```
>> xf = linspace(min(x),max(x))';  %  100 points in range of original x data
>> Af = feval('xinvpxBasis',xf);   %  Eval basis fcns at xf as columns of A
>> yf = Af*c;                      %  Evaluate the fit function at xf
>> plot(x,y,'o',xf,yf,'-');
>> legend('data','fit',2);   xlabel('x');   ylabel('y');
```

The resulting plot is shown in Figure 9.9 on page 477. To perform the same computations with an `inline` function object, use the following statements:

```
>> ...
>> Afun = inline('[1./x(:)   x(:)]');
>> [c,R2] = fitnorm(x,y,Afun)
>> xf = linspace(min(x),max(x))';
>> Af = Afun(xf);
>> ...
```

Note that once `Afun` is defined as an in-line function, it can be used just like a standard m-file function. The use of `x(:)` subexpressions takes into account that the vector x might be a row vector. In this example, `x(:)` is unnecessary, because both x and y are created from columns of the xpinvx matrix, which is read from the `xpinvx.dat` file.

The use of a matrix to compute yf exposes a subtle advantage of the procedure for evaluating A in `fitnorm`. In any curve-fitting problem, the basis functions are used (at least) twice: once to evaluate A to set up the normal equations and once again to evaluate the fit function for plotting. By defining an external routine, or an inline function object, for evaluating A, the basis functions need to be coded only once. Use of this idea to further automate the curve-fitting process is explored in Exercise 15.

Example 9.9: Curve Fit of Thermal Conductivity Data

In Example 9.2, experimental data is presented for the variation of thermal conductivity k of copper near absolute zero. We now turn to the task of obtaining a curve fits for that data. Measured values of k versus T for three different samples of copper are stored in the

files cucon1.dat, cucon2.dat, and cucon3.dat (available in the data directory of the
NMM Toolbox). The data are plotted in Figure 9.3 on page 458.

Consideration of the physical mechanisms responsible for the variation of k with T
suggests that a mathematical model for $k(T)$ is

$$k(T) = \frac{1}{\dfrac{c_1}{T} + c_2 T^2}. \tag{9.32}$$

This equation is not linear in c_1 and c_2. To fit data to this function with the linear least-
squares method, define

$$\gamma_1(T) = \frac{1}{k(T)} = \frac{c_1}{T} + c_2 T^2, \tag{9.33}$$

and fit γ_1 versus T instead of k versus T. The basis functions for Equation (9.33) are
used to define A in the cuconBasis1 m-file in the NMM Toolbox. Alternatively, the basis
functions can be evaluated with an inline function object, as demonstrated next.

The essential steps in fitting this data may be entered interactively:

```
>> fun1 = inline('[1./t  t.^2]');        %  x must be a column vector
>> [t,k] = loadColData('cucon1.dat',2,0,2);   %  read data into t and k
>> [c,r] = fitnorm(t,1./k,fun1);         %  perform the fit
>> fprintf('  %e\n',c)                    %  print coefficients
   3.616821e-01
   3.661922e-05
```

First, the routine for computing matrix A from the basis functions is defined as an inline
function object. Then, the data are read from the files with the loadColData function, an
NMM toolbox utility for reading data from a text file that contains column headings. (See
the utils directory.) The fitnorm function finds the coefficients that solve the normal
equations.

The following statements evaluate the fit at 100 points in the range of the t data and
plot a comparison of the fit with the original data:

```
>> tf = linspace(min(t),max(t))';
>> Af = feval(fun1,tf);                   %  evaluate basis fcns for gamma(t)
>> kf = 1./(Af*c);                        %  k = 1/gamma
>> plot(t,k,'o',tf,kf,'-')
```

Figure 9.10(a) shows the original data and the fit to Equation (9.32).

A better curve fit of the same data is obtained by adding a term linear in T to the
denominator of the $k(T)$ function, viz.

$$\gamma_2(T) = \frac{1}{k(T)} = \frac{c_1}{T} + c_2 T + c_3 T^2. \tag{9.34}$$

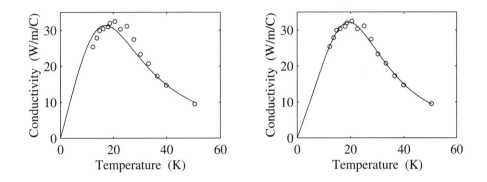

(a.) Fit of data in `cucon1.dat` to Equation (9.33).

(b.) Fit of data in `cucon1.dat` to Equation (9.34).

Figure 9.10   Least-squares fit of thermal conductivity data in file `cucon1.dat`.

The basis functions for y_2 are implemented as an inline function object:

```
>> fun2 = inline('[1./t t t.^2]');
```

Figure 9.10(b) shows the curve fit to Equation (9.34). The qualitative improvement indicated by the plot is reflected by a lower value of the residual: $\|y - Ac\|_2 = 9.6 \times 10^{-3}$ for the fit to Equation (9.33) and $\|y - Ac\|_2 = 4.5 \times 10^{-3}$ for the fit to Equation (9.34).

The `conductFit` function shown in Listing 9.5 automates the least-squares fitting of the thermal conductivity data. The `conductFit` function is designed to compare the suitability of two different sets of basis functions for fitting several k versus T data sets. In addition to performing the fit, `conductFit` plots the fit function and the original data. The `conductFit` function takes one input: the name of the file that contains the data for k versus T. Using `conductFit` with the `cucon2.dat` and `cucon3.dat` files produces the plots in Figure 9.11.

The `conductFit` function also prints the values of the fit coefficients (the c_i) and the value of $\|y - Ac\|_2$. To save space, the values of the curve fit coefficients are not printed here. The following table summarizes the $\|y - Ac\|_2$ values obtained from the two different basis functions for the three data sets:

Data set	Equation (9.33)		Equation (9.34)	
	$\|y - Ac\|_2$	R^2_{adjusted}	$\|y - Ac\|_2$	R^2_{adjusted}
`cucon1.dat`	0.01150	0.973	0.00387	0.997
`cucon2.dat`	0.00956	0.979	0.00450	0.994
`cucon3.dat`	0.00872	0.966	0.00673	0.977

```
function conductFit(fname)
% conductFit  LS fit of conductivity data for Copper at low temperatures
%
% Synopsis:  conductFit(fname)
%
% Input:  fname   = (optional, string) name of data file;
%                     Default: fname = 'conduct1.dat'
%
% Output:  Print out of curve fit coefficients and a plot comparing data
%            with the curve fit for two sets of basis functions.

if nargin<1,  fname = 'cucon1.dat';   end   % Default data file

% --- define basis functions as inline function objects
fun1 = inline('[1./t   t.^2]');            % t must be a column vector
fun2 = inline('[1./t   t   t.^2]');

% --- read data and perform the fit
[t,k] = loadColData(fname,2,0,2);      % Read data into t and k
[c1,R21,r1] = fitnorm(t,1./k,fun1);    % Fit to first set of bases
[c2,R22,r2] = fitnorm(t,1./k,fun2);    % and second set of bases

% --- print results
fprintf('\nCurve fit to data in %s\n\n',fname);
fprintf(' Coefficients of      Basis Fcns 1       Basis Fcns 2\n');
fprintf('        T^(-1)        %16.9e  %16.9e\n',c1(1),c2(1));
fprintf('        T             %16.9e  %16.9e\n',0,c2(2));
fprintf('        T^2           %16.9e  %16.9e\n',c1(2),c2(3));
fprintf('\n   ||r||_2          %12.5f       %12.5f\n',norm(r1),norm(r2));
fprintf('      R2              %12.5f       %12.5f\n',R21,R22);

% --- evaluate and plot the fits
tf = linspace(0.1,max(t))';     % 100 T values: 0 < t <= max(t)
Af1 = feval(fun1,tf);           % A matrix evaluated at tf values
kf1 = 1./ (Af1*c1);             % Af*c is column vector of 1/kf values
Af2 = feval(fun2,tf);
kf2 = 1./ (Af2*c2);
plot(t,k,'o',tf,kf1,'--',tf,kf2,'-');
xlabel('Temperature  (K)');   ylabel('Conductivity  (W/m/C)');
legend('data','basis 1','basis 2');
```

Listing 9.5 The conductFit function fits thermal conductivity data
for copper at low temperatures.

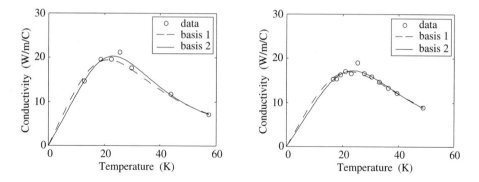

(a.) Fit of data in cucon2.dat to Equations (9.33) and (9.34).

(b.) Fit of data in cucon3.dat to Equations (9.33) and (9.34).

Figure 9.11   Least-squares fit of thermal conductivity data in files cucon2.dat and cucon3.dat.

The $\|y - Ac\|_2$ values produced by Equation (9.34) are smaller than the $\|y - Ac\|_2$ produced by Equation (9.33) for all three data sets. The R^2 values obtained with Equation (9.34) are also consistently higher than the R^2 values obtained with Equation (9.33). We conclude that Equation (9.34) fits the data better than Equation (9.33). The largest difference in the fit functions is for the cucon1.dat set, as is also apparent from Figure 9.10.

9.2.3 Least-Squares Approximation with QR Factorization

The normal equation method is widely used to solve the least-squares problem, but it is not the only way to find the c that minimizes $\|y - Ac\|_2$. The least-squares problem can also be solved via QR factorization or singular value decomposition (SVD). In this section, the QR factorization method is presented. Built-in MATLAB commands that use the least-squares method (e.g., polyfit), solve the overdetermined system of equations via QR factorization.

In exact arithmetic, the solution to a least-squares problem via normal equations, QR, and SVD is exactly the same.[3] The important differences between these approaches are in the computational cost in flops and the numerical stability of the methods.

Recall from § 8.3.3 that stability of a numerical algorithm refers to how impervious it is to perturbations in the input data. For the least-squares problem, the

---

[3]If A is an $m \times n$ matrix with $m > n$ and if rank$(A) = n$, then the linear least-squares problem has a unique solution that minimizes $\|b - Ax\|_2$. (See, for example, [28, § 6.3] or [32, § 5.3]. In the absence of roundoff, all numerical algorithms for solving the least-squares problem obtain this unique solution.

perturbations are due to inaccuracies in the measured (x, y) data that are used to form A and the right-hand-side vector of the overdetermined system. For least-squares curve-fitting, stability is important, because small changes in the measured data (e.g., those occurring on repetition of the same physical experiment), should not significantly change the curve-fit coefficients. Both the QR and SVD approaches to solving the least-squares problem are more stable than the solution via the normal equations.

The most efficient method, in terms of CPU time *and* memory, is to solve the least-squares problem via the normal equations. For many practical problems, however, the savings in CPU time and memory are not important. Similarly, when the computations are performed in double precision, the increased stability of the QR- or SVD-based least-squares solutions will not usually be noticeable. Beware that is is not too difficult to contrive situations where the time and memory savings of the normal equations are significant, or where the enhanced stability of QR or SVD methods is advantageous. So which approach is to be recommended?

It makes sense to prefer the QR method for solving the least-squares problem. Loss of significant digits in the c_i due to ill conditioning of the normal equations may occur without warning; that is, the solution may run to completion, and the user may accept the results without question. Thus, it makes sense to choose QR, because, with it, the loss of significant digits will be reduced, but not completely eliminated. In contrast, if applying the QR method results in a long execution time or if it uses too much memory, these symptoms will be immediately apparent to the user. In that case, the more efficient normal equation approach can be selected. Fortunately for MATLAB users, switching between these approaches is trivial, as is evident from a comparison of the fitnorm and fitqr m-files in the NMM toolbox.

In the following subsections, we first discuss the properties of the QR factorization and how it relates to the least-squares problem. The details of obtaining a QR factorization are not described here. Then, we describe MATLAB techniques for solving the least-squares problem via QR factorization. In particular, the use of the backslash operator for least-squares solution is demonstrated.

The essence of applying QR factorization can be exposed by considering the humble task of fitting a line to three points that are not colinear. To be specific, let us choose the points $(1, 1)$, $(2, 3)$, and $(3, 4)$. The overdetermined system for this problem is

$$\begin{bmatrix} 1 & 1 \\ 2 & 1 \\ 3 & 1 \end{bmatrix} \begin{bmatrix} c_1 \\ c_2 \end{bmatrix} = \begin{bmatrix} 1 \\ 3 \\ 4 \end{bmatrix}.$$

A Preliminary Exploration with Gaussian Elimination   To motivate the QR factorization, we will first apply Gaussian elimination to the preceding system of equations. Although Gaussian elimination *can* be applied to a system with a rectangular coefficient matrix, the result, as we shall see, is *not* the least-squares solution.

Form the augmented system (cf. § 8.2.3 on page 382) and apply Gaussian elimination without pivoting:

$$\left[\begin{array}{cc|c} 1 & 1 & 1 \\ 2 & 1 & 3 \\ 3 & 1 & 4 \end{array}\right] \longrightarrow \left[\begin{array}{cc|c} 1 & 1 & 1 \\ 0 & -1 & 1 \\ 0 & -2 & 1 \end{array}\right] \longrightarrow \left[\begin{array}{cc|c} 1 & 1 & 1 \\ 0 & -1 & 1 \\ 0 & 0 & -1 \end{array}\right].$$

At the final step of the elimination process, the last row represents the equation $0c_1 + 0c_2 = -1$, which has no solution. Put another way, the values of c_1 and c_2 that satisfy the first two equations *cannot* solve the third equation. This fact is consistent with the observation that we cannot draw a line through three-points unless they are colinear.

Recall from § 8.4.1 beginning on page 410 that Gaussian elimination can be achieved by premultiplication by an elimination matrix. For the current A, we have

$$MA = \begin{bmatrix} 1 & 0 & 0 \\ -2 & 1 & 0 \\ 1 & -2 & 1 \end{bmatrix} \begin{bmatrix} 1 & 1 \\ 2 & 1 \\ 3 & 1 \end{bmatrix} = \begin{bmatrix} 1 & 1 \\ 0 & -1 \\ 0 & 0 \end{bmatrix}.$$

The reason that Gaussian elimination does not produce the least-squares solution is that the multiplication by M does not preserve the L_2 norm of the residual

$$\|M(y - Ac)\|_2 \neq \|y - Ac\|_2.$$

This is important in seeking the least-squares solution, because the goal is to find the vector c that minimizes the residual. Unlike Gaussian elimination, QR factorization *can* be applied in a way that maintains the L_2 norm of the residual, and that is why QR, and not Gaussian, elimination is used for least-squares problems. Note that for an $n \times n$ matrix A and $n \times 1$ vectors x and b, premultiplication by the (appropriate) elimination matrix M *is* helpful, because the solution to the *square* system $MAx = Mb$ is the same as the solution to *square* system $Ax = b$.

The QR Factorization   Recall from § 8.4.1 that Gaussian elimination is equivalent to factoring A into the product of two triangular matrices L and U. An alternative factorization of A is the QR factorization.

Let A be an $m \times n$ matrix with $m > n$. The QR factorization of A is

$$A = QR \tag{9.35}$$

where Q is an $m \times m$ *orthogonal matrix* and R is an $m \times n$ upper triangular matrix.

If A is a 4×2 matrix, its QR factorization looks like

$$
\underset{4 \times 2}{A} \quad = \quad \underset{4 \times 4}{Q} \quad \underset{4 \times 2}{R}
$$

$$
\begin{bmatrix} \bullet & \bullet \\ \bullet & \bullet \\ \bullet & \bullet \\ \bullet & \bullet \end{bmatrix} = \begin{bmatrix} \bullet & \bullet & \bullet & \bullet \\ \bullet & \bullet & \bullet & \bullet \\ \bullet & \bullet & \bullet & \bullet \\ \bullet & \bullet & \bullet & \bullet \end{bmatrix} \begin{bmatrix} \bullet & \bullet \\ 0 & \bullet \\ 0 & 0 \\ 0 & 0 \end{bmatrix},
$$

where $\bullet$ indicates a nonzero value. Since Q is orthogonal, $Q^T Q = I$ and, therefore, $Q^{-1} = Q^T$. The matrix R is upper triangular. Since, in general, R is $m \times n$, the last $m - n$ rows of R are always filled with zeroes.

An important insight into the QR factorization can be obtained from the column view of the matrix–matrix product. (Cf. § 7.2.2 and Figure 7.8 in particular.) Designate $q_{(j)}$, $r_{(j)}$, and $a_{(j)}$ as the jth columns of Q, R, and A, respectively, and write out the product of Q and R as (note that Q is $m \times m$)

$$
\begin{bmatrix} \Big| & \Big| & & \Big| \\ q_{(1)} & q_{(2)} & \cdots & q_{(m)} \\ \Big| & \Big| & & \Big| \end{bmatrix} \begin{bmatrix} \\ \cdots r_{(j)} \cdots \\ \\ \end{bmatrix} = \begin{bmatrix} \\ \cdots a_{(j)} \cdots \\ \\ \end{bmatrix}.
$$

In this view of the matrix–matrix product, the third column of A, for example, is

$$
r_{1,3}\, q_{(1)} + r_{2,3}\, q_{(2)} + r_{3,3}\, q_{(3)} = a_{(3)}.
$$

In other words, $a_{(3)}$ is a linear combination of the first three columns of Q. In general, since $r_{i,j} = 0$ for $i > j$, only columns 1 through j of Q are needed to form column j of A. Thus, the entire matrix A (which is $m \times n$ with $m > n$) can be represented by only the first n columns of Q. This assumes that A has rank n, (i.e., that all n columns of A are linearly independent). If $\text{rank}(A) = k < n$, then only the first k columns of Q are needed. The last $m - n$ rows of R *must* be zero, because the columns of Q are orthogonal, and therefore linearly independent.

Since Q is an $m \times m$ matrix and the columns of Q are orthogonal, the first n columns of Q form a basis for the column space of A (i.e., range(A)). The last $m - n$ columns of Q form a basis for the subspace of $\mathbf{R}^m$ that lies outside of range(A). This space is called the orthogonal complement of range(A) and designated range(A)$^{\perp}$. As discussed next, the last $m - n$ columns of Q are not needed to solve the least-squares approximation with the QR factorization.

If $\tilde{Q}$ is the matrix composed of the first n columns of Q, and Q_c is a matrix composed of the remaining columns of Q ("c" refers to the fact that these columns form a basis for range(A)$^{\perp}$), we can write Q in block-matrix form as

$$Q = \begin{bmatrix} \tilde{Q} & Q_c \end{bmatrix}. \tag{9.36}$$

The corresponding block-matrix representation of R is

$$R = \begin{bmatrix} \tilde{R} \\ 0 \end{bmatrix}, \tag{9.37}$$

where $\tilde{R}$ is the $n \times n$ matrix consisting of the nonzero upper triangular part of R, and 0 designates an $(m - n) \times n$ matrix of zeros.

Recognizing that only the first n columns of Q are needed to create A using the coefficients in R, we can save effort and memory in the process of creating the QR factorization. The so-called *economy-size* QR factorization of A is

$$A = \tilde{Q}\tilde{R}. \tag{9.38}$$

The only substantial difference between the full QR factorization and the economy-size factorization is that the full factorization contains the additional $m - n$ columns of Q that form the basis for range$(A)^{\perp}$.

We will not discuss the various algorithms for computing the QR factorization of a matrix. Instead, we will rely on MATLAB's built-in qr function to provide Q and R from a given A. Readers wishing for additional information should consult Datta [12] and Watkins [78] for detailed, intermediate-level expositions. More concise presentations requiring greater reader sophistication are given by Gill et al. [28] and Golub and Van Loan [32]. Stewart [69] provides a thorough treatment at an advanced level. Trefethen and Bau [76] approach QR factorization and the least-squares problem in an intuitive mathematical way. Demmel [15] discusses implementation of least-squares with QR factorization in state-of-the-art numerical linear algebra codes.

The built-in qr function returns the QR factorization of a matrix. Two ways of calling qr are

```
[Q,R] = qr(A)
[Q̃,R̃] = qr(A,0)
```

where Q and $\tilde{Q}$ are orthogonal matrices, and R and $\tilde{R}$ are upper triangular matrices. The [Q,R] = qr(A) form returns the full QR factorization. (That is, if A is $m \times n$, then Q is $m \times m$ and R is $m \times n$.) The [Q̃,R̃] = qr(A,0) form returns the economy-size QR factorization where $\tilde{Q}$ and $\tilde{R}$ are the $\tilde{Q}$ and $\tilde{R}$ matrices in Equation (9.38).

Example 9.10: Using the qr Function

In this example, the built-in qr function is used to obtain the QR factorization of the 3×2 matrix from the overdetermined system of the three-point least-squares fitting problem discussed in the preceding sections, viz.,

$$A = \begin{bmatrix} 1 & 1 \\ 2 & 1 \\ 3 & 1 \end{bmatrix}.$$

Applying the built-in qr function to this matrix gives

```
>> A = [1 1; 2 1; 3 1];
>> [Q,R] = qr(A)
Q =
    -0.2673      0.8729      0.4082
    -0.5345      0.2182     -0.8165
    -0.8018     -0.4364      0.4082
R =
    -3.7417     -1.6036
         0      0.6547
         0           0
```

Although the elements of A are integers, the elements of its Q and R factors are floating-point numbers. Here only the first four digits are displayed. To within roundoff, the factorization is successful:

```
>> A-Q*R
ans =
    1.0e-15 *
      0.5551     -0.2220
      0.2220           0
      0.4441           0
```

Also Q is orthogonal (as expected):

```
>> Q'*Q - eye(3) =
ans =
    1.0e-15 *
           0     -0.0541     -0.0663
     -0.0541      0.2220      0.2034
     -0.0663      0.2034           0
```

The economy-size QR factorization of A is (cf. Equation (9.38))

```
>> [Q0,R0] = qr(A,0)
Q0 =
    -0.2673      0.8729
    -0.5345      0.2182
    -0.8018     -0.4364

R0 =
    -3.7417     -1.6036
         0      0.6547
```

As expected, Q0 and the first two columns of Q are identical, as are R0 and the first two rows of R. The economy factorization of A possesses all the necessary information in the columns of Q0 and R0 to reconstruct A.

```
>> norm(A-Q0*R0,inf)
ans =
   7.7716e-16
```

Using QR to Obtain the Least-Squares Solution   The feature of the QR factorization that makes it useful for solving least-squares problems is that multiplication by an orthogonal matrix preserves the L_2 norm of a vector; that is,

$$\|Qx\|_2 = [(Qx)^T(Qx)]^{1/2} = [(x^T Q^T)(Qx)]^{1/2} = [x^T(Q^T Q)x]^{1/2}$$
$$= [x^T x]^{1/2} = \|x\|_2.$$

Using this property of Q, we find that the least-squares curve-fitting problem of minimizing $\|y - Ac\|_2$ can be transformed as

$$\|y - Ac\|_2 = \|Q^T(y - Ac)\|_2 = \|Q^T y - Q^T Ac\|_2 = \|Q^T y - Rc\|_2,$$

where the last expression on the right-hand side is obtained by replacing A with QR. This fact is worth repeating:

> The least-squares solution to the overdetermined system $Ac = y$ is equivalent to finding the minimum of $\|Q^T y - Rc\|_2$, where $A = QR$ is the QR factorization of A.

The reason for writing the least-squares problem in this form is that once A is factored into Q and R, the c that minimizes $\|Q^T y - Rc\|_2$ is very easy to compute.

Let us return to the problem of fitting a line to the three, noncolinear points. To make the notation clear, we will work with symbols instead of numerical values. (The elements of Q and R are not integers, and working with the floating-point values does not help see the important patterns.) Writing out $\|Q^T y - Rc\|_2$ for the three-point least-squares problem gives

$$\|Q^T y - Rc\|_2 = \left\| \begin{bmatrix} q_{11} & q_{21} & q_{31} \\ q_{12} & q_{22} & q_{32} \\ q_{13} & q_{23} & q_{33} \end{bmatrix} \begin{bmatrix} y_1 \\ y_2 \\ y_3 \end{bmatrix} - \begin{bmatrix} r_{11} & r_{12} \\ 0 & r_{22} \\ 0 & 0 \end{bmatrix} \begin{bmatrix} c_1 \\ c_2 \end{bmatrix} \right\|_2$$

$$= \left\| \begin{bmatrix} z_1 \\ z_2 \\ z_3 \end{bmatrix} - \begin{bmatrix} r_{11}c_1 + r_{12}c_2 \\ r_{22}c_2 \\ 0 \end{bmatrix} \right\|_2, \qquad (9.39)$$

Implementation of Curve Fitting via QR   All the pieces are now available to create a general purpose m-file for least-squares fitting using QR factorization. The result is the `fitqr` function in Listing 9.6. `fitqr` turns out to be nearly identical to `fitnorm`. `fitnorm` and `fitqr` differ by only one line (i.e., in the solution of vector c):

```
fitnorm:   c = (A'*A)\(A'*y(:));
fitqr:     c = A\y(:);
```

```
function [c,R2,rout] = fitqr(x,y,basefun)
% fitqr   Least-squares fit via solution of overdetermined system with QR
%         Given ordered pairs of data, (x_i,y_i), i=1,...,m, fitqr
%         returns the vector of coefficients, c_1,...,c_n, such that
%              F(x) = c_1*f_1(x) + c_2*f_2(x) + ... + c_n*f_n(x)
%         minimizes the L2 norm of y_i - F(x_i).
%
% Synopsis:   c      = fitqr(x,y,basefun)
%            [c,R2]   = fitqr(x,y,basefun)
%            [c,R2,r] = fitqr(x,y,basefun)
%
% Input:    x,y    = vectors of data to be fit
%           basefun = (string) name of user-supplied m-file that computes
%                     matrix A.  The columns of A are the values of the
%                     basis functions evaluated at the x data points.
%
% Output:   c = vector of coefficients obtained from the fit
%           R2 = (optional) adjusted coefficient of determination; 0 <= R2 <= 1
%                R2 close to 1 indicates a strong relationship between y and x
%           r  = (optional) residuals of the fit

if length(y)~= length(x);   error('x and y are not compatible');   end

A = feval(basefun,x(:)); %  Coefficient matrix of overdetermined system
c = A\y(:);                  %  Solve overdetermined system with QR factorization
if nargout>1
  r = y - A*c;               %  Residuals at data points used to obtain the fit
  [m,n] = size(A);
  R2 = 1 - (m-1)/(m-n-1)*(norm(r)/norm(y-mean(y)))^2;
  if nargout>2,  rout = r;  end
end
```

Listing 9.6   The `fitqr` function uses the QR algorithm to obtain linear least-squares fit of data to an arbitrary list of functions.

The `fitqr` function uses the same basis function routines as `fitnorm`. It is easy to substitute `fitqr` for `fitnorm`, and thereby change the numerical algorithm used to solve a least-squares curve-fitting problem. For well-conditioned problems, the results obtained by these two methods will be nearly identical. The `fitqr` function is recommended for the reasons given at the beginning of this section. (See page 485.)

9.2.4 Polynomial Curve Fitting

The `fitnorm` or `fitqr` functions can be used to fit data to polynomials. Doing so requires the creation of an m-file to evaluate the monomial basis functions 1, x, x^2, ..., x^k for a polynomial of degree k. That approach will not be taken here, however. The regularity of the monomial basis allows algorithmic simplifications that lead to a more compact and convenient way of setting up the overdetermined system of equations for the fit.

Consider fitting data to a quadratic ($y = c_1 x^2 + c_2 x + c_3$). Given column vectors x and y of known data, the overdetermined system of equations for the fit is (see also Equation (9.24))

$$
\begin{bmatrix}
x_1^2 & x_1 & 1 \\
x_2^2 & x_2 & 1 \\
\vdots & \vdots & \vdots \\
x_n^2 & x_n & 1
\end{bmatrix}
\begin{bmatrix}
c_1 \\
c_2 \\
c_3
\end{bmatrix}
=
\begin{bmatrix}
y_1 \\
y_2 \\
\vdots \\
y_n
\end{bmatrix} .
\tag{9.41}
$$

Taking advantage of MATLAB's array operators the least-squares fit to a quadratic polynomial can be set up and solved in a few short lines:

```
>> x = ...      %  x and y are column vectors of known data
>> y = ...
>> A = [ x.^2  x  ones(size(x)) ];  %  Overdetermined coefficeint matrix
>> c = A\y;                         %  Least squares solution
```

The `polyfit` **Function**   The built-in `polyfit` function uses the procedure just described to obtain the least-squares curve fit for a degree n polynomial written as

$$
F(x) = p_1 x^n + p_2 x^{n-1} + \cdots + p_n x + p_{n+1}
$$

The `polyfit` function constructs the coefficient matrix and obtains the least-squares solution of the overdetermined system via QR factorization. `polyfit` can be called in the following ways:

```
function demoTcouple
% demoTcouple  Linear and quadratic fits to J-type thermocouple data
%
% Synopsis:  tcouple
%
% Input:      None
%
% Output:  Print fit coefficients and residuals.  Plot fit fcns and residuals

[v,t] = loadColData('Jtcouple.dat',2,1,3);   %  Read t = f(v) data from file

% --- Perform fits, evaluate fit function, compute residuals
vfit = linspace(min(v),max(v));
c1 = polyfit(v,t,1);   tfit1 = polyval(c1,vfit);   r1 = t - polyval(c1,v);
c2 = polyfit(v,t,2);   tfit2 = polyval(c2,vfit);   r2 = t - polyval(c2,v);
c3 = polyfit(v,t,3);   tfit3 = polyval(c3,vfit);   r3 = t - polyval(c3,v);

fprintf('\nCurve fit coefficients\n          ');
fprintf('constant        emf          emf^2          emf^3\n');
fprintf('linear   ');   fprintf('  %14.7e',fliplr(c1));   fprintf('\n');
fprintf('quadratic');   fprintf('  %14.7e',fliplr(c2));   fprintf('\n');
fprintf('cubic    ');   fprintf('  %14.7e',fliplr(c3));   fprintf('\n');

% --- Plot fit and residuals
plot(v,t,'o',vfit,tfit1,'--',vfit,tfit2,'-',vfit,tfit3,':');
legend('Data','Linear','Quadratic',2);   %  Legend in upper left corner
xlabel('emf (mV)');        ylabel('Temperature ({}^\circ F)');

f = figure;   %  new figure window for residuals
plot(v,r1,'o',v,r2,'s',v,r3,'d');   legend('Linear','Quadratic','cubic');
xlabel('emf (mV)');        ylabel('Temperature residual    ({}^\circ F)');

fprintf('\nResiduals\n                        ||r||_2      max error\n');
fprintf('linear       %8.5f      %8.5f\n',norm(r1),norm(r1,inf));
fprintf('quadratic    %8.5f      %8.5f\n',norm(r2),norm(r2,inf));
fprintf('cubic        %8.5f      %8.5f\n',norm(r3),norm(r3,inf));
```

Listing 9.7   The demoTcouple function uses the built-in polyfit
function to perform polynomial fits to thermocouple calibration data.

parabolic trend (i.e., the residual is correlated to emf). The addition of the quadratic term
significantly reduces $\|r\|_2$, because it removes the quadratic contribution in the correlation
between r and emf. The residual of the quadratic fit shows a cubic variation with emf,
and the cubic fit shows evidence of an even higher order variation. The magnitude of the
residual variation is substantially reduced as the degree of the fit polynomial is increased
from one to three.

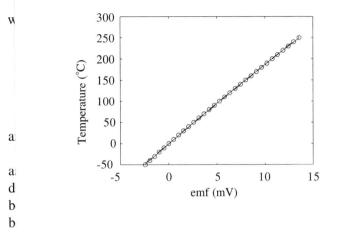

Figure 9.12 Linear, quadratic, and cubic polynomial fits of thermocouple calibration data.

In general, one seeks a combination of basis functions that result in residuals that are uncorrelated with the independent variable. For an ideal data set, this lack of correlation indicates that the fit function explains everything but the noise (errors) in the data. Real (as opposed to ideal) data sets may contain hidden correlations that cannot, and should not, be explained away by a deficiency in the set of basis functions used in the fit. For example, subsequent data points in an experiment may be correlated in time if there is an uncontrolled, and perhaps undetected, transient stimulus to the input variables.

Readers interested in further information on the examination of residuals should consult books on regression analysis. Draper and Smith [19, § 2.3] is a good place to begin.

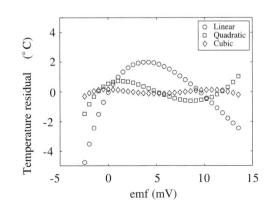

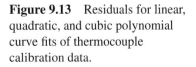

Figure 9.13 Residuals for linear, quadratic, and cubic polynomial curve fits of thermocouple calibration data.

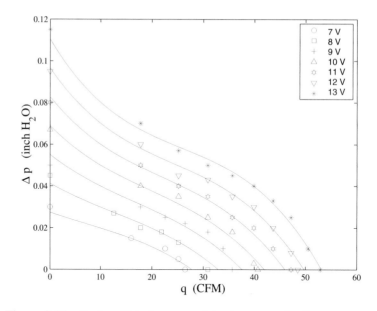

Figure 9.16   Surface fit to fan curve data at a range of voltages.

additional fan curves as a function of voltage. In other words, instead of the manufacturer's $\Delta p = F(q)$ curve, the engineers need a family of $\Delta p = F(q, v)$ curves, where v is the voltage supplied to the fan. Figure 9.16 shows data obtained from measurements on a particular fan. The symbols are experimental data and the solid lines are obtained from the least-squares fit described shortly. The data for Figure 9.16 are contained in the sequence of files `fan7v.dat`, `fan8v.dat`, ... , `fan13v.dat`, in the `data` directory of the NMM toolbox. As indicated by the file names, each file corresponds to a separate voltage. Note that the files for different voltages have different numbers of data points.

The solid lines in Figure 9.16 are obtained from a least-squares fit to

$$\Delta p = c_1 + c_2 q + c_3 q^2 + c_4 q^3 + c_5 v + c_6 v q^2 + c_7 v q^3. \tag{9.46}$$

Equation 9.46 is equivalent to the product of a polynomial that is linear in v and cubic in q; that is,

$$\Delta p = (a_1 + a_2 v)(b_1 + b_2 q + b_3 q^2 + b_4 q^3).$$

The `demoFanCurve` function in Listing 9.8 reads $\Delta p = F(q, v)$ data from the text files and performs a least-squares fit of Equation (9.46) to the data. The `demoFanCurve` function has three primary sections: (1) reading and plotting of the data, (2) formulating and solving the least-squares problem, and (3) evaluating and plotting the curve fit function at the voltages of the input data.

A $\Delta p = F(q)$ data set for each voltage is read into MATLAB variables with the `loadColData` function, which is in the `utils` directory of the NMM toolbox. The `loadColData` function reads data files with text headers and text column labels.

```
function demoFanCurve
% demoFanCurve  Multivariate fit of fan data:  dp = f(q,v).  The fit function is
%               linear in v and cubic in q, including cross products
%
% Synopsis:  demoFanCurve
%
% Input:     None, all data is read from files
%
% Output:    Print out of surface fit coefficients, and plot of data and fit

% --- Load and plot experimental data
[q7,dp7]   = loadColData('fan7v.dat',2,1);
[q8,dp8]   = loadColData('fan8v.dat',2,1);
[q9,dp9]   = loadColData('fan9v.dat',2,1);
[q10,dp10] = loadColData('fan10v.dat',2,1);
[q11,dp11] = loadColData('fan11v.dat',2,1);
[q12,dp12] = loadColData('fan12v.dat',2,1);
[q13,dp13] = loadColData('fan13v.dat',2,1);

plot(q7,dp7,'o',q8,dp8,'s',q9,dp9,'+',q10,dp10,'^',...
     q11,dp11,'h',q12,dp12,'v',q13,dp13,'*')
legend('7 V','8 V','9 V','10 V','11 V','12 V','13 V');

% --- Construct global fit function:  dp = f(q,v)
q  = [q7; q8; q9; q10; q11; q12; q13];           % q column vector
dp = [ dp7;  dp8;  dp9; dp10; dp11; dp12; dp13]; % dp column vector
v  = [ 7*ones(size(dp7));   8*ones(size(dp8));   % v column vector with
        9*ones(size(dp9));  10*ones(size(dp10)); % same length as q and dp
      11*ones(size(dp11)); 12*ones(size(dp12)); 13*ones(size(dp13)) ];

A = amatrix13(q,v);     % Assemble matrix for overdetermined system
c = A\dp;               % Solve overdetermined system
fprintf('\nc = \n');
fprintf('  %14.4e\n',c); %  Print in scientific notation, one c(i) per line

% --- Evaluate curve fit at each voltage and add plot to current figure
hold on
addQVfit('amatrix13',q7,7,c);    %  add 7V curve fit to current figure
addQVfit('amatrix13',q8,8,c);    %  add 8V curve fit, etc
addQVfit('amatrix13',q9,9,c);
addQVfit('amatrix13',q10,10,c);
addQVfit('amatrix13',q11,11,c);
addQVfit('amatrix13',q12,12,c);
addQVfit('amatrix13',q13,13,c);
hold off;   axis([0 60 0 0.12]);
xlabel('q  (CFM)');  ylabel('\Delta p   (inch H_20)');
```

Listing 9.8 The fitFanCurve function obtains the multivariate least-squares fit of fan data to Equation (9.46). The code for addQVfit and amatrix13 subfunctions is in Listing 9.9.

The basis functions for Equation (9.46) are

$$1, \quad q, \quad q^2, \quad q^3, \quad v, \quad vq^2, \quad vq^3.$$

The columns of the matrix for the overdetermined system are formed by evaluating the basis functions at each data tuple. By storing the v and q data in column vectors of equal length, matrix A can be assigned with a single line of MATLAB code, viz,

```
A = [ ones(size(q))  q  q.^2  q.^3  v  v.*q  v.*q.^2  v.*q.^3 ];
```

```
% ==========================================
function addQVfit(Afun,q,v,a)
% addQVfit  Evaluate and plot curve fit for dp = fcn(q,v) given coefficients
%           of the global polynomial fit
%
% Synopsis:  addQVfit(Afun,q,v,a)
%
% Input:   Afun = (string) name of function to evaluate matrix of
%                 the overdetermined system defined by basis functions
%          q = vector of flow rate values
%          v = scalar value of fan voltage
%          a = vector of coefficients obtained from least squares fit
%              of dp = f(q,v).  The a vector must be compatible with
%              the matrix returned by Afun
%
% Output: Plot of dp = f(q,v) is added to current figure window
qfit = linspace(min(q),1.1*max(q))';  % Note that qfit is a column vector
vfit = v*ones(size(qfit));            % Create v vector compatible with qfit
Afit = feval(Afun,qfit,vfit);         % Eval basis fcns at qfit and vfit
dpfit = Afit*a;                       % dp value obtained from fit
plot(qfit,dpfit)                      % Add line plot to current figure


% ==========================================
function A = amatrix13(q,v)
% amatrix13  Evaluate matrix of overdetermined system for fit that
%            is linear in v and cubic in q
%
% Synopsis:  A = amatrix13(q,v)
%
% Input: q = vector of flow rate values
%        v = vector of fan voltages.  Note length(q) must equal length(v)
%
% Output:  A = matrix of overdetermined system defined by basis functions
A = [ones(size(q))  q  q.^2  q.^3  v  v.*q  v.*q.^2  v.*q.^3];
```

Listing 9.9 The addQVfit and amatrix13 subfunctions of the demoFanCurve function.

Since the voltage is a scalar value for each data file, the voltage must be replicated to form the vector v. The first few entries in the v, q, and dp vectors have the following form:

file name	v	q	dp
	7	0	0.03
	7	16.0	0.015
fan7v.dat	7	22.6	0.01
	7	25.2	0.005
	7	26.5	0
	8	0	0.045
	8	12.6	0.027
fan8v.dat	8	17.8	0.02
	8	21.9	0.018
	8	25.2	0.013
	8	30.9	0
	⋮	⋮	⋮

Given vectors v and q, matrix A is evaluated in the amatrix13 subfunction. (See Listing 9.9.) Matrix A is defined by the basis functions, which are used in both setting up the least-squares problem and in evaluating the fit. By putting the evaluation of A in a separate subfunction, we need only define the basis functions once. This simplifies the task of comparing different sets of basis functions. (See Exercise 39.)

The addQVfit subfunction in Listing 9.9 evaluates the curve fit for a vector of q values and a scalar voltage. By evaluating the fit at the voltage of the original data, the quality of the fit can be visually assessed by plotting the fit function along with the original data. Running demoFanCurve gives the following output and the plot in Figure 9.16:

```
>> fitFanCurve

c =
     -6.9398e-02
      2.9203e-03
     -1.0478e-04
      1.6968e-07
      1.3831e-02
     -5.3644e-04
      1.7134e-05
     -1.3002e-07
```

The solid lines shown in Figure 9.16 indicate that the least-squares fit does a good job of following the trends in the discrete data. The agreements at the no-flow ($q = 0$) and free-air ($\Delta p = 0$) conditions are as good as one might hope. Slightly better results can be obtained with other sets of basis functions. (See Exercise 39.) Further improvement requires more sophisticated tools, such as weighted least-squares or least-squares with equality constraints.

It is a good exercise to compare this multivariate fit to separate fits of the form $\Delta p = F(q)$ for each voltage. (See Exercise 38.)

9.4 SUMMARY

This chapter presents methods for obtaining the curve fit of known data to a linear combination of functions. Given a set of m data pairs (x_i, y_i), and n basis functions $f_j(x)$, the least-squares principle is used to find the coefficients c_j that minimize $\|F(x) - y\|_2$, where $F(x) = c_1 f_1(x) + \cdots + c_n f_n(x)$ is called the fit function[4]. Writing $F(x_i) = y_i$ for each of the known data pairs, we obtain an overdetermined system of m equations in the n unknown c_j. Applying calculus to find $\|F(x) - y\|_2$ results in a system of n normal equations that can be solved by Gaussian elimination and its variants.

The simple case of fitting data to a line is used to establish the basic concepts of least-squares fitting. Some nonlinear $F(x)$ with two unknown c_j can be transformed into the equation of a line. The use of linearizing transformations is demonstrated for $y = c_1 \exp(c_2 x)$ and $y = c_1 x \exp(c_2 x)$. The R^2 statistic, also known as the coefficient of determination, is derived and related to the quality of the fit for lines and other fit functions.

The least-squares curve-fitting procedure is then applied to arbitrary, linear combinations of functions. The method of finding the c_j for these general fit functions is a direct extension of the procedure for finding the least-squares fit of data to a line. The column vectors of matrix A are formed by evaluating the basis functions at the known x_i. The overdetermined system of equations for the c_j is $Ac = y$, where y is the given y-data. Vector c is determined by solving the normal equations $(A^T A)c = A^T y$.

An alternative to solving the normal equations is to obtain a QR factorization of A, and then compute the fit coefficients from $c = R^{-1} Q^T y$. In this chapter the properties of Q and R are described, and the procedure for finding the c that minimize $\|Ac - y\|_2$ with Q and R is developed. An algorithm for computing a QR factorization of a rectangular matrix is not presented here. Instead we rely on MATLAB \ operator, which *automatically* finds the least-squares solution to $Ac = y$ with the expression c=A\y if A has more rows than columns.

The built-in `polyfit` and `polyval` functions are demonstrated for finding and then evaluating least-squares fits to polynomials. The `polyfit` function handles the details of forming the overdetermined system and obtaining the least-

---

[4] $F(x)$ is the column vector obtained by evaluating the fit function at x, where x and y are the column vectors of known data.

Sec. 9.4

File

airSat.dat
airSoundSp
airVisc.da
bearing.da
cucon1.dat
cucon3.dat

emission.(

fan8v.dat.
fan13v.da

flowsys1.
flowsys2.

GPL100.da
GPL104.da

glycerin.

H2Odensit
H2Ovisc.(
pdxTemp.(

R2.dat
thermis.
xyline.d
velocity

So
into MA
headers
variable

1. (1)
   the
2. (1)
   usir
   con

3. (1+
   197
   a fu
   in t

TABLE 9.2 FUNCTIONS FOR CURVE-FITTING INTRODUCED IN THE CHAPTER. FUNCTIONS WITH N.A. (NOT APPLICABLE) FOR A PAGE NUMBER ARE NOT LISTED IN THE TEXT, BUT ARE INCLUDED IN THE NMM TOOLBOX.

Function	Page	Description
conductFit	484	Fit thermal conductivity data for copper at low temperatures.
cuconBasis1	N.A.	Evaluate basis functions for fit of the form $y(T) = c_1/T + c_2 T^2$.
cuconBasis2	N.A.	Evaluate basis functions for fit of the form $y(T) = c_1/T + c_2 T + c_3 T^2$.
demoFanCurve	505	Multivariate least-squares fit of fan data to Equation (9.46).
demoPlaneFit	N.A.	Fit the equation of a plane $z = c_1 x + c_2 y + c_3$ to synthetic data.
demoTcouple	498	Use polyfit to perform linear and quadratic fits to thermocouple calibration data.
demoXexp	471	Demonstrate fit of synthetic data to $y = c_1 x \exp(c_2 x)$.
fitnorm	478	Least-squares fitting via solution to the normal equations.
fitqr	494	Least-squares fitting via solution of overdetermined system with QR.
linefit	464	Least-squares fit of data to $y = ax + b$.
loadColData	N.A.	Load numeric data from a file containing text and numbers. The file can contain a text header and text column labels. See the utils directory of the NMM toolbox.
xexpfit	470	Least-squares fit of data to $y = c_1 x \exp(c_2 x)$.

squares solution. The polyval function efficiently evaluates polynomials. The polyfit function is a special case of fitting an arbitrary, linear combination of functions.

In the last major section of this chapter, the case of multivariate curve-fitting is described. In a multivariate fit, the response variable y, is a function of p independent variables, $x_1, x_2, \ldots, x_p$. The new feature added by multivariate fitting is that each basis function can depend on all p independent variables, instead of just one x as in the univariate case. Two examples of multivariate fitting are provided.

Three m-file functions—linefit, fitnorm, and fitqr—contain the primary numerical methods in this chapter. linefit obtains the least-squares fit of data to a line. Both fitnorm and fitqr obtain the least-squares fit of (x, y) data to arbitrary, linear combinations of functions. fitnorm solves the overdetermined system via the normal equations, and fitqr applies QR factorization directly to the overdetermined system. To obtain least-squares fits with fitnorm or fitqr, users must supply an m-file function that evaluates A from the basis functions of the fit.

Table 9.2 lists the m-file functions developed in the chapter.

Further Reading

The least-squares data-fitting problem tends to be discussed from either a numerical or a statistical perspective. The numerical perspective, which is the one taken

concentration of solute approaches zero, the higher order terms can be neglected, and the intrinsic viscosity can be obtained from

$$\eta = \lim_{c \to 0} \left[\frac{(\mu/\mu^*) - 1)}{c} \right]. \tag{9.47}$$

The following table gives μ as a function of c for a solution of polystyrene in toluene (true value of μ is tabular value times 10^{-4}):

c (gm/L)	0	2	4	6	8	10
$\mu \times 10^4$ (kg/m/s)	5.58	6.15	6.74	7.35	7.98	8.64

Determine the value of η for this data from the $c = 0$ intercept of a curve fit of $[(\mu/\mu^*) - 1]/c$ versus c. Before performing any computations, decide on an appropriate model for the fit. Compare the value of η obtained from at least two different fit functions.

25. (2−) Assuming that data are supplied in two column vectors x and y, write *two lines* of MATLAB code that obtain the coefficients of a straight line fit. The discussion in § 9.2.4 on page 495 may be helpful. Can you write this in *one* line?

SOLUTION **26.** (3−) Write a function to fit data to $y = c_1 x^5 + c_2 x^3 + c_3 x + c_4$ without calling `polyfit`, `fitnorm`, or `fitqr`. Your function should take two column vectors x and y as input and return the coefficient vector. It should be self-contained. (That is, it should set up and solve the overdetermined system of equations without calling any auxiliary functions.) Test your solution with the following data:

x	−3.0000	−1.8571	−0.7143	0.4286	1.5714	2.7143	3.8571	5.0000
y	−4.9262	−4.4740	−3.3136	−2.9396	−2.6697	−1.3906	−0.8669	−3.3823

27. (2+) To select the appropriate fan for an air-cooled electronic enclosure, engineers need to establish the *system curve* for the enclosure. The system curve is the relationship between the flow rate q of air, and the pressure drop Δp needed to be supplied by the fan to provide the flow rate. For most flow systems, the system curve is of the form $\Delta p = c\,q^2$.

Experimental data for a particular type of electronic equipment with two different inlet grill designs are contained in `flowsys1.dat` and `flowsys2.dat` in the data directory of the NMM toolbox. The first column is the pressure drop in Pa and the second column is the flow rate in m^3/s.

Write an m-file function that uses `polyfit` to create a second order polynomial curve fit to the data in `flowsys1.dat` and `flowsys2.dat`. Evaluate the polynomial fit functions over the range $0 \le q \le q_{max}$, where q_{max} is the maximum flow rate for the data set. Superimpose the original data on the plot. What happens to the system curves as q approaches zero? Is this physically realistic?

28. (2) One way to fix the problem with the polynomial curve fit in Exercise 27 is to add the point $(\Delta p, q) = (0, 0)$ to the data sets. Modify the m-file developed in Exercise 27 to include the $(0, 0)$ point *after* the data are loaded into MATLAB variables, so that the

EXE

original data files remain intact (*Hint*: x = [0; x];). Repeat the curve fit for the data in flowsys1.dat and flowsys2.dat. Are the problems near $q = 0$ completely eliminated?

29. (2+) For turbulent flow of air in the electronic cabinet (cf. Exercises 27 and 28) the system curve should not have linear or constant terms: that is, it should be of the form $\Delta p = c\,q^2$. Write the overdetermined system of equations for the least-squares problem to find c in $\Delta p = c\,q^2$. Obtain an analytical solution of the normal equations to find a simple expression for c in terms of the known Δp and q data. Modify the m-file developed in Exercise 27 so that it uses this fit in addition to that obtained with polyfit. Apply the m-file to the data in flowsys1.dat and flowsys2.dat. Does the fit to $\Delta p = c\,q^2$ have problems as $Q \to 0$? Does adding the point $(\Delta p, q) = (0, 0)$ affect the fit? (*Hint*: Consider the solution to Exercise 7.)

30. (2+) Hart et al. (*Optical Measurement of the Speed of Sound in Air Over the Temperature Range 300-650 K*, NASA/CR-2000-210114, ICASE Report No. 2000-20, Institute for Computer Applications in Science and Engineering, NASA Langley Research Center, Hampton, VA.) report on a new technique for measuring the speed of high frequency sound waves in air using laser-induced thermal acoustics (LITA). The airSoundSpeed.dat file in the data directory of the NMM Toolbox contains data extracted from their report. The first column in airSoundSpeed.dat is the temperature of the sample in kelvins, the second column is the sound speed measured by LITA, and the third column is the sound speed predicted by another model.

For an ideal gas the sound speed is $V = \sqrt{kRT}$ where V is the sound speed, k is the ratio of specific heats, R is the gas constant, and T is the temperature of the gas. Use polyfit to create a first degree polynomial (i.e. a straight line) fit of V as a function of $\sqrt{T}$ for the LITA data. Perform another fit of the form $V = c\sqrt{T}$ to the same data, where c is the lone parameter of the fit. Compare the two fits by plotting them both on the same axes with the original data. What are the values of k deduced from the curve fit coefficients. *Hint*: The solution to Exercise 7 will be helpful.

31. (3+) (Adapted from Akai [3].) A coast-down test can be used to estimate the aerodynamic drag characteristics of a vehicle. The test begins with the vehicle moving at a known velocity. The power is cut off (transmission put in neutral), and the vehicle velocity is measured as it is allowed to slow down. The results from one such test are given in the velocity.dat file in the data directory of the NMM toolbox. A force balance on the unpowered vehicle gives

$$\sum F = F_d + F_f,$$

where F_d is the aerodynamic drag and F_f is the sum of all friction forces (tire and transmission resistance) slowing the vehicle. Suppose that F_f can be measured with a separate test. Lacking that information, we will simply neglect F_f for now. Combining Newton's law of motion with the force balance gives

$$ma = m\frac{dv}{dt} = -F_d, \quad \text{or} \quad F_d = -\frac{1}{m}\frac{dv}{dt}.$$

This equation allows us to estimate F_d from the velocity data.

(a) $\Delta p = c_1 + c_2 q + c_3 q^2 + c_4 q^3 + c_5 q^4 + c_6 v + c_7 v q + c_8 v q^2 + c_9 v q^3 + c_{10} v q^4.$

(b) $\Delta p = c_1 + c_2 q + c_3 q^2 + c_4 v + c_5 v^2 + c_6 v q^2 + c_7 v^2 q^2.$

(c) $\Delta p = c_1 + c_2 q + c_3 q^2 + c_4 q^3 + c_5 v + c_6 v q + c_7 v q^2 + c_8 v q^3 + c_9 v^2 + c_{10} v^2 q + c_{11} v^2 q^2 + c_{12} v^2 q^3.$

To facilitate a comparison, do not change the `amatrix13` subfunction. Instead, make a clone of `amatrix13` for each of the preceding fit equations. You may also want to replace the `A = amatrix13(q,v)` call in the main function of `demoFanCurve` with `A = feval(Afun,q,v)`, where `Afun` is a string containing the name of the function that evaluates matrix A. `Afun` could then be an input parameter to your modified version of the `demoFanCurve` function. For each fit equation (including Equation (9.46)), compute the residual $\|y - Ac\|_2$ of the fit for the given data points. Which fit equation do you recommend?

(a) $\Delta p = c_1 + c_2 q + c_3 q^2 + c_4 q^3 + c_5 q^4 + c_6 v + c_7 v q + c_8 v q^2 + c_9 v q^3 + c_{10} v q^4$.

(b) $\Delta p = c_1 + c_2 q + c_3 q^2 + c_4 v + c_5 v^2 + c_6 v q^2 + c_7 v^2 q^2$.

(c) $\Delta p = c_1 + c_2 q + c_3 q^2 + c_4 q^3 + c_5 v + c_6 v q + c_7 v q^2 + c_8 v q^3 + c_9 v^2 + c_{10} v^2 q + c_{11} v^2 q^2 + c_{12} v^2 q^3$.

To facilitate a comparison, do not change the `amatrix13` subfunction. Instead, make a clone of `amatrix13` for each of the preceding fit equations. You may also want to replace the `A = amatrix13(q,v)` call in the main function of `demoFanCurve` with `A = feval(Afun,q,v)`, where `Afun` is a string containing the name of the function that evaluates matrix A. `Afun` could then be an input parameter to your modified version of the `demoFanCurve` function. For each fit equation (including Equation (9.46)), compute the residual $\|y - Ac\|_2$ of the fit for the given data points. Which fit equation do you recommend?

(a) Load the data from the `airSat.dat` file.

(b) Create the coefficient matrix of the overdetermined system.

(c) Solve the overdetermined system with the backslash operator.

34. (3) Use the built-in `polyfit` function to create a variety of polynomial curve fits to the data for p versus T from in the preceding exercise. Which fit do you prefer?

35. (3−) Use the built-in `polyfit` function to perform polynomial curve fits to the thermal conductivity data in the `cucon1.dat`, `cucon2.dat`, and `cucon3.dat` files in the data directory of the NMM toolbox. (See also Example 9.9.)

(a) For each data set, find the coefficients of the polynomial fit function of degree 2, 3, 4, and 5. Evaluate and plot the fit function over the range $0 \leq T \leq 50$ K. (The `subplot` function will allow the four plots to be placed on the same page.) Superimpose the original data on each of the plots. How successful are the polynomial fits?

(b) Make copies of the `cucon1.dat`, `cucon2.dat`, and `cucon3.dat` files (changing the names). Edit the data files and add a $(0, 0)$ data point to each file. Rerun the curve-fitting of part (a). Has the additional data point improved the fit? How well does the fit meet the condition $k(T = 0) = 0$?

36. (3−) The results of part (b) of Exercise 35 can be improved by using `polyfit` to fit

$$\frac{T}{k(T)} = c_1 T^n + c_2 T^{n-1} + \cdots + c_n T + c_{n+1}. \tag{9.48}$$

Write an m-file function to fit the data in the modified files (those including the data point $(0, 0)$) to Equation (9.48). How does this fit compare with the results from Example 9.9? What values are minimized when `polyfit` is applied to Equation (9.48)?

37. (2+) Lipson and Sheth (*Statistical Design and Analysis of Engineering Experiments,* 1973, McGraw-Hill, p. 385) give data on nitrogen-oxide (NO) emission from an internal combustion engine as a function of humidity and atmospheric pressure. Their data are contained in the `emission.dat` file in the `data` directory of the NMM toolbox. Obtain a multiple linear regression of this data of the form

$$NO = c_1 + c_2 h + c_3 p,$$

where h is the humidity in *grains* per pound of dry air and p is the atmospheric pressure in inches of Mercury. What are the values of c_1, c_2 and c_3?

38. (3−) Example 9.14 on page 503 involves a multivariate fit of Equation (9.46) to performance data of a vane-axial fan. Instead of performing a multivariate fit, create separate polynomial curve fits $\Delta p = F(q)$ for each voltage. Add plots of all of the polynomial fits to a plot of all of the original data. It may be advantageous to use different-order polynomials for each voltage curve. How do these results compare with the multivariate fit in Example 9.14.

39. (3) Example 9.14 involves a multivariate fit of Equation (9.46) to performance data of a vane-axial fan. Using the `demoFanCurve` function as a starting point develop fits to

One way to compute dv/dt is by applying a finite-difference approximation to the original data:

$$\frac{dv}{dt} = \frac{v(t_i) - v(t_{i-1})}{t_i - t_{i-1}}$$

Alternatively, one could create a curve fit to the data, such as the a cubic function

$$v(t) = c_1 t^3 + c_2 t^2 + c_3 t + c_4,$$

and then differentiate the curve fit function to get dv/dt.

     Write the necessary m-files to compute and plot dv/dt as a function of time using the two methods just described. Is there a significant difference between the results obtained with the different methods?

SOLUTION **32.** (3) The pdxTemp.dat file in the data directory of the NMM toolbox contains historically averaged monthly temperatures measured at the Portland, OR, airport. The file contains four columns of data. The first column is the number of the month (1 through 12). The second through fourth columns are the historically averaged low, high, and average temperatures, respectively, for each month. Create a fit of the average temperature to the function

$$T = c_1 + c_2 \sin^2 \left[\frac{(m-1)\pi}{12} \right],$$

where m is the number of the month. Plot a comparison of the original data and the fit function. (*Hint:* (1) Replicate the January data so that the input has 13 pairs of values with January at the beginning and end of the data set, and (2) create a vector of values of $\theta = (m-1)\pi/12$.)

33. (3+) W.C. Reynolds (*Thermodynamic Properties in SI: Graphs, tables and computational equations for 40 substances*, 1979, Department of Mechanical Engineering, Stanford University, Stanford, CA) gives the following equation for the saturation pressure of air as a function of temperature:

$$\ln \left(\frac{P}{P_c} \right) = c_1 x + c_2 x^2 + c_3 \ln \left(\frac{T}{T_c} \right), \qquad \text{where} \qquad x = \frac{1}{T_c} - \frac{1}{T}.$$

$P_c = 3.77 MPa$ is the critical pressure, and $T_c = 132.5 K$ is the critical temperature. Find the values of c_i for the $p_{sat} = f(T_{sat})$ data in the airSat.dat file in the data directory of the NMM toolbox. Obtain the values of c_1, c_2, and c_3 from a linear least-squares fit of the data. Plot a comparison of the original data and the fit function. Compute the L_2 norm of the residual for the fit, $\| p - p_{fit} \|_2$.

     (*Note:* The basis functions depend on the values of T and T_c separately.) One solution is to start with a copy of the fitNorm or fitQR function and change the function so that both T and T_c are passed to the routine that evaluates the basis functions. Another solution is to write a dedicated function to perform the following steps:

original data files remain intact (*Hint*: x = [0; x];). Repeat the curve fit for the data in flowsys1.dat and flowsys2.dat. Are the problems near $q = 0$ completely eliminated?

29. (2+) For turbulent flow of air in the electronic cabinet (cf. Exercises 27 and 28) the system curve should not have linear or constant terms: that is, it should be of the form $\Delta p = c q^2$. Write the overdetermined system of equations for the least-squares problem to find c in $\Delta p = c q^2$. Obtain an analytical solution of the normal equations to find a simple expression for c in terms of the known Δp and q data. Modify the m-file developed in Exercise 27 so that it uses this fit in addition to that obtained with polyfit. Apply the m-file to the data in flowsys1.dat and flowsys2.dat. Does the fit to $\Delta p = c q^2$ have problems as $Q \to 0$? Does adding the point $(\Delta p, q) = (0, 0)$ affect the fit? (*Hint*: Consider the solution to Exercise 7.)

30. (2+) Hart et al. (*Optical Measurement of the Speed of Sound in Air Over the Temperature Range 300-650 K*, NASA/CR-2000-210114, ICASE Report No. 2000-20, Institute for Computer Applications in Science and Engineering, NASA Langley Research Center, Hampton, VA.) report on a new technique for measuring the speed of high frequency sound waves in air using laser-induced thermal acoustics (LITA). The airSoundSpeed.dat file in the data directory of the NMM Toolbox contains data extracted from their report. The first column in airSoundSpeed.dat is the temperature of the sample in kelvins, the second column is the sound speed measured by LITA, and the third column is the sound speed predicted by another model.

For an ideal gas the sound speed is $V = \sqrt{kRT}$ where V is the sound speed, k is the ratio of specific heats, R is the gas constant, and T is the temperature of the gas. Use polyfit to create a first degree polynomial (i.e. a straight line) fit of V as a function of $\sqrt{T}$ for the LITA data. Perform another fit of the form $V = c\sqrt{T}$ to the same data, where c is the lone parameter of the fit. Compare the two fits by plotting them both on the same axes with the original data. What are the values of k deduced from the curve fit coefficients. *Hint*: The solution to Exercise 7 will be helpful.

31. (3+) (Adapted from Akai [3].) A coast-down test can be used to estimate the aerodynamic drag characteristics of a vehicle. The test begins with the vehicle moving at a known velocity. The power is cut off (transmission put in neutral), and the vehicle velocity is measured as it is allowed to slow down. The results from one such test are given in the velocity.dat file in the data directory of the NMM toolbox. A force balance on the unpowered vehicle gives

$$\sum F = F_d + F_f,$$

where F_d is the aerodynamic drag and F_f is the sum of all friction forces (tire and transmission resistance) slowing the vehicle. Suppose that F_f can be measured with a separate test. Lacking that information, we will simply neglect F_f for now. Combining Newton's law of motion with the force balance gives

$$ma = m\frac{dv}{dt} = -F_d, \quad \text{or} \quad F_d = -\frac{1}{m}\frac{dv}{dt}.$$

This equation allows us to estimate F_d from the velocity data.

10

Interpolation

Interpolation is an important part of many numerical methods. Interpolating polynomials are the building blocks for the numerical integration of functions and the solution of ordinary differential equations. Interpolation theory forms the basis for the numerical approximation to partial differential equations. In both image processing and signal processing, resampling data to change resolution requires interpolation. In many fields, it is often necessary to interpolate to find intermediate values between entries in a table.

This chapter is concerned with the use of interpolation to approximate a function that is defined by a table of data. The material is developed for one-dimensional data (i.e., $y = f(x)$), although the basic ideas carry over to two and three dimensions. Figure 10.1 presents a brief summary of the organization of this chapter.

Polynomials are used to construct interpolating functions in two primary ways. In the first part of the chapter, the degree of the polynomial is increased by matching greater number of points from the discrete data set. Interpolating polynomials are constructed using monomial, Lagrange, and Newton bases, all of which are equivalent in exact arithmetic. These forms are shown to have very different numerical characteristics. Creating a polynomial of increasing degree is also shown to be of limited numerical utility, regardless of the algorithm. The basic weakness is that increasing the degree of polynomial so that it matches an increasing num-

---

Topics Covered in This Chapter

1. **Basic Ideas**
   The basic nomenclature of interpolation is introduced. Distinctions between interpolation and curve fitting, and between interpolation and extrapolation are made.

2. **Interpolating Polynomials of Arbitrary Degree**
   Methods for performing interpolation with polynomials of arbitrary degree are developed. The use of three different polynomial bases—monomial, Lagrange, and Newton—are shown to have different numerical properties. An example is given to demonstrate that polynomials of arbitrarily high degree can exhibit "wiggle" between the support points used too define the interpolant.

3. **Piecewise Polynomial Interpolation**
   High-accuracy interpolants are developed by combining non-overlapping, low-order polynomials. These piecewise interpolants are recommended for routine use. Hermite and spline interpolants are piecewise polynomials that have higher order continuities between adjacent segments. Routines for Hermite and spline interpolation are developed.

4. **MATLAB's Built-in Interpolation Functions**
   The interpolation functions included in the standard MATLAB Toolbox are briefly surveyed.

Figure 10.1   Primary topics discussed in Chapter 10.

ber of data points results in undesirable oscillations in the value of the interpolant *between* the prescribed points.

In the second half of the chapter, the interpolation problem is reformulated. Rather than building a single, high-degree polynomial over the domain of interest, an interpolating function is created by assembling a set of lower degree polynomials defined over subintervals of the domain. The overall accuracy of the resulting *piecewise* interpolant is much better than can be obtained with a single interpolating function. Routines are developed to perform interpolation with piecewise-linear functions, piecewise-cubic Hermite polynomials, and cubic-splines. The chapter ends with a brief discussion of MATLAB's built-in interpolating functions.

Example 10.1: Visual Interpolation

Figure 10.2 shows a speedometer and the face of a wristwatch, two common analog instruments. The indicators move continuously across a scale with discrete markers. When the

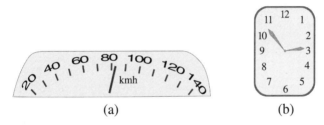

Figure 10.2   Visual interpolation of common analog instruments: (a) a speedometer and (b) the face of a wristwatch.

indicator is between markers, one can round to the nearest marker or visually estimate the value that would be indicated with a finer scale. Estimating a value between two nearby values is an essential feature of interpolation.

For the speedometer, the indicator is approximately 2/10 of the distance between 80 and 90 kmh. This suggests that the vehicle speed is approximately 82 kmh. For the watch face, the minute hand is approximately 4/5 of the distance between the 10 and the 11, so an estimate of the time is 3:54. These estimates use linear interpolation, which corresponds exactly to the underlying functions: The speed is a linear function of angular needle position, and the time in minutes past the hour is a linear function of the angular position of the minute hand.

In general, the interpolation function is not the same as the function that created the data being interpolated. The interpolating function is an approximation to the output function, $y = f(x)$. When an analog dial is read, one is making a visual estimation of the input x.

Example 10.2: Viscosity of Glycerin

Glycerin ($C_3H_5(OH)_3$) is a liquid used in the manufacture of many products from soap to (explosive) nitroglycerin. The viscosity of glycerin is a strong function of temperature, as demonstrated by the following table[1] and the plot shown in Figure 10.3:

T (°C)	0	10	20	30	40	50
μ(N · s/m)	10.60	3.810	1.492	0.629	0.2754	0.1867

The data are also available in the `glycerin.dat` file in the `data` directory of the NMM toolbox.

Using linear interpolation in the tabulated data, we can estimate the viscosity of glycerin at 22 °C:

$$\mu(22\,°C) \approx 1.492 + \frac{2}{10}(0.629 - 1.492) = 1.319.$$

As shown in Example 10.7 on page 543, using quadratic interpolation gives $\mu(22\,°C) = 1.203$, a 10% difference.

---

[1]Data adapted from E.R.G. Eckert and R.M. Drake, Jr., *Analysis of Heat and Mass Transfer*, 1972, McGraw-Hill, Table B-3, p. 779.

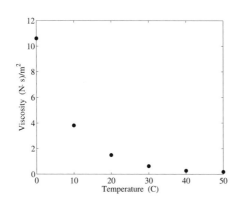

Figure 10.3   Viscosity of glycerin as a function of temperature.

10.1 BASIC IDEAS

Interpolation on a fixed set of data is the mathematical equivalent of reading between the lines. In the one-dimensional case, a set of data (x_i, y_i), $i = 1, \dots, n$ is
given as discrete samples of some known or hard-to-evaluate function $y = f(x)$.
Interpolation involves constructing and then evaluating an interpolating function,
or *interpolant*, $y = \mathcal{F}(x)$ at values of $x = \hat{x}$ that may or may not be in the (x_i, y_i)
data set. The interpolation function $\mathcal{F}(x)$ is determined by requiring that it pass
through the known data (x_i, y_i). For $\hat{x} \neq x_i$, the $\mathcal{F}(x)$ should also be a good approximation to $f(x)$, which created the tabular data in the first place.

$f(x)$ may exist as an experiment, in which case the (x_i, y_i) data represent the
input and output values of n measurements. In other cases, $f(x)$ may actually be a
known analytical function that is difficult or tedious to evaluate, especially by manual calculations. This is the case, for example, for many mathematical functions,
and for physical data presented in tabular form in handbooks. Whether or not $f(x)$
is known analytically, the interpolation procedure only uses a finite set of (x_i, y_i)
data.

In its most general form, interpolation involves determining the coefficients
$a_1, a_2, \dots a_n$ in the linear combination of n *basis functions*, $\Phi(x)$, that constitute
the interpolant

$$\mathcal{F}(x) = a_1 \Phi_1(x) + a_2 \Phi_2(x) + \cdots + a_n \Phi_n(x) \tag{10.1}$$

such that $\mathcal{F}(x_i) = y_i$ for $i = 1, \dots, n$. The basis functions may be polynomial

$$\mathcal{F}(x) = a_1 + a_2 x + a_3 x^2 + \cdots + a_n x^{n-1},$$

or trigonometric

$$\mathcal{F}(x) = a_1 + a_2 e^{ix} + a_3 e^{2ix} + \cdots + a_n e^{(n-1)ix},$$

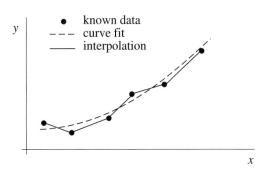

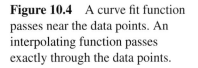

Figure 10.4 A curve fit function passes near the data points. An interpolating function passes exactly through the data points.

(where $i = \sqrt{-1}$) or some other suitable set of functions. Polynomials are often used for interpolation because they are easy to evaluate and easy to manipulate analytically.

10.1.1 Interpolation versus Curve Fitting

Given a set of data $y_i = f(x_i)$, $i = 1, \ldots, n$ obtained from an experiment or from some calculation, it is often necessary to evaluate y for x values not in the original data set. Curve fitting is an alternative to interpolation for this task. In curve fitting, the approximating function passes near the data points, but (usually) not exactly through them. The fact that the fit function and the data do not exactly agree is an implicit recognition that there is some uncertainty in the data. Figure 10.4 shows a plot of some hypothetical experimental data and a curve fit function.

In contrast to curve fitting, the interpolation process inherently assumes that the data have no uncertainty. The interpolation function passes *exactly* through each of the known data points. Figure 10.4 also shows the result of interpolating the hypothetical data with piecewise-linear functions. Whereas the curve fit function is smooth, the piecewise-linear interpolating functions have discontinuous slopes at the known data points. This lack of smoothness can be eliminated by using different interpolating functions (e.g., cubic splines).

Although there is a fundamental difference between the process of curve fitting and interpolation, the difference may not always be important. For example, in a rough engineering calculation, a linear interpolation between data points with some experimental uncertainty may yield a perfectly workable estimate. In such a situation, it is reasonable to ignore the uncertainty of the data if one also accepts that the result has inherited the uncertainty.

10.1.2 Interpolation and Extrapolation

Interpolation involves the construction and evaluation of an approximating function within the range of the independent variable of the given data set. For simplicity

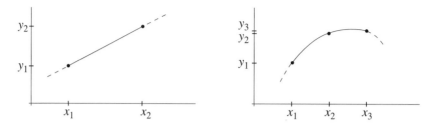

Figure 10.5 Interpolation and extrapolation for linear and quadratic polynomial interpolants. The dashed lines indicate extrapolation outside the range of the given data.

of exposition, assume that the (x_i, y_i) data are ordered such that $x_1 < x_2 < \cdots < x_n$. Interpolation provides a means of approximating $y = f(x)$ for $x_1 \leq x \leq x_n$. *Extrapolation* is the evaluation of the interpolating function outside the range of the given independent variable, i.e., for $x < x_1$ or $x > x_n$. Interpolation and extrapolation are depicted in Figure 10.5.

Example 10.3: Extrapolation of Airport Traffic Data

A robust regional economy, in addition to the continued popularity of air travel, has lead to a rapid increase in air passengers through Portland, OR during the 1990's. The pdxPass.dat file in the data directory of the NMM toolbox contains data on the number of passengers traveling through the airport between 1981 and 1998. To plan for future traffic levels, it is necessary to estimate the number of passengers that will use the airport five years into the future. Although the data apply to a particular time period, we will use them here to illustrate the perils of extrapolation.

Predicting the future is difficult. Urban planners faced with the task of estimating the future airport traffic levels use econometric models to simulate the growth in population and industrial production, as well as to simulate overall trends of the national and regional economy. In the absence of such sophisticated models, one is left only with the historic passenger data. By constructing an interpolating function through these data, it is possible to *extrapolate* into the future. The result of extrapolating the interpolation functions described later in this chapter are shown in Figure 10.6. All of the extrapolations agree for the first year or so after the known data, but then they begin to diverge significantly. An extrapolation of five years gives the numerical results presented in the following table:

Extrapolation method	Airport travelers in 2003 (millions of passengers)
linear	14.0
quadratic	13.8
cubic	53.8
cubic-spline	79.5

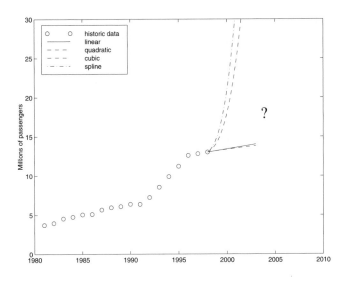

Figure 10.6   Extrapolation of airport passenger data using different interpolation functions that are described in this chapter.

The disagreement between these predictions provides a qualitative indicator of the uncertainty inherent in extrapolation.

10.2 INTERPOLATING POLYNOMIALS OF ARBITRARY DEGREE

This section presents a number of algorithms for constructing and evaluating interpolating polynomials of any degree. A set of n data points may be interpolated with polynomials of up to degree $n - 1$. Although the algorithms presented here allow construction of polynomials with any n, in practice only polynomials of low degree, say, less than 5, are useful. As n increases (i.e., as more data points are used to construct higher degree polynomials), the value of the interpolant between the data points takes on values that may deviate significantly from the nearby known data points. This is the problem of *polynomial wiggle* described in § 10.2.4.

10.2.1 Polynomial Interpolation with a Monomial Basis

Polynomial interpolation involves finding the equation of $P_{n-1}(x)$, the unique polynomial of degree $n - 1$ that passes through n known data pairs, or *support points*. A common representation of a polynomial of degree $n - 1$ is

$$P_{n-1}(x) = a_1 + a_2 x + \cdots + a_n x^{n-1}, \tag{10.2}$$

which defines the polynomial in terms of a set of *monomial basis functions*, $x^0, x^1, x^2, \ldots x^{n-1}$. Although the monomials use a familiar and compact notation, the polynomial $P_{n-1}(x)$ can be written in other formats. Consider the shifted polynomial

$$P_{n-1}(x - \xi) = b_1 + b_2(x - \xi) + \cdots + b_n(x - \xi)^{n-1}, \tag{10.3}$$

where ξ is a known offset. With appropriate definitions for the coefficients b_i, Equations (10.2) and (10.3) define the same polynomial.

The built-in MATLAB routines for evaluating polynomials (see also § 2.3.3 beginning on page 51) require that the polynomial be written in decreasing powers of x,

$$P_{n-1}(x) = c_1 x^{n-1} + c_2 x^{n-1} + \cdots + c_{n-1} x + c_n. \tag{10.4}$$

In this case the c_i are the same set of a_i values from Equation (10.2) taken in a different order.

Vandermonde Systems Given a set of n ordered pairs of (x, y) data, one can write n equations for the n unknown coefficients c_i by requiring that the polynomial pass through each of the data points. Solving the resulting system of equations determines the c_i.

Consider the construction of a quadratic interpolating function

$$y = c_1 x^2 + c_2 x + c_3 \tag{10.5}$$

that passes through the (x, y) support points $(-2, -2)$, $(-1, 1)$, and $(2, -1)$. Substituting the known points into Equation (10.5) yields a system of three equations for the c_i:

$$-2 = c_1(-2)^2 + c_2(-2) + c_3,$$

$$1 = c_1(-1)^2 + c_2(-1) + c_3,$$

$$-1 = c_1(2)^2 + c_2(2) + c_3.$$

The preceding equations may be rewritten as

$$\begin{bmatrix} 4 & -2 & 1 \\ 1 & -1 & 1 \\ 4 & 2 & 1 \end{bmatrix} \begin{bmatrix} c_1 \\ c_2 \\ c_3 \end{bmatrix} = \begin{bmatrix} -2 \\ 1 \\ -1 \end{bmatrix}. \tag{10.6}$$

For an arbitrary set of three points (x_1, y_1), (x_2, y_2), and (x_3, y_3), the matrix equation is

$$\begin{bmatrix} x_1^2 & x_1 & 1 \\ x_2^2 & x_2 & 1 \\ x_3^2 & x_3 & 1 \end{bmatrix} \begin{bmatrix} c_1 \\ c_2 \\ c_3 \end{bmatrix} = \begin{bmatrix} y_1 \\ y_2 \\ y_3 \end{bmatrix}.$$

The coefficient matrix on the left-hand side is called a *Vandermonde* matrix.

The Vandermonde matrix for Equation (10.6) can be constructed with the following MATLAB statements:

```
>> x = [-2  -1  2]';              %  transpose required, x must be a column
>> A = [x.^2  x  ones(size(x))];
```

The built-in vander function creates Vandermonde matrices from an arbitrary vector. The preceding statements can be replaced with

```
>> A = vander([-2  -1  2]);    %  vander is clever, transpose is optional
```

The vander function is smart enough to convert the input to a column vector before constructing the matrix. The dimensions of the matrix created by vander are determined by the length of the input vector. It is instructive to study the statements in the vander function.[2]

Once the Vandermonde matrix is defined, the solution to Equation (10.6) yields the coefficients of the interpolating polynomial:

```
>> y = [-2  1  -1]';
>> c = A\y
c =
   -0.9167
    0.2500
    2.1667
```

Although this procedure is straightforward, it is not the best way to construct an interpolating polynomial, because the Vandermonde system may be ill conditioned.

Example 10.4: Interpolation of Gasoline Prices

Consider the task of interpolating the (fictitious) gasoline price data (in U.S. cents) in the following table:[3]

year	1986	1988	1990	1992	1994	1996
price	113.5	132.2	138.7	141.5	137.6	144.2

Given that there are six data pairs, a simple interpolation strategy is to create a fifth-degree polynomial through the data

$$p = c_1 y^5 + c_2 y^4 + c_3 y^3 + c_4 y^2 + c_5 y + c_6, \tag{10.7}$$

---

[2]Enter type vander at the command prompt to get a listing of the function.

[3]One might reasonably object to the coarse sampling of such a volatile commodity as gasoline. Indeed, a sound scientific study would include more data, as well as an abundance of qualifications on the confidence with which the data are representative of the true population of gas prices.

where p is the price and y is the year. The following MATLAB statements set up the system of equations and solve for c:

```
>> year = [1986    1988    1990    1992    1994    1996 ]';
>> price = [133.5  132.2  138.7  141.5  137.6  144.2]';
>> A = vander(year);    % Set up Vandermonde system
>> c = A\price;         % and solve it
```

```
Warning: Matrix is close to singular or badly scaled.
         Results may be inaccurate. RCOND = 8.305426e-32
```

```
>> fprintf('%12.4e\n',c)
  3.0382e-03
 -3.0207e+01
  1.2014e+05
 -2.3890e+08
  2.3753e+11
 -9.4465e+13
```

The warning message indicates that A is ill conditioned. A very small value of RCOND[4]—an estimate of the *inverse* of the condition number—indicates that the condition number of the matrix is very large. The following statements evaluate and plot the interpolating function:

```
>> y = linspace(min(year),max(year));
>> p = polyval(c,y);                    % Eval polynomial at each y
>> plot(year,price,'o',y,p,'-')
```

The result, shown in Figure 10.7, confirms that there is a serious problem with the interpolating function. Rather than being a smooth curve, as anticipated, the interpolation function is irregular.

The preceding calculations exhibit two separate, but related, phenomena. First, matrix A is ill conditioned. For a condition number of order 10^{31} and double-precision arithmetic, Equation (8.38) on page 363 indicates that there are *no* correct significant digits in the elements of the solution vector c. Matrix A has a large condition number because there are large variations in magnitude of its elements. The smallest element is 1, and the largest element is $1996^6 \approx 3.2 \times 10^{16}$. During the forward elimination phase of the solution (i.e., when the L and U factors are computed) small roundoff errors lead to large uncertainties in the factored matrices L and U. During backsubstitution, more roundoff errors occur and are manifested as perturbations to the true c_i values. The result is the polynomial

$$\tilde{p} = \tilde{c}_1 y^5 + \tilde{c}_2 y^4 + \tilde{c}_3 y^3 + \tilde{c}_4 y^2 + \tilde{c}_5 y + \tilde{c}_6, \qquad (10.8)$$

which is different from the polynomial in Equation (10.7).

The problem of roundoff error in the computation of the c_i is inherent in polynomial interpolation with monomial bases, because Vandermonde matrices are often ill conditioned. For low-degree polynomials, say, $n \le 4$, and abscissas of magnitude $\mathcal{O}(10)$, these

---

[4]See also the built-in rcond function.

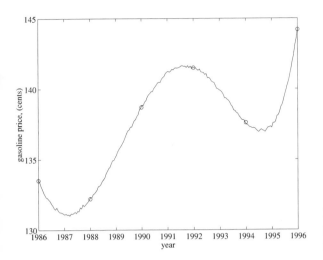

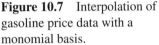

Figure 10.7   Interpolation of gasoline price data with a monomial basis.

problems will be relatively benign. Since Gaussian elimination and backward substitution produce solutions with small residuals, even for ill conditioned systems, the result of evaluating the polynomial with a monomial basis may not be problematic, even if the c_i are not exact.

The second problem with the solution to the Vandermonde system is that the coefficients of the interpolating polynomial vary over 16 orders of magnitude. Evaluating Equation (10.8) with values of y of order 1000 results in significant roundoff errors, which cause the high-frequency oscillations depicted in Figure 10.7. The roundoff errors in the evaluation of the polynomial are combined with the unreliable values of c_i to produce an interpolating function that is not an accurate approximation to the input data.

As demonstrated in this example, these problems can be important for higher degree polynomials. The following example shows how a simple change can significantly improve the interpolating function obtained with a monomial basis.

Example 10.5: Interpolation of Gasoline Prices Using Shifted Dates

The Vandermonde matrix in the preceding example is ill conditioned because the elements vary in magnitude from $\mathcal{O}(1)$ to $\mathcal{O}(10^{16})$. The condition number of the matrix can be significantly improved if the dates corresponding to the x-axis of the interpolation are rescaled. Suppose that instead of interpolating the price as a function of year, where $1986 \leq$ year ≤ 1996, the price is interpolated as a function of the shifted date, ys $=$ year $- 1991$.

```
>> year = [1986    1988    1990    1992    1994    1996 ]';    %  input data
>> price = [133.5   132.2   138.7   141.5   137.6   144.2]';
```

```
>> ys = year - mean(year);     %  Shift dates by average value (1991)
>> A = vander(ys);             %  Set up Vandermonde system
>> c = A\price                 %  and solve it
c =
     0.0030
     0.0374
    -0.0930
    -1.0237
     1.4899
   141.0863
```

The Vandermonde system for the shifted dates is not ill conditioned. (How would you quantify a comparison with the Vandermonde system from the preceding example?) In addition, the coefficients of the interpolating polynomial vary over 5 orders of magnitude, as opposed to the 16 orders of magnitude for the unshifted dates in the preceding example. Figure 10.8 presents a plot of the interpolation function, which shows none of the spurious oscillations evident in Figure 10.7.

The interpolation of gas prices with a monomial basis can be further improved if normalized instead of shifted dates are used. This is explored in Exercise 4.

10.2.2 Polynomial Interpolation with a Lagrange Basis

In a monomial basis the linear interpolating polynomial through (x_1, y_1) and (x_2, y_2) is

$$P_1(x) = c_1 x + c_2, \tag{10.9}$$

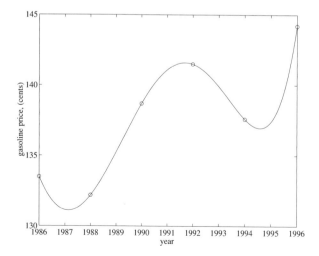

Figure 10.8 Interpolation of gasoline price data with a monomial basis and shifted dates.

where the two constants are

$$c_1 = \frac{y_2 - y_1}{x_2 - x_1} \qquad c_2 = \frac{y_1 x_2 - y_2 x_1}{x_2 - x_1}.$$

Substituting c_1 and c_2 into Equation (10.9) and rearranging gives

$$P_1(x) = y_1 \frac{x - x_2}{x_1 - x_2} + y_2 \frac{x - x_1}{x_2 - x_1}.$$

This expresses the linear interpolating polynomial in terms of a new pair of basis functions $L_1(x)$ and $L_2(x)$:

$$P_1(x) = y_1 L_1(x) + y_2 L_2(x). \qquad (10.10)$$

where

$$L_1(x) = \frac{x - x_2}{x_1 - x_2} \qquad L_2(x) = \frac{x - x_1}{x_2 - x_1}. \qquad (10.11)$$

$L_1(x)$ and $L_2(x)$ are the first-degree *Lagrange interpolating polynomials*, which are depicted in Figure 10.9. Both of these basis polynomials are linear in x, whereas the monomial basis consists of a linear function x and a constant "1". If x_i is a support point, then

$$L_j(x_i) = \delta_{ij} = \begin{cases} 0 & \text{if } i \neq j \\ 1 & \text{if } i = j \end{cases} \qquad (10.12)$$

where δ_{ij} is called the Kronecker delta.

The quadratic interpolating polynomial using a Lagrange basis and passing through (x_1, y_1), (x_2, y_2), and (x_3, y_3) is

$$P_2(x) = y_1 L_1(x) + y_2 L_2(x) + y_2 L_3(x),$$

where

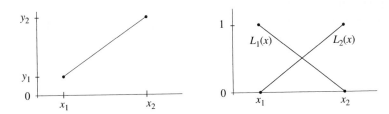

Figure 10.9 Linear interpolation and the corresponding Lagrange polynomial basis of degree one.

Equation (10.14) can be written as

$$L_j(x) = \prod_{\substack{k=1 \\ k \neq j}}^{n} \frac{x - x_k}{x_j - x_k} = \left[\prod_{k=1}^{j-1} \frac{x - x_k}{x_j - x_k} \right] \left[\prod_{k=j+1}^{n} \frac{x - x_k}{x_j - x_k} \right] \qquad (10.15)$$

Given a value of x, the numerator of each L_j, contains products of terms like

$$(x - x_1)(x - x_2) \cdots (x - x_{j-1})(x - x_{j+1}) \cdots (x - x_n).$$

Because these terms are repeated in each of the L_j, it makes sense to compute the differences once and store them. Let dxi be the vector containing all possible $(x - x_k)$ values:

```
xi  = ...         %  Evaluate interpolant at xi (given)
x   = ...         %  Tabulated x data (given)
dxi = xi - x;     %  Vector of xi - x(k) values
```

Given dxi, we can evaluate the numerator of Equation (10.15) with

```
num = prod(dxi(1:j-1))*prod(dxi(j+1:n))
```

where the built-in prod function computes the product of the elements of a vector. The subexpression prod(dxi(1:j-1)) is equivalent to $(x - x_1)(x - x_2) \cdots (x - x_{j-1})$.

The denominator in Equation (10.15) can also be constructed from precomputed quantities. This is less advantageous, because it requires storage of a lower triangular matrix whose entries are used only twice. (See Exercise 9.) If the denominators are computed only when needed, then the work will be a factor of two greater than the minimal amount of work, and there will be no additional storage. The trade-off of (less) memory for (more) computation is not critical in this application, because only modest-degree polynomials are used in practice. Taking the straightforward and marginally less efficient approach, we can evaluate the denominator of Equation (10.15) as

```
den = prod(x(j)-x(1:j-1))*prod(x(j)-x(j+1:n));
```

where, for example, x(j)-x(1:j-1) is the vector of differences x(j)-x(1), x(j)-x(2),...,x(j)-x(j-1).

The lagrint function shown in Listing 10.1 uses the preceding formulas to evaluate a Lagrange polynomial passing through a user-specified set of data. Note that the lagrint function can only interpolate one scalar xi at a time.

```
function yi = lagrint(x,y,xi)
% lagrint   Interpolation with Lagrange polynomials of arbitrary degree
%
% Synopsis:  yi = lagrint(x,y,xi)
%
% Input:   x,y = tabulated data
%          xi  = point where interpolation is to be evaluated
%
% Output:    yi = value of y at x = xi obtained via interpolation with
%                 polynomial of degree n-1, where length(y) = length(x) = n

dxi = xi - x;        %  vector of xi - x(1), xi - x(2), ... values
n = length(x);       %  degree of polynomial is n-1
L = zeros(size(y));  %  preallocate L for speed

%  Refer to section 10.2.2 in text for explanation of vectorized code
%  used to compute Lagrange basis functions, L(j)
L(1) = prod(dxi(2:n))/prod(x(1)-x(2:n));        %  j = 1
L(n) = prod(dxi(1:n-1))/prod(x(n)-x(1:n-1));    %  j = n
for j=2:n-1
   num = prod(dxi(1:j-1))*prod(dxi(j+1:n));
   den = prod(x(j)-x(1:j-1))*prod(x(j)-x(j+1:n));
   L(j) = num/den;
end
yi = sum(y.*L);      %  Evaluate Polynomial: sum of y(j)*L(j), j=1..n
```

Listing 10.1 The lagrint function for interpolation with Lagrange polynomials.

Example 10.6: Interpolation of Gasoline Prices with Lagrange Polynomials

The demoGasLag function shown in Listing 10.2 interpolates the gasoline data from Example 10.4 with Lagrange polynomials. The plot of the interpolating function (not shown here) is visually indistinguishable from that in Figure 10.8 on page 532. In particular, there are no spurious fluctuations in the interpolating function, even though the unshifted dates are used in demoGasLag. This is because the Lagrange polynomials do not require the solution of a linear system of equations and so do not suffer from the ill conditioning and roundoff that destroys the accuracy of the solution to the Vandermonde system. The reader is reminded that *in exact arithmetic*, the Lagrange interpolating polynomial is identical to the polynomial in the monomial basis. As this example demonstrates, however, polynomial interpolation with a Lagrange basis is less susceptible to roundoff than polynomial interpolation with a monomial basis.

```
function demoGasLag
% demoGasLag  Interpolate gasoline price data with Lagrange polynomials
%
% Synopsis:  demoGasLag
%
% Input:     none
%
% Output:    Plot of given data and interpolating function for gas price

year = [1986   1988   1990   1992   1994   1996 ]';    % input data
price = [133.5  132.2  138.7  141.5  137.6  144.2]';

y = linspace(min(year),max(year),200);  % eval interpolant at these dates
p = zeros(size(y));                      % Pre-allocate p for efficiency
for i=1:length(y)
  p(i) = lagrint(year,price,y(i));       % Interpolate to find p( y(i) )
end
plot(year,price,'o',y,p,'-');
xlabel('year');  ylabel('gasoline price, (cents)');
```

Listing 10.2   Use the `lagrint` function to interpolate gasoline prices.

10.2.3 Polynomial Interpolation with a Newton Basis

The Newton form of an interpolating polynomial of degree n is

$$P_n(x) = c_1 + c_2(x - x_1) + c_3(x - x_1)(x - x_2) + \cdots$$
$$+ c_{n+1}(x - x_1)(x - x_2) \cdots (x - x_n)(x - x_{n+1}),$$

where the Newton basis polynomials are

$$1, \quad (x - x_1), \quad (x - x_1)(x - x_2), \quad (x - x_1)(x - x_2)(x - x_3), \quad \cdots$$

The c_i are coefficients found by requiring that $P_n(x_i) = f(x_i)$ for $i = 1, \ldots, n+1$.
Although these basis functions may initially seem cumbersome, it turns out that
the Newton form is more computationally efficient than interpolating polynomials
written in monomial or Lagrange bases. The Newton form also has good numerical
properties, and it is very useful for theoretical analysis of interpolation schemes and
numerical integration methods described in Chapter 11.

Working with the Newton interpolating polynomials is easier with the introduction of *divided-difference* notation. Rather than first presenting divided-
difference notation in the most general form, we introduce it for the simple case of
a quadratic polynomial. The quadratic interpolating polynomial is then extended
to a cubic interpolating polynomial. The ability to easily extend the order of the

interpolation is just one advantage of working with the Newton form. After these examples are presented, the general properties of divided-differences are listed, and a MATLAB implementation of Newton polynomial interpolation is given.

Quadratic Polynomial in Newton Form   Consider a quadratic polynomial passing through (x_i, y_i), $i = 1, 2, 3$, expressed in terms of the Newton basis functions:

$$P_2(x) = c_1 + c_2(x - x_1) + c_3(x - x_1)(x - x_2). \qquad (10.16)$$

Applying the three constraints gives

$$P_2(x_1) = c_1 = y_1,$$

$$P_2(x_2) = c_1 + c_2(x_2 - x_1) = y_2,$$

$$P_2(x_3) = c_1 + c_2(x_3 - x_1) + c_3(x_3 - x_1)(x_3 - x_2) = y_3,$$

or, in matrix form,

$$\begin{bmatrix} 1 & 0 & 0 \\ 1 & (x_2 - x_1) & 0 \\ 1 & (x_3 - x_1) & (x_3 - x_1)(x_3 - x_2) \end{bmatrix} \begin{bmatrix} c_1 \\ c_2 \\ c_3 \end{bmatrix} = \begin{bmatrix} y_1 \\ y_2 \\ y_3 \end{bmatrix}. \qquad (10.17)$$

Solving this system yields the coefficients of the polynomial in Equation (10.16). Since the system is lower triangular, its solution requires only $\mathcal{O}(n^2)$ operations instead of the $\mathcal{O}(n^3)$ of a Vandermonde system, which has a full coefficient matrix.

The c_i in Equation (10.16), are given by compact formulas called divided differences. To motivate these expressions, the preceding 3×3 system of equations will be solved while keeping the system in matrix form. (See also [68, 77].) This leads to a natural introduction of the divided-difference formula.

Inspection of Equation (10.17) indicates that $c_1 = y_1$. Forward elimination yields formulas for c_2 and c_3. Begin by subtracting the first row from the second and third rows:

$$\begin{bmatrix} 1 & 0 & 0 \\ 0 & (x_2 - x_1) & 0 \\ 0 & (x_3 - x_1) & (x_3 - x_1)(x_3 - x_2) \end{bmatrix} \begin{bmatrix} c_1 \\ c_2 \\ c_3 \end{bmatrix} = \begin{bmatrix} y_1 \\ y_2 - y_1 \\ y_3 - y_1 \end{bmatrix}.$$

Next, normalize the second column by dividing the second row by $x_2 - x_1$ and dividing the third row by $x_3 - x_1$

$$\begin{bmatrix} 1 & 0 & 0 \\ 0 & 1 & 0 \\ 0 & 1 & (x_3 - x_2) \end{bmatrix} \begin{bmatrix} c_1 \\ c_2 \\ c_3 \end{bmatrix} = \begin{bmatrix} y_1 \\ \dfrac{y_2 - y_1}{x_2 - x_1} \\ \dfrac{y_3 - y_1}{x_3 - x_1} \end{bmatrix}. \tag{10.18}$$

The second row gives $c_2 = (y_2 - y_1)/(x_2 - x_1)$. Now, introduce the *first-order divided-differences*

$$f[x_1, x_2] \equiv \frac{y_2 - y_1}{x_2 - x_1} \quad \text{and} \quad f[x_1, x_3] \equiv \frac{y_3 - y_1}{x_3 - x_1}.$$

In general, the first-order divided difference involving the ordered pairs (x_i, y_i) and (x_j, y_j) is

$$f[x_i, x_j] \equiv \frac{y_j - y_i}{x_j - x_i}. \tag{10.19}$$

With this notation, $c_2 = f[x_1, x_2]$, and Equation (10.18) becomes

$$\begin{bmatrix} 1 & 0 & 0 \\ 0 & 1 & 0 \\ 0 & 1 & (x_3 - x_2) \end{bmatrix} \begin{bmatrix} c_1 \\ c_2 \\ c_3 \end{bmatrix} = \begin{bmatrix} y_1 \\ f[x_1, x_2] \\ f[x_1, x_3] \end{bmatrix}.$$

Subtract the second row from the third row to get

$$\begin{bmatrix} 1 & 0 & 0 \\ 0 & 1 & 0 \\ 0 & 0 & (x_3 - x_2) \end{bmatrix} \begin{bmatrix} c_1 \\ c_2 \\ c_3 \end{bmatrix} = \begin{bmatrix} y_1 \\ f[x_1, x_2] \\ f[x_1, x_3] - f[x_1, x_2] \end{bmatrix},$$

and divide the third row by $x_3 - x_2$

$$\begin{bmatrix} 1 & 0 & 0 \\ 0 & 1 & 0 \\ 0 & 0 & 1 \end{bmatrix} \begin{bmatrix} c_1 \\ c_2 \\ c_3 \end{bmatrix} = \begin{bmatrix} y_1 \\ f[x_1, x_2] \\ f[x_1, x_2, x_3] \end{bmatrix},$$

where

$$f[x_1, x_2, x_3] \equiv \frac{f[x_2, x_3] - f[x_1, x_2]}{x_3 - x_2}$$

is the second-order divided difference involving (x_1, y_1), (x_2, y_2), and (x_3, y_3). The solution to Equation (10.17) is, therefore,

$$c_1 = y_1,$$
$$c_2 = f[x_1, x_2], \tag{10.20}$$
$$c_3 = f[x_1, x_2, x_3].$$

The convention is to define the zeroth-order divided difference as

$$f[x_i] = y_i,$$

so that $y_1 = f[x_1]$, and the Newton form of the quadratic polynomial can be written

$$P_2(x) = f[x_1] + f[x_1, x_2](x - x_1) + f[x_1, x_2, x_3](x - x_1)(x - x_2). \quad (10.21)$$

This equation shows that *the coefficients of the Newton polynomial are divided differences.*

Cubic Polynomial in Newton Form   A cubic polynomial in Newton form can be obtained by direct extension of the quadratic polynomial. The cubic polynomial is

$$P_3(x) = c_1 + c_2(x - x_1) + c_3(x - x_1)(x - x_2) + c_4(x - x_1)(x - x_2)(x - x_3). \quad (10.22)$$

Solving for the c_i by repeating the analysis of the preceding section (see Exercise 10) yields

$$c_1 = y_1,$$
$$c_2 = f[x_1, x_2],$$
$$c_3 = f[x_1, x_2, x_3], \quad (10.23)$$
$$c_4 = f[x_1, x_2, x_3, x_4],$$

where

$$f[x_1, x_2, x_3, x_4] = \frac{f[x_2, x_3, x_4] - f[x_1, x_2, x_3]}{x_4 - x_1}$$

and

$$f[x_2, x_3, x_4] = \frac{f[x_3, x_4] - f[x_2, x_3]}{x_4 - x_2}.$$

Notice that c_1, c_2, and c_3 are identical to those in Equation (10.20). Substituting the divided difference coefficients into Equation (10.22) gives

$$P_3(x) = f[x_1] + f[x_1, x_2](x - x_1) + f[x_1, x_2, x_3](x - x_1)(x - x_2)$$
$$+ f[x_1, x_2, x_3, x_4](x - x_1)(x - x_2)(x - x_3). \quad (10.24)$$

A comparison of Equations (10.21) and (10.24) shows that

$$P_3(x) = P_2(x) + f[x_1, x_2, x_3, x_4](x - x_1)(x - x_2)(x - x_3).$$

This property extends to any pair of degree n and degree $n - 1$ polynomials, that is,

TABLE 10.1   DIVIDED-DIFFERENCE TABLE.

x_i	$f[\ ]$	$f[,]$	$f[,,]$	$f[,,,]$
x_1	$f[x_1]$			
x_2	$f[x_2]$	$f[x_1,x_2]$		
x_3	$f[x_3]$	$f[x_2,x_3]$	$f[x_1,x_2,x_3]$	
x_4	$f[x_4]$	$f[x_3,x_4]$	$f[x_2,x_3,x_4]$	$f[x_1,x_2,x_3,x_4]$

The zeroth-order differences are the known values of the function at the support points (e.g., $f[x_1] = y_1$). The recursive definition of divided-difference coefficients is compact, but it does not provide the most straightforward computational procedure for evaluating those coefficients.

A divided-difference coefficient can be manually evaluated with the aid of a divided-difference table. The table organizes the calculations in a way that shows the dependence of higher order coefficients on lower order coefficients. In the schematic representation of $f[x_1, x_2, x_3]$, the bottom row of zeroth-order differences are known. To compute $f[x_1, x_2, x_3]$, one proceeds *up* the tree of dependence. The same information is organized into columns in Table 10.1. The first two columns are the known (x_i, y_i) data. The third column contains first-order divided differences, which depend on the data in the preceding columns. Higher order differences are obtained from lower order differences in columns to the left. The arrows in Table 10.1 indicate the order in which the divided-differences must be evaluated to compute $f[x_1, x_2, x_3]$.

Example 10.8: Manual Interpolation of Current Characteristics for an FET

This example shows the detailed calculations involved in constructing a divided-difference table. The following table gives the drain current I_d as a function of the drain-to-source voltage V_{ds} for a field effect transistor (FET).

V_{ds} (V)	0	0.4	0.75	1.3	2	3	4.5	5
I_d (mA)	0	4.95	10.14	15.0	17.6	19.05	20.32	20.5

Use cubic interpolation to find the value of I_d at $V_{ds} = 1.5$ V.

The cubic Newton polynomial for current I as a function of voltage V is

$$I(V) = f[V_1] + f[V_1, V_2](V - V_1) + f[V_1, V_2, V_3](V - V_1)(V - V_2)$$

$$+ f[V_1, V_2, V_2, V_4](V - V_1)(V - V_2)(V - V_3).$$

The four nearest support points for $V = 1.5$ are at $V = 0.4, 0.75, 1.3,$ and 2. Begin construction of the divided-difference table by entering the data from the known support

The y(:
sign is ?
nth col?

D(i,j)

Note th
Th
functio

```
>> Vds
>> Id
>> D =
D =
    4.9
   10.1
   15.0
   17.6

>> c =
c =
    4.9
   14.8
   -6.
    1.

>> v =
>> Iv

Iv =
   16.
```

mials,
sectio
mials
It con
Newt

differ
differ
ences

nienc

points into the first two columns:

V_i	$f[V_i]$	$f[,]$	$f[,,]$	$f[,,,]$
0.40	4.95			
0.75	10.14	$f[V_1, V_2]$		
1.30	15.00	$f[V_2, V_3]$	$f[V_1, V_2, V_3]$	
2.00	17.60	$f[V_3, V_4]$	$f[V_2, V_3, V_4]$	$f[V_1, V_2, V_3, V_4]$

Fill in the third column with

$$f[V_{i-1}, V_i] = \frac{I_i - I_{i-1}}{V_i - V_{i-1}}.$$

For example,

$$f[V_1, V_2] = \frac{10.14 - 4.95}{0.75 - 0.4} = 14.8286.$$

Completing the calculations for the third column gives

V_i	$f[V_i]$	$f[,]$	$f[,,]$	$f[,,,]$
0.40	4.95			
0.75	10.14	14.8286		
1.30	15.00	8.8364	$f[V_1, V_2, V_3]$	
2.00	17.60	3.7143	$f[V_2, V_3, V_4]$	$f[V_1, V_2, V_3, V_4]$

The fourth and fifth columns are filled in with

$$f[V_{i-2}, V_{i-1}, V_i] = \frac{f[V_i, V_{i-1}] - f[V_{i-1}, V_{i-2}]}{V_{i-2} - V_i}$$

and

$$f[V_{i-3}, V_{i-2}, V_{i-1}, V_i] = \frac{f[V_i, V_{i-1}, V_{i-2}] - f[V_{i-1}, V_{i-2}, V_{i-3}]}{V_{i-3} - V_i},$$

respectively. For example,

$$f[V_1, V_2, V_3] = \frac{8.8364 - 14.8286}{1.3 - 0.4} = -6.6580.$$

The complete divided-difference table is

V_i	$f[V_i]$	$f[,]$	$f[,,]$	$f[,,,]$
0.40	4.95			
0.75	10.14	14.8286		
1.30	15.00	8.8364	-6.6580	
2.00	17.60	3.7143	-4.0977	1.6002

$$P_3(\hat{x}) = c_1 + c_2(\hat{x} - x_1) + c_3(\hat{x} - x_1)(\hat{x} - x_2) + c_4(\hat{x} - x_1)(\hat{x} - x_2)(\hat{x} - x_3),$$

$$(10.30)$$

where the c_i coefficients are given by the appropriate divided difference (e.g., $c_3 = f[x_1, x_2, x_3]$) and $\hat{x}$ is the value of x at which the interpolating polynomial is to be evaluated. The immediate goal is to devise an algorithm to obtain the c_i without first constructing an entire matrix and then extracting the diagonals. This is achieved by storing the intermediate (lower order) divided differences in vector c and *overwriting* appropriate elements of c as needed. The process is represented schematically in the following table:

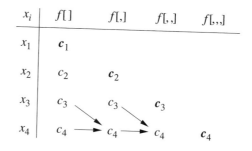

The boldface symbols on the diagonal of the table are the final values of the c_i. The c_i values below the diagonal are overwritten during execution of the algorithm.

At the start of the calculations, the c_i are assigned to the zeroth-order divided differences corresponding to the second column in the table. At the end of the calculation, the c_i contain the diagonal elements of the divided-difference table. Each successive column is processed in a for loop in which an element of c is replaced by

$$c_i \longleftarrow \frac{c_i - c_{i-1}}{x_i - x_{i-j+1}}.$$

This calculation corresponds to the computation of D(i,j) in divDiffTable. Since the values of c_i are being overwritten, it is necessary to sweep from the bottom of the table up to the diagonal. Otherwise, the value of c_{i-1} will be updated before it is used in the calculation of c_i. The preceding ideas are embodied in the following loop:

```
n = length(y);
c = y(:);        % First column is zeroth-order difference, f[x_i] = y_i
for j=2:n
  for i=n:-1:j   % Work backward to keep from overwriting unused data
    c(i) = (c(i)-c(i-1))/(x(i)-x(i-j+1));
  end
end
```

Once the c_i are available, the Newton polynomial must be evaluated. Note that the built-in `polyval` function cannot be used. (Why not?) For convenience, consider the cubic polynomial in Equation (10.30). The polynomial computation can be reorganized into a *nested multiplication* form[5] as

$$P_3(\hat{x}) = c_1 + (\hat{x} - x_1)\ (c_2 + (\hat{x} - x_2)(c_3 + c_4(\hat{x} - x_3))). \qquad (10.31)$$

This equation can be expressed in a single loop that begins with the evaluation of the innermost product, $c_4(\hat{x} - x_3)$. For a c of arbitrary length, the MATLAB implementation is

```
yhat = c(n);
for i=n-1:-1:1
  yhat = yhat.*(xhat-x(i)) + c(i);
end
```

The `newtint` function in Listing 10.4 contains the code fragments just developed. The `newtint` function can be called in one of three ways:

```
 yhat      = newtint(x,y,xhat)
[yhat,dy] = newtint(x,y,xhat)
[yhat,dy,c] = newtint(x,y,xhat)
```

The input parameters x and y are vectors that define the tabulated data to be interpolated. The `xhat` input is a scalar or vector of values at which the interpolant is to be evaluated. The result of the interpolation is returned in `yhat`. If `xhat` is a vector, then `yhat` is also a vector. This flexibility is made possible by the addition of a single array operator in the nested evaluation of `yhat`. Note that the degree of the interpolating polynomial is implicitly specified by the length of the x and y vectors. If `n = length(y)` then `yhat` is evaluated with a polynomial of degree `(n-1)`.

The optional output parameters are `dy`, the difference between `yhat` interpolated with degree $n - 1$ and degree $n - 2$ polynomials, and `c`, the coefficients of the Newton polynomial. Since the Newton polynomials are assembled recursively, the value of `dy` is easily computed from the same `c` used to obtain `yhat`.

Example 10.9: Interpolation of Gasoline Prices with Newton Polynomials

The `demoGasNewt` function shown in Listing 10.5 repeats the interpolation of gasoline data from Example 10.4 and Example 10.6. Running `demoGasNewt` produces a plot that is visually identical to that in Figure 10.8 on page 532.

---

[5]This corresponds to Horner's rule for evaluating a polynomial in a monomial basis. (See Example 3.7 on page 113.)

```
function [yhat,dy,cout] = newtint(x,y,xhat)
% newtint  Interpolation with Newton polynomials of arbitrary degree
%
% Synopsis:  yhat       = newtint(x,y,xhat)
%            [yhat,dy]   = newtint(x,y,xhat)
%            [yhat,dy,c] = newtint(x,y,xhat)
%
% Input:     x,y = vectors containing the tabulated y = f(x) data
%            xhat = (scalar or vector) x values where interpolant is evaluated
%
% Output:    yhat = value of y at each xhat obtained via interpolation
%            dy   = (optional) change in value of interpolant between
%                    polynomials of degree m-1 and m.  m = n-1 = length(x)-1
%            c    = (optional) coefficients of the Newton form of polynomial
%
% Note:      Degree of interpolating polynomial is implicitly specified
%            by the length of the x and y vectors.  If n = length(y) then
%            yhat is evaluated with a polynomial of degree (n-1)

n = length(y);   if length(x)~=n,  error('x and y are not compatible');  end

% --- Construct polynomial coefficients from diagonal of div.-diff. table
c = y(:);          % First column is zeroth-order difference, f[x_i] = y_i
for j=2:n
  for i=n:-1:j   % Work backward to keep from overwriting unused data
    c(i) = (c(i)-c(i-1))/(x(i)-x(i-j+1));
  end
end

% --- Nested evaluation of the polynomial
yhat = c(n);
for i=n-1:-1:1
  yhat = yhat.*(xhat-x(i)) + c(i);   % Array op allows vector of xhats
end

% --- optional output
if nargout>1
  yn2 = c(n-1);       % begin evaluation of polynomial of degree n-2
  for i=n-2:-1:1
    yn2 = yn2.*(xhat-x(i)) + c(i);
  end
  dy = yhat - yn2; % difference of interpolants of degree n-2 and degree n-1
  if nargout>2, cout = c;  end   % copy coefficients to output variable
end
```

Listing 10.4   The newtint function performs polynomial interpolation
with the divided-differences.

```
function demoGasNewt
% demoGasNewt  Interpolate gasoline price data with Newton polynomials
%
% Synopsis:  demoGasNewt
%
% Input:     none
%
% Output:    Plot of given data and interpolating function for gas price

year =  [1986   1988   1990   1992   1994   1996 ]';     % input data
price = [133.5  132.2  138.7  141.5  137.6  144.2]';

% --- Interpolate and plot results
y = linspace(min(year),max(year),200);  %  eval interpolant at these dates
p = newtint(year,price,y);
plot(year,price,'o',y,p,'-');
xlabel('year');  ylabel('gasoline price, (cents)');
```

Listing 10.5 The `demoGasNewt` uses Newton polynomials to interpolate ficticious gasoline data. The interpolation is performed by the `newtint` function in the NMM toolbox.

Example 10.10: Compare Work for Interpolation with Different Bases

In exact arithmetic, interpolation of a given set of data is independent of the polynomial basis used to construct the interpolant. Different polynomial bases functions may result in different numerical properties, however, as demonstrated in Examples 10.4 and 10.5. In this example, the computational work of using different polynomial bases is compared.

The `compInterp` function (not listed here, but included in the NMM toolbox) counts the flops for interpolating the gasoline prices of Example 10.4 with shifted monomial, Lagrange, and Newton polynomial bases. Given the table of six ordered pairs of gasoline price data, we evaluate fifth-order interpolating polynomials at N points. Running `compInterp` for several values of N gives the following results:

	Flop counts for $N =$				
Basis	1	10	25	100	250
Shifted monomial	520	625	820	1795	3745
Lagrange	141	1410	3525	14100	35250
Newton	106	241	466	1591	3841

The same data are depicted graphically in Figure 10.11.

For $N > 100$, the Lagrange polynomial basis takes an order of magnitude more work than the other bases. This is because the coefficients of the Lagrange polynomials must be

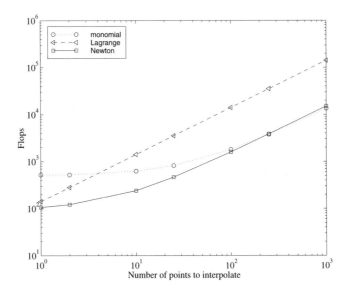

Figure 10.11 Comparison of flop counts for interpolation with different polynomial bases. A table of six data points is interpolated with a fifth-order polynomial.

reevaluated for each data point. For small-to-modest N, the Newton basis takes significantly fewer operations to achieve the same result. At small N, the work of interpolating with a monomial basis is dominated by the effort of solving the Vandermonde system. For large N the work of interpolating with monomial basis or Newton basis polynomials is dominated by the evaluation of the polynomial. Hence, these two methods take roughly the same number of flops.

These results suggest that the Newton form of the interpolating polynomial is to be preferred. It is computationally efficient, *and* it remains well conditioned as the degree of the polynomial increases. Evaluating a polynomial in a monomial basis has a slight computational advantage at large N. This advantage is easily outweighted by the ill conditioning of the Vandermonde system, which must be solved in order to evaluate the coefficients of the polynomial in the monomial basis.

10.2.4 Polynomial Wiggle

Increasing the degree of a polynomial interpolant does not necessarily increase the accuracy of the interpolation. By definition, the interpolant, $\mathcal{F}(x)$, matches the true function at the support points, (x_i, y_i), $i = 1, \ldots, n$. One cannot guarantee, however, that *between* the support points, $\mathcal{F}(x)$ will be a good approximation to the true $f(x)$ that generated the (x_i, y_i) data. If, for example, $f(x)$ is a known analytical function and the size n of the set of support points used to define $\mathcal{F}(x)$ is allowed to increase (and hence increase the degree of the polynomial $\mathcal{F}(x)$), the interpolant will likely tend to oscillate between the support points. This *polynomial wiggle* can occur even when the true $f(x)$ is smooth.

Polynomial wiggle is not responsible for the high-frequency oscillations evident in Figure 10.7 on page 531. Those oscillations are caused by roundoff errors that occur when the monomial terms are added together in evaluating the interpolating polynomial.

Sometimes, polynomial wiggle can be minimized by carefully choosing the points at which the underlying function is sampled. (See, for example, Exercises 21 and 22.) This is not an option when the data are obtained from an experiment that cannot be readily repeated. The solution is to use piecewise interpolation, as discussed in the next section. Before moving on to piecewise interpolation, consider the polynomial wiggle demonstrated in the following example:

Example 10.11: Demonstration of Wiggle in Polynomial Interpolation

A function $y = f(x)$ is created by joining two straight lines $y = -0.5x + 4$ on $1 \leq x \leq 5$ and $y = -0.4x$ on $5 < x \leq 10$. Ten samples from this function are shown in the accompanying table. There is a modest step in $f(x)$ where the two linear functions meet.

x_i	1	2	3	4	5	6	7	8	9	10
y_i	3.5	3.0	2.5	2.0	1.5	−2.4	−2.8	−3.2	−3.6	−4.0

From the sample data in the table, one could create a ninth-degree polynomial that would pass exactly through all 10 of the given data points. Due to polynomial wiggle, however, that ninth-degree polynomial will be a poor approximation to the true $f(x)$.

In the demoWiggle function (not listed here, but included with the NMM toolbox), a sequence of higher degree polynomials are created by choosing an appropriate number of points from the tabulated data. In each case, the step is located as near to the middle of the chosen data as possible. Figure 10.12 contains a sequence of plots obtained by increasing the degree of the interpolating polynomial from two to nine. Although the interpolating polynomials (solid lines) pass through the support points, each one shows significant deviation from the general trend of $f(x)$ between the support points. The magnitude of the oscillations in the interpolating function increase as the degree of the polynomial increases.

The dashed curves in each plot in Figure 10.12 show the extrapolation of the interpolating polynomials. Extrapolation with even the low-degree polynomials results in a very inaccurate approximation to $f(x)$. High-order polynomials wiggle in the range of the support points, and they diverge more rapidly than low-order polynomials outside the range of the support points.

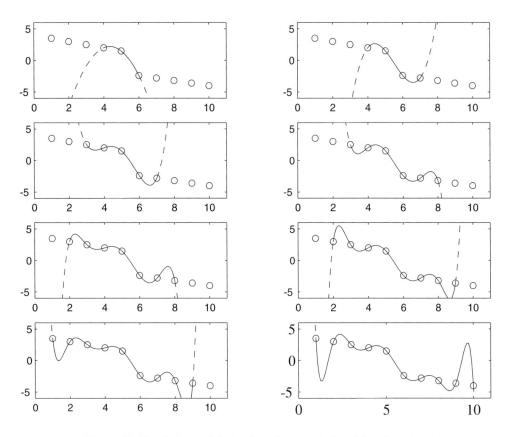

Figure 10.12   Polynomial wiggle and extrapolation. The plots show the
given data (open circles), the interpolation function (solid line) and the
extrapolation of the interpolation function (dashed lines) for increasing
degree of a polynomial interpolant.

10.3 PIECEWISE POLYNOMIAL INTERPOLATION

Interpolation with *piecewise polynomials* provides a practical solution to the short-
comings of high-degree polynomial interpolation. Instead of approximating the
function by passing a single interpolant through a large number of support points,
piecewise polynomial interpolation uses a set of lower degree interpolants, each of
which is defined on a subinterval of the whole domain. The joints between adjacent
piecewise interpolants are called the *breakpoints*, or *knots*.

The use of piecewise functions introduces new features to the interpolant.
The relationship (if there is one) between adjacent piecewise functions is of fundamental importance. In particular, the shape of adjacent interpolants is affected
by constraints on the continuity of the interpolants and its derivatives at the break-

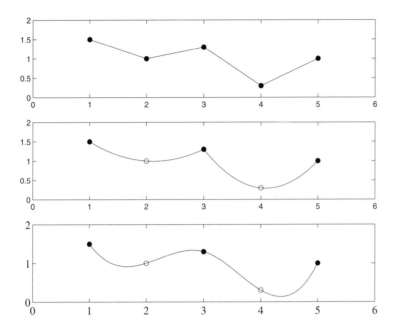

Figure 10.13 Continuity conditions for piecewise polynomial interpolants through the same five support points. The breakpoints are shown as solid dots. The top plot depicts piecewise-linear interpolation. The middle plot shows piecewise-quadratic interpolation with slope discontinuities at the breakpoints. The bottom plot shows a piecewise-cubic interpolant with continuous first and second derivatives.

points. Figure 10.13 shows common continuity constraints. The top plot depicts piecewise-linear functions that are continuous at the breakpoints. The middle plot shows two adjacent quadratic interpolants that are also continuous at the breakpoints. Although the discontinuity in slope of the piecewise-linear function seems reasonable, the slope discontinuity for the quadratic interpolants does not reflect the visual trend of the data. The bottom plot shows the interpolant that results when two adjacent cubic polynomials are required to have continuous first and second derivatives at the breakpoints. This interpolant is known as a cubic spline, which is the subject of § 10.3.5.

Change of Notation   For the rest of this chapter, $P_i(x)$ will designate a polynomial defined on the ith segment of a piecewise continuous curve. The ith segment is delimited by $x_i \leq x \leq x_{i+1}$.

Computational Tasks   As with interpolating polynomials of arbitrary degree, the use of piecewise interpolating polynomials requires one to construct and then evaluate the interpolant. Since the piecewise interpolant is not global (i.e., not a single function for all support points), the appropriate subinterval must be located before the interpolation function is evaluated. In general, the tasks required to perform a piecewise interpolation at a point $\hat{x}$ are

1. Locate $\hat{x}$ in the set of support points, (x_i, y_i), $i = 1, \ldots, n$.
2. Compute the coefficients of the *local* interpolating polynomial defined for the appropriate the support points.
3. Evaluate the local interpolating polynomial.

If the piecewise interpolants have continuity of first or higher derivatives, then adjacent interpolants may be coupled. Thus, although the individual interpolants are local, by virtue of being connected to each other at the breakpoints they exhibit some global behavior as well. This is the case for cubic-spline interpolants.

10.3.1 Piecewise-Linear Interpolation

The simplest piecewise interpolation scheme uses linear interpolants between each successive pair of breakpoints. This, in fact, is what the MATLAB plot function uses to select screen pixels (or points on a raster image of a printed page) when it draws a "curve" with solid line segments. The result is that the statements

```
>> x = linspace(0,2*pi);
>> plot(x,sin(x))
```

produce what appears to be a smooth curve representing the sine function. Because a large number of breakpoints are used, the discontinuities in the slope of the interpolant are not apparent. Repeating the plot with x = linspace(0,2*pi,10) makes the slope discontinuities easily visible.

Consider interpolation to find the value of y at $x = 0.75$ for a function defined by the following data:

x_j	0.2	0.6	1.0	1.4
y_j	0.5535	1.0173	1.0389	0.8911

The appropriate support points are $(x, y) = (0.6, 1.0173)$ and $(x, y) = (1.0, 1.0389)$. Using Lagrange basis functions (cf. Equation (10.11)) we obtain

$$L_1(0.75) = \frac{0.75 - 1.0}{0.6 - 1.0} = 0.6250 \quad \text{and} \quad L_2(0.75) = \frac{0.75 - 0.6}{1.0 - 0.6} = 0.3750,$$

$$P_1(0.75) = 1.0173\, L_1(0.75) + 1.0398\, L_2(0.75) = 1.0254.$$

The only complication in implementing piecewise-linear interpolation is in determining the appropriate pair of support points for use in constructing the interpolant. In a MATLAB function for piecewise-linear interpolation of an arbitrary data set, both the search for support points and the evaluation of the interpolating function need to be automated.

10.3.2 Searching for Support Points

Given tabulated values (x_i, y_i), $i = 1, \ldots, n$, we begin constructing a piecewise polynomial interpolant by choosing a subset of x values that bracket $\hat{x}$. For piecewise-linear interpolation, only two support points, say, x_{left} and x_{right}, are needed such that $x_{\text{left}} \leq \hat{x} \leq x_{\text{right}}$. Two selection algorithms will be discussed here: incremental search and binary search. In both cases, the x values in the data set are assumed to be monotonically increasing. After the binary search is presented, simple procedures are described for dealing with data sets having x values that are not monotonically increasing.

Incremental Search   Incremental search is a brute-force tactic to find the index of the elements in an ordered vector that bracket a test value. If the elements of vector x are monotonically increasing, the following code snippet finds the index i such that $x(i) \leq xhat < x(i+1)$ (the search occurs inside the while loop):

```
n = length(x);
if xhat<x(1) | xhat>x(n)
   error(sprintf('Test value of %g is not in range of x',xhat));
end
i = n;                      %  Search backward from n to 1
while x(i)>xhat & i>1
  i = i - 1;
end
```

The range test xhat<x(1) | xhat>x(n) is a defensive programming tactic designed to alert the user of erroneous input data.[6] For infrequent searching on short vectors, the incremental search algorithm is adequate. For long x vectors, it will be slow for two reasons: The code is not vectorized, and the algorithm is inefficient. The binary search algorithm presented in the next section will usually take fewer operations to find bracketing indices than incremental search, but it cannot be vectorized.

---

[6]To use the incremental search algorithm for extrapolation from a data set, this check will have to be removed, and some additional logic will need to be added to select the appropriate indices of the support points.

```
function yi = linterp(x,y,xi)
% linterp    Piecewise linear interpolation in a table of (x,y) data
%
% Synposis:  yi = linterp(x,y,xi)
%
% Input:     x,y = vectors containing the tabulated data
%            xi  = value of x at which function y = f(x) is desired
%
% Output:    yi = value of y at xi obtained by linear interpolation

i = binSearch(x,xi);              %  Find appropriate data pair
L1 = (x(i+1) - xi)/(x(i+1) - x(i)); %  Evaluate basis functions
L2 = (xi - x(i))/(x(i+1) - x(i));
yi = y(i)*L1 + y(i+1)*L2;          %  Evaluate interpolant
```

Listing 10.7   The `linterp` for piecewise-linear interpolation.

of emf, and emf as a function of temperature, for the same data. Figure 9.12 on page 499 shows a plot of this data.

The following statements load the data into MATLAB variables and use the `linterp` function to find the temperature at an emf of 0.8 mV.

```
>> [v,t] = loadColData('Jtcouple.dat',2,1,3);
>> linterp(v,t,0.8)
ans =
     15.7227
```

The `linterp` function can just as easily interpolate `emf` as a function of T. Given the `emf` and T vectors just defined, the emf generated at a temperature of 37 °C is

```
>> linterp(t,v,37)
ans =
     1.9024
```

10.3.4 Piecewise-Cubic Hermite Interpolation

It would be logical to follow the presentation of piecewise-linear interpolation with a presentation of piecewise-quadratic interpolation. In practice, however, the advantages of piecewise-quadratic functions over piecewise-linear functions are not compelling. For the purpose of interpolating known data, piecewise-cubic functions are much more useful. In this and the following sections, two different types of piecewise-cubic interpolating functions are considered: Hermite polynomials and cubic splines.

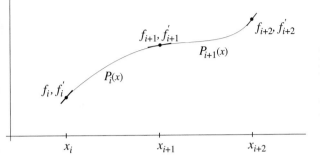

Figure 10.14 Piecewise-cubic Hermite interpolating polynomials are defined by the value of the function and the slope at each breakpoint. $P_i(x)$ is the cubic function that matches $f(x_i)$, $f'(x_i)$, $f(x_{i+1})$, and $f'(x_{i+1})$.

In all preceding derivations, a polynomial of degree n has been defined by the requirement that it pass through $n+1$ specified support points. *Hermite polynomials* are required to agree with the function *and* its first derivative at each of the support points. This results in two desirable properties:

- The segments of the piecewise Hermite polynomials have continuous first derivatives at the support points.
- The shape of the function being interpolated is better matched, because the tangent of this function and the tangent of the Hermite polynomial agree at the support points.

Because interpolating Hermite polynomials require values of both $y = f(x)$ and $f'(x)$, they are better suited to interpolation of analytical functions than discrete data, say, from an experiment. The evaluation of $f'(x)$ from discrete data is not recommended unless it is absolutely necessary. For the interpolation of discrete data with unknown $f'(x)$, splines are recommended. (See § 10.3.5 beginning on page 568.)

Figure 10.14 depicts two piecewise polynomials $P_i(x)$ and $P_{i+1}(x)$ defined on the closed intervals $[x_i, x_{i+1}]$ and $[x_{i+1}, x_{i+2}]$, respectively. The cubic form of $P_i(x)$ will be written

$$P_i(\hat{x}) = a_i + b_i(\hat{x} - x_i) + c_i(\hat{x} - x_i)^2 + d_i(\hat{x} - x_i)^3, \qquad (10.32)$$

where a_i, b_i, c_i, and d_i are coefficients for the ith segment and $\hat{x}$ is the value of x at which the Hermite polynomial is to be evaluated.[7] In MATLAB programs, Equation (10.32) will be written in the mathematically equivalent and more com-

---

[7]Recall that P_i is the polynomial defined on segment i. $P_i(x)$ is not necessarily a polynomial of degree i.

putational efficient *nested* form. (See also Example 3.7)

$$P_i(\hat{x}) = a_i + (\hat{x} - x_i)\left(b_i + (\hat{x} - x_i)\left(c_i + (\hat{x} - x_i)d_i\right)\right). \tag{10.33}$$

The four unknown coefficients a_i, b_i, c_i, and d_i in Equations (10.32) and (10.33) are defined by requiring that

$$P_i(x_i) = f(x_i), \quad P_i'(x_i) = f'(x_i), \quad P_i(x_{i+1}) = f(x_{i+1}), \quad P_i'(x_{i+1}) = f'(x_{i+1}). \tag{10.34}$$

Although $P_i(x)$ and $P_{i+1}(x)$ match at x_{i+1}, the four preceding conditions are sufficient to define a_i, b_i, c_i, and d_i independently of the values of $a_{i+1}, b_{i+1}, c_{i+1}$, and d_{i+1}. The continuity of the P_i and P_i' is guaranteed by the uniqueness of $f(x)$ and $f'(x)$.

Obtaining the Coefficients of $P_i(x)$ Divided differences can be used to define coefficients of an interpolating polynomial where the function and its derivatives are specified at the support points. The cubic polynomial meeting the conditions in Equation (10.34) can be written as (see, Conte and de Boor [11, § 2.7])

$$\begin{aligned} P_i(x) = {} & f(x_i) + f[x_i, x_i](\hat{x} - x_i) \\ & + f[x_i, x_i, x_{i+1}](\hat{x} - x_i)^2 \\ & + f[x_i, x_i, x_{i+1}, x_{i+1}](\hat{x} - x_i)^2(\hat{x} - x_{i+1}), \end{aligned} \tag{10.35}$$

where, by definition,

$$f[x_i, x_i] = f'(x_i) \quad \text{and} \quad f[x_{i+1}, x_{i+1}] = f'(x_{i+1})$$

and

$$f[x_i, x_i, x_{i+1}] = \frac{f[x_i, x_{i+1}] - f[x_i, x_i]}{x_{i+1} - x_i},$$

$$f[x_i, x_{i+1}, x_{i+1}] = \frac{f[x_{i+1}, x_{i+1}] - f[x_{i+1}, x_i]}{x_{i+1} - x_i},$$

$$f[x_i, x_i, x_{i+1}, x_{i+1}] = \frac{f[x_i, x_{i+1}, x_{i+1}] - f[x_i, x_i, x_{i+1}]}{x_{i+1} - x_i}.$$

The cubic term in Equation (10.35) involves a factor of $(\hat{x} - x_{i+1})$, which is not the desired form of Equation (10.32). Using the substitution $(\hat{x} - x_{i+1}) = (\hat{x} - x_i) + (x_i - x_{i+1})$ Equation (10.35) becomes

$$P_i(x) = f(x_i) + f[x_i, x_i](\hat{x} - x_i)$$

$$+ \{f[x_i, x_i, x_{i+1}] - f[x_i, x_i, x_{i+1}, x_{i+1}](x_{i+1} - x_i)\}(\hat{x} - x_i)^2$$

$$+ f[x_i, x_i, x_{i+1}, x_{i+1}](\hat{x} - x_i)^3. \tag{10.36}$$

Comparing Equation (10.36) with Equation (10.32) shows that a_i, b_i, c_i, and d_i are the coefficients of the $(\hat{x} - x_i)$ terms. Performing straightforward algebraic simplifications of these coefficients gives

$$a_i = f(x_i),$$

$$b_i = f'(x_i),$$

$$c_i = \frac{3f[x_i, x_{i+1}] - 2f'(x_i) - f'(x_{i+1})}{(x_{i+1} - x_i)}, \tag{10.37}$$

$$d_i = \frac{f'(x_i) - 2f[x_i, x_{i+1}] + f'(x_{i+1})}{(x_{i+1} - x_i)^2}.$$

Implementation   Interpolation with cubic Hermite polynomials is performed in three main steps. First, the coefficients of the piecewise-cubic segments are computed. Then the appropriate segment for each input x value is located. Finally, the interpolant is evaluated. The calculations are embodied in the `hermint` function in Listing 10.8. The code in `hermint` is discussed after the input and output parameters are described.

The `hermint` function is called with

```
yhat = hermint(x,f,fp,xhat)
```

For each element of vector `x`, vectors `f` and `fp` provide $y = f(x)$ and $f'(x)$, respectively. The `xhat` input parameter is a scalar or vector containing the values of x at which the interpolant is to be evaluated. The output `yhat` is the vector or scalar value of the interpolant at each element of `xhat`.

The code in `hermint` is divided into three blocks. The first block involves constructing the coefficients of the piecewise-cubic interpolants according to Equation (10.37). To guarantee the compatibility of matrices in the vectorized calculations, all input variables are converted to column vectors. Otherwise, the calculations are straightforward.

The second and third blocks of code in `hermint` deal with evaluating the interpolant at the desired $\hat{x}$ values. To evaluate the interpolant at a value of $\hat{x}$, the appropriate piecewise segment must be selected. Figure 10.15 depicts the location of a scalar $\hat{x}$ in a piecewise interpolant defined by six knots. For each element in the input `xhat` vector, a binary search is performed to find the index in `x` such that

```
function yhat = hermint(x,f,fp,xhat)
% hermint  Piecewise-cubic Hermite interpolation
%
% Synopsis: yhat = hermint(x,f,fp,xhat)
%
% Input:    x    = vector of independent variable values
%           f, fp = vectors of f(x) and f'(x)
%           xhat = (scalar or vector) x values where interpolant is evaluated
%
% Output:   yhat = scalar or vector value of cubic hermite interpolant at
%                  x = xhat.  size(yhat) = size(xhat)

n = length(x);
if      length(f)~=n,    error('x and f are not compatible');
elseif length(fp)~=n,    error('x and fp are not compatible');    end

% --- Construct coefficients of the piecewise interpolants
x = x(:);   xhat = xhat(:);    %  Convert to column vectors
f = f(:);   fp = fp(:);
dx = diff(x);                  %  Vector of x(i+1) - x(i) values
divdif = diff(f)./dx;          %  Vector of divided differences, f[x(i),x(i+1)]
a = f(1:n-1);
b = fp(1:n-1);
c = ( 3*divdif - 2*fp(1:n-1) - fp(2:n) ) ./dx;
d = ( fp(1:n-1) - 2*divdif + fp(2:n) )    ./dx.^2;

% --- Locate each xhat value in the x vector
i = zeros(size(xhat)); %  i is index into x such that x(i) <= xhat <= x(i+1)
for m=1:length(xhat)   %  For vector xhat: x( i(m) ) <= xhat(m) <= x( i(m)+1 )
  i(m) = binSearch(x,xhat(m));
end

% --- Vectorized evaluation of the piecewise polynomials
xx = xhat - x(i);
yhat = a(i) + xx.*(b(i) + xx.*(c(i) + xx.*d(i)) );
```

Listing 10.8 The hermint functions performs piecewise-cubic Hermite interpolation.

$x(i) \le \text{xhat}(m) \le x(i+1)$. To allow for a vector of xhat values, the index i is also stored in a vector.

All of the piecewise-cubic segments are constructed, even if only one *yhat* value is desired. Though this is inefficient, the advantages are that the code logic is simple and that the code is vectorized for maximum efficiency when *xhat* is a vector. The implementation in hermint is well suited for the evaluation of the

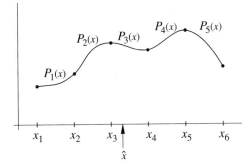

Figure 10.15 Location of the piecewise segment appropriate for interpolating $y(\hat{x})$. An interpolant constructed from six knots is shown here. The value of $y(\hat{x})$ is to be evaluated with $P_3(x)$.

interpolant over the range of all input x values. To evaluate scalar *xhat* values with higher efficiency, the hermint function should be called with x, f, and *fp* of length 2. This may require a call to binSearch before the hermint function is called.

Given the coefficients of the piecewise polynomial segments and the appropriate index to those segments for the input values of xhat, we can evaluate the interpolant with two vectorized statements:

```
xx = xhat - x(i);
yhat = a(i) + xx.*(b(i) + xx.*(c(i) + xx.*d(i)) );
```

The xx variable is a vector with the same length as xhat. The subexpression x(i) is a vector having the same length as i, regardless of the length of x. Consider the following interactive MATLAB session:

```
>> x = 0:10;                  % row vector of independent x values
>> xhat = [3.2  5.4  7.1];    % interpolate at each xhat
>> i = zeros(size(xhat))      % pre-allocate the index vector
i =
     0    0    0
```

Now, use the binSearch function to find the indices of the largest elements of x that are less than each xhat.

```
>> for k=1:length(xhat),  i(k) = binSearch(x,xhat(k));  end
>> i
i =
     4    6    8
```

The elements of x corresponding to these indices are

```
>> x(i)
ans =
     3    5    7
```

Thus, the statement xhat - x(i) returns a vector

```
>> xx = xhat-x(i)
xx =
    0.2000    0.4000    0.1000
```

Notice that length(x) = 11.

Example 10.13: Demonstration of Hermite Interpolation

The demoHermite function in Listing 10.9 creates a piecewise-cubic Hermite approximation to $y = xe^{-x}$, for $0 \leq x \leq 8$. The single input parameter n determines how many
knots are used in the range of x. The total number of piecewise-cubic segments is n − 1.
Running demoHermite produces a single plot comparing the cubic Hermite interpolant to

```
function demoHermite(n)
% demoHermite   Cubic Hermite interpolation of y = x*exp(-x) for 0 <= x <= 8
%
% Synopsis:      demoHermite
%                demoHermite(n)
%
% Input:       n = (optional) number of knots used to define the interpolant
%                    Default:  n = 4
%
% Output:      Plot of cubic Hermite approximation to y = x * exp(-x)

if nargin<1,  n = 4;  end

x = linspace(0,8,n);              %  vector of knots
y = x.*exp(-x);                   %  f(x)
yp = (1 - x).*exp(-x);            %  f'(x)
xi = linspace(min(x),max(x));     %  Evaluate interpolant at xi
ye = xi.*exp(-xi);                %  Exact f(x) for comparison

yi = hermint(x,y,yp,xi);
err = norm(yi-ye(:));
fprintf('error = %12.2e  with %d knots\n',err,n);

plot(x,y,'bo',xi,ye,'b-',xi,yi,'r--');
legend('Given','x*exp(-x)','Hermite');
text(4,0.2,sprintf('%d knots',n));
axis([0 8 0 0.5]);
```

Listing 10.9   The demoHermite function uses hermint function to
create and plot a piecewise-cubic Hermite approximation to $y = xe^{-x}$.

the original data. The absolute error defined by $E = \|\hat{y} - y_e\|_2$, where $\hat{y}$ is the value of the interpolant and y_e is the exact value of the input function, is computed. Both $\hat{y}$ and y_e are evaluated at 100 points in the range $0 \le x \le 8$.

Figure 10.16 shows a sequence of four plots created by demoHermite with increasing values of n. The interpolant rapidly approaches the original function as n increases. The quantitative variation in the error with the number of segments is summarized in the following table:

knots	$\|\hat{y} - y_e\|_2$
4	4.2×10^{-1}
8	2.2×10^{-2}
16	1.2×10^{-3}
32	6.4×10^{-5}
64	3.8×10^{-6}

The error in the interpolant decreases uniformly as the number of knots is increased. As with all types of piecewise polynomial interpolation, there is no *polynomial wiggle*. (Cf. § 10.2.4.)

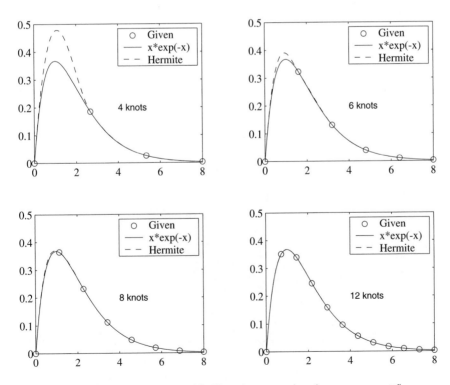

Figure 10.16   Piecewise-cubic Hermite approximations to $y = xe^{-x}$.

10.3.5 Cubic Spline Interpolation

Although piecewise-cubic Hermite polynomials produce a smoothly varying interpolant, they have the distinct disadvantage that the slope of the input function
must be specified at each breakpoint. If the data are obtained from an experiment,
for example, this slope data may not be available. Cubic-spline interpolation provides a solution to this problem, while maintaining the desired smoothness of the
interpolant.

Figure 10.17 depicts a cubic-spline interpolant through n breakpoints. Each
$P_i(x)$ is a cubic polynomial, and at each breakpoint, the $P_i(x)$, $P_i'(x)$, *and* $P_i''(x)$
are continuous. The continuity of $P''(x)$ has the effect of coupling adjacent
piecewise-cubic polynomials. As a result, the coefficients of all of the $P_i(x)$ must
be computed simultaneously, which leads to a linear system of $n - 2$ equations if
there are n breakpoints. Thus, although the cubic spline avoids the need to specify
the value of $f'(x)$ at the breakpoints, the cubic-spline interpolant is more costly to
evaluate. In many applications, this cost is not a significant problem.

Equations Defining a Cubic Spline   The equations defining cubic
splines can be obtained from the equations for piecewise-cubic Hermite polynomials. Each $P_i(x)$ for the cubic-spline is of the form of Equation (10.32), which is
rewritten here:

$$P_i(\hat{x}) = a_i + b_i(\hat{x} - x_i) + c_i(\hat{x} - x_i)^2 + d_i(\hat{x} - x_i)^3. \tag{10.38}$$

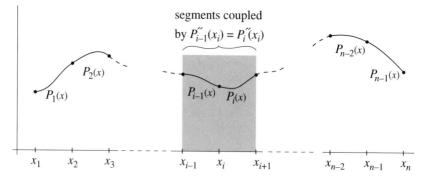

Figure 10.17   Cubic-spline interpolating functions. Continuity of
$P''(x)$ couples the adjacent piecewise polynomials.

Both the cubic-Hermite and the cubic-spline interpolating polynomials have continuous function values and continuous first derivatives (i.e., $P_{i-1}(x_i) = P_i(x_i)$ and $P'_{i-1}(x_i) = P'_i(x_i)$). The difference is in the *value* of the first derivative at the breakpoints. For the cubic Hermite polynomials, the value of $P'_i(x_i)$ is given by the input data, i.e., $P'_i(x_i) = f'(x_i)$. For the cubic spline, the value of $P'_i(x_i)$ is obtained by enforcing the continuity of $P''_i(x)$ at the breakpoints.

The formulas for a_i, b_i, c_i, and d_i in Equation (10.37) apply to the cubic spline as well, except that the values of $f'(x)$ are unknown. Notice that since

$$P'_i(\hat{x}) = b_i + 2c_i(\hat{x} - x_i) + 3d_i(\hat{x} - x_i)^2$$

and

$$P'_i(x_i) = b_i \quad \text{and} \quad P'_{i-1}(x_i) = b_{i-1},$$

we may, without any loss of generality, substitute b_i for $f'(x_i)$ and b_{i-1} for $f'(x_{i-1})$ into Equation (10.37). For the $(i - 1)$th segment, this gives

$$a_{i-1} = f(x_{i-1}),$$
$$b_{i-1} = \text{???},$$
$$c_{i-1} = \frac{3f[x_{i-1}, x_i] - 2b_{i-1} - b_i}{(x_i - x_{i-1})}, \tag{10.39}$$
$$d_{i-1} = \frac{b_{i-1} - 2f[x_{i-1}, x_i] + b_i}{(x_i - x_{i-1})^2}.$$

The b_i are unknown, and the immediate goal is to develop a procedure for computing them.[8]

The condition for determining the b_i comes from requiring that the second derivative of the spline segments be continuous at the breakpoints. From Equation (10.38),

$$P''_i(\hat{x}) = 2c_i + 6d_i(\hat{x} - x_i),$$

so that $P''_{i-1}(x_i) = P''_i(x_i)$ implies

$$2c_{i-1} + 6d_{i-1}\Delta x_{i-1} = 2c_i,$$

where $\Delta x_{i-1} = x_i - x_{i-1}$. Substituting c_{i-1} and d_{i-1} from Equation (10.39) and simplifying gives

---

[8]Many authors develop the equations for cubic splines in terms of the c_i (i.e., the value of the second derivative at the knots). The derivation used here follows that of de Boor [14].

$$\Delta x_i b_{i-1} + 2 \left(\Delta x_i + \Delta x_{i-1}\right) b_i + \Delta x_{i-1} b_{i+1}$$

$$= 3 \left(f[x_i, x_{i+1}]\Delta x_{i-1} + f[x_{i-1}, x_i]\Delta x_i\right). \tag{10.40}$$

The right-hand side of this equation is known. The left-hand side has unknowns b_{i-1}, b_i, and b_{i+1}. Equation (10.40) shows that requiring continuity of $P_i''(x)$ couples the spline coefficients in adjacent segments. The coupling is depicted graphically in Figure 10.17. Since the b_i are coupled, obtaining the coefficients of the cubic-spline interpolating polynomials requires solving a set of simultaneous equations. Once the b_i are known, the remaining coefficients a_i, c_i, and d_i are computed from Equation (10.39).

Define the following auxiliary variables to make the system of equations for b_i a bit more easy to manipulate:

$$\alpha_i = \Delta x_i, \tag{10.41}$$

$$\beta_i = 2 \left(\Delta x_i + \Delta x_{i-1}\right) = 2(\alpha_i + \gamma_i), \tag{10.42}$$

$$\gamma_i = \Delta x_{i-1}, \tag{10.43}$$

$$\delta_i = 3 \left(f[x_i, x_{i+1}]\Delta x_{i-1} + f[x_{i-1}, x_i]\Delta x_i\right). \tag{10.44}$$

Equation (10.40) becomes

$$\alpha_i b_{i-1} + \beta_i b_i + \gamma_i b_{i+1} = \delta_i. \tag{10.45}$$

How many of these equations are there?

Figure 10.17 shows a cubic spline passing through n given data pairs, (x_i, y_i), $i = 1, \ldots, n$. There are $n - 1$ piecewise-cubic polynomials, and since each of these polynomials has four coefficients, the entire spline requires the specification of $4(n - 1)$ parameters. An equal number of constraints are necessary. The following constraints were used to derive Equation (10.45):

number	type of constraint
$2(n - 1)$	each of the $n - 1$ polynomials must match the 2 given y values at the breakpoints of its segment
$n - 2$	interior points where $P_{i-1}'(x_i) = P_i'(x_i)$
$n - 2$	interior points where $P_{i-1}''(x_i) = P_i''(x_i)$
$4n - 6$	total constraints

Thus, two additional conditions are necessary to completely specify the $4(n - 1)$ parameters of the $n - 1$ piecewise-cubic polynomials that constitute the spline. These conditions can be deduced with the aid of Figure 10.17.

Recall that the unknown b_i are the values of the slope at the breakpoints. The $b_2, b_3, \ldots, b_{n-2}$ are the $n - 2$ unknown internal slopes, whereas b_1 and b_n

are slopes at the end of the spline.[9] One interpretation of the unknown conditions, therefore, is that the end slope values, b_1 and b_n, must be specified so that the $n - 2$ internal b_i can be computed. More generally, two *end conditions* must be independently prescribed in order to uniquely specify the spline. In the following sections, three types of end conditions are developed:

1. Fixed-slope end conditions
2. "Natural" spline end conditions
3. "Not-a-knot" end conditions

Before the end conditions are introduced, it is useful to write Equation (10.45) in matrix form:

$$
\begin{bmatrix}
\beta_1 & \gamma_1 & 0 \\
\alpha_2 & \beta_2 & \gamma_2 & 0 \\
0 & \alpha_3 & \beta_3 & \gamma_3 & 0 \\
& 0 & \ddots & \ddots & \ddots & 0 \\
& & 0 & \alpha_{n-1} & \beta_{n-1} & \beta_{n-1} \\
& & & 0 & \alpha_n & \beta_n
\end{bmatrix}
\begin{bmatrix}
b_1 \\
b_2 \\
b_3 \\
\vdots \\
b_{n-1} \\
b_n
\end{bmatrix}
=
\begin{bmatrix}
\delta_1 \\
\delta_2 \\
\delta_3 \\
\vdots \\
\delta_{n-1} \\
\delta_n
\end{bmatrix}
\tag{10.46}
$$

This is a tridiagonal system of linear equations for the unknown b_i. As shown here, there are apparently n equations in n unknowns. The two additional equations—those for b_1 and b_n—have been introduced as a convenient computational device for specifying the end conditions in MATLAB code. Once Equation (10.46) is solved for the b_i, the remaining coefficients are computed with Equation (10.39); that is,

$$a_i = y_i, \tag{10.47}$$

$$c_i = \frac{3f[x_i, x_{i+1}] - 2b_i - b_{i+1}}{(x_{i+1} - x_i)}, \tag{10.48}$$

$$d_i = \frac{b_i - 2f[x_i, x_{i+1}] + b_{i+1}}{(x_{i+1} - x_i)^2}. \tag{10.49}$$

The basic outline of an algorithm for computing the coefficients of a cubic spline is now complete. Given a set of data (x_i, y_i), $i = 1, \ldots, n$ and appropriate end conditions the spline coefficients are obtained with the following steps:

1. Assemble the system of Equations (10.46)
2. Solve the system for the vector of coefficients, b.

---

[9] b_n is not needed to evaluate $P_{n-1}(\hat{x})$. The value of b_n does figure into the solution of the equation for b_{n-1}, however, as is evident from setting $i = n - 1$ in Equation (10.45).

3. Compute the remaining coefficients from Equations (10.47)–(10.49) for $i = 1, \ldots, n-1$.

Given vectors a, b, c, and d of coefficients, the value of spline interpolant at a point $\hat{x}$ is obtained by

1. Determining the index i such that $x_i \le \hat{x} \le x_{i+1}$ and
2. Evaluating Equation (10.38).

Fixed-Slope End Conditions   The slopes at the end points of the cubic spline are b_1 and b_n, respectively, and Equations (10.46) are conveniently arranged to allow these values to be fixed. The first and last equations in the tridiagonal System (10.46) are

$$\beta_1 b_1 + \gamma_1 b_2 = \delta_1,$$

$$\alpha_{n-1} b_{n-1} + \beta_n b_n = \delta_n.$$

By *assigning* $\beta_1 = 1$, $\gamma_1 = 0$, $\delta_1 = f'(x_1)$, $\alpha_n = 0$, $\beta_n = 1$, and $\delta_n = f'(x_n)$ the equations for b_1 and b_n are reduced to

$$b_1 = f'(x_1),$$

$$b_n = f'(x_n).$$

Use of these formulas is demonstrated in Example 10.14. In the next section, the fixed-slope end conditions are incorporated into a MATLAB program for calculating cubic-spline coefficients.

Example 10.14: Hand Calculation of Spline Coefficients

Find the cubic-spline passing through $(x, y) = (1, 1)$, $(2, 3)$, $(3, 2)$, and $(4, 4)$ and having zero slope at $x = 1$ and $x = 4$. (Before proceeding with the calculations, it would be a good exercise to sketch the general shape of this spline.)

Directly evaluating Equations (10.41) through (10.44) for $i = 2, 3$ gives

$$\alpha_2 = x_3 - x_2 = 1,$$

$$\gamma_2 = x_2 - x_1 = 1,$$

$$\beta_2 = 2(\alpha_2 + \gamma_2) = 4,$$

$$\delta_2 = 3\left[\frac{y_3 - y_2}{x_3 - x_2}(x_2 - x_1) + \frac{y_2 - y_1}{x_2 - x_1}(x_3 - x_2)\right] = 3,$$

$$\alpha_3 = x_4 - x_3 = 1,$$

$$\gamma_3 = x_3 - x_2 = 1,$$

$$\beta_3 = 2(\alpha_3 + \gamma_3) = 4,$$

$$\delta_3 = 3\left[\frac{y_4 - y_3}{x_4 - x_3}(x_3 - x_2) + \frac{y_3 - y_2}{x_3 - x_2}(x_4 - x_3)\right] = 3.$$

Using these coefficients and the equations for b_1 and b_4 from the preceding section, the system of equations for the b_i becomes

$$\begin{bmatrix} 1 & 0 & 0 & 0 \\ 1 & 4 & 1 & 0 \\ 0 & 1 & 4 & 1 \\ 0 & 0 & 0 & 1 \end{bmatrix}\begin{bmatrix} b_1 \\ b_2 \\ b_3 \\ b_4 \end{bmatrix} = \begin{bmatrix} 0 \\ 3 \\ 3 \\ 0 \end{bmatrix}.$$

For a manual solution of this system, the trivial equations for b_1 and b_4 can be used to eliminate the b_1 and b_4 from the second and third equations:

$$\begin{bmatrix} 4 & 1 \\ 1 & 4 \end{bmatrix}\begin{bmatrix} b_2 \\ b_3 \end{bmatrix} = \begin{bmatrix} 3 - b_1 \\ 3 - b_4 \end{bmatrix} = \begin{bmatrix} 3 \\ 3 \end{bmatrix}$$

Solving the 2×2 system gives $b_2 = 3/5$ and $b_3 = 3/5$ Alternatively, a MATLAB solution of the full 4×4 system is

```
>> A = [1 0 0 0; 1 4 1 0; 0 1 4 1; 0 0 0 1];
>> d = [0; 3; 3; 0];
>> b = A\d
b =
         0
    0.6000
    0.6000
         0
```

The solution to b allows the remaining spline coefficients to be calculated from Equations (10.47)–(10.49). The result is

$$a = \begin{bmatrix} 1 \\ 3 \\ 2 \end{bmatrix}, \qquad c = \begin{bmatrix} 5.4 \\ -4.8 \\ 4.8 \end{bmatrix}, \qquad d = \begin{bmatrix} -3.4 \\ 3.2 \\ -3.4 \end{bmatrix}.$$

Note that a_4, c_4, and d_4 are not computed, because only three piecewise-cubic segments are defined for the four input data pairs. The value of b_4 is used only as a computational device to enforce the zero-slope end conditions at x_4. Creating a plot of this spline is left as Exercise 30.

MATLAB Implementation of a Spline with Fixed-Slope End Conditions

The `splintFE` function in Listing 10.10 interpolates in a set of data with a piecewise cubic spline having fixed-slope end conditions. The `splintFE` function is invoked with

```
yhat = splintFE(x,y,xhat,fp1,fpn)
```

```
function yhat = splintFE(x,y,xhat,fp1,fpn)
% splintFE  Cubic-spline interpolation with fixed slope end conditions
%
% Synopsis:   yhat = splintFE(x,y,xhat,fp1,fpn)
%
% Input:    x,y  = vectors of discrete x and y = f(x) values
%           xhat = (scalar or vector) x values where interpolant is evaluated
%           fp1  = slope at x(1), i,e., fp1 = f'(x(1))
%           fpn  = slope at x(n), i,e., fpn = f'(x(n));
%
% Output:   yhat = (vector or scalar) value(s) of the cubic spline interpolant
%                  evaluated at xhat.  size(yhat) = size(xhat)

% --- Set up system of equations for b(i)
x = x(:);   y = y(:);   xhat = xhat(:);   %  convert to column vectors
n = length(x);
dx = diff(x);                   %  vector of x(i+1) - x(i) values
divdif = diff(y)./dx;           %  vector of divided differences, f[x(i),x(i+1)]

alpha = [0; dx(1:n-2); 0];                      %  sub diagonal
beta  = [1; 2*(dx(1:n-2)+dx(2:n-1)); 1];        %  main diagonal
gamma = [0; dx(2:n-1); 0];                      %  super diagonal
A     = tridiags(n,beta,alpha,gamma);           %  Sparse, tridiagonal matrix
delta = [ fp1; ...
          3*(divdif(2:n-1).*dx(1:n-2) + divdif(1:n-2).*dx(2:n-1)); ...
          fpn ];

% --- Solve the system for b
mmdflag = spparms('autommd');       %  Store minimum degree ordering flag
spparms('autommd',0);               %  Set that flag to zero
b = A\delta;                        %  Solve the system
spparms('autommd',mmdflag);         %  Reset the minimum degree ordering flag

% --- Compute coefficients of spline interpolants
a = y(1:n-1);
c = (3*divdif - 2*b(1:n-1) - b(2:n))./dx;
d = (b(1:n-1) - 2*divdif + b(2:n))./dx.^2;
b(n) = [];                          %  discard b(n)

% --- Locate each xhat value in the x vector
i = zeros(size(xhat));   %  i is index into x such that x(i) <= xhat <= x(i+1)
for m=1:length(xhat)     %  For vector xhat: x( i(m) ) <= xhat(m) <= x( i(m)+1 )
  i(m) = binSearch(x,xhat(m));
end

% --- Nested, vectorized evaluation of the piecewise polynomials
xx = xhat - x(i);
yhat = a(i) + xx.*(b(i) + xx.*(c(i) + xx.*d(i)) );
```

Listing 10.10 The splintFE performs cubic-spline with fixed-slope end conditions.

where x and y define the tabular data to be interpolated and `xhat` is a scalar or vector of values at which the interpolant is to be evaluated. The output vector (or scalar) `yhat` has the same length as the input vector (or scalar) `xhat`. The code in the `splintFE` function is organized into five major sections:

1. Assemble the tridiagonal system of Equations (10.46) for the spline.
2. Solve the system for the slope vector b.
3. From the newly computed vector b, evaluate the remaining coefficients of the spline segments with Equations (10.47)–(10.49).
4. Find the spline segment that contains $\hat{x}$, the x value at which the spline is to be evaluated.
5. Evaluate spline interpolant at $\hat{x}$.

Each of these steps is discussed in turn.

Assemble the Tridiagonal System   The tridiagonal coefficient matrix in Equation (10.46) is sparse—for large n, most of the entries in the matrix are zero. Savings in storage, as well as execution time, can be realized by using MATLAB's sparse matrix storage format. (See Appendix B.) In `splintFE`, a sparse tridiagonal matrix is created with the NMM toolbox function `tridiags`. The inputs to `tridiags` are the size of the matrix and the three vectors that define the main, super, and sub diagonals. These diagonals are vectors β, α, and γ, respectively, as defined in Equations (10.41) through (10.43).

Solve the System   Once a sparse matrix is defined, it may be used like any other matrix in MATLAB. Specifically, a system of equations having a sparse coefficient matrix can be solved with the standard backslash operator. The solution to System (10.46) is obtained with the statement

```
b = A\delta;
```

where A is the coefficient matrix, `delta` is the right-hand-side vector, and b is the vector of slope values. In `splintFE`, the statement `b = A\delta` is surrounded by calls to the `spparms` function, which is used to control details of the sparse solution to the system. The `spparms` function is called three times: first to store the current value of the `autommd` flag, then to set the `autommd` flag "off," so that the equations are not reordered, and finally to reset the `autommd` flag to its previous value. Since matrix A for the spline system is tridiagonal, there is no advantage to reordering the equations. Telling the MATLAB kernel to avoid reordering the equations improves the overall efficiency of the solution for this system of equations.

Evaluate Remaining Spline Coefficients   Given vector b, it is relatively straightforward to compute vectors a, c, and d of spline coefficients from

Equations (10.47–10.49). The only complication is that b has n elements, where n is the number of knots, while there are only $n - 1$ cubic segments in the spline. The formulas for c_{n-1} and d_{n-1} use the value of b_n, so b_n must be retained until c and d are evaluated. The solution is to first compute c and d and then shorten the b vector to $n - 1$ elements with the statement

```
b(n) = [];
```

The result is that a, b, c, and d are all of length $n - 1$, allowing the spline evaluation to be easily vectorized.

Locate Appropriate Spline Segment and Evaluate Interpolant

To evaluate the interpolant at a point $\hat{x}$, the cubic segment containing $\hat{x}$ must be identified. This task, and the code to achieve it are the same as in the hermint function in Listing 10.8. Refer to the discussion beginning on page 563.

Evaluation of Spline Interpolant

Equation (10.38) is the formula for evaluating the ith segment of the spline interpolant. This is the same formula[10] used for a cubic Hermite interpolant. Again, refer to the discussion of the hermint function.

The splineFE function is exercised with the demoSplineFE function in the NMM toolbox. The demoSplineFE function (not listed here) creates interpolant approximations to $y = x \exp(-x)$ with different values for the slope of the spline at the end knots.

"Natural" End Conditions

The expression "natural end conditions" suggests that there are end conditions that are more intrinsically attuned to the true or ideal state of a spline. One might assume that these boundary conditions are somehow better than others. In fact, natural end conditions are less accurate than the not-a-knot end conditions presented in the next section. Natural, in this context, refers to an analogy with a draftsman's spline, which is a flexible rod used to draw smooth curves through a set of fixed reference points. Consider the shape of a draftsman's spline constrained by three points as depicted in Figure 10.18. Any part of the rod extending beyond the last constraint will have no curvature. If the shape of the rod is described by $y = f(x)$, then $y'' = 0$ for those parts of the rod between the last constraints and the free ends.

By analogy to the physical draftsman's spline, the natural end conditions for a cubic interpolating spline are $y'' = 0$. From the definition of $P_i(x)$ in Equation (10.38),

$$P_i''(\hat{x}) = 2c_i + 6d_i(\hat{x} - x_i), \qquad (10.50)$$

---

[10]The cubic Hermite will, in general, have different values of the coefficients a_i, b_i, c_i, and d_i.

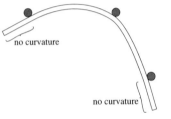

Figure 10.18   A draftsman's spline constrained by three pegs. The zero curvature between the last peg and the free ends is the reason the $y'' = 0$ end condition is called a "natural" spline.

so that a natural end condition at $x = x_1$ requires $c_1 = 0$. From Equations (10.47)–(10.49), $c_1 = 0$ in turn requires that

$$\frac{3 f[x_1, x_2] - 2b_1 - b_2}{(x_2 - x_1)} = 0,$$

or

$$b_1 + \frac{1}{2}b_2 = \frac{3}{2} f[x_1, x_2].$$

Enforcing this condition in Equation (10.46) involves setting

$$\beta_1 = 1, \quad \gamma_1 = \frac{1}{2}, \quad \delta_1 = \frac{3}{2} f[x_1, x_2] = \frac{3}{2}\frac{y_2 - y_1}{x_2 - x_1}. \tag{10.51}$$

Applying Equation (10.50) to a natural end condition at $x = x_n$ requires that

$$c_{n-1} = -3d_{n-1}(x_n - x_{n-1}).$$

Making the appropriate substitutions from Equations (10.47)–(10.49) and simplifying yields

$$b_{n-1} + 2b_n = 3 f[x_n, x_{n-1}].$$

The coefficients in the matrix from Equation (10.46) become

$$\alpha_n = 1, \quad \beta_n = 2, \quad \delta_n = 3 f[x_n, x_{n-1}] = 3 \frac{y_n - y_{n-1}}{x_n - x_{n-1}}. \tag{10.52}$$

To obtain the natural-spline interpolant, Equations (10.41) through (10.44) are used to define rows 2 through $n - 1$ in the matrix Equation (10.46). Equations (10.51) and (10.52) are used to define the first and last rows in the system.

"Not-a-Knot" End Conditions   The not-a-knot end conditions are the most accurate end conditions when information on the slope of the spline at the end points is not known. The not-a-knot condition is obtained by requiring continuity of $P'''(x)$ at the first internal knot (i.e., at x_2 or x_{n-1}). Since the spline segments are cubic polynomials and the spline already requires continuity of $P(x)$, $P'(x)$,

```
function [yhat,aa,bb,cc,dd] = splint(x,y,xhat,opt1,opt2)
% splint   Cubic-spline interpolation with various end conditions
%
% Synopsis:  yhat = splint(x,y,xhat)
%            yhat = splint(x,y,xhat,endType)
%            yhat = splint(x,y,xhat,fp1,fpn)
%            [yhat,a,b,c,d] = splint(x,y,xhat)
%            [yhat,a,b,c,d] = splint(x,y,xhat,endType)
%            [yhat,a,b,c,d] = splint(x,y,xhat,fp1,fpn)
%
% Input:   x,y  = vectors of discrete x and y = f(x) values
%          xhat = (scalar or vector) x value(s) where interpolant is evaluated
%          endType = (string, optional) either 'natural' or 'notaKnot';  used
%             to select either type of end conditions.  End conditions must be
%             same on both ends. Default: endType='notaKnot'.  For fixed slope
%             end conditions, values of f'(x) are specified, not endType
%          fp1 = (optional) slope at x(1), i,e., fp1 = f'(x(1))
%          fpn = (optional) slope at x(n), i,e., fpn = f'(x(n));
%
% Output:  yhat = (vector or scalar) value(s) of the cubic spline interpolant
%                 evaluated at xhat.  size(yhat) = size(xhat)
%          a,b,c,d = (optional) coefficients of cubic spline interpolants

% --- Process optional input arguments
   ... see complete source code of splint.m for details
% --- Set up system of equations for b(i)
   ... same as code in splintFE


% --- Modify system of equations as appropriate for the end conditions
if strncmp('not',lower(endType),3)  %  not a knot
   A(1,1) = dx(2);    A(1,2) = dx(1) + dx(2);            % Equation for b(1)
   delta(1) = ( dx(2)*(2*dx(2)+3*dx(1))*divdif(1)...
                + dx(1)*dx(1)*divdif(2) ) /(dx(1)+dx(2));
   A(n,n-1) = dx(n-2) + dx(n-1);    A(n,n) = dx(n-2);    % Equation for b(n)
   delta(n) = ( dx(n-2)*(2*dx(n-2)+3*dx(n-1))*divdif(n-1) ...
                + dx(n-1)*dx(n-1)*divdif(n-2) ) / (dx(n-2)+dx(n-1));
elseif strncmp('nat',lower(endType),3)     %  natural end conditions
   A(1,2) = 0.5;   delta(1) = 1.5*divdif(1);              %  y''(x(1)) = 0
   A(n,n-1) = 1;  A(n,n) = 2;  delta(n) = 3*divdif(n-1);  %  y''(x(n)) = 0
elseif strncmp('fix',lower(endType),3)      %  fixed-slope end conditions
   delta(1) = yp1;  delta(n) = ypn;
else
   error(sprintf('Logic error:  endType = %s',endType));
end

% --- Solve the system for b
   ... remainder of splint is same as code in splintFE
```

Listing 10.11   Excerpt from the splint function, which constructs a cubic-spline with various end conditions.

the input vector (or scalar) xhat. The first form of the splint function, in which only x, y, and xhat are specified, uses the not-a-knot end conditions. The optional endType parameter is a string that can be either natural or notKnot to select natural or not-a-knot end conditions, respectively. If the optional fp1 and fpn parameters are used, these values must be the fixed-slopes at x_1 and x_n. In other words splint(x,y,xhat,fp1,fpn) is equivalent to splintFE(x,y,xhat,fp1,fpn).

The code for the splint function does not fit on a single page of this book. As indicated by the comments in Listing 10.11, much of the code is the same as that in splintFE. Readers are encouraged to study the source code, which is included in the NMM toolbox. The significant changes from splintFE are included in Listing 10.11. These changes allow for the modification of the coefficient matrix and right-hand-side vector in equation 10.46 for the different types of end conditions.

Example 10.15: Comparison of Splines with Different End Conditions

The compSplinePlot function shown in Listing 10.12 uses different end conditions to create cubic-spline approximations to $y = xe^{-x}$ on the interval $0 \le x \le 5$. The absolute error of each spline interpolant is computed from $E = \|\hat{y} - y_e\|_2$, where $\hat{y}$ is the spline interpolant evaluated at 100 uniformly spaced points in the interval, and y_e is the exact function evaluated at these points. The choice of 100 points for the evaluation of the interpolant is arbitrary. Keeping this value constant as the number of breakpoints is increased provides a reasonable basis of comparing the end conditions.

Figure 10.19 shows the output of compSplinePlot for the default case of 6 knots. For this small number of knots the advantage of the not-a-knot end conditions is evident. The effect of enforcing zero-curvature via the natural end condition introduces more error near $x = 0$ where the slope of the function changes more quickly. The zero slope end conditions are clearly inferior, and the exact slope end conditions produce the best agreement between the interpolant and the original function.

Running the compSplinePlot function for an increasing number of breakpoints produces the following table of absolute errors:

knots	Absolute Errors: $E = \|\hat{y} - y_e\|_2$			
	natural	zero slope	not-a-knot	exact slope
4	7.0×10^{-1}	1.0	5.2×10^{-1}	1.6×10^{-1}
8	1.2×10^{-1}	3.3×10^{-1}	3.2×10^{-2}	5.4×10^{-3}
16	2.0×10^{-2}	1.1×10^{-1}	1.7×10^{-3}	2.4×10^{-4}
32	3.3×10^{-3}	3.5×10^{-2}	8.2×10^{-5}	1.3×10^{-5}
64	4.8×10^{-4}	1.0×10^{-2}	3.2×10^{-6}	7.4×10^{-7}
128	4.0×10^{-5}	1.7×10^{-3}	9.3×10^{-8}	4.4×10^{-8}

For a fixed number of knots the not-a-knot end conditions produce the smallest absolute errors if the slopes at the end of the interval are not known. This is consistent with the recommendation of de Boor [14, pp. 54–56] based on an analysis of the approximation

```
function compSplinePlot(n)
% compSplinePlot  Compare end conditions for cubic-spline interpolants
%                 Approximations to y = x*exp(-x) are constructed and plotted
%
% Synopsis:  compSplinePlot
%            compSplinePlot(n)
%
% Input:     n = (optional) number of knots in the range 0 <= x <= 5
%                Default:  n=6
%
% Output:    Plot of spline approximations to y = x*exp(-x) with not-a-knot,
%            natural, zero-slope, and exact-slope end conditions.  Normalized
%            errors for each interpolant are also computed and printed

if nargin<1, n=6;  end

x = linspace(0,5,n)';               %  Generate discrete data set
y = x.*exp(-x);
xi = linspace(min(x),max(x))';      %  Evaluate spline at these xi
ye = xi.*exp(-xi);                  %  Exact f(x) at the xi

yi = splint(x,y,xi,'natural');      %  Spline with natural end conditions
errNat = norm(yi-ye)
subplot(2,2,1);  plot(x,y,'bo',xi,ye,'b-',xi,yi,'r--');  axis([0 6 0 0.5]);
legend('knots','spline','x*exp(-x)');  title('Natural end conditions');

yi = splint(x,y,xi,0,0);            %  Spline with zero-slope end conditions
errz = norm(yi-ye)
subplot(2,2,2);  plot(x,y,'bo',xi,ye,'b-',xi,yi,'r--');  axis([0 6 0 0.5]);
legend('knots','spline','x*exp(-x)');  title('Zero-slope end conditions');

yi = splint(x,y,xi);               %  Spline with not-a-knot end conditions
errNot = norm(yi-ye)
subplot(2,2,3);  plot(x,y,'bo',xi,ye,'b-',xi,yi,'r--');  axis([0 6 0 0.5]);
legend('knots','spline','x*exp(-x)');  title('Not-a-knot end conditions');

yp1 = (1-x(1))*exp(-x(1));          %  Exact slope at x(1)
ypn = (1-x(n))*exp(-x(n));          %  and at x(n)
yi = splint(x,y,xi,yp1,ypn);        %  Spline with exact-slope end conditions
errExs = norm(yi-ye)
subplot(2,2,4);  plot(x,y,'bo',xi,ye,'b-',xi,yi,'r--');  axis([0 6 0 0.5]);
legend('knots','spline','x*exp(-x)');  title('Exact-slope end conditions');
```

Listing 10.12 The compSplinePlot function computes the accuracy of cubic spline interpolants of $y = xe^{-x}$ obtained with fixed-slope, natural, or not-a-knot end conditions.

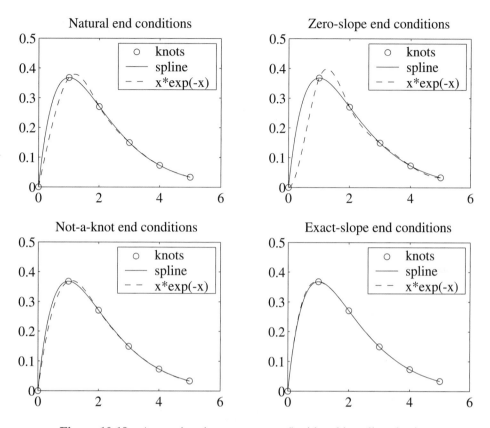

Figure 10.19   Approximations to $y = xe^{-x}$ with cubic-splines having different end conditions. Results are obtained with the compSplinePlot function in Listing 10.12.

errors. The exact slope end conditions produce the best results, since no approximation errors are introduced at x_1 and x_n. The natural end conditions are more accurate than the obviously-wrong, zero slope end conditions, but the natural end conditions are significantly less accurate than the not-a-knot end conditions.

0.4 MATLAB'S BUILT IN INTERPOLATION FUNCTIONS

Table 10.2 lists the interpolation functions in the standard MATLAB toolbox. All of these functions except interpft perform piecewise interpolation. There are no built-in equivalents for the lagrint and newtint functions for performing one-dimensional interpolation with polynomials of arbitrary degree.

TABLE 10.2   BUILT-IN MATLAB FUNCTIONS FOR INTERPOLATION OF DATA.

Function	Description
interp1	One-dimensional interpolation with piecewise polynomials.
interp2	Two-dimensional interpolation with nearest neighbor, bilinear, or bicubic interpolants.
interp3	Three-dimensional interpolation with nearest neighbor, bilinear, or bicubic interpolants.
interpft	One-dimensional interpolation of uniformly spaced data using Fourier Series (FFT).
interpn	n-dimensional extension of methods used by interp3.
spline	One-dimensional interpolation with cubic-splines using not-a-knot or fixed-slope end conditions.

10.4.1 One-dimensional Interpolation with interp1 and spline

The built-in interp1 function performs one-dimensional interpolation with one of the following four methods:

- *Nearest-neighbor* interpolation uses piecewise-constant functions (polynomials of degree zero). The interpolant is discontinuous at the midpoint between two adjacent knots.
- *Linear* interpolation uses piecewise-linear polynomials.
- *Cubic* interpolation uses piecewise-cubic polynomials such that the interpolant and its first derivative are continuous.
- *Spline* interpolation uses cubic splines with not-a-knot or fixed slope boundary conditions. This option performs the same interpolation as the built-in spline function.

A sample of these interpolation methods is given in Figure 10.20. The interp1 function can be called in the following ways:

```
yhat = interp1(y,xhat)
yhat = interp1(x,y,xhat)
yhat = interp1(x,y,xhat,method)
```

In each form of the interp1 function, y is the value of the tabulated function to be interpolated and xhat is a scalar or vector of values at which the interpolant is to be evaluated. The vector x, if it is given, supplies the value of the independent variable for the tabulated function; that is, x is the vector of x values in the $y = f(x)$ table. If x is not an input parameter, the table is assumed to have x values defined by x = 1:n, where n = length(y). The optional fourth parameter *method* takes one of the string values "nearest", "linear", "cubic" or "spline", which

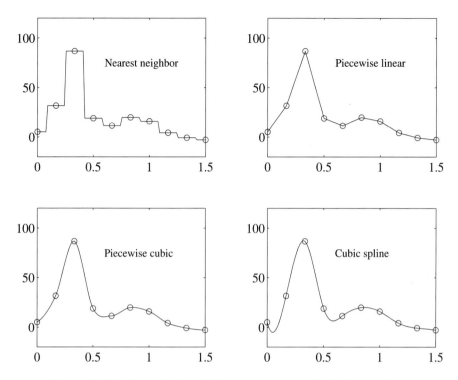

Figure 10.20   Interpolation of the same data set with the four methods provided by the built-in `interp1` function. Results are obtained with the `demoInterp1` function in the NMM toolbox.

correspond to the four methods described in the preceding list. The output *yhat* is a vector (or scalar) of the same length as *xhat* and contains the value of the interpolant at each element of *xhat*.

The following statements demonstrate how `interp1` might be used to perform a nearest-neighbor interpolation:

```
>> x = linspace(0,1.5,10);          %  define knots
>> y = humps(x);                    %  humps is a built in function
>> xi = linspace(min(x),max(x));    %  eval interpolant at xi
>> yn = interp1(x,y,xi,'nearest');
>> plot(x,y,'o',xi,yn,'-');
```

The result is the plot in the upper left corner of Figure 10.20. The four plots in Figure 10.20 are created with the `demoInterp1` function in the NMM toolbox.

Cubic-spline interpolation can be performed with either `interp1` or `spline`. The statement

```
yhat = interp1(x,y,xhat,'spline')
```

is equivalent to

```
yhat = spline(x,y,xhat)
```

The input parameters x and y provide the data table that defines the function to be interpolated. The value of the interpolant $yhat$ is evaluated at each $xhat$. By default, interp1(...,'spline') and spline(...) use not-a-knot end conditions. If input vector y has two more elements than the input x, then the first and last elements of y are taken to be the values of $y'(x_1)$ and $y'(x_n)$, respectively.

Notice that in the lower right corner of Figure 10.20 the cubic-spline interpolant has a dip near $x = 0$. This does not reflect the local trend of the humps function. The error is caused by the rather coarse spacing of knots and the not-a-knot end condition. The approximation could be improved by adding knots near $x = 0$ or by using the exact-slope end conditions. (See Exercise 33.)

10.5 SUMMARY

Two major themes are discussed in this chapter: interpolation with polynomials of arbitrary degree and interpolation with piecewise polynomials. Piecewise polynomial interpolation is generally more useful for practical applications because it is less likely to encounter numerical difficulties.

Table 10.3 lists the m-file functions for interpolation developed in this chapter. Interpolation functions supplied with the standard MATLAB toolbox are listed in Table 10.2 on page 584.

Interpolating Polynomials of Arbitrary Degree

When constructing interpolating polynomials of arbitrary degree, one has a choice of basis functions. In this chapter we considered interpolation in monomial, Lagrange, and Newton bases.

Finding the coefficients of a monomial basis requires the solution of a Vandermonde system. The Vandermonde matrix can be ill conditioned, which leads to uncertainties in the coefficients of the monomial. In addition, the terms in the monomial representation (the coefficients times their respective powers of x) may have large differences in magnitude, leading to roundoff errors in the evaluation of the polynomial. These numerical complications can be ameliorated by shifting and scaling the x data before the Vandermonde system is constructed. (See Example 10.5 and Exercise 4.)

TABLE 10.3 FUNCTIONS FOR INTERPOLATION DEVELOPED IN THIS CHAPTER. FUNCTIONS WITH N.A. (NOT APPLICABLE) FOR A PAGE NUMBER ARE NOT LISTED IN THE TEXT, BUT ARE INCLUDED IN THE `interpolate` DIRECTORY OF THE NMM TOOLBOX.

Function	page	Description
binSearch	558	Binary search to find index i such that $x_i \leq \hat{x} \leq x_{i+1}$.
compInterp	N.A.	Compare flops for interpolation with different polynomial bases. (See Example 10.10.)
compSplinePlot	582	Compare the accuracy of cubic-splines with different end conditions by approximating $y = xe^{-x}$.
demoGasLag	538	Use Lagrange polynomial basis to interpolate gasoline price data.
demoGasNewt	N.A.	Use Newton polynomial basis to interpolate gasoline price data.
demoGasVand	N.A.	Interpolate gas price data using monomial basis functions. This involves the solution of a poorly scaled Vandermonde system.
demoGasVandShift	N.A.	Interpolate gas price data using monomial basis functions and shifted dates. The Vandermonde system has better scaling and lower condition number.
demoHermite	566	Piecewise-cubic Hermite interpolation of $y = xe^{-x}$ on the interval $0 \leq x \leq 5$.
demoInterp1	N.A.	Use the built-in `interp1` function to interpolate data sampled from the `humps` function.
demoWiggle	N.A.	Plot wiggle caused by increasing the order of a polynomial interpolant. (See Example 10.11.)
divdiffTable	546	Construct a table of divided-difference coefficients.
hermint	564	Perform piecewise-cubic Hermite interpolation.
lagrint	537	Interpolate with Lagrange polynomials of arbitrary degree.
linterp	560	Perform piecewise-linear interpolation in a table of (x, y) data.
newtint	550	Interpolate with Newton polynomials of arbitrary degree.
splint	580	Perform cubic-spline interpolation with various end conditions.
splintFE	574	Perform cubic-spline interpolation with fixed-slope end conditions.

Interpolation with a Lagrange basis is most useful for theoretical analysis. Polynomial interpolants formed with a Lagrange basis are relatively immune to roundoff errors, but the computational formulas are inefficient.

For numerical computation, interpolation with a Newton basis is preferable to using monomial or Lagrange bases. The Newton polynomials are relatively immune to roundoff errors, and are computationally efficient. The `newtint` function in Listing 10.4 is recommended for interpolation with polynomials of arbitrary degree. The coefficients of the Newton interpolating polynomial are divided differences of the input data set. Divided-differences are also useful in the development of computational formulas for piecewise Hermite polynomials and cubic splines.

When interpolating with polynomials of arbitrary degree on data with equally spaced support points, one must guard against errors introduced by polynomial wiggle. Polynomial wiggle affects polynomials defined in any basis.

Piecewise Polynomial Interpolation

Piecewise polynomial interpolation involves the use of relatively low-degree polynomials that are locally defined over subsets of the input data. For one-dimensional data ($y = f(x)$), the interpolant consists of a set of interpolants that are joined at points along the x-axis called breakpoints, or knots. Evaluation of a piecewise interpolant at a point $\hat{x}$ involves additional code logic to search for the appropriate local interpolant in the set of piecewise interpolants defined over all of the knots.

Piecewise-linear interpolation may be performed with the built-in `interp1` function or the `linterp` function in Listing 10.7. The `interp1` function also provides nearest-neighbor, piecewise-cubic, and cubic-spline interpolants.

Piecewise-cubic Hermite interpolation requires the specification of both the function $y = f(x)$ and its first derivative $f'(x)$ at each of the knots. This is most feasible for functions that are available analytically. When the derivative of the tabulated function is not available, cubic-spline interpolation is recommended. Cubic splines are smooth because the interpolant and its first two derivatives are continuous at the knots. Although cubic splines consist of a set of locally defined piecewise-cubic segments, the continuity of the second derivative at the knots links adjacent segments. Thus, the construction of a cubic-spline interpolant requires the solution of a system of equations. In addition, conditions on the slope at the end of the spline must be supplied. The built-in `interp1` and `spline` functions only allow for the construction of cubic splines with not-a-knot and fixed slope end conditions. The `splint` function in Listing 10.11 can be used to construct cubic splines with not-a-knot, fixed-slope, or natural end conditions.

Recommendations

The first step in choosing an interpolation scheme is to decide what the application requires. Do you need to look up values in a table? Or do you need to construct a routine that will repeatedly evaluate the approximation? Piecewise interpolation is likely to be a good choice in either case. In limited situations, constructing an interpolating polynomial of fixed degree might offer a more compact (i.e., self-contained) solution. For the later case, the Newton form of the polynomial is recommended. One could construct the coefficients of the interpolant with `divDiffTable` and then hard-code these into a small m-file that evaluates the interpolant. In doing so, one should be sure to use all the digits of the coefficients returned by `divDiffTable`.

For routine interpolation of tabulated data, the built-in `interp1` and `interp2` functions are recommended.[12] The built-in routines also support extrapolation.

---

[12]For three and higher dimensions, `interp3` and `interpn` should be used, but this would hardly be considered routine interpolation. You might ask if there is an interpolation strategy more closely linked with your data before blindly using these higher dimensional functions.

If global smoothness of the interpolant is important, then cubic splines or piecewise-cubic Hermite interpolation should be considered. The accuracy of the spline interpolant can be strongly influenced by the end condition. Lacking knowledge of the slope at the ends of the data the not-a-knot end conditions should be used. If the slope at the end points is known, use the fixed-slope form of the `splint` function in the NMM toolbox, the built-in `interp1( ... ,'spline')` function, or the equivalent `spline` function. Users needing more sophisticated interpolation tools should consider the *Spline Toolbox* sold by the MathWorks.

For interpolation in two or higher dimensions, the `interp2` and `interp3` functions should be used. These functions require that the data be defined on a rectangular grid. The grid need not be uniform. The `griddata` function is used to interpolate scattered data defined by $z = f(x, y)$, where the x- and y-coordinates do not lie on a rectangular grid.

Further Reading

Interpolation is a staple in the literature of numerical analysis. The presentation in this chapter follows most closely that of Conte and de Boor [11]. Some of the material presented here is also similar to that provided by Van Loan [77]. Cheney and Kincaid [10] cover the same material in more detail, although the derivation of splines in Cheney and Kincaid is based on solving for the second-derivative coefficients instead of the first derivatives at the knots. For a rigorous mathematical treatment of interpolation, refer to de Boor [14], and Stoer and Bulirsch [70]. For applications of splines in computer-aided design (CAD) consult the book by Farin [21]. For applications of splines in curve fitting, see de Boor [14] and Dierckx [17].

Two important topics not covered in this chapter are *B splines* and *Neville's algorithm* for evaluation of an interpolant. B splines are spline functions that form the mathematical basis for all splines. For an introduction to computing with B splines, see [10, 14, 21, 43]. Neville's algorithm is a procedure for evaluating a polynomial interpolant of arbitrary order without explicitly constructing the coefficients of the polynomial. Neville's algorithm is very efficient for interpolation and extrapolation where only one value of the interpolant is needed. In particular, Neville's algorithm is used in *Romberg integration*, another important topic not covered here. (See [10, 61, 64, 70] for more information.)

EXERCISES

The number in parenthesis at the beginning of each exercise indicates the degree of skill and amount of effort necessary to complete the exercise. See § 1.4 on page 10 for a description of the rating system.

1. (1−) What are the basis functions for the linear interpolating polynomial $P_1(x) = c_1 x + c_2$?

2. (2) Eckert and Drake (*Analysis of Heat and Mass Transfer*, 1972, McGraw-Hill, Table B-13, p. 790) give the following data for the surface tension of water as a function of temperature:

T (°C)	0	10	20	30	40	50	60	70	80	100
$\sigma \times 10^3$ (N/m)	78.2	74.8	73.4	71.6	70.2	68.5	66.7	64.9	63.2	59.3

The value of σ at $0\,°C$, for example, is 78.2×10^{-3} N/m. Plot σ versus T. Are these data suitable for interpolation? What other means of approximating these data might be more appropriate?

SOLUTION 3. (1+) What are the condition numbers for the two Vandermonde matrices in Examples 10.4 and 10.5? How does the change in $\kappa(A)$ relate to the different results obtained in Example 10.5?

4. (2) Perform the monomial basis interpolation of gasoline prices from Examples 10.4 and 10.5 using normalized years instead of shifted years. The normalized year is $y_n = (y - \bar{y})/(y_{max} - y_{min})$, where $\bar{y}$ is the average value of y. What is the range of y_n values? Compare the magnitude of the interpolating coefficients and the condition number of the resulting Vandermonde matrix with those obtained in Examples 10.4 and 10.5.

5. (2−) In Example 10.4, will converting the gas prices from cents to dollars improve the condition of the system of equations? Why or why not?

SOLUTION 6. (2+) In Example 10.4, the coefficients of the interpolating polynomial are evaluated and printed to five significant digits. Evaluate the gasoline prices and the errors in the interpolant using the truncated coefficients and the following definitions: Let (y_i, p_i) be the year and price in the given tabulated data. Let $\hat{p}_i$ be the price interpolated with the untruncated polynomial coefficients at the y_i, and $\tilde{p}_i$ be the price interpolated with the truncated coefficients at the y_i. In the absence of numerical errors we expect $p_i = \hat{p}_i = \tilde{p}_i$ from the definition of interpolation. Compute and print p_i, $\hat{p}_i - p_i$, $\|\hat{p} - p\|_2$, $\tilde{p}_i$, $\tilde{p}_i - p_i$, and $\|\tilde{p} - p\|_2$. How many digits of the c coefficients need to be retained in order to get $\|p - \tilde{p}\|_\infty$ comparable to $\|p - \hat{p}\|_\infty$? (*Hint:* The chop10 function in the utils directory of the NMM toolbox will be helpful.)

7. (2+) Repeat the preceding Exercise for the coefficients of the shifted polynomial interpolant described in Example 10.5.

8. (1+) Write out the Lagrange basis functions for the cubic interpolating polynomial passing through (x_j, y_j), (x_{j+1}, y_{j+1}), (x_{j+2}, y_{j+2}), and (x_{j+3}, y_{j+3}).

9. (3) In the discussion of implementing Lagrange interpolation on page 536, it is asserted that the denominator of Equation (10.15) could be precomputed and stored in a lower triangular matrix whose entries are used only twice. Prove both that the storage requirement is a lower triangular matrix and that the entries in this matrix are used only twice.

10. (2) Set up the 4×4 system of equations for coefficients of the cubic interpolating polynomial in Newton form. (See Equation (10.22).) Solve this system by hand, showing all intermediate steps, to obtain the coefficients in Equation (10.23).

11. (1+) Manually construct the divided-difference table for the interpolation problem in Example 10.7.

SOLUTION 12. (1+) Manually perform the quadratic interpolation in Example 10.7 using instead the following support points.
    (a) $T_1 = 20$, $T_2 = 30$, $T_3 = 40$
    (b) $T_1 = 0$, $T_2 = 10$, $T_3 = 20$
    Compare the results to the interpolant using $T_1 = 10$, $T_2 = 20$, and $T_3 = 30$.

13. (2) Manually compute the third- and fourth-degree polynomial interpolants of the viscosity data at 22 °C in Example 10.7. Which support points should you use? Is the answer significantly different from the result obtained with quadratic interpolation in the example?

SOLUTION 14. (2) The H2Osat.dat file in the data directory of the NMM toolbox contains saturation data for water. Use this data and quadratic polynomial interpolation to manually compute p_{sat} in the range $30 \leq T \leq 35\ °C$.
    (a) *Manually* construct the divided-difference table. Use the divDiffTable function to check your calculations.
    (b) Extract the coefficients of the Newton interpolating polynomial from the divided-difference table.
    (c) Evaluate the interpolant at $T = 32$, 33, and 34 °C. Verify you calculations with newtint.

15. (2) Repeat Exercise 14 using a cubic polynomial interpolant. What is the difference in the p_{sat} values obtained with quadratic and cubic interpolants?

16. (3) Build a custom, self-contained routine that returns the viscosity of glycerine as a function of temperature. The data are provided in Example 10.7. The routine should evaluate a cubic polynomial in a Newton basis. First, use the divDiffTable function to compute the coefficients of the interpolating polynomial. Store the *values* of these coefficients in a vector in your routine, and then evaluate the Newton polynomial. In other words, the coefficients are evaluated only once by you, the programmer, not every time your routine is executed. The advantage of this approach is that the viscosity computations would not require knowledge of any other routines in the NMM toolbox. It could also be easily translated to another language, such as C, Java, or Fortran.

17. (3) Consider the following code snippet, which uses interpolation with Newton polynomials to approximate the sine function on the interval $0 \leq x \leq 2\pi$:

```
x = 0:pi/6:2*pi;    y = sin(x);    %  original data
xi = linspace(min(x),max(x));      %  eval interpolant at xi

yi2 = newtint(x(1:3),y(1:3),xi);   %  2nd degree interpolant
yi3 = newtint(x(1:4),y(1:4),xi);   %  3rd   "    "     "    "
yi4 = newtint(x(1:5),y(1:5),xi);   %  4th
yi5 = newtint(x(1:6),y(1:6),xi);   %  5th
yi6 = newtint(x(1:7),y(1:7),xi);   %  6th
```

```
plot(x,sin(x),'o',xi,yi2,'.',xi,yi3,'--',xi,yi4,':',xi,yi5,'-',...
    xi,yi6,'-.');
legend('original','degree 2','degree 3','degree 4','degree 5',...
      'degree 6');
axis([0 2*pi -5 5]);
```

Executing these statements reveals that the attempted interpolation gives poor results for larger values of x. Increasing the degree does not uniformly improve the accuracy of the calculations. (The fourth-degree interpolation appears to work better than the fifth-degree interpolation.) The user has made an error in applying `newtint`. What's wrong with this code? Write a corrected sequence of statements that yields good interpolation results over the entire range $0 \le x \le 2\pi$. The correct result will show very little difference with the degree of interpolation above five. (*Hint:* Does `newtint` allow extrapolation?)

SOLUTION **18.** (3+) The degree of the polynomial interpolant used by `lagrint` and `newtint` is determined by the length of the input vectors to these functions. Suppose one wished to specify the order of the interpolant, regardless of the length of the input data. In other words, suppose the objective was to perform a local interpolation of degree n in a table of length m, where $m > n$. This requires selecting an appropriate subset of the input data table and passing this subset to `lagrint` or `newtint`. For example, a quadratic interpolation could be performed with

```
x = ...     % define tabular data
y = ...
xhat = ...    % interpolate at this value
ibeg = ...    % beginning index for support points of interpolant
yhat = newtint(x(ibeg:ibeg+2),y(ibeg:ibeg+2),xhat)
```

Write an m-file function called `quadinterp` that automatically selects an appropriate subset of vectors x and y, and returns the value of the quadratic interpolant using those support points. The function definition statement for `quadinterp` is

```
function yhat = quadinterp(x,y,xhat)
```

The `quadinterp` function calls `newtint` to perform the interpolation. The `binSearch` function in Listing 10.6 will be useful. Use your `quadinterp` function to generate data for smooth plot of the glycerin viscosity data in Example 10.2.

19. (3+) Use the results of Exercise 18 to develop a `polyinterp` function to perform polynomial interpolation of degree n in a table of more than $n + 1$ data pairs. The function definition statement for `polyinterp` is

```
function yhat = polyinterp(x,y,xhat,n)
```

where n is the degree of the polynomial interpolant. Verify that the results of `polyinterp( ... ,2)` are identical to `quadinterp( ... )`. Use your `polyinterp` function to generate a cubic interpolant for the the glycerin viscosity data in Example 10.2. Plot the original data and the interpolant. Note that an elegant solution to this problem is called *Neville* interpolation.

20. (2+) Consider the problem of interpolation in the given table with repeated data. One interpretation of the interpolant is the curve in the accompanying plot. The data in the table are problematic, because when the data are represented by $y = f(x)$, $f(x)$ is not unique for some x. This problem also exists if the data are considered to be $x = g(y)$. This type of interpolation is important, for example, in describing the shape of an object with a CAD program.

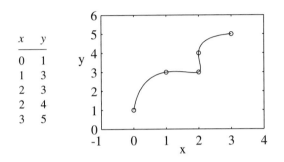

x	y
0	1
1	3
2	3
2	4
3	5

(a) Set up the Vandermonde system for these data. What is the rank of the coefficient matrix? What is the rank if the fourth point is changed from $(2, 4)$ to $(2, 3)$?

(b) Will the problems identified in part (a) be fixed by using a Lagrange or Newton basis? (Direct experimentation with `lagrint` and `newtint` will be informative.) Does using the built-in `interp1` function solve the problem?

(See Exercise 37 for a method to generate the curve in the plot.)

21. (3) The classic example of polynomial wiggle is the so-called *Runge* function

$$r(x) = \frac{1}{1 + 25x^2},\qquad (10.55)$$

named after German mathematician Carl Runge (1856–1927), who used this function to study the behavior of high-degree polynomial interpolation. Write a function m-file called `runge` to perform the following tasks.

(a) Compute n equally spaced x_k values ($k = 1, \ldots, n$) on the interval $-1 \le x \le 1$. Let n be an input parameter to `runge`.

(b) Evaluate $r(x_k)$ from Equation (10.55) for $k = 1, \ldots, n$.

(c) Use the n pairs of $(x_k, r(x_k))$ values to define a degree $n - 1$ polynomial interpolant, P_{n-1}. Evaluate the interpolant at $\hat{x}_j$, $j = 1, \ldots, 100$ points in the interval $-1 \le x \le 1$.

(d) Plot a comparison of the original data, $(x_k, r(x_k))$, the interpolant, $(\hat{x}_j, P_{n-1}(\hat{x}_j))$, and the true value of the function at the interpolating points $(\hat{x}_j, r(\hat{x}_j))$. Use open circles for $r(x_k)$, a dashed line for $P_{n-1}(\hat{x}_j)$, and a solid line for $r(\hat{x}_j)$.

(e) Print the value of $\|r(\hat{x}) - P_{n-1}(\hat{x})\|_2$.

Run your runge function for n=5:2:15, and discuss the behavior of $\|r(\hat{x}) - P_{n-1}(\hat{x})\|_2$ as n is increased.

22. (3) Write a `rungec` function based on the `runge` function developed in the preceding exercise. Instead of equally spaced x_k values, use the Chebyshev points

$$x_k = -\cos\left(\frac{(2k-1)\pi}{2n}\right), \qquad k = 1, \ldots, n.$$

Compare the behavior of $\|r(\hat{x}) - P_{n-1}(\hat{x})\|_2$ when n Chebyshev support points are used instead of n equally spaced support points to define the interpolant.

23. (2) Rewrite the `H2Odensity` function in Listing 3.12 so that density is interpolated from the data in the `H2Odensity.dat` file in the `data` directory of the NMM toolbox.

SOLUTION **24.** (2) The `stdatm.dat` in the `data` directory of the NMM toolbox gives the properties of the so-called standard atmosphere as a function of elevation above sea level. Write a routine that uses piecewise-linear interpolation to return the values of T, p, and ρ, at any elevation in the range of the table. Write your m-file function so that it does not read the data from this file when it is executed; that is, store the data in matrix variables in your m-file. What are the values of T, p, and ρ at $z = 5500$ m and $z = 9023$ m? Plot the variation of T and ρ in the range $0 \leq z \leq 15$ km.

25. (2+) Remove the range check from the `binSearch` function (by turning those statements into comments), and run the modified `binSearch` function with x=0:10 and xhat=11 for inputs. Describe in words what happens. Comment on how this result will affect a subsequent interpolation step.

26. (2) Modify the `binSearch` function so that it returns ia = 1 when xhat < x(1), and ia = n - 1 when xhat > x(n). These changes allow `binSearch` to return indices to be used for extrapolation as well as interpolation.

27. (2+) Add an additional check to the `binSearch` function to verify that the data are monotonic. (*Hint*: Use the `diff` function compute a vector of dx values. Checking the sign of the dx elements determines monotonicity.) Devise at least two sets of non-monotonic input data to verify that your modifications to `binSearch` is working.

28. (2+) Carry out the algebraic manipulations necessary to obtain the coefficients a_i, b_i, c_i, and d_i in Equation (10.37).

29. (2+) By direct evaluation, verify that $P_{i-1}(x_i) = P_i(x_i)$ and $P'_{i-1}(x_i) = P'_i(x_i)$ for the cubic-spline interpolant. (*Hint*: Use the coefficients in Equation (10.39) and the definitions of $P(x)$ and $P'(x)$.)

30. (2+) Use the `splintFE` function to repeat the calculations in Example 10.14. Plot the spline.

31. (2+) Consider the case of evaluating either a piecewise-cubic Hermite or a cubic-spline interpolant at just one value. The `hermint` function computes the equations for all of the cubic segments before finding the appropriate segment needed in the interpolation. A routine that is more efficient for evaluating the cubic Hermite interpolant at a single point would only construct the interpolant for the appropriate segment. Is a similar efficiency savings possible for a cubic-spline interpolant? Why or why not?

SOLUTION **32.** (1+) Plot the spline interpolant of the following data:

x_i	0.2	0.6	1.0	1.4	1.8	2.2
y_i	0.5535	1.0173	1.0389	0.8911	0.7020	0.5257

On the same plot, compare the spline interpolant to $y = \sqrt{12.5}\,x\exp(-\sqrt{1.5}\,x)$, which was used to create the data in the table.

33. (2+) In the lower-right-hand plot of Figure 10.20 the cubic-spline interpolant of the humps function has an inaccurate dip near $x = 0$. For reference, evaluate and plot the humps function at 100 points in the interval $0 \le x \le 1.5$. On the same axes as the plot of humps, add plots of the cubic-spline interpolants obtained with exact-slope and not-a-knot end conditions. Use the built-in spline function, and create the splines with 10 equally-spaced knots. Repeat the comparison when the splines are created with 17 equally-spaced knots. Based on the results of your computations and plots, recommend a procedure for creating a qualitatively accurate spline interpolant of humps.

34. (2+) The following statements construct a cubic-spline interpolant to the built-in humps function on the interval $0 \le x \le 1.5$:

```
x = linspace(0,1.5,10)';
y = humps(x);
xhat = linspace(min(x),max(x),36)';
yhat = spline(x,y,xhat);
plot(x,y,'o',xhat,yhat,'r-')
```

Viewing the plot reveals that the solid line does not pass through the knot near the primary peak of humps. (The discrepancy can be made clear by adding an axis([0 0.5 80 90]) statement.) Is the disagreement between the interpolant due to the end conditions on the spline? Or is there a bug in the built-in spline routine? Or is there another reason for the disagreement? Implement a correction for this problem.

35. (3−) The following statements construct a cubic-spline interpolant of the rational function $y = (1 - x^2)/(2 + x^3)$ on the interval $0 \le x \le 10$:

```
n = 5;
x = linspace(0,10,n);
y = (1 - x.^2)./(2 + x.^3);
xhat = linspace(min(x),max(x));
[yhat,a,b,c,d] = splint(x,y,xhat,'natural');
...
```

Add more statements to compute and print $y''(x_1)$ and $y''(x_n)$ of the spline using the coefficient vectors a, b, c, and d. What should the values of $y''(x_1)$ and $y''(x_n)$ be? If the values of $y''(x_1)$ and $y''(x_n)$ are not what you expect, is there a bug in splint?

36. (3+) Write a modified form of `splint` (and any other functions as needed) that allows extrapolation for `xhat < x(1)` and `xhat < x(n)`. Use your modified function to perform cubic extrapolation of the air passenger data in Example 10.3.

37. (3) Exercise 20 contains a data set with repeated x and y values. The plot in the problem statement of Exercise 20 was created with a *parametric spline*. Instead of interpolating $y = f(x)$, a parametric spline uses $x = x(t)$ and $y = y(t)$, where t is a parameter of the curve, as the following depicts:

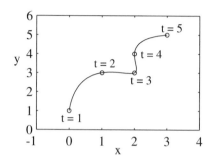

For the data in the plot, t was chosen simply to be the index of the data points in the table. This is not necessary as long as t is single-valued and monotonically increasing or decreasing. Furthermore, t need not be an integer.

(a) Develop a `paramSpline` function using the following prologue

```
function [xi,yi,ti] = paramSpline(x,y,n)
% paramSpline   Parametric spline interpolation.
%
% Synopsis:    [xi,yi,ti] = paramSpline(x,y)
%              [xi,yi,ti] = paramSpline(x,y,n)
%
% Input:   x,y = vectors of data defining a curve in (x,y) plane
%          n   = (optional) number of points to generate on the
%                interpolated curve.  Default:  n = 100
%
% Output: xi,yi = vectors of points on parametric curves x = xi(ti)
%                 and y = yi(ti) obtained from separate cubic spline
%                 interpolations of x and y.  Plotting (xi,yi)
%                 produces a smooth curve through the (x,y) data
%
%            ti = vector computed with ti = linspace(min(t),max(t),n)
%                 where t = 1:length(x) is vector of indices for x and
%                 y, and n is an optional input parameter.
```

(b) Use your `paramSpline` and the data in Exercise 20 to create the plot in Exercise 20.

11

Numerical Integration

The value of the definite integral

$$I = \int_a^b f(x)\, dx \tag{11.1}$$

must be approximated numerically if a closed-form expression for $\int f(x)dx$ involving elementary functions (not other integrals) cannot be found or when $f(x)$ is known only at discrete values of x (e.g., if $f(x)$ is from experimental data or is the output of a computer simulation). Numerical integration is also advantageous when an analytical formula for an integral is known, but is difficult or inconvenient to evaluate.

The choice of numerical integration method depends somewhat on the nature of $f(x)$. Several m-file functions that implement different integration schemes are provided in this chapter. All numerical integration methods require that $f(x)$ can be evaluated at any x in the interval $a \le x \le b$. If the function has singularities (i.e., $f(x^*) = \pm\infty$ for some x^* in the interval), then special precautions must be taken. If at least one of the limits of integration is infinite, then other procedures must be applied. There are well-established solutions for these special cases, but there is no one numerical integration scheme that applies to all integrals.

Example 11.3: Integration of a Polynomial

The definite integral of $P_n(x) = c_1 x^n + c_2 x^{n-1} + \cdots + c_{n+1}$ is

$$\int_a^b \left[c_1 x^n + c_2 x^{n-1} + \cdots + c_{n+1} \right] dx = \left[\frac{c_1}{n+1} x^{n+1} + \frac{c_2}{n} x^n \; \cdots \; c_{n+1} x \right]_{x=a}^{x=b}.$$

In MATLAB, the integral is easily evaluated from the polynomial coefficients with the `polyval` function. (See Exercise 2.) There is no approximation, of course, in the integration of $P_n(x)$. Throughout this chapter, $P_n(x)$ will be used to approximate some $f(x)$ that appears in the form of Equation (11.1).

11.1 BASIC IDEAS AND NOMENCLATURE

Numerical integration is also called *numerical quadrature*. The term quadrature originally referred to the process determining the dimension of a square having the same area as some other planar shape. This suggests a basic computational strategy of numerical integration: To evaluate $I = \int f(x)\,dx$, approximate the curve $y = f(x)$ with a simpler function that is easy to integrate. The area under the simple curve is approximately equal to the area under $f(x)$.

Figure 11.3, for example, shows a piecewise-linear approximation to a function. The area under this approximation can be computed by summing the areas of the trapezoidal regions between the piecewise approximation and the x-axis. Polynomials are very easy to integrate, and the theory of polynomial interpolation is well understood. Most numerical integration schemes, therefore, involve constructing a polynomial interpolant to $f(x)$ and then integrating the interpolant to obtain an approximation to the integral of $f(x)$.

The integrand $f(x)$ is evaluated at n points, called *nodes*, in the interval defined by the limits of the integral. The nodes are designated x_i and are assumed to be ordered and distinct (i.e., $a \le x_1 < x_2 < \cdots < x_n \le b$). If $x_1 = a$ and $x_n = b$, the interval is said to be *closed* and is identified with the symbol $[a, b]$. If $x_1 > a$ and $x_n < b$, the interval is *open* and is identified with the symbol (a, b).

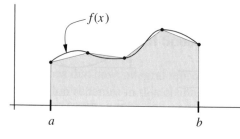

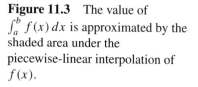

Figure 11.3 The value of $\int_a^b f(x)\,dx$ is approximated by the shaded area under the piecewise-linear interpolation of $f(x)$.

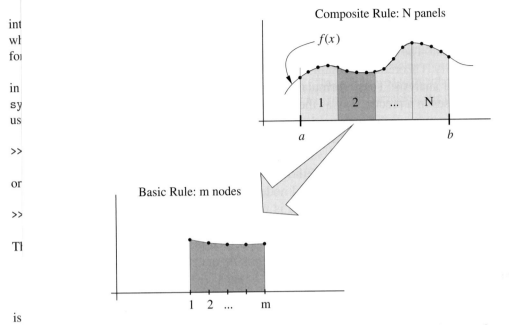

Figure 11.4   Basic and composite rules for numerical quadrature of $f(x)$.

In Chapter 10, piecewise polynomial interpolation is demonstrated to be superior to global interpolation with a single polynomial. This result also applies to numerical integration schemes. Figure 11.4 shows a global interval $[a, b]$ divided into N panels.[1] On each panel, a relatively low-degree polynomial approximation to $f(x)$ is created. Integrating the polynomial approximation on the panel gives what is called a *basic rule*. A basic rule involves just enough $(x, f(x))$ pairs to define one segment of the piecewise polynomial. Applying the basic rule to each of the N panels and adding together the results gives what is called a *composite rule*, or an *extended rule*.

The location and number of the nodes within a panel determine many important characteristics of the basic rule. When the nodes are equally spaced, the resulting integration formulas are known as *Newton–Cotes rules*. In contrast, *Gaussian quadrature rules* use nodes chosen as the zeros of orthogonal polynomials. Gaussian quadrature rules have a much smaller truncation error than the corresponding Newton–Cotes rules using the same number of nodes. Although the Gaussian quadrature rules are more complex to derive, they are not significantly harder to implement in a program.

---

[1] In the on-line help for the quad8 function, a panel refers to the spacing between the nodes, not the width of the subinterval.

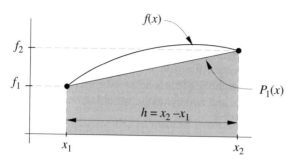

Figure 11.5 The basic trapezoid rule for numerical integration is applied to two nodes on an interval.

Lagrange interpolating polynomial for the interval in the figure is

$$P_1(x) = \frac{x - x_2}{x_1 - x_2} f_1 + \frac{x - x_1}{x_2 - x_1} f_2. \tag{11.4}$$

Using $P_1(x)$ as an approximation to $f(x)$, we can estimate the integral of $f(x)$ from x_1 to x_2 with

$$I = \int_{x_1}^{x_2} f(x)\, dx \approx \int_{x_1}^{x_2} P_1(x)\, dx.$$

Substituting Equation (11.4) for $P_1(x)$ in the integral and simplifying yields

$$\int_{x_1}^{x_2} P_1(x)\, dx = \int_{a}^{b} \left(\frac{x - x_2}{x_1 - x_2} f_1 + \frac{x - x_1}{x_2 - x_1} f_2 dx \right)$$

$$= -\frac{f_1}{h} \int_{x_1}^{x_2} (x - x_2)\, dx + \frac{f_2}{h} \int_{x_1}^{x_2} (x - x_1)\, dx$$

$$= \frac{1}{2}(f_1 + f_2)h,$$

where $h \equiv x_2 - x_1$. Therefore,

$$I = \int_{x_1}^{x_2} f(x)\, dx \approx \frac{1}{2}(f_1 + f_2)h. \tag{11.5}$$

An error analysis (see, for example, [10, 70]) shows that the truncation error for the basic trapezoid rule is $\mathcal{O}(h^3)$

$$I = \int_{x_1}^{x_2} f(x)\, dx = \frac{1}{2}(f_1 + f_2)h + Ch^3 f''(\xi), \tag{11.6}$$

where C is a constant, ξ is some point in the interval $x_1 < \xi < x_2$, and $f''(x) = d^2 f/dx^2$.

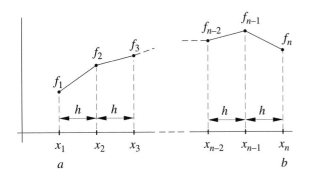

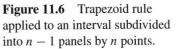

Figure 11.6   Trapezoid rule applied to an interval subdivided into $n-1$ panels by n points.

Composite Rule   The composite trapezoid rule is obtained by subdividing an interval into several subintervals, or *panels*, and applying the basic rule to each panel. The composite trapezoid rule is depicted in Figure 11.6. The value of the integral for the entire interval is obtained from the sum of the integrals for each panel:

$$\int_a^b f(x)\,dx = \int_a^{x_2} f(x)\,dx + \int_{x_2}^{x_3} f(x)\,dx + \cdots + \int_{x_{n-1}}^{x_n} f(x)\,dx.$$

Let x_i be a sequence of uniformly spaced points on the closed interval $[a, b]$:

$$x_i = a + (i-1)h, \quad i = 1, \dots, n, \quad \text{and} \quad h = \frac{b-a}{(n-1)}. \tag{11.7}$$

Applying Equation (11.6) to each of the panels in Figure 11.6 gives

$$\int_{x_1}^{x_n} f(x)\,dx = \frac{1}{2}(f_1 + f_2)h + C_1 h^3 f''(\xi_1),$$

$$+ \frac{1}{2}(f_2 + f_3)h + C_2 h^3 f''(\xi_2),$$

$$\vdots$$

$$+ \frac{1}{2}(f_{n-1} + f_n)h + C_{n-1} h^3 f''(\xi_{n-1}),$$

where $x_i < \xi_i < x_{i+1}$. If $K = \max[C_i f''(\xi_i)]$ is finite, then the sum of the unknown truncation errors is bounded by $(n-1)Kh^3$, and

$$(n-1)Kh^3 = (n-1)K \left(\frac{b-a}{n-1}\right)^3 = K\frac{(b-a)^3}{(n-1)^2} = K'h^2,$$

where $K' = K(b - a)$. The composite trapezoid rule is, therefore,

$$\int_{x_1}^{x_n} f(x)\, dx = h \left[\frac{1}{2} f_1 + f_2 + f_3 + \cdots + f_{n-2} + f_{n-1} + \frac{1}{2} f_n \right] + \mathcal{O}\left(h^2\right).$$

(11.8)

The K' constant is fixed for a given integrand and limits of integration. The only part of the truncation error that is under user control is the number of nodes, n.

Example 11.5: Manual Calculation with the Trapezoidal Rule

Use the trapezoid rule to evaluate erf(1):

$$I = \text{erf}(1) = \frac{2}{\sqrt{\pi}} \int_0^1 e^{-x^2}\, dx$$

For $n = 5$, the stepsize is $h = (1 - 0)/4 = 0.25$. The following table lists the values of $\exp(-x_i^2)$ at $x_i = (i - 1)h$

x_i	0	0.25	0.50	0.75	1.00
$\exp(-x_i^2)$	1.0000	0.9394	0.7788	0.5698	0.3679

Adding up the terms in the composite trapezoid rule gives

$$I = \frac{2}{\sqrt{\pi}} (0.25) \left[(0.5)(1.0) + 0.9394 + 0.7788 + 0.5698 + (0.5)(0.3679) \right]$$

$$= \frac{2}{\sqrt{\pi}} (0.7430)$$

$$= 0.8384.$$

To four decimal places, the exact value of erf(1) is 0.8427, so the error in the trapezoid rule approximation with $n = 5$ is -0.0043.

Implementation of Trapezoid Rule for Arbitrary $f(x)$ The trapezoid function in Listing 11.1 uses the composite trapezoid rule to numerically integrate a user-defined function. First, the input and output parameters of trapezoid are summarized. Then, the code in the function is discussed. The trapezoid function is invoked with

I = trapezoid(fun,a,b,npanel)

where fun is the name of the m-file that evaluates the integrand, a and b are the lower and upper limits of integration, and npanel is the number of panels used in the integration. The accuracy of the numerical integral is strongly influenced by the value of npanel so, in general, one should use trapezoid with several values of

```
function I = trapezoid(fun,a,b,npanel)
% trapezoid   Composite trapezoid rule
%
% Synopsis:   I = trapezoid(fun,a,b,npanel)
%
% Input:      fun    = (string) name of m-file that evaluates f(x)
%             a, b   = lower and upper limits of the integral
%             npanel = number of panels to use in the integration
%                      Total number of nodes = npanel + 1
%
% Output:     I = approximate value of the integral from a to b of f(x)*dx

n = npanel + 1;      % total number of nodes
h = (b-a)/(n-1);     % stepsize
x = a:h:b;           % divide the interval
f = feval(fun,x);    % evaluate integrand

I = h * ( 0.5*f(1) + sum(f(2:n-1)) + 0.5*f(n) );
```

Listing 11.1 The trapezoid function evaluates a definite integral with the trapezoidal rule.

npanel to be sure that the integral is evaluated to within a desired tolerance. This procedure is demonstrated in Example 11.6.

The m-file specified by the *fun* parameter must accept a single *vector x* as input and return a single vector $y = f(x)$. The natural way to perform the calculations in this m-file is to use array operators. (See page 36).

The code in trapezoid is straightforward. Notice that the input parameter is npanel, the total number of panels, instead of n, the total number of points used in the composite rule. To evaluate the sum in the composite trapezoid rule, Equation (11.8) is written as

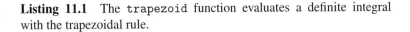

$$I = h \left[\frac{1}{2} f_1 + \sum_{i=2}^{n-1} f_i + \frac{1}{2} f_n \right]$$

and directly translated into a single line of MATLAB code:

```
I = h * (0.5*f(1) + sum(f(2:n-1)) + 0.5*f(n));
```

Use of the trapezoid function is demonstrated in the following example.

Example 11.6: Trapezoid Rule Evaluation of $\int_0^5 xe^{-x}\, dx$

This example shows how to use the trapezoid function to approximate the value of

$$I = \int_0^5 xe^{-x}\, dx = -e^{-x}(1+x)\big|_0^5 = 1 - 6e^{-5}.$$

Because the exact value of the integral is known, the truncation error produced by the code can be compared with the theoretical prediction for the truncation error.

The xemx function shown in the lower part of Listing 11.2 evaluates $f(x) = xe^{-x}$. The use of the .* array operator allows the input variable x to be a vector or scalar. This

```
function demoTrap
% demoTrap   Use composite trapezoidal rule to integrate x*exp(-x) on [0,5]
%
% Synopsis:  demoTrap
%
% Input:     none
%
% Output:    Table of integral values for increasing number of intervals

a = 0;   b = 5;    Iexact = -exp(-b)*(1+b) + exp(-a)*(1+a);
fprintf('\n\tIexact = %14.9f\n',Iexact);

fprintf('\n   n      h            I                error        alpha\n');
errold = [];
for np = [ 2 4 8 16 32 64 128 256]
  I = trapezoid('xemx',a,b,np);
  err = I - Iexact;
  n = np + 1;    h = (b-a)/(n-1);      %  number of nodes and stepsize
  fprintf(' %4d %9.5f %14.9f %14.9f',n,h,I,err);

  if ~isempty(errold)
    fprintf('  %9.5f\n',log(err/errold)/log(h/hhold));
  else
    fprintf('\n');
  end
  hhold = h;   errold = err;          %  prep for next stepsize
end
```

```
function y = xemx(x)
% xemx   Evaluate x*exp(-x), where x is a scalar or vector
y = x.*exp(-x);
```

Listing 11.2   demoTrap and xemx function for trapezoidal rule evaluation of $\int_0^5 xe^{-x}\, dx$.

is crucial if `xemx` is to be used with any of the numerical integration routines described in this chapter.

Instead of using an external function such as `xemx` to define the integrand, one could use an `inline` function object. (See also, §3.6.4 on page 137.) The following statements define an inline function object and then pass it to `trapezoid` to evaluate the integral

```
>> f = inline('x.*exp(-x)')
f =
    Inline function:
    f(x) = x.*exp(-x)

>> trapezoid(f,0,5,4)
ans =
    0.8355
```

Note that when passing an inline function object to another function, no quotes are used around the name of the object. Contrast this to the statement

```
>> trapezoid('xmex',0,5,4)
ans =
    0.8355
```

which passes the external function in the file `xemx.m` to `trapezoid`.

The `demoTrap` function also shown in Listing 11.2 uses the `trapezoid` and `xemx` functions to evaluate the composite trapezoid rule approximation to $\int_0^5 xe^{-x}\,dx$ for a sequence of decreasing h values (increasing n). For each h, the approximate value of the integral and the absolute error are printed. Running `demoTrap` gives the following output:

```
>> demoTrap

Iexact =    0.959572318
```

n	h	I	error	alpha
3	2.50000	0.555143410	-0.404428908	
5	1.25000	0.835474884	-0.124097434	1.70441
9	0.62500	0.926771814	-0.032800504	1.91968
17	0.31250	0.951254724	-0.008317594	1.97948
33	0.15625	0.957485472	-0.002086846	1.99484
65	0.07812	0.959050139	-0.000522179	1.99871
129	0.03906	0.959441744	-0.000130574	1.99968
257	0.01953	0.959539673	-0.000032645	1.99992

The meaning of the `alpha` column is explained shortly. One might be tempted to conclude that the `trapezoid` function is correct, since the error decreases as n increases. A more careful test for correctness involves examining the quantitative behavior of the truncation error.

becomes

$$\int_{x_1}^{x_n} f(x)\,dx = \sum_{i=1}^{n-1} \frac{1}{2}\,(f_i + f_{i+1})\,(x_{i+1} - x_i)\,.$$

The calculations in `trapzDat` are contained in just three lines of MATLAB code:

```
dx   = diff(x);                    %  vector of x(i+1)-x(i) values
avef = f(1:n-1) + 0.5*diff(f);     %  vector of average f values
I = sum(avef.*dx);                 %  avef(1)*dx(1) + avef(2)*dx(2) + ...
```

The `avef` vector is defined with vectorized code based on the following identity:

$$\frac{1}{2}(f_i + f_{i+1}) = f_i + \frac{1}{2}(f_{i+1} - f_i).$$

Use of the `trapzDat` function is demonstrated in Example 4.3 beginning on page 163. The `testTrapzDat` function for testing `trapzDat` is developed in Example 4.4 beginning on page 170.

11.2.2 Simpson's Rule

Simpson's rule approximates $f(x)$ with a quadratic interpolating polynomial. The higher order polynomial produces a numerical integration scheme with a truncation error that is smaller than that of the trapezoid rule.

As depicted in Figure 11.8, let x_1, x_2, and x_3 be three equally spaced points on the x-axis, and let f_1, f_2, and f_3 be the values of $f(x)$ at those points. The second-order Lagrange interpolating polynomial passing through these points can

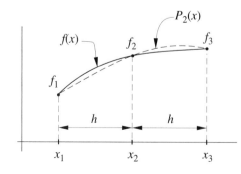

Figure 11.8 Simpson's rule applied to a panel of three nodes. The interpolating polynomial $P_2(x)$ (dashed line) will not, in general, match the true $f(x)$ (solid line).

be written as

$$P_2(x) = \frac{1}{h^2}(x - x_2)(x - x_3)f_1 + \frac{1}{h^2}(x - x_1)(x - x_3)f_2$$

$$+ \frac{1}{h^2}(x - x_1)(x - x_2)f_3, \tag{11.9}$$

where $h = (x_3 - x_1)/2$.

Using $P_2(x)$ to interpolate $f(x)$, the integral of $f(x)$ is approximately

$$I = \int_{x_1}^{x_3} f(x)\,dx \approx \int_{x_1}^{x_3} P_2(x)\,dx = h\left(\frac{1}{3}f_1 + \frac{4}{3}f_2 + \frac{1}{3}f_3\right). \tag{11.10}$$

An error analysis (see, for example, [10, 70]) shows that

$$I = h\left(\frac{1}{3}f_1 + \frac{4}{3}f_2 + \frac{1}{3}f_3\right) + Ch^5 f^{(4)}(\xi), \tag{11.11}$$

where C is a constant, $f^{(4)} = d^4 f/dx^4$ and ξ is some point in the interval $x_1 < \xi < x_3$. Note that the C in Equation (11.11) is not the same value as the C in Equation (11.6).

Composite Rule   Figure 11.9 shows an x interval of arbitrary length divided into $n - 1$ subintervals of equal size $h = (b - a)/(n - 1)$. The basic rule in Equation (11.11) requires a panel consisting of three nodes (two subintervals). The composite rule is obtained by adding together the basic rules for each panel. For this to work, there must be an even number of subintervals of width h. *Simpson's composite rule requires that $n - 1$ be an even number.* The total number of nodes n must be odd.

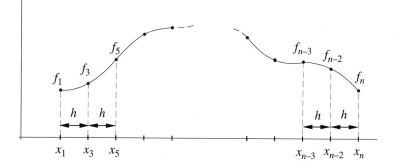

Figure 11.9 Simpson's rule applied to an interval subdivided into $(n - 1)/2$ panels by n points.

Adding together the basic rules for each panel gives

$$\int_{x_1}^{x_n} f(x)\, dx = h\left(\frac{1}{3}f_1 + \frac{4}{3}f_2 + \frac{1}{3}f_3\right) + C_1 h^5 f^{(4)}(\xi_1)$$

$$+ h\left(\frac{1}{3}f_3 + \frac{4}{3}f_4 + \frac{1}{3}f_5\right) + C_2 h^5 f^{(4)}(\xi_2)$$

$$\vdots$$

$$+ h\left(\frac{1}{3}f_{n-2} + \frac{4}{3}f_{n-1} + \frac{1}{3}f_n\right) + C_{n-1} h^5 f^{(4)}(\xi_{n-1}),$$

where $x_i < \xi_i < x_{i+1}$. Assume that $K = \max[C_i f^{(4)}(\xi_i)]$ exists, so that an upper bound on the truncation error for the composite Simpson's rule is

$$(n-1)Kh^5 = (n-1)K\left(\frac{b-a}{n-1}\right)^5 = K\frac{(b-a)^5}{(n-1)^4} = K'h^4,$$

where $K' = (b-a)K$. The composite Simpson's rule becomes

$$\int_{x_1}^{x_n} f(x)dx = \frac{h}{3}[f_1 + 4f_2 + 2f_3 + 4f_4 + 2f_5 + \cdots \qquad (11.12)$$

$$+ 2f_{n-4} + 4f_{n-3} + 2f_{n-2} + 4f_{n-1} + f_n] + \mathcal{O}(h^4).$$

Example 11.7: Manual Calculation with Simpson's Rule

The truncation error for Simpson's rule is much smaller than that of the trapezoid rule. This example verifies the expectation that for the same n, Simpson's rule will produce a more accurate estimate of an integral.

In Example 11.5 (see page 606), the value of erf(1) was estimated using the trapezoid rule with $n = 5$. Applying the composite Simpson's rule to the same data gives

$$I = \frac{2}{\sqrt{\pi}}\frac{0.25}{3}[1.0 + 4(0.9394) + 2(0.7788) + 4(0.5698) + 0.3679]$$

$$= \frac{2}{\sqrt{\pi}}(0.7469)$$

$$= 0.8428.$$

The error in the Simpson's rule approximation with $n = 5$ is 0.0001. For the same number of evaluations of $f(x)$, Simpson's rule produces a significantly more accurate result than the trapezoid rule, which gives and error of -0.0043.

Implementation of Simpson's Rule for Arbitrary $f(x)$ The simpson function in Listing 11.4 evaluates Simpson's composite rule for a user-defined inte-

```
function I = simpson(fun,a,b,npanel)
% simpson     Composite Simpson's rule
%
% Synopsis:   I = simpson(fun,a,b,npanel)
%
% Input:      fun    = (string) name of m-file that evaluates f(x)
%             a, b   = lower and upper limits of the integral
%             npanel = number of panels to use in the integration
%                      Total number of nodes = 2*npanel + 1
%
% Output:     I = approximate value of the integral from a to b of f(x)*dx

n = 2*npanel + 1;    %  total number of nodes
h = (b-a)/(n-1);     %  stepsize
x = a:h:b;           %  divide the interval
f = feval(fun,x);    %  evaluate integrand

I = (h/3)*( f(1) + 4*sum(f(2:2:n-1)) + 2*sum(f(3:2:n-2)) + f(n) );
%            f(a)          f_even             f_odd           f(b)
```

Listing 11.4   The simpson function evaluates a definite integral with Simpson's rule.

grand. The input and output parameters are identical to the trapezoid function. Note that the third input parameter to simpson is npanel, the number of panels, not n, the total number of nodes. If instead n were the input parameter, its value would have to be checked to make sure that n-1 is even, as required by Simpson's rule. Using npanel as the input parameter avoids this potential source of error and confusion.

The formula for the composite Simpson's rule is programmed by exploiting the even–odd pattern of the terms with multipliers of 4 and 2. Equation (11.12) can be written

$$ I = \frac{h}{3} \left[f_1 + 4 \sum_{i=2,4,\ldots}^{n-1} f_i + 2 \sum_{i=3,5,\ldots}^{n-2} f_i + f_n \right] $$

Assuming that the discrete $f(x)$ are stored in the vector f, the expression inside the square brackets can be evaluated with

```
f(1) + 4*sum(f(2:2:n-1)) + 2*sum(f(3:2:n-2)) + f(n)
```

where f(2:2:n-1) is a vector of terms in f with even indices, and f(3:2:n-2) is a vector of terms with odd indices.

Example 11.8: Simpson's Rule for Evaluating $\int_0^5 xe^{-x}\,dx$

This example repeats the calculations in Example 11.6 using Simpson's Rule. The demoSimp uses the simpson and xemx functions to evaluate $\int_0^5 xe^{-x}\,dx$. The demoSimp function is not listed here, because it is identical to the demoTrap function, except that the line

```
I = trapezoid('xemx',xmin,xmax,np);
```

is replaced by

```
I = simpson('xemx',xmin,xmax,np);
```

Running demoSimp gives the following results:

```
>> demoSimp

Iexact =    0.959572318
```

n	h	I	error	alpha
3	2.50000	0.712116434	-0.247455884	
5	1.25000	0.928918708	-0.030653610	3.01304
9	0.62500	0.957204124	-0.002368194	3.69420
13	0.41667	0.959084588	-0.000487730	3.89706
17	0.31250	0.959415695	-0.000156623	3.94852
65	0.07812	0.959571695	-0.000000623	3.98702
129	0.03906	0.959572279	-0.000000039	3.99870
257	0.01953	0.959572316	-0.000000002	3.99967

As expected, the errors are much smaller than those produced by the trapezoid rule. In addition, the α exponent of the truncation error approaches 4 as n is increased, in accordance with Equation (11.12).

Figure 11.10 graphically depicts Simpson's rule integration of $\int_0^5 xe^{-x}\,dx$ for $n = 7$, 9, and 11. The plot in the figure was created with the plotSimpInt function, which is included in the NMM toolbox, but not listed here.

11.2.3 Catalog of Newton–Cotes Rules

A basic rule for the approximate value of

$$I = \int_a^b f(x)\,dx$$

is obtained by substituting $f(x) \approx P_{n-1}(x)$ and evaluating the resulting integral. Using the Lagrange representation of $P_{n-1}(x)$ (see page 532):

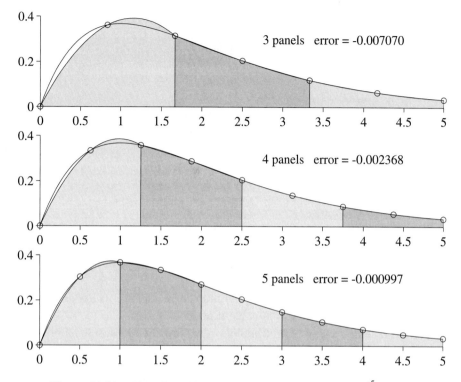

Figure 11.10   Plot of the Simpson's rule approximation to $\int_0^5 xe^{-x}\, dx$ for increasing number of points.

$$\int_a^b P_n(x)\, dx = \int_a^b [L_1(x)f_1 + L_1(x)f_1 + \cdots + L_n(x)f_n]\, dx$$

$$= \left[\int_a^b L_1(x)\, dx\right] f_1 + \left[\int_a^b L_2(x)\, dx\right] f_2 + \cdots + \left[\int_a^b L_n(x)\, dx\right] f_n$$

$$= c_1 f_1 + c_2 f_2 + \cdots + c_n f_n$$

$$= \sum_{j=1}^n c_j f_j,$$

where c_j are coefficients called the *weights* and $f_j = f(x_j)$ are the values of the integrand evaluated at the *nodes* x_j in the interval $a \le x_j \le b$. The preceding derivation shows that the weights are obtained from

$$c_j = \int_a^b L_j(x)\, dx, \tag{11.13}$$

where

$$L_j(x) = \prod_{\substack{k=1 \\ k \neq j}}^{n} \frac{x - x_k}{x_j - x_k}.$$

For large n, it is more convenient to derive the values of c_j with an equivalent procedure called the method of undetermined coefficients (see, for example, [10, 13]) than by direct evaluation of Equation (11.13).

The Newton–Cotes rule given by

$$I = \sum_{j=1}^{n} c_j f_j$$

is said to have *precision* of order n if it produces the exact value of the integral for $f(x)$ that are polynomials of degree n or less. Based on the accuracy of the underlying interpolating polynomial, it would seem that the precision of a quadrature rule through n nodes can not be greater than $n - 1$. This is the case for Newton–Cotes rules.[3] It is possible, using Gaussian quadrature (see § 11.3), to obtain precision greater than n with a quadrature rule using n nodes.

Next is presented a short list of higher order Newton–Cotes rules. For a larger catalog, see Abramowitz and Stegun [1] or Davis and Rabinowitz [13]. The discussion in the remainder of this section only concerns the basic rules that define the numerical integration formula with the minimum number of points. It is straightforward to develop composite rules for each of the basic rules presented here. The exact formulas for the truncation errors of each rule is also listed. The truncation error is of the form

$$C h^{\alpha} f^{(\beta)}(\xi),$$

where C is a constant, α is an integer referred to as the order of the scheme, β is an integer indicating the order of a derivative

$$f^{(\beta)} \equiv \frac{d^{\beta} f}{dx^{\beta}},$$

and ξ is some point in the interval $a < \xi < b$. Remember that the order of a composite rule is one less than the order of the basic rules listed below.

All Newton–Cotes rules use nodes that are equally spaced in the interval. Closed and open rules differ in whether the endpoints of the interval are included as nodes. Figure 11.11 depicts the closed three-point rule (Simpson's Rule) and the corresponding open three-point rule. A closed rule using n nodes defined on the

---

[3]A Newton–Cotes rule using n nodes is not guaranteed to have a precision of $n - 1$. Compare Simpson's rule and Simpson's 3/8 rule on page 619.

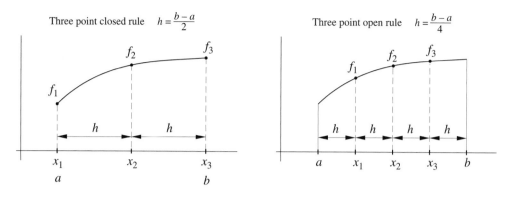

Figure 11.11   Closed and open intervals for three-point Newton–Cotes rules.

interval $[a, b]$ has $x_1 = a$ and $x_n = b$. An open rule using n nodes has $x_1 > a$ and $x_n < b$.

Rules for Closed Intervals   For each of the following formulas, the nodes are equally spaced in the interval according to

$$x_i = a + (i - 1)h.$$

The trapezoid rule is

$$\int_a^b f(x)\,dx = \frac{h}{2}(f_1 + f_2) - \frac{h^3}{12}f''(\xi), \quad h = b - a.$$

Simpson's rule is

$$\int_a^b f(x)\,dx = \frac{h}{3}(f_1 + 4f_2 + f_3) - \frac{h^5}{90}f^{(4)}(\xi), \quad h = \frac{b-a}{2}.$$

Simpson's $\frac{3}{8}$ rule is

$$\int_a^b f(x)\,dx = \frac{3h}{8}(f_1 + 3f_2 + 3f_3 + f_4) - \frac{3}{80}h^5 f^{(4)}(\xi), \quad h = \frac{b-a}{3}.$$

The six-point rule is

$$\int_a^b f(x)\,dx = \frac{5h}{288}(19f_1 + 75f_2 + 50f_3 + 50f_4 + 75f_5 + 19f_6)$$
$$- \frac{275}{12096}h^7 f^{(6)}(\xi), \quad h = \frac{b-a}{5}.$$

The nine-point rule is

$$\int_a^b f(x)\,dx = \frac{h}{14175}(3956f_1 + 23552f_2 - 3712f_3 + 41984f_4 \qquad (11.14)$$

$$-18160f_5 + 41984f_6 - 3712f_7 + 23552f_8 + 3956f_9)$$

$$-\frac{2368}{467775}h^{11}f^{(10)}(\xi),$$

$$h = \frac{b-a}{8}.$$

Note that the nine-point rule has negative weights. This can be a disadvantage, because weights of opposite sign can lead to cancellation roundoff errors for an $f(x)$ that is always positive. Other high-order Newton–Cotes rules also have negative weights.

    Rules for Open Intervals   Open rules have a slight advantage in the evaluation of integrals with mild singularities at the endpoints. Specifically, if $f(x)$ is not defined (or is infinite) at a or b *and* if $f'(x)$ is bounded at the endpoints, then an open rule may produce a good approximation, whereas a closed rule would not. The open rules are not a panacea, however. (See [13, p.71].) Press et al. [61] recommend avoiding the open rules and instead suggest that "semiopen" rules should be used only at the end panels of the interval if these rules help to avoid mild singularities.

    The three-point open rule is

$$\int_a^b f(x)\,dx = \frac{4h}{3}(2f_1 - f_2 + 2f_3) + \frac{14h^5}{45}f^{(4)}(\xi),$$

$$h = \frac{b-a}{4} \qquad x_i = a + ih.$$

Note that this rule has a negative weight, which leads to the possibility of cancellation errors in the evaluation of the integral.

11.3 GAUSSIAN QUADRATURE

The basic rule for Gaussian quadrature uses the same computational formula as Newton–Cotes rules. For n nodes,

$$I = \int_a^b f(x)\,dx \approx \sum_{j=1}^n c_j f(x_j). \qquad (11.15)$$

Gaussian quadrature optimizes the accuracy of numerical integration by choosing special combinations of nodes (x_j) and weights (c_j) in Equation (11.15). The resulting quadrature rules are optimal in the following sense. If $f(x)$ is a polynomial of degree k, then the Gaussian quadrature rule using n nodes is exact for $k \leq 2n - 1$. This is the highest possible precision for n evaluations of the integrand. The choice of the nodes and weights for Gaussian quadrature relies on the properties of orthogonal polynomials. An outline of this theory is provided in the next section. Although the theoretical development of Gaussian quadrature is more involved than the development of Newton–Cotes rules, the implementation of Gaussian quadrature is not significantly more complicated. At the end of this section, the gaussQuad function is provided for numerical integration of a user-defined $f(x)$ with Gauss–Legendre quadrature.

Before delving into the underlying theory, consider the following example, which shows that Gaussian quadrature can obtain accurate results with very few evaluations of the integrand:

Example 11.9: Demonstrate the Accuracy of Gaussian Quadrature

This example provides a "computation by recipe" for the evaluation of erf(1). The goal is not to encourage the rote use of formulas, but to provide motivation for learning why Gaussian quadrature rules can be so effective. Following this example, we reveal the theory of Gaussian quadrature.

A surprisingly accurate approximation for $\text{erf}(x) = (2/\sqrt{\pi}) \int_0^x \exp -z^2 \, dz$ can be obtained with the two-node Gaussian quadrature formula

$$I = \int_a^b f(x) \, dx \approx \frac{b-a}{2} \left(c_1 f(x_1) + c_2 f(x_2) \right),$$

where

$$x_1 = \frac{b+a}{2} - \left(\frac{b-a}{2} \right) \frac{1}{\sqrt{3}}, \quad x_2 = \frac{b+a}{2} + \left(\frac{b-a}{2} \right) \frac{1}{\sqrt{3}}, \quad c_1 = 1, \quad c_2 = 1.$$

Notice that the approximate value of the integral has the same form as the Newton–Cotes rules. What is most strikingly different is that the expressions for the location of the nodes, x_j, have rather complicated form and the weights, c_j, have rather special values. Evaluating the approximation to I to seven decimal places gives

$$x_1 = \frac{1}{2} - \left(\frac{1}{2} \right) \frac{1}{\sqrt{3}} = 0.2113249, \quad x_2 = \frac{1}{2} + \left(\frac{1}{2} \right) \frac{1}{\sqrt{3}} = 0.7886571,$$

$$f_1 = \exp(-x_1^2) = 0.9563243, \quad f_2 = \exp(-x_2^2) = 0.5368803,$$

$$\text{erf}(1) \approx \frac{2}{\sqrt{\pi}} \frac{1}{2} [(1.0)(0.9563243) + (1.0)(0.5368803)] = 0.8424504.$$

The approximation has an error of 2.5×10^{-4}, which is a factor of 100 smaller than the error produced by the trapezoid rule with 5 (not 2) function evaluations. This exceptional accuracy results from the carefully chosen nodes and weights used in the Gaussian quadrature formula.

11.3.1 Theoretical Basis

Polynomials are used as models for $f(x)$ in the development of Gaussian quadrature rules. The hope is that if the basic quadrature rule does a good job at integrating a high-order polynomial, then it is likely—though not guaranteed—to do a good job of approximating the integral of other functions. This is also true of Newton–Cotes rules, but the connection between polynomials and Gaussian quadrature is even deeper.

This section develops the rationale behind Gaussian quadrature. Although we present no formal proofs, there is a fair level of mathematical detail. The primary steps of this development are:

1. Derive a theoretical formula for the truncation error of quadrature rules based on polynomial interpolants of the integrand.

2. Show that the truncation error can be made exactly zero for integrands that are polynomials of degree m when the integrands are interpolated with polynomials of degree n. Identify the condition that enables a zero truncation error for $m > n$.

3. Summarize the properties of orthogonal polynomials that make them the best candidates for interpolating the integrand.

An Expression for the Error   It is useful to first establish an expression for the error in the numerical integration of an arbitrary function $f(x)$. Following [11, 40], begin by deriving an expression for the error in a polynomial interpolant of $f(x)$ and then integrating the interpolation error.

Let $P_{n-1}(x)$ be a polynomial of degree at most $n-1$ that interpolates $f(x)$ at n points, $x_1, \ldots, x_n$. From the definition of the Newton interpolating polynomial, Equation (10.26),

$$P_{n-1}(x) = f[x_1] + (x - x_1)f[x_1, x_2] + \cdots$$
$$+ (x - x_1)(x - x_2) \cdots (x - x_{n-1})f[x_1, x_2, \ldots, x_n].$$

Let $\hat{x}$ be any point not equal to one of the $x_1, \ldots, x_n$, and let $P_n(x)$ be the polynomial of degree n that interpolates $f(x)$ using values of f at $x_1, \ldots, x_n$ and $\hat{x}$;

$$P_n(x) = f[x_1] + (x - x_1)f[x_1, x_2] + \cdots$$
$$+ (x - x_1)(x - x_2) \cdots (x - x_n)f[x_1, x_2, \ldots, x_n, \hat{x}],$$

or, using the recursive form of Equation (10.27),

$$P_n(x) = P_{n-1}(x) + f[x_1, x_2, \ldots, x_n, \hat{x}] \prod_{j=1}^{n} (x - x_j).$$

By definition, $P_n(\hat{x}) = f(\hat{x})$, so that

$$f(\hat{x}) = P_{n-1}(\hat{x}) + f[x_1, x_2, \ldots, x_n, \hat{x}] \prod_{j=1}^{n} (\hat{x} - x_j),$$

and the error in the interpolant $P_{n-1}(x)$ at $x = \hat{x}$ is

$$e_{n-1}(\hat{x}) = f(\hat{x}) - P_{n-1}(\hat{x}) = f[x_1, x_2, \ldots, x_n, \hat{x}] \prod_{j=1}^{n} (\hat{x} - x_j). \qquad (11.16)$$

The only restriction on $\hat{x}$ is that it must not equal one of the nodes that define the interpolant. This is hardly a restriction, since, by definition of the interpolant,

$$e_{n-1}(x_j) \equiv 0 \quad \text{for any} \quad j = 1, \ldots, n.$$

Equation (11.16), therefore, gives the interpolation error for any x not in the set of nodes that define the interpolant.

The numerical integral of $f(x)$ using n nodes is obtained by integrating the $P_{n-1}(x)$ that interpolates $f(x)$:

$$\int_a^b f(x) \, dx \approx \int_a^b P_{n-1}(x) \, dx.$$

The error in numerically integrating $f(x)$ with n nodes is

$$E_n\{f\} = \int_a^b f(x) \, dx - \int_a^b P_{n-1}(x) \, dx$$

$$= \int_a^b f[x_1, x_2, \ldots, x_n, x] \prod_{j=1}^{n} (x - x_j) \, dx, \qquad (11.17)$$

where the second line is obtained by substituting Equation (11.16) for $f(x) - P_{n-1}(x)$.

Toward Maximum Precision   Recall that the *precision* of a numerical integration rule is the maximum degree of a polynomial that is integrated exactly. The precision of the trapezoid rule is one, the precision of Simpson's rule is two. Gaussian quadrature provides the maximum precision by allowing the location of the nodes as well as the values of the weights to be chosen.

For convenience, let

$$\psi(x) = (x - x_1)(x - x_2) \cdots (x - x_n),$$

so that Equation (11.17) can be written

$$E_n\{f\} = \int_a^b f[x_1, x_2, \ldots, x_n, x]\psi(x)\,dx. \tag{11.18}$$

If $f(x)$ is a polynomial of degree $k < n$, then $f[x_1, \ldots, x_n, x] = 0$. (See property 3 on page 542), so that $E_n\{f\} = 0$. This is not new information, since it defines the limit on the accuracy of Newton–Cotes schemes applied to polynomial integrands. If $f(x)$ is a polynomial of degree $k \geq n$, the error can be made zero if the nodes in the integration rule are the zeros of special $\psi(x)$. This is a critical result and is the basis for choosing the nodes in Gaussian quadrature rules. Note that $\psi(x)$ is not the polynomial used to interpolate $f(x)$ in the integration rule. A complete specification for $\psi(x)$ is yet to be determined.

To make $E_n\{f\} = 0$ for $k > n$, additional conditions must be placed on $\psi(x)$. Assume that $f(x)$ is a polynomial of degree at most $n + m$. The nth order divided difference of f then is at most a polynomial of degree m, so

$$f[x_1, \ldots, x_n, x] = \sum_{\ell=0}^m \sigma_\ell x^\ell,$$

for some coefficients σ_ℓ, the values of which are unimportant. Under these assumptions, Equation (11.18) becomes

$$E_n\{f\} = \int_a^b f[x_1, \ldots, x_n, x]\psi(x)\,dx$$

$$= \int_a^b \left[\sum_{\ell=0}^m \sigma_\ell x^\ell \right] \psi(x)\,dx$$

$$= \sigma_0 \int_a^b \psi(x)\,dx + \sigma_1 \int_a^b x\,\psi(x)\,dx + \cdots + \sigma_m \int_a^b x^m \psi(x)\,dx.$$

Regardless of values of the σ_ℓ, $E_n\{f\} = 0$ as long as

$$\int_a^b x^\ell \psi(x)\,dx = 0, \quad \text{for all } \ell = 0, 1, \ldots, m. \tag{11.19}$$

If the conditions in Equation (11.19) are met, then the approximation to the integral will be exact when $f(x)$ is a polynomial of degree $k \leq n + m$. The upper limit on k for which the numerical integral is exact is $2n - 1$.

Orthogonal Polynomials   The inner product of two scalar functions $g(x)$ and $h(x)$ is defined as

$$\langle g, h \rangle = \int_a^b w(x)g(x)h(x)\,dx, \tag{11.20}$$

where $w(x)$ is called the *weight function*. Two functions are *orthogonal* with respect to the weight function if

$$\int_a^b w(x)g(x)h(x)\,dx = 0 \qquad \text{whenever } g(x) \neq h(x). \tag{11.21}$$

For example, direct calculation shows that $g(x) = 1$ and $h(x) = x$ are orthogonal on $[a, b] = [-1, 1]$ if $w(x) = 1$ or $w(x) = (1 - x^2)^{-1/2}$. (See Exercise 17.)

For some $w(x)$, there are sequences of polynomials, $\Phi_n(x)$, that are orthogonal and that are exactly of degree n. The polynomials are orthogonal if

$$\langle \Phi_i(x), \Phi_j(x) \rangle = \int_a^b w(x)\Phi_i(x)\Phi_j(x)\,dx = 0, \qquad \text{for } i \neq j. \tag{11.22}$$

Equation (11.19) requires that the $\psi(x)$ polynomial in the error term be orthogonal for a weight function $w(x) = 1$. $E_n\{f\} = 0$, therefore, if *the nodes of the Gaussian quadrature rule are the zeros of an orthogonal polynomial*. Other properties of orthogonal polynomials guarantee that the nodes defined by the zeros of $\psi(x)$ will be useful for interpolating $f(x)$. In particular, the zeros (roots) of an orthogonal polynomial with real coefficients are real, simple, (i.e., each zero is distinct) and located on the *interior* of $[a, b]$, the interval on which they are defined. (See, for example, [70, Theorem 3.6.10].) In addition, sequences of orthogonal polynomials may be generated with a three-term recurrence relationship of the form

$$\Phi_n(x) = (\rho_n x + \tau_n)\Phi_{n-1}(x) - \zeta_n\Phi_{n-2}(x)$$

for some scalar coefficients ρ_n, τ_n, and ζ_n.

The *Legendre polynomials* are defined on the interval $[-1, 1]$ with $w(x) = 1$. The first four Legendre polynomials are

$$\Phi_0 = 1,$$

$$\Phi_1 = x,$$

$$\Phi_2 = \frac{1}{2}(3x^2 - 1),$$

$$\Phi_3 = \frac{1}{2}(5x^3 - 3x).$$

The recurrence relationship for Legendre polynomials is

$$\Phi_n(x) = \frac{2n-1}{n} x \Phi_{n-1}(x) - \frac{n-1}{n} \Phi_{n-2}(x), \qquad n \geq 2.$$

Use of Legendre polynomials in Gaussian quadrature is called Gauss–Legendre quadrature.

11.3.2 The Basic Rule for Gauss–Legendre Quadrature

The background is now in place for developing the algorithm for Gauss–Legendre quadrature. The location of the nodes are given by the roots of the Legendre polynomial of degree n. This choice of nodes guarantees that the precision of the integration rule will be $2n - 1$. Since the orthogonal property of Legendre polynomials exists only on the interval $-1 \leq x \leq 1$, the quadrature rule must be expressed as an integral with those limits. In § 11.3.5, a procedure is developed for applying the basic rule defined for $-1 \leq x \leq 1$ to integrals with arbitrary, finite limits of integration.

The Gauss–Legendre quadrature rule involving n nodes is

$$\int_{-1}^{1} f(x)\,dx \approx \int_{-1}^{1} P_{n-1}(x)\,dx = \sum_{j=1}^{n} c_j f(x_j),$$

where $P_{n-1}(x)$ interpolates $f(x)$ at the n nodes of the quadrature rule. The $P_{n-1}(x)$ cannot also be the Legendre polynomial of degree $n - 1$, because that polynomial will always be zero at the nodes—the same points that are needed to interpolate $f(x)$. The interpolating polynomial is expressed in a Lagrange basis, and the weights are obtained with the same procedure used for the Newton–Cotes rules (cf. Equation (11.13))

$$c_j = \int_{-1}^{1} L_j(x)\,dx. \tag{11.23}$$

The weights will not be equal to those from the Newton–Cotes rule of the same order, because the nodes are at the zeros of the Legendre polynomials. Example 11.11 shows the details of evaluating x_j and c_j for $n = 2$.

Given a procedure for obtaining the nodes and weights, Algorithm 11.1 performs Gauss–Legendre quadrature to approximate $I = \int_{-1}^{1} f(x)\,dx$.

Algorithm 11.1   Basic Rule for Gauss–Legendre Quadrature

specify n, the number of nodes
obtain n node locations, x_j, and weights, c_j, for $-1 \leq x \leq 1$
evaluate $f(x_j)$, $j = 1, \ldots, n$

initialize: $I = 0$
for $j = 1, \ldots, n$
  $I \leftarrow I + c_j f(x_j)$
end

Apart from the process of obtaining the values of x_j and c_j that maximize the accuracy of I, the procedure for computing I is very simple. § 11.3.4 describes a method for calculating the x_j and c_j of any order. § 11.3.5 discusses how Gauss–Legendre quadrature can be applied to integrals with arbitrary, finite limits.

Example 11.10: Manual Calculation with Gauss–Legendre Quadrature Rule

The cumulative distribution function of a normally distributed random variable with a mean of zero and a standard deviation of one is

$$F(x) = \frac{1}{\sqrt{2\pi}} \int_{-\infty}^{x} e^{-z^2/2} \, dz,$$

and the probability that a random x will occur within one standard deviation of the mean is

$$F(1) - F(-1) = \frac{1}{\sqrt{2\pi}} \int_{-1}^{1} e^{-z^2/2} \, dz.$$

Since the limits of this integral are -1 and 1, it may be evaluated by direct application of a Gauss–Legendre rule.

The nodes and weights for a five-node Gauss Legendre rule are:

j	x_j	c_j
1	-0.9061798459386640	0.2369268850561890
2	-0.5384693101056830	0.4786286704993660
3	0.0000000000000000	0.5688888888888890
4	0.5384693101056830	0.4786286704993660
5	0.9061798459386640	0.2369268850561890

Evaluating the terms in the sum gives

j	$\exp(-x_j^2/2)$	$c_j \exp(-x_j^2/2)$
1	0.6632648101210487	0.1571452654293647
2	0.8650442658532125	0.4140349868884232
3	1.0000000000000000	0.5688888888888890
4	0.8650442658532125	0.4140349868884232
5	0.6632648101210487	0.1571452654293647

$$\sum c_j \exp(-x_j^2/2) = 1.7112493935244650,$$

so that

$$F(1) - F(-1) = \frac{1.7112494}{\sqrt{2\pi}} = 0.6826897.$$

11.3.3 Table Lookup for Nodes and Weights

Values of nodes and weights for Gauss–Legendre quadrature are tabulated in several reference books. Abramowitz and Stegun [1], for example, give tables of nodes and weights for selected Gauss–Legendre rules up to order 96. Computing the nodes and weights for large n is is not a trivial task. One approach is described in § 11.3.4.

Figure 11.12 is a graphical representation of the nodes and weights for Gauss–Legendre quadrature of order two through six. From this figure, or from a table of nodes and weights, one observes the following properties:

- The weights for any order n are positive.
- The nodes are located symmetrically about $x = 0$.

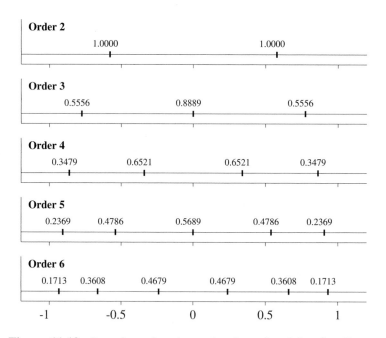

Figure 11.12 Location of nodes and value of weights for Gauss–Legendre quadrature of order two through six. For each order, the locations of the nodes are indicated by a heavy vertical tick mark. Above the tick mark for each node is the value of the corresponding weight.

- The value of the weights are equal for nodes that are equal distances from $x = 0$.

The `GLtable` function shown in Listing 11.5 provides the nodes and weights for Gauss–Legendre quadrature of order one through eight. Using `GLtable` is efficient, because (almost all) the values are created by assignment, not by computation. To use higher order rules, one could modify `GLtable` by adding the values of nodes and weights from a handbook, such as [1]. Though tedious, this approach is straightforward. Alternatively, one could use the NMM toolbox routine `makeGLtable`, which is described in the next section.

11.3.4 Computing the Nodes and Weights

In this section, we present two ways of finding the nodes and weights for Gauss–Legendre Quadrature. First, a manual procedure is described that is only suitable for low-order rules. Then, a more sophisticated method first suggested by Golub and Welch [33] is presented.

Manual Computation for Low-Order Rules   The nodes of a Gauss–Legendre quadrature rule are located at the zeros of the corresponding Legendre polynomial. Once the zeros are known, the weights can be computed by direct evaluation of Equation (11.23). Although this two-step procedure is straightforward, it does not scale well to high-order quadrature rules. The following example demonstrates the calculations for a rule of order two:

Example 11.11: Compute Gauss–Legendre Nodes and Weights of Order Two

This example demonstrates how the nodes and weights for low-order Gauss–Legendre rules may be directly computed. The nodes are the zeros of the appropriate Legendre polynomial. The Legendre polynomial of degree 2 is $\Phi_2(x) = (1/2)(3x^2 - 1)$. The zeros are the solutions to $3x^2 - 1 = 0$, viz.,

$$x_1 = -\frac{1}{\sqrt{3}}, \qquad x_2 = \frac{1}{\sqrt{3}}.$$

Here the nodes are obtained with simple algebra. See, for example, [13] for methods of finding the zeros for higher degree Legendre polynomials.

The weights are computed from Equation (11.23), where L_j are the Lagrange interpolating polynomials of degree $n - 1$. For $n = 2$,

$$L_1 = \frac{x - x_2}{x_1 - x_2}, \qquad L_2 = \frac{x - x_1}{x_2 - x_1}.$$

Given x_1 and x_2 as just defined, we get

$$L_1 = \frac{x - 1/\sqrt{3}}{-2/\sqrt{3}} = -\frac{\sqrt{3}}{2}\left(x - \frac{1}{\sqrt{3}}\right), \qquad L_2 = \frac{x + 1/\sqrt{3}}{2/\sqrt{3}} = \frac{\sqrt{3}}{2}\left(x + \frac{1}{\sqrt{3}}\right),$$

```
function [x,w] = GLTable(n)
% GLTable  Nodes and weights for Gauss-Legendre quadrature of order n<=8
%
% Synopsis:  [x,w] = GLTable(n)
%
% Input:     n = number of nodes in quadrature rule, maximum: n = 8
%
% Output:    x = vector of nodes
%            w = vector of weights

% Numerical values from "Handbook of Mathematical Functions",
% Abramowitz and Stegun, eds., 1965 Dover (reprint), Table 25.4, p. 916

nn = fix(n);                 %  Make sure number of nodes is an integer
x = zeros(nn,1);  w = x;     %  Preallocate x and w vectors

switch nn
  case 1
    x = 0;   w = 2;

  case 2
    x(1) = -1/sqrt(3);     x(2) = -x(1);
    w(1) =  1;             w(2) =  w(1);

  case 3
    x(1) = -sqrt(3/5);     x(2) =  0;      x(3) = -x(1);
    w(1) =  5/9;           w(2) =  8/9;    w(3) =  w(1);

  case 4
    x(1) = -0.861136311594053;     x(4) = -x(1);
    x(2) = -0.339981043584856;     x(3) = -x(2);
    w(1) =  0.347854845137454;     w(4) =  w(1);
    w(2) =  0.652145154862546;     w(3) =  w(2);

  case 5
    x(1) = -0.906179845938664;     x(5) = -x(1);
    x(2) = -0.538469310105683;     x(4) = -x(2);
    x(3) =  0;
    w(1) =  0.236926885056189;     w(5) =  w(1);
    w(2) =  0.47862867049366;      w(4) =  w(2);
    w(3) =  0.568888888888889;
```

Listing 11.5   The GLtable function returns the nodes and weights for
Gauss–Legendre quadrature of order less than or equal to eight.

```
case 6
  x(1) = -0.932469514203152;    x(6) = -x(1);
  x(2) = -0.661209386466265;    x(5) = -x(2);
  x(3) = -0.238619186083197;    x(4) = -x(3);
  w(1) =  0.171324492379170;    w(6) =  w(1);
  w(2) =  0.360761573048139;    w(5) =  w(2);
  w(3) =  0.467913934572691;    w(4) =  w(3);

case 7
  x(1) = -0.949107912342759;    x(7) = -x(1);
  x(2) = -0.741531185599394;    x(6) = -x(2);
  x(3) = -0.405845151377397;    x(5) = -x(3);
  x(4) =  0;
  w(1) =  0.129484966168870;    w(7) =  w(1);
  w(2) =  0.279705391489277;    w(6) =  w(2);
  w(3) =  0.381830050505119;    w(5) =  w(3);
  w(4) =  0.417959183673469;

case 8
  x(1) = -0.960289856497536;    x(8) = -x(1);
  x(2) = -0.796666477413627;    x(7) = -x(2);
  x(3) = -0.525532409916329;    x(6) = -x(3);
  x(4) = -0.183434642495650;    x(5) = -x(4);
  w(1) =  0.101228536290376;    w(8) =  w(1);
  w(2) =  0.222381034453374;    w(7) =  w(2);
  w(3) =  0.313706645877887;    w(6) =  w(3);
  w(4) =  0.362683783378362;    w(5) =  w(4);

otherwise
  error(sprintf('Gauss quadrature with %d nodes not supported',nn));

end
```

Listing 11.5   (*Continued*)

and

$$c_1 = \int_{-1}^{1} L_1 \, dx = -\frac{\sqrt{3}}{2} \int_{-1}^{1} \left(x - \frac{1}{\sqrt{3}} \right) dx = -\frac{\sqrt{3}}{2} \left(\frac{x^2}{2} - \frac{x}{\sqrt{3}} \right)_{x=-1}^{x=1} = 1,$$

$$c_2 = \int_{-1}^{1} L_2 \, dx = \frac{\sqrt{3}}{2} \int_{-1}^{1} \left(x + \frac{1}{\sqrt{3}} \right) dx = \frac{\sqrt{3}}{2} \left(\frac{x^2}{2} + \frac{x}{\sqrt{3}} \right)_{x=-1}^{x=1} = 1.$$

Automatic Computation for High-order Rules   We now describe a method for obtaining the Gauss–Legendre nodes and weights of any order. The computation involves solving a numerical eigenvalue problem, which requires attention to numerical details, as well as concern for computational efficiency. The curious reader should refer to Appendix A for an introduction to the algebraic eigenvalue problem. We will rely on the built-in `eig` function to compute the eigenvalues. The `eig` function is efficient and reliable, making the approach described next suitable for routine work. The procedure for computing the nodes and weights originated with Golub and Welsch [33] and was refined by Gautschi [26]. The presentation here is an abridged version of that provided by Schwarz [64].

The zeros (roots) of the degree-n Legendre polynomial $\Phi_n(x)$ are the eigenvalues of the symmetric, tridiagonal matrix

$$
J =
\begin{bmatrix}
0 & \beta_1 & & & & \\
\beta_1 & 0 & \beta_2 & & & \\
& \beta_2 & 0 & \beta_3 & & \\
& & \ddots & \ddots & \ddots & \\
& & & \beta_{n-2} & 0 & \beta_{n-1} \\
& & & & \beta_{n-1} & 0
\end{bmatrix},
\tag{11.24}
$$

where

$$
\beta_k = \frac{k}{\sqrt{4k^2 - 1}} \qquad k = 1, 2, \ldots, n - 1.
$$

Given the $n \times n$ matrix J, the eigenvalue problem is to find eigenvalue λ and the corresponding eigenvector v such that

$$
Jv = \lambda v.
$$

An $n \times n$ matrix will have at most n eigenvalue–eigenvector pairs. The eigenvalues of J in Equation (11.24) are real, distinct, and come in pairs of values with opposite sign. The eigenvectors of J are orthonormal. Since the nodes of the Gauss–Legendre rule of order n are the zeros of the Legendre polynomial of degree n, obtaining the eigenvalues of J_n gives the nodes. The corresponding weights are given by

$$
c_k = 2(v_1^{(k)})^2, \qquad k = 1, 2, \ldots, n,
\tag{11.25}
$$

where $v^{(k)}$ is the normalized ($\|v\|_2 = 1$) eigenvector corresponding to λ_k and $v_1^{(k)}$ is the first element of that normalized eigenvector.

The MATLAB statements that follow compute the nodes and weights of the Gauss–Legendre quadrature rule of order four. First, construct the J matrix:

```
>> n = 4;
>> beta = (1:n-1)./sqrt(4*(1:n-1).^2 - 1)
beta =
    0.5774    0.5164    0.5071
```

```
>> J = diag(beta,-1) + diag(beta,1)
J =
         0    0.5774         0         0
    0.5774         0    0.5164         0
         0    0.5164         0    0.5071
         0         0    0.5071         0
```

The two-parameter form the `eig` function, `[V,D] = eig(A)` returns the eigenvectors as columns of the matrix V, and the eigenvalues as the diagonal entries of the diagonal matrix D:

```
>> [V,D] = eig(J)
V =
    0.5710   -0.4170   -0.5710   -0.4170
    0.3363   -0.6220    0.3363    0.6220
   -0.4170   -0.5710    0.4170   -0.5710
   -0.6220   -0.3363   -0.6220    0.3363
D =
    0.3400         0         0         0
         0    0.8611         0         0
         0         0   -0.3400         0
         0         0         0   -0.8611
```

The nodes are the diagonal entries in D:

```
>> x = diag(D)
x =
    0.3400
    0.8611
   -0.3400
   -0.8611
```

For use with Gauss–Legendre quadrature rules, the nodes need to be stored in increasing order. This is easily arranged with the built-in `sort` function. The two-parameter form of `sort` is needed, because any rearrangement of D needs to be applied to V in order to maintain the relationship between the eigenvalues and their eigenvectors.[4] In the following lines of code, the elements of x are stored in increasing order, and the sort order is stored in a vector `ix`, which is then used to reorder V by columns:

```
>> [x,ix] = sort(diag(D)); % sort order is saved in the ix vector
>> V(:,1:n) = V(:,ix)       % shuffle columns of V according to ix
```

---

[4]The kth eigenvalue is stored in (D(k,k)), and its corresponding eigenvector is in $V(:,k)$.

```
V =
   -0.4170   -0.5710    0.5710   -0.4170
    0.6220    0.3363    0.3363   -0.6220
   -0.5710    0.4170   -0.4170   -0.5710
    0.3363   -0.6220   -0.6220   -0.3363
```

The weights are obtained by squaring and multiplying by two the first element of each normalized eigenvector. (Cf. Equation (11.25).) These elements are found in the first row of V:

```
>> V(1,:)
ans =
    0.5710   -0.4170   -0.5710   -0.4170
```

MATLAB automatically normalizes the eigenvectors:

```
>> norm(V(:,1))
ans =
    1.0000

>> norm(V(:,2))
ans =
    1.0000
```

Thus, it is unnecessary to do so before computing the weights:

```
>> w = 2*V(1,:).^2
w =
    0.3479    0.6521    0.6521    0.3479
```

The preceding sequence of statements are the basis of the GLNodeWt function in Listing 11.6. The MATLAB code is adapted from the gaussint code of Wilson and Turcotte [79, § 5.2]. Although the computational work performed by GLNodeWt grows rapidly with the order of the quadrature rule, the execution time is negligible for a single invocation of GLNodeWt. If it is desired, one could use GLNodeWt to generate values for nodes and weights that could be copied into GLtable. The makeGLtable function in the NMM toolbox is provided to automate this process.

11.3.5 Composite Rule for Gauss–Legendre Quadrature

As with the Newton–Cotes rules, Gaussian Quadrature can be applied to a large interval that is divided into several panels. There are important differences implementation, however, owing to the need to locate the nonuniformly spaced integration nodes within each panel.

```
function [x,w] = GLNodeWt(n)
% GLNodeWt  Nodes and weights for Gauss-Legendre quadrature of arbitrary order
%           obtained by solving an eigenvalue problem
%
% Synopsis:  [x,w] = GLNodeWt(n)
%
% Input:     n = order of quadrature rule
%
% Output:    x = vector of nodes
%            w = vector of weights


%  Algorithm based on ideas from Golub and Welsch, and Gautschi.  For a
%  condensed presentation see H.R. Schwarz, "Numerical Analysis: A
%  Comprehensive Introduction", 1989, Wiley.  Original MATLAB
%  implementation by H.W. Wilson and L.H. Turcotte, "Advanced Mathematics
%  and Mechanics Applications Using MATLAB", 2nd ed., 1998, CRC Press

beta   = (1:n-1)./sqrt(4*(1:n-1).^2 - 1);
J      = diag(beta,-1) + diag(beta,1);   % eig(J) needs J in full storage
[V,D]  = eig(J);
[x,ix] = sort(diag(D));  % nodes are eigenvalues, which are on diagonal of D
w      = 2*V(1,ix)'.^2;  % V(1,ix)' is column vector of first row of sorted V
```

Listing 11.6   The GLNodeWt function computes the nodes and weights for Gauss–Legendre quadrature of any order.

To obtain a numerical approximation to

$$I = \int_a^b f(x)\,dx, \tag{11.26}$$

divide the interval $[a, b]$ into N panels of equal size $H = (b - a)/N$. In this section, N is used to denote the number of panels, and n is retained as the number of nodes in each panel. The panel width is H and should not be confused with h, the spacing between nodes used in Newton–Cotes rules. The use of equal-sized panels is a convenience, not an absolute requirement. The starting point of each panel is

$$x_i = a + (i - 1)H, \qquad i = 1, \dots, N.$$

A Gauss–Legendre quadrature rule is applied to each panel to approximate

$$I_i = \int_{x_i}^{x_{i+1}} f(x)\,dx. \tag{11.27}$$

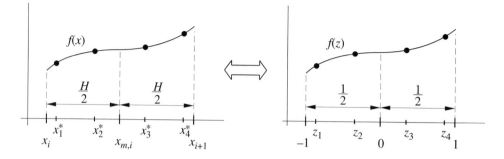

Figure 11.13   Transformation of an arbitrary panel $x_i \leq x \leq x_{i+1}$ to one with $-1 \leq z \leq 1$ suitable for Gauss–Legendre quadrature. The four node quadrature rule is depicted here.

The value of the integral in Equation (11.26) is obtained by adding together the contributions from each panel:

$$I = \sum_{i=1}^{N} I_i. \tag{11.28}$$

To apply a Gauss–Legendre quadrature rule, the limits of the integral in Equation (11.27) must be transformed from $[x_i, x_{i+1}]$ to $[-1, 1]$. This is achieved with the following change of variables:

$$z = \frac{x - x_{m,i}}{H/2}, \qquad x_{m,i} = \frac{1}{2}(x_i + x_{i+1}), \tag{11.29}$$

as depicted in Figure 11.13. The variable of integration must also be changed with the limits. Since

$$x = x_{m,i} + \frac{zH}{2} \quad \Longrightarrow \quad dx = \frac{H}{2}\,dz,$$

Equation (11.27) becomes

$$I_i = \int_{-1}^{1} f(x)\,\frac{H}{2}\,dz = \frac{H}{2}\int_{-1}^{1} f\left(x_{m,i} + \frac{zh}{2}\right)\,dz. \tag{11.30}$$

Equations (11.27) through (11.30) apply to a quadrature rule with any number of nodes. The algorithm for Gauss–Legendre quadrature on the interval $[a, b]$ is:

Algorithm 11.2   Composite Rule for Gauss–Legendre Quadrature

input: $f(x), a, b, N, n$

$H = (b - a)/N$
compute (or look-up) z_j, and w_j, for $-1 \leq z \leq 1$
$I = 0$
for $i = 1, \ldots, N$ (loop over panels)
  $I_i = 0$
  for $j = 1, \ldots, n$ (loop over nodes)
   $x_j^* = x_{m,i} + z_j\,H/2$
   $I_i \leftarrow I_i + c_j f(x_j^*)$
  end
  $I \leftarrow I + I_i$
end

The symbol x_j^* refers to the x location of the jth node in the current panel. The superscript * is used to avoid confusion with x_i, the location of the starting edge of the ith panel. Refer to Figure 11.13 for a graphical representation of the x_i and x_j^* locations.

The truncation error for the composite Gauss–Legendre composite rule using n nodes on panels of size H is [11, 40, 70]

$$E_{n,H}\{f\} = \frac{1}{2}C_n \left(\frac{H}{2}\right)^{2n} f^{(2n)}(\xi) = \mathcal{O}\left(H^{2n}\right), \qquad (11.31)$$

where C_n is a factor depending on n only, $f^{(2n)}$ is shorthand for $d^{(2n)} f/dx^{(2n)}$, and ξ is some point in (a, b).

Example 11.12: Gauss–Legendre Quadrature for Evaluation of erf(x).

This example demonstrates the computations involved in applying the composite rule for Gauss–Legendre quadrature to the evaluation of

$$\mathrm{erf}(1) = \frac{2}{\sqrt{\pi}} \int_0^1 e^{-x^2}\, dx.$$

For convenience, let

$$I = \int_0^1 e^{-x^2}\, dx,$$

so that

$$\mathrm{erf}(1) = 2I/\sqrt{\pi}.$$

Now, we compute the numerical value of I with the Gauss–Legendre quadrature rule of order two, for one panel, $H = 1$, and two panels, $H = 1/2$. From a table of nodes and weights, or from Example 11.11, the nodes and weights for the Gauss–Legendre quadrature

```
function I = gaussQuad(fun,a,b,npanel,nnode,varargin)
% gaussQuad  Composite Gauss-Legendre quadrature
%
% Synopsis:  I = gaussQuad(fun,a,b,npanel)
%            I = gaussQuad(fun,a,b,npanel,nnode)
%            I = gaussQuad(fun,a,b,npanel,nnode,arg1,arg2,...)
%
% Input:  fun    = (string) name of m-file that evaluates f(x)
%         a,b    = lower and upper limits of the integral
%         npanel = number of panels in interval [a,b]
%         nnode  = (optional) number of nodes on each subinterval
%                  Default:  nnodes=4
%         arg1,arg2,... = (optional) parameters passed through to fun
%
% Output: I = approximate value of the integral from a to b of f(x)*dx

if nargin<5,  nnode = 4;  end

if nnode<=8
  [z,wt] = GLTable(nnode);          %  Look up nodes and weights,
else                                %  or if n is too big for the table,
  [z,wt] = GLNodeWt(nnode);         %  compute the nodes and weights
end
H = (b-a)/npanel;                   %  Size of each panel
H2 = H/2;                           %  Avoids repeated computation of H/2
x = a:H:b;                          %  Divide the interval

I = 0;                              %  Initialize sum
for i=1:npanel
  xstar = 0.5*(x(i)+x(i+1)) + H2*z; %  Evaluate 'fun' at these points
  f = feval(fun,xstar,varargin{:});
  I = I + sum(wt.*f);               %  Add contribution of this subinterval
end
I = I*H2;                           %  Factor of H/2 for each subinterval
```

Listing 11.7 The gaussQuad function implements composite Gauss–Legendre quadrature for an arbitrary integrand and range of integration.

```
function demoGauss(np,nn)
% demoGauss  Use Gauss-Legendre quadrature to integrate x*exp(-x) on [0,5]
%
% Synopsis:  demoGauss
%            demoGauss(np)
%            demoGauss(np,nn)
%
% Input:   np = (optional) panels used in node refinement test.  Default: np=1
%          nn = (optional) nodes used in panel refinement test.  Default: nn=3
%
% Output:  Tables integral values obtained with Gauss-Legendre quadrature
%          as function of increasing nodes and increasing number of panels

if nargin<1;  np = 1;  end
if nargin<2;  nn = 3;  end
a = 0;  b = 5;  Iexact = -exp(-b)*(1+b) + exp(-a)*(1+a);

% --- Truncation error as function of number of nodes
H = (b-a)/np;
fprintf('\nGauss-Legendre quadrature with %d panels, H = %f\n',np,H);
fprintf('\n nodes        I              error\n');
for n = 1:8
  I = gaussQuad('xemx',a,b,np,n);
  fprintf('%4d  %14.10f %12.2e\n',n,I,I - Iexact)
end

% --- Truncation error as function of panel size
fprintf('\nGauss-Legendre quadrature with %d nodes\n',nn);
fprintf('\n panels    H              I              error       alpha\n');
k = 1;    % alpha is computed only if k>1
for npanel = 1:8
  I = gaussQuad('xemx',a,b,npanel,nn);
  err = I - Iexact;
  H = (b-a)/npanel;                % Compute H for output only
  fprintf(' %4d %10.5f %14.10f %12.2e',npanel,H,I,err);

  if k>1,  fprintf('  %8.2f\n',log(err/errold)/log(H/HHold));
  else,    fprintf('\n');  end
  HHold = H;  errold = err;  k = k + 1; % prep for next stepsize
end
```

Listing 11.8 The demoGauss function shows how the truncation error Gauss–Legendre quadrature decreases with the number of panels and the number of nodes per panel.

Running demoGauss with the default arguments gives

```
>> demoGauss

Gauss-Legendre quadrature with 1 panels, H = 5.000000

  nodes       I           error
    1    1.0260624828    6.65e-02
    2    1.1093615949    1.50e-01
    3    0.9744587198    1.49e-02
    4    0.9601822632    6.10e-04
    5    0.9595862620    1.39e-05
    6    0.9595725226    2.05e-07
    7    0.9595723201    2.10e-09
    8    0.9595723180    1.58e-11

Gauss--Legendre quadrature with 3 nodes

  panels     H          I          error      alpha
    1     5.00000   0.9744587198   1.49e-02
    2     2.50000   0.9600305785   4.58e-04     5.02
    3     1.66667   0.9596190800   4.68e-05     5.63
    4     1.25000   0.9595811126   8.79e-06     5.81
    5     1.00000   0.9595746842   2.37e-06     5.88
    6     0.83333   0.9595731218   8.04e-07     5.92
    7     0.71429   0.9595726395   3.22e-07     5.94
    8     0.62500   0.9595724631   1.45e-07     5.96
```

The second test gives $\alpha \simeq 6$, which is consistent with the truncation error estimate of Equation (11.31) for $n = 3$. In general, the truncation errors are much smaller than those produced by the trapezoid rule or simpson's rule for the same number of function evaluations. A quantitative comparison of these methods is performed in the next example.

Example 11.14: Compare Computational Efficiency of Integration Rules

In this example, the truncation error formulas for the composite trapezoid, Simpson, and Gauss–Legendre rules are used to estimate the relative computational efficiency of these integration methods. Let n_f be the number of evaluations of the integrand, and let N be the number of panels used in a composite integration rule. For each of the three methods, the size of the panel used in the composite rule is

$$H = \frac{b - a}{N}.$$

The number of nodes per panel (n_f) for the trapezoid rule, Simpson's rule, and Gauss–Legendre rules is $n_f = N + 1$, $n_f = 2N + 1$, and $n_f = Nn$, respectively.

The truncation error of the trapezoid rule is $\mathcal{O}(h^2)$, where $h = H$ is the spacing between the nodes. For Simpson's rule, $h = H/2$. Substituting $H = (b - a)/N$ and

$N = n_f - 1$ and retaining only the highest order terms the truncation error of the trapezoid rule becomes $\mathcal{O}(n_f^{-2})$. Making similar manipulations for the other integration methods gives the following results:

Method	Truncation Error dependency on h	dependency on n_f
Trapezoid	$\mathcal{O}(h^2)$	$\mathcal{O}(n_f^{-2})$
Simpson's	$\mathcal{O}(h^4)$	$\mathcal{O}(n_f^{-4})$
Gauss–Legendre	$\mathcal{O}(H^{2n})$	$\mathcal{O}(n_f^{-2n})$

These expressions are sufficient to show that for $n > 2$, the Gauss–Legendre rule is the most computationally efficient and that the Gauss–Legendre rules become even more efficient as n is increased. One might conclude from this that it makes more sense to increase the order of the Gauss–Legendre rule instead of the number of panels used in an interval. However, this is not always true, since the expressions in the preceding table do not include the $f^{(2n)}(\xi)$ term in Equation (11.31). It is usually a good idea to subdivide the integration interval into at least a few panels and then increase the order of the quadrature rule.

A quantitative comparison of computational efficiency can be made by measuring the truncation error as a function of n_f for a known integral. The compIntRules function (available in the NMM toolbox, but not listed here) computes the truncation error produced by the trapezoid, Simpson's and four-node Gauss–Legendre rules in the evaluation of $\int_0^5 xe^{-x}\, dx$. Running compIntRules gives

```
>> compIntRules

Truncation error versus number of function evaluations
```

Trapezoid		Simpson		GL 4 node	
nf	error	nf	error	nf	error
2	-8.75e-01	3	-2.47e-01	2	1.50e-01
4	-2.09e-01	5	-7.07e-03	4	6.10e-04
8	-4.26e-02	9	-2.66e-04	8	4.59e-06
16	-9.46e-03	17	-1.28e-05	16	2.18e-08
32	-2.22e-03	33	-7.07e-07	32	8.99e-11
64	-5.39e-04	65	-4.15e-08	64	3.56e-13
128	-1.33e-04	129	-2.51e-09	128	1.22e-15
256	-3.29e-05	257	-1.55e-10	256	0.00e+00

The two columns under each method are the number of function evaluations and the truncation error, respectively. The same information is plotted in Figure 11.14. The tabulated results and the plot in Figure 11.14 confirm the comparison of theoretical truncation error estimates for these three schemes. The four-node Gauss–Legendre rule is significantly more efficient than the trapezoid rule or Simpson's rule. For the same cost—the same

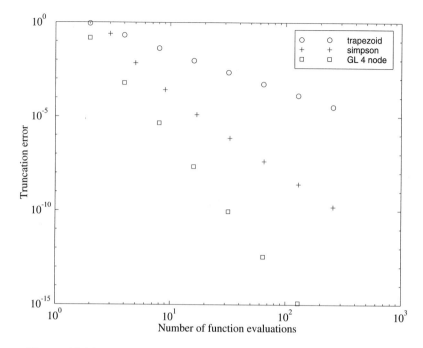

Figure 11.14 Truncation error as a function of the number of function evaluations in computing $\int_0^5 xe^{-x}\,dx$ with the trapezoid rule, Simpson's rule, and fourth-order Gauss–Legendre quadrature.

number of evaluations of the integrand—the four-node Gauss–Legendre rule obtains an estimate of the value of the integral with much smaller truncation error. In addition, the four-node Gauss–Legendre rule has a far greater rate of reduction of the truncation error as the number of evaluations of the integrand increases.

If the preceding computations were repeated for Gauss–Legendre rules using two and eight nodes, how would the plot in Figure 11.14 change? (See Exercise 20.)

11.4 ADAPTIVE QUADRATURE

Adaptive quadrature attempts to both automate and optimize the numerical evaluation of an integral. Automation results in relieving the user of the need to specify the size (or number) of panels into which the limits of integration are subdivided. Starting with an initial distribution of panels, the adaptive quadrature algorithm increases the number of panels where an estimation of the truncation error for the integral exceeds a user prescribed tolerance. The optimization occurs when the panels are allowed to vary in size over the interval defined by the limits of the integral. In this way, small panels, which require more evaluations of the integrand, are used only where needed.

If all goes well, the result of the adaptive quadrature is a value for the integral to within a user-specified tolerance. Furthermore the numerical result is obtained in a shorter execution time than if the entire domain were subdivided into uniformly small panels. Adaptive schemes should not be considered completely automatic. Although the use of a tolerance eliminates the need to specify the number of panels, users should be sure that the tolerance is suitable for the problem at hand. Confirming the value of the integral by repeating the computation with smaller (and perhaps larger) tolerances is a good idea. With reasonable effort, adaptive methods do offer a useful tool in dealing with numerical integration problems.

The adaptive schemes developed in this section use local refinement of panel size. An alternative approach to adaptive quadrature is based on a systematic, *uniform* refinement of the panel size. A popular method using uniform refinement is Romberg integration. Romberg integration can be effective for smooth integrands (i.e., where there is no strong advantage to refining the panel size in a limited number of subranges of the limits of integration). See [10, 64, 70] for development of the theory of Romberg integration. Press et al. [61] give C programs for Romberg integration. Mathews and Fink [53] and Fausett [22] provide MATLAB implementations.

QUADPACK [59] is a Fortran library of adaptive quadrature methods. The adaptive methods in QUADPACK are more sophisticated than the routines presented here, including the built-in quad and quad8 functions. A significant advantage of (most of) the QUADPACK routines is that they perform refinement based on *global adaptation* of the subintervals in which the basic rules are applied. The adaptive schemes presented later use only *local adaptation*.

A locally adaptive scheme successively refines a given subinterval until either the contribution to the integral on the finest refinement of the subinterval meets a tolerance or until a recursion limit is reached. For some integrands, for which the value of the integral over a subinterval approaches zero, local refinement can cause the recursion limit to be reached, even if the numerical value of the integral is accurate. The local adaption scheme has no way of knowing that the true value of the integral is approaching zero on the local subinterval being refined. In this situation, the local error will make a negligible contribution to the global error.

A globally adaptive scheme monitors an error estimate for the entire integral by summing the error estimates for all of the subintervals. The program logic for a global scheme is more complex. The advantage is that the computational effort is directed towards ranges of x that contribute to the global error. In this way, a globally adaptive scheme avoids being confounded by a local subinterval having a negligible contribution to the global integral.

11.4.1 Adaptive Integration Based on Simpson's Rule

In this section, an adaptive numerical integration routine is developed based on Simpson's rule. The resulting m-file function is similar to the built-in quad function.[5] The theory of the method and the logic of the program are based on the presentation of Cheney and Kincaid [10]. A similar development is given by Conte and de Boor [11].

The Adaptive Algorithm   The numerical approximation to the integral

$$I = \int_a^b f(x)\, dx \qquad (11.32)$$

is computed by applying Simpson's basic rule over subintervals. Each subinterval is then independently refined by further subdivision. Figure 11.15 shows a sequence of four levels of refinement for the adaptive Simpson's rule. The computations begin with an application of Simpson's rule on level 1. The midpoint $c = (a+b)/2$ of the interval for level 1 is computed, and Simpson's rule is applied to each of the *half-sized* intervals, $[a, c]$ and $[c, b]$. The truncation error for the interval of size $H = b - a$ is compared with the sum of the truncation errors for the two intervals

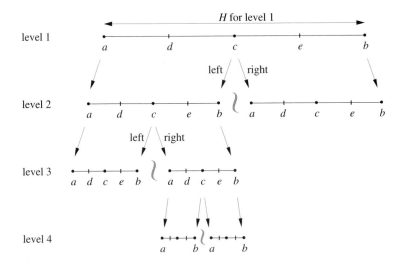

Figure 11.15 Four levels of refinement for the adaptive Simpson quadrature algorithm.

[5]MATLAB version 6 uses a more sophisticated algorithm for quad although its core integration scheme is still Simpson's rule.

of size $H/2$. If the difference is greater than a user-prescribed tolerance, the two half-sized intervals are each taken as starting points for another level of refinement.

In Figure 11.15 the refinement step is depicted by the left and right arrows from level 1 to level 2. At level 2, point b on the left segment is the same x value as point a on the right segment. Once the refinement is initiated, the left and right segments are processed separately, so we can reuse the a, b, c, d, and e symbols.

The decision of whether or not to refine an interval hinges on an estimate of the truncation error. Simpson's basic rule is

$$I = \int_a^b f(x)\,dx = \frac{h}{3}(f(a) + 4f(c) + f(b)) - \frac{h^5}{90}f^{(4)}(\xi), \qquad h = \frac{b-a}{2}.$$

$$(11.33)$$

The point ξ, where $a < \xi < b$, is unknown, but it is a constant as long as a and b are fixed. Note that $h = H/2$ is the spacing between the three nodes that define Simpson's rule and that $H = b - a$ is the width of the panel over which Simpson's basic rule is applied.

Equation (11.33) can be rewritten as

$$I_1 = S_1(h) + E_1(h), \tag{11.34}$$

where the subscript 1 indicates that this is the value of the integral for level 1. S_1 is the numerical approximation of the integral on level 1

$$S_1(h) = \frac{h}{3}(f(a) + 4f(c) + f(b)), \tag{11.35}$$

and E_1 is the truncation error corresponding to S_1:

$$E_1(h) = -\frac{h^5}{90}f^{(4)}(\xi). \tag{11.36}$$

Equation (11.34) is exact because the truncation error is included.

The integral in Equation (11.32) may also be evaluated (exactly) as the sum of two integrals at level 2 of the algorithm

$$I_2 = I_\ell + I_r = \int_a^c f(x)\,dx + \int_c^b f(x)\,dx, \tag{11.37}$$

where the subscripts ℓ and r refer to the left and right subintervals, respectively. Applying Simpson's rule to the two half-sized intervals gives

$$I_\ell = \int_a^c f(x)\,dx = S_\ell(h/2) + E_\ell(h/2)$$

and

$$I_r = \int_c^b f(x)\,dx = S_r(h/2) + E_r(h/2),$$

where

$$S_\ell(h/2) = \frac{h}{6}(f(a) + 4f(d) + f(c)), \qquad E_\ell(h/2) = -\frac{(h/2)^5}{90} f^{(4)}(\xi_\ell),$$

$$S_r(h/2) = \frac{h}{6}(f(c) + 4f(e) + f(b)), \qquad E_r(h/2) = -\frac{(h/2)^5}{90} f^{(4)}(\xi_r).$$

Notice that the derivatives in the truncation error terms are evaluated at points in their respective intervals: $a < \xi_\ell < c$ and $c < \xi_r < b$.

Define S_2 and E_2 as the values of the numerical integral and its truncation error at level 2:

$$S_2 = S_\ell(h/2) + S_r(h/2) \quad \text{and} \quad E_2 = E_\ell(h/2) + E_r(h/2).$$

So, Equation (11.37) can be rewritten as

$$I_2 = S_2 + E_2. \tag{11.38}$$

I_1 and I_2 are exactly equal, but, in general, $S_1 \neq S_2$ because the truncation errors on level 1 and level 2 are not the same. S_1 and S_2 are evaluated numerically, but E_1 and E_2 can only be estimated because, in general, ξ, ξ_ℓ, and ξ_r are not known. The adaptive scheme continues refinement until $|S_1 - S_2|$ is less than a user-prescribed tolerance. To develop this convergence test we obtain an estimate of the relative magnitudes of E_1 and E_2.

The truncation errors on the two levels are

$$E_1 = -\frac{h^5}{90} f^{(4)}(\xi) \quad \text{and} \quad E_2 = -\frac{(h/2)^5}{90} f^{(4)}(\xi_\ell) - \frac{(h/2)^5}{90} f^{(4)}(\xi_r).$$

Assuming that

$$f^{(4)}(\xi) = f^{(4)}(\xi_\ell) = f^{(4)}(\xi_r) = C, \tag{11.39}$$

where C is an unknown constant, we get

$$E_2 \approx -\frac{2}{2^5} \frac{h^5}{90} C = -\frac{1}{16} \frac{h^5}{90} C = \frac{E_1}{16}. \tag{11.40}$$

This is an estimate of how much improvement can be expected if the integral is evaluated at level 2 instead of level 1.

Equation (11.40) can also be used to estimate how close the numerical integral is to the true value of the integral. Set the right-hand side of Equation (11.34) equal to the right-hand side of Equation (11.38) and rearrange terms to get

$$S_1 - S_2 = E_2 - E_1.$$

Introduce the approximation of Equation (11.40) and solve for E_2:

$$E_2 = \frac{1}{15}(S_1 - S_2).$$

Substituting this result into Equation (11.38) and rearranging terms yields

$$I_2 - S_2 = \frac{1}{15}(S_1 - S_2). \tag{11.41}$$

This equation is an estimate of the error in the integral under the assumption that $f^{(4)}(x) = C$ in $[a, b]$. In practice, the user supplies an absolute tolerance δ on the acceptable error in the integral. Then, if

$$\frac{1}{15}|S_1 - S_2| < \delta, \tag{11.42}$$

the value of S_1 can be accepted as the value of the local contribution to the integral. If not, the refinement is recursively applied to level 2. (That is, each subinterval of level 2 is treated in the same way as the original interval in level 1.)

The preceding manipulations may be applied to an arbitrary number of re-finement levels. The key ingredients are a formula for evaluating the integral over a subinterval—Equation (11.35)—and a formula for estimating the error in the value of the integral—Equation (11.41).

A recursive, two-level version of the adaptive quadrature algorithm to evalu-ate Equation (11.32) is:

Algorithm 11.3   Two-level Adaptive Simpson's Rule Quadrature

$I = \text{adaptSimp}(f, a, b, \delta)$

input: f, a, b, δ (f is the *name* of the routine to evaluate $f(x)$)

$S_1 = \text{simpson}(f, a, b, (b-a)/2)$ (Simpson's rule on level 1)
$S_2 = \text{simpson}(f, a, b, (b-a)/4)$ (Simpson's rule on level 2)
if $(1/15)|S_1 - S_2| < \delta$, accept $I = S_2$
otherwise, refine:
    $c = (a+b)/2$
    $I_{\text{left}} = \text{adaptSimp}(f, a, c, \delta/2)$
    $I_{\text{right}} = \text{adaptSimp}(f, c, b, \delta/2)$
    $I = I_{\text{left}} + I_{\text{right}}$
return

The statement, f = feval(fun,a:h2:b), evaluates $f(x)$ at all five points used by both S_1 and S_2. This requires that the *fun* m-file be vectorized: that is, given a vector of x values, the *fun* function returns a vector of $f(x)$ values.

Example 11.15: Adaptive Integration of humps

The built-in humps function evaluates

$$f(x) = \frac{1}{(x-0.3)^2 + 0.01} + \frac{1}{(x-0.9)^2 + 0.04} - 6. \qquad (11.43)$$

As shown in the upper half of Figure 11.16, $f(x)$ has local maxima at $x = 0.3$ and $x = 0.9$. This function is interesting, because it contains both flat and steep regions over a fairly short range of x values, so it is a good candidate for testing adaptive quadrature methods.

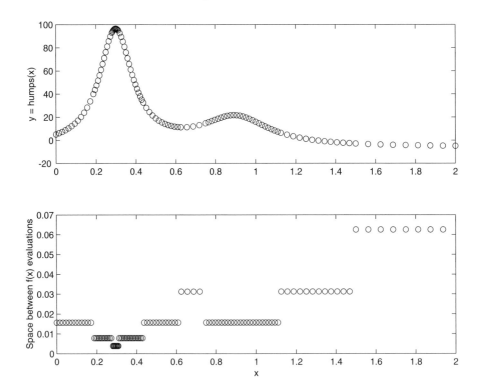

Figure 11.16 Plot of the one-dimensional humps function and the output distance between adjacent evaluations of $f(x)$ when humps is integrated with demoSimpson. These plots were created with demoAdaptSimp(5e-4), which uses a modified version of adaptSimpson called adaptSimpsonTrace.

```
function demoAdaptSimp(tol)
% demoAdaptSimp   Integrate humps(x) with adaptive Simpson's rule
%
% Synopsis:   demoAdaptSimp
%             demoAdaptSimp(tol)
%
% Input:  tol = (optional) absolute tolerance on truncation error in
%               evaluation of the integral.  Default:  tol = 5e-3
%
% Output: Value of numerical approximation to the integral and the error;
%         Min and max spacing of points along x used in evaluating integrand
if nargin<1,  tol=5e-3;   end
a = 0;   b = 2;   Iexact = humpInt(a,b);

flops(0);    [s,x] = adaptSimpsonTrace('humps',a,b,tol);   f = flops;
dx = diff(x);
fprintf('\n\tMinimum and maximum spacing    = %g    %g\n',min(dx),max(dx));
fprintf('\tExact value of the integral    = %g\n',Iexact);
fprintf('\tNumerical value of the integral = %g\n',s);
fprintf('\tError (I - Iexact)             = %g\n',s-Iexact);
fprintf('\tFlops                          = %g\n',flops);

subplot(2,1,1);    plot(x,humps(x),'o');    ylabel('y = humps(x)');
subplot(2,1,2);    plot(x(1:end-1),abs(diff(x)),'o');
xlabel('x');       ylabel('Space between f(x) evaluations');
```

Listing 11.10   The demoAdaptSimp function applies adaptive Simpson's rule integration to the humps function.

The demoAdaptSimp function in Listing 11.10 applies the adaptive Simpson's rule integration scheme to the humps function. The exact value of the integral is readily available. (Cf. Exercise 3.) A modified version of adaptSimpson called adaptSimpsonTrace (cf. integrate directory of the NMM toolbox) is used in demoAdaptSimp. The adaptSimpsonTrace function makes it easier to study the behavior of the adaptive Simpson's rule. adaptSimpsonTrace builds a vector of all x values at which the integrand is evaluated. The list of x values is unnecessary, except as a diagnostic, so this feature is not included in the adaptSimpson function. The x values are returned to demoAdaptSimp, which reports the minimum and maximum spacing between adjacent evaluations of $f(x)$. Running demoAdaptSimp with the default tolerance gives the following output and the plots shown in Figure 11.16:

```
>> demoAdaptSimp

Minimum and maximum spacing    = 0.0078125    0.125
Exact value of the integral    = 29.3262
Numerical Value of the integral = 29.3159
Error (I - Iexact)             = -0.0102954
Flops                          = 1875
```

The upper plot shows where Equation (11.43) was evaluated during the adaptive quadrature. The lower plot shows space between adjacent evaluations of $f(x)$. As expected, the smallest spacing between $f(x)$ evaluations occurs in ranges of x where $f(x)$ changes most rapidly.

The printout from demoAdaptSimp indicates that the magnitude of the absolute error exceeds the default tolerance (5×10^{-3}) by a factor of two. Although this is bothersome, it is to be expected, since the decision to stop refinement of the interval in adaptSimp size is based on an estimate of the truncation error, not the true error. As shown next, this strict violation of the error tolerance occurs only at relative large values of tol.

Running demoAdaptSimp for a range of tolerances gives the following table of results:

tol	min(dx)	max(dx)	error	flops
5×10^{-2}	0.0156	0.125	-2.8×10^{-2}	1125
5×10^{-3}	0.00781	0.125	-1.0×10^{-2}	1875
5×10^{-4}	0.00391	0.0625	-1.5×10^{-5}	3975
5×10^{-5}	0.00195	0.0625	-7.0×10^{-6}	6825
5×10^{-6}	0.00195	0.0313	-7.4×10^{-7}	12675

As the tolerance is reduced, the absolute error decreases. Note that the absolute error exceeds the tolerance only for tol $= 5 \times 10^{-3}$. As expected, the work to obtain the integral, as measured by the flop count, increases as the tolerance decreases. More evaluations of the integrand are required to improve the estimate of the integral.

When adaptive quadrature is applied to an integral with an unknown value, it is wise to use a sequence of tighter convergence tolerances. As the tolerance is reduced, the numerical value of the integral should approach a constant, which is a reasonable indication that the refinement of accuracy in the solution is successful.

Other adaptive integration algorithms use more sophisticated criteria to terminate local refinement and thereby improve the probability that the user's tolerance will be met [59, 25].

11.4.2 Built-in quad and quad8 Functions

In MATLAB version 5 and earlier, the built-in quad and quad8 functions use adaptive numerical quadrature to obtain the numerical value of an integral to within a specified tolerance. The quad function is similar to the adaptSimpson function, discussed in the preceding section. An important difference between quad and adaptSimpson is that quad does not use a direct estimate of the truncation error. Rather, the integral over a subinterval is refined until the change between two subsequent refinement levels is less than a tolerance. The quad8 function uses the same logic as quad, but with the nine-point Newton–Cotes rule[6] (see Equation (11.14)), instead of Simpson's rule. The quad8 function can be expected to obtain an integral within a desired tolerance with fewer evaluations of the integrand than either quad or adaptSimpson.

The syntax for quad and quad8 are identical. Either function can be called in any of the following ways (substitute "quad8" for "quad" as desired):

```
I = quad(fun,a,b)
I = quad(fun,a,b,tol)
I = quad(fun,a,b,tol,trace)
I = quad(fun,a,b,tol,trace,arg1,arg2, ... )
```

The minimum input parameters are *fun*, a string containing the name of the m-file that evaluates $f(x)$, and the lower and upper limits of integration a and b, respectively. The optional *tol* parameter is either a scalar or a vector. A scalar value of *tol* specifies the relative tolerance on the value of integral. A vector value of *tol* prescribes both a relative tolerance and an absolute tolerance on the error, or

```
tol = [rel_tol abs_tol]
```

Any nonzero value for the optional parameter *trace* causes a plot of the integrand to be created. The plot, which is similar to the upper plot in Figure 11.16, shows the points at which the adaptive scheme evaluated $f(x)$. The *arg1*, *arg2*, ... , values are not directly used by quad or quad8. Rather, these parameters are passed on to the user-defined m-file specified by the parameter *fun*.

Once the $f(x)$ function is coded in an m-file or as an inline function, both quad and quad8 can be used and the results compared. In addition, the value of the integral should be checked for sensitivity to the parameter *tol*. If the value of the integral varies with the value of *tol*, then the relative and absolute tolerances should be systematically reduced until the value of the integral approaches a limit.

---

[6]The prologue to quad8 refers to it as an "an adaptive recursive Newton–Cotes 8 panel rule." The panel referred to is the distance between the nodes in the rule, (i.e., $h = (b - a)/8$ when the basic rule is evaluated at nine points). Throughout this chapter the term "panel" has been used to refer to the width of the subinterval for the basic rule of a quadrature method, $H = (b - a)/N$.

Example 11.16: Demonstration of the built-in quad **function**

In this example, the humps function described in Example 11.15 is integrated with the quad and quad8 functions. Using the default tolerance parameters gives

```
>> format long              %  show lots of digits
>> quad('humps',0,2)
ans =
   29.32622038887953

>> quad8('humps',0,2)
ans =
   29.32621734123175
```

The two methods agree to six significant figures. The exact value of the integral is

```
>> format long
>> humpInt(0,2)
ans =
     29.32621380439114
```

and both quad and quad8 give the correct answer to six significant figures.

Repeating the computations with a tighter convergence tolerance changes the seventh and eighth digits, in the values returned by quad and quad8, respectively:

```
>> quad('humps',0,2,1e-4)
ans =
   29.32621406442962

>> quad8('humps',0,2,1e-4)
ans =
   29.32621386300150
```

At this tighter tolerance quad8 gains three more correct digits, and quad gains two more correct digits.

For these sample computations, the quad and quad8 functions return nearly identical estimates of the value of the integral. There are some integrands, however, that may cause one or even both of these routines to fail to meet the user-specified error tolerance. Thus, being able to compare the results of the two methods is an important step in the evaluation of an integral.

For well-behaved integrals, the difference between quad and quad8 is not in the accuracy with which these methods compute the value of the integral, but in the effort expended to obtain the integral to within a specified tolerance. In general, quad8 will obtain the result with fewer calls to the routine that evaluates the integrand. The demoQuad function in Listing 11.11 evaluates the numerical integral of the humps function with a systematic refinement of the relative tolerance parameter. The difference between the exact value of the integral and values returned by quad and quad8 is reported. The built-in flops

```
function demoQuad(a,b)
% demoQuad   Use built in quad and quad8 to integrate 'humps' on [0,2]
%
% Synopsis:   demoQuad
%             demoQuad(a,b)
%
% Input:   a,b = (optional) upper and lower limits of integral
%               Default:  a = 0;   b = 2
%
% Output: Tables of absolute error and flops as function of tol parameter
%             input to quad and quad8.  Plots of error vs. tol and error vs. flops

if nargin<2,   a=0; b=2;   end

tol = [5e-2  5e-3  5e-4  5e-5];     %  sequence of relative tolerances
for k = 1:length(tol)
  flops(0);   q(k)  = quad('humps',0,2,tol(k));    f(k) = flops;
  flops(0);   q8(k) = quad8('humps',0,2,tol(k));   f8(k) = flops;
end
Iexact = humpInt(0,2);   e = abs(q - Iexact);   e8 = abs(q8 - Iexact);

fprintf('                  ----- quad -----     ----- quad8 -----\n');
fprintf('      tol          error      flops      error       flops\n');
for k = 1:length(tol)
  fprintf('%11.2e  %11.2e  %6d   %11.2e   %6d\n',tol(k),e(k),f(k),e8(k),f8(k));
end

subplot(2,1,1);
loglog(e,tol,'o--',e8,tol,'^-');
legend('quad','quad8',2);   xlabel('Absolute error');   ylabel('tol');

subplot(2,1,2);
loglog(e,f,'o--',e8,f8,'^-');
legend('quad','quad8');     xlabel('Absolute error');   ylabel('flops');
```

Listing 11.11   The demoQuad function demonstrates use of quad and quad8 by integrating the humps function defined in Equation (11.43).

function is used to measure the computational effort in evaluating the integral. Running
demoQuad gives

```
>> demoQuad
    ----- quad -----        ----- quad8 -----
        tol          error      flops        error      flops
      5.00e-02      2.91e-02      914        6.56e-01      608
      5.00e-03      2.54e-05     2552        5.06e-05     1577
      5.00e-04      3.30e-06     5009        3.54e-06     2223
      5.00e-05      1.94e-07    10924        1.60e-08     3192
```

The plots in Figure 11.17 provide a graphical summary of this performance data. Reducing the value of tol reduces the absolute error in the numerical value of the integral. Remember that tol is a parameter used to control refinement. In general, there is no way to guarantee that either the relative or the absolute error in the integral will meet the criteria implied by the value of tol, because quad and quad8 *cannot know* the true value of the integral. Indeed, the real reason for using quad, quad8, or any numerical integration scheme is that the true value of the integral is unknown.

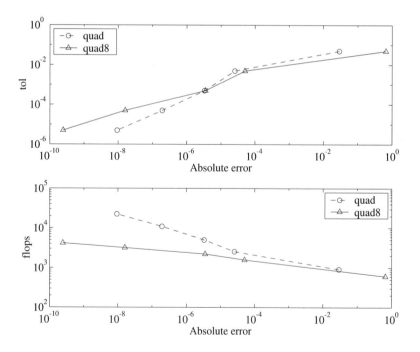

Figure 11.17   Performance of built-in quad and quad8 functions in integrating the one-dimensional humps function. Plots are produced by the demoQuad function.

Although quad and quad8 both obtain improved estimates of the integral, the tabular output of demoQuad and the lower plot in Figure 11.17 show that quad8 does so more efficiently. The flop count for quad8 is substantially lower than the flop count for quad at the same tolerance level. The reason is that quad8 requires fewer calls to $f(x)$ than quad to achieve convergence to within the same tolerance.

11.4.3 New quad and quadl Functions

MATLAB version 6, which is in preparation as this book goes to press, will have two new adaptive quadrature routines based on the adaptsim and adaptlob functions recently developed by Gander and Gautschi [25]. The new built-in functions will be called quad and quadl and will replace the (old) quad and quad8 functions. The new quad is still based on Simpson's rule, but it includes improved stopping criteria and a Romberg extrapolation step. The stopping criteria involves making a quick initial approximation of the integral to establish an appropriate order of magnitude for the refinement error tolerance. This, and other details of the stopping criteria as described by Gander and Gautschi, help to prevent the adaptive scheme from getting stuck in a subinterval that does not meet the local error tolerance, but does not contribute significantly to the magnitude of the integral.

The quadl function uses the same improved stopping criteria as the new quad. The integration scheme in quadl is based on a four-point Gauss–Labatto rule with a three-point Kronrod extension. A second Kronrod extension provides the error estimate that controls the adaptive refinement. The Kronrod technique is a modification to the basic Gaussian quadrature scheme to make it efficient for adaptive refinement. Recall that Gaussian quadrature uses nodes that are not equally-spaced in a panel. A Kronrod extension selects the location of the nodes to satisfy the optimal accuracy property of the Gaussian rule, *and* provide as many common nodes as possible for the next refinement level. The new quad and quadl functions have been shown by Gander and Gautschi to be more efficient than the old quad and quad8. The new functions are also significantly more reliable in the sense that they obtain the value of the integral to within the user-specified error tolerance for a wide variety of test integrals. Note that no adaptive quadrature scheme can be guaranteed to meet a user-specified error tolerance because the convergence criteria are based on estimates of the truncation error—the true value of the integral is, in general, unknown.

The new quad and quadl functions will have the same input and output parameters as the old (version 5 and earlier) quad and quad8 functions. When MATLAB version 6 is released, the (new) quad and quadl functions should be used instead of the old quad and quad8 functions.

11.5 IMPROPER INTEGRALS AND OTHER COMPLICATIONS

An improper integral has either one or more limits that are infinite or has a singularity inside the range of integration or at one of the limits of the integration. The common characteristic is unboundedness, either in the value of the integrand or the limits of the integral. Such integrals can often be evaluated numerically after applying a mathematical transformation of one sort or another that removes the unboundedness. The transformations are rather specific to each type of complication, so that instead of a general prescription for improper integrals, one is left with a set of techniques.

Another complication for numerical quadrature is an integrand that oscillates between positive and negative values. In this case, the problem is not unboundedness, but loss of precision due to cancellation.

Davis and Rabinowitz [13] discuss a variety of methods for dealing with these complications. The QUADPACK routines provide several strategies for dealing with improper integrals. These include the use of coordinate transformation, special weight functions, and combinations of different basic quadrature rules. In this section, we demonstrate only a small sample of the available techniques.

11.5.1 Integrals with Infinite Limits

Integrals of the form

$$\int_a^\infty f(x)\,dx$$

are considered in this section. The lower limit a is a finite scalar, and often $a = 0$. The integral is well defined only if $f(x)$ is bounded and it approaches zero as x approaches infinity. The obvious difficulty with this integral is that the upper limit cannot be represented in finite precision arithmetic. A quick fix is to use a large number $x^* <$ realmax instead of infinity as the limit. The problem with the quick fix is that it does not, in general, lead to an efficient computation of the integral.

Approaching an Infinite Limit   An integral with an infinite upper limit can be written as

$$I = \int_0^\infty f(x)\,dx = \int_0^{z_1} f(x)\,dx + \int_{z_1}^{z_2} f(x)\,dx + \int_{z_2}^{z_3} f(x)\,dx + \dots,$$

$$(11.44)$$

where $z_1 < z_2 < z_3 < \dots$. For convenience, let

$$I_j = \int_{z_{j-1}}^{z_j} f(x)\,dx, \qquad (11.45)$$

so that Equation (11.44) becomes

$$I = \lim_{k \to \infty} \sum_{j=1}^{k} I_j.$$

When the contributions to I decrease with x, it is possible to economize the numerical approximation. The simplest economization is to truncate the sum of partial integrals. Additional savings in computation can be realized if the size of the interval is increased. One can choose, for example,

$$z_{j+1} - z_j = \rho \left(z_j - z_{j-1} \right), \tag{11.46}$$

where $\rho \geq 1$ is a factor controlling the rate of growth of the intervals. The final refinement of this strategy is to stop adding intervals when

$$|I_{k+1}| < \delta \left| \sum_{j=1}^{k} I_j \right|,$$

with δ a relative tolerance. These ideas are incorporated in the quadToInfinity function in Listing 11.12. The partial integrals I_j can be evaluated by any numerical quadrature scheme for finite intervals. The quadToInfinity function allows the user to select between gaussQuad, quad, and quad8. Other schemes can easily be added by editing the quadToInfinity source code.

Example 11.17: Application of quadToInfinity

The following MATLAB session uses quadToInfinity function to evaluate

$$I = \int_0^{\infty} \exp(-x^2) \, dx = \frac{\sqrt{\pi}}{2}$$

```
>> fun = inline('exp(-x.^2)');
>> I = quadToInfinity(fun);
```

j	dx	x2	I_j	Isum
0	0.5	0.5	0.46128101	0.46128101
1	1.0	1.5	0.39490739	0.85618839
2	2.0	3.5	0.03003787	0.88622627
3	4.0	7.5	0.00000066	0.88622693
4	8.0	15.5	0.00000000	0.88622693
5	16.0	31.5	0.00000000	0.88622693
6	32.0	63.5	0.00000000	0.88622693

```
>> err = I-sqrt(pi)/2
err =
   1.1102e-16
```

```
function Isum = quadToInfinity(fun,a,dx0,tol,method)
% quadToInfinity  Integral from a to infinity evaluated as sum of integrals
%                 Size of subintervals increases geometrically.  Sum is
%                 terminated when change in integral is less than tolerance
%
% Synopsis:  I = quadToInfinity(fun)
%            I = quadToInfinity(fun,a)
%            I = quadToInfinity(fun,a,dx0)
%            I = quadToInfinity(fun,a,dx0,tol)
%            I = quadToInfinity(fun,a,dx0,tol,method)
%
% Input:  fun = (string) name of m-file that evaluates the integrand, f(x)
%         a   = (optional) lower limit of the integral.  Default: a = 0
%         dx0 = (optional) size of first interval of x axis used to
%               evaluate the partial integrals.  Default:  x = 0.5
%         tol = (optional) relative tolerance.  Sum is terminated when
%               abs(I_{k+1}/I_k) < tol, where I_k = sum(I_j), j=1,...,k.
%               and I_j is integral over subinterval j.  Default: tol=5e-4
%         method = (optional) integral rule used for subintervals. method=1
%               for composite Gauss-Legendre quadrature with 8 panels and 6
%               nodes per panel; method=2 for built-in quad; method=4 for
%               built-in quad8.  Default:  method = 1
%
% Output:  I = estimate of the integral of f(x) dx from x=a to x=infinty
if nargin<2,     a = 0;  end
if nargin<3,   dx0 = 0.5;  end
if nargin<4, tol = 5e-4;  end
if nargin<5, method = 1;  end
j = 0;  dx = dx0;   Isum = 0;   x1 = a;   maxint = 35;   %  Initialize

fprintf('\n    j        dx      x2         I_j           Isum\n');
while j<maxint
  x2 = x1 + dx;
  switch method
    case 1,      I = gaussQuad(fun,x1,x2,8,6);
    case 2,      I = quad(fun,x1,x2);
    case 3,      I = quad8(fun,x1,x2);
    otherwise,   error(sprintf('method = %d not allowed',method));
  end
  Isum = Isum + I;
  fprintf(' %4d %8.1f %8.1f  %12.8f   %12.8f\n',j,dx,x2,I,Isum);
  if j>5 & abs(I/Isum) < tol,  break;  end
  j = j + 1;   x1 = x2;   dx = 2*dx;  % prepare for next interval
end
```

Listing 11.12 The quadToInfinity function evaluates an integral with an infinite upper limit.

The integrand rapidly decays with x, so few subintervals are needed. Furthermore, the Gaussian quadrature scheme provides good accuracy near $x = 0$ with the default value of dx0.

A more difficult integral is (see [59, problem 16, page 84])

$$I = \int_0^\infty \frac{x^{1/5}}{(1 + 10x)^2}\, dx = \frac{-10^{-6/5}\pi}{5\sin(6\pi/5)} = 0.0674467742.$$

The next MATLAB session uses the default parameters of the quadToInfinity function to evaluate this integral

```
>> fun = inline('x.^(1/5)./(1+10*x).^2');
>> I = quadToInfinity(fun)
```

j	dx	x2	I_j	Isum
0	0.5	0.5	0.04896325	0.04896325
1	1.0	1.5	0.00998439	0.05894765
2	2.0	3.5	0.00405910	0.06300675
3	4.0	7.5	0.00201032	0.06501707
4	8.0	15.5	0.00107734	0.06609441
5	16.0	31.5	0.00059835	0.06669275
6	32.0	63.5	0.00033803	0.06703078
7	64.0	127.5	0.00019256	0.06722334
8	128.0	255.5	0.00011015	0.06733348
9	256.0	511.5	0.00006313	0.06739661
10	512.0	1023.5	0.00003622	0.06743284
11	1024.0	2047.5	0.00002079	0.06745363

```
I =
   0.0675

>> Iexact = 10^(-6/5) * (-1/5)*pi/sin(pi*6/5)
Iexact =
   0.0674

>> err = I-Iexact
err =
   6.8584e-06
```

Improving the numerical approximation to this integral is the goal of Exercise 29.

Gauss–Laguerre Quadrature   Laguerre polynomials are orthogonal polynomials defined on $[0, \infty)$ with a weight function $w(x) = e^{-x}$. (Cf. Equation (11.22).) (Recall that $w(x) = 1$ for Gauss–Legendre quadrature.) When Laguerre polynomials are used to define the nodes and weights in a Gaussian quadrature scheme, the result is a *Gauss–Laguerre rule*

$$\int_0^\infty e^{-x} f(x)\, dx \approx \sum_{j=1}^n c_j f(x_j), \qquad (11.47)$$

where x_j are the zeros of the Laguerre polynomial of degree n and c_j are the corresponding weights. Tables of nodes and weights for Gauss–Laguerre quadrature are available. (See, for example, [1].) Once c_j and w_j are available, the implementation of the Gauss–Laguerre scheme is straightforward. Note that there is no composite Gauss–Laguerre rule, because the nodes and weights are defined over the entire interval $[0, \infty)$.

For integrals without an e^{-x} weight function appearing explicitly in the integrand, we can write

$$\int_0^\infty f(x)\,dx = \int_0^\infty e^{-x} e^x f(x)\,dx \approx \sum_{j=1}^n c_j e^{x_j} f(x_j). \qquad (11.48)$$

In other words, the modified weights $c_j e^{x_j}$ replace the c_j in Equation (11.47). Davis and Rabinowitz [13] warn that Equation (11.48) should only be used when $e^x f(x)$ is well approximated by a polynomial.

Equation (11.48) is useful as a computational rule, and it also reveals that Gauss–Laguerre quadrature is likely to be more successful with rapidly decaying $f(x)$. (For additional information on Gauss–Laguerre quadrature, see [13].)

The rules in Equations (11.47) and (11.48) are implemented in the function gaussLagQuad in Listing 11.13. The nodes and weights are provided either as a lookup table in GLagTable or computed in GLagNodeWt by solving a related eigenvalue problem. GLagTable and GLagNodeWt are not listed here, but are included in the integrate directory of the NMM toolbox.

Example 11.18: Application of Gauss–Laguerre Quadrature

In this example, Gauss–Laguerre quadrature using the guassLagQuad function is demonstrated with two test integrals. The first test integral is

$$I = \int_0^\infty x^4 e^{-x}\,dx = 24.$$

The following statements define the $f(x)$ in accordance with Equation (11.47) and use Gauss–Laguerre rules of increasing order:

```
>> fun = inline('x.^4');
>> I = gaussLagQuad(fun,2)
I =
   20.0000

>> I = gaussLagQuad(fun,3)
I =
   24.0000
```

```
function I = gaussLagQuad(fun,nnode,wtype,varargin)
% gaussLagQuad  Gauss-Laguerre quadrature for integrals on [0,infinity)
%
% Synopsis:   I = gaussLagQuad(fun,node)
%             I = gaussLagQuad(fun,node,wtype)
%             I = gaussLagQuad(fun,node,wtype,arg1,arg2,...)
%
% Input:      fun   = (string) name of m-file that evaluates f(x)
%             nnode = number of nodes on each subinterval
%             wtype = (optional) flag indicating how weight function is applied
%                     If wtype = 1 (default) the integrand is of the form
%                     exp(-x)*f(x) and the quadrature rule is sum(w(i)*f(x(i))).
%                     If wtype = 2 the integrand is of the form f(x)
%                     and the quadrature rule is sum(w(i)*exp(x(i))*f(x(i))).
%             arg1, arg2 = (optional) parameters passed through to fun
%
% Output:     I = approximate value of the integral

if nargin<3,  wtype = 1;  end

if nnode<=25
   [x,w] = GLagTable(nnode);      %  Look up nodes and weights,
else                             %  or if n is too big for the table,
   [x,w] = GLagNodeWt(nnode);     %  compute the nodes and weights
end

f = feval(fun,x,varargin{:});
if wtype == 1
   I = w'*f;                      %  int(exp(-x)*dx) = sum(w*f)
else
   we = w.*exp(x);               %  Use rule in the form int(f*dx) = sum(w*exp(x)*f)
   I = we'*f;                     %  not int(exp(-x)*dx) = sum(w*f)
end
```

Listing 11.13 The gaussLagQuad function uses Gauss–Laguerre quadrature to evaluate integrals of the form $\int_0^\infty e^{-x} f(x)dx$ (wtype = 1) or $\int_0^\infty f(x)dx$ (wtype = 2).

```
>> I = gaussLagQuad(fun,4)
I =
     24.0000
```

The exact value of the integral is obtained for the third-order rule. This is consistent with the theory of Gaussian quadrature. For the orthogonal polynomial defined with the appropriate weight function (e^{-x} for Laguerre polynomials), a Gaussian quadrature rule of order n obtains the exact value of the integral for polynomials of degree $2n - 1$. This test integral gives us confidence that the gaussLagQuad function is a correct implementation of Gauss–Laguerre quadrature.

The second test integral is

$$I = \int_0^\infty \exp(-x^2)\,dx = \frac{\sqrt{\pi}}{2},$$

which is also evaluated in Example 11.17. Since e^{-x} cannot be factored from the integrand, the rule in Equation (11.48) must be used. This is affected by using $f(x) = e^{-x^2}$ and wtype = 2 as inputs to gaussLagQuad:

```
>> fun = inline('exp(-x.^2)');  Iexact = sqrt(pi)/2;
>> I = gaussLagQuad(fun,5,2),   err = I-Iexact
I =
    0.8558
err =
   -0.0304

>> I = gaussLagQuad(fun,15,2),  err = I-Iexact
I =
    0.8864
err =
    1.2449e-04

>> I = gaussLagQuad(fun,25,2),  err = I-Iexact
I =
    0.8862
err =
    3.7225e-06
```

The error is not quickly reduced as the order of the Gauss–Laguerre rule is increased. The reason is that e^{-x^2} is not well approximated by a polynomial. An accurate value of this integral is more readily obtained with the quadToInfinity function.

11.6 SUMMARY

Several basic and composite rules for numerical quadrature are presented in this chapter. Basic rules are building blocks for the composite rules that approximate the value of an integral over an arbitrary, finite interval. Table 11.1 lists the names of m-file functions developed in this chapter.

The accuracy of composite rules is demonstrated via numerical experiment in several examples. For the trapezoid rule, Simpson's rule, and Gauss–Legendre rule, increases in accuracy correspond to greater efficiency, since the value of the integral can be obtained to a desired accuracy with fewer evaluations of the inte-

TABLE 11.1 FUNCTIONS FOR NUMERICAL INTEGRATION DEVELOPED IN THIS
CHAPTER. FUNCTIONS WITH N.A. (NOT APPLICABLE) FOR A PAGE NUMBER ARE
NOT LISTED IN THE TEXT, BUT ARE INCLUDED IN THE NMM TOOLBOX.

Function	page	Description
adaptSimpson	651	Adaptive numerical integration based on Simpson's rule.
compIntRules	NA	Compare computational efficiency of the trapezoid rule, Simpson's rule, and Gauss–Legendre quadrature rule.
demoGauss	641	Use Gauss–Legendre quadrature to evaluate $\mathrm{erf}(x)$.
demoGaussLag	NA	Use Gauss–Laguerre quadrature to evaluate two integrals on $[0, \infty)$.
demoSimp	NA	Demonstrate use of Simpson's rule by integrating $f(x) = xe^{-x}$.
demoTrap	608	Demonstrate use of trapezoid rule by integrating $f(x) = xe^{-x}$.
expmx2	641	Evaluate $\exp(-x^2)$, where x is a scalar or vector. Used to compute $\mathrm{erf}(x)$.
gaussLagQuad	665	Perform Gauss–Laguerre quadrature of user-specified function on $[0, \infty)$.
gaussQuad	640	Composite Gauss–Legendre quadrature of user-specified function.
GLagTable	NA	Look up numerical values of nodes and weights for Gauss–Laguerre quadrature of order $n \leq 15$.
GLTable	630	Look up numerical values of nodes and weights for Gauss–Legendre quadrature of order $n \leq 8$.
GLagNodeWt	NA	Compute values of nodes and weights for Gauss–Laguerre quadrature of any order.
GLNodeWt	635	Compute values of nodes and weights for Gauss–Legendre quadrature of any order.
humpInt	NA	Calculate the exact value of a definite integral of the built-in humps function defined by Equation (11.43).
makeGLtable	NA	Create a table of Gauss–Legendre nodes and weights. The output is formatted so that it may be directly copied and pasted into GLtable.m.
plotSimpInt	NA	Create a graphical display of Simpson's rule integration.
plotTrapInt	NA	Create a graphical display of trapezoid rule integration.
recursiveIndent	NA	Demonstrate the use of a recursive function call.
simpson	615	Use Simpson's rule to integrate a user-defined function.
trapezoid	607	Use the trapezoid rule to integrate a user-defined function.
trapzDat	611	Use the trapezoid rule to integrate discrete data.
xemx	608	Evaluate $x \exp(-x)$, where x is a scalar or a vector.

grand. Of these, the Gauss–Legendre rule is the most accurate and efficient, while the trapezoid rule is the least.

Further gains in efficiency are obtained by incorporating the basic rules in an adaptive scheme. The user specifies a tolerance on the estimated error in the integral, and the adaptive algorithm chooses points at which the integrand is to be evaluated so that the tolerance is met. The built-in quad and quad8 functions are examples of adaptive schemes.

At the end of the chapter, a small sample of special techniques for integrals with an infinite upper limit is presented.

When faced with a new numerical integration problem, it is wise to try more than one quadrature rule and to vary the parameters controlling the computations of each rule. In this way, a sequence of estimates on the value of the integral are computed, thereby increasing the likelihood that a close estimate of the true value of the integral can be obtained. For nonadaptive schemes, the refinement strategy is to increase the number of panels used to evaluate the integral. For adaptive schemes, the refinement strategy involves systematic reduction of the tolerance on the numerical value of the integral.

Further Reading

Most elementary numerical analysis books cover numerical integration. Introductory expositions are given by Cheney and Kincaid [10] and Burden and Faires [9]. Acton [2] stresses careful examination of the properties of the integrand *before* a numerical method is applied. For an emphasis on mathematical analysis of the methods themselves, consult Isaacson and Keller [40] or Stoer and Bulirsch [70]. For an emphasis on implementation and, in particular, for tracing the origins of quad and quad8, see Forsythe et al. [24] and Kahaner et al. [43]. Press et al.[61] provide source code in C.

Davis and Rabinowitz [13] provide a comprehensive survey of numerical integration methods along with several Fortran codes. The QUADPACK library [59] of Fortran codes[7] implements a variety of numerical integration schemes for the evaluation of definite integrals of a single variable. Kahaner et al. [43] provide a subset of QUADPACK routines for adaptive Gauss–Kronrod quadrature and piecewise-cubic Hermite integration of discrete data. The curious reader may also want to experiment with the adaptGK and demoAdaptGK functions provided in the integrate directory of the NMM toolbox. The adaptGK function is an adaptive quadrature scheme based on the Gauss–Kronrod 7-15 rule presented in [59].

The book by Krommer and Ueberhuber [48] includes coverage of recent developments in numerical integration, including implementations on parallel computers, the use of symbolic software packages, and integration in two or more dimensions.

EXERCISES

The number in parenthesis at the beginning of each exercise indicates the degree of skill and amount of effort necessary to complete the exercise. See § 1.4 on page 10 for a description of the rating system.

---

[7]The QUADPACK source code is available at www.netlib.org.

1. (1) Manually compute the values of the following integrals:

$$I_1 = \int_{-\pi/2}^{\pi} (x^2 + x + 1)\, dx, \qquad I_2 = \int_{\sqrt{3}}^{-5} (x^3 - 1)\, dx.$$

2. (2) Write a `polyInt` function that uses the built-in `polyval` function to evaluate the definite integral of a polynomial. The inputs to `polyInt` should be a vector of polynomial coefficients and the lower and upper limits of integration. Test your function by evaluating the two integrals in the preceding exercise.

3. (1+) Use the symbolic capability of the *Student Edition of* MATLAB or the *Symbolic Mathematics Toolbox* to find the definite integral of the generalized humps function

$$f(x) = \frac{1}{(x - c_1)^2 + c_2} + \frac{1}{(x - c_3)^2 + c_4} + c_5.$$

4. (1+) Manually (i.e., with pencil and paper) evaluate the following integrals with the trapezoid rule using two panels, and compare the results with the exact analytical value of the integrals, as well as with the results obtained with the `trapezoid` function.

(a) $I = \int_0^2 x \exp(-x)\, dx.$

(b) $I = \int_0^{\pi} \cos(x)\, dx.$

5. (1+) Repeat the preceding problem using Simpson's rule instead of the trapezoid rule.

6. (3) Write a `quadSpline` function that evaluates the integral of a cubic-spline approximation obtained with the `splint` function from Listing 10.11. The prologue for `quadSpline` should be:

```
function I = quadSpline(x,y)
% quadSpline    Evaluate integral of a 1D cubic-spline
%
% Synopsis:    I = quadSpline(x,y)
%
% Input:       x,y = vectors of data defining the knots of the spline
%
% Output:      I = integral of cubic-spline passing through knots used
%                  to create the spline.  Uses the splint function.
```

Verify that your `quadSpline` function works by testing it with a modified version of the `trapzDatTest` function in Listing 4.3 on page 172. What is the value of α for `quadSpline`?

7. (2) Make a copy of the `trapezoid.m` file. (See Listing 11.1 and the corresponding file in the NMM toolbox) called `trapezerr.m`. In `trapezerr.m`, change the last line to

```
I = h * (0.5*y(1) + sum(y(2:n)) + 0.5*y(n));
```

In other words, replace the y(2:n-1) subexpression with y(2:n) and thereby introduce a bug in the code. Modify the demoTrap function in Listing 11.2 so that it calls
trapezerr instead of trapezoid. Run the modified demoTrap function. Does the
absolute error decrease with increasing n? What happens to value of α? If α was not
computed, might it be possible to conclude that the trapezerr function was actually
working correctly?

SOLUTION   **8.** (2+) F. M. White (*Fluid Mechanics*, fourth edition, 1999, McGraw-Hill, New York,
problem 6.57) gives the following data for the velocity profile in a round pipe

r/R	0.0	0.102	0.206	0.412	0.617	0.784	0.846	0.907	0.963
u/u_c	1.0	0.997	0.988	0.959	0.908	0.847	0.818	0.771	0.690

r is the radial position, $R = 12.35$ cm is the radius of the pipe, u is the velocity at
the position r, and u_c is the velocity at the centerline $r = 0$. The *average* velocity in a
round pipe is defined by

$$
V = \frac{1}{\pi R^2} \int_0^R u 2\pi r\, dr, \qquad \text{or} \qquad \frac{V}{u_c} = \int_0^1 2\frac{u}{u_c} \eta\, d\eta,
$$

where $\eta = r/R$. What is the value of V for the given data if $u_c = 30.5$ m/s? Do not
forget to include the implied data point $u/u_c = 0$ at $r/R = 1$. The data in the table is
in the vprofile.dat file in the data directory of the NMM toolbox.

9. (2) Use the trapezoid function to evaluate erf(1) for a sequence of increasing n
(decreasing h). What value of h is required to get an absolute error less than 5×10^{-8}?

10. (2) Repeat Exercise 9 using the simpson function instead of the trapezoid function.

11. (2) Repeat Exercise 9 using the gaussQuad function instead of the trapezoid function.

SOLUTION   **12.** (2+) Use the Trapezoid rule to evaluate

$$
\beta(m, n) = \int_0^1 x^{m-1}(1 - x)^{n-1}\, dx
$$

for any m and n and for a sequence of decreasing panel sizes h. Print the value of
$\beta(m, n)$, and the error relative to the value returned by the built-in beta function. Use
your function to evaluate $\beta(1, 2)$, $\beta(1.5, 2.5)$, $\beta(2, 3)$, and $\beta(2, 5)$. Comment on the
convergence rate. (*Hint:* The values of m and n can be passed around (not through)
trapezoid with global variables.)

13. (2) Repeat Exercise 12 using Simpson's rule.

14. (2) Repeat Exercise 12 using Gauss–Legendre quadrature.

15. (2+) Write an m-file to return the value of

$$
p(s) = \frac{1}{\sqrt{2\pi}} \int_{-s}^s e^{-z^2/2}\, dz
$$

Use composite Gauss–Legendre quadrature with six panels and four nodes per panel.
$p(s)$ is the probability that a sample from a normally distributed, random population

with unit standard deviation and zero mean will fall with $\pm s$ of the standard deviation. Compute $p(s)$ for $s = 1$, $s = 2$, $s = 2.5$, and $s = 3$.

16. (2) Evaluate

$$I = \int_0^1 \sqrt{x}\, dx$$

using the NMM routines `trapezoid`, `simpson`, and `gaussQuad`. For each routine, evaluate the integral for at least three different panel sizes. Present a table comparing the measured truncation error as a function of panel size. Report any problems in obtaining values of I. Which routine works best for this problem?

17. (2+) Show (see § 11.3.1 on page 625) that $g(x) = 1$ and $h(x) = x$ are orthogonal on $(a, b) = (-1, 1)$ if $w(x) = 1$ or $w(x) = (1 - x^2)^{-1/2}$.

18. (3) A sequence of *orthonormal* polynomials, $\tilde{\Phi}_n(x)$ is defined by

$$\langle \tilde{\Phi}_i(x), \tilde{\Phi}_j(x) \rangle = \int_a^b w(x) \tilde{\Phi}_i(x) \tilde{\Phi}_j(x)\, dx = \delta_{i,j} = \begin{cases} 0 & \text{if } i \neq j \\ 1 & \text{if } i = j \end{cases}$$

Given a sequence of orthogonal polynomials $P_i(x)$, we can generate an orthonormal sequence by multiplying each $P_i(x)$ by an appropriate constant, so that the preceding condition holds. Note that only the $i = j$ case is important in determining the constant.

(a) Given the Legendre polynomials on page 625, find the first three orthonormal Legendre polynomials.

(b) Use Gaussian quadrature to prove that your derivation in part (a) satisfies the condition for $i = j$.

19. (2+) Following the calculations in Example 11.11, compute the nodes and weights for the Gauss–Legendre quadrature rule of order three.

20. (2+) Write a function m-file that evaluates $\int_0^5 x \exp(-x)\, dx$ using composite Gauss–Legendre quadrature with a fixed number of nodes on an increasing number of panels. What is the value of α for the truncation error expression $\mathcal{O}(h^\alpha)$ for the two-node Gauss–Legendre rule using 1, 2, 3, 4, 6, and 8 panels? How does your computed value compare with the theoretical prediction of truncation error?

21. (3) Repeat the preceding Exercise using four- and eight-node Gauss–Legendre rules. Discuss any problems you might have in computing α.

22. (2+) Write an m-file function that evaluates $\int_0^{2\pi} \sin^2(x)\, dx$ using the composite trapezoid rule, composite Simpson's rule, and composite Gauss–Legendre quadrature with two nodes per panel. Place the calls to `trapezoid`, `simpson`, and `gaussQuad` inside a loop, and repeat the calculations for `np = [1 2 4 8 16 32]`, where `np` is the number of panels. Record the number of function evaluations `n` for each method. Print the absolute error $|I - I_{\text{exact}}|$ for the three methods versus n. (See, for example, [13, § 2.9] for help in explaining the results.)

23. (2) (Kahaner et al. [43]) Use the following integral to estimate the value of π:

$$\pi = \int_0^1 \frac{4}{1 + x^2}\, dx.$$

Compare the convergence behavior of the composite trapezoid rule, composite Simpson's rule, and composite Gauss–Legendre quadrature rule with 2, 4, 8, 16, 32, 64, and 128 panels.

24. (2) Choose an integration method, and write the necessary MATLAB code to evaluate

$$E = \int_0^{2\pi} \sqrt{1 - k^2 \sin^2 x}\, dx,$$

the elliptic integral for any value of k. Compare your results with those produced by the ellipke function for $a = 2$ and $b = 1$ and for $a = 12$ and $b = 1$. What technique is used by ellipke to obtain the value of the integral?

25. (2+) Test the performance of the adaptive quadrature routines adaptsimpson, quad, and quad8 (or quadl) on

$$I = \int_0^1 \sqrt{x}\, dx$$

For each routine, evaluate the integral for at least three different error tolerances. Present a table comparing the measured truncation error as a function of error tolerance. Report any problems in obtaining values of I. Which routine works best for this problem? Compare the behavior of these adaptive routines with the behavior of the nonadaptive schemes in Exercise 16.

26. (2+) (Assuming you have access to MATLAB version 6) Modify the demoQuad function in Listing 11.11 to compare the performance of the new quad and quadl functions for integrating the built-in humps function. Is the relationship between the performance of the new quad and quadl similar to the relationship between the performance of the old quad and quad8?

27. (3) The thermal radiation emitted from an object is a function of its absolute temperature. A blackbody emitter is an ideal surface that emits radiation uniformly in all directions and absorbs all radiation incident on its surface. (See, for example, F.P. Incropera, and D.P. Dewitt, *Fundamentals of Heat and Mass Transfer*, fourth edition, 1996, Wiley, New York.) The variation of the emissive power as a function of wavelength of a blackbody emitter is described by the Planck distribution

$$E_{\lambda,b} = \frac{c_1}{\lambda^5 [\exp(c_2/\lambda T) - 1]}$$

where λ is the wavelength in μm, T is the absolute temperature in kelvins, $c_1 = 3.7418 \times 10^8 \ \mu\mathrm{m}^4/\mathrm{m}^2$ and $c_2 = 1.4388 \times 10^4 \ \mu\mathrm{m}\cdot\mathrm{K}$. The energy emitted in the wavelength range $0 \le \lambda \le \lambda^*$ is

$$F_{0 \to \lambda^*} = \int_0^{\lambda^* T} \frac{E_{\lambda,b}}{\sigma T^5} d(\lambda T)$$

where $\sigma = 5.6696 \times 10^{-8} \mathrm{W}/(\mathrm{m}^2\mathrm{K})$. The integrand that defines $F_{0 \to \lambda^*}$ depends on the product λT, not on λ and T separately.

Write the MATLAB function(s) to evaluate $F_{0 \to \lambda^*}$ for any input value of λT. Evaluate $F_{0 \to \lambda^*}$ for $\lambda^* T = 1000, 5000, 8000, 10000$, and 20000. (*Answer:* at $\lambda^* T = 5000$, $F_{0 \to \lambda^*} = 0.633766$.) Note that the computed value of $F_{0 \to \lambda^*}$ depends on the numerical values of the constants c_1, c_2, and σ. Discrepancies with other tabulated values of the $F_{0 \to \lambda^*}$ function will ultimately depend more on the constants used to define $F_{0 \to \lambda^*}$ than on the integration scheme. Nonetheless, you should strive for high accuracy in the numerical evaluation of the integral.

28. (2+) Evaluate the following integrals numerically

(a) $I = \displaystyle\int_0^\infty \frac{2\,dx}{1 + x^2} = \pi.$

(b) $I = \displaystyle\int_0^\infty x^2 e^{-x}\,dx = 2.$

(c) $I = \displaystyle\int_0^\infty \frac{\ln(x)\,dx}{1 + 100x^2}\,dx = \frac{-\pi}{20}\ln(10).$

29. (2+) Find an improved approximation to the second integral in Example 11.17 by changing the input parameters to `quadToInfinity`. Which option has the most effect on the accuracy?

30. (3+) Stanley Middleman (*An Introduction to Mass and Heat Transfer*, 1998, Wiley, New York, p. 221) analyzes the dissolution of a solid residue by a solvent flowing in a tube. To find the time to dissolve a given thickness of residue, one needs to find the value of τ satisfying

$$\int_0^\tau \frac{du}{(1 - u^3)^{1/3}} = 1$$

Writing the preceding equation as

$$f(\tau) = \int_0^\tau \frac{du}{(1 - u^3)^{1/3}} - 1$$

turns this into a root-finding problem: Find the value of τ that makes $f(\tau) = 0$. Use the built-in `fzero` function and an adaptive quadrature method to solve this problem. Note that the m-file that evaluates $f(\tau)$ needs to accept a vector of τ values and return a vector of $f(\tau)$ values. A simple way to provide this functionality is to use something like the following code.

```
f = zeros(size(tau));
for k=1:length(tau)
    f(k) = ...              %  evaluate f( tau(k) )
end
```

What is the value of τ that satisfies the integral equation? *Hint:* τ is less than 1.

12

Numerical Integration of Ordinary Differential Equations

Differential equations are mathematical models that describe the rate of change of one variable with respect to another. Many fundamental physical laws, including the conservation of mass, momentum, and energy are naturally expressed as differential equations. There are many types of differential equations, and solutions procedures tend to be specialized accordingly. This chapter is concerned with what are called initial-value problems. Given a differential equation and the appropriate initial condition(s), the solution to an initial-value problem obtains the future evolution of the dependent variable(s). Initial-value problems arise in the analysis of electrical circuits, dynamics of machinery, heat transfer, chemical kinetics, population dynamics, and economics, as well as many other areas of science and technology.

The primary topics covered in this chapter are summarized in Figure 12.1. We begin with some examples of differential equations as motivation for studying numerical solution algorithms. Euler's method, the simplest algorithm for numerical integration of ordinary differential equations (ODEs), is described in some detail. A MATLAB implementation of Euler's method is given, along with an analysis of its discretization error. The more accurate midpoint method and Heun's method are presented next, followed by the fourth-order Runge–Kutta method. These methods are developed as extensions to Euler's method. Euler's, the midpoint, Heun's,

674

Topics Covered in This Chapter

1. **Basic Ideas and Nomenclature**

   Ordinary differential equations (**ODEs**) and the prototype **initial-value problem** are defined. The distinguishing features of exact (analytical) and numerical solutions to ODEs are identified.

2. **Euler's Method**

   The simple scheme known as **Euler's method** is developed, implemented in MATLAB, and analyzed. Expressions for the **local discretization error** and the **global discretization error** are developed and verified with numerical experiments. Euler's method is the simplest type of **one-step method**: Values of the dependent variable at time t_j are computed only from values of the dependent variable at one preceding step.

3. **Higher Order One-step Methods**

   The **midpoint method**, **Heun's method**, and the fourth-order **Runge–Kutta method** are presented. Order-of-magnitude expressions for discretization error and numerical experiments show that these are all more efficient than Euler's method.

4. **Adaptive Stepsize Algorithms**

   Adaptive stepsize algorithms adjust the changes in the independent variable so that the numerical solution to the ODE is estimated to have an accuracy within a user-specified tolerance. The built-in ode23 and ode45 functions are adaptive stepsize methods. The basic ideas embodied in adaptive stepsize algorithms are described, and the use of the ode23 and ode45 functions is demonstrated by example.

5. **Coupled ODEs**

   Many practical initial-value problems involve **coupled ODEs** or **higher order ODEs**. Higher order ODEs are equivalent to a system of coupled, first-order ODEs. The numerical solution to coupled, first-order ODEs and the conversion of higher order ODEs to a system of first-order ODEs are demonstrated.

6. **Additional Topics**

   Numerical techniques not discussed in earlier sections are briefly described. The built-in methods for **stiff equations** are identified.

Figure 12.1   Primary topics covered in Chapter 12.

and the Runge–Kutta methods serve as preparation for using MATLAB's built-in ODE integration routines ode23 and ode45, which use adaptive stepsize control to obtain more accurate solutions. By progressing through the simpler routines presented in the beginning of the chapter, the reader is acquainted with the accuracy issues and input–output parameters that also apply to the built-in, adaptive stepsize routines.

Routines for integrating a single ordinary differential equation are extended to systems of equations in the second half of the chapter. The general procedure for integrating a system of equations is discussed first in the context of the fourth-order Runge–Kutta algorithm. An example system consisting of two coupled, first-order ODEs—the two-species predator–prey model—is presented. A solution to this system is implemented using the built-in ode45 function. The procedure for integrating a single higher order ODE by converting it to a system of first-order ODEs is demonstrated next. A simulation of a second-order mass–spring–damper system is used as an example. A general procedure for any higher order ODE is also described. The chapter concludes with a brief discussion of additional topics in the study of numerical solutions to ODEs.

12.1 BASIC IDEAS AND NOMENCLATURE

This section provides a brief review of ordinary differential equations and a preview of the numerical techniques presented in this chapter. Common nomenclature is defined.

12.1.1 Ordinary Differential Equations

A prototypical *ordinary* differential equation (ODE) is

$$\frac{dy}{dt} = f(t, y), \tag{12.1}$$

where $f(t, y)$ is a function of the *independent variable* t and the *dependent variable* y. The dy/dt is an *ordinary* derivative because y is a function of t alone. Contrast this to a *partial* differential equation, which describes how a dependent variable, say, u, depends on two or more variables (e.g., $u = u(x, y)$).

The rate relationship in Equation (12.1) does not completely specify y. In fact, Equation (12.1) has an infinite number of solutions. To specify a unique $y(t)$, one must also supply an *initial condition*

$$y(t_0) = y_0.$$

The preceding equations are usually written together as

$$\frac{dy}{dt} = f(t, y), \qquad y(t_0) = y_0. \tag{12.2}$$

Equation (12.2) is referred to as an *initial-value problem*. To make this complete, we must also specify the range of t over which the equation is to be solved (e.g., $t_0 \le t \le t_N$).

Throughout this chapter, the independent variable will be t, which can often be interpreted as time. Indeed, many initial-value problems are models of transient behavior, so t is a natural choice for the independent variable. The reader should be aware that there are many initial-value problems that are not time dependent. The independent variable for a physical problem could be x, the distance from some reference location. In that case, the initial values are values of the dependent variable (and perhaps its derivatives) that are imposed on the physical boundary $x = 0$.

Equation (12.1) is called a first-order ODE, because it involves only the first derivative of y. Ordinary differential equations exist with second-, third-, and higher order derivatives. The *order* of a differential equation is the order of the highest derivative of the dependent variable that appears in the equation.

Some ODEs exist in coupled systems with other ODEs. In that case, each dependent variable y_1, y_2, $\ldots$, y_m has its own differential equation, and those equations can contain expressions involving the other dependent variables. For example, the following defines a system of two, coupled, first-order ODEs:

$$\frac{dy_1}{dt} = \alpha y_1 + \beta y_2 + g_1(t), \qquad y_1(t_0) = y_{1,0},$$

$$\frac{dy_2}{dt} = \gamma y_1 + \delta y_2 + g_2(t), \qquad y_2(t_0) = y_{2,0}.$$

In the preceding pair of equations, α, β, γ, and δ are known coefficients, and the $g_i(t)$ are known functions of t.

All of the numerical methods presented in this chapter are developed for solving first-order ODEs. As described in § 12.5.2, higher order ODEs are solved numerically by first converting them to a mathematically equivalent system of coupled, first-order ODEs.

Example 12.1: Newton's Law of Motion

The motion of an object under the action of an applied force is governed by

$$F = ma,$$

where F is the magnitude of the force, m is the mass, and a is the resulting acceleration of the object. This is really an ODE, because

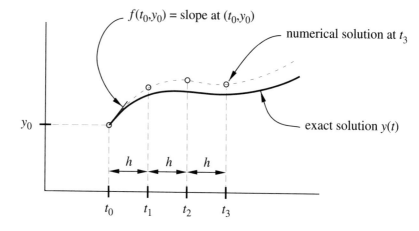

Figure 12.3 Conceptual idea behind the numerical approximation to the exact solution of $dy/dt = f(t, y)$, $y(t_0) = y_0$.

be defined by

$$t_j = t_0 + jh, \qquad j = 0, 1, 2, \ldots, N, \tag{12.6}$$

where the spacing parameter h is called the stepsize. For now, h will be assumed to be a known constant. In the more advanced techniques considered later in the chapter, h will be variable. The numerical solution to Equation (12.2) is obtained by computing a series of y_j at the corresponding t_j.

Throughout this chapter, the exact but unknown solution to Equation (12.2) is designated $y(t)$, or simply y. The exact solution at a discrete t_j is $y(t_j)$. The numerical approximation to $y(t_j)$ is y_j. This nomenclature is summarized in Table 12.1. The use of these symbols allows the error in the numerical solution at t_j to be written $e_j = y_j - y(t_j)$.

A Problem with Subscripts Figure 12.3 and Equation (12.6) define the sequence of discrete t values as $t_0, t_1, \ldots, t_N$. In a computer program, it is natu-

TABLE 12.1 NOMENCLATURE USED IN THE NUMERICAL SOLUTION TO ORDINARY DIFFERENTIAL EQUATIONS.

Symbol	Meaning
t_j	Discrete value of independent variable t.
$y(t)$	Exact solution to the differential equation.
$y(t_j)$	Exact solution evaluated at $t = t_j$.
$e_j = y_j - y(t_j)$	Error in the approximate numerical solution at $t = t_j$.

ral to store the values of t_j in an array. A direct translation to MATLAB code is not possible, however, since all MATLAB arrays begin with an index of 1, not 0. This is a small detail that can trip up the unwary. The correspondence between the mathematical t_j and the MATLAB variables t(j) is summarized in the following table:

mathematical symbol:	t_0	t_1	$\dots$	t_N
MATLAB variable:	t(1)	t(2)	$\dots$	t(n)

This translation requires

$$\text{n} = N + 1.$$

The value of h must be the same with either indexing notation. For a uniform h we have

$$h = \frac{t_N - t_0}{N} = \frac{\text{t(n)} - \text{t(1)}}{\text{n} - 1} \qquad \text{(uniform } h \text{ only)}.$$

Usually, the value of h is specified, and the t_j are calculated from Equation (12.6). In MATLAB, the entries of a uniformly spaced vector t can be computed with

```
tn = ...          % Specify the final value of t
h = ...           % and the stepsize
t = (0:h:tn)';
```

where the transpose of (0:h:tn) creates a column vector.

12.2 EULER'S METHOD

The Taylor Series expansion of the unknown solution to Equation (12.2) about the point $t = t_0$ is

$$y(t) = y(t_0) + (t - t_0)\, y'(t_0) + \frac{(t - t_0)^2}{2}\, y''(t_0) + \cdots, \qquad (12.7)$$

where $y' = dy/dt$, $y'' = d^2y/dx^2$, etc. Retaining only the first derivative term and using the right-hand side of Equation (12.1) to evaluate $y'(t_0)$, Equation (12.7) becomes

$$y(t) \approx y(t_0) + (t - t_0)\, f(t_0, y_0). \qquad (12.8)$$

With this formula, the numerical approximation to $y(t_1)$ is

$$y_1 = y_0 + h\, f(t_0, y_0), \qquad (12.9)$$

where $h = t_1 - t_0$. Figure 12.3 provides a graphical interpretation of this equation. Given the value of $y_0 = y(t_0)$, an approximate solution to $y(t_1)$ is obtained by extrapolating from (t_0, y_0) with the slope of the $y(t)$ curve evaluated at (t_0, y_0). From the sketch in Figure 12.3, it is apparent that the accuracy of this approximate solution is affected by the size of h and by the curvature of the true $y(t)$ function between $t = t_0$ and $t = t_1$. These issues are examined in § 12.2.2.

Equation (12.9) gives an explicit formula for computing y_1 from the known values of t_0, y_0, and h. Since an approximate numerical value for y_1 is available, y_2 can be computed with the same procedure, namely,

$$y_2 = y_1 + h\,f(t_1, y_1),$$

and so on. In general,

$$y_j = y_{j-1} + h\,f(t_{j-1}, y_{j-1}), \qquad j = 1, 2, \ldots, N, \qquad (12.10)$$

This simple integration strategy is known as *Euler's method*, or *Euler's explicit method*. It is called an explicit method because the value of y at the next step is calculated only from the value of y at the previous step. Given the approximate formula, one can solve for y_j explicitly in terms of t_{j-1}, y_{j-1}, and $f(t_{j-1}, y_{j-1})$, all of which are known.

Equation (12.10) is an approximation, because it is obtained by truncating the Taylor series in Equation (12.7). One expects, therefore, that use of Equation (12.10) will result in a numerical solution that differs from the exact solution. An analysis of this approximation is given after presenting an example calculation and a general purpose MATLAB implementation of Euler's method.

Example 12.3: Manual Calculation with Euler's Method

The initial-value problem

$$\frac{dy}{dt} = t - 2y, \qquad y(0) = 1 \qquad (12.11)$$

will be used to test Euler's method. The exact solution is

$$y = \frac{1}{4}\left[2t - 1 + 5e^{-2t}\right].$$

Because the exact solution is known, it is not necessary, of course, to find a numerical solution. Nevertheless, solving the problem both ways allows us to study the behavior of the numerical method, and it provides a benchmark for checking a computer program for bugs.

The following table shows the results of manual calculations for the first few steps with $h = 0.2$. For comparison, the exact solution $y(t_j)$ and the error $y_j - y(t_j)$ are also tabulated.

j	t_j	$f(t_{j-1}, y_{j-1})$	Euler $y_j = y_{j-1} + h\, f(t_{j-1}, y_{j-1})$	Exact $y(t_j)$	Error $y_j - y(t_j)$
0	0.0	NA	(initial condition) 1.0000	1.0000	0
1	0.2	$0 - (2)(1) = -2.000$	$1.0 + (0.2)(-2.0) = 0.6000$	0.6879	-0.0879
2	0.4	$0.2 - (2)(0.6) = -1.000$	$0.6 + (0.2)(-1.0) = 0.4000$	0.5117	-0.1117
3	0.6	$0.4 - (2)(0.4) = -0.400$	$0.4 + (0.2)(-0.4) = 0.3200$	0.4265	-0.1065

The approximate solution with Euler's method follows the general trend of the exact solution. The error introduced at any one step is affected by errors from preceding steps. As is the case for the $t_3 = 0.6$ step, the magnitude of the error may actually decrease from one step to the next.

12.2.1 Implementation of Euler's Method

Given a differential equation $dy/dt = f(t, y)$, we can code the right-hand-side function into Equation (12.10) and evaluate it repeatedly with a loop. Equations (12.10) and (12.11), for example, can be combined as follows:

```
y(1) = ...  % initial condition
for j=2:n
    y(j) = y(j-1) + h * (t(j-1) - 2*y(j-1));
end
```

Recall that $j = 1$ corresponds to the initial condition $t(1) = t_0$. Obviously, this code only applies to the numerical integration of Equation (12.11). Since Euler's method can be applied to any first-order ODE, it is useful to create a general-purpose routine that contains the logic of Euler's method, without the code for a particular ODE. Such a general-purpose routine needs some way of evaluating the right-hand side of the ODE supplied to it. This is easily implemented by calling the right-hand-side function *indirectly* with the `feval` function. (See § 3.6.3 on page 134.)

The `odeEuler` function in Listing 12.1 is a general implementation of Euler's method. The first input argument to `odeEuler` is `diffeq`, a string that stores the name of an m-file that evaluates the right-hand side of the ODE for any values of t and y. The statement

```
y(j) = y(j-1) + h*feval(diffeq,t(j-1),y(j-1));
```

is equivalent to Equation (12.10) with $f(t_{j-1}, y_{j-1})$ replaced by `feval(diffeq,` `t(j-1),y(j-1))`.

To use `odeEuler` with a particular ODE, simply create a short m-file or an inline function object that evaluates the right-hand side of the differential equation. As an example, the `rhs1` function in the lower half of Listing 12.2 evaluates the

```
function [t,y] = odeEuler(diffeq,tn,h,y0)
% odeEuler  Euler's method for integration of a single, first order ODE
%
% Synopsis:    [t,y] = odeEuler(diffeq,tn,h,y0)
%
% Input:       diffeq = (string) name of the m-file that evaluates the right
%                       hand side of the ODE written in standard form
%              tn   = stopping value of the independent variable
%              h    = stepsize for advancing the independent variable
%              y0   = initial condition for the dependent variable
%
% Output:      t = vector of independent variable values:  t(j) = (j-1)*h
%              y = vector of numerical solution values at the t(j)

t = (0:h:tn)';            % Column vector of elements with spacing h
n = length(t);            % Number of elements in the t vector
y = y0*ones(n,1);         % Preallocate y for speed

%   Begin Euler scheme; j=1 for initial condition
for j=2:n
   y(j) = y(j-1) + h*feval(diffeq,t(j-1),y(j-1));
end
```

Listing 12.1   The odeEuler function for integration of a first-order
ODE with Euler's explicit method.

right-hand side of Equation (12.11). Given odeEuler.m and rhs1.m the results
obtained manually in the preceding example are reproduced with the following
statements:

```
>> [x,y] = odeEuler('rhs1',0.6,0.2,1);
>> disp([x,y])
```

Try it for yourself!

The same results are obtained with the following statements that define the
code to evaluate dy/dt as an inline function object:

```
>> dydt = inline('t - 2*y','t','y')
>> [x,y] = odeEuler(dydt,0.6,0.2,1);
>> disp([x,y])
```

The input variables to the dydt object must be explicitly identified (i.e., dydt
= inline('t - 2*y','t','y') not dydt = inline('t - 2*y')) to avoid
a runtime error when the feval function is executed in odeEuler. Explicit identi-

```
function demoEuler(h)
% demoEuler  Integrate dy/dt = t - 2*y;  y(0) = 1 with Euler's method
%
% Synopsis:  demoEuler(h)
%
% Input:     h  = (optional) stepsize, Default:  h = 0.2
%
% Output:    A table comparing the numerical and exact solutions

if nargin<1,  h = 0.2;  end

tn = 1;  y0 = 1;                       %  stopping time and IC
[t,y] = odeEuler('rhs1',tn,h,1);       %  Euler integration
yex = ( 2*t - 1 + 5*exp(-2*t) )/4;     %  Exact solution

fprintf('     t      y_Euler     y_exact      error\n');
for k=1:length(t)
  fprintf('%9.4f  %9.6f  %9.6f  %10.2e\n',t(k),y(k),yex(k),y(k)-yex(k))
end
fprintf('\nMax error = %10.2e for h = %f\n',norm(y-yex,inf),h);
```

```
function dydt = rhs1(t,y)
% rhs1   Evaluate right hand side of dy/dt = t - 2*y
dydt = t - 2*y;
```

Listing 12.2 The demoEuler function for comparing the numerical solution from Euler's method solution with the exact solution of Equation (12.11). The rhs1 function evaluates the right-hand side of the ODE.

fication of the input variables allows feval to know both the number and order of the input variables.

A comparison of Equations (12.7) and (12.8) shows that Euler's method involves neglecting terms with coefficients of order h^2 and higher. The neglected terms are responsible for what is called the *discretization error*[1] of the scheme. As h is reduced, the discretization error at each step will also be reduced. An exact analysis of this effect is presented in the next section. Let us first proceed with an experimental investigation of the effect of stepsize on the accuracy of Euler's method.

---

[1]The term *truncation error* is also used, although the two terms have slightly different meaning in this context. (See § 12.2.2.)

Example 12.4: Effect of Reducing the Stepsize

The demoEuler function in Listing 12.2 creates a comparison between the solution by
Euler's method and the exact solution to Equation (12.11). Here are the results of running
demoEuler with $h = 0.2$ and $h = 0.1$ (to save space, some steps of the $h = 0.1$ case are
not shown):

```
>> demoEuler
    t      y_Euler   y_exact     error
 0.0000   1.000000  1.000000    0.00e+00
 0.2000   0.600000  0.687900   -8.79e-02
 0.4000   0.400000  0.511661   -1.12e-01
 0.6000   0.320000  0.426493   -1.06e-01
 0.8000   0.312000  0.402371   -9.04e-02
 1.0000   0.347200  0.419169   -7.20e-02

Max error =  1.12e-01 for h = 0.200000

>> demoEuler(0.1);
    t      y_Euler   y_exact     error
 0.0000   1.000000  1.000000    0.00e+00
 0.1000   0.800000  0.823413   -2.34e-02
 0.2000   0.650000  0.687900   -3.79e-02
 0.3000   0.540000  0.586015   -4.60e-02
    ...
 0.8000   0.359715  0.402371   -4.27e-02
 0.9000   0.367772  0.406624   -3.89e-02
 1.0000   0.384218  0.419169   -3.50e-02

Max error =  5.02e-02 for h = 0.100000
```

These results confirm the hunch that h reduces the error. The ratio of the maximum
error in the $h = 0.1$ solution to the error in the $h = 0.2$ solution is

$$\frac{\max(y_j - y(t_j))_{h=0.1}}{\max(y_j - y(t_j))_{h=0.2}} = \frac{0.502}{1.12} = 0.45 \approx \frac{1}{2}.$$

Reducing h by a factor of one-half reduces the accumulated error by a factor of (roughly)
one-half. This is consistent with a theoretical analysis, which shows that the accumulated
error is proportional to h.

Figure 12.4 shows the results of applying Euler's method to Equation (12.11) for a
larger range of t and for three stepsizes ($h = 0.2$, $h = 0.1$, and $h = 0.05$). Reducing h
results in smaller errors at each time step.

12.2.2 Analysis of Euler's Method

The preceding example demonstrates that the error in applying Euler's method is
reduced when h is reduced. This result is intuitively reasonable, since the accuracy

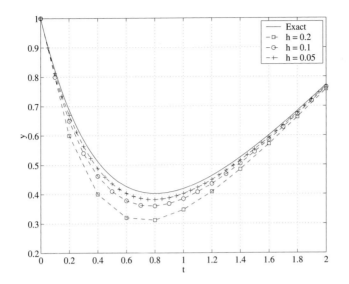

Figure 12.4   Comparison of the exact solution of equation (12.11) with solutions obtained with Euler's method using step sizes of $h = 0.2$, $h = 0.1$, and $h = 0.05$.

of using the slope at (t_{j-1}, y_{j-1}) to predict future changes in $y(t)$ will deteriorate as $h = t_j - t_{j-1}$ increases. It is also intuitively reasonable that the accuracy of the prediction depends on the $f(t, y)$ in the right-hand side of Equation (12.2). If $f(t, y)$ is slowly changing, or, more precisely, if $|f'(t, y)| = |y''(t)|$ is small, then one expects the value of $f(t_{j-1}, y_{j-1})$ to be a reliable estimate of $f(t, y)$ in a larger neighborhood around (t_{j-1}, y_{j-1}) than if $|y''(t)|$ is large. These intuitive ideas are quantified in this section. It is impossible to compute the exact magnitude of the error in a numerical solution to an initial-value problem unless the exact solution is known. The goal of the current analysis is not to precisely measure the error, but to determine how quickly the *order of magnitude* of the error decreases as h decreases.

There are two perspectives in evaluating the behavior of a numerical approximation to Equation (12.2). One can consider the size of the error made during any one step, or one can consider the errors in the entire interval $t_0 \le t \le t_N$ over which the solution is sought. Both perspectives will be used here. The error at any one step is called the *local discretization error* (LDE), and the error for the entire solution is called the *global discretization error* (GDE). The term *discretization error* is used instead of *truncation error*, because it is more suggestive of how the theoretical expressions for the error are obtained. Rather than focusing on the terms that are dropped in a Taylor series expansion, the expression for the local discretization error is obtained by comparing the equation satisfied by the discrete approximation to the original ODE.

Local Discretization Error   The computational formula for Euler's method (Equation (12.10)), can be rearranged as

$$\frac{y_j - y_{j-1}}{h} = f(t_{j-1}, y_{j-1}), \tag{12.12}$$

which is the discrete analog to the original ODE in Equation (12.2). The left-hand side is an approximation to the derivative dy/dt. The numerical solution produced by Euler's method is the discrete function y_j that satisfies the so-called *Difference Equation* (12.12).

It is not surprising that the exact and the approximate solution disagree, since they are governed by two different equations (Equations (12.2) and (12.12), respectively). In fact, at any one time step, if the exact solution is substituted into the difference equation, the equality in Equation (12.12) does not hold; that is,

$$\frac{y(t_j) - y(t_{j-1})}{h} - f(t_{j-1}, y(t_{j-1})) \neq 0. \tag{12.13}$$

The local discretization error is a measure of how far the left-hand side of the preceding equation is from zero.

A technical problem with using Equation (12.13) to measure the local discretization error is that the exact solution is unlikely to coincide with (t_{j-1}, y_{j-1}) for any step except $j = 0$. To remedy this problem, introduce an auxiliary family of functions $z_j(t)$, which are the exact solutions to the initial-value problems (compare $z_j(t)$ with Equation (12.2)):

$$\frac{dz_j}{dt} = f(t, y), \quad z_j(t_{j-1}) = y_{j-1}, \quad j = 1, \ldots, n - 1. \tag{12.14}$$

The $z_j(t)$ are the continuous functions that satisfy Equation (12.14) in the jth subinterval *and* pass through the preceding numerical solution point (t_{j-1}, y_{j-1}). The relationship between $y(t)$, $y_j(t_j)$, and $z_j(t)$ for Equation (12.11) is shown in Figure 12.5.

The local discretization error $\tau(t, h)$ can now be precisely defined by substituting $z_j(t)$ into Equation (12.12):

$$\tau(t, h) = \frac{z_j(t_j) - z_j(t_{j-1})}{h} - f(t_{j-1}, z_j(t_{j-1})). \tag{12.15}$$

The local discretization error (LDE) is simply the residual when the difference equation is evaluated with the exact solution to Equation (12.14). The notation $\tau = \tau(t, h)$ is a reminder that the discretization error depends on h, which is under

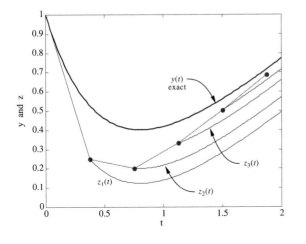

Figure 12.5   Exact solution $y(t)$ and numerical solution (solid dots) obtained from Euler's method for $dy/dt = t - 2y$, $y(0) = 1$, and $h = 0.4$. The $z_j(t)$ are the exact solutions to $dz_j/dt = t - 2z_j$, $z_j(t_{j-1}) = y_{j-1}$.

user control, and t, the position in the interval, which determines the magnitude of derivatives of the function $z_j(t)$ (or $y(t)$).

Equation (12.15) is not in the most useful form, because it does not clearly indicate how the discretization error depends on h. A little additional manipulation makes that dependency explicit. Expanding $z_j(t)$ in a Taylor series about the point (t_{j-1}, y_{j-1}) gives

$$z_j(t_j) = z_j(t_{j-1}) + hz'_j(t_{j-1}) + \frac{h^2}{2}z''_j(\xi), \qquad (12.16)$$

where ξ is some point in the closed interval $[t_{j-1}, t_j]$. The preceding equation can be rearranged as

$$\frac{z_j(t_j) - z_j(t_{j-1})}{h} = z'_j(t_{j-1}) + \frac{h}{2}z''_j(\xi). \qquad (12.17)$$

Substituting the right-hand side of the ODE in Equation (12.14) into Equation (12.17) and rearranging terms gives

$$\frac{z_j(t_j) - z_j(t_{j-1})}{h} - f(t_{j-1}, z_{j-1}) = \frac{h}{2}z''_j(\xi).$$

Comparing this expression with Equation (12.15) shows that the LDE for Euler's method for the jth interval is

$$\tau(t_j, h) = \frac{h}{2}z''_j(\xi).$$

The LDE is influenced by h, which is under control of the user, and $z''_j(\xi)$, which is determined by the ODE being integrated. All that we know about ξ is that it lies somewhere in the jth interval. The value of $z''_j(\xi)$, therefore, can not be computed.

reduced at the expense of more calculations per step. It should be remembered that although $f(t, y)$ is evaluated at more than one point in the interval $t_{j-1} \leq t \leq t_j$, the methods are still one-step methods, because only the *solution* at one previous step, (i.e., y_{j-1}), appears on the right-hand side of Equation (12.22).

The discretization errors of one-step methods can be analyzed with the techniques presented in § 12.2.2. For the initial-value problem of Equation (12.2), any one-step method with a LDE (cf. Equation (12.15))

$$\tau(t, h) \leq Ch^p = \mathcal{O}(h^p), \tag{12.24}$$

where $p \geq 1$, has the GDE

$$\max |y(t_j) - y_j| = \mathcal{O}(h^p). \tag{12.25}$$

(See, for example, [9, 31, 65, 70] for a proof.) In other words, a one-step method with LDE that is $\mathcal{O}(h^p)$ has a GDE that is also $\mathcal{O}(h^p)$.

12.2.4 Summary of §12.2

Euler's method has been used to illustrate important features of numerical methods for ODEs. These features are:

- The numerical integration scheme is derived from a truncated Taylor series approximation of the ODE.
- The implementation separates the logic of the ODE integration scheme from the evaluation of the right-hand side $f(t, y)$. A general-purpose ODE solver requires the user to supply a small m-file for evaluating $f(t, y)$.
- The local discretization error (LDE) accounts for the error at each time step. In general, for one-step methods, the LDE is of the form

  $$LDE = \mathcal{O}(h^p),$$

  where h is the stepsize and p is an integer $p \geq 1$.
- The global discretization error (GDE) includes the accumulated effect of the LDE when the ODE integration scheme is applied to an interval using several steps of size h. Using the definition of LDE in this text, the GDE is

  $$GDE = \mathcal{O}(h^p).$$

12.3 HIGHER ORDER ONE-STEP METHODS

In the preceding section, Euler's method was used to develop many basic ideas—in particular, to establish the characteristics of one-step methods. In this section, a sequence of progressively more accurate one-step methods is discussed. The presentation moves more quickly, as each method can be viewed as an enhancement to the ideas embodied in Euler's method. The methods are presented in order of increasing accuracy (larger GDE to smaller GDE).

12.3.1 Midpoint Method

The only way to increase the accuracy of Euler's method is to reduce h. The effect of doing this is to evaluate the numerical solution more frequently along the t-axis. An alternative procedure is to evaluate the slope more than once per step, with the goal of reducing the LDE. The midpoint method uses a tentative Euler step to the midpoint of the interval, where the slope for the entire interval is reevaluated.

Figure 12.6 illustrates one step of the midpoint method. The value, y_{j-1}, of the dependent variable is assumed to be known at t_{j-1}. Define k_1 as the value of the slope evaluated at (t_{j-1}, y_{j-1}):

$$k_1 = f(t_{j-1}, y_{j-1}).$$

Then, use k_1 to estimate the solution at the midpoint of the interval:

$$y_{j-1/2} = y_{j-1} + \frac{h}{2} f(t_{j-1}, y_{j-1}).$$

In other words, $y_{j-1/2}$ is the value of y at $t_{j-1} + h/2$ that would be predicted by Euler's method. Next, estimate the slope at the midpoint and call its value k_2:

$$k_2 = f\left(t_{j-1} + \frac{h}{2}, y_{j-1} + \frac{h}{2}k_1\right).$$

Finally, compute the value of y at the end of the full interval with

$$y_j = y_{j-1} + h k_2.$$

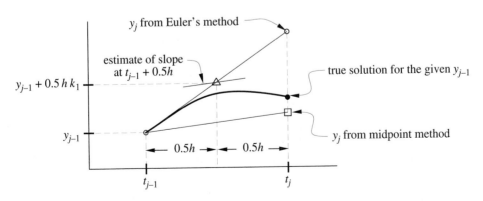

Figure 12.6   Graphical representation of the midpoint method.

```
function [t,y] = odeMidpt(diffeq,tn,h,y0)
% odeMidpt   Midpoint method for integration of a single, first order ODE
%
% Synopsis:  [t,y] = odeMidpt(diffeq,tn,h,y0)
%
% Input:     diffeq = (string) name of the m-file that evaluates the right
%                     hand side of the ODE written in standard form
%            tn = stopping value of the independent variable
%            h  = stepsize for advancing the independent variable
%            y0 = initial condition for the dependent variable
%
% Output:    t = vector of independent variable values:  t(j) = (j-1)*h
%            y = vector of numerical solution values at the t(j)

t = (0:h:tn)';            %  Column vector of elements with spacing h
n = length(t);            %  Number of elements in the t vector
y = y0*ones(n,1);         %  Preallocate y for speed
h2 = h/2;                 %  Avoid repeated evaluation of this constant

%   Begin Midpoint scheme; j=1 for initial condition
for j=2:n
   k1 = feval(diffeq,t(j-1),y(j-1));
   k2 = feval(diffeq,t(j-1)+h2,y(j-1)+h2*k1);
   y(j) = y(j-1) + h*k2;
end
```

Listing 12.3   The odeMidpt function for integrating a first-order ODE with the midpoint method.

The local and global discretization errors of the midpoint method are $\mathcal{O}(h^2)$. The increase in accuracy is achieved by doubling the number of times $f(t, y)$ must be evaluated at each step. Is the effort worth it? The answer is yes, as demonstrated in Example 12.5.

Implementation of the midpoint method requires only a slight variation on the code used to implement Euler's method. The result is the odeMidpt function in Listing 12.3.

Example 12.5: Comparison of Midpoint and Euler Methods

Consider the choice of integrating an ODE with either Euler's method or the midpoint method. For a given h, the midpoint method is clearly more accurate—its global discretization error is $\mathcal{O}(h^2)$, whereas Euler's global discretization error is $\mathcal{O}(h)$. On the other hand, the midpoint method also makes twice as many calls to the $f(t, y)$ routine. Suppose the solutions are to be evaluated at a sequence of smaller and smaller h. Let the h used for one solution be half of the value of the h for the previous solution. On subsequent runs, the

```
function compEM
% compEM      Compare Euler and Midpoint for solution of dy/dt = -y;  y(0) = 1
%
% Synopsis:  compEM
%
% Input:     none
%
% Output:    Flops and global trunc errors for a sequence of stepsizes

tn = 1;  y0 = 1;        % Length of interval and initial condition

fprintf('\n   h      flopsE    errE      flopsM    errM\n');
for h = [0.2  0.1  0.05  0.025  0.0125  0.00625]
   flops(0);  [te,ye] = odeEuler('rhs2',tn,h,1);  flopse = flops;  % Euler
   flops(0);  [tm,ym] = odeMidpt('rhs2',tn,h,1);  flopsm = flops;  % Midpoint
   % --- global discretization errors
   yex = y0*exp(-te);        % Exact solution at discrete t
   erre = max(abs(ye-yex));   errm = max(abs(ym-yex));
   fprintf('%8.5f %7d %11.2e %7d %11.2e\n',h,flopse,erre,flopsm,errm);
end
```

> **Listing 12.4**   The compEM function for comparing the numerical solu-
> tion to Equation (12.26) obtained with Euler's method and the midpoint
> method.

GDE for the midpoint method is reduced by a factor of four, whereas for Euler's method, the GDE is reduced by only a factor of two.

To quantify the advantage of reduced discretization error, the midpoint method and Euler's method are used to solve

$$\frac{dy}{dt} = -y, \qquad y(0) = 1, \qquad 0 \le t \le 1. \tag{12.26}$$

The numerical results are compared to the exact solution, $y = e^{-t}$.

The compEM function in Listing 12.4 obtains the numerical solutions to Equation (12.26) with a progression of smaller h. The computational effort is measured with the built-in flops function. For each h, the flops and global discretization errors for the two methods are printed. Running compEM produces the following results:

```
>> compEM
   h         flopsE    errE      flopsM    errM
0.20000       31     4.02e-02     57     2.86e-03
0.10000       61     1.92e-02    112     6.62e-04
0.05000      121     9.39e-03    222     1.59e-04
0.02500      241     4.65e-03    442     3.90e-05
0.01250      481     2.31e-03    882     9.67e-06
0.00625      961     1.15e-03   1762     2.41e-06
```

As expected, at a given h, Euler's method takes roughly half as much work as the midpoint method. It also obtains a significantly less accurate solution. For Equation (12.26), Euler's method requires $h = 0.0125$ to obtain roughly the same accuracy, that the midpoint method achieves with $h = 0.2$. For the same accuracy, Euler's method requires more than eight times the effort effort (481 flops as opposed to 57 flops) needed by the midpoint method. Clearly, the midpoint method is a superior technique.

The gain in accuracy of the midpoint method is consistent with its formal accuracy of $\mathcal{O}(h^2)$. For example, reducing the step size from 0.025 to 0.0125 results in a factor-of-four reduction in the error:

$$\frac{\max(|e_j|)_{h=0.025}}{\max(|e_j|)_{h=0.0125}} = \frac{3.90e-05}{9.67e-06} = 4.03 \approx 2^2.$$

12.3.2 Heun's Method

Heun's method, also called the modified Euler method, is similar to the midpoint method in that it involves two slope evaluations per step. Heun's method is represented graphically in Figure 12.7. As with the midpoint method, define k_1 as the value of the slope at (t_{j-1}, y_{j-1}):

$$k_1 = f(t_{j-1}, y_{j-1}).$$

Next, use k_1 to make a tentative estimate of the slope at the *end* of the interval:

$$k_2 = f(t_{j-1} + h, y_{j-1} + hk_1).$$

This value of k_2 is not the same as the k_2 for the midpoint method. Finally, compute y_j with the average of slopes k_1 and k_2:

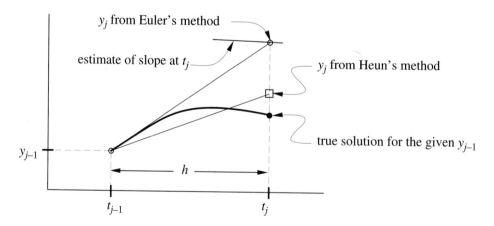

Figure 12.7   Graphical representation of the Heun's method.

$$y_j = y_{j-1} + h\frac{k_1 + k_2}{2}.$$

The local and global discretization errors of Heun's method are $\mathcal{O}(h^2)$, and it requires two function evaluations per step of size h. Thus, both the formal accuracy and work requirements of Heun's method are equivalent to the midpoint method. Implementation of Heun's method is the goal of Exercise 10.

12.3.3 Fourth-order Runge–Kutta Method

Heun's method uses an average of two slope values in the interval $t_{j-1} \le t \le t_j$ to predict the value of y_j. One might suspect that using an average of more than two slopes could result in greater accuracy (i.e., lower discretization error). This is the case, although a simple-minded average of more slopes is not as effective as a *weighted* average. A general formula for computing y_j from a number of slope estimates is

$$y_j = y_{j-1} + \sum_{\ell=1}^{m} \gamma_\ell k_\ell,$$

where γ_ℓ are weighting coefficients and k_ℓ are slopes evaluated at different points in the jth interval. For Heun's method $\gamma_1 = \gamma_2 = 0.5$. In general, the weights must satisfy

$$\sum_{\ell=1}^{m} \gamma_\ell = 1.$$

There is a formal procedure for obtaining γ_ℓ and k_ℓ such that the final approximation has a desired discretization error. The resulting schemes are referred to as Runge–Kutta methods, named after the two people who independently developed this approach.

   A very popular and straightforward method that embodies this idea is the fourth-order Runge–Kutta method, which we will refer to as "RK-4." The order of a Runge–Kutta method is equal to the order of its GDE. For RK-4, the local and global discretization error are $\mathcal{O}(h^4)$. At each h-size step of RK-4, four estimates of the slope are used as indicated in Figure 12.8. These slope estimates, k_1, k_2, k_3, and k_4, are calculated as follows:

$$k_1 = f(t_{j-1}, y_{j-1}),$$

$$k_2 = f\left(t_{j-1} + \frac{h}{2}, y_{j-1} + \frac{h}{2}k_1\right),$$

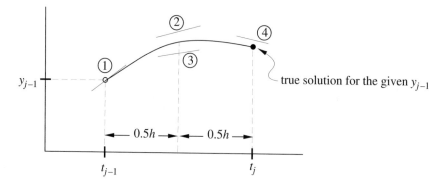

Figure 12.8 Graphical representation of the four points at which the slope is evaluated in fourth-order Runge–Kutta method.

```
function [t,y] = odeRK4(diffeq,tn,h,y0)
% odeRK4   Fourth order Runge-Kutta method for a single, first order ODE
%
% Synopsis:  [t,y] = odeRK4(fun,tn,h,y0)
%
% Input:     diffeq = (string) name of the m-file that evaluates the right
%                     hand side of the ODE written in standard form
%            tn  = stopping value of the independent variable
%            h   = stepsize for advancing the independent variable
%            y0  = initial condition for the dependent variable
%
% Output:    t = vector of independent variable values:  t(j) = (j-1)*h
%            y = vector of numerical solution values at the t(j)

t = (0:h:tn)';                     %  Column vector of elements with spacing h
n = length(t);                     %  Number of elements in the t vector
y = y0*ones(n,1);                  %  Preallocate y for speed
h2 = h/2;  h3 = h/3;  h6 = h/6;    %  Avoid repeated evaluation of constants

%  Begin RK4 integration; j=1 for initial condition
for j=2:n
   k1 = feval(diffeq, t(j-1),    y(j-1)       );
   k2 = feval(diffeq, t(j-1)+h2, y(j-1)+h2*k1 );
   k3 = feval(diffeq, t(j-1)+h2, y(j-1)+h2*k2 );
   k4 = feval(diffeq, t(j-1)+h,  y(j-1)+h*k3  );
   y(j) = y(j-1) + h6*(k1+k4) + h3*(k2+k3);
end
```

Listing 12.5 The odeRK4 function for integration of a first-order ODE with the fourth-order Runge–Kutta method.

$$k_3 = f\left(t_{j-1} + \frac{h}{2}, y_{j-1} + \frac{h}{2}k_2\right),$$

$$k_4 = f(t_{j-1} + h, y_{j-1} + hk_3).$$

A weighted average of the k_i are used to compute the next value of y:

$$y_j = y_{j-1} + h\left(\frac{k_1}{6} + \frac{k_2}{3} + \frac{k_3}{3} + \frac{k_4}{6}\right). \tag{12.27}$$

The odeRK4 function in Listing 12.5 implements the RK-4 scheme using the same code structure as the odeEuler and odeMidpt functions. The primary difference is the computation of additional slope values for each step. The RK-4 method requires four times as much work per step as Euler's method and twice as much work per step as the midpoint method. Though the work per step is greater, the reduced discretization error makes the RK-4 method a more efficient way to achieve a desired accuracy in the solution.

Example 12.6: Comparison of Euler, Midpoint and RK-4 Methods

This example extends the comparison in Example 12.5 (see page 694) to include the RK-4 method. The compEMRK4 function (not listed here, but included in the NMM toolbox) contains the code to measure the flops and global discretization errors when the Euler, midpoint, and RK-4 methods are used to solve Equation (12.26) with a sequence of decreasing h.

```
>> compEMRK4
  h          flopsE    errE        flopsM    errM        flops4    err4
  0.20000    31        4.02e-02     57       2.86e-03     129      5.80e-06
  0.10000    61        1.92e-02    112       6.62e-04     254      3.33e-07
  0.05000    121       9.39e-03    222       1.59e-04     504      2.00e-08
  0.02500    241       4.65e-03    442       3.90e-05    1004      1.22e-09
  0.01250    481       2.31e-03    882       9.67e-06    2004      7.56e-11
  0.00625    961       1.15e-03   1762       2.41e-06    4004      4.70e-12
```

As expected from the discretization error estimate, the errors from RK-4 are much smaller than those produced by Euler's method or the midpoint method. The effort, as measured by the number of flops, for the RK-4 method is also greater than for the midpoint method or Euler's method, though the work increase buys a significant reduction in discretization error.

The following table reorganizes some of the output from compEMRK4 in a way that allows a comparison of the effort necessary to obtain roughly equal accuracy with each of the methods:

	Error	h	flops
Euler	1.2×10^{-3}	0.00625	961
Midpoint	6.6×10^{-4}	0.1	112
Midpoint	2.4×10^{-6}	0.00625	1762
RK-4	3.3×10^{-7}	0.1	254

For comparable accuracy (error of $\mathcal{O}(10^{-3})$), the midpoint method requires roughly one eighth the number of flops needed by Euler's method. The RK-4 method achieves the same accuracy (error of $\mathcal{O}(10^{-6})$) as the midpoint method with one seventh as many flops. We conclude that the midpoint method is much more efficient than Euler's method, and the RK-4 method is much more efficient than either the midpoint or Euler's method. This comparison is strictly applicable to the model problem in Equation (12.26), although qualitatively similar results can be expected for other ODEs.

Finally, the output from compEMRK4 can be used to verify the theoretical discretization error estimate for RK-4. At $t = 1.0$, the ratio of the error in the $h = 0.00625$ RK-4 solution to the error in the $h = 0.0125$ RK-4 solution is

$$\frac{\max(|e_j|)_{h=0.00625}}{\max(|e_j|)_{h=0.0125}} = \frac{4.7 \times 10^{-12}}{7.56 \times 10^{-11}} = 0.0622 \approx (0.499)^4.$$

Thus, reducing the h by a factor of one-half reduces the maximum error by a factor of (approximately) one-half raised to the fourth power. This is consistent with the theoretical analysis that shows that the global discretization error for RK-4 is $\mathcal{O}(h^4)$.

12.4 ADAPTIVE STEPSIZE ALGORITHMS

As demonstrated in the preceding sections, there are two basic strategies for increasing the accuracy of the numerical solution to an ODE: reducing h and choosing a more accurate scheme. The dramatic success obtained by increasing the order from Euler's method to the RK-4 method unfortunately does not continue above order four for Runge–Kutta-type methods. The accuracy can be improved, but the cost in increased evaluations of the ODE right-hand side renders these higher order methods less attractive. The key to further efficiency is to make more selective use of the solution effort. Specifically, the overall number of steps necessary to achieve a solution can (usually) be reduced by *adaptively* varying h. Although the methods presented up to this point have used a fixed h, there is no reason why h cannot be changed from one step to the next during the numerical solution. The only complication is in devising a criterion for automatically choosing the size of h.

To be efficient, an algorithm for adjusting h must relate changes in h to the local accuracy of the solution. The objective is to reduce h when smaller h is necessary to meet a user-specified error tolerance and to increase h when doing so will not cause the error tolerance to be exceeded. In order for this to work, the ODE integration scheme must somehow measure the errors it is making during the solution. This may seem impossible, because the exact solution is unknown, or otherwise we would not need the numerical solution. It turns out that an *estimate* of the LDE is sufficient for controlling the size of h.

One way of estimating the LDE is to compute the approximate solution with two different h and compare the results. If there is no difference between the solution produced by a large and a small value of h, then there is no advantage to decreasing the h. If there is a significant difference between the solutions produced by the two h, then we assume the solution obtained with the large h is inaccurate. Such a procedure obviously requires evaluations of two numerical solutions for each step that is completed.

Another way to estimate the discretization error is to simultaneously advance the solution using one value of h with two different schemes having different LDE. If the less accurate scheme gives (close to) the same result as the more accurate scheme, there is no reason to decrease the h. If, on the other hand, there is a significant difference between the y_j predicted by the two schemes, then the h should be reduced. This is the approach taken by the built-in routines ode23 and ode45.

12.4.1 The ode23 and ode45 Routines

The built-in ode23 and ode45 functions use adaptive stepsize algorithms known as Runge–Kutta–Fehlberg methods. With a carefully chosen set of substeps in the interval of size h, Runge–Kutta–Fehlberg methods simultaneously obtain two solutions with different discretization errors at each step. Computing two solutions per step allows the accuracy of the solution to be monitored *and* the h to be adjusted according to a user-prescribed tolerance on the error.

The ode23 routine simultaneously uses second- and third-order Runge–Kutta formulas to advance the solution and monitor the accuracy. Similarly, ode45 simultaneously uses fourth- and fifth-order formulas. The Runge–Kutta–Fehlberg methods are elegant, because, in addition to providing a mechanism for monitoring the accuracy, the two formulas share some of the intermediate slope values (k_1, k_2, etc.). The ode45 routine, for example, requires only six slope evaluations instead of the nine (four for the RK-4 method plus five for the RK-5 method) slope evaluations that might be expected from a simplistic implementation. See [61, 65] for a discussion of the Runge–Kutta–Fehlberg method and its implementation in a working code. The ode45 routine is based on the algorithm of Dormand and Prince [18].

The ode45 function can be called in the following ways:[2]

---

[2]Other variations are possible. Enter help ode45 at the MATLAB prompt for additional information.

```
[t,Y] = ode45(diffeq,tn,y0)
[t,Y] = ode45(diffeq,[t0 tn],y0)
[t,Y] = ode45(diffeq,[t0 tn],y0,options)
[t,Y] = ode45(diffeq,[t0 tn],y0,options,arg1,arg2, ... )
```

ode23 uses the same parameter sequence. The first argument `diffeq` is the name of an m-file that returns the right-hand side of the differential equation. The `t0` and `tn` parameters define the overall interval for which the solution is sought. If both `t0` and `tn` are provided, the values must be stored in a single vector hence the notation [`t0 tn`]. If `t0` is not given, it is assumed to be zero. The initial condition is supplied as `y0`. The `options` parameter is described in the following subsection. The `arg1`, `arg2`, ... , parameters are passed through to the user-defined `diffeq` routine without being used by ode45. The use of such pass-through parameters is described below and demonstrated with examples.

Unlike the routines presented up to this point, neither ode23 or ode45 require specification of h. Instead, ode23 and ode45 adjust h so that

$$\tilde{\tau} < \max(\texttt{RelTol} \times |y_j|, \texttt{AbsTol}),$$

where $\tilde{\tau}$ is an estimate of the LDE, `RelTol` and `AbsTol` are the error tolerances, and y_j is the computed value of y at the jth time step. The default values of error tolerances are

$$\texttt{RelTol} = 1 \times 10^{-3}, \quad \text{and} \quad \texttt{AbsTol} = 1 \times 10^{-6}. \qquad \text{(default values)}$$

The max( ) operation in the condition for $\tilde{\tau}$ means that the *larger* of the tolerances controls the step size adjustment.

Suppose, for instance, that $|y_j| \sim 100$. The default values for `RelTol` and `AbsTol` mean that the largest acceptable error estimate is $0.1 = 1 \times 10^{-3} \times 100$. The absolute tolerance (1×10^{-6}) is much smaller than `RelTol` $\times y_j$ in this case. The relative tolerance of 1×10^{-3} corresponds to an uncertainty in the computed solution of the order of 0.1%. In contrast, if $|y_j| \sim 10^{-5}$, then the (default) absolute tolerance of 1×10^{-6} would be applied, and the uncertainty in the computed solution is of order 10%. Thus, when the magnitude of the solution is small or when the value of y_j near zero-crossings in important, `AbsTol` should be adjusted accordingly. The values of `RelTol` and `AbsTol` are changed with the `options` argument of ode45.

The various features of ode45 are explored through a sequence of examples. First, we demonstrate the simplest usage of ode45.

Example 12.7: Solve an ODE with ode45

The following statements obtain the solution to Equation (12.26) with ode45. The exact solution at the chosen values of t are is compared to the numerical solution.

```
>> tn = 1; y0 = 1;              % stopping time and initial condition
>> [t,y] = ode45('rhs2',tn,y0); % ode45 solution
>> yex = y0*exp(-t);            % Exact solution
>> norm(y-yex,inf)
ans =
     5.7038e-09
```

The GDE of 6×10^{-9} is comparable to the GDE obtained with a fixed-size RK-4 method with $h = 0.025$. (Cf. Example 12.6 on page 699). For this simple ODE, there is little advantage to using the sophisticated computational machinery of ode45. For general use, however, ode45 is highly recommended.

Controlling ode45 **with** odeset   The built-in ODE integration routines (see also Table 12.3 on page 726) have several parameters controlling their execution. Default values of these parameters provide a reasonable starting point for a solution to an ODE. The odeset function is the user interface for adjusting these parameters. It is not possible to change the control parameters directly in the call to ode45.

Adjusting the control parameters is a two-step process. First, a *data structure*[3] variable is created that contains the parameter values to be changed. This data structure is then passed to ode45. A typical usage of odeset looks like

```
options = odeset('parameterName',parameterValue, ... );
[t,y] = ode45(diffeq,tn,y0,options);
```

parameterName is the name of the parameter to be changed and *parameterValue* is the numerical value to be assigned. The input to odeset lists *parameterName* and *parameterValue* pairs. The possible parameters can be obtained by entering odeset at the command prompt.

```
>> odeset
        AbsTol: [positive scalar or vector 1e-6 ]
           BDF: [on | off ]
        Events: [on | off ]
   InitialStep: [positive scalar ]
      Jacobian: [on | off ]
     JConstant: [on | off ]
      JPattern: [on | off ]
          Mass: [on | off ]
  MassConstant: [on | off ]
```

---

[3]A data structure is a special variable type that can contain an arbitrary collection of other variables. The options variable output from odeset is a data structure that contains pairs of strings and numeric values. Data structures are advanced features of MATLAB version 5 and later. Enter help struct at the command prompt for more information. With the odeset function, you do not need, and should not try, to directly alter the contents of the options data structure.

```
   MaxOrder: [1 | 2 | 3 | 4 | 5 ]
    MaxStep: [positive scalar ]
  OutputFcn: [string ]
  OutputSel: [vector of integers ]
     Refine: [positive integer ]
     RelTol: [positive scalar 1e-3 ]
      Stats: [on | off ]
 Vectorized: [on | off ]
```

Not all of these parameters apply to every ODE solver. Values of the ODE solver options can be set individually or in groups. For example, to reset the InitialStep parameter to 0.001, use

```
>> options = odeset('InitialStep',0.001)
```

To set InitialStep to 0.001 and MaxStep to 0.2, use

```
>> options = odeset('InitialStep',0.001,'MaxStep',0.2)
```

After values in the options data structure are assigned, the data structure is passed as the fourth input parameter of ode45, as in

```
>> [t,y] = ode45('myODE',tn,y0,options);
```

Examples 12.8 and 12.9 demonstrate how odeset is used. For additional information, enter help odeset at the MATLAB command prompt.

Example 12.8: Using odeset with ode45

This example shows how the odeset function is used to control the solution obtained by ode45. The demoODE45opts function in Listing 12.6 compares the solution to Equation (12.26) obtained with ode45 to the exact solution. Input values of rtol and atol override the default values of RelTol and AbsTol used by ode45. If no inputs are supplied to demoODE45opts, the original defaults for RelTol and AbsTol are used.

The odeset function is also used to change the Refine parameter, which controls whether or not the output from ode45 is interpolated to finer increments on the t-axis. The interpolation is desirable in many problems because ode45 can produce highly accurate results with fairly large h. The h can be so large that a plot of the results would not be visually acceptable, even though the solution is obtained well within the user-specified error tolerances. The Refine parameter defines how many interpolated values are created between the solution values (t_j, y_j). For ode45, the default value of Refine is 4, meaning that the arrays t and y returned by ode45 will have four times as many points as were actually used to obtain the numerical solution. The extra output points are interpolated between the numerical solution values so that the value of Refine has no effect on the accuracy of the solution. In demoODE45opts, the default value of Refine is set to 1, so that the printed results can be directly compared with the results from Examples 12.5 and 12.6.

```
function demoODE45opts(rtol,atol,nref)
% demoODE45opts  Integrate dy/dx = -y;  y(0) = 1 with ode45 and options
%
% Synopsis:  demoODE45opts
%            demoODE45opts(rtol)
%            demoODE45opts(rtol,atol)
%            demoODE45opts(rtol,atol,nref)
%
% Input: rtol = (optional) relative tolerance used by ode45
%               Default: rtol = 1e-3 (internal default used by ode45)
%        atol = (optional) absolute tolerance used by ode45
%               Default: atol = 1e-6 (internal default used by ode45)
%        nref = (optional) ratio of the number of solution steps returned
%               by ode45 to those actually computed with the RK-45 method.
%               Default: nref = 1, meaning all returned values are from
%               steps of the RK-45 algorithm.  nref>1 causes ode45 to
%               interpolate nref additional "solution" values per step
%
% Output:   A table comparing the numerical and exact solutions

if nargin<1, rtol = 1e-3;  end
if nargin<2, atol = 1e-6;  end
if nargin<3, nref = 1;     end

%  Set tolerance and output refinement options.
options = odeset('RelTol',rtol,'AbsTol',atol,'Refine',nref);
tn = 1;  y0 = 1;
flops(0);  [t,y] = ode45('rhs2',tn,y0,options);  f = flops;
yex = y0*exp(-t);   emax = norm(y-yex,inf);

fprintf('      t      y_ode45   y_exact     error\n');
for k=1:length(t)
  fprintf('  %7.4f  %8.6f  %8.6f  %9.2e\n',t(k),y(k),yex(k),y(k)-yex(k));
end
fprintf('\nMax error =%12.4e rtol = %9.2e atol = %9.2e\n',emax,rtol,atol);
fprintf('%g flops\n',f);
plot(t,yex,'-',t,y,'o');
title(sprintf('Solution to dy/dt = -y;  Refine = %d',nref));
xlabel('t');  ylabel('y');
```

Listing 12.6 The demoODE45opts uses ode45 to solve Equation (12.26) with user-selectable tolerance parameters.

Running demoODE45opts with the default error tolerances produces the following results:

```
>> demoODE45opts
   x        y_ode45    y_exact    error
0.0000    1.000000   1.000000   0.00e+00
0.1000    0.904837   0.904837   2.97e-10
0.2000    0.818731   0.818731   5.38e-10
 ...
0.8000    0.449329   0.449329   1.18e-09
0.9000    0.406570   0.406570   1.20e-09
1.0000    0.367879   0.367879   1.21e-09

Max error = 1.21e-09 for rtol = 1.00e-03 atol = 1.00e-06
3450 flops
```

The maximum error of 1.2×10^{-9} is two orders of magnitude smaller than the maximum error obtained by the fixed-stepsize odeRK4 routine (see Example 12.6 on page 699) for the same ODE. The increase in accuracy in this case is not caused by changes in h as the solution is computed. ode45 uses $h = 0.1$ for each step. Since ode45 monitors the LDE by comparing fourth- and fifth-order Runge–Kutta solutions, it has a fifth-order solution available at each time step. The difference between the fourth- and fifth-order solutions is used to correct the fourth-order solution, thereby rendering a result with a GDE smaller than $\mathcal{O}(h^4)$.

Note that the flop count for ode45 using the default tolerances and Refine = 1 is three times larger than that required by odeRK4 to obtain the same accuracy (see Example 12.6 again), but with a time step of $h = 0.025$ instead of $h = 0.1$. For this simple ODE the fixed stepsize algorithm has the advantage, but that will not be the case for more complicated ODEs.

Passing Extra Parameters Through ode45   Most ODEs contain parameters that affect the solution. For example, the ODE describing an exponential decay (cf. Equation (12.26))

$$\frac{dy}{dt} = -\alpha y \tag{12.28}$$

has the parameter α, which is the inverse of the time constant. A simple, but *incorrect*, function for evaluating the right-hand side of this ODE is the following rhsDecayNot function:

```
function dydt = rhsDecayNot(t,y)
% rhsDecayNot Incorrect attempt to define rhs of dydt = -alpha*y
dydt = -alpha*y;
```

The problem with this m-file, of course, is that alpha is not defined.

The built-in ODE routines have the capability to pass parameters through to the ODE-defining function. The general syntax of the call to ode45 is

```
[x,y] = ode45(diffeq,tn,y0,options,args ... )
```

where `args` ... is a list of comma-separated parameters. These additional `args` are simply passed through ode45 to the `diffeq` m-file. The `options` parameter (see the preceding section) is *required* if the optional parameters are to be passed through ode45. If no `options` are to be set, a null matrix [] is used for the `options` parameter. In the ODE-defining routine, additional input arguments must be provided to accept the pass-through parameters. The general syntax of the ODE-defining routine is

```
function dydt = rhsFunction(t,y,flag,args ... )
```

where `args` is the list of the input parameters passed from ode45. The `flag` parameter is *required* whenever additional parameters are to be passed through ode45. The `flag` supports more sophisticated capabilities of ode45 that will not be described here.[4]

With the (correct) rhsDecay function shown in Listing 12.7, the following statements invoke ode45 for the solution to Equation (12.28) with an initial condition of $y_0 = 10$:

```
>> tn = 4; y0 = 1; alpha = 5;
>> [t,y] = ode45('rhsDecay',tn,y0,[],alpha);
```

The advantage of this approach is that the ODE can be solved with another value of alpha simply by changing the value of alpha sent to ode45.

Example 12.9 shows how several features of the ode45 function can be combined to solve a more substantial and more interesting first-order ODE.

Example 12.9: Heat Treating of Metal Rods

This example demonstrates how the automatic stepsize capabilities of ode45 make it easy to solve complicated ODEs. The effect of changing the refinement of the solution via interpolation is also shown. Before the numerical solution is presented, some background information of the physical problem is given.

The material strength of metals is controlled by their chemical composition and the mechanical forming processes used in their production. After the molten metal is solidified, but before it has completely cooled, it is shaped into bars, sheets, or rods. The metal is allowed to cool and is then subjected to carefully controlled changes in temperature in a

---

[4]Enter help odefile at the MATLAB prompt for more information.

```
function demoODE45args(alpha)
% demoODE45args  Integrate dy/dt = -alpha*y;  y(0) = 1 with variable alpha
%
% Synopsis:   demoODE45
%             demoODE45(alpha)
%
% Input       alpha = (optional) decay rate coefficient.  Default:  alpha = 5
%                     Default: rtol = 1e-3 (internal default used by ode45)
%
% Output:   A table and plot comparing the numerical and exact solutions

if nargin<1, alpha = 2;  end

tn = 1;  y0 = 1;
[t,y] = ode45('rhsDecay',tn,y0,[],alpha);
yex = y0*exp(-alpha*t);
fprintf('     t      y_ode45    y_exact     error\n');
for k=1:length(t)
  fprintf('  %7.4f  %8.6f  %8.6f  %9.2e\n',t(k),y(k),yex(k),y(k)-yex(k));
end
fprintf('\nMax error = %10.2e for alpha = %9.2e\n',norm(y-yex,inf),alpha);
plot(t,yex,'-',t,y,'o');
title(sprintf('Solution to dy/dt = -%g*y',alpha));  xlabel('t');  ylabel('y');
```

```
function dydt = rhsDecay(t,y,flag,alpha)
% rhsDecay  Evaluate rhs of dy/dt = -alpha*y with a variable alpha.
%           "flag" parameter is required for compatability with ode45
dydt = -alpha*y;
```

Listing 12.7   The demoODE45args function uses ode45 or to integrate
a first-order ODE with optional pass-through parameters. The rhsDecay
function defines the right-hand side of a system of ODEs, which depends
on the value of the extra parameter alpha.

process called heat treating. A simple model of heat treating yields a nonlinear, first-order
ODE for the temperature of the solid metal as a function of time.[5]

Figure 12.9 is a schematic of a particular type of heat treating. In this scenario, the
steel has been formed into long bars that are heated to relieve the stresses introduced during
the forming process. Removing mechanical stresses by heating or other means is called
annealing. In this particular annealing process, the steel bars are heated by passing an

---

[5]This example is based on an end-of-chapter exercise in Chapter 5 of [39].

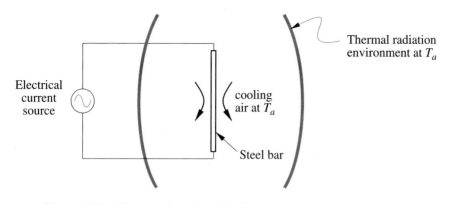

Figure 12.9   Heat treating of steel rods.

electric current through them. After the bars reach a desired temperature, the current is shut off, and fans are turned on to blow cooling air over the bars.

During both the heating and cooling phases, the bars are exchanging heat by *convection* and *radiation*. The convective heat transfer is due to air movement around the bars and is modeled as

$$Q_c = \mathcal{H} A_s (T - T_a),$$

where $\mathcal{H}$ is an empirical constant called the heat transfer coefficient, A_s is the surface area of the bar, T is the temperature of the bar (assumed to be internally uniform), and T_a is the air temperature.

Radiation heat transfer is due to electromagnetic radiation in the infrared spectrum. The bars exchange heat with any surface they can "see." In this example, we assume that all surfaces surrounding the bars are at temperature T_a, the temperature of the ambient air. The rate of radiative cooling is then

$$Q_r = \epsilon \sigma A_s (T^4 - T_a^4),$$

where ϵ is the emissivity of the rod surface ($0 \leq \epsilon \leq 1$) and $\sigma = 5.67 \times 10^{-8} \text{W/m}^2 \text{ K}^4$ is the Stefan–Boltzmann constant. When radiation heat transfer is involved, all calculations must use an absolute temperature scale (i.e, kelvins (K) or degrees Rankine (°R)). In the m-files developed for this problem, the calculations are performed in kelvins and the output is converted to degrees Celsius with $T(\text{K}) = T(°\text{C}) + 273.15$.

At any instant, the energy balance is

$$mc \frac{dT}{dt} = \dot{Q}_V - \dot{Q}_c - \dot{Q}_r,$$

where t is time, m is the mass of a bar, c is its specific heat, Q_V is the rate of electrical heat generation, Q_c is the rate of convective cooling, and Q_r is the rate of radiative cooling. Substituting the preceding relationships for the Q's into the energy balance and rearranging terms gives

$$\frac{dT}{dt} = \frac{1}{mc} \left\{ \dot{Q}_V - A_s \left[\mathcal{H}(T - T_a) + \epsilon \sigma (T^4 - T_a^4) \right] \right\}. \tag{12.29}$$

To make this problem more interesting and realistic, the heat-treating process is assumed to occur during two phases. In the first phase, the electrical current is on, and the fans supplying the flow of cooling air are turned off. In the second phase, the electrical current is turned off, and the fans are turned on. When the cooling fans are turned off, the convective cooling rate is greatly reduced. Without the fans, the motion of the air is only due to the increased buoyancy (lower density) of the air adjacent to the bars. This is known as *free convection*, and is distinct from the forced convection that occurs when the fans are on. A reasonable model of the transition from free convection (no fan) to forced convection for this geometry is

$$\mathcal{H} = \begin{cases} 15 \ W/(m^2 °C) & \text{if } t < t_c \quad \text{(free convection)} \\ 100 \ W/(m^2 °C) & \text{if } t > t_c \quad \text{(forced convection)} \end{cases} \tag{12.30}$$

where t_c is the time at which the heating is stopped and the cooling fans are turned on.

The heat-treating model is implemented in the demoSteel function in Listing 12.8, and the rhsSteelHeat function in Listing 12.9. The main program, demoSteel, sets up the initial conditions and control parameters, calls ode45 to obtain the solution, and plots the results. rhsSteelHeat evaluates the right-hand side of Equation (12.29). An inspection of the call to ode45 in demoSteel and the input parameter list of rhsSteelHeat reveals that a number of the problem parameters are passed through ode45. (Cf. the discussion on page 706.) The two heat-transfer coefficients in Equation (12.30) that are used to simulate the transition from free to forced convection are stored in a vector for input to rhsSteelHeat.

Running the simulation with the default parameters gives the following result and the plot in the left half of Figure 12.10:

```
>> demoSteel
rtol = 1.00e-03 atol = 1.00e-06 Tmax = 656.86
```

Rerunning the simulation without interpolation of the output (i.e., with nref = 1) gives the following result and the plot in the right half of Figure 12.10:

```
>> demoSteel(1)
rtol = 1.00e-03 atol = 1.00e-06 Tmax = 656.86
```

The two results are identical, except for the number of points output from ode45.

12.5 COUPLED ODEs

The algorithms presented thus far are applicable to individual, first-order ODEs. With slight modification, the same algorithms work for coupled *systems* of first-

```
function [tout,Tout] = demoSteel(nref,rtol,atol)
% demoSteel  Solve ODE describing heat treating of a steel bar using ode45
%
% Synopsis:  demoSteel                     [t,T] = demoSteel
%            demoSteel(nref)               [t,T] = demoSteel(nref)
%            demoSteel(nref,rtol)          [t,T] = demoSteel(nref,rtol)
%            demoSteel(nref,rtol,atol)     [t,T] = demoSteel(nref,rtol,atol)
%
% Input:     nref = (optional) number of interpolations between steps.
%                   Default:  nref = 4 (internal default used by ode45)
%            rtol = (optional) relative tolerance used by ode45
%                   Default: tol = 1e-3 (internal default used by ode45)
%            atol = (optional) absolute tolerance used by ode45
%                   Default: tol = 1e-6 (internal default used by ode45)
%
% Output:    Plot of temperature of the bar versus time.
%            t = (optional) vector of times at which solution is obtained
%            T = (optional) vector of temperatures from numerical solution

if nargin<1,  nref = 4;      end    % Process optional input arguments
if nargin<2,  rtol = 1e-3;   end
if nargin<3,  atol = 1e-6;   end

len = 1;       dia = 1e-2;       % bar length and diameter, meters
rho = 7822;    c = 444;          % density (kg/m^3) and heat capacity (J/kg/K)
As = pi*dia*len;                 % surface area of bar, m^2, neglect ends
mc = len*0.25*pi*dia^2*rho*c;    % mc = rho*volume*c
emiss = 0.7;                     % emissivity of bar
htc = [15; 100];                 % heat transfer coefficients, W/m^2/C
Ta = 21 + 273.15;                % ambient temperature, K
tcool = 70;                      % begin cooling at tcool seconds
tf = 3*tcool;                    % total simulation time, seconds
QV = 3000;                       % rate of electrical heat generation, W

% --- Set tolerance and refinement options and solve the ODE
options = odeset('RelTol',rtol,'AbsTol',atol,'Refine',nref);
[t,T] = ode45('rhsSteelHeat',tf,Ta,options,mc,QV,tcool,htc,As,Ta,emiss);

T = T - 273.15;              % convert kelvins to Celsius
f = figure;  plot(t,T,'+');  % open new figure window and plot
xlabel('Time  (s)');  ylabel('Temperature (C)');
title(sprintf('nref = %d,  rtol = %9.1e,  atol = %9.1e',nref,rtol,atol));
fprintf('rtol = %9.2e  atol = %9.2e  Tmax = %7.2f\n',rtol,atol,max(T));

if nargout>1,   tout = t; Tout = T;   end    % Optional return variables
```

Listing 12.8 The demoSteel function used to simulate heat treating
of steel bars. (See also rhsSteelHeat in Listing 12.9.)

```
function dTdt = rhsSteelHeat(t,T,flag,mc,QV,tcool,htc,As,Ta,emiss)
% rhsSteelHeat  Right hand side of first order ODE for heat treating simulation
%
% Synopsis  dTdt = rhsSteelHeat(t,T,flag,mc,QV,tcool,htc,As,Ta,emiss)
%
% Input:    t     = time (sec)
%           T     = current estimate of bar temperature (K)
%           flag  = (not used) placeholder for compatibility with ode45
%           mc    = product of mass and specific heat capacity (J/K)
%           QV    = rate volumetric heat addition (W)
%           tcool = time (sec) at which heating is stopped and cooling begins
%           htc   = vector of convective heat transfer coefficients (W/m^2/C)
%           As    = surface area of the bar (m^2)
%           Ta    = ambient tempeature (K)
%           emiss = emissivity of the bar (dimensionless)
%
% Output:   dTdt = rate of increase of temperature with time.

if t<tcool
  QVol = QV;  hh = htc(1);    %  heating phase, natural convection
else
  QVol = 0;   hh = htc(2);    %  cooling phase, forced convection
end
dTdt = (1/mc)*( QVol - As*( hh*(T - Ta) + emiss*(5.67e-8)*(T^4 - Ta^4) ) );
```

Listing 12.9   The rhsSteelHeat function to define the right-hand side of the ODE for simulating the heat treating of steel bars.

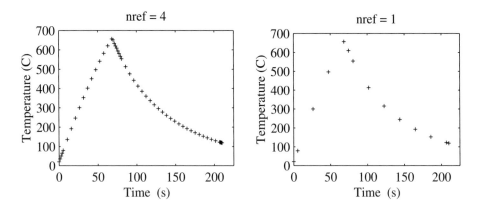

Figure 12.10   Heat-treating simulation results. The plot on the left shows the ode45 solution obtained with the default "options" parameters. The plot on the right shows the ode45 solution obtained with nref = 1 (i.e., no interpolation of the output). The numerical solution is obtained at the same points in both plots.

order ODEs. Consider the following pair of ordinary differential equations

$$\frac{dy_1}{dt} = f_1(t, y_1, y_2) \tag{12.31}$$

$$\frac{dy_2}{dt} = f_2(t, y_1, y_2) \tag{12.32}$$

These equations are coupled, because the equation for y_1 explicitly depends on y_2 and vice versa.

This section is concerned with coupled first-order systems. The fourth-order Runge–Kutta method is used to demonstrate the basic technique. Higher order ODEs are equivalent to a system of first-order ODEs. The technique for solving higher order ODEs is also covered in this section.

12.5.1 The RK-4 Algorithm for Coupled ODEs

The fourth-order Runge–Kutta method requires the evaluation of four slope estimates (values of dy/dt) per step. For Equation (12.31), the value of dy_1/dx at any t depends on both y_1 and y_2. It is important, therefore, that the intermediate slope estimates for both equations be made *simultaneously*. In other words, the basic RK-4 method uses values of k_1, k_2, k_3, and k_4 for each equation, but each k_i ($i = 1, \ldots, 4$) depends on t and potentially all of the y values. Properly applying the technique requires that the k_1 values for all differential equations in the system are computed before the k_2 values are computed.

Consider the integration of two coupled equations where the values at step $(j - 1)$ are known. Let $k_{1,i}$ be the the first Runge–Kutta coefficient (slope) for the ith equation, let $k_{2,i}$ be the second Runge–Kutta coefficient, etc. To advance to the jth step, first compute

$$k_{1,1} = f_1 \left(t_j, \ y_{j,1}, \ y_{j,2} \right),$$
$$k_{1,2} = f_2 \left(t_j, \ y_{j,1}, \ y_{j,2} \right).$$

Then

$$k_{2,1} = f_1 \left(\left(t_j + \frac{h}{2} \right), \ \left(y_{j,1} + \frac{h}{2} k_{1,1} \right), \ \left(y_{j,2} + \frac{h}{2} k_{1,2} \right) \right),$$
$$k_{2,2} = f_2 \left(\left(t_j + \frac{h}{2} \right), \ \left(y_{j,1} + \frac{h}{2} k_{1,1} \right), \ \left(y_{j,2} + \frac{h}{2} k_{1,2} \right) \right),$$

and so on

$$k_{3,1} = f_1 \left(\left(t_j + \frac{h}{2} \right), \ \left(y_{j,1} + \frac{h}{2} k_{2,1} \right), \ \left(y_{j,2} + \frac{h}{2} k_{2,2} \right) \right),$$

$$k_{3,2} = f_2\left(\left(t_j + \frac{h}{2}\right), \left(y_{j,1} + \frac{h}{2}k_{2,1}\right), \left(y_{j,2} + \frac{h}{2}k_{2,2}\right)\right),$$

$$k_{4,1} = f_1\left((t_j + h), (y_{j,1} + hk_{3,1}), (y_{j,2} + hk_{3,2})\right),$$

$$k_{4,2} = f_2\left((t_j + h), (y_{j,1} + hk_{3,1}), (y_{j,2} + hk_{3,2})\right).$$

The dependent variables are advanced to the next step only after all of the intermediate slope values are obtained:

$$y_{j,1} = y_{j-1,1} + h\left(\frac{k_{1,1}}{6} + \frac{k_{2,1}}{3} + \frac{k_{3,1}}{3} + \frac{k_{4,1}}{6}\right),$$

$$y_{j,2} = y_{j-1,2} + h\left(\frac{k_{1,2}}{6} + \frac{k_{2,2}}{3} + \frac{k_{3,2}}{3} + \frac{k_{4,2}}{6}\right).$$

These calculations are easily organized into loops, as shown in the odeRK4sys function in Listing 12.10. The odeRK4sys function is written for clarity, not as an example of optimal MATLAB code. The odeRK4sysv function (not shown here, but included with the NMM toolbox) improves the efficiency by writing all of the for k=1:neq loops as vector expressions. Note that odeRK4sysv also supports the varargin facility, thereby eliminating the need to use global variables to pass parameters to the ODE-defining routine.

The odeRK4sys and odeRK4sysv functions are general enough to handle any number of differential equations. The number of equations in a system, neq, is determined from the length of y0, the vector containing the initial conditions. To advance the system of equations, the user-supplied routine that defines the right-hand side of the ODEs must process vectors. The input is the scalar t and a vector of y values. The output is a vector of dy/dt values. The length of the y and dy/dt vectors must be equal to neq.

The built-in ode45 function handles systems of equations in the same way as odeRK4sys. In fact, an important reason for creating odeRK4sys was to show how to write the ODE-defining routine for use with ode45 when integrating a system of equations. The details of the ODE-defining routine are demonstrated in Examples 12.10 and 12.11.

Example 12.10: A Coupled System of Equations

In this example, a numerical solution to the following system is obtained:

$$\frac{dy_1}{dt} = -y_1 e^{1-t} + 0.8y_2, \qquad y_1(0) = 0,$$

$$\frac{dy_2}{dt} = y_1 - y_2^3, \qquad y_2(0) = 2.$$

```
function [t,y] = odeRK4sys(diffeq,tn,h,y0)
% odeRK4sys  Fourth order Runge-Kutta method for systems of first order ODEs
%            Nonvectorized version
%
% Synopsis:  [t,y] = odeRK4sys(diffeq,tn,h,y0)
%
% Input:     diffeq = (string) name of the m-file that evaluates the right
%                       hand side of the ODE system written in standard form.
%            tn     = stoping value of the independent variable
%            h      = stepsize for advancing the independent variable
%            y0     = vector of the dependent variable values at t = 0
%
% Output:    t = vector of independent variable values:  t(j) = (j-1)*h
%            y = matrix of dependent variables values, one column for each
%                state variable.  Each row is from a different time step.

t = (0:h:tn)';           %  Column vector of elements with spacing h
nt = length(t);          %  number of steps
neq = length(y0);        %  number of equations that are simultaneously advanced
y = zeros(nt,neq);       %  Preallocate y for speed
y(1,:) = y0(:)';         %  Assign IC. y0(:) is column, y0(:)' is row vector

h2 = h/2;  h3 = h/3;  h6 = h/6;  %  Avoid repeated evaluation of constants
k1 = zeros(neq,1);  k2 = k1;     %  Preallocate memory for the Runge-Kutta
k3 = k1;  k4 = k1;  ytemp = k1;  %  coefficients and a temporary vector

%  Outer loop for all steps:  j = time step index;  n = equation number index
for j=2:nt
    told = t(j-1);    yold = y(j-1,:)';  %  Temp variables, yold is column vector
    k1 = feval(diffeq,told,yold);      %  Slopes at the starting point
    for n=1:neq
      ytemp(n) = yold(n) + h2*k1(n);   %  Estimate all y's at midpoint
    end
    k2 = feval(diffeq,told+h2,ytemp);  %  1st estimate of slopes at midpoint
    for n=1:neq
      ytemp(n) = yold(n) + h2*k2(n);   %  2nd estimate of all y's at midpoint
    end
    k3 = feval(diffeq,told+h2,ytemp);  %  2nd estimate of slopes at midpoint
    for n=1:neq
      ytemp(n) = yold(n) + h*k3(n);    %  Estimate y at end point
    end
    k4 = feval(diffeq,told+h,ytemp);   %  Estimate of slopes at endpoint
    for n=1:neq                        %  Simultaneously advance all y's
      y(j,n) = yold(n) + h6*(k1(n)+k4(n)) + h3*(k2(n)+k3(n));
    end
end
```

Listing 12.10 The odeRK4sys function, a nonvectorized implementation of the fourth-order Runge–Kutta method for systems of differential equations. See also the vectorized version, odeRK4sysv, in the ode directory of the NMM toolbox.

```
function demoSystem
% demoSystem  Solve system of two coupled first order ODEs
%
% Synopsis:  demoSystem
%
% Input:     none
%
% Output:    Plot of solution

y0 = [0; 2];    % Initial conditions stored in a column vector
tn = 3;
%  [t,y] = ode45('rhsSys',tn,y0);                 %  ode45 solution
[t,y] = odeRK4sysv('rhsSys',tn,0.1,y0);  %  odeRK4sys solution
plot(t,y(:,1),'+',t,y(:,2),'o');
xlabel('t');  ylabel('y_1  and  y_2');  legend('y_1','y_2');
```

```
function dydt = rhsSys(t,y)
% rhsSys  Right hand side vector for two, coupled, first order ODEs
dydt = [ -y(1)*exp(1-t) + 0.8*y(2);
          y(1) - y(2)^3];               %  a column vector
```

Listing 12.11   The demoSystem function uses ode45 or odeRK4sysv
to integrate a system of coupled, first-order ODEs. The rhsSys function
defines the right-hand side of a system of ODEs.

The rhsSys function shown in the lower part of Listing 12.11 evaluates the right-hand
side of the system. Notice that the return variable, dydt, is a column vector as required by
ode45. The solution to the system is obtained and plotted with

```
>> y0 = [0; 2];                       % ICs are stored in a *column* vector
>> [t,y] = ode45('rhsSys',3,y0);     % Solution on interval 0 <= t <= 3
>> plot(t,y(:,1),'+',t,y(:,2),'o');
```

The result is shown in Figure 12.11.

Example 12.11: Predator–Prey Equations

This example demonstrates how to solve a coupled system of ODEs that constitute a simple
model of a biological system. Some background information is given on the system before
its solution is described. The numerical solution itself is straightforward.

Consider the population dynamics of two interdependent species of animals. One
species, the prey, is the primary food source for the other species, the predator. This model
would describe, for example, the populations of rabbits and wolves on an isolated island.
Let the population of the the prey be $p_1(t)$ and the population of the predator be $p_2(t)$. The

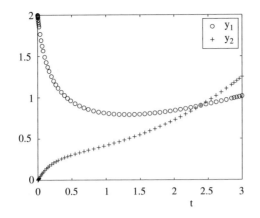

Figure 12.11 Plot of solution to the coupled system of first-order ODEs $dy_1/dt = -y_1 \exp(1-t) + 0.8y_2$, $dy_2/dt = y_1 - y_2^3$.

rate of increase in the two populations can be modeled as

$$\frac{dp_1}{dt} = \alpha_1 p_1 - \delta_1 p_1 p_2, \tag{12.33}$$

$$\frac{dp_2}{dt} = \alpha_2 p_1 p_2 - \delta_2 p_2, \tag{12.34}$$

where α_1 and α_2 are growth-rate coefficients and δ_1 and δ_2 are death-rate (mortality) coefficients for the two populations.

The first term on the right-hand side of Equation (12.33) describes the fertility of the prey, which is assumed to be controlled only by the availability of mates. The prey is assumed to have no shortage of food. The second term on the right-hand side of Equation (12.33) is the death rate of the prey. Prey mortality increases with the number of predators (who are eating the prey) and the size of the prey population. The δ_1 coefficient reflects the hunting efficiency of the predators.

Equation (12.34) is the differential equation for the growth in population of the predator. The predators reproduce in proportion to their numbers, but their reproduction rate is also limited by the available food (p_1). The α_1 coefficient describes both the fertility of the predators and the nutritional value of the prey. The mortality of the predator increases in direct proportion to its own population, and it is independent of the population of prey. As the predator population grows, it more rapidly consumes its own food supply, and the importance of starvation, either as a primary or secondary cause of death, increases.

A solution of this system of differential equations requires initial conditions $p_1(0)$ and $p_2(0)$; the fertility and mortality coefficients α_1, α_2, δ_1, and δ_2; and a method for integrating the system of differential equations. The initial conditions and the growth and mortality coefficients come from an understanding of the species being studied. The numerical integration scheme must be capable of integrating a system of differential equations.

The problem-specific code for the predator–prey model is contained in two m-files. The driver routine, demoPredPrey in Listing 12.12, defines the initial conditions, calls ode45, and plots the results. The ODE-defining routine rhspop2 in the lower part of Listing 12.12 evaluates the right-hand sides of Equations (12.33) and (12.34), given the time stored in the scalar variable t, the populations p_1 and p_2 stored in the vector p, and the vectors of parameters alpha and delta. The values of dp_i/dt are returned to ode45 in the vector dpdt. The time t does not appear as an explicit parameter in Equations (12.33) and (12.34), but it must be an input parameter of rhspop2 to be compatible with ode45. The unused flag parameter is also required for compatibility with ode45.

Results from a trial run of the predator–prey model are shown in Figure 12.12. These results are obtained with the default values of p1start, p2start, and tstop, by entering

```
>> demoPredPrey
```

In demoPredPrey, the odeRK4sysv integration routine can be used instead of ode45 by removing the comment character % in front of the call to ode45 and changing the call to ode45 to a comment statement. Beware that the results of the integration with odeRK4sysv are sensitive to h. In general, ode45 is to be preferred over odeRK4sysv, because it uses an adaptive stepsize algorithm to maintain a higher accuracy during each step.

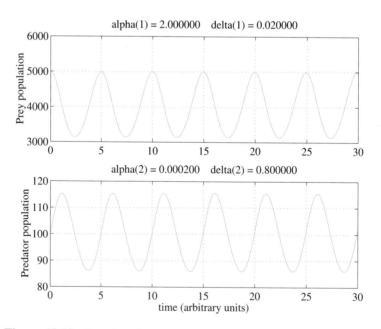

Figure 12.12   Results of the predator–prey model for $\alpha_1 = 2$, $\delta_1 = 0.02$, $\alpha_2 = 0.0002$, and $\delta_2 = 0.8$ with initial population of prey at 5000 individuals and initial population of predators at 100 individuals.

```
function demoPredprey(p1start,p2start,tstop)
% demoPredprey   Coupled ODEs for a two-species predator-prey simulation
%
% Synopsis:   demoPredprey
%             demoPredprey(p1start,p2start,tstop)
%
% Input:      pstart1 = (optional) initial population of species 1
%             pstart2 = (optional) initial population of species 2
%             tstop   = (optional) duration of the simulation
%
% Output:     Plot of populations versus time

if nargin<1,  p1start = 5000;  end
if nargin<2,  p2start = 100;   end
if nargin<3,  tstop = 30;      end

% ---  Parameters to be passed to rhspop2
alpha = [ 2.0  0.0002 ];      delta = [ 0.02   0.8 ];

p0 = [p1start; p2start];                      %  Initial conditions
[t,p] = ode45('rhspop2',tstop,p0,[],alpha,delta);  %  Solution with ode45
% [t,p] = rk4sysv('rhspop2',tstop,tstop/500,p0,alpha,delta);   % with rk4sysv

% --- Plot the results
subplot(2,1,1);   plot(t,p(:,1));    grid;   ylabel('Prey population');
title(sprintf('alpha(1) = %f    delta(1) = %f',alpha(1),delta(1)));

subplot(2,1,2);   plot(t,p(:,2));    grid;
xlabel('time (arbitrary units)');    ylabel('Predator population');
title(sprintf('alpha(2) = %f    delta(2) = %f',alpha(2),delta(2)));
```

```
function dpdt = rhsPop2(t,p,flag,alpha,delta)
% rhsPop2   Right hand sides of coupled ODEs for 2 species predator-prey system
%
% Synopis:  dpdt = rhsPop2(t,p,flag,alpha,delta)
%
% Input:    t = time. Not used in this m-file, but needed by ode45
%           p = vector (length 2) of populations of species 1 and 2
%           flag  = (not used) placeholder for compatibility with ode45
%           alpha = vector (length 2) of growth coefficients
%           delta = vector (length 2) of mortality coefficients
%
% Output:   dpdt = vector of dp/dt values
dpdt = [ alpha(1)*p(1)      - delta(1)*p(1)*p(2);
         alpha(2)*p(1)*p(2) - delta(2)*p(2);       ];
```

Listing 12.12 The demoPredPrey function uses ode45 or odeRK4sysv to integrate the system of differential equations for the two species predator–prey model. The rhsPop2 function defines the right-hand side of system of ODEs.

719

12.5.2 Higher Order Differential Equations

To numerically integrate a higher order ODE, the equation must be mathematically transformed to an equivalent system of first-order ODEs. Consider the second-order ODE

$$\frac{d^2u}{dt^2} + \alpha\frac{du}{dt} + \beta u = f(t) \tag{12.35}$$

governing $u = u(t)$. Introduce two new *state variables* y_1 and y_2 defined by

$$y_1 \equiv u \qquad y_2 \equiv \frac{du}{dt}.$$

Taking the derivative of y_1 and y_2 with respect to t gives

$$\frac{dy_1}{dt} = \frac{du}{dt} = y_2,$$

$$\frac{dy_2}{dt} = \frac{d^2u}{dt^2} = f(t) - \alpha\frac{du}{dt} - \beta u = f(t) - \alpha y_2 - \beta y_1.$$

Thus, the two coupled first-order ODEs

$$\frac{dy_1}{dt} = y_2, \tag{12.36}$$

$$\frac{dy_2}{dt} = f(t) - \alpha y_2 - \beta y_1 \tag{12.37}$$

are equivalent to the single second-order ODE in Equation (12.35).

Any nth order ODE can be transformed into a system of mathematically equivalent n first-order ODEs. Given

$$\frac{d^n u}{dx^n} = f(t, u),$$

the transformation is

Define y_i	ODE for y_i
$y_1 = u$	$\dfrac{dy_1}{dt} = y_2$
$y_2 = \dfrac{du}{dt}$	$\dfrac{dy_2}{dt} = y_3$
$y_3 = \dfrac{d^2u}{dt^2}$	$\dfrac{dy_3}{dt} = y_4$
$\vdots$	$\vdots$
$y_n = \dfrac{d^{n-1}u}{dt^{n-1}}$	$\dfrac{dy_n}{dt} = f(t, u)$

The y_i are usually called the state variables for the system. When the system arises from a single higher order ODE, the right-hand sides for all but one differential equation contains only one other state variable.

Example 12.12: Second-order Mechanical System

This example shows how a second-order ODE can be converted to a system of two first-order ODEs. The mathematical system used here comes from a model of a common mechanical system. The equation for the mechanical system is derived first. Then, a numerical solution with `ode45` is implemented.

Consider the spring–mass–damper system shown in Figure 12.13. An external, time-varying force is applied to the object of mass m causing it to move. The spring applies a restoring force, and the damper dissipates energy. A force balance on the object requires that

$$\sum F = ma,$$

where $\sum F$ is the sum of all forces acting on the object and a is the object's acceleration. The spring force acts in the negative x direction, and it is proportional to the distance the spring is compressed. The damper opposes the motion of the object, and the damping force increases with the velocity of the object. The standard damper model assumes that the force is proportional to the velocity of the object. The equations for the spring and damper forces are

$$F_{\text{spring}} = -kx \quad \text{and} \quad F_{\text{damper}} = -c\dot{x},$$

where k is the spring constant and $\dot{x} \equiv dx/dt$ is the instantaneous velocity of the mass. Substituting the preceding equations into the force balance gives

$$F(t) - kx - c\dot{x} = m\ddot{x},$$

where $\ddot{x} \equiv d^2x/dt^2$ is the acceleration of the object. The preceding equation is usually written as

$$\ddot{x} + 2\zeta\omega_n\dot{x} + \omega_n^2 x = \frac{F}{m}, \tag{12.38}$$

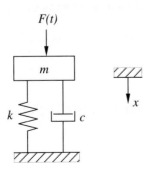

Figure 12.13   A generic spring–mass–damper system.

where ζ is the dimensionless damping coefficient and ω_n is the natural frequency:

$$\zeta \equiv \frac{c}{2\sqrt{km}}, \qquad \omega_n \equiv \sqrt{k/m}.$$

Equation (12.38) can be written as an equivalent system of first-order ODEs with the following transformation:

$$y_1 \equiv x, \qquad y_2 \equiv \dot{x}.$$

Thus,

$$\frac{dy_1}{dt} = y_2, \tag{12.39}$$

$$\frac{dy_2}{dt} = \frac{F}{m} - 2\zeta\omega_n y_2 - \omega_n^2 y_1. \tag{12.40}$$

Equations (12.39) and (12.40) are a system of coupled, first-order ODEs.

There are many possible forcing functions. For simplicity, a step function is used to demonstrate how this model of the second-order system works. A step function is equivalent to placing an additional mass m_s on top of the object shown in Figure 12.13 at an instant in time. In that case, the magnitude of the applied force is $m_s g$, where g is the acceleration of gravity (9.8 m/s^2 in SI units). The mathematical description of a step function applied at time t_0 is

$$F(t) = \begin{cases} 0, & \text{if } t < t_0 \\ F_0, & \text{if } t \geq t_0 \end{cases}$$

where F_0 is the magnitude of the step.

The numerical model for the second-order system in Equations (12.39) and (12.40) is implemented in the demoSmd and rhssmd functions in Listing 12.13. The driver routine demoSmd sets the initial conditions, calls ode45, and plots the results. The rhssmd routine defines the system of equations to be integrated. Given values of t, y_1, and y_2, rhssmd evaluates the right-hand sides of Equations (12.39) and (12.40). The zeta, omegan, and a0 $= F_0/m$ parameters are passed through ode45 to rhssmd as described in § 12.4.1 on page 706.

Entering

```
>> demoSmd
```

in the command window produces the plots shown in Figure 12.14. The transient response of the system to a step function depends on the values of the system parameters ζ and ω_n. After the transient response decays, the system achieves a new equilibrium position that corresponds to the static deflection of the spring by the new mass $m + m_s$.

```
function demoSmd(zeta,omegan,tstop)
% demoSmd    Second order system of ODEs for a spring-mass-damper system
%
% Synopsis:  smdsys(zeta,omegan,tstop)
%
% Input:     zeta  = (optional) damping ratio;  Default:  zeta = 0.1
%            omegan = (optional) natural frequency;  Default: omegan = 35
%            tstop = (optional) stopping time;  Default:  tstop = 1.5
%
% Output:    plot of displacement and velocity versus time

if nargin<1,  zeta = 0.1;   end
if nargin<2,  omegan = 35;  end
if nargin<3,  tstop = 1.5;  end

y0 = [0; 0];   a0 = 9.8;     %  Initial conditions and one g force/mass
[t,y] = ode45('rhssmd',tstop,y0,[],zeta,omegan,a0);

subplot(2,1,1);
plot(t,y(:,1));  ylabel('Displacement');  grid;
title(sprintf('zeta = %5.3f    omegan = %5.1f',zeta,omegan));
subplot(2,1,2);
plot(t,y(:,2));  xlabel('Time (s)');  ylabel('Velocity');  grid;
```

```
function dydt = rhsSmd(t,y,flag,zeta,omegan,a0)
% rhsSmd  Right-hand sides of coupled ODEs for a spring-mass-damper system
%
% Synopsis:  dydt = rhsSmd(t,x,flag,zeta,omegan,a0)
%
% Input:     t     = time, the independent variable
%            y     = vector (length 2) of dependent variables
%                    y(1) = displacement and y(2) = velocity
%            flag  = dummy argument for compatibility with ode45
%            zeta  = damping ratio (dimensionless)
%            omegan = natural frequency (rad/s)
%            a0    = input force per unit mass
%
% Output:    dydt = column vector of dy(i)/dt values

if t<=0, fonm = 0.0;
else,    fonm = a0;    % Force/mass (acceleration)
end

dydt = [ y(2);  fonm - 2*zeta*omegan*y(2) - omegan*omegan*y(1)];
```

Listing 12.13 The demoSmd and rhssmd functions for solving the
ODEs describing a spring–mass–damper system.

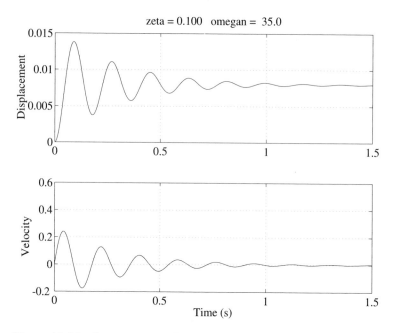

Figure 12.14   Step response of a second-order mechanical system with $\zeta = 0.1$ and $\omega_n = 35$ (rad/s). Initial conditions are $x = \dot{x} = 0$.

12.6 ADDITIONAL TOPICS

This chapter is just an introduction to the numerical solution of ordinary differential equations. Some important topics not covered here are the stability of ODE integration methods, multistep methods, and stiff equations. The stability of a method refers to its tendency (or lack thereof) to produce a numerical solution that grows in magnitude when the exact solution does not grow. All of the one-step methods presented in this chapter will produce unstable results if given a large enough time step.

Multistep methods use values of the numerical solution at several steps to predict the value at the next step. All of the methods presented in this chapter are one-step methods, even though for most of these methods the slope is evaluated more than once per step. The built-in ode115 routine is a multistep method that adaptively chooses the number of previous steps to incorporate in the solution for a given step.

The stiffness of an ODE refers to presence of multiple scales of change. Some mathematical models of chemical reactions, for example, exhibit phenomena with both fast and slow rates of change with time. To track the fast processes, small time steps are required, and to resolve the slow processes, a large overall time integration period is required. A system is said to be stiff if the rates of change are so different that standard methods, such as RK-4, become inefficient at meeting both the short and long time-scale requirements. The stability of an ODE integration scheme becomes important for stiff problems if the time step required to keep the method stable is so small that the numerical solution becomes impractical. The ode23s and ode115s routines in the MATLAB toolbox are designed to treat stiff problems.

For more information on stability and multistep methods, see the introductory book by Shampine et al. [65]. Moler [56] gives a concise description of stiffness and the MATLAB routines designed to treat it. Many introductory numerical analysis texts give a brief treatment of stiffness. Finlayson [23] provides a more complete discussion, along with examples of stiff systems arising in chemical engineering.

12.7 SUMMARY

In this chapter, several methods are presented for the numerical solution of ordinary differential equations (ODEs). Euler's method is the simplest and least accurate of a family of techniques called one-step methods.

Because of its simplicity, it is easy to analyze the local and global discretization errors of Euler's method. The same type of analysis can be applied to other one-step methods. The local discretization error establishes the order of the method as defined by Equations (12.15) and (12.24). The global discretization error is more informative for practical purposes, because it provides an estimate for the largest error in an interval for which the solution is obtained. For one-step methods, the order of the local discretization error is equal to the order of the global discretization error.

The midpoint method and the fixed stepsize RK-4 method have smaller discretization errors than Euler's method. The increase in accuracy is obtained by evaluating the slope more than once per step. The extra computational effort is worthwhile, because the smaller discretization errors allow larger time steps to be taken, while maintaining the same accuracy. Numerical experiments in this chapter demonstrate that given the goal of achieving a specified accuracy, the midpoint method is much more efficient than Euler's method, and the fixed stepsize RK-4 method is much more efficient than the midpoint method. Table 12.2 lists a number of m-files used demonstrate simple methods and compare the performance of different methods.

The MATLAB toolbox contains several routines for solving ODEs. The built-in routines listed in Table 12.3 are highly recommended for solving practical problems. The ode23 and ode45 functions contain sophisticated implementations of variable stepsize Runge–Kutta methods. Rather than specifying a stepsize for use

EXERCISES

The number in parenthesis at the beginning of each exercise indicates the degree of skill and amount of effort necessary to complete the exercise. See § 1.4 on page 10 for a description of the rating system.

1. (1+) Obtain the analytical solution to Equation (12.5) with the initial condition $T(t = 0) = T_0$.

2. (1) How is the initial condition stored in $y(1)$ in the odeEuler function in Listing 12.1?

SOLUTION   3. (1) Manually perform three steps of Euler's method to solve

$$\frac{dy}{dt} = \frac{1}{t + y + 1}, \qquad y(0) = 0,$$

with $h = 0.2$.

4. (1) Use odeEuler to solve the ODE in the preceding Exercise for $0 \le t \le 1$ with $h = 0.2$.

5. (2) Using demoEuler.m as a starting point, write an m-file to solve

$$\frac{dy}{dt} = \cos(t), \quad y(0) = 0, \quad 0 \le t \le 4\pi,$$

with Euler's method. This will require a simple function (e.g., rhscos.m) to evaluate the right-hand side of the ODE. Why won't the built-in cos function work? Plot a comparison of the exact solution and the solution obtained with Euler's method for $h = 4\pi/100$ and $h = 4\pi/1000$. For both h values, what is the absolute error at $t = 4\pi$, and what is the maximum (absolute) error over $0 \le t \le 4\pi$.

6. (2) Extend the preceding Exercise by creating a log–log plot of the error at $t = 4\pi$ and the maximum (absolute) error over $0 \le x \le 4\pi$ for $h = 4\pi/n$, where $n = 10, 10^2, 10^3, 10^4$. Plot both errors on the same axes, and discuss the results. Do you expect the trend to continue indefinitely for increasing n?

SOLUTION   7. (2+) (Stoer and Bulirsch [70]) Use Euler's method with $h = 0.05$ to solve

$$\frac{dy}{dt} = \sqrt{y}, \quad y(0) = 0, \quad 0 \le t \le 2.$$

Plot a comparison of the numerical solution with the exact solution. Does the plot indicate that there is an error in odeEuler? If there is no error in odeEuler, can you explain the peculiar results? Recompute the solution with odeMidpt and odeRK4. (*Hint*: What happens if the initial condition $y(0) = \varepsilon_m$ is used instead of $y(0) = 0$?)

8. (2) A MATLAB implementation of Heun's method is used to integrate

$$\frac{dy}{dt} = \frac{2(1 - t)}{(0.05 + (t - 1)^2)^2}, \qquad y(0) = 1.x$$

The plot on the left shows the results of numerically integrating the ODE with a succession of smaller step sizes. The table on the right lists the maximum error between the numerical solution and the known exact solution. Is the MATLAB implementation correct? Why or why not? *Do not* write a program to answer these questions.

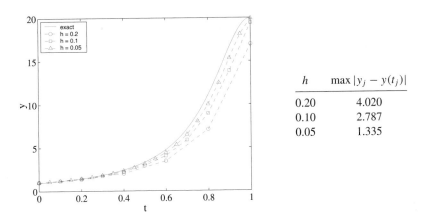

h	max $|y_j - y(t_j)|$
0.20	4.020
0.10	2.787
0.05	1.335

9. (2−) Use the built-in `flops` function to measure the number of flops required to integrate Equation (12.11) over the interval $0 \le t \le 2$ with $h = 0.2$, $h = 0.1$, $h = 0.05$, and $h = 0.025$ using Euler's method and the midpoint method. Can the midpoint method achieve comparable accuracy to Euler's method for less work? give a quantitative justification for your answer.

SOLUTION 10. (2+) Using `odeEuler.m` as a guide, write an m-file to implement Heun's method for an arbitrary, first-order ODE. Use your function to solve Equation (12.11) for $h = 0.2$, $h = 0.1$, $h = 0.05$, and $h = 0.025$. Compare the global discretization error of your program with the theoretical prediction of the global discretization error for Heun's method.

11. (2) Using the `compEMRK4` function in the NMM toolbox as a guide, compare the flops and accuracy of solving Equation (12.26) with the fixed-step-size RK-4 method and the built-in `ode23` and `ode45` routines.

12. (1+ each) For each of the following initial-value problems, verify that the given $y(t)$ is the solution.

SOLUTION (a) $\dfrac{dy}{dt} = \dfrac{t^2}{\alpha} - y$; $y(0) = 1$; $\implies$ $y(t) = \dfrac{1}{\alpha}\left[t^2 - 2t + 2 + (\alpha - 2)e^{-t}\right]$.

(b) $\dfrac{dy}{dt} = 2t - 1 - \dfrac{1}{x + \alpha}$; $y(0) = -\ln(\alpha)$; $\implies$ $y(t) = t^2 - t - \ln(t + \alpha)$.

(c) $\dfrac{dy}{dt} = \alpha t + \beta t y$; $y(0) = 1$; $\implies$ $y(t) = -\dfrac{1}{\beta}\left[\alpha - (\alpha + \beta)e^{\beta t^2/2}\right]$.

(d) $\dfrac{dy}{dt} = \dfrac{2(\beta - t)}{\left[\alpha + (t - \beta)^2\right]^2}$; $y(0) = \dfrac{1}{\alpha + \beta^2}$; $\implies$ $y(t) = \dfrac{1}{\alpha + (t - \beta)^2}$.

(e) $\dfrac{dy}{dt} = \alpha y - \beta y^2$ $y(0) = y_0$ $\implies$ $y(t) = \dfrac{\alpha y_0}{\beta y_0 + (\alpha - y_0 b)\exp(-\alpha t)}$.

13. (1+ each) Solve the initial-value problems in Exercise 12 for $0 \le t \le t_n$. Use Euler's method with a sequence of decreasing h. Plot the exact and numerical solutions, and report the largest error at the discrete values of t. Use the following values of α, β, y_0, and t_n.

   (a) $\alpha = 3$, $y_0 = 1$, $t_n = 2$.
   (b) $\alpha = 1/20$, $t_n = 2$.
   (c) $\alpha = 1$, $\beta = -2$, $y_0 = 1$, $t_n = 4$.
   (d) $\alpha = 1/20$, $\beta = 1$, $t_n = 2$.
   (e) $\alpha = 2$, $\beta = 1/50$, $y_0 = 1$, $t_n = 8$.

14. (1+ each) Repeat Exercise 13 using the midpoint method to solve the equations.

SOLUTION 15. (1+ each) Repeat Exercise 13 using the built-in ode23 method and ode45 methods to solve the equations. Do not attempt to run the sequence of decreasing h values. (Why not?) Instead, compare the solutions from ode23 and ode45 using the default convergence parameters.

16. (2+) Solve the heat-treating model from Example 12.9 using odeRK4v instead of ode45. Using the odeRK4v function (included in the ode directory of the NMM toolbox) will avoid the need to make changes in the rhsSteelHeat function. What h is needed to obtain T_{max} within 1 °C of the value predicted by ode45 using its default parameters?

17. (2+) Solve the ODE in Exercise 7 with the built-in ode45. Compare the numerical solutions obtained with $y(0) = 0$ (exactly) and $y(0) = \varepsilon_m$ with the exact solution. Explain the difference in the computed solutions.

18. (1+) Run the demoPredPrey program with the following inputs
   (a) $p_1(0) = 5000$, $p_2(0) = 10$
   (b) $p_1(0) = 500$, $p_2(0) = 10$
   (c) $p_1(0) = 50$, $p_2(0) = 10$
   (d) $p_1(0) = 5000$, $p_2(0) = 300$
   (e) $p_1(0) = 50000$, $p_2(0) = 300$
   What qualitative behavior is common to the population time histories for all of these initial conditions?

19. (1+) Use the odeRK4sysv function to solve the predator-prey system of ODEs in Example 12.11. Use the same initial conditions and values for α and δ, and run the simulation for $h = 0.5, 0.1, 0.05$. Are the population histories predicted with the fixed stepsize scheme different from the population histories predicted with ode45?

20. (3) Starting with the odeEuler function, write an odeEulerSys function that can integrate systems of ODEs. Test your program by repeating the predator-prey simulation in Example 12.11. The α and δ parameters will need to be communicated to the m-file that evaluates the right-hand side of the ODE system. The recommended way to do this is with the varargin facility. (See, for example, the code in odeRK4sysv.) Alternatively, one can use global variables. Use the same initial conditions and values for α and δ, and run the simulation for $h = 0.05, 0.02, 0.01$. How are the population

histories predicted with the Euler scheme qualitatively different from the population histories predicted with ode45?

21. (3) Repeat the preceding exercise using the midpoint method to integrate the system of equations.

22. (2) The Rössler system of equations is (See, e.g. Moon [57], Problem 5–9.)

$$\dot{x} = -y - z, \qquad \dot{y} = x + ay, \qquad \dot{z} = b + z(x - c)$$

Obtain numerical solutions to this system for $a = 0.398$, $b = 2$, $c = 4$, and $0 \le t \le 100$. Start with random intial conditions (y0=rand(1,3)) and repeat the simulation four times. Use the built-in plot3 function to create a three-dimensional plot of the solution trajectory $(x(t), y(t), z(t))$. Use subplot(2,2,i), i=1:4 to put the plots from the four runs in same figure window. Do the initial conditions have a strong influence on the trajectories?

23. (2+) The demoODE45opts function allows experimentation with the Refine option for the ode45 function. For example, the following statments superimpose two solutions with the same error tolerances on the same plot.

```
>> demoODE45opts(1e-3,1e-6,1)
>> hold on; demoODE45opts(1e-3,1e-6,4); hold off
```

The two solution curves appear to be identical except for the extra points created by interpolation. The value of Max error reported by the demoODE45opts function is different for the two runs. If the two solutions truly are identical, then the Max error should be the same. Explain why the Max error values are different. Suggest a change to the code in demoODE45opts that yields values of Max error that are independent of nref. *Hint*: The necessary change only affects the values used to compute emax not the solution parameters sent to ode45.

24. (3) The exact solution for the position x, and velocity $\dot{x}$ of the mass in Example 12.12 are

$$x_e(t) = \frac{a_0}{\omega_n^2}\left[1 - e^{-\zeta t}\left(\cos \omega_d t - \gamma \sin \omega_d t\right)\right]$$

$$\dot{x}_e(t) = \frac{a_0}{\omega_n}\sqrt{1 - \zeta^2}\, e^{-\zeta \omega_n t} \sin \omega_d t$$

where

$$\omega_d = \omega_n\sqrt{1 - \zeta^2} \qquad \gamma = \frac{\zeta}{1 - \zeta^2}$$

Modify the demoSmd function to add the exact solutions for the displacement and velocity to the plots, and to print the total number of time steps used in the numerical solution. Add statements to compute and print $\|x - x_e\|_\infty$ and $\|\dot{x} - \dot{x}_e\|_\infty$, where x and $\dot{x}$ are the numerical solutions returned by ode45. Add statements to find

x_{max}, $t(x_{max})$, v_{max}, and $t(v_{max})$ from the numerical solution, where x_{max} is the maximum displacement of the mass, and v_{max} is the maximum velocity of the mass. (*Hint:* `[xmax,ixmax] = max(x(:,1)))`

Run the modified `demoSmd` function for `tstop` $= 0.2$ s with the default convergence tolerance. Rerun `demoSmd` while reducing `RelTol` and `AbsTol` from their default values to $1/1000$ of their default values. (Eight to ten runs will be sufficient to establish a clear trend.) Summarize your simulation results in a table showing how the values of $\|x - x_e\|_\infty$, $\|\dot{x} - \dot{x}_e\|_\infty$, x_{max}, $t(x_{max})$, v_{max}, and $t(v_{max})$ depend on the convergence tolerances. Is the numerical solution sensitive to the values of `RelTol` and `AbsTol`? Comment on the plots of the exact and numerical solutions.

25. (2+) Create a modified version of the `rhsSmd` function (see Listing 12.13 on page 723) to implement the following forcing functions for the second-order spring–mass–damper system of Example 12.12.

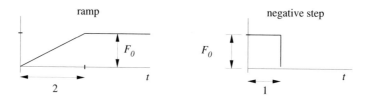

(a) Sinusoidal force input. $F(t) = F_0 \sin(\omega t)$, where $\omega \neq \omega_n$.
(b) Ramp force input from 0 to 2 seconds, then constant at F_0.
(c) Constant force of F_0 for a duration of 1 second, then zero force (negative step).

Compare the system responses for $F_0 = 1$. (*Hint:* Write a separate m-file function to evaluate each $F(t)$ for parts (a), (b), and (c). A particular $F(t)$ function is then chosen at run-time, not by repeated editing of `rhsSmd`. One way to do this is to pass the *name* of the chosen $F(t)$ m-file through `ode45` to the modified `rhsSmd` function, where the $F(t)$ function is then called with the built-in `feval` function. In this implementation, the name of the $F(t)$ function should also be an input to the modified `demoSmd` function.)

26. (3−) The following is a simplified model of the suspension system of one wheel of an automobile:

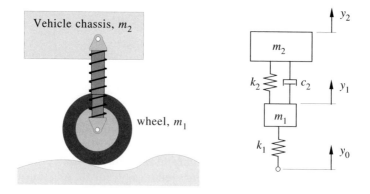

The input to the system is the time-varying displacement $y_0(t)$ corresponding to changes in the terrain. The shock absorber is characterized by its spring rate k_2 and damping coefficient c_2. Damping in the tire is neglected. (There is no c_1 term.)

Applying Newton's law of motion and force balances to the wheel and vehicle chassis yields the following system of equations:

$$m_1\ddot{y}_1 + c_2(\dot{y}_1 - \dot{y}_2) + k_2(y_1 - y_2) + k_1 y_1 = k_1 y_0(t),$$

$$m_2\ddot{y}_2 - k_2(y_1 - y_2) - c_2(\dot{y}_1 - \dot{y}_2) = 0.$$

(a) Convert these two second-order equations into an equivalent system of first-order equations. (How many first-order equations are required?)

(b) Use an appropriate ODE integration routine to solve this system for $m_1 = 110kg$, $k_1 = 136$ N/m, $m_2 = 1900$, $k_2 = 16$ N/m, $c_2 = 176$ N s/m and a forcing function $y_0(t) = 0.05 \sin(3\pi t)$.

(c) Repeat the solution with c_2 reduced by a factor of 5. Describe the change in behavior of the system caused by reducing c_2.

SOLUTION **27.** (2+) Duffing's equation

$$\frac{d^2x}{dt^2} + kx + x^3 = B \cos t$$

describes the chaotic dynamics of a circuit with a nonlinear inductor. (See, for example, Moon [57], Chapter 6). Convert this equation to a system of two first-order ODEs, and solve the system for $k = 0.1$ and $B = 12$ and $0 \le t \le 100$. Create the *Poincaré* map of the system by plotting dx/dt versus x.

Bibliography

[1] M. Abramowitz and I. A. Stegun. *Handbook of Mathematical Functions*. Dover, New York, 1965.

[2] F. S. Acton. *Numerical Methods That Work*. The Mathematical Association of America, Washington, D.C., 1990.

[3] T. J. Akai. *Applied Numerical Methods for Engineers*. Wiley, New York, 1994.

[4] E. Anderson, Z. Bai, C. Bischof, J. Demmel, J. Dongarra, J. Du Croz, A. Greenbaum, S. Hammarling, A. McKenney, S. Ostrouchov, and D. Sorenson. *LAPACK User's Guide*. SIAM, Philadelphia, 1992.

[5] B. M. Ayyub and R. H. McCuen. *Probability, Statistics, and Reliability for Engineers*. CRC Press, Boca Raton, FL, 1997.

[6] P. R. Bevington and D. K. Robinson. *Data Reduction and Error Analysis for the Physical Sciences*. McGraw-Hill, New York, 1992.

[7] A. Björk. *Numerical Methods for Least Squares Problems*. SIAM, Philadelphia, 1996.

[8] R. P. Brent. *Algorithms for Minimization without Derivatives*. Prentice-Hall, Englewood Cliffs, NJ, 1973.

[9] R. L. Burden and J. D. Faires. *Numerical Analysis*. PWS Publishers, New York, 3d edition, 1985.

[10] W. Cheney and D. Kincaid. *Numerical Mathematics and Computing*. Brooks/Cole Publishing Co., Pacific Grove, CA, 3d edition, 1994.

[11] S. D. Conte and C. de Boor. *Elementary Numerical Analysis: An Algorithmic Approach*. McGraw-Hill, New York, 3d edition, 1980.

[12] B. N. Datta. *Numerical Linear Algebra and Applications*. Brooks/Cole, Pacific Grove, CA, 1995.

[13] P. J. Davis and P. Rabinowitz. *Methods of Numerical Integration*. Academic Press, New York, 2d edition, 1984.

[14] C. de Boor. *A Practical Guide to Splines*. Springer-Verlag, New York, 1978.

[15] J. W. Demmel. *Applied Numerical Linear Algebra*. SIAM, Philadelphia, 1997.

[16] J. Dennis, Jr. and R. B. Schnabel. *Numerical Methods for Unconstrained Optimization and Nonlinear Equations*. SIAM, Philadelphia, 1996.

[17] P. Dierckx. *Curve and Surface Fitting with Splines*. Clarenden Press, Oxford, 1993.

[18] J. Dormand and P. Prince. A family of embedded Runge–Kutta formulae. *Journal of Computational and Applied Mathematics* **6**:19–26, 1980.

[19] N. R. Draper and H. Smith. *Applied Regression Analysis*. Wiley, New York, 3d edition, 1998.

[20] A. Edelman. The mathematics of the Pentium division bug. *SIAM Review* **39(1)**:54–67, Mar 1997.

[21] G. Farin. *Curves and Surfaces for Computer Aided Geometric Design: A Practical Guide*. Academic Press, Inc., Boston, 2d edition, 1990.

[22] L. V. Fausett. *Applied Numerical Analysis Using* MATLAB. Prentice Hall, Upper Saddle River, NJ, 1999.

[23] B. A. Finlayson. *Nonlinear Analysis in Chemical Engineering*. McGraw-Hill, New York, 1980.

[24] G. Forsythe, M. Malcolm, and C. Moler. *Computer Methods for Mathematical Computations*. Prentice-Hall, Englewood Cliffs, NJ, 1977.

[25] W. Gander and W. Gautschi. Adaptive Quadrature—Revisited. *BIT*, **40(1)**:84–101, 2000.

[26] W. Gautschi. On the construction of Gaussian quadrature rules from modified moments. *Mathematics of Computation*, **24(110)**:245–260, Apr. 1970.

[27] J. R. Gilbert, C. Moler, and R. Schreiber. Sparse matrices in MATLAB: Design and implementation. *SIAM Journal on Matrix Analysis and Applications* **13(1)**:333–356, Mar 1992.

[28] P. E. Gill, W. Murray, and M. H. Wright. *Numerical Linear Algebra and Optimization*, volume 1. Addison-Wesley, Redwood City, CA, 1991.

[29] D. Goldberg. What every computer scientist should know about floating-point arithmetic. *ACM Computing Surveys* **23(1)**:5–48, March 1991.

[30] H. H. Goldstine. *The Computer: from Pascal to von Neumann*. Princeton University Press, Princeton, NJ, 1972.

[31] G. Golub and J. M. Ortega. *Scientific Computing and Differential Equations: An Introduction to Numerical Methods*. Academic Press, Inc., Boston, 1992.

[32] G. H. Golub and C. F. Van Loan. *Matrix Computations*. The John Hopkins University Press, Baltimore, MD, 3d edition, 1996.

[33] G. H. Golub and J. H. Welsch. Calculation of Gauss quadrature rules. *Mathematics of Computation* **23**:221–230, 1969.

[34] D. Hanselman and B. Littlefield. *Mastering* MATLAB *5: A Comprehensive Tutorial and Reference*. Prentice Hall, Upper Saddle River, NJ, 1998.

[35] M. T. Heath. *Scientific Computing: An Introductory Survey*. McGraw-Hill, New York, 1997.

[36] N. J. Higham. *Accuracy and Stability of Numerical Algorithms*. SIAM, Philadelphia, 1996.

[37] R. R. Hocking. *Methods and Applications of Linear Models: Regression and the Analysis of Variance*. Wiley, New York, 1996.

[38] R. A. Horn and C. R. Johnson. *Matrix Analysis*. Cambridge University Press, Cambridge, 1985.

[39] F. P. Incropera and D. P. DeWitt. *Introduction to Heat Transfer*. Wiley, New York, 2d edition, 1990.

[40] E. Isaacson and H. B. Keller. *Analysis of Numerical Methods*. Dover, New York, 1994.

[41] M. Jenkins and J. Traub. A three-stage variable-shift iteration for polynomial zeros and its relation to generalized Rayleigh iteration. *Numerical Mathematics* **14**:252–263, 1970.

[42] M. Jenkins and J. Traub. Zeros of a complex polynomial. *Communications of the ACM* **15(2)**:97–99, Feb 1972.

[43] D. Kahaner, C. Moler, and S. Nash. *Numerical Methods and Software*. Prentice Hall, Englewood Cliffs, NJ, 1989.

[44] Kelley. *Iterative Methods for Linear and Nonlinear Equations*. SIAM, Philadelphia, 1995.

[45] Kelley. *Iterative Methods for Optimization*. SIAM, Philadelphia, 1999.

[46] B. W. Kernighan and R. Pike. *The Practice of Programming*. Addison-Wesley, Reading, MA, 1999.

[47] B. W. Kernighan and P. J. Plauger. *The Elements of Programming Style*. McGraw-Hill, New York, 2d edition, 1978.

[48] A. R. Krommer and C. W. Ueberhuber. *Computational Integration*. SIAM, Philadelphia, 1998.

[49] C. L. Lawson and R. J. Hanson. *Solving Least Squares Problems*. SIAM, Philadelphia, 1995.

[50] G. Lindfield and J. Penny. *Numerical Methods Using* MATLAB. Ellis Horwood, New York, 1995.

[51] P. Marchand. *Graphics and GUIs with* MATLAB. CRC Press, Boca Raton, FL, 2d edition, 1999.

[52] R. L. Mason, R. F. Gunst, and J. L. Hess. *Statistical Design and Analysis of Experiments: with Applications to Engineering and Science*. Wiley, New York, 1989.

[53] J. H. Mathews and K. D. Fink. *Numerical Methods Using* MATLAB. Prentice Hall, Upper Saddle River, NJ, 3d edition, 1999.

[54] C. Moler. A tale of two numbers. *SIAM News* **28(1)**:1,16, Jan 1995.

[55] C. Moler. Floating points: IEEE standard unifies arithmetic model. MATLAB *News and Notes*, Fall 1996:11–13, 1996.

[56] C. Moler. Golden ODEs: New ordinary differential equation solvers for MATLAB and SIMULINK. MATLAB *News and Notes*, Summer 1996:11–13, 1996.

[57] F. C. Moon. *Chaotic and Fractal Dynamics: An Introduction for Applied Scientists and Engineers*. Wiley, New York, 1992.

[58] B. N. Parlett. *The Symmetric Eigenvalue Problem*. SIAM, Philadelphia, 1998.

[59] R. Piessens, E. de Doncker-Kapenga, C. Überhuber, and D. Kahaner. *QUADPACK: A Subroutine Package for Automatic Integration*. Springer-Verlag, Berlin, 1983.

[60] J. C. Polking. *Ordinary Differential Equations Using* MATLAB. Prentice Hall, Englewood Cliffs, NJ, 1995.

[61] W. H. Press, B. P. Flannery, S. A. Teukolsky, and W. T. Vetterling. *Numerical Recipes in C*. Cambridge University Press, New York, 2d edition, 1992.

[62] W. C. Reynolds. *Thermodynamic Properties in SI*. Stanford University, Department of Mechanical Engineering, Stanford, CA, 1979.

[63] T. P. Ryan. *Modern Regression Methods*. Wiley, New York, 1997.

[64] H. R. Schwarz. *Numerical Analysis: A Comprehensive Introduction*. Wiley, New York, 1989.

[65] L. Shampine, R. Allen, Jr., and S. Preuss. *Fundamentals of Numerical Computing*. Wiley, New York, 1997.

[66] L. Shampine and M. W. Reichelt. The MATLAB ODE suite. *SIAM Journal on Scientific Computing* **18(1)**:1–22, Jan 1997.

[67] G. Stewart. Gauss, statistics, and Gaussian elimination. Technical Report TR-3307, University of Maryland, Department of Computer Science, College Park, Maryland, 1994.

[68] G. Stewart. *Afternotes on Numerical Analysis*. SIAM, Philadelphia, 1996.

[69] G. Stewart. *Matrix Algorithms, Volume 1: Basic Decompositions*. SIAM, Philadelphia, 1996.

[70] J. Stoer and R. Bulirsh. *Introduction to Numerical Analysis*. Springer-Verlag, New York, 2d edition, 1993.

[71] G. Strang. *Linear Algebra and Its Applications*. Harcourt Brace Jovanovich, Fort Worth, TX, 3d edition, 1988.

[72] G. Strang. *Introduction to Linear Algebra*. Wellesley-Cambridge Press, Wellesley, MA, 1993.

[73] The Mathworks, Inc. Using MATLAB. The Mathworks, Inc., Natick, MA, 1996.

[74] The Mathworks, Inc. Using MATLAB Graphics. The Mathworks, Inc., Natick, MA, 1996.

[75] The Mathworks, Inc. MATLAB Language Reference Manual. The Mathworks, Inc., Natick, MA, 1996.

[76] L. N. Trefethen and D. Bau, III. *Numerical Linear Algebra*. SIAM, Philadelphia, 1997.

[77] C. F. Van Loan. *Introduction to Scientific Computing: A Matrix Vector Approach Using* MATLAB. Prentice Hall, Upper Saddle River, NJ, 1997.

[78] D. S. Watkins. *Fundamentals of Matrix Computations*. Wiley, New York, 1991.

[79] H. B. Wilson and L. H. Turcotte. *Advanced Mathematics and Mechanics Applications Using* MATLAB. CRC Press, Boca Raton, FL, 2d edition, 1997.

A

Eigenvalues and Eigensystems

The reader has, no doubt, encountered eigenvalue problems before. In the solution of homogeneous, linear differential equations, for example, the acceptable form of the solution is determined by an eigenvalue problem. The building block solutions are called eigenfunctions. To solve the differential equation, one must find the eigenvalue–eigenfunction pairs, which, in general, are infinite in number. This is different from the matrix, or *algebraic*, eigenvalue problem considered in this chapter. The matrix eigenvalue problem arises from discrete models of physical systems. Such discrete models have finite number of degrees of freedom, and the resulting eigenvalue problem involves determining a finite number of eigenvalue–eigenvector pairs. The eigenvectors are discrete—they consist of a finite number of elements—as are the vectors considered elsewhere in this book.

The matrix eigenvalue problem is a large and important part of numerical analysis. This appendix provides a very brief introduction to matrix eigenvalues and eigenvectors. Use of the built-in `eig` function for finding eigenvalues and eigenvectors of a matrix is demonstrated.

Computing the eigenvalues of a matrix is important in a number of applications.

- In numerical analysis, the convergence of an iterative sequence involving matrices is determined by the size of the eigenvalues of the iterated matrix.
- In dynamic systems, the eigenvalues indicate whether the system is oscillatory, stable (decaying oscillations), or unstable (growing oscillations).
- In oscillatory systems, the eigenvalues of the differential equation (for a continuous model) or the coefficient matrix of a finite element model are directly related to the natural frequencies of the system.
- In regression analysis, eigenvectors of the correlation matrix are used to select new predictor variables, or *principle components*, that are linear combinations of the original predictor variables.

The built-in `eig` function is useful in these applications. If only a few of the discrete eigenvalues are of interest, the built-in `eigs` function is appropriate.

A.1 EIGENVECTORS MAP ONTO THEMSELVES

The matrix–vector product $y = Ax$ can be interpreted as the rotation and elongation of the vector x by the matrix A. The resulting vector y clearly depends on both x and A. It turns out that there are special vectors associated with A that are not rotated by A; they are merely stretched (or shrunk) by the action of A. These special vectors are the eigenvectors of A.

Consider the `iterMult` function in Listing A.1. Given a matrix A and a compatible vector x, `iterMult` carries out a variation on the following sequence:

$$u_{(0)} = x,$$

$$u_{(1)} = A\,u_{(0)},$$

$$u_{(2)} = A\,u_{(1)} = A\,A\,u_{(0)},$$

$$\vdots$$

$$u_{(k)} = A\,u_{(k-1)} = \underbrace{A\,A\,\ldots A}_{k \text{ times}}\,x.$$

The notation of subscripts in parenthesis reinforces the idea that $u_{(0)}, u_{(1)}, \ldots, u_{(k)}$ is a sequence of k vectors and *not* the $1, \ldots, m$ elements of the vector u. The `iterMult` function evaluates the preceding sequence with the exception that at each step the vector $u_{(k)}$ is scaled by its L_∞ norm. The `iterMult` function exhibits an interesting behavior. For many matrices, the sequence of vectors

$$x, \ Ax, \ A^2x, \ A^3x \ldots$$

converges to a vector that depends only on A, not the starting vector x.

```
function [u,lambda] = iterMult(A,x,nit)
% iterMult  Iterated multiplication of a vector by a matrix: u = A*A*...*A*x
%
% Synopsis:  u          = iterMult(A,x,nit)
%            [u,lambda] = iterMult(A,x,nit)
%
% Input:    A = an n by n matrix
%           x0 = n by 1 (column) vector to start the iterations
%           nit = number of iterations
%
% Output:   u = A*A* ... A*x, result of m multiplications of A on x
%               scaled by the max norm of the result at each step
%               The max norm of u is printed at each step
%           lambda = (optional) infinity norm of the scaled u
u = x;
fprintf('  k     norm(u,inf)\n');
for k=1:nit
  u = A*u;
  r = norm(u,inf);
  u = u/r;
  fprintf('%3d     %f\n',k,r);
end
if nargout==2, lambda = r; end
```

Listing A.1   The `iterMult` function repeatedly multiplies a vector x_0
by a matrix A and scales the result.

Here is the (edited) result of 50 `iterMult` iterations for the $(-1, 2, -1)$ tridiagonal matrix:

```
>> A = tridiag(5,2,-1);    % tridiag from linalg directory of NMM toolbox
>> x = rand(5,1);
>> u = iterMult(A,x,50)
   k     norm(y,inf)
   1     1.190089
   2     2.214240
   3     3.650440
   :     :
  49     3.732051
  50     3.732051

   u =
      -0.5000
       0.8660
      -1.0000
       0.8660
      -0.5000
```

```
lambda =
    3.7321
```

You can easily test to see whether the results of this example depend on the starting vector by generating another random x or by picking special vectors like $x = [1, 0, 0, 0, 0]^T$ and $x = [0, 1, 0, 0, 0]^T$.

The output of `iterMult` indicates that the L_∞ norm of $A^k u$ has converged to a constant value. An additional manual iteration shows that $A^k u$ also becomes constant:

```
>> w = A*u;
>> lambda = norm(w,inf)
lambda =
    3.7321

>> unew = w/lambda;
>> disp([w  u  unew])
    -1.8660    -0.5000    -0.5000
     3.2320     0.8660     0.8660
    -3.7321    -1.0000    -1.0000
     3.2321     0.8660     0.8660
    -1.8661    -0.5000    -0.5000
```

As expected, `unew` is (nearly) the same as u from the previous iteration. Due to roundoff and the convergence properties of `iterMult`, `unew` and u will not be exactly equal. (How close are they?)

The preceding calculations may be summarized as follows. Given a matrix A and a random starting vector u_0, the sequence of vectors $u_{(k)} = Au_{k-1}$, $k = 1, 2, \ldots$, converges to $v = \lim_{k\to\infty} u_{(k)}$. The vector v has the property that Av gives a scalar multiple of v itself. In other words,

$$Av = \lambda v. \tag{A.1}$$

In general, Equation (A.1) defines a special scalar–vector pair, where λ is the *eigenvalue* and v is the *eigenvector* of A. Since the product Av only differs from v by a scalar multiplier, we conclude that A cannot rotate its eigenvectors.

The eigenvectors and eigenvalues of A are characteristics of A. The iterations in the `iterMult` function are just a simple way to create a pair of (λ, v) values. This technique, called the power method, is developed in a later section. Computing the eigenvalues and eigenvectors of an arbitrary matrix A is a substantial numerical task, which requires more sophisticated techniques that the power method. Consult [12, 78] for introductions to the computation of matrix eigenvalues.

A.2 MATHEMATICAL PRELIMINARIES

This section is a brief summary of the mathematical nomenclature used in working with the matrix eigenvalue problem.

A.2.1 Characteristic Polynomial

Equation (A.1) defines the matrix eigenvalue problem. For hand calculations and theoretical analysis, it is helpful to work with an equivalent form. Subtracting λv from both sides of the equation gives

$$(A - \lambda I)v = 0,$$

where I is the identity matrix. The solution to this equation requires that either $v = 0$ (the trivial solution), or

$$\det(A - \lambda I) = 0, \tag{A.2}$$

where $\det(\bullet)$ is the *determinant* of its matrix argument. Evaluating Equation (A.2) for an $n \times n$ matrix A results in a degree-n polynomial in λ called the *characteristic polynomial* of A:

$$\det(A - \lambda I) = p(\lambda) = \lambda^n + \alpha_{n-1}\lambda^{n-1} + \alpha_{n-2}\lambda^{n-2} + \cdots + \alpha_0. \tag{A.3}$$

The roots of this polynomial are the eigenvalues of A. This suggests that solving the matrix eigenvalue problem can be converted into a root-finding problem. Though this is theoretically possible, it is an approach that is complicated by the occurrence of repeated roots and ill conditioning of the polynomial root-finding problem. In general, it is not a good idea to find the eigenvalues of A by trying to find the roots of $p(\lambda)$.

Example A.1: Characteristic Polynomial of a Matrix

Evaluate the characteristic polynomial of

$$A = \begin{bmatrix} 3 & -2 & 1 \\ -2 & 4 & -1 \\ 1 & -1 & 5 \end{bmatrix}.$$

The desired result is obtained from a straightforward computation of

$$\det(A - \lambda I) = \begin{vmatrix} (3 - \lambda) & -2 & 1 \\ -2 & (4 - \lambda) & -1 \\ 1 & -1 & (5 - \lambda) \end{vmatrix},$$

which gives

$$\det(A - \lambda I) = \lambda^3 - 12\lambda^2 + 41\lambda - 37. \tag{A.4}$$

The built-in `poly` function computes the characteristic polynomial of a matrix:

```
>> A = [3 -2  1; -2 4 -1; 1 -1 5];
>> p = poly(A)
p =
    1.0000  -12.0000   41.0000  -37.0000
```

The elements of vector p are arranged in decreasing powers of λ, and they agree with Equation (A.4).

A.2.2 Companion Matrix

Before proceeding with the general problem of finding the eigenvalues of a matrix, we will take a brief detour to reconsider the problem of finding the roots of a polynomial. Although using a root-finding method to determine the eigenvalues of a matrix is not a good idea, it turns out that the reverse problem, namely, finding the roots of a polynomial by solving an eigenvalue problem, *is* a good idea. (Cf. § 6.7 beginning on page 279.)

     If the characteristic polynomial of A is given by Equation (A.3), then a companion matrix of A is

$$C = \begin{pmatrix} -\alpha_{n-1} & -\alpha_{n-2} & -\alpha_{n-3} & \cdots & -\alpha_1 & -\alpha_0 \\ 1 & 0 & 0 & \cdots & 0 & 0 \\ 0 & 1 & 0 & \cdots & 0 & 0 \\ \vdots & \vdots & \ddots & \ddots & \vdots & \vdots \\ 0 & 0 & \cdots & 1 & 0 & 0 \\ 0 & 0 & \cdots & 0 & 1 & 0 \end{pmatrix}.$$

Direct evaluation (try a 3×3 example) shows that the characteristic polynomial of C is the same as Equation (A.3).

A.2.3 Eigenfacts

The following facts are useful in working with eigenvalue problems (see, for example, [12, 58, 71, 78], for more detailed development of these ideas):

- The eigenvalues of a matrix may be repeated. For example,

$$A = \begin{bmatrix} 1 & 1 \\ -1 & 3 \end{bmatrix}$$

has repeated eigenvalues of $\lambda = 2$.

- If A is an $n \times n$ matrix, it has at least one distinct eigenvalue and at most n eigenvectors.
- The sum of the diagonal elements of any square matrix is equal to the sum of the eigenvalues of the matrix

$$\sum_{i=1}^{n} a_{ii} = \sum_{i=1}^{n} \lambda_i,$$

where λ_i are the eigenvalues of A. The sum of the diagonal elements of a matrix is also called the *trace* of the matrix (i.e., trace$(A) = \sum_{i=1}^{n} a_{ii}$).

- The product of the eigenvalues of any matrix is equal to the determinant of that matrix

$$\prod_{i=1}^{n} a_{ii} = \det(A).$$

- If A has real elements and is nonsymmetric, its eigenvalues may be real or complex. Complex eigenvalues exist in conjugate pairs. For example,

$$B = \begin{bmatrix} 1 & 1 \\ -2 & 3 \end{bmatrix}$$

has the complex eigenvalues $\lambda = 2 \pm i$.

- If A is symmetric, its eigenvalues are real.
- If the eigenvalues of A are all positive real numbers, then A is positive definite, and

$$\psi(x) = x^T A x > 0.$$

for any column vector x with n real elements. ψ is called a *pure quadratic form* (*quadratic* because the element of x appear in second-order terms (e.g., x_1^2, $x_1 x_2$, ...) and *pure* because the *only* second-order terms appear in the expression for $\psi(x)$ (e.g., no x_1, x_2, ..., or constant terms).

- If a matrix has n distinct eigenvalues, then it has a set of n linearly independent eigenvectors.
- If an $n \times n$ matrix A has n distinct eigenvalues, then A can be factored as

$$A = X \Lambda X^{-1}, \tag{A.5}$$

where

$$\Lambda = \begin{bmatrix} \lambda_1 & 0 & 0 & 0 \\ 0 & \lambda_2 & & \vdots \\ \vdots & & \ddots & 0 \\ 0 & \cdots & 0 & \lambda_n \end{bmatrix}$$

and the columns of X are the eigenvectors of A. Equation (A.5) is sometimes called the *eigenvalue decomposition*, or *spectral decomposition*, of A. Since the existence of the decomposition in Equation (A.5) *requires* that A have n distinct eigenvalues, it is important to remember that for a general matrix A, the eigenvalue decomposition *may not exist*. If A can be factored as in Equation (A.5), then it is said to be *diagonalizable*.

- The eigenvectors of a matrix are determined only to within a scalar multiple. To prove this, let $w = v/\sigma$, where σ is any scalar. Substituting $v = \sigma w$ into Equation (A.1) gives

$$A(\sigma w) = \lambda(\sigma w),$$

$$\sigma A w = \sigma \lambda w,$$

$$A w = \lambda w.$$

Therefore v and w are both eigenvectors associated with the eigenvalue λ.

The preceding list of facts is helpful in at least two ways. When working on a practical problem that can be formulated as a matrix eigenvalue problem, the properties of the matrix may be used to deduce the properties of the solution. For example, if the matrix eigenvalue problem is derived from a system of differential equations, and if the matrix involved is symmetric, then without any further analysis, one can conclude that the system will not oscillate, since oscillatory systems correspond with matrices with eigenvalues that exist in complex conjugate pairs. On the other hand, when working on a numerical methods for finding eigenvalues and (possibly) eigenvectors, encountering a matrix that is not symmetric means that some shortcuts applicable only to symmetric matrices cannot be applied.

In the context of this book, the list of eigenfacts should be considered as a convenient reference. It is not a substitute for a more systematic and thorough discussion of matrix eigenvalue problems.

A.3 THE POWER METHOD

The `iterMult` function in Listing A.1 implements the so-called power method for computing the largest or *dominant* eigenvalue of a matrix. The power method is useful when only the largest eigenvalue is desired *and* when the largest eigenvalue is distinct from the other eigenvalues. When it works, the power method is quite efficient. It can be attractive for large sparse matrices, since the bulk of the computational work is expended in computing a matrix–vector product. If the (large and sparse) matrix is stored in sparse matrix format (see Appendix B), the matrix–vector product can be performed efficiently. The power method is derived in this section because it is a simple algorithm and the algorithm exposes some properties of matrix eigenvalues. The power method is also closely related to the study of convergence of stationary iterative methods for solving $Ax = b$. For an arbitrary matrix, the power method may fail, or it may converge very slowly.

A.3.1 Power Iterations

Assume that the matrix A has n linearly independent eigenvectors $v_{(1)}, v_{(2)}, \dots, v_{(n)}$. Remember that the subscripts on v are placed in parenthesis to indicate a sequence of vectors, not the selections of vector elements. According to Watkins [78, following Corollary 4.2.11] if one considers the universe of all random matrices, the assumption of linearly independent eigenvectors is met by "most," but not all, matrices. Let's take that observation and the knowledge that the power method has proven useful in a number of practical applications as the motivation for proceeding.

For convenience, let the n eigenvalues of A be ordered such that

$$|\lambda_1| > |\lambda_2| > \cdots > |\lambda_n|. \tag{A.6}$$

Since the n eigenvectors of A are linearly independent, they form a basis for n-dimensional space and any n-dimensional vector x can be written as

$$x = \alpha_1 v_{(1)} + \alpha_2 v_{(2)} + \cdots + \alpha_n v_{(2)},$$

where the α_i are scalar coefficients. For the current application, the magnitude of the α_i are unimportant as long as $\alpha_1 \neq 0$. Given this representation of x, the product Ax is

$$Ax = A\left[\alpha_1 v_{(1)} + \alpha_2 v_{(2)} + \cdots + \alpha_n v_{(2)}\right] = \alpha_1 A v_{(1)} + \alpha_2 A v_{(2)} + \cdots + \alpha_n A v_{(n)}.$$

From Equation (A.1), each of the $Av_{(i)}$ terms may be replaced by $\lambda_i v_{(i)}$, where $(\lambda_i, v_{(i)})$ is an eigenvector–eigenvalue pair. Thus,

$$Ax = \alpha_1 \lambda_1 v_{(1)} + \alpha_2 \lambda_2 v_{(2)} + \cdots + \alpha_n \lambda_n v_{(n)}.$$

Multiplying on the left by A and replacing the $Av_{(i)}$ terms by $(\lambda_i, v_{(i)})$ gives

$$A\,Ax = A^2 x = \alpha_1 \lambda_1^2 v_{(1)} + \alpha_2 \lambda_2^2 v_{(2)} + \cdots + \alpha_n \lambda_n^2 v_{(n)}$$

and, in general,

$$A^k x = \alpha_1 \lambda_1^k v_{(1)} + \alpha_2 \lambda_2^k v_{(2)} + \cdots + \alpha_n \lambda_n^k v_{(n)},$$

where $A^k = \underbrace{A\,A \ldots A}_{k \text{ times}}$.

Factoring λ_1^k from the right-hand side of the preceding expression gives

$$A^k x = \lambda_1^k \left[\alpha_1 v_{(1)} + \alpha_2 \left(\frac{\lambda_2}{\lambda_1} \right)^k v_{(2)} + \cdots + \alpha_n \left(\frac{\lambda_n}{\lambda_1} \right)^k v_{(n)} \right]. \qquad (A.7)$$

Two observations that follow from the preceding equations reveal how the power method works. From Equation (A.6), one sees that $(\lambda_i / \lambda_1) < 1$, for all $i > 1$. Thus, all terms inside the square brackets in Equation (A.7) except $\alpha_1 v_{(1)}$ go to zero as k increases:

$$A^k x \longrightarrow \lambda_1^k \alpha_1 v_{(1)} \qquad \text{as } k \longrightarrow \infty. \qquad (A.8)$$

Furthermore, as k increases, the right-hand side of Equation (A.7) approaches a vector in the same direction as the eigenvector $v_{(1)}$. In fact, because eigenvectors are only determined up to an arbitrary multiplicative constant, $\lambda_1^k \alpha_1 v_{(1)}$ *is* the $v_{(1)}$ eigenvector associated with λ_1.

It appears, therefore, that computing $A^k x$ for an arbitrary x and a sufficiently large k will yield the dominant eigenvector of A. While this is true in exact arithmetic (and as long as there is a dominant eigenvalue of A), for large n or large λ_1, the magnitude of the coefficients in $A^k x$ will quickly grow enough to cause overflow. Overflow may be avoided by scaling the product $A^k x$ at each iteration. A convenient scale factor is the L_∞ norm of $A^k x$ itself, since this yields a vector with its largest element equal to one.[1]

The basic computation of the power method is summarized as

$$u_{(k)} = \frac{A^k x_0}{\| A^k x_0 \|_\infty}, \qquad k = 1, 2, \ldots, \qquad (A.9)$$

where x_0 is an arbitrary initial vector. For large enough k, the value of $u_{(k)}$ becomes (via Equation (A.8))

$$u_{(k)} = \frac{A^k x_0}{\| A^k x_0 \|_\infty} = \frac{\lambda_1^k \alpha_1 v_{(1)}}{\| \lambda_1^k \alpha_1 v_{(1)} \|_\infty} = \frac{\lambda_1^k \alpha_1 v_{(1)}}{\lambda_1^k \alpha_1 \| v_{(1)} \|_\infty} = \frac{v_{(1)}}{\| v_{(1)} \|_\infty} \qquad \text{as } k \longrightarrow \infty.$$

---

[1]The L_2 norm may also be used with the result that the sequence of vectors produced by the power method will have length one instead of having their largest elements equal to one. Either norm may be used, although using the L_∞ norm will take fewer floating-point computations.

In words, the power iterations produce the normalized eigenvector corresponding to the dominant eigenvalue. An efficient program to implement the power method does not compute $A^k x_0$ from scratch on each iteration. Rather, the sequence of $u_{(k)}$ vectors is computed recursively with

$$u_{(k)} = \frac{Au_{(k-1)}}{\|Au_{(k-1)}\|_\infty} \quad \text{and} \quad \lim_{k \to \infty} u_{(k)} = v_{(1)}.$$

where $v_{(1)}$ is the dominant eigenvector of A.

The eigenvalue corresponding to the dominant eigenvector is obtained from the power iterations with no additional effort. Define a temporary vector $w = Au_{(k-1)}$. Then, at convergence, $w = Au_{(k-1)} = \lambda_1 u_{(k-1)}$, so that

$$\frac{\|w\|_\infty}{\|u_{(k-1)}\|_\infty} = \lambda_1,$$

but since $\|u_{(k-1)}\|_\infty = 1$ (see Equation (A.9)),

$$\lambda_1 = \|w\|_\infty.$$

Organizing the preceding ideas into a sequential procedure gives the following algorithm for the power method:

Algorithm A.1   Power Iteration

initialize $u_{(0)}$
for $k = 1, 2, \ldots$
  $w = Au_{(k-1)}$
  $\lambda = \|w\|_\infty$
  $u_{(k)} = (1/\lambda)w$
end

In Algorithm A.1, w is a temporary vector. Since the iteration history is not of interest, the intermediate $u_{(k)}$ need not be stored, and the u vector can be overwritten to avoid creating the temporary w vector. Note that inside the power algorithm, $u_{(k)}$ is an eigenvector of A only at convergence.

The `iterMult` function in Listing A.1 performs power iterations. The `powerit` function (not listed here) in the NMM toolbox is a modified version of the `iterMult` function that is more suitable for eigenvalue computations.

A.3.2 Inverse-Power Iterations

The *inverse-power method* may be applied to find the smallest eigenvalue of a matrix. Multiplying both sides of Equation (A.1) by A^{-1} on the left gives

$$A^{-1}Av = \lambda A^{-1}v,$$

$$\lambda^{-1}v = A^{-1}v.$$

If we define a new matrix $B = A^{-1}$ and a new scalar $\mu = \lambda^{-1}$ then the preceding equation is equivalent to

$$Bv = \mu v.$$

Therefore, if (λ, v) is an eigenvalue–eigenvector pair of A, then (λ^{-1}, v) is an eigenvalue–eigenvector pair of A^{-1}. Applying power iterations to $B = A^{-1}$ (if the method converges) will yield the smallest eigenvalue of A.

A simplistic implementation of the power method would involve a literal computation of $B = A^{-1}$ and then applying Algorithm A.1 to B. Instead, consider the matrix multiplication step $w = Au_{(k-1)}$ in Algorithm A.1. With the inverse-power method matrix A is replaced by $B = A^{-1}$, and the statement $w = Bu_{(k-1)} = A^{-1}u_{(k-1)}$ is equivalent to solving

$$Aw = u_{(k-1)}$$

for w, given $u_{(k-1)}$. For the reasons discussed on page 373, solving the preceding system is preferable to computing $w = A^{-1}u_{(k-1)}$. Furthermore, since A is unchanged during the iterations, an LU factorization of A can be performed once at the beginning of the iterations. Thus, the expression "solve $Aw = u_{(k-1)}$" is interpreted as applying a sequence of two triangular solves (backward substitution and then forward substitution) at each iteration. The following Algorithm specifies these details:

Algorithm A.2　　Inverse-power Iteration

initialize $u_{(0)}$
factor: $A = LU$
for $k = 1, 2, \ldots$
　　solve: $Lw = u_{(k)}$
　　solve: $Uu_{(k+1)} = w$
　　$\mu = \|w\|_\infty$
　　$u_{(k)} = (1/\mu)w$
end
$\lambda = 1/\mu$

In practice, the convergence of inverse iteration is accelerated by a simple manipulation that shifts the eigenvalues so that the smallest eigenvalue is close to zero. (See, for example, Watkins [78].) The `powerit` and `poweritInv` functions in the `eigen` directory of the NMM toolbox implement shifted power iterations and shifted inverse-power iterations, respectively.

A.4 BUILT-IN FUNCTIONS FOR EIGENVALUE COMPUTATION

The power method is useful only when a few of the eigenvalues of a matrix are to be computed, *and* when the desired eigenvalues are real, *and* when the desired eigenvalues differ sufficiently in absolute value. For a general matrix, these conditions are unlikely to be met, and more sophisticated methods for finding eigenvalues are needed.

The *QR algorithm* is a powerful method for computing all the eigenvalues of a matrix. The QR algorithm iteratively transforms a given matrix into another matrix that is equivalent in the sense that it has the same eigenvalues. The eigenvalues and, if desired, the eigenvectors can then be efficiently extracted from the transformed matrix. Although the QR algorithm for computing eigenvalues uses the *QR factorization* of a matrix (cf. § 9.2.3), solving the eigenvalue problem is more subtle and involved than merely computing the QR factorization. Consult [12, 15, 32, 76, 78] for discussions of how the QR algorithm is used to solve the algebraic eigenvalue problem.

A.4.1 The `eig` Function

The `eig` function uses the QR algorithm to find all of the eigenvalues and optionally all of the eigenvectors of a matrix. In MATLAB version 5 and later, the input matrix may be dense or sparse. Two ways of calling the `eig` function are

```
lam = eig(A)
[V,L] = eig(A)
```

where A is a square matrix, `lam` is a column vector of eigenvalues, L is a diagonal matrix with the eigenvalues of A on the diagonal (i.e., `lam = diag(L)`), and V is a matrix with columns equal to the eigenvectors of A. Enter `help eig` to see other options for using `eig`.

Example A.2: Using `eig`

The built-in `eig` function makes it easy to find the eigenvalues and eigenvectors of a tridiagonal matrix. For example, consider the following:

```
>> A = tridiag(5,2,-1)     %  tridiag is an NMM toolbox function
A =
     2    -1     0     0     0
    -1     2    -1     0     0
```

```
    0    -1    2    -1    0
    0     0   -1     2   -1
    0     0    0    -1    2
>> lam = eig(A)
lam =
    3.0000
    1.0000
    2.0000
    3.7321
    0.2679
```

Notice that the largest eigenvalue is the same as that produced by the power iterations on page 743. The complete set of eigenvectors and eigenvalues of A are

```
>> [V,L] = eig(A)
V =
  -0.5000    0.5000    0.5774    0.2887    0.2887
  -0.5000   -0.5000    0.0000    0.5000   -0.5000
        0   -0.0000   -0.5774    0.5774    0.5774
   0.5000    0.5000    0.0000    0.5000   -0.5000
   0.5000   -0.5000    0.5774    0.2887    0.2887
L =
   1.0000         0         0         0         0
        0    3.0000         0         0         0
        0         0    2.0000         0         0
        0         0         0    0.2679         0
        0         0         0         0    3.7321
```

It is important to remember that eigenvalues and eigenvectors come in pairs. Accordingly, the kth eigenvalue of A is L(k,k), and the corresponding eigenvector is V(:,k). Thus, the dominant eigenvalue/eigenvector pair is obtained with

```
>> [lmax,imax] = max(abs(diag(L)))
lmax =
    3.7321
imax =
    5

>> V(:,imax)
ans =
    0.2887
   -0.5000
    0.5774
   -0.5000
    0.2887
```

The `eigSort` function in the NMM toolbox (not listed here) obtains the eigenvalues and eigenvectors of a matrix and returns the V and L matrices sorted in order of ascending or descending magnitude of λ_i.

A.4.2 The `eigs` Function

The `eigs` function finds a limited number of the eigenvalues of a matrix. The `eigs` function is much more efficient than `eig` when the coefficient matrix is sparse (cf. Appendix B) and when only a few eigenvalues are needed.

A.5 SINGULAR VALUE DECOMPOSITION

Any real $m \times n$ matrix A with $m \geq n$ can be factored into the product of three matrices

$$A = U \Sigma V^T, \tag{A.10}$$

where U is an orthogonal $m \times m$ matrix, Σ is an $m \times n$ diagonal matrix, and V is an orthogonal $n \times n$ matrix. This rather forbidding expression provides a way to examine the underlying properties of A. Equation (A.10) is the Singular Value Decomposition (SVD) of A.

The elements of matrix Σ are the *singular values* of A. A visual representation of Σ is

$$\Sigma = \begin{bmatrix} \sigma_1 & & & \\ & \sigma_2 & & \\ & & \ddots & \\ & & & \sigma_n \\ 0 & 0 & \cdots & 0 \\ \vdots & & & \vdots \\ 0 & 0 & \cdots & 0 \end{bmatrix}, \tag{A.11}$$

where $\sigma_1 \geq \sigma_2 \geq \cdots \geq \sigma_n$. In exact arithmetic, the number of nonzero singular values of A is equal to the rank of A. In floating-point arithmetic, a matrix can be nearly singular if σ_n, the smallest singular value, is much smaller than σ_1. In fact, the L_2 norm condition number of a square matrix $(m = n)$ is

$$\kappa_2(A) = \|A\|_2 \|A^{-1}\|_2 = \frac{\sigma_1}{\sigma_n} \quad \text{where } A \text{ is } n \times n. \tag{A.12}$$

By convention, $\kappa_2 = \sigma_1/\sigma_n$ is also used for rectangular matrices (i.e., when $m > n$). In the special case where A is a symmetric matrix, the SVD and the eigenvalue decomposition (see § A.2.3) are related. In particular, when A is symmetric the singular values of A are the absolute values of its eigenvalues. In general, whether or not A is square and whether or not A is symmetric, the singular values of A are the eigenvalues of $A^T A$ if $m \geq n$ or AA^T if $m < n$. Rather than focus on the correspondence of the SVD and the eigenvalue problem in these special cases, it is useful to consider the differences between these decompositions.

The eigenvalue decomposition in Equation (A.5) only applies to square matrices, and it exists for a particular A only if all of the eigenvalues of A are distinct (no repeated eigenvalues). In contrast, the SVD exists for *all* matrices, square or rectangular, independent of the number and kind (positive, real, complex) of the eigenvalues.

Eigenvalues are useful in analyzing algorithms that involve repeated multiplication by A or where e^A is computed. Singular values are useful in the study of the properties of A. The SVD is also useful in some computational tasks, such as in solving rank-deficient least squares problems.

A.5.1 The svd Function

The built-in svd function performs the SVD of a matrix. It may be called in the following four ways:

```
S = svd(A)
S = svd(A,0)
[U,S,V] = svd(A)
[U,S,V] = svd(A,0)
```

Here, A is any matrix, S is the diagonal matrix Σ in Equation (A.10), and U and V are unitary matrices in Equation (A.10). When the second argument of 0 is passed as input to svd, the result is an economy-size SVD. The economy-size decomposition is useful when A is an $m \times n$ matrix with $m > n$. The economy-size SVD gives the first n columns of U and a square $(n \times n)$ Σ. Note that when $m > n$ the full SVD of A gives a Σ matrix with only zeros in the last $m - n$ rows.

The built-in svds function computes a limited number of singular values of a sparse matrix.

B

Sparse Matrices

Sparse matrices have many more zeros than nonzeros. The fraction of nonzeros is so low that a considerable advantage can be gained by using more complicated techniques for storing and retrieving the matrix elements.

Sparse matrices do not introduce any new mathematical features of linear algebra. Their creation and use is an important implementation issue that is usually addressed with a specialized programming library. To benefit from sparse matrices, special data structures are used to store only the nonzero entries. This is in contrast to a conventional, or full storage scheme in which all elements of a matrix are stored, regardless of whether the elements are zero. The terms *sparse matrix* and *full matrix*, therefore, refer to the storage scheme only. A sparse matrix is mathematically equivalent to a full matrix.

MATLAB provides built-in support for sparse matrices. Once a sparse matrix is created, it may be used in MATLAB expressions in the same way that a full matrix is used. Not all built-in functions work on both sparse and full matrices. In these cases, a specialized sparse matrix version is provided. Thus, the advantages of using sparse matrices can often be obtained with little additional effort. The goal of this appendix is to introduce sparse matrix storage ideas and the built-in sparse matrix format in MATLAB. Readers wanting additional information, including details about the internal representations of MATLAB sparse matrices, should consult *Using* MATLAB [73] and the article by Gilbert et al. [27].

B.1 STORAGE AND FLOP SAVINGS

Consider the benefits of storage savings when sparse matrix techniques are used. Let δ be the storage density of a sparse matrix:

$$\delta = \frac{\text{number of nonzero elements}}{\text{total number of elements}}. \tag{B.1}$$

The storage density for an $n \times n$ tridiagonal matrix, for example, is

$$\delta = \frac{3n - 2}{n^2} \approx \frac{3}{n}.$$

As n increases, the storage density decreases, or the *sparsity* increases. By storing only nonzero elements of a matrix, the use of computer memory is kept to a minimum. This enables larger matrices to be stored in a given amount of memory (RAM).

In addition to reduced memory requirements, there are significant computational advantages to using sparse storage. When the matrix is stored as a full matrix, the work to perform a matrix–vector multiplication is $\mathcal{O}(n^2)$ flops. When the matrix is stored in sparse format, a matrix–vector multiplication requires $\mathcal{O}(n_{nz})$ flops, where n_{nz} is the number of nonzeros. For a tridiagonal matrix, $n_{nz} \approx 3n$, so the cost of a matrix–vector multiplication can be reduced from $\mathcal{O}(n^2)$ to $\mathcal{O}(n)$. The savings in operations are significant, especially for large n.

B.2 MATLAB SPARSE MATRIX FORMAT

The tridiagonal matrix is an example of a special class of sparse matrices with diagonal structure. Other examples of sparse matrices are depicted in Figure B.1. These include matrices with five (pentadiagonal) or more diagonals, banded matrices, and sparse matrices with arbitrary patterns of nonzeros.

It is important to realize that when utilizing a sparse matrix format, it is possible that some of the *stored* values are zeros. These zeros may arise, for example, in special cases of input data to an algorithm. There is no need to guarantee that all of the values stored in the sparse matrix data structure are nonzero. The important distinction is that due to the structure of the problem, for example, numerical solution to partial differential equations, there is a large number of matrix elements that will *always* be zero.

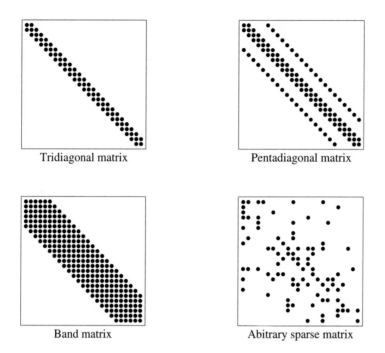

Tridiagonal matrix

Pentadiagonal matrix

Band matrix

Abitrary sparse matrix

Figure B.1   Four examples of sparse matrices: tridiagonal, pentadiagonal, banded, and arbitrary. The nonzero entries are represented by solid
dots.

B.2.1 Creating Sparse Matrices

MATLAB does not automatically create sparse matrices. Once a sparse matrix is
created, however, it may be used just like the full matrices that have been used
up to this point. Table B.1 lists some of the built-in sparse matrix functions. Enter
"help sparfun" at the command prompt for a list of additional functions.

An arbitrary sparse matrix in MATLAB is created from a list of the row and
column indices (i and j) of the nonzero elements, along with of the values of those
elements. Thus, a sparse matrix can be represented by a table where each row of
the table identifies the i and j indices along with the value of element $a_{i,j}$. As an
example, the matrix

$$A = \begin{bmatrix} 1 & 0 & 1 \\ 0 & 2 & 0 \\ 3 & 3 & 0 \end{bmatrix} \tag{B.2}$$

TABLE B.1   BASIC SPARSE MATRIX FUNCTIONS. TYPE `HELP` `SPARFUN` FOR A COMPLETE LIST OF BUILT-IN SPARSE MATRIX FUNCTIONS.

Functions for Creating Sparse Matrices

`spalloc`	Allocate memory for a sparse matrix that will then be defined with subsequent calls to other sparse matrix functions.
`sparse`	Convert a full matrix to sparse storage format *or* assemble a sparse matrix from vectors of indices and elements.
`spdiags`	Assemble a sparse matrix from diagonal vectors or extract the diagonal elements of a sparse matrix.
`speye`	Create a sparse identity matrix.
`sprand`	Create a sparse matrix with random entries.

Functions for Manipulating Sparse Matrices

`full`	Convert a sparse matrix to full matrix.
`nnz`	Return the number of nonzero elements in a sparse or full (dense) matrix.
`nonzeros`	Extract the nonzero elements of a sparse matrix. Result is a vector.
`nzmax`	Return the maximum number of nonzero elements allocated for a sparse matrix. In general $\mathtt{nzmax(A)} \geq \mathtt{nnz(A)}$.
`spparms`	Set parameters of a sparse matrix that control how it is manipulated by other sparse matrix routines.
`spones`	Replace all nonzero elements of a sparse matrix with ones.
`spy`	Visualize a sparse matrix by plotting nonzero entries as dots in a two-dimensional array.

is described with the following table:

row index	column index	value
1	1	1
3	1	3
2	2	2
3	2	3
1	3	1

Any element not listed in the table is assumed to be zero and is therefore not stored. The built-in `sparse` function can be used to construct a sparse matrix from just such a tabular description of the elements.

The `sparse` function can be called in the following ways

```
S = sparse(A)
S = sparse(is,js,as)
S = sparse(is,js,as,nrows,ncols)
S = sparse(is,js,as,nrows,ncols,nonzeros)
```

Here, S is the sparse matrix to be created. In the first form of sparse, the input A is a full matrix. This usage of sparse is not effective at economizing memory utilization since the full A needs to be created in the first place. Creating a sparse matrix directly from a full matrix is useful, however, in debugging sparse matrix calculations when a working code using full matrix storage is available.

In the second form of the sparse function, is, js, and as are vectors containing the three columns of the tabular representation of the sparse matrix. The optional parameters $nrows$ and $ncols$ explicitly define the number and rows and columns, respectively, in S. If $nrows$ and $ncols$ are not specified, an $m \times n$ sparse matrix is created with $m = \max(is)$ and $n = \max(js)$. If the optional $nonzeros$ parameter is not given, S is created with enough memory to hold length(as) nonzero elements. This is useful, for example, when all the elements needed to create S are available before sparse is called. In some applications, for example in assembling the stiffness matrix of a finite element model, the S matrix is constructed by adding small groups of elements at a time. In these situations the optional $nonzeros$ parameter tells the sparse function to allocate sufficient memory to hold the final S.

Sometimes, it may not be convenient to create a sparse matrix by first creating the vectors of indices and elements. In that case, an empty sparse matrix can be created with the spalloc function, and elements of the matrix can be added one at at time or in groups with assignment operations. The syntax of spalloc is

```
S = spalloc(m,n,nonz)
```

where m and n are number of rows and columns, and $nonz$ is the total number of nonzeros in S. The value of $nonz$ need not be a precise. If $nonz$ is less than the ultimate number of nonzeros needed to store the matrix, MATLAB will allocate more memory for S as necessary. If $nonz$ is greater than necessary, memory reserved for nonzeros will go unused. For maximum computational efficiency, it is better to oversize, than undersize a sparse matrix when it is first allocated.

Example B.1: Creating and Displaying a Simple Sparse Matrix

A sparse version of matrix A defined in Equation (B.2) can be created with

```
>> is = [ 1 3 2 3 1];
>> js = [ 1 1 2 2 3];
>> as = [ 1 3 2 3 1];
>> S = sparse(is,js,as)
S =
    (1,1)        1
    (3,1)        3
    (2,2)        2
    (3,2)        3
    (1,3)        1
```

The default display of a sparse matrix is in the form of a table defining the locations and values of the nonzero elements. Each row of the output corresponds to one entry in the sparse matrix. The numbers in parentheses are the row and column indices of an element, and the last number is the value of the element.

Individual elements of S can be referred to and assigned with the subscript notation used for full matrices:

```
>> S(1,3)
ans =
     1
```

Even though the value of S(1,2) is not stored—it is one of the zeros that is skipped in the sparse storage scheme—its value can be returned with subscript notation:

```
>> S(1,2)
ans =
     0
```

The full function converts a matrix from sparse to full format. It provides a convenient way to display a (small) sparse matrix as an array of numbers.

```
>> full(S)
ans =
     1   0   1
     0   2   0
     3   3   0
```

Example B.2: Creating a Sparse Matrix with `spalloc`

The following statements use the `spalloc` function to allocate memory for a sparse 5×5 tridiagonal matrix. The individual elements are then added one element at a time.

```
S = spalloc(5,5,13);        % 5 x 5 matrix with 13 nonzero elements
S(1,1) = 2; S(1,2) = -1;    % first row
for i=2:4
  S(i,i-1) = -1; S(i,i) = 2; S(i,i+1) = -1;
end
S(5,4) = -1; S(5,5) = 2;    % last row
```

The built-in nnz and nzmax functions return the actual and maximum number of nonzero elements in the sparse matrix, respectively. It is possible, for example, to oversize the tridiagonal matrix created in the preceding example.

```
>> S = spalloc(5,5,18);    % 5 x 5 sparse matrix with room for 18 nonzeros
>> S = ...                 % assign tridiagonal entries as above
>> nnz(S)
ans =
     13
```

```
>> nzmax(S)
ans =
    18
```

At any point after S created in sparse format, more elements can be added to it. Doing so does not alter the type of S—it is still sparse:

```
>> S(1,5) = -1;    S(5,1) = -1;
>> nnz(S)
ans =
    15

>> nzmax(S)
ans =
    18
```

To obtain maximum code efficiency (minimum total execution time), you should avoid building a sparse matrix one element at a time, unless sufficient memory for the entire sparse matrix is allocated before elements are added. When additional memory needs to be allocated to insert elements in a sparse matrix, MATLAB needs to reorganize the internal data structures used to store the matrix. The CPU time to reorder the data structures can become measurable for very large sparse matrices. The most efficient procedure for building a sparse matrix is to first create vectors of row index, column index, and element values, and then assemble the sparse matrix with one call of the form S = sparse(is,js,as), as previously demonstrated.

Sparse Matrices with Diagonal Structure   The spdiags function creates and extracts diagonal elements of sparse matrices. It is the sparse counterpart of the diag function for full matrices, although the input parameters are significantly different for the two functions. To create a sparse matrix with spdiags use

```
sparseMatrix = spdiags(diagElements, diagIndices, nrows, ncols)
```

where *diagElements* is an *nrows* $\times$ *p* matrix of elements to be inserted into *sparseMatrix*, and *p* is the total number of diagonals having nonzero elements. The *diagIndices* parameter is a row vector of length *p* indicating the diagonal location in *sparseMatrix* of each column of *diagElements*. The *sparseMatrix* is created with *nrows* rows and *ncols* columns. The number of diagonals *p* is not specified explicitly. It is defined by the number of columns in both *diagElements* and *diagIndices*.

Using the spdiags function, a sparse matrix representation of the $(-1, 2, -1)$ tridiagonal matrix can be created as follows:

```
>> n = 5;                               % Size of the n-by-n matrix to create
>> a = 2*ones(n,1);                     % Main diagonal entries
>> b = -ones(n,1);                      % Sub- and super-diagonal entries
>> S = spdiags([b a b],[-1 0 1],n,n);
```

The diagonal elements are assembled into an $n \times 3$ matrix with the expression [b
a b]. The expression [-1 0 1] indicates that b is to be stored in the -1, or first
subdiagonal, and the $+1$, or first superdiagonal, and a is to be stored in the main
diagonal.

Example B.3: Arbitrary Tridiagonal Matrices in MATLAB Sparse Format

Assuming that a, b, and c are MATLAB column vectors having n elements, the following
statements construct a tridiagonal matrix using the notation of Equation (7.31):

```
a = ...; b = ...; c = ...;      % define a, b, and c
n = length(a);                  % must equal length(b) and length(c)
A = spdiags([ [c(2:n); 0] a [0; b(1:n-1)] ], [-1 0 1], n,n);
```

The first argument to the spdiags function is the three column matrix

$$\begin{bmatrix} c_2 & a_1 & 0 \\ c_3 & a_2 & b_1 \\ \vdots & \vdots & \vdots \\ c_n & a_{n-1} & b_{n-2} \\ 0 & a_n & b_{n-1} \end{bmatrix}$$

which is constructed by shifting the locations of elements in vectors b and c. The shifts are
necessary to create the matrix in Equation (7.31) because the spdiags function inserts the
elements of the input matrix into the sparse matrix by columns.

The tridiags function in Listing B.1 provides additional automation for the creation of sparse tridiagonal matrices. The tridiags function is in the linalg directory
of the NMM toolbox. With tridiags, the diagonals of the matrix can be specified as either vectors or scalars. If the inputs are scalars, the scalar values are replicated along the
diagonals of the sparse matrix.

The following statements contrast two ways of interpreting the input vectors used to
create a sparse tridiagonal matrix:

```
>> a = 1:5; b = a; c = a;              >> a = 1:5; b = a; c = a;
>> A = tridiags(5,a,b,c);             >> B = spdiags([c a b],[-1 0 1],5,5);
>> full(A)                            >> full(B)
ans =                                 ans =
     1    1    0    0    0                 1    2    0    0    0
     2    2    2    0    0                 1    2    3    0    0
     0    3    3    3    0                 0    2    3    4    0
     0    0    4    4    4                 0    0    3    4    5
     0    0    0    5    5                 0    0    0    4    5
```

```
function A = tridiags(n,a,b,c)
% tridiags   Create sparse tridiagonal matrix from two or three scalars or
%            vectors
%
% Synopsis:   A = tridiags(n,a,b)
%             A = tridiags(n,a,b,c)
%
% Input:     n     = size of desired (n by n) matrix
%            a,b,c = scalar or vector values for the main, super and sub
%                    diagonals.  If a, b, or c are scalars, they are
%                    replicated to fill the diagonals.  If c is not supplied,
%                    c = b is assumed
%
% Output:    A = sparse, tridiagonal matrix of the form
%
%                    a  b  0  0              a(1)  b(1)   0     0
%                    c  a  b  0      or      c(2)  a(2)  b(2)   0
%                    0  c  a  b               0    c(3)  a(3)  b(3)
%                    0  0  c  a               0     0    c(4)  a(4)

if nargin<4,  c = b;  end

if length(a)==1,  a = a*ones(n,1);  end    % replicate scalars
if length(b)==1,  b = b*ones(n,1);  end
if length(c)==1,  c = c*ones(n,1);  end
if length(a)<n | length(b)<n | length(c)<n
  error(sprintf('a,b,c must be scalars or have length >= %d',n));
end

a = a(:);  b = b(:);  c = c(:);   % guarantee column vectors
A = spdiags([ [c(2:n); 0] a [0; b(1:n-1)] ],[-1 0 1], n,n);
```

Listing B.1   The tridiags function creates sparse tridiagonal matrices using MATLAB's built-in sparse format.

Since $A = B^T$, the shifted columns trick used in tridiags could be avoided by using the statement

```
A = spdiags( [c a b], [-1 0 1], 5, 5)';
```

Transposing the output of spdiags requires a careful understanding of how that function works. It is less obvious than using the less elegant tridiags function.

B.2.2 Operations on Sparse Matrices

Once a sparse matrix is defined, it may be used like any other matrix. MATLAB understands how to perform mixed algebra involving both full and sparse matrices. Consider, for example, the following MATLAB session involving the sparse matrix created in Example B.1

```
>> S = sparse(...);   % see Example B.1
>> A = full(S);
>> A-S
ans =
     0      0      0
     0      0      0
     0      0      0
```

The result of mixed matrix addition or subtraction is always a full matrix. An operation involving two sparse matrices will generally result in another sparse matrix. MATLAB tries to preserve sparsity when it can:

```
>> B = S/2;
>> C = S-B
C =
   (1,1)        0.5000
   (3,1)        1.5000
   (2,2)        1.0000
   (3,2)        1.5000
   (1,3)        0.5000
```

Example B.4: Computational Savings Due to Sparse Storage

Sparse storage is used in the `splint` function, which creates a spline interpolant to a set of (x, y) data pairs. (See § 10.3.5 beginning on page 568.) Obtaining the coefficients of the spline requires solving a tridiagonal system of equations. In this example we demonstrate the computational savings realized by storing the tridiagonal matrix in sparse format.

    As a basis for comparison, the `splintFull` function performs the same numerical task as `splint`, but it does so using full storage for the coefficient matrix. The `splintFull` function is not listed here, but is included in the `interpolate` directory of the NMM toolbox. The following display shows the lines that are different for `splint` (on the left) and `splintFull` on the right.

Sparse storage:

```
% --- Set up system of equations
...
A = tridiags(n,beta,alpha,gamma);
...
% --- Solve the system for b
mmdflag = spparms('autommd');
spparms('autommd',0);
b = A\delta;
spparms('autommd',mmdflag);
```

Full storage:

```
% --- Set up system of equations
...
A = tridiag(n,beta,alpha,gamma);
...
% --- Solve the system for b
b = A\delta;
```

The tridiags and tridiag functions from the NMM toolbox create sparse and full tridiagonal matrices, respectively. The calls to the spparms function suppress row reordering that is normally performed before a sparse system is solved. The row reordering attempts to reduce fill-in during the LU factorization. Since the coefficient matrix in this problem is tridiagonal, the L and U factors will not have additional storage due to fill-in, so suppressing the row reordering saves effort without affecting the flop count.

The compSplintFlops function (included in the interpolate directory of the NMM toolbox, but not listed here) compares the flop counts for interpolating (x, y) data pairs with splint and splintFull functions. The computational effort is measured as a function of the number of knots used to defined the spline. Running compSplintFlops gives the following results

```
>> compSplintFlops
```

knots	sparse flops	full flops	relative effort
4	214	292	0.7329
8	401	859	0.4668
16	772	2838	0.2720
32	1511	10281	0.1470
64	2986	39020	0.0765
128	5933	151599	0.0391
256	11824	598066	0.0198
512	23603	2376245	0.0099

The first column is the number of knots used to construct the spline. The second and third columns are the number of flops to construct and evaluate the spline interpolant. The third column is the ratio of the sparse flops to the full flops. Although other tasks are performed in splint and splintFull, solving the coefficient matrix is the dominanting factor in determining the flop count for the spline interpolation code. Clearly, the sparse matrix format provides substantial savings as the size of the problem grows.

MATLAB Toolbox Functions

\, 382, 404e, **396–426**, 443, 454x, 530e, 532e, **493–573**

abs, 46t, 47
addpath, 59
angle, 46t, 47
axis, 66t

bessel, 599
beta, 599, 670x
break, 115–117

chol, 410t, **424–426**, 453x
clear, 53, 92
close all, 90e
cond, 403e
condest, 409
conj, 46t, 47
contour, **74**, 512x
conv, 51t
cos, 39

datevec, 141x
dbtype, **176**
dec2bin, 192, 234x
deconv, 51t
det, **345–346**, 362x
diag, 27t, 330, **346**, 350, 380, 763
diff, 594
disp, **101**
dot, 38, 300

eig, 281, 632, 633, **753–755**
eigs, 755
ellipj, 599
ellipke, 672e
else, 109
elseif, 109
end, 108–115
erf, 80, 81x, 177, 599
error, 127, **177–178**, 557
exp, 23, 47
expint, 599
eye, **27**, 27t

fclose, 60
feval, 128, **134–136**, 479, 683, 684
fgetl, 61e, 61
fgets, 61
find, **125–128**, 146x
fliplr, 559
flipud, 559
flops, 332, 454x, 656e, 695
fopen, **60**, 61e, 104
for, 105, **110–113**, 114
format, **102**
fprintf, 51, 61, 101, **102–105**, 109, 117, 530
fscanf, 61, 61e
full, 760, **762**
fzero, 241t, 268e, **273**, 284, 673x

gamma, 22, 599
global, 133–134
grid, **66**, 66t
griddata, 589
gtext, 66t

help, **23–24**, 157–159
humps, 585, 652, 656e, 667t, 669x

if, 108–109
imag, 46t, 47
inline, **137–138**, 148x, 479, 481e
input, 100
int, 602e
interp1, 183x, 292x, 559, **584–586**, 588, 593x
interp2, 584t
interp3, 584t
interpft, 584t
interpn, 584t
inv, **348**, 449x

keyboard, 178

legend, 66t, **66**, 145x
length, 27t, **32**, 112, 121
linspace, 27t, **29**, 33
load, **53–58**, 165e, 511
log, 23
log10, 23
loglog, 65
logm, 23
logspace, 27t, **30**, 78x

lookfor, 24, 157, 158
lu, 410t, **420–422**, 454x

max, 394
mesh, 69
meshc, 69, 512x

nargin, 129, 131
nargout, 129, 131
nnz, 760, **762**
nonzeros, 760
norm, 77, 78x, 237x, **303**, 321e, **334**, 358x, 744
null, 340
num2str, 50, 101
nzmax, 760, **762**

ode113, 726
ode115, 724
ode115s, 725
ode15s, 726
ode23, 701–710, 730x
ode23s, 725, 726
ode45, **701–710**, 714, 718, 722, 730x
    controlling with odeset, 703
    output interpolation, 704e, 710e
    pass-through parameters, 706
odeset, 703
ones, 17, 27t, **29**, 120, 330, 350

path, 59
pause, 178
plot, **63–69**, 90e, 129, 556
poly, 51t
polyder, 51t
polyfit, 51t, 457, 475, 485, **495–499**, 516, 517x, 519x
polyval, 51t, **51**, 113, 143x, 283e, 475, 549
polyvalm, 51t
prod, 359x, 362x, 536

qr, 410t, 489, 493e
quad, 646, **654–655**, 661, 667, 668
quad8, 601n, **654–655**, 661, 667, 668

rand, 27t, 123, 470e
rank, 336, 342, 360x, 373
rcond, 409, 530n
real, 46t, 47
reshape, 42

residue, 51t
return, 117
roots, 51t, 241t, **280**

save, 53–56
semilogx, **65**
semilogy, **65**
sign, 110, 246
sinh, 235x
size, 27t, **32**
sort, 559, 633
spalloc, 760, **761**
sparse, **760**, 760
spdiags, 760, 763, 764e
speye, 760
spline, 584t, **585–586**, 588, 589
spones, 760
spparms, 575, 760
sprand, 760
sprintf, 50, 127, 178, 557
spy, 760
str2mat, 50
subplot, 68–69
surf, **69**
surfc, 69

surfl, 69
svd, 410t, **756**
svds, 756
switch, 109
sym, 603e
syms, 603e

text, 66t
tic/toc, 358x
title, 66t, **66**
trapz, 611
type, 176

vander, 529
view, 71

while, **114–115**, 213
who, 52, 92
whos, 52

xlabel, **66**, 66t

ylabel, 66t, **66**

zeros, 27t, **29**, 120

Listings for NMM Toolbox m-files

adaptSimpson, 651
addmult, 95
Archimedes, 228

binSearch, 558
bisect, 260
brackPlot, 247

Cholesky, 425
compEM, 695
compSplinePlot, 582
conductFit, 484
cvcon, 111

dailyAve, 167
demoAdaptSimp, 653
demoArgs, 130
demoBisect, 255
demoBreak, 116
demoEuler, 685
demoFanCurve, 505

demoGasLag, 538
demoGasNewt, 551
demoGauss, 641
demoHermite, 566
demoNewton, 264
demoNewtonSys, 435
demoODE45args, 708
demoODE45opts, 705
demoPredPrey, 719
demoQuad, 657
demoReturn, 118
demoSmd, 723
demoSSub, 431
demoSteel, 711
demoSystem, 716
demoTaylor, 223
demoTcouple, 498
demoThreeRes, 441
demoTrap, 608
demoXcosx, 138
demoXexp, 471
divDiffTable, 546

epprox, 207
expSeriesPlot, 220

fidiff, 230
fitnorm, 478
fitqr, 494
fsum, 136
fx3, 249
fx3n, 267

gaussLagQuad, 665
gaussQuad, 640
GEPivShow, 395
GEshow, 388
GLNodeWt, 635
GLtable, 630, 631

H2Odensity, 132, 175
halfDiff, 200
hermint, 564

inputAbuse, 100
iterMult, 743

JfReservoir, 442

lagrint, 537
legsn, 269, 278
linefit, 464
linterp, 560
luNopiv, 417
luPiv, 418

multiply, 173
myCon, 87

newtint, 550
newton, 266
newtonSys, 437
newtsqrt, 214
noneg, 177, 178
nonegp, 178

odeEuler, 684
odeMidpt, 694

odeRK4, 698
odeRK4sys, 715

plotData, 98
polyGeom, 99
pumpCurve, 397

quadroot, 179
quadToInfinity, 662

rhs1, 685
rhsDecay, 708
rhsPop2, 719
rhssmd, 723
rhsSteelHeat, 712
rhsSys, 716
riverReport, 168
rotvec, 320

simpson, 615
sincos, 136
sinser, 218
splint, 580
splintFE, 574

tablen, 269, 278
takeout, 88
testsqrt, 215
threesum, 95
trapezoid, 607
trapzDat, 611
trapzDatTest, 172
tridiags, 765
trigplot, 92
twosum, 95

vecSeq, 306

weeklyAve, 167

xemx, 608
xexpfit, 470

Subject Index

[ ], 35–36, 168e

\, 382, **396**, 404e, 409–410, 419, 420, 422, **426**, 426, 443, 454x, 530e, 532e, **493–573**

%, 93, 156

abs, 46t, 47
adaptive
  adaptSimpson function, 651
  demoAdaptSimp function, 653
  numerical integration, 644–659
  quad8 function, 654–655
  quad function, 654–655
  stepsize for ODE solution, 700–701
adaptSimpson, 650, 654
adaptSimpsonTrace, 653
addmult, 96
addpath, 59
adjoint, 312
algorithm
  Backward Substitution, 381

Basic Rule for Gauss–Legendre
  Quadrature, 626
Bisection, 253
Bracketing, 245
Composite Rule for Gauss–Legendre
  Quadrature, 636
Conversion from Floating-Point to Binary,
  198
definition of, 4
Diagonal System Solution, 380
Fixed-Point Iteration, 250
Forward Substitution, 381
Gaussian Elimination with Partial
  Pivoting, 394
Gaussian Elimination, 387
Interval Halving to Oblivion, 199
Inverse-power Iteration, 752
Iterative Solution of Nonlinear Systems,
  428
LU Factorization in Place, 415
LU Factorization, 415

Least-Squares Solution via QR, 492
Matrix–Matrix Multiplication by
    Columns, 327
Matrix–Matrix Multiplication by Inner
    Products, 328
Matrix–Vector Multiplication by
    Columns, 315
Matrix–Vector Multiplication by Rows,
    318
Newton's Method for Scalar Equations,
    262
Newton's Method for Systems, 433
Power Iteration, 751
Secant, 270
Solve $Ax = b$ with Cholesky
    Factorization, 422
Solve $Ax = b$ with LU factorization, 411
Successive Substitution, 430
Two-level Adaptive Simpson's Rule
    Quadrature, 649
Vector–Matrix Multiplication by
    Columns, 324
Vector–Matrix Multiplication by Rows,
    323
angle, 46t, 47
ans, 18, 21
Archimedes, 228
array indexing, **121–122**, 353, 417
array operators, **39–42**, 249e, 300e, 304e
arrays, **24**
augmented matrix, 370
axis, 66t

B splines, 589
backslash, 382, **396**, 404e, 409–410,
    419–420, 422, **426**, 443, 454x, **493**,
    495, 529, 530e, 532e, **573**
backward stable, 406
backward substitution, 379–395, 399, 411
basic rule for numerical integration, 601
basis functions, 455, 473–475, **524**
bessel, 599
beta, 599, 670x
"big-oh" notation, 225, 690, 692
binSearch, 559, 565
bisect, 259, 265, 286x
bisection, 253–262, 558
    analysis of, 256–257
    bisect function, 260
    convergence rate, 256

demoBisect function, 255
bit, 191–192
Boolean, 105
bracketing roots, 245–250
brackPlot, 246, 248e, 274
break, 115–117
breakpoints, 554
bugs
    definition of, 151
    FDIV, 190e
    first usage of "computer bug", 187n
    preventing, 174–176
byte, 191–192

catastrophic cancellation, 206e, 207e, 271
chol, 410t, **424–426**, 453x
Cholesky, 424
Cholesky factorization, 422–426
clear, 53, 92
close all, 90e
closed interval, 600, 619–620
coefficient of determination, 464–467, 480
    adjusted, **480**
coffee algorithm, 4
colon notation, **33–35**, 119
    as wildcard to select rows or columns, 34
    convert matrix to column vector, 43, 547
column space, 339, 369
comment statements, 17, **93**, 156–157
companion matrix, 280, 746
compatible, 370n
compEM, 695
compEMRK4, 699, 729x
compInterp, 551
compIntRules, 643
complete pivoting, 391
complex numbers, **45–48**, 179e
composite rule for numerical integration,
    601
compSplinePlot, 581
concatenate strings, 49
cond, 403e
condest, 409
condition number, 398, 402–410, 443, 530e,
    590x
    meaning of large, 408
conductFit, 483e
conj, 46t, 47
conjugate transpose, 312
consistent, 370, 374

contour, **74**, 512x
conv, 51t
convergence
    absolute criterion, 216–217
    of bisection method, 256–257
    criteria for roots, 257–259
    of fixed-point iteration, 253
    of Newton's method for scalar equations,
        264–265
    newtsqrt function, 214
    relative criterion, 216–217
    testing, 213–217
cos, 39
cubic spline, 555, 568–583
cuconBasis1, 482e
curve-fitting
    basis functions, 474–475
    conductFit function, 484
    demoFanCurve function, 505
    demoTcouple function, 498
    demoXexp function, 471
    fitnorm function, 478
    fitqr function, 494
    linefit function, 464
    meaning of least-squares, 460
    nonlinear, via transformation, 468–472
    R^2 statistic, 464–467
    residuals, examination of, 497x
    to $y = c_1 e^{c_2 x}$, 468
    to $y = c_1 x e^{c_2 x}$, 469
    to $y = c_1 x^{c_2}$, 469
    to a line, 458–464
    to arbitrary $f(x)$, 473
    to polynomials, 495–499
    via normal equations, 475–485
    via QR, 485–495
    xexpfit function, 470
cvcon, 110e

dailyAve, 166e
data structure, 703, 757
datevec, 141x
dbtype, **176**
debugging
    MATLAB tools, 176–180
    defensive programming, 174–176
    definition of, 151
dec2bin, 192, 234x
deconv, 51t
defensive programming, 174–176

delete
    matrix and vector elements, 35–36
    variables from workspace, 53
demoArgs, 129e
demoBisect, 254
demoBreak, 116
demoFanCurve, 504e, 519x
demoGasLag, 537
demoGasNewt, 549
demoGauss, 639e
demoHermite, 566
demoInterp1, 585
demoNewton, 263
demoNewtonSys, 434e, 454x
demoODE45opts, 704, 731x
demoPlaneFit, 503e
demoPredPrey, 718
demoQuad, 656e
demoSimp, 616e
demoSmd, 722, 731x
demoSplineFE, 576
demoSSub, 431e
demoSsub, 453x
demoSteel, 710
demoTcouple, 497
demoTrap, 609
demoWiggle, 553
det, **345–346**, 362x
determinant, 342–346, 745
    expansion by minors, 342
diag, 27t, 330, **346**, 350, 380, 763
diagnostic printing with verbose flag,
        170
diagonal matrix, **346–347**, 379
diagonalizable, 748
diff, 594
difference equation, 688
direct methods, 427
discretization error
    Euler's method, 685
    global, 690–691
    local, 688–690
    order of, 690
disp, **101**
divDiffTable, 546, 548, 588, 591x
divide and conquer, 160
divided-difference, 538–551, 562
    table, 544
dot, 38, 300
double precision, **194**, 209, 195t

`eig`, 281, 632, 633, **753–755**
eigenvalue, 744
   `eig`, 753–755
   `eigs`, 755
   inverse-power method, 751–753
   of companion matrix, 280, 746
   power method, 748–751
eigenvalue decomposition, 748
eigenvalue problem, 631
eigenvector, 744
`eigs`, 755
`eigSort`, 755e
`ellipj`, 599
`ellipke`, 672e
elliptic integral, 599x
`else`, 109
`elseif`, 109
`end`, 108–115
   as subscript, 35
`eps`, 21, 210
`erf`, 80, 81x, 177, 599
`error`, 127, **177–178**, 557
errors
   absolute, 211
   relative, 211
Euclidean norm, 302
Euler's method, 681–691
   `demoEuler` function, 685
   discretization error, 688–691
   `odeEuler` function, 684
   truncation error, 690
   vs. midpoint method, 694e
   vs. RK-4 methods, 699e
`exp`, 23, 47
`expint`, 599
extended rule, 601
extrapolation, 526, 553e
`eye`, **27**, 27t

`false`, 105
fatal error, 173
`fclose`, 60
FDIV bug, 190e
`feval`, 128, **134–136**, 479, 683, 684
   inline function object, 684
`fgetl`, 61, 61e
`fgets`, 61
file identifier, 60, 103
`find`, **125–128**, 146x
`fitnorm`, **477–480**, 482e, 486, 514x

`fitqr`, 480, 486, **494–495**
fixed-point iteration, 250–253, 263
   convergence, 253
   definition of fixed-point, 250
`fliplr`, 559
`flipud`, 559
floating-point numbers
   arithmetic, 202–204
   precision limits, 197–200
   range limits, 194–197
   storage in computer memory, 193–194
flops, 331–333, 343, 398
   for interpolation in different bases,
      551e
   matrix–matrix product, 332
   savings with sparse storage, 758
   vector inner product, 331
`flops`, 332, 454x, 656e, 695
`fopen`, **60**, 61e, 104
`for`, 105, **110–113**, 114
formal solution
   linear system of equations, 373
   to first-order ODE, 679
`format`, **102**
forward substitution, 381, 399, 411
`fprintf`, 51, 61, 101, **102–105**, 109,
      117, 530
`fscanf`, 61e, 61
`fsum`, 138, 156
`full`, 760, **762**
full pivoting, 391
full rank, 341
full storage scheme, 757
function hiding, 22
function m-files, **93–100**, 162
   advantages over scripts, 94
   input/output parameters, 94–100
   prologue, 157, 159
`fx3`, 249e
`fzero`, 241t, 268e, **273**, 284, 673x

`gamma`, 22, 599
Gauss, C.F., 379n
Gaussian elimination, 379–395
   flop count, 399t
   sensitivity to inputs, 399–402
   stability, 405–406
   used to determine rank, 341
   with pivoting, 387–395
   without pivoting, 382–387

Gaussian quadrature, 620–642
    basic rule, 626
    composite rule, 634–642
    demoGauss function, 641
    Gauss–Laguerre rule, 663–665
    Gauss–Legendre nodes, 626–634
    gaussQuad function, 640
    GLNodeWt function, 635
    GLtable function, 630, 631
gaussLagQuad, 664
gaussQuad, 621, 639, 661, 670x
GDE, 687
GEPivShow, 394
GEshow, 387, 447e, 452x
GLagNodeWt, 664
GLagTable, 664
GLnodes, 126
GLNodeWt, 634, 639e
global, 133–134
global variables, 93, **133–134**, 268e, 714
    avoiding use of, 275, 714
GLtable, 629, 634, 639
grid, **66**, 66t
griddata, 589
growth factor for Gaussian elimination, 406
gtext, 66t

H2Odensity, 131, 156, 157
help, **23–24**, 157–159
help browser, 23
hermint, 563
Hermite interpolation, 560, 567
Hermite polynomials, 561
hermitian conjugate, 312
Heun's method, 696–697
    discretization error, 697
Horner's Rule, 113e
humps, 585, 652, 656e, 667t, 669x

i, 21, **45–48**
identity matrix, 347
if, 108–109
ill conditioned, 376x 398, 443
    matrix, **402**, 529, 530, 531e, 586
imag, 46t, 47
inconsistent, 370
indexing
    array, **121–122**, 417
    logical, 122–125
Inf, 21, 196, 263n, 303

initial condition, 676
inline, **137–138**, 148x, 479, 481e
inline function object, 128, **137–138**, 479,
        481, 655, 683
    calling with feval, 684
inner product, 37–39, **299–301**, 329
input, 100
inputAbuse, 100
int, 602e
integers
    computer arithmetic with, 202–203
    storage in computer memory,
        192–193
integrated circuit cooling, 366–368x
interp1, 183x, 292x, 559, **584–586**, 588,
        593x
interp2, 584t
interp3, 584t
interpft, 584t
interpn, 584t
interpolation
    binSearch function, 558
    compSplinePlot function, 582
    cubic spline, 555
    demoGasLag function, 538
    demoGasNewt function, 551
    demoHermite function, 566
    divDiffTable function, 546
    hermint function, 564
    Lagrange basis, 532–538
    lagrint function, 537
    linterp function, 560
    monomial basis, 527–532
    newtint function, 550
    Newton basis, 538–551
    piecewise polynomial, 554–583
    piecewise-cubic Hermite, 560, 567
    splintFE function, 574
    spline, 568–583
    splint function, 580
    support points, 527
    vs. curve fitting, 525
    vs. extrapolation, 525–526
interval
    closed, 600, 619–620
    open, 600, 620
inv, **348**, 449x
inverse-power method, 751–753
invertible, **348**, 374, 443
iteration function, 250

iterative method
   contrast with direct method, 427
iterMult, 743, 748, 751

j, 21, **45–48**
Jacobian, 433

keyboard, 178
Kirchhoff's Law
   of currents, 377
   of voltages, 377
knots, 554, 566e, 577–579
Kronecker delta, 533

L_1 norm, 303
L_2 norm, **302**, 308, 750n
Lagrange polynomials, 532–538, 551e
lagrint, 536, 583, 592, 593x
Laguerre polynomials, 663
LDE, **687**
least squares, 369, 371e, **460**
   solution via normal equations, 463,
        475–480
   solution via QR Factorization, 491–493
left division, 382, **396**, 404e, 409–410,
        419–420, 422, **426**, 443, 454x, **493**,
        495, 529, 530e, 532e, 573
left null space, 339
legend, 66t, **66**, 145x
Legendre polynomials, 625
   zeros of, 632
legsNG, 268
legz, 277
length, 27t, **32**, 112, 121
linear combination, 297–298, 335
linear independence, 369
linear systems of equations
   condition number, 402–410
   consistent, 370
   direct methods, 427
   Gaussian elimination, 379–395
   inconsistent, 370
   matrix formulation, 365–368
   overdetermined, 461–463, 485–495
   solving via matrix factorization, 410–426
   solving with \, 396, **426**
linearly dependent, **335–336**, 372–374
linearly independent, **335–336**, 372–374
linefit, 467, 512x
L_∞ norm, **303**, 742, 744, 750

linspace, 27t, **29**, 33
linterp, 588
load, **53–58**, 97e, 165e, 511
loadColData, 62e, 482e, 504e, 511
local variables, 93
log, 23
log10, 23
logical indexing, 122–125
loglog, 65
logm, 23
logspace, 27t, **30**, 78x
lookfor, 24, 157, 158
loops
   for, 110–113
   while, 114–115
lu, 410t, **420–422**, 454x
LU factorization, 410–422
luPiv, 417

machine precision, 209, 258
makeGLtable, 629, 634
mat files, 53–56
MATLAB path, 58
MATLAB variables, built-in
   ans, 18, 21
   eps, 21, 210
   i, 21, 45
   Inf, 21, 196, 263n, 303
   j, 21, 45
   NaN, 21, 263n
   pi, 19, 21
   realmax, 21, 195, 346
   realmin, 21, 195
   varargin, 268e, 714
matrix
   Cholesky factorization, 422–426
   column space, 339, 369
   companion, 746
   creating, 26–30
   deleting elements, 35–36
   determinant, 342–346
   diagonal, **346–347**, 379
   eigenvalues, 280
   identity, the, 347
   ill conditioned, 376x, **402**, 529, 530, 531e,
        586
   inverse, **348**, 373, 396
   invertible, **348**, 374
   LU factorization, 410–422
   minor of, 342

noninvertible, 374
nonsingular, **348**, 374
norms, 333–334
null, 35–36, 168e
null space, 339–340
orthogonal, **351–352**, 487, 755
permutation, **352–353**, 416–417,
　　421–422
positive definite, 351
range, 339
rank, 341–342, 373
rank one, 301
singular, 301, **348**, 374
sparse, 331e, 350, 575, 749, **757–767**
　　condition number, 409
strings, 48–51
symmetric, 312, **349**
symmetric positive definite, 351, 406
triangular, 380–382, 410–426
tridiagonal, 79x, 142x, **349–350**, 571,
　　575, 578n, 632, 743, 763–765
Vandermonde, 528–532
matrix factorization, 410–426
　Cholesky, 422–426
　LU, 410–422
　QR, 426, **485–495**
　SVD, 755–756
matrix norms, 333–334
　spectral, 334
matrix operations, 310–333
　addition and subtraction, 311
　flop counts, 331–333, 398
　matrix–matrix product, 325–333
　matrix–vector product, 313–316
　scalar multiplication, 311
　transpose, 27, 30, 44, 312
　vector–matrix product, 313–316
max, 394
mesh, 69
meshc, 69, 512x
methods, for objects in object-oriented
　　programming, 137
midpoint method, 693–696
　discretization error, 694
　odeMidpt function, 694
　vs. Euler's method, 694e
　vs. RK-4 methods, 699e
minor, 342
multiple linear regression, 500
multiply, 173

myArrow, 362x
myCon, 87e, 93

NaN, 21, 263n
nargin, 129, 131
nargout, 129, 131
nested multiplication, **113**, 549, 562, 566
Neville's algorithm, 589
newtint, 583, 587, 591x, 592, 593x
newton, 265, 267, 286x, 436
Newton polynomials, 538–551, 551e
　nested multiplication, 549
Newton's Law
　of cooling, 678e
　of motion, 677e
Newton's method
　convergence, for scalar equations,
　　264–265
　demoNewton function, 264
　divergence of, 263
　for one variable, 261–268
　for systems of equations, **432–442**
　fx3n function, 267
　general implementation, 265
　legsn function, 269, 278
　newton function, 266
　tabln function, 269, 278
Newton–Cotes rules, 601
newtonNG, 268
newtonSys, 436, 454x
NMM toolbox, 59
nnz, 760, **762**
nodes, 600
　Gauss–Legendre, 626–634
noneg, 177
noninvertible, 374
nonlinear
　newtonSys, 436
　curve fit via transformation, 468–472
　systems of equations, 427–434
nonsingular, **348**, 374, 443
nonzeros, 760
norm
　matrix, 333–334
　vector, 301–308
norm, 77, 78x, 237x, **303**, 321e, **334**, 358x,
　　744
normal equations, 457, 461, 463, 474
not-a-knot end condition, **577–579**, 581e,
　　586

null, 340
null matrix, 35–36, 168e
null space, 339–340
num2str, 50, 101
numerical analysis, 5
numerical calculation, 1–3
numerical integration
   adaptive, 602, 644–659
   adaptSimpson function, 651
   basic rule, **601**, 603, 612, 619, 626
   composite rule, **601**, 605, 613, 634
   demoAdaptSimp function, 653
   demoGauss function, 641
   demoTrap function, 608
   extended rule, 601
   Gauss–Laguerre quadrature, 663–665
   Gauss–Legendre, 634–642, 642e
   Gaussian quadrature, 601, **620–642**
   gaussQuad function, 640
   GLNodeWt function, 635
   GLtable function, 630, 631
   Newton–Cotes rules, 601, **616–620**
   nodes, 617
   panel, 601
   precision, 618, 621, 623
   Romberg, 589, 645
   simpson function, 615
   Simpson's rule, 612–616, 642e
   trapezoid function, 607
   trapezoid rule, 166e, **603–612**, 642e
   trapzDat function, 611
   truncation error, 602
   weights, 617
   xemx function, 608
numerical method
   definition of, 4
numerical quadrature, 600
   global adaptation, 645
   local adaptation, 645
nzmax, 760, **762**

$\mathcal{O}(\,)$, 223–229, 690, 692
object-oriented programming, 137
objects, **45**, **137**
ODE
   coupled, 710–718
   higher order, 720–724
ode113, 726
ode115, 724
ode115s, 725

ode15s, 726
ode23, 701–710, 730x
ode23s, 725, 726
ode45, **701–710**, 714, 718, 722, 730x
   controlling with odeset, 703
odeEuler, 683, 728x
odeMidpt, 694, 728x
odeRK4, 699, 706, 728x
odeRK4sys, 714
odeRK4sysv, 714, 718
odeset, 703
on-line help, 157–159
one step methods, 675, 691–692
ones, 17, 27t, **29**, 120, 330, 350
open interval, 600, 620
operator precedence, 33, **107**
order notation
   truncation error, 223–229
orthgonal matrix, 755
orthogonal
   functions, 625
   matrix, **351–352**, 487
   polynomials, 625–626
   vectors, 308
orthonormal
   polynomials, 671x
   vectors, **308–309**
outer product, 37, **301**, 329
overdetermined, 369
overflow, **195–197**, 218, 232, 234x, 345, 750

panel, 601
parametric spline, 596x
partial pivoting, 387–395
path, 58, 158
path, 59
pause, 178
permutation
   matrix, **352–353**, 416–417
   vector, 353
permutation matrix, 421–422
permutation vector, 417
pi, 19, 21
picnic table design, 240e, 267e
piecewise polynomial interpolation, 554–583
pivot, 384
pivot row, 384

pivoting
   complete or full, 391
   partial, 387–395
plot, **63–69**, 90e, 129, 556
plotData, 145x
plotData, 97e
plotSimpInt, 616
plotTrapInt, 611
poly, 51t
polyder, 51t
polyfit, 51t, 457, 475, 485, **495–499**, 516,
   517x, 519x
polyGeom, 99e
polynomial wiggle, 553, 567, 587
polynomials, 51–52
   MATLAB functions, 51
   interpolating with, 527–583
   Lagrange basis, 532–538, 551e
   Laguerre, 663
   monomial basis, 527–532, 551e
     shifted, 528
   nested multiplication, **113**, 562, 566
   Newton basis, 538–551, 551e
polyval, **51**, 51t, 113, 143x, 283e, 475,
   549
polyvalm, 51t
positive definite, **747**
power method, 748–751
powerit, 751, 752
poweritInv, 752
preallocation of matrices, **120–121**
precision
   double, **194**, 195t, 209
   of quadrature rule, 618, **621**, 623
   single, **194**, 195t, 203, 209
   used by MATLAB, 195
primary function, 98
prod, 359x, 362x, 536
prologue, 157, 159
pump curve, 363x
pumpCurve, 397x, 451

qr, 410t, 489, 493e
QR algorithm, 753
QR factorization, 426, 457, 485–495, 753
   economy-size, 489
quad, 646, **654–655**, 661, 667, 668
quad8, 601n, **654–655**, 661, 667, 668
quadratic form, 747
quadrature, **600**

quadroot, 179
quadToInfinity, 661, 661e, 673x

R^2, 464–467, 480
   adjusted, 480
rand, 27t, 123, 470e
range, 339, 488
rank, 341–342, 374
   deficient, 341
   determining via Gaussian elimination,
     341
   full, 341
   role in solution of linear systems, 372–373
rank, 336, 342, 360x, 373
rcond, 409, 530n
real, 46t, 47
realmax, 21, 195, 346
realmin, 21, 195
recursion, 218e, 219e
recursive function calls, 650
recursiveIndent, 650
regression, 456
reshape, 42
reshape matrices
   with colon notation, 43, 547
   with reshape, 42
residual, 407
   minimizing with least-squares, 460–461
   minimizing with QR Factorization,
     491–492
residue, 51t
return, 117
rhs1, 683
rhsDecay, 707
rhsDecayNot, 706
rhspop2, 718
rhssmd, 722
rhsSteelHeat, 710
rhsSys, 716
RK-4 method
   discretization error, 697
   vs. Euler and midpoint methods, 699e
Romberg integration, 589, 645
root finding
   bisect function, 260
   bisection, 253–261
   bracketing roots, 245–250
   brackPlot function, 247
   convergence criteria, 257–259
   demoBisect function, 255

root finding (*continued*)
  demoNewton function, 264
  divergence of, 251e, 263, 272, 273
  fixed-point iteration, 250–253
  fx3 function, 249
  fx3n function, 267
  hybrid methods, 273–279
  legsn function, 269, 278
  newton function, 266
  Newton's method, 261–268
  of polynomials, 279–283
  secant method, 268–273
  tablen function, 269, 278
  with fzero, 273–279
  with roots, 280–283
roots, 51t, 241t, **280**
rotation matrices, 319e
roundoff error, 113, **191–210**, 229e, 271,
      530, 531e, 553, 586
  cancellation, 206x, 271, 620
  epprox function, 207
  fidiff function, 230
  halfDiff function, 200
  in convergence test, 258
  minimizing effect of, 253
  solving linear systems, 374
row space, 339, 340e
rules of thumb for solution to linear system,
      407–408
Runge–Kutta methods, 697–701
  demoODE45opts function, 705
  ode23 function, 701–702
  ode45 function, 701–724
  odeRK4sysv function, 714
  odeRK4sys function, 715
  odeRK4 function, 698
  adaptive, 700–710
  for coupled ODEs, 713–718

save, 53–56
script m-files, **86–93**, 162
  use function m-files instead, 94
search
  binSearch, 558
  binary, 558–559
  for interpolation support points, 557
  incremental, 127e, 557–558
search path, 58
secant method, 268–273
  divergence of, 272

Seebeck effect, 496e
semilogx, **65**
semilogy, **65**
side effect, 91
sign, 110, 246
simpson, 616, 670x
Simpson's rule, 612–616
  adaptive, 646–654
  adaptSimpson function, 651
  demoAdaptSimp function, 653
  demoSimp function, 616
  simpson function, 615
sincos, 137
single precision, **194**, 195t, 203, 209
singular, 374
singular matrix, 348
singular value decomposition, 340, 342, 485,
      755–756
singular values, 755
sinh, 235x
size, 27t, **32**
software design
  defining modules, 162–168
  divide and conquer, 160
  stepwise refinement, 160–162
  top-down, 160
sort, 559, 633
spalloc, 760, **761**
sparse, 760, **760**
sparse matrix, 331e, 350, 575, 749, **757–767**
  condition number, 409
sparse storage scheme, 757
sparsity, 758, 766
  inverse of storage density, 758
spdiags, 760, 763, 764e
spectral decomposition, 748
spectral norm, 334
speye, 760
spline, 568–583
  fixed-slope end condition, 572–576, 581e
  natural end condition, 576–577, 581e
  not-a-knot end condition, **577–579**, 581e,
      586
  parametric, 596x
spline, 584t, **585–586**, 588, 589
splint, 579, 588, 589, 766e
splintFE, 573
splintFull, 766e
spones, 760
spparms, 575, 760

sprand, 760
sprintf, 50, 127, 178, 557
spy, 760
square root, iterative calculation of, 213,
    286x
stability, 406
Statbox, 510
state variables, 720
stepsize, 680
    adaptive, 700–701
    effect of reducing, 686
stepwise refinement, 160–162
Stixbox, 510
str2mat, 50
string
    concatenation, 49
strings, 24, **48–51**
subfunctions, 98
subplot, 68–69
subscripts
    matrix elements, 31
    using colon notation, 34
subspace, 337
    span of, 337
successive substitution
    for systems of nonlinear equations,
        429–432
support points, 527
surf, **69**
surfc, 69
surfl, 69
SVD, 340, 342, **755–756**
svd, 410t, **756**
svds, 756
switch, 109
sym, 603e
symbolic calculation, 1–3, 201–202,
    325
    integration, 602–603
symmetric matrix, 312, **349**
    positive definite, 351, 406
syms, 603e
systems of equations
    consistent, 370
    inconsistent, 370
    nonlinear, 427–434

tablen, 268
tablenNG, 268
tablez, 277, 291x

Taylor Series, **221–223**, 681
testTrapzDat, 612
TEX notation, 90
text, 66t
thermocouple, 496e
threesum, 96
thumb, rules of, for solution to linear system,
    407–408
title, **66**, 66t
toolbox
    NMM, vi
    Spline, 589
    Statbox, 510
    Statistics, 510
    Stixbox, 510
    Symbolic Math, 201
top-down, 160
trace, 359x, 747
transpose
    matrix, 27, 30, 44, 312
    operator, 26
    string matrix, 49
    vector, 26, 33, 44, 297
trapezoid, 606, 669e, 670x
trapezoid rule, 166e, **603–612**
    demoTrap function, 608
    trapezoid function, 607
    trapzDat function, 611
trapz, 611
trapzDat, 166e, 611
triangular matrix, 380–382, 410–426
tridiag, 350, 767x
tridiagonal matrix, 79x, 142x, **349–350**, 571,
    575, 578n, 632, 743, 763–765
tridiags, 575, 764e, 767x
true, 105
truncation error, **217–232**, 602
    Archimedes function, 228
    demoTaylor function, 223
    fidiff function, 230
    ODE solvers, 685n, 690
    order notation, 223–229
    sinser function, 218
two's-complement, 193
twosum, 94
type, 176

underdetermined, 369
underflow, **195–197**, 200, 232, 246
unit roundoff, 209

vander, 529
Vandermonde matrix, 397, 528–532
varargin, 268e, 714
variables
  global, 93, **133–134**, 268e
    avoiding, 275, 714
  local, 93
vector
  deleting elements, 35–36
  Euclidean norm, 302
  inner product, 329
  L_1 norm, 303
  L_2 norm, 302
  L_∞ norm, 303
  linear combination, 297–298, 335
  linearly dependent, **335–336**, 372–374
  linearly independent, **335–336**,
    372–374
  norms, 301–308
  orthogonal, 308
  orthonormal, **308–309**, 351
  outer product, 329
  p norms, 303
  permutation, 353
  subspace, 337
vector operations, 296–301
  addition and subtraction, 296
  dot product, 299–301
  inner product, 299–301
  outer product, 301
  scalar multiplication, 296
  transpose, 26, 33, 44, 297

vector space, 336–338
  basis of, 337–338
  column, 339
  null, 339
  dimension of, 337–338
  row, 339
vectorization, 39, **118–128**
  with array operators, 39–42
verbose flag for diagnostic printing, 170
view, 71

weeklyAve, 166e
weight function, 625
weights
  Gauss–Legendre, 626–634
  numerical integration, 617
Wheatstone bridge, 376–379x
while, **114–115**, 213
whitespace, 154
who, 52, 92
whos, 52
wiggle, polynomial, 553, 567, 587
word, of computer memory, 191
workspace, 52–53

xemx, 608, 616
xinvpxBasis, 480e
xlabel, 66t, **66**

ylabel, **66**, 66t

zeros, 27t, **29**, 120